HUNTING
HUMANS

BOOKS BY ELLIOTT LEYTON

The Compact:
Selected Dimensions of Friendship (ed., 1974)

Dying Hard:
The Ravages of Industrial Carnage (1975)

The One Blood:
Kinship and Class in an Irish Village (1975)

Bureaucracy and World View:
Studies in the Logic of Official Interpretation
(with Don Handelman, 1978)

The Myth of Delinquency:
An Anatomy of Juvenile Nihilism (1979)

Sole Survivor:
Children Who Murder Their Families (1990)

Violence and Public Anxiety: A Canadian Case
(with William O'Grady and James Overton, 1992)

Men of Blood:
Murder in Modern England (1995)

Touched by Fire:
Doctors Without Borders in a Third World Crisis (1998)

Serial Murder:
Modern Scientific Perspectives (ed., 2000)

HUNTING HUMANS

THE RISE OF THE MODERN
MULTIPLE MURDERER

ELLIOTT LEYTON

SECOND EDITION:
Completely Revised and Updated

CARROLL & GRAF PUBLISHERS
NEW YORK

HUNTING HUMANS

Carroll & Graf Publishers
An Imprint of Avalon Publishing Group Inc.
245 West 17th Street • 11th Floor
New York, NY 10011

First Carroll & Graf trade paperback edition 2003

Lyric taken from one of the best-selling albums of the mid-1980s,
SYNCHRONICITY, by The Police, permission from A & M Records
of Canada, copyright 1983, Magnetic Publishing Co.

Library of Congress Cataloging-in-Publication Data is available.

ISBN: 0-7867-1228-7

Printed in the United States of America
Design by Kathy Lake, Neuwirth & Associates
Distributed by Publishers Group West

FOR THOSE WHO TAUGHT ME HOW TO LIVE
*. . . especially Bonnie Leyton, Sam Feinstein,
and the Clary Family*

FOR THOSE WHO TAUGHT ME HOW TO THINK

*. . . especially Elliot Liebow and
Philip Jenkins*

AND IN MEMORY OF MY BELOVED LATE AUNT

*Tillie Feinstein, who talked with me late
into the dry prairie night*

Contents

Preface to the 2003 Edition

When the manuscript for *Hunting Humans* was
completed in 1984, it was to be one of the first few
books in the modern world to recognize multiple murder as a significant social phenomenon, not just an isolated psychopathological incident. The book stirred controversy everywhere among those whose
interests it threatened—especially orthodox criminologists, forensic
psychiatrists, radical feminists, and academics who thought the subject
was too vulgar for the Senior Common Room. Still, Philip Jenkins, the
dean of contemporary homicide studies, later paid me the ultimate
compliment when he wrote, "Elliott Leyton did more than anyone else
to place the study of multiple murder on a sound academic footing."
Criminologist Steve Egger was kind enough to add that the book had
made me "the father of serial murder studies."

Hunting Humans was first published in the United States by New
York University Press (initially—and confusingly—under the title,
Compulsive Killers); by McClelland and Stewart in Canada; and by
Penguin Books in Britain. Since then, *Hunting Humans* has gone
through dozens of reprintings and translations into many languages,
including Japanese and Polish. It has remained in print in the United

Kingdom, Canada, and Japan, but it has been unavailable for some time in the USA. While each new printing permitted minor changes in the manuscript, the exigencies of modern publishing did not give me the chance to revise the book fully—neither to account for changes in my own thinking, nor to acknowledge the work of other researchers who had refined the issues and improved the quality of available data.

The publication of this entirely revised, expanded, and updated second edition has given me the opportunity to incorporate fresh material from the many scholars who have enriched the study of multiple murder since the mid-1980s. It has also given me the chance to share some of the insights gleaned from my association with international police forces—especially New Scotland Yard in London and the South Yorkshire police, as well as the FBI Academy in Quantico, Virginia, the Royal Newfoundland Constabulary, and Dutch Interpol in The Hague. I am exceedingly grateful to my American publishers, Carroll & Graf, and to Philip Turner for giving this new edition of *Hunting Humans* the opportunity to surface in America.

I am an anthropologist, and this book is very much a piece of anthropology, yet the book is not written in a style that will be familiar to many social scientists. I make no apology for this, for although I admire the insights of the social sciences, I am able to keep my passion for their style of exposition well under control. Long ago, renowned McGill University archaeologist Bruce Trigger and I agreed that the ugly and impenetrable specialist jargon commonly used by modern social scientists is more than just an intellectual disaster. It is a betrayal of the democratic spirit that founded the modern university and an abandonment of the mandate of that university—to make the results of scholarly research accessible to the informed general reader.

In this regard, I merely try to emulate the literacy and grace of sociologically inclined historians such as Douglas Hay or Hugh Thomas. A union among historians, psychologists, novelists, historical sociologists, and anthropologists is long overdue; for it is only with the special gifts of all of them that we can hope to join George Eliot's scientists in piercing "the obscurity of those minute processes which prepare human misery and joy, those invisible thoroughfares which are the first lurking places of anguish, mania and crime, that delicate poise and transition which determine the growth of happy or unhappy consciousness." Although I remain scrupulously wedded to empirical fact throughout this book, treating interviews and published material as if they were my field notes, I feel free to take my intellectual pleasures where and when I find them—necessarily so, since this is as much an exercise in historical reconstruction as it is anything else.

Finally, I must apologize to my readers around the world for forcing them to read about so much human suffering and degradation. We can only bear it if we remind ourselves that the eradication of a disease requires the intensive study of all its pus and blood and deformed tissue. So far, the only reliable cure we have discovered is *madame guillotine*. Regrettably, while her use may provide us with some arcane satisfaction, she can do nothing to staunch the outbreak of this most modern and virulent of social epidemics.

Elliott Leyton, PhD
Professor of Forensic Anthropology
Memorial University of Newfoundland

1 The Great Multiple Murder Panic

"For murder, though it have no tongue, will speak
With most miraculous organ."

Hamlet

The Panic

A great wave of anxiety hit the North American public during the mid-1980s. New incarnations of serial and mass killers seemed to be among us everywhere, and we were no longer safe. The newspapers, television, magazines, books, films, and the Internet all dwelt in frenzied detail on these "new" killers while, as always, providing no context for understanding the phenomenon. To compound matters, the hysteria was legitimized by a U.S. Department of Justice proclamation that there were as many as one hundred multiple murderers killing in America at any given time, stealing the lives of thousands each year.

It was as if a bloodthirsty race of space aliens had come to live among and prey upon us. The intensely publicized cross-country rampages of kidnapping and sexual murder perpetrated by Ted Bundy on young university women (or believed to have been committed by Henry Lee Lucas), or by the lesbian killer Aileen Wuornos as she prowled the highways of Florida, or by James Huberty's murderous siege of the McDonald's restaurant in San Ysidro, all seemed a declaration that what had in the past been a rare and isolated event was now the norm. We lived in an ugly new moonscape in which cold and remorseless killers stalked the land, invaded our homes, and murdered our loved ones.

To make the killers even more memorably frightening, the media, police and public together often gave them nicknames. To Jack the Ripper, the Zodiac Killer, the Boston Strangler, and the Moors Murderers we now added the Nightstalker, the Green River Killer, the Hollywood Freeway Killer, the Son of Sam, the Vampire Killer, the Yorkshire Ripper, the Hillside Strangler, and the Singing Strangler, to name but a few. Thus the names sensationalized the unthinkable and contributed to the emerging national panic about crime—an anxiety that would be skillfully manipulated by both radical special interest groups and conservative "law and order" politicians.

Yet these claims of a new kind of menace were misleading. Far from being a new phenomenon, multiple murder had been with us for centuries; and far from suddenly and exponentially increasing, there had been a modest but consistent increase in rates throughout the twentieth century. But all was now brought to life by officialdom, television, and film.

Within a few years, the Department of Justice responded to criticism and renounced the inflammatory claims (for which there had been no evidence); but for many years gullible scholars, social activists, and popular writers continued to deploy these figures, finding that these inflated rates bolstered their political case. Politics makes strange bedfellows: In this instance, police, radical feminists, black activists, and conservative political and religious fundamentalist groups all found themselves using the same wildly distorted claims to justify their political arguments and make their cases for greater power and funding.

I first embarked upon this awful journey into the dead souls of modern multiple murderers because I was unable to understand the motivations that drove these multiple murderers or the satisfactions they seemed to derive from their killings. But after years of total immersion in the killers' diaries, confessions, psychiatric interviews, statements to the press, videotapes, and photographs, I see the cultural origins of their motives as obvious and their deformed gratifications as intense. The uncomfortable conclusion reached in this book is that there will be many more such killers before this epoch in the social history of our civilization draws to a close.

Multiple murderers may in fact be statistically rare, responsible for approximately one percent of all murders, but I shall try to show that the killers are not mere freaks. Rather, they can only be fully understood as representing the logical extension of many of the central "masculine" themes in their culture—of worldly ambition, of success and failure, and of "manly" avenging violence. Although they take several forms—the *serial killer* whose murders provide both revenge and a lifelong celebrity career; and the *mass killer* who often no longer wishes to live and whose murders constitute his suicide note—they can only be accurately and objectively perceived as the prime embodiment of deforming aspects of their civilization, not mere drooling derangement.

Still, it *seemed* at the time that the 1980s were years of unprecedented growth, experimentation, and innovation among multiple murderers, years in which all previous "records" were broken and sacrosanct social barriers were pierced. In 1984 alone, a fortyish drifter named *Henry Lee Lucas* appeared on national television and terrified the nation with his bogus attention-seeking confessions in which he claimed to have tortured and murdered hundreds of women, a number far in excess of any previous claimant's. In the end it mattered little that most of his claims came from his twisted imagination, not reality, because his impact on the nation was so profound: He perfectly fit the temper of his times. His claims were so sensational that he polevaulted into national television shows and intimate interviews with great stars, yielding him great infamy. It seems likely that in fact he killed "only" three—his mother, his girlfriend, and his landlady—but his convincing and widely-disseminated lies were what mattered. Lucas lived with his fifteen-year-old common-law wife in a trailer parked in The House of Prayer For All People campground, a former chicken farm operated as a Pentecostal retreat in a small town in Texas.

He was brought to the attention of the police when he was suspected of murdering an elderly local woman who had befriended him. Jailed on little more than suspicion, he passed a note to a deputy claiming that "I have done something terrible, and I want to talk to sheriff." It was only then that inquisitive police began the lengthy interrogations and checking of his claims (at first sensationally confirming them and capturing a worldwide audience, before realizing later that they had been duped). Lucas outlined his fiction to police, spinning an unrivaled tale of rape, torture, dismemberment and murder, while conceding only that "I know it ain't normal for a person to go out and kill a girl just to have sex with her."

The thirteenth child of a prostitute mother, Lucas began his criminal career in 1960 when, at the age of twenty-three, he stabbed his mother to death in her bed. He said he spent the following fifteen years in prisons and mental hospitals in Michigan without obtaining any relief from his homicidal "needs." "I have been to the Ionia State Hospital for the Criminally Insane in Michigan," he told a Texas judge. "I have been to a mental hospital in Princeton, West Virginia. And I tell them my problems, and they don't want to do nothing about it, but there is a hundred, oh, about a hundred women out there that says different." He claimed that he had been released over his protestations: "I told them before I ever left prison that I was going to commit crimes, told them the type of crimes I was going to commit, and they wouldn't believe it. They said I was going regardless of whether I liked it or not. And the day I got out of jail is the day I started killing." He said he killed two women that day.[1]

"I was death on women," he told a television reporter and a credulous world. "I didn't feel they need to exist. I hated them, and I wanted to destroy every one I could find. I was doing a good job of it. I've got [killed] 360 people, I've got 36 states, in three different countries. [Later, when he was losing the attention of the media, Lucas claimed he had killed 600.] My victims never knew what was going to happen to them. I've had shootings, knifings, strangulations, beatings, and I've participated in actual crucifixions of humans. All across the country, there's people just like me who set out to destroy human life." For eight years, he said, he had crossed the continent, looking for women alone and defenseless—hitchhikers, runaways, women whose cars had broken down on lonely roads. He even explained his behavior in intellectual constructs borrowed from his culture, which is to say in terms of his abused childhood. "That's the way I grew up when I was a child—watching my mom have sexual acts. She wouldn't go into different rooms, she'd make sure I was in the room before she started anything, and she would do it deliberately to make me watch her, you know. I got so I hated it. I'd even leave the house and go out and hide in the woods and wouldn't even go home. And when I'd go home, I'd get beat for not coming home. I don't blame Mom for what she done, I don't blame her for that. It's the idea of the way she done it. I don't think any child out there should be brought up in that type of environment. In the past, I've hated it. It's just inside hate, and I can't get away from it." Lucas's fanciful tales had captured the culture.[2]

Nineteen eighty-four was also the year in which genuine "records" were broken and new depths plumbed. The then-highest total of victims in a mass murder (killing in one explosive burst) occurred when *James Oliver Huberty* burst into a McDonald's restaurant in San Ysidro, California, and began to shoot. During the course of an eighty-two-minute siege he walked through the restaurant and fired some 245 shots at terrified and dying customers, killing twenty-one and wounding nineteen more before a police bullet finally struck him in the chest and killed him. Huberty was no homeless and uneducated drifter. It is true that he had come from a "broken home" and that his only friend during his lonely childhood had been his dog, but such minor anguish has been the lot of millions. His mother, who abandoned her son and his only sister when they were very young, could only say that "I knew he needed help."[3]

The adult Huberty was married and had two daughters. Reportedly, he was a graduate in sociology from a small Quaker college in Ohio and he owned his own home, which is to say that he possessed some of the exterior hallmarks of the stable family man. Nevertheless, he lost his job as a welder when the plant closed, and he never practiced embalming, for which he had received a license in 1965 from the Pittsburgh Institute of Mortuary Science. According to one news magazine, many of his friends thought he was a communist when he blamed the capitalist system for the closure of his plant. However, his wife said, "If anything, he was a Nazi." Huberty decided to move west and start a new life, but he lost a great deal of money on the sale of his home. Then, inexplicably, he moved to the Mexican border town of Tijuana where, unable to speak the language and feeling (according to his wife) "hopeless, lost and rejected," his hatred of the rejecting Hispanics began to grow. He then moved back to the U.S., settling in San Ysidro within sight of a McDonald's restaurant much frequented by young Hispanics. He could find work only as a part-time security guard but was laid off within a few weeks.[4]

In what seems to have been a last attempt to salvage what remained of his life, he tried to obtain an appointment at a mental health clinic but was unable to obtain one in the understaffed institution. On the day of the killings he visited the San Diego Zoo with his family. Staring at the caged animals, perhaps feeling not unlike them, Huberty told his wife, "Society's had their chance!" He drove his family to their home and, announcing that "I'm going hunting . . . hunting humans," he armed himself and drove to the nearby McDonald's in his battered Mercury.

The reaction of the state following the massacre was almost as tragic and misguided as the event itself. If television coverage can be taken as meaningful (and it is surely *the* prime cultural disseminator in modern America), the state and its agencies intervened only to express bewilderment regarding the killer's motive, and to offer the services of therapists who would help victims (present and future) to "adjust" to the shock of such tragedies. The state thus moved to avoid the question: Are such killings truly inevitable? Why did Huberty choose to kill and die among the many Hispanic customers of that restaurant? Was there in fact any connection between his precipitous decline in the social hierarchy and his assault on the newly successful, the struggling Hispanics who moved too freely in "his" white, middle-class restaurant? Was there deep social meaning to this act, or only bizarre psychopathology? In the immediate aftermath of the killings, scientists were dispatched to find answers to the Huberty case. Typically, however, they were instructed to look in the wrong direction and told to dissect his brain to search for mysterious "lesions" among its folds rather than analyzing the social meaning of his acts.

If others raised the murderous ante of lives destroyed and minds and bodies maimed, *Christopher Wilder* raised the social ante, for he was among the first to prey exclusively on upper-middle-class and upper-class targets. Wilder's case is especially fascinating, although it must remain an enigma since he was killed during his capture and he left nothing behind to explain himself—except his murders. Yet he was no enraged lumpen proletarian taking out his rage upon the class that suppressed him; nor was he a dispossessed petit bourgeois like Huberty, protesting his disenfranchisement. Born to reputedly wealthy Australian parents, Wilder emigrated to the United States in 1970 and established his own moderately successful contracting business. He owned Florida real estate worth at least a half million dollars, skied in chic resorts, raced cars, and kept a luxury home—according to many reports. Yet there are suggestive contradictions in his life. His business partner has disputed the authenticity of his wealth, claiming that Wilder's diamond rings were fakes, his Porsche seventeen years old, and his home a "junk-heap" that he repaired with the construction company's left-over materials. His partner insisted that Wilder was "just an easy-going quiet guy who watches a lot of TV because he has nothing else to do." As the contradictions multiplied during the investigation, Wilder was found to be an animal lover: this rapist, torturer, and murderer had made donations to Save The Whales and the Seal Rescue Fund. Moreover, he always braked when turtles crossed the road. Nevertheless, after an international career in sexual assault (for which he went virtually unpunished) this easygoing watcher of television, this lover of whales, seals, and turtles, abducted eleven beautiful and elegant women, only three of whom survived the ordeal. Using a

standard ruse, he approached young women, some of whom were
aspiring models, and offered them careers in modeling. If they refused
to accompany him "for photographs," he would abduct them by force
and subject them to electric shocks and other tortures before killing
them. Not unlike Theodore Bundy, whom we examine in great detail
later in this book, Wilder began his cross-country rampage shortly
after a beautiful young woman, a teacher of mentally disturbed children and herself a member of an established Florida family, refused his
offer of marriage. The authorities were bewildered by the entire case,
but a racing partner of Wilder's put the critical question when he
insisted there was no obvious logic to Wilder's sex crimes: "If you
want to act out a pornographic scene, you just go out and hire a bunch
of hookers. He had no reason to subject himself [or, presumably, his
victims] to this." Precisely. Why should Wilder indulge in such life-
destroying activities when, if his motivation was only sexual, he could
have safely satisfied it on a commercial basis? This book is an attempt
to answer that coarse and inelegant question in full and to follow its
ramifications wherever they might lead us. We must study them well,
for there will be many more such killers—and it should be clearly
understood that their intent is to steal our daughters and sons and to
snuff out their lives.[5]

The D.C. Snipers

The Next Generation

> "I like killing people because it is so much fun."
> ... *attributed to Lee Boyd Malvo*

The world was riveted by their murder spree in October 2002, in the
course of which they shot and killed ten people and wounded three
more in the Washington, D.C., area alone. They seemed to be invisible
and appeared out of nowhere, then killed and disappeared as if by

magic. All the experts had been flummoxed, mystified by the killers' identities and motives: Few had guessed there were two snipers, and fewer still had thought they might be anything other than the usual angry white males. Yet the dominant male suspect in the killing team was a raging African-American from the slums of Baton Rouge, a decorated veteran from the Gulf War who had converted to Islam; and his enthusiastic accomplice was allegedly an insecure West Indian boy desperate for a father.

They seem to have thought of themselves as heroic rebels striking a blow against the oppressive and racist white state, and there seemed a certain logic in the spawn of the slums of Baton Rouge and Kingston striking at the heart of middle-class America. Lofty yet entirely bogus political motives are a common self-serving justification among these remorseless killers who—just like the savage *Columbine* school killers—prey on the innocent while venting their anger and indulging their own exalted sense of superiority. Similar illusions accompanied black activist Mark Essex when he shot a honeymooning couple as an alleged blow against the racist state; when DeSalvo killed "to put something over on high class people"; when Starkweather murdered to erase his position at what he thought was the bottom of society, collecting other people's garbage; and when both Bundy and Kemper killed young women students to get even with the upper class and its "brats" and to make their "little social statement." But the fact of the matter appears to be that they were merely acting out their rage as part of a clumsily designed terrorist campaign to extort ten million dollars from the American taxpayer.

If Muhammad and Malvo were an unlikely pair, their motives seemed more focused. There had been some 500 sniper attacks in the U.S. between 1976 and 2000, and the motives for them had typically seemed vague, even trivial. Thomas Dillon, for example, killed five hunters and fishermen in Ohio between 1989 and 1992, his only apparent motive an adolescent fantasy in which he would escape from his dull life as a draftsman for the water department in Canton, Ohio, to fulfill a dream he had had since high school—to kill someone. Personal and subpolitical protests, often over minor provocations and slights, are not just confined to the juvenile murderers who terrorized Columbine High School.

The D.C. Snipers seemed indifferent to the race of their victims, but most serial killers (like most killers in general) prey upon their own race, like *Wayne Williams*, the black disc jockey in Atlanta who murdered black children, or Ted Bundy, who murdered white women. Although Malvo seems to have been abandoned by his parents for much of his life, the role of child abuse in the creation of serial killers remains unclear: Many killers have relatively normal childhoods, and many who were abused as children go on to lead normal lives. Regardless, most criminologists would agree that a sexualized lust for revenge, power, and control is the most common motive for serial killings; although criminologist Eric Hickey thought the snipers' killings were also a kind of communiqué to American society: "It wasn't the process of killing so much, it was about eliciting a response from the community."

In fact, the D.C. Snipers appear to have been motivated by a vague hostility toward America and a strong desire for extortion. Investigators believe that the motive for the shootings was a bizarre plan to terrorize the region in order to intimidate the government into giving them $10 million to stop the shootings. Whatever their motives, they began shooting long before they arrived in Washington, D.C.: In all, they would be suspects in twenty-one shootings, including thirteen deaths, in Alabama, Georgia, Louisiana, Maryland, Virginia, Washington state, and the District of Columbia.

The Killing Time

> "Your children are not safe anywhere at any time."
> *Note left by sniper*

1. February 16, 2002, Tacoma, Washington: The Beginning. Isa Nichols, a former employee of Muhammad, had backed Muhammad's ex-wife in a bitter custody dispute over the couple's three children.

When Isa's niece opened the door, she was shot to death in what now appears to have been a case of mistaken identity.

2. Early May, 2002, Tacoma, Washington: Racist Terrorism. Ballistic evidence suggests that Muhammad and Malvo were responsible for the drive-by shooting in which a .44 Magnum revolver was fired twice into a Tacoma synagogue. There were no casualties.

3. September 21, 2002, Montgomery, Alabama: Robbery and Murder. Claudine Parker, 52, was killed and Kellie D. Adams, 24, shot through the head during a bungled robbery at the ABC Beverages store. The attackers were interrupted while rifling through the purse of one of the victims and fled, but a fingerprint left at the liquor store would later—*much later*—be matched with Malvo. Similarly, ballistics tests would tie the Bushmaster .223 rifle to many of the shootings.

4. September 23, 2002, Baton Rouge, Louisiana: Robbery and Murder. Hong Im Ballenger, 45, a beauty supply shopkeeper, was shot in the head as she walked to her car. The attackers escaped with her purse, paycheck, and cell phone. Ballenger had been afraid of being robbed and habitually carried pepper spray in her pocket but had no chance to use it.

5. October 2, 2002, Aspen Hill, Maryland: Vandalism. No one was hurt when a window was shot out of a crafts store with a .223 rifle, narrowly missing a child at play.

6. October 2, 2002, Wheaton, Maryland: Murder. Less than an hour later, at 6:04 P.M., James D. Martin, 55, was shot dead in a grocery store parking lot.

7. October 3, 2002, White Flint, Maryland. Early in the morning, James L. "Sonny" Buchanan, 39, was shot dead while cutting grass at an automobile dealership. Malvo is reported to have laughed when he recalled this killing: The mower continued to move while its operator lay dying.

8. October 3, 2002, Rockville, Maryland. A few minutes later, taxi driver Prem Kumar Walekar, 54, was shot dead at a gas station.

9. October 3, 2002, Silver Spring, Maryland. Twenty-five minutes elapsed before Sarah Ramos, 34, was killed outside a post office.

10. October 3, 2002, Kensington, Maryland. A little more than one hour later, Lori Ann Lewis-Rivera, 25, became the next target of opportunity for the snipers. She was shot dead as she vacuumed her van at a gas station.

11. October 3, 2002, Washington, D.C. That evening, Pascal Charlot, 72, was murdered while standing on a Washington street.

12. October 4, 2002, Fredericksburg, Virginia. In mid-afternoon, a 43-year-old woman was shot in the back and wounded in a crafts store parking lot.

13. October 7, 2002, Bowie, Maryland. In the early morning, a 13-year-old boy was shot and wounded as he was dropped off at school. Malvo allegedly told a prison guard it had to be done "to make Chief Moose upset, to make him emotional so he wouldn't think straight, and it worked!"

14. October 9, 2002, Manassas, Virginia. In the early morning, Dean Harold Meyers, 53, was shot dead at a gas station.

15. October 11, 2002, Fredericksburg, Virginia. In the early morning, Kenneth H. Bridges, 53, was shot dead at a gas station.

16. October 14, 2002, Falls Church, Virginia. Linda Franklin, 47, an analyst for the FBI, was shot and killed at a home improvement store. The shooting panicked the other shoppers: "Screaming, yelling, people started running," said one bystander. Malvo is reported to have laughed when recalling this killing.

17. October 19, 2002, Ashland, Virginia. In the early evening, a 37-year-old man was shot and wounded outside a steakhouse. The man collapsed, telling his wife, "I've been shot." This time the killer left a message at the scene, suppressed by the police: The message spelled out their demands and added, "Your children are not safe anywhere at any time." The killer also telephoned two priests, one in Bellingham, Washington, and the other in Ashland, Virginia, but abruptly ended the conversations when told the priests were not available. The killers were now trying to talk to their public, as well as negotiate their demands with the authorities.

18. October 22, 2002, Aspen Hill, Maryland: The Last Victim.

Conrad Johnson, a 35-year-old bus driver, was shot and fatally wounded while standing on the steps of the bus. According to reports in the British press, the snipers left a note at the scene of the bus driver's shooting: "For you, Mr. police, call me God. Do not release to the press. Can you hear us now! Do not play these childish games with us. You know our demands."

During this period, Chief of Police Charles Moose engaged in cryptic one-way televised conversations with the snipers, who contacted him by telephone and by notes. For several days, he stated on television: "To the person who left us a message at the Ponderosa last night: You gave us a telephone number. We do want to talk to you. Call us at the number you provided. Thank you." Later, he announced, "The message that needs to be delivered is that we are going to respond to a message that we have received. We are preparing our response at this time." Soon Moose was asking them to call back: "The person you called could not hear everything you said. The audio was unclear and we want to get it right. Call us back so that we can clearly understand." Still later, urging further dialogue with the snipers, Moose said: "It is important that we do this without anyone else getting hurt. We have researched the options you stated and found that it is not possible electronically to comply in the manner that you requested. However, we remain open and ready to talk to you about the options you have mentioned," and Moose offered to set up a secure method for them to communicate. "You indicated that this is about more than violence. . . . We understand that you communicated with us by calling several different locations. Our inability to talk has been a concern to us, as it has been for you. You have indicated that you want us to do and say certain things. You've asked us to say, 'We have caught the sniper like a duck in a noose.' We understand that hearing us say this is important to you."

Fin. October 24, Meyersville, Maryland. Police arrest Muhammad and Malvo asleep in their car at a rest stop. Police then revealed the method the snipers had used to evade notice and capture: Their car's back seat and trunk had been hollowed out to provide a shooting platform for a prone gunman firing through a hole in the trunk. Once the muffled shot was made, the car could easily pull undetected into traffic.

A senior law enforcement official noted that Muhammad had in the past made "angry statements about the United States" and expressed sympathy for the 9/11 hijackers, making comments like, "The United States had it coming to them."

The Unlikely Pair

The Obedient Servant: Lee Boyd Malvo (aka John Lee Malvo)

Washington Post reporters Serge F. Kovaleski and Mary Beth Sheridan noted that Malvo was born in 1985 in Kingston, Jamaica's violent working-class slum, where entire families live on the streets in cardboard boxes. The rootless young man had later attended school in the poverty-stricken mountains of Jamaica. By the time he was fourteen, Malvo was seen by his school vice-principal as a charming and entertaining but insecure youngster "who had been repeatedly uprooted as his mother changed jobs" and often was deposited for extended periods with people he hardly knew—strangers, friends, or relatives. When the teacher asked Malvo's mother why she continually relocated her fatherless child, the mother assured her that they would soon be moving together to a better life. But less than three years later, Malvo had become a silent and brooding young man, apparently roaming the Washington, D.C., Beltway with a sniper rifle, searching for targets of opportunity.

Despite dozens of interviews with Malvo's associates in Jamaica, Antigua, and the United States, Kovaleski and Sheridan were unable to establish to their own satisfaction how a "bright and bubbly youngster became a sullen and submissive drifter" or whether his subservience to the commands of his "dad," John Muhammad, was "respect more than fear." Yet the former seemed rather more likely since, as the vice-principal had seen so clearly: "Any child exposed to that kind of instability would crave security and acceptance: He wanted a positive man," and that is precisely what he was to find in John Muhammad.

In Jamaica, the infant Malvo had first lived with his father, Leslie Malvo, a mason, and his mother, Una, a seamstress; but within a few years the elder Malvo left to work in the Cayman Islands. Upon returning two years later, he found that his wife and son had gone, and the mother had made no efforts to arrange further contact. She continued her pattern of frequent movement among the Caribbean islands, only occasionally accompanied by her child. When Malvo was eight or nine, he was left with his mother's sister in Jamaica for a few years; the young Malvo was remembered as a studious, pious, and obedient little boy with a passion for reading. One friend said that Malvo "was all about God and his schoolwork: he wanted to have a good career and help his family." He was eager to please, staying behind to help his teachers after classes—so much so that his former vice-principal thought that "I can see people manipulating him."

Then in July of 1999, Malvo flew to Antigua to join his mother, earning money by selling roadside chicken and drinks, yet excelling in school at the same time. Ten months later, Muhammad arrived in Antigua and began to make a living selling fraudulent U.S. travel documents; not long after that, Malvo's mother returned to Jamaica and left him on his own in Antigua. But his rent was unpaid, and Malvo soon moved in with John Muhammad and his three children. The unholy relationship quickly solidified between the insecure young man searching for a solid father figure and the former Desert Storm soldier. Following in his hero's footsteps, Malvo converted to Islam by the spring of 2001; he began bringing his Koran to school and reciting Islamic scripture. His grades began to fall.

Muhammad told the school that he was now Malvo's guardian. Carrying false identification papers in May of 2001, the two of them flew to Fort Myers, Florida, to be temporarily reunited with Malvo's mother, who was working at a restaurant there. But within months, Malvo and Muhammad were living in a shelter for the homeless in Bellingham, Washington. The pair presented themselves to everyone as father and son, although Malvo's mother made a fruitless journey by bus to Bellingham to try to take her son away from Muhammad. "The thing that stood out to us was that [Malvo] was a follower of John's, that his purpose was to please John and always be in John's favor and do whatever John wanted him to do," the director of the shelter said. Those who watched him thought Malvo was being "trained" rather than raised, on a strict regimen of religion, exercise, and nutrition.

At school in Bellingham, Malvo was a quiet young man who kept to himself; but he had no school transcripts, a fact that did not pass unnoticed by his counselors. "As far as anyone could tell," said a Bellingham police officer, "the kid never existed on paper," although his name appeared in the high school yearbook with the caption, "Photo unavailable." "Nobody paid much attention to him," said the mother of one his fellow students. However, he had previously been fingerprinted by Bellingham police following a domestic abuse case when he had struck his mother.

Just after his seventeenth birthday, not long after what appears to have been a murder in Bellingham, the penniless pair left Washington state on a meandering journey through the southern and eastern United States. Arriving in Baton Rouge, Lousiana, in the summer of 2002, David Halbfinger and Sarah Kershaw noted in the *New York Times*, the pair stayed with a cousin of Muhammad's. While they appeared to be destitute, Muhammad told his cousin that "he was on a secret government mission to track down stolen Army explosives; and he introduced Lee Malvo to her as a 'highly trained' member of his undercover team," calling him by a nickname, "Sniper." That night, Muhammad gestured at Malvo and told his cousin: "He's highly trained. He works with us. He's not my son—I just pass him off as my son."

The Stern Master: John Allen Muhammad (a.k.a. John Allen Williams)
    New York Times reporters Blaine Harden and Tim Golden noted that Muhammad "was known to friends for his crushing handshake, his deft touch in repairing fast cars—and his temper." He had grown up in the teeming black slums of Baton Rouge in the poor neighborhood known as The Avenues. His cousin recalled a conversation with Muhammad shortly before his killing spree: Pretending to be a

government agent, Muhammad had asked his cousin where he could find a "high-crime drug area." She thought it an odd question. "I told him, 'You grew up in one.'"

In 1981, a few years after his graduation from high school, Muhammad had joined the Louisiana National Guard and married his high school sweetheart, Carol Kaglear, with whom he had one son. "He was a good, caring man," another cousin remembered. "He coached a football team and liked kids. He was well-mannered and friendly. Real clean cut." But others saw a different Muhammad: A classmate described him as "a loner" with a nasty temper. "He was one of the quiet ones, [but] if you got him mad, you got him up." He was a problem in the National Guard, being disciplined for failing to appear for duty and for striking a non-commissioned officer—for which he was demoted from sergeant and sentenced to seven days in military prison.

Not all the transforming details of his life are known, but in November of 1985 he left his wife and son, converted to Islam, and joined the army. After conversion, his ex-wife complained that he would still issue commands on what to feed their child: "I told him as long as he lived with me, it was up to me." Yet he seemed to thrive in the army: He trained primarily as a combat engineer, serving at Fort Lewis in Washington state, in Germany, and at Ford Ord, California. He was described by military officials as a "competent but not extraordinary soldier" who had won his marksmanship badge for the use of the M-16. In 1988 he remarried and had a son and two daughters.

He left the army in 1994 but remained in Tacoma and joined the National Guard. He started an automotive repair business and opened a martial arts school; but the mechanic service was "erratic" and the martial arts studio collapsed in a financial dispute with his partner. Muhammad "was manipulative and would do anything to get his way," the former partner recalled. He was also fighting with his first wife over custody of their son, then twelve: After visiting his father for the summer, the boy converted to Islam and was not returned to his mother until she had obtained a court order.

Although Muhammad attended a mosque in Seattle, the only thing his friends at the time remember truly exciting him was when he worked in security for the "Million Man March" for Louis Farrakhan, leader of the Nation of Islam. "When he came back," a friend told the reporters, "he told me that it was a great experience and he really enjoyed the camaraderie and the feeling and all that stuff." But by that time, his second marriage was falling apart, and his wife was granted a restraining order against him for his alleged abuse of the children. She had become terrified of him. "He was a demolitions expert in military," she wrote to the court. "He is behaving very irrational. Whenever he does talk with me he always says that [he] is going to destroy my life." A federal weapons charge filed against him at the time stated that he had threatened his wife and children.

Soon after, Muhammad abducted the three children and relocated briefly to Prince George's County, Maryland, before moving to the Caribbean Island of Antigua with the children. Writing in the *New York Times*, David Gonzalez said Muhammad was well known in St. John's, Antigua, usually accompanied by his three children. Not long after, they were joined by Malvo. Muhammad seems to have returned to the United States frequently, returning to the island with easily shoplifted items that local people had requested—discs, batteries, medicines, power tools, cameras. He also set up a thriving business helping West Indians get bogus Antiguan passports and fake American birth certificates, and he helped Malvo's mother get the documentation to enter the U.S. Always, he tried to be a role model, one young man he'd befriended recalled: "He always talked to me about keeping my body fit. He said a fit body develops a good mind. He mainly helped me with my self-esteem. He told me to stay in school and finish my education so I could reach my dreams in life."

Malvo and Muhammad returned to the U.S. and began their peripatetic life after a brief period in Tacoma, where Malvo was taught to shoot the M-16 clone, the Bushmaster .223 semi-automatic rifle. Their relationship appeared to be that of father and son. Writing in the *New York Times*, Andrew Jacobs noted that they always carried with them their guide to life, Daniel Reid's *The Tao of Health, Sex and Longevity*, an introduction to Taoist philosophy which emphasized nutrition, breathing, "sex therapy" and herbal aphrodisiacs. Armed spiritually and literally, they were ready for their mission.

The Aftermath

Muhammad was silent in the months after his capture, although at first, a law enforcement official told CBS News correspondent Bob Orr, it looked as if Muhammad, not Malvo, would be the one to confess. "It looked like Muhammad was ready to share everything, and these guys were going to get a confession." But then everything reversed itself. Malvo allegedly "made some nonverbal admissions," and then under skillful interrogation he began to speak openly to officials. At once, according to reports in the Associated Press, he implicated Muhammad in the shootings, describing them as equal partners—Muhammad had acted as a spotter while Malvo had done the actual shooting, although either of them had the right to call off a shot. Malvo allegedly admitted to many of the shootings in detail and expressed no remorse. He is alleged to have told a prison guard how he customarily fasted before "killing people" on his "missions," because "if you don't eat, you get more oxygen to your brain."

On November 16, 2002, in an act not likely to yield widespread public sympathy, Malvo's defense attorneys lodged complaints that Malvo was "under constant scrutiny and being denied basic rights" in prison, adding that "his right to privacy was being infringed by the guards, his mattress was too thin, he had been denied reading material, his cell lights glared 24 hours a day and he was being denied vegetarian meals." "This is about the right to human dignity," one of his lawyers told the court.

During the hearing to decide whether Malvo should face the death penalty, he was told of the pain he had caused his victims and their loved ones. Malvo stared expressionlessly, sitting with his chin on his hand, as William Franklin told of his wife being shot and killed. Yet what could be expected from such a rootless young man, bonded only to the raging Muhammad? Malvo was briefly given access to magazines and books and a copy of the Koran, but prison deputies found the word "Muhammad" written on Malvo's cell floor and other scrawls on his shoes. Malvo was charged with destroying county property and lost his access to all non-religious and non-legal reading materials. On February 24, 2003, when a female deputy walked past Malvo's cell, she heard him laugh and say, "I would like to cut her throat." Until these incidents, jail officials had considered Malvo a "model inmate."[6]

Insanity and Multiple Murder

Are such multiple murderers merely "insane"? Can such bizarre behavior be dismissed as simple psychiatric or genetic freakishness? There is an ancient chord in our civilization which insists that such terrible acts be interpreted in terms of possession by evil spirits or by witchcraft (an explanation which reverberates today in the media's frequent, and inaccurate, speculation that occultism is a motive for these crimes). A more modern variation of this theme similarly dismisses the acts with notions of "possession" by mental disease. It would be most comforting if we could continue to accept such explanations, for they satisfyingly banish guilt beyond our responsibility. Yet to do so would beg the question—why does modern America produce so many more of these "freaks" than any other industrial nation? Moreover, if the killers are merely insane, why do they in fact so rarely display the cluster of readily identifiable clinical symptoms (including disorders of thought and affect) which psychiatrists agree mark mental illness? In one important sense, of course, any person who murders another human being has abandoned all reason and sanity; yet such a position is essentially *moral*, not scientific, and does not help us in an objective attempt to understand the cause and meaning of such a phenomenon.

How can we begin to explain these modern multiple murderers who, whether in a campaign lasting many months or in one that can be measured in minutes, launch premeditated assaults upon a single social category (not mere "random" targets, as is so often believed)? The killers appear to defy the social laws by coming not just from the bottom classes, for they are often upper working class or lower middle class in their origins. Perhaps they are victims—as courtroom psychiatry has argued so powerfully—of obscure mental disorders? Perhaps they are, but if so, why should there be so many more victims of this particular type of mental disease in the last quarter of the twentieth and early years of the twenty-first centuries? Is there something in our modern toilet-training practices, or some strange change in our biochemistry, which is producing so much of this disorder? Perhaps not, for the whole notion of mental disease as defined by modern psychiatry (which teaches that mental illness is a disease much like, say, tuberculosis) becomes tenuous when subjected to the anthropological, cross-cultural evidence. The apparently immutable mental diseases of schizophrenia, manic depression, and so on often disappear or take quite different forms in other cultures. Thus a troubled person's leave-taking from conventional reality (which we call "psychosis") may take a form, violent or otherwise, that the culture prescribes. For example, according to historical ethnological records, madness could take the form of Windigo Psychosis—a belief in Ojibwa traditional culture that persons could be possessed by spirits and that they would then have an uncontrollable desire to eat human flesh. Believing what they were taught, the victims are reported to have killed humans, sometimes their own families, and devoured their flesh. Similarly, in the pressure cooker of Inuit life, the madness sometimes took a special northern form known as Arctic Hysteria, in which the victims would rip off their clothing and, insensible to danger, race out onto the ice floes.

In his splendid but little-known study of a schizophrenic, *Oscar*, Peter J. Wilson concludes that madness is the individual's response to the obliteration of his identity by others. "The only recourse available to those who are so overwhelmed is to banish such tyranny from their lives—to a hospital, an asylum, any ship of fools." Thus madness can be a creative and self-protecting act, and a program of the culture—for the South American "primitives," the *Yanomamo*, do not experience

Arctic Hysteria, and Americans do not encounter Windigo Psychosis. In our own society, an increasing number of people seem to kill for the pleasure it gives them. Are they merely insane, or are they acting out some coded social message? The lesson here is that the psychiatric analogy is an imperfect one: Madness is not exactly like cancer or any other physical ailment. Rather, it can usefully be seen as a culturally programmed dialogue. It should not therefore be surprising that no matter how hard psychiatrists have searched, they have been unable to discover much mental disease among our captured multiple murderers (except in the unthinkable nature of their acts). Therein lies the special horror, for the killers are apparently "normal," excepting only their utter lack of remorse and human feeling for others (a profound character flaw nowadays glossed as "psychopathy"); and they kill without mercy—they kill to make a statement.

If multiple murderers cannot be dismissed as biological or psychological freaks, neither can they be regarded simply as manifestations of America's astonishingly high homicide rate (the highest by far in the developed Western industrial world). When the U.S. general homicide rate finally began to fall in the mid-1990s, there was no accompanying collapse in multiple murder rates—nor an increase when the homicide rate began a faltering resurgence in the early years of the new century. Thus a rise or fall in the overall homicide rate is *not necessarily* related to similar fluctuations in the multiple murder rate. Similarly, in Canada, where the overall homicide rate has been declining for a quarter of a century, the multiple murder rate seems relatively stable (if periodically inflated by sensational killings). More interestingly, nations such as Britain or Germany, which have very low overall homicide rates, appear to produce rather more multiple murderers than we might expect, while nations such as Switzerland have both low overall homicide and multiple murder rates.

The point should be clear: These are different phenomena. The multiple murderer, who sacrifices his own life and that of the innocent to make an art form out of killing strangers, is qualitatively a very different man from the most common form of murderer—the slum husband who, harassed by poverty or humiliation, beats his neighbor or lover to death in some drunken brawl. A sophisticated quantitative debate still rages in social science over whether the ultimate cause of homicide lies in absolute poverty, relative inequality, or in regional subculture; but clearly all three embrace their share of truth, for all deprivation provokes frustration, and culture is ever the programmed maze instructing individuals how best to display their emotions.

In any case, the multiple murderer is quite a different person: Most often on the margins of the working or lower middle classes, he is usually a profoundly conservative figure who comes to feel excluded from the class or social group he so devoutly wishes to join. In an extended campaign of vengeance, he murders innocent strangers, taking targets of opportunity from the social type (in their behavior, their appearance, or their location) that he feels has rejected or excluded him.

With varying degrees of explicitness, multiple murderers see themselves as soldiers on a mission. Small wonder then that they feel neither remorse for their victims nor regret for launching their bloody crusades. Moreover, the public treats them as major celebrities, following their every deed. No one ever became famous by beating his wife to death in an alley, but virtually all our multiple murderers achieve true and lasting fame. For the remainder of their lives, they are the subjects of articles and books, radio and television shows, and Internet web sites; and they thus attain an immortality denied the "unenterprising" common man in our deformed civilization. During their celebrated trials, they may well be surrounded by admiring women who press their affections upon the killer, radiating admiration and even love as they do so. Sometimes, as with Theodore Bundy, a reverent member of the public will marry the killer during his trial— and even conceive his child during his incarceration. He will be besieged with letters and communications from special-interest groups who will see in him some weighty philosophical point or an opportunity to test their theories of rehabilitation. Tragically, the Son of Sam was not so very wrong when he thought the public was almost urging him on during his killing spree, for the media chronicled his every

deed in a state of mounting excitement. Should any killer fail to grasp
the cultural message that this is a certain route to celebrity and fulfillment, a brilliant popular song by The Police spells it out:

> Once that you've decided on a killing
> First you make a stone of your heart
> And if you find that your hands are still willing
> You can turn a murder into art
>
> Well if you have a taste for this experience
> You're flushed with your very first success
> Then you must try a twosome or a threesome
> Before your conscience bothers you much less
>
> Then you can join the ranks of the illustrious
> In history's great dark Hall of Fame
> All our greatest killers were industrious
> At least the ones that we all know by name.

Murder for Its Own Sake

It was never my intention in this book to study all forms of multiple
murder. A paucity of data made it difficult or impossible for me to
examine the so-called "Tylenol" murders, the many recent hospital
murders, the plunging of automobiles onto crowded sidewalks, or
even the common homosexual multiple murderers (who rarely leave
any confessions behind them). One can only speculate that they might
be similar to those studied here. Additionally, I rule out of our
province those who kill for *profit*, like Charles Sobhra who was implicated in the murder and robbery of dozens of tourists in Asian resorts.
This is merely one form of making a living, one in which the murder
is incidental to the goal. Those who practice this barbaric "profession" would undoubtedly follow another if they were offered more

money. We are concerned only with those who appear to kill *for its own sake*, those for whom killing alone is the apparent goal.

Neither are we studying the professional state-employed torturers and murderers who are essentially career bureaucrats, wreaking havoc on their fellows on behalf of the rulers of modern governments. They kill far more than those we study here, for these bureaucratic killers are *apparatchiks*, killing with the latest technology as part of their career strategies and primarily (or even entirely) for career advancement. Transfer them with a solid promotion to the Board of Weights & Measures and they would be just as happy, although some might miss the shuddering of their victims. These killers find their perfect embodiment in Adolf Eichmann, the efficient ruler of the Nazi death camp, but his emulators have appeared everywhere. Modern death squads pursue their terror on behalf of the ruling elites, and sometimes do so with the enthusiastic assistance of the general population, but they are not the individual entrepreneurs pursuing their private goals who are the objects of our study.

Perhaps the most successful government-sponsored mass-murder programs since the Second World War have been in Rwanda, where the Hutu-dominated government ordered its peoples to massacre the Tutsi minority; or in Indonesia, where right-wing Islamic fundamentalists annihilated the political left; and in Cambodia, where left-wing revolutionaries destroyed anyone not seen as an untainted candidate for the perfect socialist state. In Indonesia, where hundreds of thousands were murdered, the Islamic government's decision to eliminate the opposition communist party (PKI) began in 1965 with mass executions by government troops and then spread to a general slaughter of all party members and their families. Amnesty International's *Political Killings By Governments* records in its dry prose how in many regions "local army commanders loaded lorries with captured PKI members—their names checked off against hastily prepared lists—and drove them to isolated spots nearby for execution, usually by bullet or knife." Elsewhere in Indonesia, however, and spurred on by government approval, "most people were executed [by common citizens] with long sugar-cane knives and sickles and the slaughter often assumed a ritualistic and ceremonial character. In several places the killers held feasts with their bound victims present. After the meal each guest was invited to decapitate a prisoner."[8]

In Cambodia, the slaughter was conceived by the communist government as a means of stopping any potential counterrevolutionary activity. Only high-ranking officers were killed at first, but death was soon extended to anyone merely *suspected* of resistance to the new regime. One Khmer Rouge soldier who tired of the killing testified: "In 1975, we were made to change policy. The victory of the revolution had been too quick. If the population was not wiped out immediately, the revolution would be in danger because the republican forces, the forces of Sihanouk, the capitalist forces would unite against it. It was therefore necessary to eliminate all these forces and to spare only those of the Communist Party. It was necessary to eliminate not only the officers but also the common soldiers as well as their wives and children. This was based on revolutionary experience. In the past, Sihanouk had killed revolutionaries, but their wives, children and relatives had united against him and had joined us. That must not be repeated against us now. At the beginning of 1976, however, the families of common soldiers were also killed. One day at Choeung Prey, I cried for a whole day on seeing women and children killed. I could no longer raise my arms [to kill]. Comrade Saruoeun said to me: 'Get on with it.' I said: 'How can I? Who can kill women and children?' Three days later I was arrested."

But these wretched creatures with their extermination camps, all prisoners of their own systems and the empires that dehumanize and manipulate them, are not the stuff of this book.

The men (and, occasionally, the women) of whom I write seek neither profit nor bureaucratic advancement. On the contrary, they are what the Germans call the practitioners of *lustmord*, "joy-murderers" who act quite independently, killing simply because of the personal satisfaction they seem to derive from the act. However, I shall try to show that their killings are not just mere pleasure: They are also a kind of personal subpolitical and conservative protest, sometimes cloaked in a bogus political ideology, which nets the killers a substantial social profit of revenge, extortion, celebrity, identity and sexual relief. They conceive of the killings as a kind of mission, task, or crusade—sometimes only dimly perceived (as with DeSalvo and David Berkowitz), and sometimes expressed with great clarity (as with the D.C. Snipers, Essex, Panzram, and Starkweather). In either case it is the same phenomenon, a kind of *primitive rebellion against the social order* which has become an increasingly fashionable form of social "art."

If the murders can only be understood as personalized social protest, it must be emphasized that these killers are no radicals: They have enthusiastically embraced the established order only to discover that it does not offer them the place they demand or can endure. Their rebellion is a protest against their perceived exclusion from society, not an attempt to alter it as would befit the revolutionary identity so many of them claim. This fundamentally rebellious, not revolutionary, nature of their protest is undoubtedly why so few government and police resources are allocated to their capture (compared, say, to the huge police apparatus that monitors political dissidents), for they pose little threat to the established order—neither in their ideology nor in their acts. Thus in this book we discuss the D.C. Sniper extortionists, Huberty the "Nazi," Essex the racist, Kemper of the Junior Chamber of Commerce, Bundy the Young Republican, Berkowitz the avenging rebel, DeSalvo the social climber, and Starkweather who slaughtered those who had him assigned to the "bottom." These were no more "blows for the people" than they were the acting out of some dreaded mental disease. To the contrary, they were the revenge of those who had looked upon their own lives and pronounced them unendurable, then made the decision to exact a fearful revenge upon the innocent and in the process risk their own lives.

The killings are thus also a form of *suicide note* (literally so with many mass murderers, who expect to die before the day or week is out; metaphorically so for many serial murderers, who dedicate the remainder of their lives to their meaningless "cause"), in which the killer states clearly which social category has excluded him. Our task is to learn to read the note, to pore over the killings and the speeches of the killers, searching for meaning. We must not be content with superficial explanations that focus merely on personal and short-term satisfactions, however compelling they may appear to be, for they avoid coming to terms with the ultimate cause of these abominations. This warning is necessary, for even society's most perceptive spokesmen can fall into this error—as when the astute Judge Ronald George, who presided over the Hillside Strangler trials, neglected the role of society and culture in unconsciously "authorizing" violence when he otherwise correctly concluded that "Angelo Buono and Kenneth Bianchi terrorized this city for several months, haunting the community like the ultimate in evil spirits as they abducted children and young women, torturing, raping and sodomizing them, and finally depriving their families and friends of them forever . . . and all for what? The momentary sadistic thrill of enjoying a brief perverted sexual satisfaction, and venting their hatred of women." While this book must *not* be taken as a plea for the serious consideration of the killers' "philosophies," it does argue that if we are to understand the forces that create them, we must look beyond their vile pleasures to the source of their deformation.[9]

The Settling of Accounts

> "There comes a point when the only way you can make a statement is to pick up a gun."
>
> *Sara Jane Moore*[10]

I thus intend to argue the case that these killers are not alien creatures with deranged minds so much as they are alienated people with a disinterest in continuing the dull lives in which they feel entrapped. Reared in a civilization that legitimatizes violence as a response to frustration, provided by the mass media, the Internet and violent pornography with both the advertising announcing the *normalization of sadism* and the instruction manual outlining correct procedures, they grasp the "manly" identity of pirate and avenger. If they no longer wish to live, they will stage a mass killing whose climax is their execution; but should they wish to live, and to achieve notoriety—even celebrity—they will prepare for careers in serial murder. In doing so, they settle old scores in a manner which often yields a double dividend of sexual pleasure and defiance of the authorities. The killings are a kind of vituperative monologue with the social order—sometimes literally so, as when the macabre British homosexual serial murderer, *Dennis Nilsen,* stood in front of the corpses of the young men he had killed and tied to chairs in his apartment and lectured at them for hours, apparently on subjects as diverse as civil service regulations and modern social issues. More often, however, the killer's message is whispered too low to comprehend unassisted, or it is expressed in garbled riddles. What did Nilsen mean when he wrote to the investigating officers after his arrest that "The evil was short-lived and it cannot live or breathe for long inside the conscience"? The evil was nothing of the kind, for he would have continued to kill indefinitely had he not been unmasked by complaints from neighbors. "I have slain my own dragon," wrote this killer of sixteen defenseless young men, but he offered no apology and no further explanation when asked what form the dragon took or precisely why he killed. "I don't know," he told police. "I've been trying to work it out. I'm not a headshrinker but everyone keeps walking out on me [a reference to the fact that his friends invariably abandoned him, colossal bore that he was]. There might be a lot of individual reasons. Being a professionally perfect person I hate the establishment. I am under great pressure. I drink to relieve the pressure." Is this mere madness, or some garbled message delivered in an indecipherable code by this professionally perfect person who hates the establishment?[11]

One of the most disturbing (yet the most vital) acts the killers perpetrate is when, after their capture, they so often indulge in the cheapest kind of moralizing—lecturing society or even the families of their victims, accusing the parents of the basest behavior. The records of the trial of the fifteenth-century pedophile torture-murderer, *Baron Gilles de Rais*, document the preposterous manner in which he instructed the parents of those he had murdered on how best to raise their surviving children. In a California court, the man who kidnapped and killed young *Polly Klaas* basely accused her father of the vilest sexual crimes; while in Canada, the child-murderer *Clifford Olson* sat in prison and composed philosophical essays on subjects about which he knew nothing, sending letters to journalists, judges and professors of sociology. "I have always enjoyed sociology myself," he wrote, "as its [*sic*] a science of human society. In the last 18 months I have been doing some extenive [*sic*] writings on a vast amount of my own personal reflections on my own views on many subjects which I believe in myself. . . . Some of my topicts [*sic*] and papers I have completed are as follows. (1) immortality: (2) good and evil: (3) beauty: (4) emotion: (5) love: (6) logic: (7) happiness: (8) family: (9) knowledge: (10) art: these have all been completed." We do ourselves a great disservice if we simply dismiss this for the pretentious and illiterate prattle that it is—the same disservice that a mediocre general does for his army if he ignores the thinking of his enemy (for whom he has too much contempt)—for we ensure the killers' triumph if we do not struggle to understand their motives and goals. If we are to excise this abomination from the universe, we must listen studiously to what they say, despite their insufferability. Some of the killers unknowingly speak a form of truth.[12]

Who are these modern American multiple murderers? They refuse to meet our expectations. I have already suggested that very few of them are insane or delusional in any observable or scientific sense. They are most commonly white, male, and from the working class or lower middle class. Most important, in their thoughts and behavior they are among the most *class-conscious* people in America, obsessed with every nuance of status, class, and power. This sensitivity expresses itself variously among different types of multiple murderers. Among serial murderers, their truncated sense of self and identity (only partly a reflection of disordered childhoods) pushes them toward finding their identity and their personal fulfillment in the killings, and all their ambitions in the international celebrity that attends their capture. This contrasts strikingly with mass murderers like Essex, Huberty, and Starkweather, who are much more likely to come from relatively solid familial situations but find themselves unable to maintain the social position they covet: The gap between their expectations and their achievements is so wide that they can only vent their rage upon the hated group in one brief suicidal purple explosion. Huberty felt himself too annulled to yearn for the public spotlight that so bedazzled Berkowitz and Bundy. Yet both serial and mass murderers are overwhelmed with a profound sense of alienation and frustration stemming from their feelings that no matter how fierce their ambitions may be (and they are often among the most ambitious of men), no matter what they might do, they cannot achieve the place in society to which they aspire. They aim high, these multiple murderers: They have not, like Durkheim's contented man, accepted their station in life. Sometimes, as with Bundy and perhaps Wilder, they *do* achieve the position they covet, but their uncertain social origins and the stress of upward mobility render them unable to feel at ease with themselves while sitting upon this lofty throne. In such a milieu, a sense of a vengeful personal mission can begin to incubate.

Typically, their victims are drawn from a single social type, community or category. Sometimes this takes the form of those who are members (or who appear to be) of a specific social class above the killer, as when Kemper preyed upon those uppity "snobby brats" or when Wilder marauded among those who appeared to be models and socialites. Typically too, unless their sexuality is undeveloped (as was Berkowitz's and Kemper's) or overwhelmed by a deformed sexual sadism, they prey upon members of that social group whom they find sexually attractive. Sex does not appear to be the prime motivator, but it is vital to their enterprise—a bonus or an extra dividend to their adventure. Despite the fact that neither Berkowitz nor the D.C. Snipers touched their victims, or that Starkweather made only a few fumbling attempts to do so, we should not dismiss the sexual component of the sprees but merely emphasize its secondary position to the "Prime Mission," which is to wreak vengeance upon the established order. Thus the D.C. Snipers appeared to be giving the heart of the American establishment what it "had coming"; the Boston Strangler was "putting things over on high-class people"; Starkweather was showing how "dead people are all on the same level"; Kemper was making "a demonstration to the authorities"; Bundy was stealing the most valuable "possessions" of the established classes, their beautiful and talented young women; and Essex was killing white people who, he had decided, were the "beasts of the earth." In this limited sense then, the killers know precisely what they are doing and why they are doing it. If we are to understand them, rather than just dismiss them, their acts must be seen as a kind of grotesque and loathsome creativity, not a consequence of some drooling derangement.

Our purpose in this book is to determine the source of this deformation, demonstrating through the intensive examination of illustrative cases the fundamentally social nature of their creation and the deep social meaning of their acts. Along our path we shall encounter many lies and half-truths, but we shall attempt a dissection with surgical precision. En route, we will occasionally assess the behavior of the social institutions charged with the responsibility for dealing with multiple murderers: Here too we shall encounter surprises, for the police, who are commonly regarded as stupid and brutal, often appear in these pages to possess more intelligence and insight into the killers than do the "professionals." Moreover, as the distinguished American psychiatrist Willard Gaylin has freely admitted, "Most of us are aware of how trivial, ephemeral, descriptive, and meaningless are psychiatric diagnoses." Unfortunately, some of his colleagues overlook these ambiguities when trying to squeeze psychiatric theory to fit courtroom practice.[13]

The Mass Media and Multiple Murder

We should understand that the serial killer has now assumed the symbolic mantle once worn by in our civilization by "monsters, demons, ghouls, vampires, werewolves, and zombies." When a new killer or killings come to light, the mass media focus upon them in a way that is an as-yet uncharted combination of loathing and fascination. Thus the killers come to occupy a central position in our nightmares; and their social role appears to be to embody, display and define all evil. We should remind ourselves that the fear so generated erodes the social fabric, transforms public life from the joyous communal experience it might be to a savage zero-sum encounter, and demeans the humanity of all.[14]

In addition, there is a real measure of exploitation in the role often taken by the media. The criminologist Ratner wondered to what extent "media depictions of women as available sex objects encourage [future] serial killers to believe that women exist solely in order to gratify their bizarre fantasies?" He is also concerned that the media's glorification of serial killers endlessly rehearses "the confusion between normal and pathological currents in mass culture." Moreover, he argues that it is an error to dismiss "as mere commercialism" items such as serial killer web sites and trading cards, which he feels intensify "the association of serial murder with youthful recreation" and subtly encourage similar acts. He emphasizes that serial murder should not provide the media with further opportunities for degrading, titillating, and frightening the public; rather, we should mount a "dispassionate analysis of the cause of split families, the scale of domestic violence and the effects of abuse and neglect."[15] It is not an insignificant thing that after Karla Homolka was convicted of joining her husband in the multiple rape and murder of abducted young women in Canada, an admiring web site appeared entitled "Karla's a Babe!"

We draw so many of our ideas about the world from what we see in the mass media and mass culture. One of the most disturbing aspects of this is the manner in which serial killers are often glorified and glamorized—through a process in which they are depicted as Super Males, even Supermen. As an illustration of the way this happens, note the currently popular books and films about "*Hannibal the Cannibal*" by Thomas Harris. Thomas is a master storyteller but Dr. Hannibal

Lecter bears no resemblance to the defective, limited, unfeeling, and ungifted persons who are the overwhelming majority of multiple killers. Moreover, in the portrayal of Hannibal's enemies as less glamorous and more evil than himself, we inevitably come to identify with, and feel sympathy for, the killer Hannibal. This is a profound cultural problem because in glorifying and validating what is deformed in the human psyche, the popular thrillers may lead our most vulnerable young people in directions we would not wish them to go.

The Mythology

The primary nonsense dispensed by this genre lies in its consistent portrayal of killers as supremely intelligent, glamorous, cosmopolitan, cultivated, physically powerful, and sexually gifted. No wonder women sometimes "fall in love" with imprisoned serial killers, for they are presented by the media as the ultimate sexualized celebrity males. Dr. Lecter, for example, is portrayed as a *European aristocrat* who spent his childhood playing in the vast forests on his family's estate in Lithuania. His "father was a count, title dating from the tenth century." So natural is his aristocratic bearing that he is intuitively respected by everyone—even the wild boars that have been trained to eat him. He is also an *international financier*, able to move his monies around the world through secret accounts: Naturally, he has the most *exquisite and impeccable taste* and can only bear to drive Jaguars, and only the finest food and wine will do. It goes without saying that he is an *accomplished classical musician and musicologist* and a *multilingual historical scholar* who wins the competition for the curatorship of a great museum by reading and commenting upon Dante with detailed erudition and in perfect Italian. He is also a *distinguished psychiatrist*, with a once lucrative private practice, who routinely reviews scholarly books in the *American Journal of Psychiatry*. He is of course a *master criminal* who, with his genius for disguise, moves freely across international borders despite intensive police surveillance. Naturally too, he is *immensely powerful*: "Size for size he is as strong as an ant," and he is *highly trained in lethal combat*, killing deftly with teeth and knives.

An unarmed Lecter dispatches an armed policeman, "seizing him around the neck with terrible strength," then disemboweling him and breaking his neck.

Naturally he is *exceedingly intelligent*, and has complete control over his mind and body; his self-control is so perfectly pitched that he shows utter indifference when he is being hideously tortured. For his own vile murders and depredations, Lecter is given a *legitimizing excuse*, a cultural "justification." It seems that there is a terrible thing in his past that he can neither forgive nor forget, and it is all because he loved his sister so. The starving Nazi soldiers who had found him and his young sister hiding in their estate had killed and eaten the little girl. Since that terrible day, Lecter "had not been bothered by any considerations of deity, other than to recognize how his own modest predations paled beside those of God, who is in irony matchless, and in wanton malice beyond measure." Needless to add, Lecter is a *skillful lover* able to sexually enchant a beautiful woman half his age. He drugs and kidnaps Starling, but inevitably she falls in love with him and they escape to Argentina. Years later, a couple is glimpsed in Buenos Aires entering the opera: The woman is so beautiful that her mere presence "raised an admiring murmur in the crowd." The man's "head was sleek as an otter." Who else could it be but the perfect cannibal couple?

The Reality

Multiple murderers are usually without intellectual or physical attainments; they are often uneducated and sometimes virtually illiterate. Their purported brilliance at evading the police is simply based upon the difficulty in finding an assailant who has no social or material links to the victim: In fact, the murder of strangers is as easy to get away with as is sneaking up behind someone and stabbing him in the back. There hasn't been an aristocratic serial murderer in half a millennium. Neither are there any distinguished psychiatrists, musicologists, or financiers in their midst, although physicians or nurses mad with power have "terminated" the patients they deem worthless. Women do not find them irresistible: They are defective and limited persons whose only means of relating to others is to trap, humiliate, and kill them—clumsy and pathetic sexual sociopaths acting out their sadistic primitive fantasies. Do they have "legitimate" excuses for their rampages? All of them have a personal myth which paints them as "victims" of society; all of them imagine their victims provoked violence and "asked for it"; all of them have a grudge against society for real or imagined slights. None of them has any excuse for what he does. Are they always male? Recent research makes it clear that something like fifteen percent of serial killers are female, although women are more likely to embrace multiple murder for economic rather than obviously sexual motives (killing, for example, to collect on insurance policies). Are they experts in combat? Most of them surrender to the police without a struggle and are incapable of engaging someone who is not half their strength or heavily drugged. Are they intelligent like Hannibal Lecter? Most of them are on the dull side of normal intelligence; and the few who were moderately intelligent, such as Panzram and Kemper, are the exceptions to the rule. Big lies can make great films, just as they make great politicians; but they do nothing to further our understanding of the deviant human being, and such killers are too easily transformed into subterranean Super Heroes, ripe for imitation.

A Warning

A caution should be issued here. There is a pitfall that entraps researchers and readers alike when venturing into this kind of territory. I refer to the propensity, brilliantly attacked by Willard Gaylin, to become so emotionally involved with the killers as to minimize, or even entirely forget, the evil that these men have done. This selective amnesia takes many forms, but all are pernicious. I do not speak here only of the kind of sycophantic and grotesque affection that Flora Rheta Schreiber oozes over her informant, the torture-murderer Joseph Kallinger, in her book *The Shoemaker* (a syrup so thick that it inspires the killer to send poems to his biographer). I also refer to the kind of shift of sympathy that warps books even as beautifully crafted as Daniel Keyes's *The Minds of Billy Milligan*. Keyes, so enraptured by his subject, was unable to control his righteous rage at the "rednecks" who interrupted the multiple rapist's "rehabilitation" by shooting at him as he walked on the grounds of the mental hospital. I do not approve of shooting anyone, but author and reader must maintain some perspective and remind themselves that Milligan was a brutal rapist who destroyed the peace and contentment of his victims. The victims deserve more sympathy than Billy, and a society that does not understand this provides fertile ground for the sowing of more rapists and murderers.

Willard Gaylin has written with great insight about the process whereby the victims, not the killers, are diminished and denied their humanity in order to put the killer on trial in the best possible light. A similar infection invades the description of the killer and his murders, and some scholars are no more resistant to this disease than anyone else. If we insist upon the right to understand the dark forces that propel a person into launching a war upon the innocent, we must also assume the responsibility of recognizing the unholiness of his acts and the tragedies that he perpetrates. A cultural system that does otherwise, as does our own, is guilty of much more than misplaced tenderness: It must be charged with encouraging the repetition of such acts. Conversely, a legal system such as ours that sometimes makes a mockery of natural justice for violent offenders, releasing them back into society without any sense of wrongdoing, commits a grave error. To avoid these problems, I have tried very hard, while seeking to understand the motives of the killers, to *de-glamorize the actors and to humanize their victims*. We are all human beings, but the innocent deserve more than the guilty.

Many of us are programmed by our social system to displace our rage upon others, but why do many individuals with equally tragic (or far more so) backgrounds choose not to kill? The fundamental act of humanity is to refuse to kill. Our murderers have consciously rejected that humanity. They are not robots programmed by some machine to do exactly what they do: They know precisely what they are doing, they take a warped pleasure in it, and an expression of genuine remorse is rare indeed. For their betrayal of humanity, they deserve no better fate than to be permanently excised from the social order. Their only value is as objects of study.

2 The Modern Serial Murderer

Data: The Lost "Diary" of the "Vampire of Silesia"

While languishing in prison awaiting his execution, Poland's most infamous serial killer, Zdzislaw Marchwicki, created a remarkable document. Serial killers rarely write about their crimes, and when they do so it is usually to justify themselves, not to provide the curious mixture of richness of detail and poverty of all human feeling that is so fully revealed in this otherwise monotonously barbaric memoir. It has not been previously published in English, but the stumbling and half-literate memoir has been translated from internal police documents by Polish criminologist Kacper Gradon. Marchwicki's spree seems to have begun with a series of unsolved assaults and murders in the 1950s, but they did not come to the attention of the police and the public until November of 1964. These assaults continued until March of 1970, during which time he attacked at least twenty-one women, eleven of them in 1965 alone. At least fourteen women died as a result of his attacks. "His modus operandi was almost identical in each case," Gradon observed. "He would follow his victim, hit her on the head with a blunt object, then repeatedly strike the unconscious woman until he crushed her skull." After that he would toy with her body, finally having sexual intercourse with her corpse.

Because his crimes took place in the industrialized and urbanized mining region of southern Poland, with its network of rail and road connections, it was easy for Marchwicki to travel unnoticed over a large area. The first murder victim to be noted by police and public was Anna Mycek in 1964. In the following year, Marchwicki attacked and killed so many that police created a Special Operations Group charged with the coordination of police, criminologists, court experts, and psychiatrists (including American expert Dr. James A. Brussel). The Group also created one of the very earliest scientific profiles, which singled out nearly 500 psychological and physical characteristics that could be used to eliminate suspects in the region. Despite this, their offer of a very large reward, and the dispatch of decoy policewomen to the streets, their pursuit was in vain. In 1966, the case became even more high-profile when Marchwicki murdered Jolanta Gierek, the eighteen-year-old niece of the soon-to-be head of the communist state, Edward Gierek. Police efforts intensified and eventually a suspect list of some 250 men was compiled; Marchwicki was on that list, but he was not arrested. Marchwicki's fourteenth and last murder was committed in March of 1970, when, along with his brother and nephew, he killed and robbed Dr. Jadwiga Kucia, an academic from Silesian University.

He was not to be captured by conventional means. In the end, it was his wife who turned him in, but not for the murders. In January of 1972, his wife had telephoned the police and reported that her near-impotent husband had savagely beaten her and their children. The moment Marchwicki was arrested for this abuse, he began without prompting to pour out his confessions to the police: "Hey, so many of you, as you caught that Vampire, eh? You've got me," he said. Then he changed his story and denied the killings, not confessing again until he was on trial. Strong material evidence linked him directly to the murders that had terrorized Silesia for eight years (especially the possession of "trophies" from his victims, including an unusual fountain pen and a unique watch); and he was found guilty of fourteen murders and six attempted murders. Despite his plea of insanity, he was sentenced to death; and while awaiting execution in prison he wrote a brief account of his childhood and his time as a slave laborer for the Nazis. Most of the text, says Gradon, "consists of the graphic descriptions of compulsive masturbation, rapes, sexual intercourse with animals such as cows and hens, and incest; but he also writes about the severe beatings, hunger and physical violence in his family." At the end of the manuscript, Marchwicki apologizes for his sins and asks for death (which he would soon receive), but not without egomaniacally patronizing his readers. "His last words," notes Gradon, "constitute a kind of paternal advice to his audience": "Let them who read this diary know that it's no good to kill. They will avoid the suffering that I go through by observing the Fifth Commandment." Aside from the fact that he confuses the Fifth with the Sixth Commandment, he, like most other serial killers, makes precious little mention of the infinitely greater suffering of his victims.

I Marchwicki Zdzislaw write about me life and I'm gonna start with, that I was born in Dabrowa Gornicza on a day of October 18 1927. So, as a young boy I went to the primary school in Bedzin, learning ain't no good to me, I was a no good student and that's why I skipped school and kept watching girls. For being no good, for humiliation, the teacher man or woman used the punishment forced us to sit with the girls. It ain't no punishment to me, I was kinda happy with that. It often happen to me that during the break I goed to the toilet, played with my penis. When war began, they took me to Germany for slave work. There I had sex with a woman older than me, the married one, Eva was her name. Her husband was with the army that time, and there was no one to work in the field, so they gave me to that farm. One day when working, Eva offered me to go with her upstairs to home I lived. She offered me the inter coorse, it went this way that Eva took out my penis herself and then she

put it in her and then it went like that in every further inter
coorse. . . .

Then they took me to the different farmer in Celiny where I
worked at Gaborka's. One day the idea come to my head to perform the inter coorse with cow. It looked sorta like with that
woman, but I had to stay on chair and it was kinda not comfortable. I climbed on chair, took cow's tail on the back, took my
penis and put the penis into vagina and I moved my ass till I
cummed. To next inter coorse it came on the meadow. I remember I picked hay that time and I felt a need of inter coorse. So I
looked a round if no one isn't there and I took cow by the chain
and I stayed her in the place that she was lower and I was on the
hill and I performed the inter coorse like before; but Gaborka
catched me. Close she came and she cursed on me: "You Pig!" I
cursed her: "you whore, you rag!" After that argyment, I escaped
and went home. Gaborka went to the gendarmerie to inform
them about the situation I mentioned: on the same day the
policeman came and took me to the police and then they took me
in the beginning to Gestapo where they cursed on me and beat
me and then took me to jail. In jail was I for month and then they
took me to the camp in Kedziezyn.

After sorta 3 or 4 weeks I escaped from there and headed to
home: I knew that war is ending and Front is coming and that's
why I didn't hide. After I went out I started to work in the coal
mine. I was 20 years old in that time. In 1954 I lived with wife;
my life with wife was no good. Wife and I were nervous and for
nothing we've got fights. Like for lack of money, like for me not
talking to her much enough, and finally because I was weak in
sexual matters and because my wife became whore. Then the
fight exploded. After fights with wife I escaped and lived with
[my] sister or father; then wife took the lover and lived with him
for a longer time. After that separation I would come back to
wife because I was thinkin' about our children. It often hap-

pened like I had the inter coorses with wife during her period. I liked to have a lick of her female organs at that time.

When I lived with father, I met that women who fixed the shoes at father's place, Helena. At the time I had fight with wife and I lived with Helena I had performed the inter coorses with her during her period and I also tried to lick her female organs. We did it to each other. Helena is in love with me, she is very glad from my love. I loved her too, but in spite of that some kind of force was leading me to my wife. Probably I loved her more than Helena. As I stated before that I licked her organs during her period, I need to add that my wife also tried that forbidden love, but only for a few times: I didn't allow her more because it didn't bring especial pleasure. Among others that was one of the reasons of our fights.

I'd like to also mention my childhood. When I was two years old my mother died, some time after birthing my younger brother, Jan. Because we didn't have no care, Father married a few times more, but he ain't lived long with them wifes [and] after a bunch of years he divorced with them. Father worked in the mines till the time of death, and that is all on the subject of me childhood.

And now I return to the older years; I realy wasn't a good father and husband for wife, because I don't care for them children. Little time spent at home because I worked, because I drove for crimes, or drunk with friends, so I was a guest in da house and I luved to piss her off. And then one day wife gave me the chicken soup, so I throwed them chicken out. When wife called me to be in peace, I smiled deep in my soul and I caused the fight and in this way I pissed her off, for she cheated on me, for she fighted the time I drinked that I come home late. I didn't talk much to wife and children. Five children I have. To wife I didn't talk even when I took her during inter coorse, and after inter coorse, as I mentioned, to wife I didn't talk much; she asked me sumthing I just mumbled sumthing or nodded me head. I did it for purpoos, though I know that I shouldn't do that, but I did that, pissed her off with that and got happy from that.

In 1951 I attaked woman in forest. Drove me there me phriend I worked with. I goed there in the purpoos of attaking sum woman, cause I wanted to try other love and that's what I did. After attacking her and ouverpowering her I made the inter coorse to her and then I taked her money and watch and I goed away. After doing that crime I went home; in home I thinked about it and about what it was to me and I comed to think that I feeled the better satisfaction than with wife and with Ema. From that cause, this first crime gived the start to the next ones. I dared to make the next crime in 1952 and in Wysoka I did it. I remember I wus there for the cement from the cement factoree; I walked away from tha driver 'cause I had the plan to attack sum woman. At one moment I saw the woman that I followed. In one moment when noone was around us I hit her few times in tha head with the iron rod. When she falled down I took her panties off and I played with her feemail organs, then I taked her money from her handbag in amount of 400 zlotys and quickly walked away.

In 1954 I commited the crime in Dabrowa Mala on the woman aged 30 years. Crime happened near the cemetery. I attacked there tha woman, beating her with the iron rod in the head as always, taked off her panties and played wit' her organs, taked her monee and I think her watch, and aftur that I quickly goed away back to home. Next crime I did in 1956 in Michalkowice near the pond and the fort. I wus der wit' me brother Heniek. In the end of Summer I met Heniek in town and then I proposed to him that he goes with me to Michalkowice. I told brother that we both will attack woman. Brother agreed on me proposishun and we both goad to tha aforementioned town, toward pond where we meeted woman. With Heniek we both carried her to tha other place wher I had a sexual inter coorse, I taked her 500 zlotys; after the crime we with brother goed back on our way. Me brotha' proposed that we drop by to tha reestaurant; we went to "Popularna" ordered a liter [of vodka] and shared them moneys, talk about the murter and left going home. Few days layter we met again and in short talk I tolded him that it would be yousful to go to Strumieszyce. Brother also agreed and we goed to his home; brother dressed up and in tha after noon we went to the aforementioned town. After coming we met woman; I attacked her hitting with tha crowbar. Heniek helped me to drag her to the bushes and waited for me on the side. I stripped her halfway, played with her feemail organs, looked at all of this, taked her monee. We quickly goed away, droped by to the restaurant when we drinked half liter of vodka and then we went our ways.

Next crime I did in Dabrowka Mala, near railways in 1959. I met woman whom I attacked. Hit her in tha head with the crow bar, performed the inter coorse wit'er, taked her ring and moneys; after the incident I taked tha bus and goed home. Next I did in Lagisza in 1965, goed there wit tha car. After getting out I went on foot to the place where there wer no buildings; I meeted woman there, she walked in front of mc, she was kinda 40 years old. I attacked her, had an inter coorse with her, taked ring and moneys, got into bus and goed home. Four days layter I selled the ring to the stranger on the market. Next crime I did in Dabrowka Mala in 1964 I went there to that town; woman I attacked I hit few times with tha rawhide. When the woman falled down I stripped her to played with her organs, taked moneys and run away. Next crime I did in Bedzin in 1964 near railway, I goed there with tha streetcar for the poorpose of cumitting murder of some woman. Walking I meeted her woman in front of me. From the back I hited her few times in tha head she falled down I started to search her taked her moneys taked her ring and goed away. That woman was sorta 40 years old. Next craym I did in Dabrowka Mala in tha park when coming back from me mother in law I meeted woman who was returning in front of me. I hit her from behind few times in the head with tha rawhide taked her monee taked her ring leaved her and goed away. I selled it on the market to tha stranger—and ring and watch. I skipped to say that it was in 1964. Next I did the same year in town of Rogoznik. On place I got with the bus. I went there with the purpoos to attack some woman. After coming I went toward forest it was kinda dark; behind buildings I met tha woman. I coming from behind her hit her few times in the head she falled down I searched her, found her money with her, taked her ring too, that I selled leyter time. That woman counted sorta 40 years of age. After the incident I goed away goed home, latur I selled the taken stuff.

A year layter I made a murder on them meadows in Lagisza. I wus there alone, I went for the poorpose to attack some woman. When I got there it was already dark. I meeted her woman she was not young; I attacked her, taked her money, taked her other thinks like her ring and wedding ring. I selled it to one stranger on the market. I mention that I performed the inter coorse to that woman. Next crime I did in 1965. In Wojkowice I did ther the murder on the woman 30 years old. To Wojkowice I goed with tha bus in evening time. After I goed from the bus in front of me I meeted woman, I attacked her hit her few times in the head with rawhide. Whan woman falled down I stripped her to half, played with her feemail organs, taked moneys and goed away. In tha year of 1966 in Lagisza I attacked woman in the age of 30 years, so after coming to Lagisza I goed myself to tha bushes where I met woman. After checking nobody seeing me I hit woman in tha head with tha iron rod, then I stripped her to half, played with her orguns taked money golden ring and goed toward bus. Selled taken objects. In 1967 I commiteed tha crime in Strumieszyce in the evening hours. After I goed to that town I met woman. I followed 'er at one moment we were in the empty place with no buildings, me hitting'er in tha head with the iron rod when she falled down. I stripped her to half, played with her parts and aftur that taked moneys and ring. I would like to mention that when playing with her orguns she probublee wanted to fight, 'cause she waved her paws and then I musted to kill her finally. I mention that I taked the handbag from she woman, I left the woman after all, took items from tha handbug I gave to me sis and I sold the bag and the ring to tha stranger fella'.

I described all me life and I think that everything. I got arrested in that case; arrested me when I goed to work in morning hours and taked me to the police station in Katowice, presented me the murder charge. Before they taked me to the police station in and presented me tha charge of violence to da family. Wife accused me that I beat'er don't give'er moneys, that I catch me daughter by her feemail orguns, that I was a no-good father— as it is true, but I denied it. They presented me tha charge of killing them women I described; to them killings I didn't admit 'cause I was scared. I didn't admit it in court. Then as I mentioned I found meself in the Police Headquarters and when I didn't admit they taked me to the General Headquarters in Warsaw and then I didn't admit for three months. Then I breaked down and I started to explain, then I was examined by few speshyalists and aftur that they taked me to the mental hospital and I was there a few months and then they finished me investigation.

After few months there was first court and first them examined me brotha Janek, didn't admit to guilt and often fighted with tha prosecutor and cursed on witnesses and on other people in court. He cursed tha prosecutor "the red Ukrainian." Second they examined me sis, they told her she gut stuff from them murders. Sis admiited to some things but she ain't no know where 'em comed from but really she knowed 'cause I told her dat. Then they examined J.K., he admitted to the incident near Televison [the final murder]. Next one was examined Flak Zdzislaw, son of me sis, they told him that he heared us talkin' bout them murders. He ain't admit that, but sure he heard it. Next was brotha Heniek, 'bout tha incident near Television and he admitted. Last was I and I didn't admit to them murders, just in the end

I ain't got nerves and I stand up and said I confess to them murders I am the killer and the big one, killed 20 or maybe 26 I don't exactly remember and please send me where I should go even when me is so scared. Aftur the examination of them witnesses they gived us them sentences and sis got 4 years, her son too 4, J.K. 12 years got—so few 'cause he told 'bout tha murder near Television.

Heniek my brotha got 25 years, brother Janek and meself gut death penalty. I thought that they give me 25 years or in worst kinda' death penalty and I thought 'bout I will write to them Government and they will pardon me and I'm gonna get out one day. Just after the court I ain't no write to them Government 'cause I didn't knou how to give the reasons for that and how to put it. Although my phriends cheered me up, I couldn't go thru me breakdown and I went apeshit for that. Many times I stood up and comed and ringed to them guards and asked 'em to lead me where I hafta go—that means to hang me, but me pleas ain't had no effect. And every time them guard opened the door and telled me to go to sleep and don't scream at nite, and even then I goed apeshit and I did it 'cause I wanted and I didn't wanted 'em to hang me. Before that decision to die I always thinked how much is me life worth and how much pain I gived to them people and to me family and in that nastee way I hafta leave this world. When I comed to that thinking there was something weird happenin' and I can't deescribe it; then I kneeled and stayed up and this way I sayed goodbye to the world. I didn't pray 'cause I don't know how. When I kneeled something was talking to me ear that I hafta decide to go down and though I was scared that weird power forced mee to that. I remember dat one nite I begged that they lead me out the same day. And not only this was a cause, because I am the perverted one. In young age I already had the drive to them sexual things, it's in me diary that I'm shy and that I did good to meself thru jerking off, and looked for me sexual satisfaction in tha inter coorse with cow and hen. The inter coorse with hen didn't go 'cause I ain't have no luck to do that, simply.

I deescribed all mee life and it looks like to me that every craym too. It was hard to deescribe that but I did well and I wanna finish it with the words, and all of them who read me diary know that it's no good to kill. They gotta avoid the suffering that I go thru by observing the God's Fifth Commandment. Marchwicki Zdzislaw, the Vampire of Silesia.

Theory: Overview of Serial Murder

The multiple murder of strangers is conventionally divided into serial murders (killings over an extended period of time, usually but not always with a sexual component, for example, Ted Bundy), and mass murder (killings during a few minutes or days, in which the killer soon expects to be captured or die, for example, the McDonald's Massacre). The murder of one person differs in important ways from multiple murder. In most homicides, there is some form of previous relationship between killer and victim—they are family, acquaintances, associates or lovers. In multiple murder, however (except in the obvious case of those who murder their families), the victims are more likely to be strangers (as in the McDonald's Massacre). A second major difference is that most killers tend to be drawn from the least successful strata of society—the under-educated, the chronically unemployed, those living on welfare benefits and with chronic drug and/or alcohol problems. But multiple murderers come from a wider range of backgrounds: Indeed, they are often gainfully employed and sometimes have reasonable expectations of conventional futures. Their problem is more likely to be internal: They live by a "narrative," a story of their own histories, in which they see themselves as unjustly maltreated heroes wreaking vengeance on their oppressors.

Typologies of Serial Murder

Holmes and De Burger based their influential typology on 110 cases. Drawing on ideas that had emerged from the FBI Academy, they developed their typology of the "dominant motives" of serial murderers. They rejected purely social explanations: Poverty, poor neighborhoods, unstable families, and a subculture of violence could not be the cause of serial murder since only a few of those who are exposed to such social stresses become serial killers. They concluded that the explanation for the behavior must therefore lie in psychological factors, i.e., "in the psyche of the killer." Their categories include the *Visionary Type*, whose killings are "committed in response to 'voices' or 'visions' that demand that a person or category of persons be destroyed"; the *Mission-Oriented Type*, who typically decides to "go on a 'mission' to rid the world of a category of people" he has branded as beneath contempt (for example, prostitutes); the *Hedonistic Type*, who kills for thrills, seeking only "pleasure or a sense of well-being." Finally, there is the *Power/Control-Oriented Type*, whose primary satisfaction comes from his complete domination over the life and death of the victim.[1]

Psychobiological Perspectives

The psychobiological tradition assumes that the causes of all human behavior are rooted one way or another in human biology. Perhaps the best-known variation of this tradition looks to specific biological/chemical/neurological flaws in the killer, such as the overblown XYY chromosome research that Fox criticized for "premature speculation and, consequently, much confusion." In fact, only three percent of prisoners were found to have the extra Y chromosome, and these actually "displayed, in their criminal behavior, *less* violence against persons." Subsequently, XYY has only been correlated with non-aggressive characteristics—mild retardation, tallness, and resistance to corrective training.[2] While few scientific researchers would argue that biological differences alone account for murder, some biological factors are being looked at as "vulnerability factors" which might well contribute to an increased susceptibility to violent behavior.

For example, in one study, low serotonin production has been found "in the majority of subjects with a history of impulsive violent behavior." Still, as one distinguished researcher admitted in private, "the circumstantial evidence may be considerable, but the smoking gun has yet to be found."[3]

Psychiatric/Psychological Perspectives

The assumption here is that the origins of behavior lie in the psychological makeup of each individual, and the classic work here is Lunde's *Murder and Madness*. Lunde concluded that such multiple killers "are almost always insane" and that their insanity takes the form of selecting as victims those who have "certain attributes which torment him." The victims themselves "are unaware of their psychological or symbolic significance to the killer," which may include the killer's belief that they send telepathic messages to him. In addition, Lunde thought that the insanity of these multiple killers takes two primary forms— one a hostile paranoid schizophrenia, and the other a sexual sadism, in which the killer only achieves sexual fulfillment through "torture and/or killing and mutilation."[4]

The most widely accepted contemporary concept is that of *psychopathy* (sometimes called sociopathy or antisocial personality disorder), which describes a remorseless and unfeeling personality that cannot respond to the humanity in other people. Many scholars have written extensively on the "common core of attributes" of psychopathy. These include "pathological lying," "impulsivity," "a lack of remorse, guilt and shame; [and an] inability to experience empathy or concern for others," or even to establish affectionate relationships.[5]

Giannangelo's *The Psychopathology of Serial Murder* tried to strike a balanced perspective: He suggested that a history of "physical, sexual, or mental abuse" might be the most important trait shared by "most" serial killers, although there are no conclusive data to confirm this belief. As a result of their abusive childhoods, serial killers developed "a pervasive lost sense of self and intimacy, an inadequacy of identity, [and] a feeling of no control," which manifested themselves in what may be "the ultimate act of control," the murder of many people. He maintained that despite the abusive histories of serial killers, they would not become serial killers without a "biological ingredient that makes the mix an explosive one." His "serial killer diagnosis," then, outlines such a predatory person as having congenital or trauma-induced physiological anomalies, a personal life history of severe abuse, an early display of antisocial and/or criminal behavior, evidence of pervasive sexual deviance, and a tendency to live in a state of fantasy.[6]

Although the concept of psychopathy is now widely used in criminal psychiatry and psychology, it has several flaws which have been extensively criticized. Although it accurately describes many of the behavioral characteristics associated with multiple murderers, it does not explain why many who have these qualities do not kill. Indeed, psychiatrist J. Reid Meloy has written that such a diagnosis is "too descriptive, inclusive, criminally based, and socioeconomically skewed to be of much clinical or research use." Steven Egger concludes that while the notion of psychopathy is a useful label and category, its inability to predict whether a victim will be a remorseless killer or a corporate executive merely reminds us "that we in fact don't know why these people act as they do."[7]

Feminist Issues and Perspectives

If feminist thought has been one of the more liberating products of the twentieth century, its position on multiple murder is flawed by baseless accusations, a contempt for evidence, and even what sometimes appears to be an ugly sexism. Indeed, the basic radical feminist text on serial murder insists that far from being a perversion of the male sexual impulse, rape and sexual murder are the *essence* of the male. This is entirely compatible with radical feminist beliefs that modern gender relations constitute a patriarchal "war against women," that "there is a [male] worldwide conspiracy for the mass extermination of women," and that serial murder is merely the control of women through their organized international execution. Cameron and Frazer argue incorrectly that such killers are *always male*; and that far from being seen as a deviant, the sex killer "is [seen as] a hero, at the centre of literary and philosophical celebration." In this view, then, the rape and murder of women is *normal* for men.[8]

However, Hickey's extensive data made it clear that *fully seventeen percent of serial killers are female*. He does not argue that serial killer Nurse Jane Toppan's motives were in any way typical when she claimed that her ambition had been to "have killed more people—more helpless people—than any man or woman who has ever killed." In fact, the motives of female serial killers are more likely to be concerned with material gain (as when women serially murder their children, husbands, or tenants to collect their life insurance) than an obviously perverted sexuality. Female serial killers prey primarily on the most vulnerable—patients in hospitals and nursing homes or children. Finally, Hickey observed that serial killing is not just a crime perpetrated by men on women: While more than one-third of male serial killers preyed exclusively on women, just under one half killed both males and females, and a fifth killed only men.[9]

In *Using Murder*, Philip Jenkins adds that in order to maximize their political and emotional impact, hard-line radical "feminists have stuck to the original grossly inflated and long-discredited [U.S.] Department of Justice estimates of the number of serial killers and victims," when in fact women "are by far the *least likely* segment of the population to fall victim to homicide." Indeed, in contemporary America, *while black men have a 1 in 21 chance of falling victim to homicide, the chances for black women are 1 in 104, while white men have a 1 in 131 chance, and white women 1 in 369*. Jenkins concludes that if the radical feminist analysis is lacking in "scholarly merit," the theories have been a significant rhetorical device for underlining the injustices inflicted everywhere upon women and other "relatively powerless groups." Similarly, Julie Cluff and her colleagues criticized feminist theorizing for dismissing even "the possibility that women could be serial killers." Cluff underlined the limitations of studying only male sexual predators and suggested that the remedy will lie in the serious study of the female serial killer.[10]

Such a search might begin with the very large number of *"medical"* serial killers, typically nurses and nurses' aides but occasionally also doctors: They are far more prolific murderers than the stereotypical "ripper" sexual sadist, and they dominate the ranks of serial killers who have claimed forty or more victims (with some, like Dr. Shipman in England, suspected of involvement in as many as 200 murders of their patients). The ease with which a nurse or doctor can kill patients without any fear of detection is aided by the fact that death in a hospital setting is expected and does not arouse suspicion and that hospital and medical bureaucracies tend to be closed to external examination.

The Frequency of Serial Killing

There are so many difficulties in the collection of reliable statistics on serial murder that the precise frequency of serial murder is not known. Early commentators followed the lead of the U.S. Justice Department and wildly overestimated the number of such killers, but it appears that these "increases" are really increases in public interest and attention from journalists. In the period between 1880 and 1990, when the U.S. produced a minimum of six or seven hundred serial killers, Jenkins found only twenty-five officially recognized cases of serial murder in England and Wales. Serial murder in the U.S. has also taken a cyclical pattern, and its history falls into three periods: a rather high rate until 1940, when there were at least twenty-four "extreme" serial killers who killed a minimum of ten; followed by "a time of relative tranquility in the mid-century"; and then a renewed "murder wave" that has continued from the mid-1960s to the present. Thus the increase of serial killing since 1965 was not "a wholly new phenomenon," but merely "a return to earlier historical patterns."[11]

In the light of all this controversy, we can only echo Egger's conclusion that as yet we have "no decisive answers," except that American rates of serial killing are exceptionally high—like all American homicides. Still, the victims of serial murderers comprise "only" one percent of the all homicides each year, i.e., between 150 and 250 annually in the United States.

It should be noted that such killers do not appear only in the developed industrial world: Third World countries also produce serial killers, but their inadequate justice systems undoubtedly overlook many of their killers. Javed Iqbal was arrested in Pakistan for the sex murders of an estimated 100 boys; Alfredo Garavito is suspected of claiming 140 victims in Colombia; and there have surely been many more.

Social Perspectives

The primary and unresolved question remains that of *causation*. What could cause a person to take the life of a number of innocent human beings, often people of whom he has neither prior knowledge nor personal hatred? What are the *social forces* that might determine, underlie, or shape the production of such a remorseless killer? Do certain types of cultures or specific historical epochs incubate or encourage such violence?

Many commentators now argue that the killers appear most frequently in unstable epochs or periods of cultural dislocation. The killers themselves may come from abusive homes, "dysfunctioning families, [whose children] suffer flagrant abuse and neglect." The abused children then become more likely to seek solutions to their predicaments through a vindictive "individual fantasy" that is "bereft of scruples." "Scripted eroticized violence" becomes the means for fulfilling these fantasies, in the course of which the powerlessness of the child is "symbolically neutralized and avenged." R. S. Ratner speculated that in an orgy of serial murder, victims are ritually captured, possessed, defiled, and disposed of, affording the killer "brief vengeance against the rejecting family/society." Unfortunately, the absence of reliable statistics means we do not know if the claims of abusive childhoods are correct.[12]

3 A Demonstration to the Authorities

EDMUND EMIL KEMPER III

"I had thought of annihilating the entire block that I lived on."

Edmund Kemper[1]

Raised by a shrilly belittling university administrator (and her succession of husbands, none of whom could measure up to her fierce social ambitions) who locked him in a cellar and endlessly berated him for his social failures, and incarcerated throughout his adolescence in a mental hospital for sex offenders, he grew up to be a young man who believed in all the conventional values, but lacked the confidence to be anything other than a flagman for the California Department of Highways. His task first drifted into his consciousness well before he was ten. He grew fascinated with execution, the means by which the authorities legally punished and eliminated evildoers. His younger sister remembered that "he would stage his own execution in the form of a childhood 'game' in which he had her lead him to a chair, blindfold him, and pull an imaginary lever, after which he would writhe about as if dying in a gas chamber." One Christmas, her grandparents gave her a doll: When she looked for it one day she discovered it decapitated and handless, a mutilation theme that was to recur within the developing mentality of Edmund Emil Kemper III.[2]

Still younger than ten, his task shifted hesitantly to living things. To transform a separate life-form into his true and exclusive possession, he later explained, he made his first kill. He buried the family cat alive in his yard. When it had suffocated, he brought it into his room and cut off its head, which he stuck on a spindle. His mingled satisfaction and fascination expressed themselves in the prayers he intoned over the head. At about the same time, one of his psychiatrists later reported, he began embroidering fantasies which celebrated the deaths of people— his sisters, mother, and others. "It was mainly his older sister," a court psychiatrist said many years later. "She had friends, got more attention, respect, and affection from the mother. In general, she had the things he didn't have."[3]

First he had feigned killing himself in his ceremonial executions; then he had killed a symbol of a person by mutilating a doll; then he had killed a living thing in order to possess it; and working ever closer to what would be his prime task, his *raison d'être* (but gradually, for he was a cautious man), his thoughts had been filled with killing people. The purpose of the killing was to demand redress for the injustices that he thought had been perpetrated against him. Still a child, his fantasy matured into what would be his life's work. It blended mutilation, murder, possession, justice, and revenge with his own developing sexuality. The psychiatrist Lunde tells us that Kemper began to "sneak out of the house at night and from a distance stare at women walking down the street, fantasizing about his desire to love and be loved by them. Even at this early age, however, he felt that relationships with women would be impossible for him" unless he had killed them. During this period, Kemper confided to his younger sister that he would like to kiss his second-grade teacher. "She taunted him by saying, 'Why don't you go and kiss her,' and was puzzled at his reply: 'If I kiss her I would have to kill her first.'" He was unable to communicate or satisfy his desire: Instead, carrying his stepfather's bayonet, he stood one night outside his teacher's house, "imagining himself killing her and carrying her off to make love to her."[4]

His presentation of self was already growing so bizarre, with his silences and his stares, that his peers shrank from him. By the time he was thirteen, he was suspected of shooting a neighborhood pet dog.

After that, he was excommunicated by the other boys, "being taunted, intimidated, and chased even more than before," once so "threateningly that he fled into a nearby house, where a woman called the police in his behalf." He considered killing men, but fear of male reprisal and the absence of any sexual promise blurred the fantasy enterprise. His execution reveries temporarily abated when one of his several stepfathers treated him with kindness, taking him fishing and hunting; yet there came a time when Kemper, holding an iron bar, stood behind his stepfather, ready to spring. "His plan," writes his biographer Margaret Cheney, "after bashing him over the head, was to steal his car and drive to southern California for a reunion with his natural father." However, courage failed him and he ran away instead.[5]

Upon his return, now thirteen, he killed again in order to possess a fickle cat that preferred his sister, this time killing with a more complex ritual. He sliced off the top of the cat's skull with a machete, exposing its brain. The convulsing cat showered Kemper with blood while he held one of its forelegs and stabbed it repeatedly with his knife. Terrified that he would be discovered and punished, he buried the cat in his yard and cleaned his room. "Parts of the cat, for reasons that he did not fully understand, he decided to hide in his closet." It would not be the last time that a mammalian head would be his secret trophy and glittering prize, his just revenge and sensual reward. His mother later discovered parts of the cat and confronted Edmund with them. But, as Lunde tells us, "when confronted with accusations of such behavior by his mother or others, Ed would usually deny the charges and blame someone else."[6]

The Killing Time

Now described by his mother as "a real weirdo," Kemper spent a period shuttling between the homes of his mother and his remarried father, and then was sent against his wishes to live with his paternal grandparents on their isolated California ranch. In late summer, now fourteen, he was sitting with his grandmother at her kitchen table as she went over the proofs of her latest children's story. Kemper rose and took his .22 rifle from its rack, telling his grandmother he was going to hunt rabbits. Suddenly, he felt the same anger that had overwhelmed him when he had killed the cats, and this time too its resolution was clear. Without conscious thought, he sighted the rifle on his grandmother's head and fired. Blood spurted from her nose and mouth, and he shot her twice more in the back. Lunde says Kemper stabbed her many times as if to kill her repeatedly, just as he had done in rehearsal with the cats. When his grandfather drove up to the house, Kemper shot and killed him before he had the opportunity to discover his wife's murder.[7]

After a few moments' hesitation, he telephoned his mother and asked her what he should do. When the police arrived, he briefly denied the crimes but then admitted that "I just wondered how it would feel to shoot Grandma." The court psychiatrist reported that during Kemper's brief detention in Juvenile Hall, he had regretted the lost opportunity of undressing his grandmother, "but felt that was an unnatural thought and did not want to talk about it." Kemper spent the following four years in a maximum security mental hospital, Atascadero, and in 1969 at the age of twenty-one was returned to the care of the California Youth Authority, who paroled Kemper to his mother—against the advice of the psychiatrists.[8]

Now free, there began an interregnum during which he formed and then rehearsed his final plan of action. Kemper had grown to six feet nine inches tall and weighed close to 300 pounds, and this massive person began to go on endless drives in his car. In the years 1970–'71, he picked up dozens of pretty young women hitchhikers, developing his "gentle-giant" presentation of self, exploring his ability to deal with the women, talking to them and putting them at their ease, and training for his task. He was not alone, for the same town was incubating Herbert Mullin and John Frazier, two other Santa Cruz mass murderers, whom Kemper would later come to despise for their lack of "legitimacy" and competence. Finally, at the age of twenty-three, he felt he was ready to begin his ultimate adventure. It was to last eleven months, with eight more dead, before he turned himself in to the police.[9]

On May 7, 1972, two eighteen-year-old Fresno State College roommates, Mary Ann Pesce, an expert skier from an affluent California suburb, and Anita Luchessa, the eldest daughter of a farming family, were hitchhiking to visit friends at Stanford University. Standing on a ramp leading to the freeway, they stepped into Kemper's stopped car. Because they did not know the area well, he was able to take them east instead of south, confusing them with what he later called "a few loopy-loops around freeways and bypasses," until he pulled into a quiet rural cul-de-sac. Pesce tried to reason with him, searching for a chord of empathy and, remarkably, finding it: "I was really quite struck by her personality and her looks, and there was just almost a reverence there," Kemper recalled. He handcuffed Pesce to the back seat with great delicacy: "I think once I accidentally—this bothers me too, personally—I brushed, I think with the back of my hand when I was handcuffing her, against one of her breasts, and it embarrassed me. I even said, 'whoops, I'm sorry' or something like that." He locked Luchessa in the trunk.[10]

Returning to Pesce, he drew a plastic bag over her head, and wrapped a bathrobe's rope-tie around her neck; but the rope snapped when he pulled hard on it, and meanwhile Pesce had bitten a hole in the plastic bag, frustrating his efforts. With her back to him, he later recalled, he "poised the blade over her back, trying to decide where her heart was, and struck and hit her in the middle of the back." He continued "thrusting hard," striking her several more times in the back. In her terror, Pesce twisted around and he was able to knife her in the side: then "she turned completely over to see . . . or to get her back away from me, and I stabbed her once in the stomach." At this point, "she turned back over on her stomach, and I continued stabbing." Kemper remembered worrying that the blows were not working. "I felt I was getting nowhere," so "I reached around and grabbed her by the chin and pulled her head back and slashed her throat. . . . She lost consciousness immediately."[11]

Leaving Pesce dead or dying in the backseat, he stepped out of the car and pulled Luchessa from the trunk, stabbing her in a flurry of cuts to the throat, the heart, the eyes, and the forearms: "What surprised me was how many blows she took. They were all heavy blows." Kemper drove back to his home and carried the bodies into his apartment. In privacy, taking Polaroid photographs of his actions, he decapitated Luchessa, disrobed and dissected Pesce, and sexually assaulted various body parts. Later, he drove into the mountains with Pesce's body in a plastic bag, and buried it, disguising the site with techniques he had learned from the Boy Scouts of America. He kept the heads of both women for a time, but then threw them into a ravine. He never forgot Pesce, nor the "reverence" he felt toward her. "Sometimes, afterward," he later told the court, "I visited there . . . to be near her . . . because I loved her and wanted her."[12]

His task was held in abeyance for four months after the killings, and he contented himself with feasting on the Polaroid photographs he had made of his last mission. On September 14, 1972, Kemper was hunting again. He observed fifteen-year-old Aiko Koo hitchhiking at a bus stop, on her way to an advanced dance class in San Francisco. Koo entered his car and was whisked through the usual bewildering array of freeway ramps, until the car pulled into a rural lane invisible from the main road. Kemper taped her mouth, closed her nostrils with his fingers, and began to suffocate her. Koo struggled violently. When her struggling seemed to cease, Kemper removed his hand from her face to find that she was still breathing: "I guess she became conscious enough to where she remembered what was happening, and went back into the extreme panic." Now he would make certain that he stopped her breathing. Her back arched as her lungs fought for air, but she lost consciousness. She was still breathing slightly as he carried her from the car and laid her body on the ground, removed her underclothing, and began intercourse. She started to breathe again, for the last time. "I took the muffler that she had around her neck and . . . choked her for a moment," he recalled. Sexually satisfied, and convinced that she was dead, he put her body in the trunk of the car, stopping at a bar for a few bottles of beer on the way home—after all, "I was hot, tired, and thirsty."[13]

On his way back to the car, he reopened the trunk to take another look at Koo, "admiring my catch like a fisherman." Satisfied, he drove to his mother's house for a visit, then took Koo's body back to his apartment, decapitated her, and dissected the body. The following day, with Koo's head in the trunk of his car parked in the psychiatrists' lot, two psychiatrists interviewed Kemper and agreed that he was now "safe." They recommended that his juvenile record be sealed to permit him to live a normal adult life. Kemper then buried Koo's head and hands near a religious camp in the mountains.[14]

Four months passed again before his urge reasserted itself. On January 8, 1973, he picked up hitchhiking Cindy Schall, a student at Cabrillo College who had not yet decided whether to become a school teacher or a policewoman. Using his usual stratagems, he whisked her to a secluded side road. Brandishing his new .22 Ruger pistol, he forced her into the trunk. Out of the corner of her eye, Kemper remembered, she saw him raise the gun. He marveled at the speed with which the bullet struck her skull and took her life: "One second she's animated and next second she's not. Just a noise and absolute, absolute stillness." Together they drove to his mother's house, where he placed her body in a closet and went to bed. When his mother had gone to work at the university (where she held an administrative position) the following morning, he removed Schall from the closet and carried her to his bed, where he made love to her corpse. Afterwards, he placed her in the bathtub and, using his Buck knife and his California Department of Highways axe, dissected her. Washing away all traces of blood, he placed the body parts in plastic bags and took them for a drive along the coast, stopping to throw the bags off a cliff. A few days later, when Schall's body parts were discovered by the police, Kemper still had her head in a box in his closet. Later, he buried her head in his mother's back yard.[15]

Schall had been his first kill he had picked up in his own town. It bolstered his confidence that he would not be unmasked before his mission was completed. With growing assurance, he moved his operations to the campus where his mother worked and increased the rate of his kills. Less than a month passed before the opportunity presented itself once more. On February 5, 1973, twenty-three-year-old Rosalind Thorpe, a student at Santa Cruz's Merrill College, was hitchhiking on campus. Kemper picked her up and, a little further along the campus drive, yet another hitchhiker, Alice Liu, entered his car and sat in the back seat. With no one visible on the campus's broad road, he turned to his front seat passenger and shot Thorpe just above her left ear: "She had a rather large forehead and I was imagining what her brain looked like inside, and I just wanted to put it right in the middle of that." Liu's response to the explosive assault in front of her was to cover her face in fear. Kemper tried to shoot through her hands, but missed twice. The third shot "hit her just right around the temple area." He shot her several more times. The firing ceased when a car came into view. He drove through the campus's guard station, with Liu gurgling in the back seat. When they had passed the campus and reached the edge of town, "I slowed down very slow, turned her head to the side, and fired point-blank at the side of her head." Pulling over to the side of the road, he was able to put both bodies in the trunk without being seen.[16]

Kemper drove to his mother's home, but he left the bodies in the trunk while he talked with his mother until bedtime. Then he went out-side to the car and decapitated both corpses, his knife flashing in the trunk. He stopped to buy cigarettes at a bar and then went to bed at his mother's. When his mother left for work the following morning, he car-ried Liu's headless body into the house, placed it on the floor and made love to her torso. As "an afterthought" when carrying her torso back to the car, he severed her hands while she lay in the trunk. He then took Thorpe's head into the house and meticulously removed the bullet from it: "I cleaned the blood off both of them in the bathroom . . . so I wouldn't get all bloody." Later, with both bodies in the car, he drove to Alameda to visit a friend, but he was unable to eat dinner that night. He went to a film, bought gas, and dumped the bodies miles from Santa Cruz.[17]

The task was now nearing completion. He would kill no more young university women. For a time he toyed with alternatives, even giving serious consideration to the idea of killing everyone on his block: "I thought of making this a demonstration to the authorities in

Santa Cruz—how serious this was, and how bad a foe they had come
up against. . . . I had thought of annihilating the entire block that I lived
on. . . . Not only the block that I lived on but the houses approaching
it, which would have included as many as ten or twelve families. And
it would be a very slow, a very slow, quiet attack." But it was not
essential to his mission, and it came to nothing. It seems that, in entertaining the possibility, he was merely half-consciously delaying what
he knew must come next, shirking his responsibilities by pretending to
fabricate new ones.[18]

By Easter weekend he could no longer pretend. At 4 A.M., he lay in
bed "thinking about it. It's something hard to just up and do," he later
admitted. "But I was pretty fixed on that issue because there were a lot
of things involved. Someone just standing off to the side, watching,
isn't really going to see any kind of sense, or rhyme or reason." But his
sense of responsibility and commitment prevailed. "I had done some
things, and I felt that I had to carry the full weight of everything that
happened. I certainly wanted for my mother a nice, quiet, easy death
like I guess everyone wants."[19]

Determined thus to be responsible, and claiming to be kind (one of
the few instances where he claims to be moral), he carried a hammer into
his mother's bedroom at 5:15 A.M. "She moved around a little bit, and I
thought maybe she was waking up. I just waited and she was just laying
there. So I approached her right side . . . and I hit her just above the temple on her right side of the head . . . with a very hard blow. . . . Blood
started running down her face from the wound, and she was still breathing." With his usual passion for detail, he later described how he had then
turned his mother over on her back, held her chin up with his right hand
and slashed her throat. While she bled profusely, he decided that "what's
good for my victims was good for my mother." He decapitated her,
handcuffed her wrists, and put her in the closet. Rumors suggest that he
placed his mother's head on the mantel and either threw darts at it, or
punched it, or both; but he did cut out her larynx and push it down the
garbage disposal, and then sexually attack her headless body.[20]

Even now his mission was not entirely fulfilled. He felt ill and could neither eat nor enjoy his surroundings: "I couldn't stand being around the house any more." Still in a murderous rage, he drove through town and encountered an acquaintance, Robert, who owed him ten dollars. He could not help "chortling" at what Robert did not know—that he had buried Koo's head behind his chum's house, as a kind of joke. They decided to do some drinking and drove to a liquor store where Robert offered him the ten dollars: "To tell you the truth [that] saved his life, because with his little excuses, I needed to kill somebody at that point, and I think he deserved it more than anybody."[21]

Yet if Robert "deserved" to die in the sense that he had delayed his repayment of Kemper's loan, he was insufficiently central to Kemper's emotional life. Kemper decided that the "someone else" to die would be his mother's friend, Sally Hallet, who had enjoyed the affection and confidence that had been denied him. He telephoned Mrs. Hallet and invited her to a "surprise" dinner with his mother. When she arrived at the house exhausted from her day's work, Mrs. Hallet said, "'Let's sit down, I'm dead.' And I kind of took her at her word there," said Kemper, who punched her in the stomach and finally choked her to death. He severed her head and left her body on his bed as a final trophy, but spent that night in his mother's bed.[22]

Now his task had been discharged and his homicidal energy almost spent. He had killed ten people in almost perfect symmetry, by strangulation, stabbing, and shooting: first, two kin (his grandparents); then, six beautiful young women; and concluding with a kinswoman and quasi-kin (his mother and her intimate friend). He had eaten the flesh of two of his victims. According to journalist Don West, "He finally admitted having cut flesh from their legs, freezing it and then cooking it in a macaroni casserole." He ate them, he said, because "I wanted them to be a part of me—and now they are." Later, under police questioning, he would confess many of the details of how he had mutilated his victims—removing their teeth and keeping bits of skin and hair as keepsakes.[23]

Yet having completed his task, he did not know quite what to do. He left a note for the police in his mother's house, assuming they would soon find it.

Appx. 5:15 a.m. Saturday. No need for her to suffer any more at the hands of this horrible "murderous Butcher." It was quick—asleep—the way I wanted it.

Not sloppy and incomplete, gents. Just a "lack of time." I got things to do!!![24]

But he did not know what the "things to do" were. At 10 A.M. on Easter Sunday, he began driving relentlessly east. He drove to Reno, Nevada, where he rented a car and continued racing away from the coast. After eighteen hours, he was pulled over by police in Colorado and given a speeding ticket. He was surprised and then disappointed to realize that an All Points Bulletin had not been put out for him. In fact, the police knew nothing of his activities.

He continued driving east, stuffing himself with No-Doz tablets to maintain the pace. Then, in eastern Colorado, explicitly signaling that he felt his previous behavior to have been rational, he grew afraid of becoming irrational. "I felt I was losing control, and I was afraid that anything could cause me to go off the deep end, and I didn't know what would happen then. I had never been out of control in my life," Kemper said, and this fear moved him to pull over to a public telephone booth. The Santa Cruz police, some of whom were his drinking companions, would not take his confession seriously, and it took several calls and an extended vigil at the telephone booth before Colorado police arrived and arrested him. In his terms, his responsibilities had been discharged with honor: Soon he would sleep and eat like a fulfilled man. He would never be out of protective custody again.[25]

The Talking Time

What a remarkable creature was Edmund Emil Kemper III, not only in that his murders combined two usually separate homicidal themes— killing both relatives *and* young women—but also in his personal attributes. He was immense; so much so that his size disqualified him from

his dream of joining the police. Yet this was no deranged Franken-
stein's monster, for his IQ measured a gifted 136, and his conversation
was textured with wit and irony (even if its content was monotonously
homicidal, its purpose narrowly to shock). Neither was he delusional
like the killers Mullin and Berkowitz claimed to be, building uncon-
ventional and therefore "false" worlds. His mind perceived the world
clearly and conventionally, and did not fill it with fantasies of demons
and spirit forces. We must pay serious attention to Kemper.

It is the jumbled messages given off by the ideological conformity
of a Kemper and the pseudoradicalism of a Charles Manson that create the public perplexity about multiple murderers. Why do they do
the terrible things they do? What kind of an explanation can we expect
from this John Wayne-glorifying giant (he grew up worshiping and
identifying with the American hero-actor, John Wayne, whom his
rival, Mullin, grew up hating*), sporting his bloodstained buckskin
jacket, his prized Junior Chamber of Commerce pin (hard-won during his years in Atascadero mental hospital) adorning his lapel and
proclaiming his utter conventionality? Can we expect a thoughtful
answer from this freak whose childhood was little more than a sustained torrent of verbal abuse from his much-married mother? Fortunately we can, not only because he described and justified his acts in
such detail, and not only because he was so intelligent, but also
because, as Cheney reminds us, although a troubled person may make
a "poor autodiagnostician," nevertheless "Kemper with his years of
psychoanalysis had greater insight than most."[26]

We cannot, however, expect a *straightforward* answer from him.
Perhaps we might have had we not stared for so long into the photographs of his face and been struck by his ill-concealed contempt for
everyone and everything around him. He loved to toy with his simple-
minded inquisitors, first offering one explanation, then denying it, and
bringing forth another; leaving his audience always feeling that he "was
holding back the real key to his behavior." He would play with the

---

* Wayne's grip on the psyches of American multiple murderers is both deep and consistent. See also John Wayne Gacy, the homosexual torturer and multiple murderer.

court psychologists, starting interviews by trying to give *them* the Minnesota Multiphasic Personality Inventory (a test which he had learned and administered to others during his years in the mental hospital). He never, thought his interrogators, told the whole truth; and whenever he was in danger of telling more than he wished, he would simply begin to describe dismemberment in detail, riveting the attention of his interviewers and leading the conversation in other directions.[27]

Moreover, his black humor would continually resurface, partly to amuse himself, but more, it seems, to shock his audience. Thus he would satirize both the California dialect and himself, claiming he dreamed of decapitating hitchhikers as a means of "finding out where their heads were at"; or claiming that cutting off the hands of two of his victims had been "an afterthought." He used the standard rules of Hollywood humor to shock a woman reporter for a detective magazine who tried to sound him out on his attitudes toward women: "What do you think now when you see a pretty girl walking down the street? One side of me says, 'Wow, what an attractive chick, I'd like to talk to her, date her.' The other side of me says, 'I wonder how her head would look on a stick.'" Surely this is playing the game for all that it is worth.[28]

This amused malice also typified his behavior toward his rival and fellow multiple murderer, Herbert Mullin, who for a time occupied a cell adjacent to him. Kemper insisted upon calling him "Herbie," a diminutive Mullin hated. When a reporter asked him why he continued to ridicule and torment Mullin, Kemper replied: "Well, he had a habit of singing and bothering people when somebody tried to watch TV. So I threw water on him to shut him up. Then, when he was a good boy, I'd give him peanuts. Herbie liked peanuts. That was effective, because pretty soon he asked permission to sing. That's called behavior modification treatment."[29]

Yet we should not be lulled into thinking Kemper's purpose was mundane, for he felt he was on a kind of crusade, and despised those (like Mullin) who killed without any apparent ideological justification. "He [Mullin] was just a cold-blooded killer . . . killing everybody he saw for no good reason." Kemper laughed when he realized that his audience would not understand his own "good reason," and added: "I guess that's kind of hilarious, my sitting here so self-righteously talking like that, after what I've done." When asked if Mullin was insane, Kemper replied with a mixture of pomposity and self-satire: "Yes, judging from my years in Atascadero, I would say he is mentally ill." We shall see if this is all mere rationalization and persiflage.[30]

If Kemper found the act of contrition unthinkable, he sometimes claimed he found the act of confession disturbing. "This is a bummer. Which is why I get depressed in that damn cell 'cause I realized earlier today after talking to you guys that I . . . make a very strong attempt not to think about any of this stuff, anything related to it, and especially my mother while I'm in that cell, because I just get super depressed. I'm just sitting there, I still haven't slept in four days. I tried two more times back there to sleep, and I'd lay down—and the first thing, I'd start thinking about this last weekend. And I get super torqued-up and I'm wide awake; just absolutely not drowsy. And this is including 1,500 miles of driving almost constantly. And the last nine hundred miles of it was nothing but gas—a bottle of pop once in a while, and a lot of No-Doz."[31]

Unlike the killers Bundy, who tells us nothing, or Panzram, who puts it too succinctly, Kemper talks freely, with mingled embarrassment and delight, despite protestations, reservations, and contradictions. In the end, he leaves us with not one, but five explanations. Taken separately, as they were by his examiners, they seem to contradict one another and cancel each other out. That is why his interrogators complained that he could neither stop complaining nor tell the "whole truth. We always felt he was holding something back," said one. I think not. The examiners did not see that they were being handed a complete and consistent package, merely delivered in superficially contradictory bundles, and sometimes wrapped in Atascadero's flimsy psychology.[32]

Again and again, Kemper patiently explained that the murder spree was an organized "operation," subject to specific "rules," and that the murders were formal "executions," for which his childhood games had been mere rehearsals. He repeatedly denied police suggestions that the murders had been "spontaneous urges," and insisted that they had deep meaning. It would, he said, be "kind of hard to go around killing somebody just for the hell of it. . . . It's not a kicks thing, or I would have ceased doing it a long time ago. It was an urge. I wouldn't say it was on the full of the moon or anything, but I noticed that no matter how horrendous the crime had been or how vicious the treatment of the bodies after death . . . still, at that point in my crimes the urge to do it again coming as often as a week or two weeks afterwards—a strong urge, and the longer I let it go the stronger it got, to where I was taking risks to go out and kill people—risks that normally, according to my little rules of operation, I wouldn't take because they could lead to arrest."[33]

He did not plunge cavalierly into such reckless behavior; in fact, he procrastinated for months. At first, he admitted, "I was scared, and kept telling myself I didn't really want to do it. But I was determined. I was very frustrated, because it was like a game to me. Up to that point, it always had been. It was a big adventure, a big thrill. But I never permitted myself to follow through." Once committed, however, his operation was conducted flawlessly, so much so that "if I had kept my mouth shut, I would have gotten away with them, I think, forever."[34]

To what intent does he refer when he said that after the tenth kill, "the original purpose was gone"? Which plan had been fulfilled, which force released, to allow him "to burn out the hate and fear"? What had changed so much that now "the need that I had for continuing death was needless and ridiculous. It wasn't serving any physical or real or emotional purpose. It was just a pure waste of time"? Our quest requires a detailed explication of his statements.[35]

Sexual Mania

The "natural" or common-sense explanation for Kemper's behavior, much preferred by police, psychiatrists, journalists, and the public, is of course a sexual one, and Kemper himself offered this for our titillation from time to time. After all, it does make a certain sense: He was primarily engaged in killing beautiful young women and sexually assaulting their corpses. Sometimes he even went so far as to claim he was little more than an especially brutal rapist who killed merely to eliminate the only witnesses to his sexual exploits. He explained that he learned this tactic during his adolescence in the mental hospital, when his fellow patients had warned him that too many rapists were identified and caught. Arguing logically from this, he said: "I had decided from my past stay at Atascadero and listening to a lot of stories, that what I thought was my past experience—it seemed to me a lot more efficient not to have someone, unless you're absolutely sure that they weren't going to go to anybody. I decided to kind of mix the two and have a situation of rape and a murder and no witness and no prosecution." All of this would make sense if he had systematically raped his victims. But he did not. In some cases, he hardly touched them sexually. Perhaps other needs were being satisfied?[36]

To pursue this even further: On the one hand he claimed that rape without murder was "just way too chancy"; but on the other hand he wondered if the murders had been necessary at all, allowing himself to speculate: "Thinking back on it, I really honestly think I could have gotten away with doing exactly what I told them I was going to do, which was rape. I didn't say that word. But one of them asked me, 'What do you want?' And I pointed the gun. I just lifted it up between the two of them, and I told her, 'You know what I want.'"[37]

Yet this overlooks his sexual incapacities. He insisted that he had a "very strong sensual drive, a weird sexual drive that started early, a lot earlier than normal, before I was aware of the phallic responsibilities." His sexual fantasies "were usually around women and rather than just having an orgasm it was having it with a dead woman. That was my fantasy. It would be more along the lines of a not so forceful rape." Still, we search in vain for any clear indication that sexuality was his strongest impulse. In places, he came close to denying his own claim of an all-powerful sexuality. He admitted that he "felt very inadequate sexually and sensually and socially," and that his fantasies of making passionate love to people "became dissatisfying because part of me knew that I couldn't really carry these things out. I couldn't follow through with the male end of the responsibility, so my fantasies became . . . if I killed them, you know, they couldn't reject me as a man. It was more or less making a doll out of a human being . . . and carrying out my fantasies with a doll, a living human doll."[38]

He insisted that he would have preferred to have raped Mary Ann Pesce and Anita Luchessa, his first victims, but "I had full intentions of killing them both. I would love to have raped them. But not having any experience at all in this area . . . this is one of the big problems I had." Yet his murders were always associated with an extraordinary, lace-curtain kind of sexual delicacy. He emphasized that he had attempted "no hanky-panky" with Cynthia Schall before he killed and dissected her; and recalled that he had apologized to Mary Ann when his hand had accidentally brushed against her breast while he was smothering her with a plastic bag: "There was absolutely no contact with improper areas," he insisted absurdly. Is this some sort of insane lower-middle-class sense of "refinement," some lunatic Puritanism that concerns itself with touching "improper areas" while murdering a young woman? Conversely, if he killed his mother to spare her the "embarrassment" of learning that he was a multiple murderer, then why was it necessary for him to sexually and symbolically assault her corpse?[39]

There are too many contradictions here, and the most fundamental one is surely that of his claimed super-sexuality. Despite all his protestations about his powerful sexual drive, he did not appear to be driven to exercise it very often. Moreover, the only act he seems genuinely to have found sexually exciting was decapitation. "I remember there was actually a sexual thrill," he said, for he loved to hear the "pop" when the head was separated from the body. "You hear that little pop and pull their heads off and hold their heads up by the hair. Whipping their heads off, their body sitting there. That'd get me off." Undoubtedly, but in what sense was that a sexual experience?[40]

For Kemper, *death*, not sex, was the ecstasy. Death, not sex, was much closer to the prime goal, for he knew "there was always a disappointment in not achieving a sexual rapport, let's say, with the victim. That's why the sex after death sometimes, because it's through frustration." Thus sex seemed to be a secondary benefit, and this suggestion is made even more explicit in his explanation of why he killed no men (other than his grandfather, who was in the way): "I suppose I could have been doing this with men, but that always posed more of a threat. They weren't nearly as vulnerable. . . . Plus, like in the case where sex is involved, or the thrill of having a woman around, alive and dead, wasn't there with a man." In sum, he "could have" killed men, and to have done so would not have violated his prime purpose; but they were physically less vulnerable and infinitely less exciting. Thus sex was the secondary, not the primary, benefit. If death, not sex, was a more important motive, then why?[41]

Possession

Possession is a second major motivational theme running through Kemper's monologue to the authorities. On the witness stand, he claimed he had killed women for the same reason that, as a child, he had killed cats—"to make it mine." He killed the women because, "Alive, they were distant, not sharing with me. I was trying to establish a relationship, and there was no relationship. . . . When they were being killed, there wasn't anything going on in my mind except that they were going to be mine. . . . That was the only way they could be mine."[42]

Here Kemper was arguing, in a vein commonly found in "primitive" cultures, that certain acts allowed an individual to possess the body and spirit of his victims. "I wanted the girls for myself—as possessions. They were going to be mine; they are mine!" In this spirit too, he ate the flesh of several of his victims: "I wanted them for my own. I wanted them to be a part of me—and now they are."[43]

The process of possession as he described it is to turn something human and animate, which he could neither own nor control, into something material and inanimate (yet of the very stuff of life), which he could control. In his words, "It was more or less making a doll out of a human being. Taking life away from them, a living human being, and then having possession of everything that used to be theirs. All that would be mine. Everything . . . I was swashbuckling." Precisely. With their torsos in his closet, their heads in his trunk, or their last photographs in his bedroom, he came into possession of their material form and their spirit: swashbuckling, like a pirate ransacking golden galleons. We shall return to this theme.[44]

Trophy Hunting

Kemper offered an additional explanation, often misinterpreted by observers as yet another contradiction, which stressed the exhilaration of this ultimate triumph. "The head trip fantasies were a bit like a trophy. You know, the head is where everything is at, the brain, eyes, mouth. That's the person. I remember being told as a kid, you cut off the head and the body dies. The body is nothing after the head is cut off. . . . [At this point in the confessions, according to West, Kemper paused and chuckled] Well, that's not quite true. With a girl, there's a lot left in the girl's body without a head. Of course, the personality is gone."[45]

Once again, Kemper marshaled his thoughts to sort out what had been his goals. He tried to emphasize that the blood and gore were not central to his enterprise, dismissing it as a deviation that only emerged later. "I had started to really get into gear toward the end there. I was getting what I think is sicker, and it was much more of a need for more of the blood—and the blood got in my way. It wasn't something I desired to see. Blood was an actual pain in the ass. What I wanted to see was the *death*, and I wanted to see the *triumph*, the exultation over the death. It was like eating, or a narcotic, something that drove me more and more and more," he said. "I just wanted the exultation over the other party. In other words, winning over death. They were dead and I was alive. That was a victory in my case." Moreover, the victory was a double one, for the triumph was not only over the lifeless victim, but also over his own fear—the latter triumph enhanced by his use of the pistol, which "made it much simpler, much easier, much quicker, less of a threat to me personally. I was less afraid to attack."[46]

Mother Rage

A fourth explanatory thread is the notion, obviously heavily influenced by his years of "therapy" in the mental hospital, that the killings were a kind of displacement to safer objects of the rage he felt toward his mother. More than any other, this explanation was seized upon by the psychologically oriented public as the True Version of Events. "Had he killed her [his mother] first, perhaps the others might have been spared," mused Cheney, ignoring the fact that he killed another after his mother. Still, there is plenty of evidence that mother rage was a profound reality in his life, and the theory is not to be dismissed.[47]

Kemper described his troubled childhood with considerable insight. "Very early, my natural parents were always loud and very pushy. As I was growing up, I shied away from loud noises and arguments. My mother was very strong and she wanted a man who was very strong. My father was very big and very loud, but he was very weak and she wanted the opposite. . . . You know, wooing and dating, you're one thing, but after you're married you let it all hang out. She was just too powerful. She would drive them away, attack them verbally, attack their manhood."[48]

Cheney touched on an important point when she observed that Kemper's mother felt her husband's work was menial, and the two often argued over money. In addition, Mrs. Kemper had claimed her husband "never spanked the children and they never had any respect for him. All he ever gave Ed was his medals and war stories." In an earlier letter, she recalled that his father "favored the son and was overprotective. . . . He resented my disciplining the boy at even an early age and sometimes blames the girls for letting him get in trouble." For his part, the father reported alarming maternal practices: "His mother made him at the age of eight years sleep in the cellar of the house for about eight months. He was terrified of this place. There was only one way out. Someone had to move the kitchen table and lift the trapdoor. I put a stop to it and threatened her with the law." Kemper's mother justified this behavior in terms of her reluctance to be "overprotective"—a stance her sister had taken with her own son, and had been disappointed to learn that she had produced a homosexual.[49]

Kemper's parents had separated in 1957, and Mrs. Kemper moved with her three children to Helena, Montana, where she found work as a bank secretary. She was divorced from Kemper in 1961, and two months later married a German immigrant. This second husband soon left, and a year later, divorced once more, she married a forty-five-year-old plumber named Turnquist. "I found out," Kemper later recalled, "that she didn't need any protection at all. She used always to tell me how much I reminded her of my father, whom she dearly hated, of course." Turnquist was a kindly stepfather, taking Kemper on fishing trips and teaching him to hunt; but it was Turnquist whom Kemper had stood behind with an iron bar, planning to knock him unconscious and steal his car in order to visit his natural father. About that time, his mother wrote: "I was deeply worried during the years about the lack of a father relationship, and so I tried everything I could to compensate for that." But, according to Lunde, she interpreted this as *carte blanche* to "punish and ridicule him in order to 'make him a man.'"[50]

After his first incarceration for the murder of his grandparents, Kemper rapidly internalized the psychological definitions of self dispensed by the staff at Atascadero, a process which revealed itself clearly in his later remarks: "I found out in the hospital that I really killed my grandmother because I wanted to kill my mother." But why then was he still in a murderous rage after killing his mother? Why then go on to kill her friend? "My grandmother was worse than my mother. I had this love-hate complex with my mother that was very hard for me to handle and I was very withdrawn—withdrawn from reality because of it. I couldn't handle the hate, and the love was actually forced upon me, you know. It was a very strong family-tie type love. There was a constant battle inside me that was the major thing of my whole life. I didn't have any social attitude, any social personality at all." This echoes a theme especially common among those who annihilate their own families. At Atascadero, he "learned" that he "really" hated his mother: surely true, but insufficient cause for what was to come.[51]

When he was released from Atascadero, the authorities ignored the psychiatrists' sound advice and "They paroled me right back to Mama.

Well, my mother and I started right in on horrendous battles, just horrible battles, violent and vicious. I've never been in such a vicious verbal battle with anyone. It would go to fists with a man, but this was my mother and I couldn't stand the thought of my mother and I doing these things. She insisted on it, and just over stupid things." And what were these epic struggles about? They were the classic obsessive concerns of those gripped by status insecurity, by the fear of downward mobility, expressed in fears that their work is too menial, their income is too low, their personal styles inappropriate to their class aspirations: "I remember one roof-raiser was over whether I should have my teeth cleaned."[52]

Kemper tried to flee. He took a job with the state's Department of Highways and rented his own apartment. But in early 1972, he broke his arm in a motorcycle accident and began spending more time at his mother's home, recuperating. West recorded that their neighbors knew when Kemper was visiting from the shouts and loud arguments reverberating through the walls, during which Kemper would be "upbraided for lazing about drinking beer and *not making something of himself*. . . . She had been known to reduce Guy [her pet name for Kemper] to tears in front of his friends with her sharp tongue." At the time, Kemper denied that the fights were important, insisting to a neighbor that the vehement quarrels were simply his family's means of expression. Parading his Atascadero psychology, he told the neighbor: "We like to get things out in the open. My mother and I are really very close and we know these fights don't mean anything."[53]

In the meantime, Kemper appeared to struggle for her love, showering her with presents on social occasions such as Easter, or her birthday. But there was nothing that this beer-swilling, ex-mental patient and flagman for the Department of Highways could possibly do to please this university administrator. When he fled back to his own apartment, she continued to pursue him. "I couldn't stay away from my mother. . . . She would get madder than cat shit, got my phone number, calling me up wanting to come up and visit all the time. The hassle with my mother made me very inadequate around women, because they posed a threat to me. Inside I blew them up very large.

You know, the little games women play, I couldn't play, meet their demands, so I backslid. . . . With my Atascadero learning, I kept trying to push her toward where she would be a nice motherly type and quit being such a damned manipulating, controlling vicious beast. She was Mrs. Wonderful up on the campus, had everything under control. When she comes home, she lets everything down and she's just a pure bitch, bust her butt being super nice at work and come home at night and be a shit."[54]

He occasionally attributed the murders of Rosalind Thorpe and Alice Liu to an argument with his mother. "I was mad that night. My mother and I had a real tiff. I was pissed. I told her I was going to a movie and I jumped up and went straight to the campus, because it was still raining and ideal [hunting weather]. I decided that the first girl I picked up who looked halfway decent, I'm going to blow her brains out." Most students of Kemper supported this view, painting the killings exclusively as a kind of dialogue with his mother. After he shot Cynthia Schall, West said Kemper "felt pleased with his choice of the long hollow-point slugs, because she had died more quickly and easily than anyone. He had a sudden impulse to go home and tell his mother, so she could know that there were some things he could do right." Yet Kemper himself explained it in subtly different terms, emphasizing broader issues than his disordered relationship with his mother: "The real me was somewhat bolstered at Atascadero to where I wouldn't let anyone push me over the brink any more to just self-destruction. In the case of the girls, it was fantasy coming back. Rather than fight my mother, fight the world, finally I decided, well, screw it. I'm going to play their little game." Exactly, but what was this game of theirs, and in what sense was he playing it?[55]

Kemper told the psychiatrist Lunde of his "recurring fantasies of killing women, his mother in particular"; and he had often considered killing her, entering her bedroom at night, carrying a weapon. But Kemper rationalized the actual murder of his mother as an attempt to spare her embarrassment. "I felt . . . that I was going to be caught pretty soon for the killing of these girls. . . . A long time ago, I had thought about what I was going to do in the event of being caught for the other crimes, and the only choices I saw were just accept it and go to jail, and let my mother carry the load and let the whole thing fall in her hands, like happened the last time with my grandparents, or I could take her life." Kemper rationalized as much as any human being, especially one caught in such a persona-degrading circumstance as he was in, but he rarely did so with such transparent self-serving naivety as here: Undoubtedly he did so because nothing else he had done was so unequivocally taboo in his civilization.[56]

When asked why he had taken so long to actually kill his mother, he confessed his fear of her: "I never had the nerve. You would have to understand the gap I had to bridge the way people had been manipulating me." When it was finally done, her killing was more than he could have wished, for it both reduced her in his eyes and released him from her prison. "I had always considered my mother very formidable, very fierce and very foreboding. She had always been a very big influence in my life and whether I hated her or loved her, it was amazing to me how like every other victim of mine had died, how vulnerable, how human she was. It shocked me for quite some time. I'm not sure it still doesn't shock me [but] I felt quite relieved after her death." During his last run, through Colorado, Kemper thought deeply of the biblical symbolism associated with his acts. The Bible had always fascinated him, and the severing of his mother's left hand was "symbolic, I suppose. I think it is like the left-hand-of-God thing," God's punishing hand, of which the cutting from his mother's body freed him from all retribution.[57]

Revenge

The biblical eye-for-an-eye is the fifth and final explanatory theme running through Kemper's ambiguous confessions—an Old Testament theme that he spelled out in great detail, most convincingly, and then repudiated during his trial. Still, the central emphasis is clear: He wished both to "make a demonstration to the authorities" and to "even up the Accounts Receivable to match the Accounts Payable." But what did he wish to demonstrate to the authorities, and what were the missing payments in the accounts ledger? This phrase "demonstrate to the authorities" is peculiar wording, resonant more of political proclamation than of private act. And a demand for payment is an odd position for Kemper to take: He was no impoverished black proletarian denied forever a place in the social order. To the contrary, with his intelligence and his mother's marginal middle-class membership, he could have easily made good his deficiencies in a junior college, then transferred to university and entered the middle-class world himself. But he did not do so: Unlike so many false rebels, his acts confirmed his advertised disdain. He chose instead to wage a complex vendetta as the only means to validate himself and seize control of his own destiny (even if in doing so he transferred the remainder of his life to the state).[58]

What *was* this John Wayne-worshiping laborer's conception of his society? "I consider it a very phony society, a very phony world, where people are too busy copping out to so many things to exist and fit into a group that they had lost sight of their individual aims and goals. I had become completely lost, and very bitter about what I considered these phony values and phony existence, and decided that I was going, not necessarily to weed things out—because I would have ended up killing most of the world if I weeded out—but I was striking out at what was hurting me the worst, which was the area, I guess, deep down, I wanted to fit in the most, and I had never fit in, and that was the in-group." This statement begins with a measure of accuracy and coherence, if expressed in most childish terms, but soon degenerates into a contradictory Atascadero group-therapy form of analysis—where he first claims to reject society (and especially those who abandon their principles in order to "fit in") and then "admits" that all he really wanted was to be a part of it.[59]

We would be foolish to expect consistency in any human being, let alone in a multiple murderer engaged in the enterprise of justifying his existence. Nevertheless, a man of intelligence is talking here about the ultimate purpose of his life, a purpose he embraced so passionately that he sacrificed all else for it. His thoughts deserve careful scrutiny. He edged toward a truth when he discussed his unfulfilled plan of "anni-hilating" his neighborhood. "Yeah. That was one of my things. I'd feel inadequate there, feel like everybody's catching up with me, and I'm not doing anything. Considering the abilities I did have, in say cre-ating a calm about me where people weren't excited or suspicious or nervous . . . I believed and I still believe that had I wanted to, just as a demonstration—and I thought of making this a demonstration to the authorities in Santa Cruz—how serious this was, and how bad a foe they had come up against."[60]

This "foe" of the authorities wanted more than just to exult in the possession of his trophies, or to punish his mother. "It wasn't just deaths I wanted. It was, like I said, somewhat of a *social statement* in there too." Entirely congruent with this was his discussion of why he did not prey on children, despite their vulnerability. "There are two things against that. One is the most important—that is that children are innocent. Children are unknowing. And I have always been very pro-tective of children for that reason." But of *what* are their elders guilty? He continued: "These girls weren't much more than children, I sup-pose, but I felt . . . that they were old enough to know better than to do the things they were doing . . . out there hitchhiking, when they had no reason or need to. They were flaunting in my face the fact that they could do any damn thing they wanted, and that society is as screwed up as it is. So that wasn't a prime reason for them being dead. It was just something that would get me a little uptight, the thought of that, them feeling so safe in a society where I didn't feel safe." But of what could a 300-pound, six-foot-nine-inch giant be afraid?[6]

Kemper preyed only on those he felt shared the guilt (either directly in their power over him, or indirectly via their apparent social associ-ation with the authorities): the dominant class, and most especially on that class's beautiful and desired young women whose "flaunted" indifference toward him hurt him most. Thus he could say with hon-esty that "I had some Accounts Payable and I closed my Accounts Receivable, and so I had to balance the accounts." The targets for his "little game" were to be young women who were appropriately upper class, at least in appearance. Hitchhiking was the only mechanism that made such targets vulnerable: "I couldn't entice young, well-to-do smart asses whom I dearly hated into my car to go for a ride any other way." He did not consider himself a meaningless "bubble that burst all over society—I was more organized than that." He knew where to find his victims, and why he was destroying them. "I was swashbuckling, I was destroying only society's finest young girls. I was not interested in the ragged, dirty little hippies, that would have been simple. I could have run up a huge score that way."[62]

This foe of the authorities made his coherent plan, organized his demonstration, and decided to attack. "I was frustrated in my dreams and desires totally. It was sad, really. I didn't blame society for me not being able to be a policeman, but . . ." society seemed so utterly *indifferent* to him. Even when he was returning Liu's torso to the car, "I just wandered right out there with her and put her in the trunk right under the window. That's one thing that amazes me about society. That is, that you can do damn near anything and nobody's gonna say anything or notice. Rather than fight my mother, fight the world, finally I decided, well, screw it. I'm going to play their little game. They are going to see what they want to see—Ed out working, Ed doing this and that. Meanwhile Ed is deep in deciding how he can get back at society for putting him in this hellhole in the first place."[63]

Within this dweller in hellholes crystalized a new identity, undoubtedly his first agreeable one: the Swashbuckling Avenger. Only through the series of intellectual twists and transformations we have charted could an intellect so conventional that it embodied all the mainstream themes of his civilization—John Wayne and policemen, the Boy Scouts, the National Rifle Association, and the Atascadero branch of the Junior Chamber of Commerce—commit itself to the slaughter of women. He would annihilate a sample of the excluding class, women who kept him in his hellhole literally, as in locking him in a cellar, or by offering him only contempt, disrespect, and bland indifference.

Kemper was too proud to spend his life as a flagman for the Department of Highways, too obsessed with his inadequacies to do anything about them, too rattled by his mother and Atascadero to devote his energy to anything but staying alive. The choice made a certain sense: Now, if he picked up women in his car, it would be only for an entirely serious purpose: "It was for possible execution . . . and it would only be if they were young, reasonably good looking, not necessarily well-to-do, but say, of a better class of people than the scroungy, messy, dirty, smelly, hippy types I wasn't at all interested in. I suppose they would have been more convenient, but that wasn't my purpose. *My little social statement was, I was trying to hurt society where it hurt the worst,* and that was by taking its valuable . . . future members of the working society; that was the upper class or the upper-middle class, what I considered to be snobby or snotty brats, or persons that was actually—that ended up later being better equipped to handle a living situation than I was, and be more happily adjusted."[64]

With the commitment sealed, he still yearned to communicate with these snobby, happy brats. During their drive, he tried to establish a kind of relationship with his first victims, Pesce and Luchessa, but his sense of social incompetence so overwhelmed him that "I felt like a big bumblebutt. . . . They were both eighteen at the time, I think, and I was twenty-three, which isn't that much of a gap, but it was just like a million years."[65]

After killing them, he made scrupulous attempts to ensure that they had been suitably upper class (for if they had been otherwise, his protest would have been pointless), especially Mary Ann Pesce, to whom he had been most attracted. He went through her wallet and noted the middle-class college student card and the Bear Valley ski-patrol card. Obtaining her family's address, he drove the hundreds of miles to ensure that it was in a "country club district" (for had it not been, his plan would surely have been malfunctioning). Later, he allowed himself to fabricate a close relationship with Pesce: "I was quite struck by her personality, her looks, almost a reverence," but it was a frustrated one, for even "with me in control of the situation there, I still wasn't in control of her and it made me mad."[66]

Ted Bundy consciously eliminated all emotional contact with his prospective victims, speaking to them as little as possible to avoid the development of any inhibiting social bond. Kemper did the opposite and tried to cultivate a relationship—not to make the kill more difficult, but largely to obtain the necessary social information to be sure the girls were of the targeted upper class. "This was something I usually tried—to talk to the girls about, and gently probe about, different things; to find out their life-style, their living conditions, whatever." At first he was not certain that Aiko Koo was from the correct background: "She was very free and prolific in her speech, and I believed from her speech that she came from a home of meager means, that her parents had either divorced or her father had left her at an early age. . . . And there was no family car. The only transportation that she had was a bus to and from where she would go. Her clothing was rather plain and she apparently had taken pains to dress herself . . . as clean-cut as possible." If she was a marginal case, she was available; her *style* was suitably upper class, and Kemper correctly sensed that she came from "an aristocratic type of family" in a state of genteel poverty. Still, it troubled him that Koo had not been a proper choice.[67]

In essence then, this evidence paints Kemper as a swashbuckling pirate who boards the upper-class galleon and carries off its most valuable possessions, its beautiful young women. But in court, under questioning from his own attorney, Kemper denied the entire theory he had constructed so painstakingly during the interrogations. Now he claimed he killed only to possess them (theory two): "When the girls were alive, they were distant and not sharing with me. I was trying to establish a relationship." Is this a legitimate denial, or mere frustration at trying to explain his story so often? Or was it a bored accommodation with his attorney to the kind of sentence they wished to receive? I think it was the latter. It takes no great imagination to sketch in the hurried conversations, during which the virtues of a "crazy" plea (of some psychic need to possess his victims) would be pressed in order to ensure the relative comfort and safety of a mental hospital. A statement of revenge might have ensured only the tender mercies of a prison.[68]

At the close of the trial, the swashbuckling pirate showed his true ideological affinity: He was leading a brief rebellion, not a revolution. The only relationship he established during the trial was with Deputy Sheriff Colomny, who was his jailer. "He's more like a father to me than anyone I have ever known. He's like the father I wish I had had," Kemper said at his sentencing. With that, he removed his precious Junior Chamber of Commerce pin from the lapel of his buckskin jacket. Deputy Colomny watched as "Ed looked at it for a long time and tears came to his eyes. Then he handed it to me and said, 'Here, I want you to have it.'" Like so many swashbuckling pirates before him, once his rampage was stopped, he embraced the social order, and counted his booty.[69]

Tales from Psychiatry

> "I see no psychiatric reason to consider him [Kemper] to be a danger to himself or any other member of society."
>
> *Kemper's psychiatrist*

Psychiatry's unrivaled access to the court system makes it the heir to the richest data on all criminal behavior. What insights did the psychiatrists construct about Kemper during the many years he was in their care? Kemper first came to their attention after killing his grandparents. The psychiatrists immediately disagreed about him. The court psychiatrist, one of the few mental health professionals ever to understand how dangerous Kemper was, found him to be "psychotic, confused and unable to function." His notes continued with the observations that Kemper "has paranoid ideation, growing more and more bizarre. It is noteworthy that he is more paranoid toward women, all except his mother, who is the real culprit. He is a psychotic and danger to himself and others. He may well be a very long-term problem," he predicted with eerie prescience. Whether or not the court psychiatrist's "diagnosis" of "psychotic" was accurate, he was to be the last professional whom Kemper could not fool about his threat to the world.[70]

The California Youth Authority social workers and medical staff, responding presumably to Kemper's articulate and duplicitous intelligence, disagreed with the court psychiatrist and found Kemper's thinking to be neither confused, bizarre, nor psychotic. One report stressed that he showed "no flight of ideas, no interference with thought, no expression of delusions or hallucinations, and no evidence of bizarre thinking." Their diagnosis was that while Kemper had poor ego strength and suffered from passivity and a fear of injury by other boys, he merely suffered from "personality trait disturbance, passive-aggressive type." Just before his sixteenth birthday—and despite the non-sexual nature of his killings—Kemper was admitted to Atascadero mental hospital for sex offenders, a "learning experience" in which he would be immersed for five years.[71]

In the mental hospital, Kemper established a relationship with a Dr. Vanasek, and began earning his good opinion by working for him, administering psychological tests to patients in the psychology laboratory. "He was a very good worker," Vanasek remembered, "and this is *not* typical of a sociopath. He really took pride in his work." Taking pride in his work, passing through adolescence in a milieu of violent rapists encouraged to broadcast their crimes and fantasies in group "therapy," Kemper internalized both their disordered sexuality and the hospital's psychological theories—although he seems to have used his psychological knowledge primarily to conceal his own developing ideas, and to dupe his examiners.[72]

Still, his tests revealed the rage that was still boiling inside him. When he was nineteen, the usual Rorschach inkblots provoked from him a response of nonhuman and violent images—"two bears running into each other"; "alligator's jaws—his mouth is wide open"; "oil fire in the distance, black smoke going up in the air, reflecting in water"; "a trapdoor with a spider at the bottom, sitting down in the hole waiting to snatch an insect." The testing psychologist's conclusions, based on the results of the Rorschach and TAT tests, were that: "Emotionally, Mr. Kemper is somewhat immature and volatile. The prevailing mood is that of moderate depression accompanied by generalized anxiety. There is evidence of a rather substantial amount of latent hostility. . . .

He gives the impression of a rather passive, dependent person rather than one who is overtly aggressive. The possibility of explosiveness is certainly evident, however." The collection of his personality traits revealed the following profile: "Intelligent, emotionally unstable, easily upset, shy, suspicious, self-opinionated, artless, apprehensive, noncritical, careless, follows own urges, tense, driven, overwrought, and fretful"—a set of traits which might, one speculates, belong to half the human race. Still, this nonaggressive, "rather passive, dependent person" was soon to be released.[73]

Paroled to his mother over the objections of his psychiatrists, Kemper left Atascadero with a rapidly coalescing vision of what his life task might be. But his bland manner reassured the parole psychiatrist who, months later, released him from parole after the satisfying and intimate interview. The psychiatrist did not look in Kemper's trunk, where lay a victim's head. In an evaluation that may well stand for all time as the least prescient, the psychiatrist wrote: "I see no psychiatric reason to consider him to be a danger to himself or any other member of society. His motorcycle and driving habits would appear to be more of a threat to his own life and health than any threat he is presently to anyone else."[74]

Later, after his murderous task had been completed and he had turned himself in, having made his demonstration to the authorities, Kemper received even closer psychiatric scrutiny. Psychiatric specialist on sexual deviation, Dr. Joel Fort, examined Kemper and concluded that he was a "sex maniac": "The two central themes were an overwhelming sexual curiosity and obsession with sex, to such an extent that, insofar as we use lay language or concepts that have been widely circulated in society, I think he could best be described as a sex maniac, certainly to a greater degree than anyone else I have seen in working with sexual and criminal problems in the past twenty years. The second theme was a tremendous range of hatred, rage, or aggressiveness that stemmed from a series of childhood experiences and subsequent experiences, and that involved or included getting back at a society that he felt wronged him, getting back at his mother and father that he felt had wronged him." But was Kemper's *sexual* obsession really much stronger than that of any lonely and frustrated virgin? And, in a world replete with wrongs, was he not wronged far less than many, perhaps most?[75]

Fort concentrated with gusto on Kemper's bizarre sexual practices, dwelling on his "oral copulations with several of his victims," and the "violent, extremely exciting acts of penile vaginal intercourse where he rapidly had orgasms and ejaculation, taking Polaroid photographs of them and of the heads of several after he beheaded them, then followed in a sort of a declining . . . sense of sexual pleasure by collecting their clothing, keeping some of it for varying periods of time, and collecting objects like books or other paraphernalia that they were carrying with them, and keeping them for varying periods of time, and glancing at them sometimes."[76]

Fort rejected a diagnosis of paranoid schizophrenia, a label that was much in the air after Kemper's capture, on the reasonable grounds that "a paranoid schizophrenic should have marked feelings of unreality, depersonalization—meaning that you lose your sense of identity, and lose the boundaries between yourself and other people in your environment [but why is this a sign of some mental disease, and not a response to his niche in society?], and most of all, has delusions, meaning false beliefs, beliefs that you are being persecuted." Similarly, Fort rejected a paranoid label, since Kemper's mother and grandmother had in fact appeared to reject him and deny him affection. Unfortunately, Fort insisted on merely labeling Kemper with a diagnosis that signals a mere sense of social disengagement: "I would place him in the broader category of personality disorder, specifically antisocial personality, which is no more, and no less, than the old diagnosis of psychopath or sociopath." Fort said the characteristics of those in this mental state include "not operating by any recognized or accepted moral code"; not profiting "from experience in the usual sense, that is, does not modify his behavior to conform to societal standards." Here Fort is simply describing some of the characteristics of any eccentric or non-conformist, not providing any useful insight into the mind of a multiple murderer. A more canny observation was that Kemper had achieved the celebrity status commonly granted multiple murderers in

America (even being asked for his autograph). Fort noted that Kemper "gets a considerable amount of pleasure and satisfaction from his status as a mass killer," but rather than looking for possible meaning in this, he explained it in terms of Kemper's inadequacy—it was all "the recognition that he sometimes desperately sought as a child, the attempt to overcome rejection."[77]

In the most scholarly assessment Kemper was to receive, the psychiatrist and writer Donald Lunde dismissed the applicability of the "criminal chromosome" theory, the profoundly unscientific product of the Harvard Medical School and elsewhere which suggests that "XYY boys are more impulsive than XY boys." Lunde noted that Kemper "fits one proposed description of the XYY—unusually tall, above average intelligence, and unusually violent" (along with a substantial minority of the American male population), but concluded that tests performed at Stanford University's Medical Center revealed that Kemper's chromosomes, like those of all our multiple murderers, were normal. Lunde went on to reject the categories of paranoid schizophrenia, sociopath, and personality disorder, but inserted his own: the "sadistic murderer. In rare individuals, for reasons that are not well understood, sexual and violent aggressive impulses merge early in the child's development, ultimately finding expression in violent sexual assaults, and in the most extreme cases, sadistic murders or sex murders." Interesting, but we are left wondering why some individuals should link sexuality and violence, and why they must kill to be satisfied, and whether that satisfaction is sexual or social.[78]

Kemper's Task

"I didn't want to kill *all* the co-eds in the world."

Edmund Kemper[79]

It is our responsibility, of course, to offer proof of our assertions: that it helps us little to know that "psychotics" or "sadists" may have a desire to humiliate and destroy their victims; that Kemper's rampage is more than the expression of a mental disease or the egomaniacal indulgence of a deranged sexuality; and that his task or mission permitted him to construct a crisp identity and terminate his alienation from society. Where then do we begin to decipher Kemper's code? One logical place is where he ended—with his conscious decision to shut down his "operation" and capitulate to the authorities: It was through this action that Kemper made the point most forcefully that his murder spree had been a task, and that the task had been fulfilled.

His Capitulation

Kemper reasoned, using his knowledge of police techniques garnered through his friendships with many officers, that so long as he followed his carefully considered procedures, he could have continued murdering: "If I had kept my mouth shut, I would have gotten away with them, I think, forever." He knew that the police were trying to capture the killer, but he also knew that "with the tools the police have to work with and with the basic concept that society isn't as cold-blooded and ruthless and back-stabbing as I am, they didn't really have [a chance]. I was being rather cunning about the whole thing." This statement alone would surely disqualify any literal application of the "sex maniac" theory, for why should he cease for all time (and he knew that once he confessed, he would be incarcerated for the remainder of his life) an activity he found so necessary and enjoyable (unless he was riddled with guilt and remorse, which he was not)?[80]

A partial explanation might lie in the strain he was feeling. "I was fairly agitated," he said. "I was kidding around a lot and was very nervous. My stomach was killing me. I think I'm developing ulcers because of all this. Not so much now, but I was in a great tension whenever something like that was happening, especially people in the trunk and having to dispose [of their bodies]. I'd get close to the point of panic until it was done. Shit," he said, "I couldn't keep on going forever. . . . I really couldn't have. Emotionally, I couldn't handle it much longer. Toward the end there, I started feeling the folly of the whole damn thing, and at the point of near exhaustion, near collapse, I just said the hell with it and called it all off. Let's say . . . I wore out of it." Kemper said of his last run, the frenzied drive away from the coast before he made the decision to capitulate: "It was very late at night. I was exhausted. . . . I was past exhaustion. I was just running on pure adrenaline. My body was quivering . . . and my mind was slowly just beginning to unravel." However, this explanation overlooks the fact that if he was under terrible tension before and during a kill, once it was done and the body disposed of, he experienced something verging on euphoria: "I would just completely relax." What was different now? Why would the ecstasy of total relaxation no longer return to him? Could it be because his task was finished, his point made, and he could no longer justify his killings?[81]

A second partial explanation of why Kemper capitulated is contained in his remark that, during his drive to Colorado, he began to feel that for the first time in his life he "was losing control" of himself. "I had never been out of control in my life," he said, a remarkable statement coming from someone we are taught to think of as quintessentially out of control, a rabid mad dog killer. Kemper explained this by distinguishing between mental and physical control: "I had lost control of my body. I had experienced this in the killing of my grandparents when I was fifteen. I just completely lost control of myself. But as far as my mind went, I had realized what was going on and I couldn't stop it. In this case my body was just exhausted and my mind was starting to go. I was hallucinating."[82]

Continuing with this illumination of his perspective, Kemper said: "I finally had a thought. I was trying to think, 'Wow, I have got to stop this because it is getting so far out of hand. I am not going to be responsible for what happens any further' . . . and I didn't like that idea." In other words, he accepted full responsibility for what to us is madness but to him was not—the murder of ten human beings—but he was concerned that he might do something that was not justifiable, to kill without meaning or awareness. "The original purpose was gone. It was starting to weigh kind of heavy. Let's say I started returning to some lucid moments where I—where I started to burn out the hate and fear . . . and the need that I had for continuing death was needless and ridiculous. It wasn't serving any physical or real or emotional purpose. It was just a pure waste of time." To kill without meaning was unacceptable to him; and when he had killed ten times, his quota had been filled. Further killings would have been without purpose, and he did not wish to leave that charge in his wake. If he submitted to the authorities then because he had achieved his objectives, what were those objectives?[83]

Unfinished Business

The most remarkable thing about Kemper's life—like that of many multiple murderers—is how unremarkable it was, at least before he began his homicidal career. It is true that being locked in the cellar by his appalling mother must have been deeply traumatic for him, but many people have experienced similar deprivation and yet still grow to a healthy maturity. It seems to be true that his mother, endlessly and maniacally picking at him, was an impossible woman to live with, for she could not control her status hysteria or her unloading of that insecurity upon her son. But he was not living with her when he began to kill; and even if he had been, a more plausible solution to his dilemma would have been to run away. It is true that his mother was much-married during his childhood, a practice which profoundly disorients a child, but from all accounts, including his own, his stepfathers seemed exceptionally kind to him. This is not at all the stuff of legend. Indeed, it seems misleading to look only to his family and childhood for the causes of his murderous career since his childhood was, by modern standards, not that appalling.

The reader may feel that in doing so we have closed the doors to understanding, for our civilization is entrapped in the mental custom of explaining the adult *exclusively* in terms of the child. But we have not closed all doors, and Kemper has opened still others. In his confessions, Kemper gave five "theories" to explain his behavior, theories which, the reader will remember, often contradicted one another—or seemed to. They were his frustrated sexuality, his need to possess, his exultant trophy hunting, his rage toward his mother, and the lust for revenge. If we take him only partly at his word, and see these not as separate and contradictory theories, but as insufficiently articulated *elements* of a single theory, we can then edge closer to the truth— which is that they were all part of his motive and his profit, all incorporated in a single plan.

Baldly stated, the question "Why did Kemper kill?" is the wrong one. The truth is that many humans have in them the capacity to terminate life (ask any psychiatrist or police officer)—to eliminate opposition, say, or for sadistic pleasure—but few choose to do so. Most avoid such an act, not because they are morally superior, as they so commonly claim, but because they are imprisoned in a web of responsibilities, commitments, beliefs, and sentiments which would render murder either an absurd gamble or ridiculous self-destruction. As inalienable parts of family, community, and society, most humans either already receive sufficient satisfactions in their lives, or they have been convinced that further prayer, work, or luck may bring them about. All of which is to say that most humans have too much to lose, and unless they are burdened by an ill-considered rashness, they will not embark on any homicidal venture, let alone a sustained campaign.

But imagine another man, perfectly sane, but one who has from his earliest beginnings found himself to be set aside from all the life that swirls around him; a boy who comes to feel that he could neither love nor be loved; and whose identity begins to coalesce around an adolescent fantasy of a pirate adventurer, or perhaps a cowboy who rights all exclusionary wrongs. It makes a certain sense that, rejected by both parents, living with a grandmother he found even more punitive, and obsessed with his growing violent fantasies (the only way he could retaliate against the constant assaults on his *persona*), he might explode and kill, and lose control of his body but not his mind, as Kemper would put it. Imprisoned then through steamy adolescence in an all-male institution, he had no opportunity to accidentally experience a

loving sexual relationship (or even to hear of one, given his sex-crim-
inal companions), or to discover that he might be more than he had
come to believe. It makes sense that, with an identity so stunted and
abridged that he could later confess he had "no personality at all," he
might be easy prey for any fantasy that would offer him a measure of
identity. Similarly, his incapacity for forming relationships resulted in
a personal alienation so complete that there was no one in his life
except his raging mother. Here was a man with very little to lose.
Hardly surprising then that the mature cowboy/pirate/adventurer
might elect to swashbuckle, to form a game plan that would confront
all the major issues in his life—and do so with a forcefulness and final-
ity in keeping with the spirit of a true adventurer.* What were these
major issues? His rage at his mother, his frustrated sexuality, and his
utter alienation from all humanity.

Putting the flesh of reality to his fantasy through a conscious decision to swashbuckle would deal not only with the ghosts of his childhood, but with the empty promise of his adult life (for he could not
bring himself to believe that anything would change—and perhaps he
was right). Yet Kemper was no revolutionary, had no desire to transform the social order under the banner of some brave new ideology:
On the contrary, he identified with its most conservative symbols.
And yet he knew that he could never be a part of life unless he revoked
his excommunication through some extravagant act, establishing
thereby a social niche for himself and a firm identity: a simple desire,
but a necessary one, for only if he has his own borders can a man
negotiate with adjacent entities.

Thus Kemper's motive was clear: "I had been frustrated in my

---

* With the special gift of hindsight, it is easy to see that the signs were there much earlier: in his TAT test at the age of nineteen. When shown a photograph of a boy and an
older man, he replied: "In this situation we've got a young man who's got problems, and
his dad is counseling him. . . . He wanted to follow in his father's footsteps, but then he
had a lot of other interests he couldn't really follow if he did take a position in his
father's corporation. . . . He decides he really doesn't like that kind of work. It's holding him down, so he sells out and joins the Merchant Marines and goes tearing off
around the world."[84]

dreams and desires totally." A remedy soon crystalized in the form of a task: He must make a demonstration to the authorities, confronting the social order with the fact of his excommunication. He would not beg for admission like some sniveling coward. No, like his adventurer, he merely exacted revenge coolly, acting out his "social statement" by "destroying society's finest." Why young women? Partly, it is their vulnerability that makes them so easy to subdue, and, partly, their flamboyant sexuality which he could now exploit; but primarily because they were the front line, as it were, of the class that humiliated him daily through their acts of indifference, their refusal to accept him.

The task of this foe of the authorities is now clear. In performing it, his lowly flagman status would disappear, his identity would fuse and, paradoxically, his alienation cease. As he slipped into the social niche of celebrated multiple murderer, he cured society's indifference to him, and did so while exacting his fearful revenge and indulging all his repressed sexuality. Thus one single all-encompassing task yielded many profits—of revenge, of triumph, and of ecstasy.

Yet Kemper stopped when he had killed six young women: "I didn't want to kill *all* the co-eds in the world." Having made his social statement and indulged his sexual fantasies, having created his identity and his niche, it went without saying that his "purpose was gone." Soon it would be time to retire, but not before he had completed the trilogy of communal, sexual, and familial revenge. In killing his mother and her best friend—and doubly violating the most fundamental taboos by doing it with the utmost savagery—this once-alienated man without any identity or sexuality established himself in the world. Not a man to be trifled with is the bearer of such a crisp and powerful masculine identity. He had come to terms with that "total frustration" which all our multiple murderers remedy in their crusades. After his lengthy confessions had staked his claim to greatness for all time, his task was utterly discharged: *Now* he could rest and sleep (not while he was confessing, but only when he was finished).

Although we should grieve for his victims and their bereaved families, we must not grieve for him. If his recent photographs are anything to go by, he sits in his institution a happy man. This should not be any surprise, for he has confronted all the major issues in his life, and resolved them. Kemper has, in his own terms, rewritten his personal history, and in the lunacy of destruction, created himself.

4 Owning a Female Person

THEODORE ROBERT BUNDY*

"What's one less person on the face of the earth
anyway?"

Ted Bundy[1]

O ne cannot be precise about how many beautiful
young women he killed, for he has never made a full
confession. It is generally accepted that he killed at least twenty, and he
is suspected of killing close to forty, making him among the most "successful" of all modern multiple murderers. Like Edmund Kemper, he
preyed only on the middle class and the desirable. Because he was
both handsome and intelligent, the notion became widespread that he
was some kind of "enigma," but he was no such thing, although he
often spoke cryptically. The mandate here is to show how his killings
were all of a piece, and a comprehensible one at that—part of a logical
and systematic campaign. We know that he was conceived in what he
thought was the terrible shame of illegitimacy, and that he was raised
in a lower-middle-class household whose possessions and style he

---

* Bundy's own comments in letters and transcripts are of some use, and they are recorded
in many books written about him. The most revealing is *The Only Living Witness*, by
Stephen C. Michaud and Hugh Aynesworth; but I was also helped a great deal by Ann
Rule's *The Stranger Beside Me* (which so fascinated me that it brought me to the study
of this phenomenon); as well as Steven Winn and David Merrill's *Ted Bundy: The Killer
Next Door*, Richard W. Larsen's *Bundy: The Deliberate Stranger*, and Elizabeth Kendall's
The Phantom Prince: My Life with Ted Bundy.

despised. His increasingly frantic desire to rise in the social hierarchy revealed itself during childhood in the humiliation he felt as he and his stepfather harvested vegetables for a pittance in the Seattle market gardens; during adolescence in his theft of cars and luxury goods that gave him the upper-middle-class style he so desperately coveted; and during early adulthood in his powerful need for the dual social validation of marriage to a socialite and the status of an attorney. In the final event, he did not feel comfortable in carrying off this impersonation of an upper-middle-class person; but in an important way, his serial killings provided him with his desired union with upper-middle-class women, and launched him in his "career" as an attorney.

His task began to struggle to the surface in 1972. Making love to a casual date, he shoved his forearm against her neck, tightening it until she could not breathe. She shouted at him, but he did not respond. He removed his arm only after he had climaxed and, according to the woman, he seemed to have had no idea what he had been doing. Within a few months of this incident, he began tying up his lover during their lovemaking, an experiment she terminated after he began to strangle her, as if in a trance. Soon Bundy was stalking a woman who had left a bar to walk along a darkened side street. He found a piece of two-by-four in an alley and scurried ahead of her, hiding in a spot where he estimated their paths would intersect; but to his disappointment, she turned into her house before she reached him. Overwhelmed with the desire that the experience had kindled in him, he began following other women, finally striking one woman with a wooden club as she fumbled nervously for her keys at the door to her house. She screamed and fell, causing him to panic at the enormity of what he had done, and to run off.[2]

It was not until early January of 1974 that he had both mastered technique and conquered fear sufficiently to become a more effective assailant. He attacked a young woman asleep in her windowed basement apartment in his own neighborhood, the university district in Seattle, Washington. She was sound asleep when the heavy metal rod crashed into her skull, and unconscious when a medical instrument was thrust roughly into her vagina, causing severe internal injuries. "Mary" was in a coma for months. She recovered, but could remember nothing of the attack.[3]

The Killing Time

He made his first kill a few weeks later. On the night of January 31, 1974, Lynda Ann Healy, a twenty-one-year-old psychology student at the University of Washington, a worker with retarded children, was asleep in the basement apartment of the home she shared with four other young women. He crept into the house, apparently through an unlocked door, knocked Lynda unconscious and gagged her, removed her nightgown and hung it in the closet, remade the bed to give the impression it had not been slept in, and carried her out of the window. Describing the abduction in the curious "as-if" third-person style he later adopted with his biographers Michaud and Aynesworth, he said: "He'd probably put her in the back seat of the car and cover her with something. . . . Let's say that he decided to drive to a remote location that he just picked out. Once he had arrived at this point where he didn't have a fear of alarming anyone in the neighborhood with shouts or screams or whatever, [he would] untie the woman. . . . He would have the girl undress and then, with that part of himself gratified, he found himself in a position where he realized that he couldn't let the girl go. And at that point he would kill her and leave her body where he'd taken her." It is not clear how long he kept the body before disposing of it in his burial ground in the woods near Seattle, but it is unlikely that it was for long.[4]

It took him six weeks to recover from the fear engendered by the first murder, and to regain the confidence to kill again. On March 12, 1974, he talked nineteen-year-old college student Donna Gail Manson into his car as she walked the short distance from her college dormitory to a jazz concert on the campus of Evergreen State College in Olympia, Washington. Her body was never recovered.

The technique he was developing to abduct intelligent university women was first revealed in a failed attempt he made on yet another college campus, Ellensburg's Central Washington State College. On the evening of April 14, 1974, wearing a cast and splint on his left arm and fumbling with a load of books, he induced a nineteen-year-old college student to help him get his books to his car. He asked her to unlock the door, but she was alert and refused. When he unlocked the door and ordered her to get into the car, she later told police, "I sort of ran away. Kind of fast." Three days later on the same campus, he approached another woman student. This time he had a sling on one arm and a brace on the other, and was dropping his books. She volunteered to help him, but was too wary to bend over and search for the keys he had "dropped" beside the car, and she left him there. Moments later, however, he was luckier. Biology major Susan Rancourt had left her meeting of prospective dormitory counselors and was heading back toward her own room. He intercepted her somewhere along her route, presumably using the same ruse. He cracked her skull with a blunt instrument, then kidnapped, raped, and murdered her, eventually dumping her body beside Lynda Healy on the forested slope. Susan Rancourt was his third kill.[5]

Less than three weeks later, on May 6, 1974, he killed again. Kathy Parks, a major in world religions at Oregon State University in Corvallis, Oregon, was leaving her dormitory to meet friends for coffee in the Student Union Building. He approached her as she walked the short distance, then kidnapped, raped, and murdered her. He had traveled the 260 miles to Corvallis, he suggested to Michaud and Aynesworth, as "an attempt to commit a crime without it being linked to other crimes." He described meeting Kathy, once more in his curious nonculpable third person: "Let's say she was having a snack in the cafeteria and [he] just sat down next to her and began talking, and representing himself to be a student there, and suggested that they go out somewhere to get a bite to eat or to get a drink. Either he was convincing enough or she was depressed enough to accept his invitation. Of course, once she got in his car, then he had her in a position where he wanted her, and could then assume control over her. . . . Let's say that as he travels further and further away from a populated area, she probably is becoming uncomfortable . . . and, of course, by the time he pulled up and stopped, there would be virtually nothing she could do about it. . . . She would submit to whatever instructions he gave her, out of fear." After the rape, Bundy suggested that Parks was driven to Seattle alive. He drove her to his burying ground, raped her once more, and "at that point he killed [Kathy]. Either in the car or he marched her off the road and killed her in a more secluded location."[6]

He altered his method to make his fifth kill. He picked up twenty-two-year-old Brenda Ball in the early hours of June 1, 1974, in a working-class tavern in Seattle, drove her back to his apartment, and kept her there. As he described it to Michaud and Aynesworth: "He was interested in varying his M.O. [method of operation] in such a way as not to fan the flames of community outrage or the intensity of the police investigation. That is why this girl found herself to be the next victim. . . . [H]e picked her up hitchhiking and they got to talking and she had nothing to do. He would ask her if she wanted to go to a party at his place and take her home. . . . The initial sexual encounter would be more or less a voluntary one, but one which did not wholly gratify the full spectrum of desires that he had intended. And so, after the first sexual encounter, gradually his sexual desire builds back up and joins, as it were, these other, unfulfilled desires, this other need to totally possess her. After she'd passed out [from the alcohol], as she lay there somewhere in a state between coma and sleep, he strangled her to death." He kept her body in his apartment for several days, moving her between his bed and the closet: "There wouldn't be any urgency [in disposing of the body] since she was in a place that was private. Ultimately, he'd have to bundle her up in some fashion and take her out to his car when it's late one night." While her body was with him in his apartment, there is evidence that he re-applied her makeup and shampooed her hair.[7]

Less than two weeks later, on the night of June 11, 1974, he returned to the University of Washington campus in Seattle to abduct former cheerleader Georgeann Hawkins as she walked the few yards from her boyfriend's dormitory to her own. She would be his sixth known rape and murder. At about the time Georgeann disappeared other students saw a man in the vicinity wearing a leg cast and using crutches.[8]

He seems to have waited a full month before he struck again, killing two in one day, as if to make up for lost time. On July 14, 1974, a summer Sunday with sunbathers converging on the beach at Lake Sammamish, he used a variation on his earlier ruse and approached a woman with his left arm in a sling. He struck up a casual conversation with her and asked if she would help him with his boat. She agreed to do so and accompanied him to the parking lot, but balked when she saw no boat there. "Where is it?" she asked. "It's at my folks' house," he replied. "It's just up the hill." She was too wary to accompany him, but shortly after, twenty-three-year-old Janice Ott agreed. As Bundy later told his biographers: "He would not be able to drive a great distance without arousing the suspicions of the girls in the car. And so he would seek a secluded space, a secluded area, within a fairly short driving distance of the Lake Sammamish area. Somewhere where there were no cars, no traffic, or whatever. [He'd] be acting a role. Talking about the weather, reinforcing the ruse, just chitchat. He had a house somewhere in the area, and took them there, one girl to the house and came back and got the other one. . . . Once the individual would have her in a spot where he had, you know, security over her, then there would be a minimum amount of conversation which would be, you know, designed to avoid developing some kind of a relationship. . . . Had he been cautious, he would've probably killed the first individual before leaving to get the second girl. But in this instance, since we've agreed he wasn't acting cautiously, he hadn't killed the first girl when he abducted the second. . . . He'd follow the same pattern with the second girl as the first. . . . Then the normal self would begin to re-emerge and, realizing the greater danger involved, would suffer panic and begin to think of ways to conceal the acts—or at least his part in them. So he'd kill the two girls, place them in his car, and take them to a secluded area and leave them." In this fashion, both Janice Ott and Denise Naslund were abducted and transformed into his seventh and eighth possessions. When he was finished with them and their bodies, he dumped them at one of his burying grounds, and went out for the evening with his mistress, the pseudonymous "Elizabeth Kendall." He complained of a cold that night, but ate voraciously, consuming several large hamburgers.[9]

Nineteen days later, on August 2, 1974, he abducted Carol Valenzuela, twenty, in downtown Vancouver, Washington. When he was finished with her, he strangled her and dumped her body at another one of his burial grounds near the Oregon border. She was his ninth confirmed kill. The body of his tenth, another young woman, was never identified, but her corpse was found near Valenzuela's.[10]

The people of Washington heaved a collective sigh when there were no further disappearances in September or October, and police began to speculate that the killer might have left the state. They were correct. He had moved to Salt Lake City to enter the University of Utah's Law School. He waited until October 2, 1974, before making his first confirmed Utah kill, taking sixteen-year-old high school cheerleader Nancy Wilcox. On October 18, 1974, he stole his twelfth, Melissa Smith, the seventeen-year-old daughter of the Chief of Police of Midvale, Utah. He raped and sodomized her, strangled her with one of her own knee-length stockings, and left her nude corpse by the road, her vagina stuffed with dirt and twigs. There is some medical evidence that he kept her captive for as long as a week before killing her, although she was probably unconscious for that period from the heavy blow that fractured her skull.[11]

Three nights later, he took his thirteenth victim, Laura Aime, apparently while she was hitchhiking. It is clear from her autopsy report that he followed his usual pattern with her—breaking Laura's jaw and fracturing her skull with a blunt instrument, then committing anal and vaginal rape before strangling her with her own stocking. Laura Aime also suffered a vaginal puncture wound and her hair appeared to have been freshly shampooed, suggesting that he kept her body for a period after her death, as he had done with Melissa Smith.

On November 8, 1974, he made the critical fumble that would, in due course, end his homicidal career. Posing as a policeman, he talked Carol DaRonch into his car on a pretext, but she had the wit to fight back when he tried to handcuff her. In her frantic struggle, she escaped from his car and took shelter with a couple in another car. He drove off and left her there, but her testimony as the only survivor of a Bundy assault would soon convict him on the charge of kidnapping. For the moment, however, all that lay in the future. That same night, after his aborted attack on Carol DaRonch, he continued his murderous efforts and talked Debra Kent out of a high school drama concert in Salt Lake city. She was his fourteenth victim.

The ensuing uproar in Utah caused him to become slightly more circumspect in his operations, and he moved his Killing Ground to Colorado, driving endlessly in his beloved Volkswagen—hunting. On January 11, 1975, he stole his fifteenth victim, twenty-three-year-old vacationing nurse Caryn Campbell, as she walked from the lobby to her room in her luxury hotel in Aspen. He killed her in his usual manner, crushing her skull with a blunt instrument. On March 15, 1975, he took his sixteenth victim, young ski instructor Julie Cunningham. Her body was never recovered. On April 6, 1975, he stole twenty-five-year-old Denise Oliverson, as she rode away from her boyfriend's home on her bicycle. Most often after these murders, he would ease his tensions in extended and emotional long-distance calls to his mistress in Seattle, Elizabeth Kendall.[12]

His momentum was broken suddenly in August of 1975 when an alert and intuitive Utah police officer saw Bundy driving uncertainly through a suburb late at night, and pulled the car over for inspection. Inside the Volkswagen, the officer found handcuffs, an ice pick, a pantyhose mask, a ski mask, several lengths of rope, and some torn pieces of white sheet. The police officer impounded the material as evidence, and warned Bundy to expect a warrant against him for the possession of burglary tools, an all-purpose charge that often (as in this case) yields bigger dividends. From now on, Bundy would be always under the scrutiny of the police. If he could still kill with near-impunity, he did so now with great difficulty. He was soon charged with Carol DaRonch's kidnapping and sentenced to the Utah State Prison for a short term. Not long after that, he was transferred to Colorado because the evidence against him was beginning to mount. He was to stand trial for the murder of Caryn Campbell. After two years in jails with abysmal security, a second ingenious escape attempt was successful. He made his way across America, looking for an appropriate university town in which to settle—for it was only in such an academic atmosphere that he could feel comfortable. He considered Columbus and its Ohio State campus, examined the University of Michigan at Ann Arbor, but finally settled on Florida. He took a room in Tallahassee and posed as a graduate student at the city's Florida State University.[13]

He seems to have tried to hold his task in abeyance, for had he been able to resign from it (and from his reckless and constant petty thefts) he might have remained free for the rest of his life since the police were searching for him thousands of miles away. Yet within a few weeks he was hunting humans again. In his penultimate outrage, in the early hours of January 15, 1978, dressed in dark clothing and armed with a log club, he took advantage of a faulty lock on the door of the university's Chi Omega sorority house and ran from room to room, silently attacking the sleeping women. His eighteenth victim was Lisa Levy: He crushed her skull with his club and bit deep into her buttocks as he raped her, and then sodomized her with an aerosol can. He crossed the hall to another room, wielding his club with such force upon his victims that the "room was spattered and smeared with their blood; even the ceiling was dotted with red drops that had sprayed up from their attacker's thrashing club." He was unable to kill the two women in this room, but he broke Karen Chandler's jaw, right arm, and one finger, fractured her skull, the orbit of her right eye and both her cheekbones, and left deep gouges and cuts on her face. He turned at some point to Karen's sleeping roommate, Kathy Kleiner, and broke her jaw with such force that several of her teeth were later found in her blood-soaked bedclothes. Moving to another room, he clubbed and then strangled Margaret Bowman to death: She was his nineteenth confirmed victim. At this point, his energies remarkably unabated, he was interrupted from his carnage, probably by one of the sorority sisters returning late to the house, and he fled. Racing back toward the safety of his room, he stopped outside the apartment of Cheryl Thomas, a twenty-one-year-old student of dance, who was asleep in her bed. Having broken in, he smashed her jaw with several blows from his club, left a pantyhose mask and a large semen stain on her blood-soaked bed, and escaped. Cheryl Thomas did not die, but she lost the hearing in one ear permanently and suffered a partial loss of balance that put an end to her career as a dancer.[14]

With the community and state in an uproar over the Chi Omega attack, Bundy began his confused and meandering last run. Had he simply made for another state, he might never have been captured. But his behavior suggests that he could no longer sustain the task: He roamed in circles through Florida, finding time only for heavy drinking and his twentieth kill. On February 9, 1978, he talked twelve-year-old Kimberly Leach out of her school playground. He kidnapped her, raped her vaginally and anally, and either strangled her or cut her throat (by the time the body was found, it was in too advanced a stage of decomposition to be certain of the cause of death). He dumped her body in an abandoned hogshed after keeping her in his possession for an undetermined length of time. Within a few days, he was behaving so erratically that yet another alert and suspicious police officer pulled his car over, this last time on the night of February 14–15. After a scuffle, he was arrested. He asked the arresting officer to shoot him. He would never be free again.[15]

Bundy and Psychology

"I'm a psychologist, and it really gives me insight."

Ted Bundy[16]

Bundy seems always to have been tortured by what he felt were the dual social stigmas of his illegitimacy and his "common" lower-middle-class upbringing, but he did not become a patient of psychologists and psychiatrists until his criminal acts had deeply embroiled him in the judicial system. Even that contact proved futile, since he used his intelligence to dissemble and obfuscate, hampering all efforts to determine his inner condition. Inevitably for one so uncommunicative, the diagnosis was singularly unenlightening, except insofar as it revealed some of the difficulties experienced by the forensic psychological sciences. Most notable among these are the inability to predict an individual's potential for future violence, or to diagnose a condition, despite being expected to do so by the judicial system.

This occasional inability to perceive the nature of what is sitting in front of them was made apparent by Bundy's happy passage through the bachelor's degree program in psychology at the University of Washington (before he embarked upon his career in law). His psychology professors there thought the world of him, one writing at the time that: "He conducts himself more like a young professional than a student. I would place him in the top one per cent of the undergraduates with whom I have interacted." And a second wrote about Bundy in 1972: "It is clear that other students use him as a standard to emulate. . . . His personal characteristics are all of the highest standards. Ted is a mature young man who is very responsible and emotionally stable (but not emotionally flat as many students appear—he does get excited or upset appropriately in various situations). . . . I am at a loss to delineate any real weakness he has." During his summer employment at Seattle's Crisis Clinic, charged with the task of counseling individuals who were emotionally troubled, he passed smoothly among the staff, except for only a few who noted his wooden and rigid presentation of self. "Ted," one suspicious colleague told Larsen, "always seemed to respond to the callers with sort of a cold lecture, telling them they should learn to discipline their emotions, to take charge. He didn't seem to have . . . the compassion, the understanding that these people were unable to take control." This woodenness reflected his own uncertain passage through the social order, and it is unclear whether the fact that he was trained in psychology, and was actually practicing a form of it while his homicidal resolve was hardening, constitutes any testimony against the profession.[17]

Indeed, until the eminent forensic psychiatrist Tanay interviewed him in his Florida cell, the only astute attention he had received was from the Seattle psychiatrists who, interviewing *in absentia* the killer they knew only as "Ted," early in the investigation prepared a profile for the police. Journalists Winn and Merrill summarized the profile: "His actions and demeanor tend to categorize him as a sociopath and it is fair to say he is also a sexual psychopath, [a type of person] characterized by certain typical traits, including a lack of emotion and an absence of remorse, yet strangely, such people tend to be extroverts: likable, engaging, often deliciously hedonistic. . . . In short, the experts said, such a person appears perfectly normal. But . . . untroubled by feelings of guilt, a psychopathic killer tends to repeat his act again and again." Yet even this analysis, however astute it may have been, failed to transcend mere categorization, and it was based typically upon the retrospective knowledge of the disordered behavior (the murders), rather than upon any examination of the qualities of a person.[18]

The first professional actually to examine Bundy was Dr. Gary Jorgensen, a clinical psychologist at the University of Utah, whose diagnosis must rank with that of Edmund Kemper's psychiatrist as among the least prescient of all time. Jorgensen was retained by Bundy's lawyer to offer a diagnosis. He spent several hours with Bundy and administered the inevitable battery of psychological tests, including a Rorschach and the Minnesota Multiphasic Personality Inventory. He concluded that Bundy was a "normal person. Mr. Bundy," he wrote, "is an extremely intelligent young man who is intact psychologically. In many regards he is the typical young Republican that he has been in the past." Jorgensen compounded his error by listing what he saw as Bundy's psychological attributes—"good social presence, ego strength and good self-concept, positive self-identity, highly intellectual, independent, tolerant, responsible." Bundy also seemed to him to have "a normal psychosexual development." It would appear that Jorgensen's constructions were based upon an assumption of Bundy's innocence and an "analysis" of his carefully constructed middle-class mask. Many others were to make the same mistake and to pay a much higher price—with their lives. Meanwhile, the only people who had had the wit to suspect Bundy's presentation of self were the much-maligned police. As one intuitive deputy put it, shortly after Bundy's arrest for possession of burglary tools: "I don't know. Bundy is the strangest man I've ever met. . . . It's just a gut reaction. This man's into something big."[19]

After Bundy's conviction for the kidnapping of Carol DaRonch, he was given an intensive ninety-day medical examination at Utah State Prison. The medical staff searched for some biological flaw that might explain his violence but, as with all of our multiple murderers, were unable to find one. X-rays of his skull discovered nothing untoward, and a brain scan was negative. Electroencephalograms were "completely unremarkable," and there was "no evidence of organic brain disease" or any form of mental impairment. The psychological tests seemed more revealing, but they were so primarily because the psychologists now *knew* from his conviction that he was capable of violence toward women. Since he had just been convicted for kidnapping, this knowledge now enabled them to "find" some problems. Thus the prison psychiatrist, Dr. Van O. Austin, felt that Bundy "does have some features of the anti-social personality, such as a lack of guilt feelings, callousness, and a very pronounced tendency to compartmentalize and methodically rationalize his behavior. . . . At times he has lived a lonely, somewhat withdrawn, seclusive existence which is consistent with, but not diagnostic of, a schizoid personality."[20]

On the basis of the psychological tests they directed at Bundy, the prison staff contrasted the positive and negative sides of his personality. On the positive side, they thought, were his "high intelligence, no severely traumatizing influences in childhood or adolescence, no serious defects in physical development, habits, school adjustment, emotional maturation, or sexual development, adequate interest in hobbies and recreational pursuits, average environmental pressures and responsibilities," and "no previous attacks of emotional illness"—observations which reveal rather dramatically how much the tests rely upon the individual's presentation of self and the tester's notion of the immutability of what are essentially middle-class values. On the negative side, the staff complained that "when one attempts to understand Mr. Bundy he becomes evasive," but this insight seemed to be based on their prior knowledge of his kidnapping charge, rather than on any psychological insight—as was their additional remark that Bundy was "somewhat threatened by people unless he feels he can structure the outcome of the relationship."[21]

Finally, what seemed on the surface to be significant may well have been merely characteristics of a large proportion of the human race: For example, the staff's comments on the one "fairly strong conflict . . . evidence in the testing profile, that being the subject's fairly strong dependency on women, yet his need to be independent. Mr. Bundy would like a close relationship with females, but is fearful of being hurt by them. In addition, there were indications of general anger, and more particularly, well-masked anger toward women." Alas, all we really learn from this is that a conviction in court tells us more about a human being than any number of Minnesota Multiphasic Personality Inventories. Perhaps we must speculate that the art of the police officer and the judge is at least as revealing and accurate as that of the psychologist's science. Regardless, the prison psychiatrist concluded on June 7, 1976, that "I do not feel that Mr. Bundy is psychotic. In fact he has a good touch with reality, knows the difference between right and wrong, has no hallucinations or delusions."[22]

Bundy's observation about his observers was at least as insightful. In a letter to his friend Ann Rule, he wrote: ". . . after conducting numerous tests and extensive examinations, [they] have found me normal and are deeply perplexed. Both of us know that none of us is 'normal.' Perhaps what I should say is that they find no explanation to substantiate the verdict or other allegations. No seizures, no psychosis, no dissociative reactions, but in no way, crazy. The working theory is now that I have completely forgotten everything, a theory which is disproved by their own results. 'Very interesting,' they keep mumbling." Presumably he was also unimpressed by the results of his California

Life Goals Evaluation Schedules Test which showed, rather unhelp-
fully, that he had six rather common goals in life: "To have freedom
from want. To control the actions of others. To guide others with their
consent. To avoid boredom. To be self-fulfilled. To live one's life one's
own way."[23]

Yet if the tests produced little but nonsense, his letter to Rule regarding his feelings about his trial while experiencing the psychiatric evaluation was immensely revealing: "I was whistling in the wind," he wrote,
"yet in a curious sort of way, I felt a deep sense of fulfillment. I felt
relaxed but emphatic; controlled, but sincere and filled with emotion."
What manner of man talks about "fulfillment" as his life is draining
away in prison? What was there in the judicial and psychological process
that "filled" him "with emotion"? These were profoundly significant
statements of Bundy's, and we shall return later to their substance.[24]

His last known contact with the professionals was when he stood
trial for his life in Tallahassee. There, he was examined by the distinguished psychiatrist, Dr. Emanuel Tanay, who "thought Bundy had an
anti-social personality, was characterized by bad judgment, 'thrilled'
at the chance of defying authority, and could be dangerous." Tanay
himself wrote that Bundy "has an incapacity to recognize the significance of evidence held against him [although] it would be simplistic to
characterize this as merely lying inasmuch as he acts as if his perception of the significance of evidence was real. He makes decisions based
upon these distorted perceptions of reality. Furthermore, he maintains
an attitude and mood consistent with his perception of reality, namely,
he is neither concerned nor distressed in an appropriate manner by the
charges facing him." Tanay wrote that "transcripts of the many hours
of his conversations with police officers constitute a variety of "confession" [but that] when this is pointed out to him by me, he does not
dispute my inference, he merely provides a different explanation."
Tanay felt strongly that "this behavior was not, in my opinion, the
result of rational reflection and decision-making process but a manifestation of the psychiatric illness from which Mr. Bundy suffers."
Thus Tanay thought Bundy's refusal to accept the weight of evidence

against him was in itself indicative of a mental disease. "It is his view that the case against him is weak or even frivolous. This judgment of Mr. Bundy's is considered to be inaccurate by his defense counsel and, most likely, represents a manifestation of his illness." Tanay concluded with the important insight that, "It is my impression that a major factor is his deep-seated need to have a trial, which he views as an opportunity to confront and confound various authority figures." *Precisely.* But why should Bundy have such a deep-seated need? What could he possibly gain from it?[25]

Public Pronouncements

"I don't feel guilty for anything . . . I feel sorry for people who feel guilt."

Ted Bundy[26]

Bundy never *quite* confessed his murders. Indeed, during his trials in Utah and Colorado, he loudly protested his innocence. In an impassioned letter written at the time to his friend Rule, he wrote: "I want you to know, I want the whole world to know that I am innocent. I have never hurt another human being in my life. God, please believe me." Even then, however, there was often the curious element of dissociation and confusion in his denials, as in the bizarre statement he made before the television cameras in Colorado: "More than ever, I'm convinced of my own innocence." More than ever?[27]

He dropped his fervent claims of innocence after his final capture in Florida, texturing his comments with a kind of scrupulously honest ambiguity. He did not deny the charge of murder, but criticized instead the quality of the state's evidence against him. Throughout this Florida period, whether in exhausting interviews with the police or in intimate letters to his friends, he would maintain this brand of crypticism. When asked by Florida police about his role in the Chi Omega murders, for example, he told them, "The evidence is there. Don't quit digging for it." Similarly, in a letter to a friend he said, "I dreamt of freedom. I had it and lost it through a combination of compulsion and stupidity," an apt judgment on his final murders—yet no admission. He talked vaguely about his "problem," about his "anti-social acts," and told detectives that, "I want to talk to you, but I've built up such a block so that I could never tell." So too, rather than answer an incriminating question, he would say instead, "I don't want to have to lie to you."[28]

When he admitted to police that he preferred Volkswagens because the passenger seat could be removed easily, he elaborated: "Well, I can carry things easier that way."

"You mean you can carry bodies easier that way?" asked a detective.

"Well, let's just say I can carry cargo better that way," Bundy replied.

"That cargo you carried, was it sometimes damaged?"

"Sometimes it was damaged, sometimes it wasn't," Bundy replied. When he felt himself edging too close to making an admission, he would back off: "Laying in bed," he said to police, "I said to myself, 'Shoot, it's going to be easier than the dickens and it would all come out.' Again, I know what you want, but I'm interested in the whole thing, in everything. It's the whole ball of wax, and it's got to be dealt with. . . . I'm interested in clearing up everything . . . and in giving answers to questions that would be helpful. . . . [but] What is it I wanted to do? It's not as clear to me now as it was before."[29]

For a time he implied that he was holding back in order to negotiate the most favorable terms for himself. Undoubtedly this is partly true, but since he maintained that position long after he had received three death sentences, it is legitimate to conclude that more was involved than mere haggling. Still, he haggled. "My attorney's position," he said, "is that all the state and you all want to do, besides solve these cases, is to execute me. And that would be the logical result of anything you were attempting to get from me, if indeed that's what you wanted. There's no doubt in their minds, given the laws of the state of Florida, that's what would happen if the guilty party were captured. They advocate a different point of view: going right down the line and eventually securing my freedom. I like these kinds of situations because it allows me to take—well, it doesn't allow me really anything. Now if I had my choice—and I don't necessarily—but if I sit back and think about how I would like the thing to resolve itself, everybody satisfied by getting all the answers to all the questions they want to ask, then after that was all over, I would like to be back in Washington state, because that's where my mother is, that's where my family is, and that's where I'm from. . . . It's just being home, back where I was raised, being close to my family. I know it sounds rather complex," he continued, "but it just seems to work for me now. OK, Ted Bundy wants something out of this and maybe that's not right and maybe he doesn't deserve it—and in a way that's true. But still I've got to take care of my own survival. Ted Bundy wants to survive, too. I have many responsibilities, as I've told you before, to my parents—and that's part of it. The second part is getting out of the limelight as quickly as possible without all these horrendous trials. . . . And getting close, back close to my parents, and giving the knowledge and peace of mind that can be returned to people who don't know what happened . . . to their loved ones." Here Bundy is posing, in an incredibly unconvincing way, as a kind of dispossessed homebody, devoted to little but his parents, and whose prime concern is to give "peace" to the parents of his victims. Why such a pose? I think it obvious that at the time he could not overcome his stage fright for what would be his greatest performance, the Florida murder trials. Time and rest would heal his anxiety.[30]

For the time being, he could merely claim to police that "I'm trying to avoid infuriating you, believe me. I don't mean to be saying this is the way it's going to be, because I can't do that. There's one thing I know for sure: that I've got the answers here and they're for me to give. I want to get to the point where it would be the best all around, not excluding me. I still place a value on myself." Yet when detectives begged him to tell them where his last victim's body was hidden, he seemed overwhelmed with embarrassment: "But I'm the most cold-hearted son of a bitch you'll ever meet." Again, the detective asked, "Ted, if you will tell me where the body is. . . . " Bundy replied: "I can't do that to you, because the sight is too horrible to look at." Recovering quickly, he reminded the detectives that "I've got the answers, and the answers are mine to give."[31]

He continued this charade long after his convictions, even with his literary interrogators, Michaud and Aynesworth, speaking only in "as-ifs" and in the third person, and bridling if the queries came too close to indicting him: "I'm not going into that," he told Michaud. "This is already too thinly disguised. I've gone further now than I wanted to." He insisted that he was a victim of a malicious judicial system and the media, trapped by what was entirely circumstantial evidence and a venal, incompetent press. But his *definition* of innocence was not whether he had in fact committed the murders, but whether the state had marshaled sufficient evidence against him: "I am not convinced, in any objective sense, of the strength of the state's case," he said in court in Miami. He embraced sheer legalism with a passion that is rarely encountered, and this puzzling quality demands explanation.[32]

Biographies

"I've always felt somehow lost in my life."

Ted Bundy[33]

The apparent paradoxes that litter Bundy's life have engaged the imaginations of the many who knew him and who have written about him: the crisis center counselor who raped women . . . the potential governor of the state who was driven by secret urges to kill . . . the law student who threw away his life rather than accept the reality of his own incompetence as an attorney. Bundy did not fit the shape that the public requires from its multiple murderers. Yet there were many Bundys. In one of the ironies that dot this case, the daughter of the police chief who would pursue him had worked with him and found him "the kind of guy a girl my age would look at and just say wow! Sort of Kennedy-like. He was a champion of causes," she recalled. "He was concerned about the situation of the blacks, of all minorities. And the poor. He was unhappy with the injustices of society, and he wanted to do something about them." On the other hand, a widowed pastry cook found his friendship and his dedicated rhetoric a mixed blessing: "He was always borrowing money from me," she told Bundy's biographer Larsen, and not always paying it back. A young woman who dated him glimpsed his contradictions. Although they were close friends, Bundy would not visit her parents in their middle-class home: "It was funny," she commented. "Ted was always so self-confident, so sure of himself, but I got the feeling that he felt terribly inferior at times."[34]

Many loved him, including his mother, who seemed to have doted on her love-child, seeing him perhaps as the family's potential for re-entry into the respectable middle class. Louise Bundy did what she could for all her children. She told Winn and Merrill: "They had the best we could give them on a middle-class income. The most we could give them was lots of love. . . . Many a night we stayed up well past midnight. He'd have a big test coming up the next day, and I'd go through with him and ask the questions . . . I've always had a very special relationship with all my children. . . . But Ted being my oldest, and you might say my pride and joy, our relationship was very special. We talked a great deal together." Admiring women and a loving family? There seemed to be little unusual in his background: Certainly it defied all assumptions of an abused childhood, and revealed nothing to suggest the growth of such a disordered creature.[35]

The Official Autobiography: Bundy the Young Republican

Like many public men and women's best efforts, Bundy's autobiography presented him as he wished to be seen, and this performance was unwavering in its studied banality, at least until his capture in Florida. If an undistinguished career in school was followed by an equally undistinguished career at college, he was able to reminisce about his boyhood in pleasant, if ambiguous, terms: "I haven't blocked out the past. I wouldn't trade the person I am, or what I've done—or the people I've known—for anything. So I do think about it. And at times it's a rather mellow trip to lay back and remember."

At college, he avoided the fraternity/sorority life with even greater zeal than he avoided studying, claiming that he "wasn't interested in the social politicking, the emphasis on clothes and parties. It was shallow and superficial."[36]

If his own commitment to scholarship was similarly superficial, he seemed to have thrived in the college atmosphere. "People are great anyway, but college students are beautiful people. Good-looking people. Healthy people. Exciting people." In particular, he loved the life of the university district—the district where the killings began—and the special feeling it gave him: "I love the district. I have never become so attached to any other place that I lived. I never felt so totally a part of the eco-system." Indeed, and therein lay the problem.[37]

He spent the late 1960s putting together his image as a confident and upper-middle-class young Republican. His social adeptness grew, as did that air-of-a-Kennedy about him. He was admired by many men and women (although many also distrusted his facade, which struck them as bumbling and artificial). He even won a commendation from the Seattle police for chasing a purse snatcher and returning the purse to its rightful owner. In 1970, he saved a young girl from drowning. What stopped this guardian of the moral order from continuing this trajectory? Ideologically, he was conservative in the extreme. His applications to the law schools are models of the dedicated young establishmentarian—"a believer in the system," as his Republican Party employer called him. He wished to be a lawyer, he wrote one law school, "to arbitrate questions between individuals and institutions; to search for the facts; and ultimately, to provide for the orderly resolution of conflict and the avoidance of 'violence'—these activities have attracted me to a program of legal study. I see the legal profession engaged in a quest for order."[38]

How remarkable that this future multiple murderer would be so concerned with "order," with the "resolution of conflict," and with the "avoidance of violence." How odd that this rebel-to-be should be so committed to change in government through legislative, not revolutionary, means. "His stance made him something of a loner," wrote his friend Rule, "among the work-study students working at the Crisis Clinic. They were semi-hippies . . . and he was a conservative Republican." Moreover, he was infuriated by the student riots. "On more than one occasion, he had tried to block the demonstrations, waving a club and telling the rioters to go home. He believed there was a better way to do it, but his own anger was, strangely, as intense as those he tried to stop." He argued with Rule at the time that his conservatism was really a progressive stratagem: "Anarchy isn't going to solve anything," she remembered him saying. "You just end up scattering your forces and getting your head broken."[39]

Even after he was arrested, he stuck to his version of his autobiography. "When I first came under attack by the legal system," he wrote, "I was twenty-eight, a bachelor, a law student, engaged to be married, and enjoying the brightest period of my life. I had come to terms with many things . . . and one thing I had come to terms with long ago was the circumstances of my birth," a reference to his illegitimacy. He insisted that there was nothing abnormal about him or his life, and continued to describe himself as a kind of quintessential middle-class young man with excellent prospects, concerned only with discovering himself and his place in society. "I am still too young to look upon my life as History," he wrote to a Seattle magazine. "I am at a stage in life, an egocentric stage, where it matters only that I understand what I am and not what others may think of me."[40]

The Revised Autobiography: Bundy the "Entity"

After his capture in Florida, his autobiography was extensively, if hesitantly, "rewritten." It revealed a glimpse of what lay underneath the Young Republican. "In an even, professorial tone," Michaud and Aynesworth recalled, "he began to speak of themes in modern society—violence, the treatment of women, the disintegration of the home, anonymity, stress. Finally, he turned from the sociological to the specific, and began describing the killer. Within 'this individual,' he explained, there dwelt a being—Ted sometimes called it 'an entity,' 'the disordered self,' or 'the malignant being.' The story of 'the entity's' birth came slowly, chronologically, a consistent tale of gathering psychopathy that nurtured itself on the negative energy around it. Protected by his use of the third person, he forged ahead in detail to explain how thoughts about sex in general came to concentrate on sexual violence, how pornography shaped and directed the 'entity,' how the illness inside him drew him toward ever-increasing shows of violence, and how the killer managed to mask his disordered self from his unsuspecting friends. He took pains in his explanations lest I develop overly simplistic ideas. . . . The killer was not a schizophrenic, Bundy iterated and reiterated. 'It is truly more sophisticated than that,' he cautioned. Ted called it 'a hybrid situation,' a psychopathology in which the 'entity' is both in and of the killer, not some alien presence but a purely destructive power that grew from within."[41]

Bundy's third-person self-analysis was studded with the psychological euphemisms so characteristic of psychology graduates— "inappropriate acting out" for murder, and "satisfying that part of himself" for rape. Yet his thoughts on the internal struggle he experienced seemed real enough: "This person was constantly attempting to be objective and to determine whether or not any of his psychopathological tendencies were being exposed. He was constantly assessing that probability and trying to keep a sense of proportion within himself. Not just for a surface kind of demonstration, but also in the hopes of keeping on an even keel, rationally, normally. Not isolating himself too much from the mainstream. Not simply to preserve conditions under which the malignant part of him could survive, but also sometimes to overcome those desires."[42]

He frequently reminded Michaud and Aynesworth that the gratification he sought lay in the possession of the victim, not in the violence or in the sex. But what bothered his interrogators most was their important insight that there were "elements of will, *conscious will,* taking part in the creation of this entity, as if Ted had wanted to become a killer." *Precisely*: This was no uncontrollable compulsion. Bundy made a decision, a solemn commitment, and then reaped the whirlwind. Tracing the growth of his linkage of sexuality with violence,

Bundy recalled: "This condition is not immediately seen by the individual or identified as a serious problem. It sort of manifests itself in an interest concerning sexual behavior, sexual images. It might simply be an attraction such as *Playboy*, or a host of other normal, healthy sexual stimuli that are found in the environment. But this interest, for some unknown reason, becomes geared toward matters of a sexual nature that involve violence. I cannot emphasize enough the gradual development of this. It is not short-term." Bundy thus argued for a kind of sexual origin for the killings, suggesting that he began to focus on "pornography as a vicarious way of experiencing what his peers were experiencing in reality. Then he got sucked into the more sinister doctrines that are implicit in pornography—the use, abuse, the possession of women as objects." Sucked in?[43]

Then, Bundy continued, came the fantasies in which "this person" began to see himself as an actor. "He was walking down the street one evening and just totally by chance looked up into the window of a house and saw a woman undressing. He began, with increasing regularity, to canvass, as it were, the community he lived in. He peeped in windows and watched women undress or whatever could be seen during the evening. He approached it almost like a project, throwing himself into it, literally, for years. . . . He gained, at times, a great amount of gratification from it. And became increasingly adept at it, as anyone becomes adept at anything they do over and over again."[44]

Bundy thought his interrogators might "make a little more sense out of much of this if you take into account the effect of alcohol. It's important. It's very important as a trigger. When this person drank a good deal, his inhibitions were significantly diminished." One evening he found himself trailing a woman with the intention of attacking her: "The revelation of the experience and the frenzied desire that seized him really seemed to usher in a new dimension to that part of him that was obsessed with violence and women and sexual activity—a composite kind of thing not terribly well defined but more well defined as time went on. This particular incident spurred him on succeeding events to hunt this neighborhood, searching." Finally, he struck one woman, as recounted earlier, and fled in panic. "What he had done terrified him," Bundy surmised, "purely terrified him. Full of remorse and remonstrating with himself for the suicidal nature of the activity, the ugliness of it all, he quickly sobered up. He was horrified by the recognition that he had the capacity to do such a thing. He was fearful, terribly fearful, that for some reason or another he might be apprehended. But slowly, the pressures, tensions, dissatisfactions which, in the very early stages, fueled this thing had an effect. Yet it was more self-sustaining and didn't need as much tension or as much disharmony externally as it did before. It sort of reached a point where this condition would generate its own needs, and wouldn't need that reservoir of tension or stress that it seemed to thrive on before."[45]

He learned to conquer his fear. "The next time, it took him only three months to get over it," said Bundy. "What happened was this entity inside him was not capable of being controlled any longer, at least not for any considerable period of time. It began to try to justify itself, to create rationalizations for what it was doing. Perhaps to satisfy the rational, normal part of the individual. One element that came into play was anger, hostility. But I don't think that was an overriding emotion when he would go out hunting, or however you want to describe it. On most occasions it was a high degree of anticipation, of excitement, or arousal. It was an adventuristic kind of thing."[46]

Bundy insisted that he "received no pleasure from harming or causing pain to the person he attacked. He received absolutely no gratification. He did everything possible within reason—considering the unreasonableness of the situation—not to torture these individuals, at least not physically. The fantasy that accompanies and generates the anticipation that precedes the crime is always more stimulating than the immediate aftermath of the crime itself. He should have recognized that what really fascinated him was the hunt, the adventure of searching out his victims. And, to a degree, possessing them physically as one would a potted plant, a painting, or a Porsche. Owning, as it were, this individual."[47]

The particular victims he selected would be images of "the idealized woman," he said, which for him meant the upper-middle-class woman:

Because he wished to maintain them as images, and not develop relationships, he avoided talking to them. "They wouldn't be stereotypes necessarily. But they would be reasonable facsimiles to women as a class. A class not of women, per se, but a class that has almost been created through the mythology of women and how they are used as objects." He selected a particular woman if the opportunity was there and if he found her handsome; but even that beauty was *socially* defined—"The person's criteria would be based upon those standards of attractiveness accepted by his peer group." When the female object had been spotted and captured, he "would not want to engage in a great deal of serious conversation" with her. "Once the individual would have her in a spot where he had, you know, security over her, then there would be a minimum amount of conversation which would be, you know, designed to avoid developing some kind of relationship."[48]

After his arrest and escape from the Colorado jail, he made his way across the country and experienced an immense sense of fulfillment and peace, when other fugitives might have felt only fear of apprehension. Within days of arriving in Florida, however, that special feeling disappeared. "All of a sudden, I just felt smaller and smaller and smaller. And more insecure too. And more alone. Bit by bit by bit. I felt something drain out of me. I felt it slip away from me like in the old movies where you see the ghost lift out of the body lying on the ground. And by the time I got off the bus in Tallahassee, things just didn't seem right. From the time I first set foot on Tennessee Street, I kept saying to myself, 'I gotta leave here.'" Just as his sense of self disappeared, so did his resolution to steer clear of the law. But why? What made him feel so lifeless again, and so small?[49]

Michaud and Aynesworth, and many others, thought all this was clear evidence of "an unconscious need to return to confinement," but I think not. In fact, his task was incomplete. Within five weeks he would kill the women in Chi Omega's sorority house. He would never discuss these murders, but he did once boast to Aynesworth that "I'm the only one that can do it. The only one." Similarly, he was boasting to his rooming-house fellows within hours of the massacre. Neither was this a form of self-destruction in the psychiatric sense, for his task was now completed: Once he accepted that, in the state of mental and physical exhaustion that followed his murder of Kimberly Leach, he would be free to find a measure of personal happiness in incarceration, to develop his own philosophy, and to revel in the fame that was now his. "There is no true answer," he concluded during his final trial, "only controversy." The statement reflected his constant delight in mystifying his audience.[50]

The Demystification of Ted Bundy

Theodore Robert Bundy was no "enigma." He spoke to us only in lies and riddles because such obfuscation and insult were central to his task. Even then, long after the trials, when he consented to read us chapter and verse, he elected to do so only in that third-person style to further tantalize and antagonize us and, perhaps, not forswear the possibility of a stay of execution. To understand the man, we need merely to examine two of his personal qualities—his relentless snobbery and his uncivil behavior toward the authorities—and the two central events in his personal history: his illegitimacy, and his inability to love the woman he wanted to love.

Bundy the Snob

> "Personalized stationery is one of the small but truly necessary luxuries of life."
>
> *Ted Bundy*[51]

"Even the little Teddy was deeply class-conscious," observed Michaud and Aynesworth. Younger than ten, when Edmund Kemper was burying alive the family cat, Bundy was already "humiliated" to be seen in his stepfather's "common" Rambler automobiles. Indeed, the only relative who did not inspire disdain in him was a cultivated uncle who taught music at Tacoma's College of Puget Sound. The uncle's professorial home, with its gleaming grand piano, emitted for him an aura of substance and middle-class refinement. He daydreamed of being adopted by Roy Rogers and Dale Evans, a common enough fantasy among eight-year-olds, to be sure, but with him the prime motive was to have his own pony and to be rich, and so escape from what the precociously ambitious Ted Bundy seemed to feel so profoundly beneath him. So intense was this premature materialism that, according to his mother, the little Teddy would always pull her to the most expensive sections of clothing stores.[52]

The snobbery of the adult Bundy was so extreme as to suggest an exceptional degree of status anxiety, however smoothly it might have been articulated in his daily performances. How many awaiting trial for murder would concern themselves with the bourgeois niceties of personalized stationery, or trouble to comment so affectedly on its worth? How many would retain a food and wine snobbery in prison, writing to a friend: "Yet, whatever supernatural force guides our destinies . . . I must believe this invisible hand will pour more chilled Chablis for us in less treacherous, more tranquil times to come." Certainly, he used his snobbery to impress others. His rather simple mistress, Elizabeth Kendall, wrote disarmingly of the breathless manner in which she watched him select a wine from France for their first meal together, at a time when she confessed she "was impressed by any wine that had a cork in the bottle." Later, in a darker time, when urged to recall terrible things about ghastly murders he had committed, he said instead to his interrogators: "How do you describe the taste of *bouillabaisse*? Some remember clams, others mullet." These were carefully assembled and exquisitely constructed snobberies, quite out of character for a lower-middle-class Tacoma upbringing—as was his loathing for everything he thought (and he used the word) "common." Again, why was his psyche so colonialized that he felt it essential to affect an "English," or at least a mid-Atlantic, accent?[53]

The status anxiety seemed particularly intense in his relationships with women. Was it a youthful prank, or a symptom of a deep sense of status deprivation, that drove him to the bother of borrowing a friend's best china and silver for a dinner he orchestrated for a girlfriend—and dressing for that dinner in a waiter's jacket and satin-striped trousers? What made it impossible for him, despite many invitations, to visit the home of an early girlfriend from the middle class? "He didn't feel that he fit in with . . . my 'class,'" she later recalled. "I guess that's the only way to describe it. He wouldn't come to my parents' home because he said he just didn't fit in." Most important of all, when he did ultimately fall in love so deeply—with a California socialite, long-haired and graceful like his victims, who was a fellow student at the University of Washington—why, after years of ardently pursuing her, did he coldly reject her the moment she accepted his proposal of marriage? "I just wanted to prove to myself," he later wrote, "that I could have married her." But is this not an extravagant means of proof? "She moved like something out of *Vogue*," Bundy continued, "and anything she wore looked like a million dollars. I, on the other hand, possessed the innocence of a missionary, the worldliness of a farm boy. . . . She and I had about as much in common as Sears and Roebuck has with Saks."[54]

There can be no doubt that he was obsessed with what he called his "social deficits." It was this profound feeling of social inferiority and personal worthlessness that made him turn away from his college's fraternity and sorority life—an otherwise appropriate niche for a person of his pretensions—and rendered hollow his claim that he spurned them because the Greek Row life was "shallow and superficial." It was inevitable that by his first year in college, as he later told a psychiatrist, he would be obsessed with a "longing for the beautiful coed," and a frustrating foreknowledge that "I didn't have the skill or social acumen to cope with it." Perhaps it now becomes more apparent why he ultimately captured and killed sorority girls, or their "idealized models," for it was an obvious way in which his class-scarred soul could conceive of their possession.[55]

Bundy the snob immersed himself in *classless* material possessions and activities. The only car he loved was the Volkswagen Bug, an automobile remarkable for little other than its classless image (so unlike those detested lower-middle-class Ramblers of his stepfather). In these classless vehicles, he transported the idealized sorority girls to their deaths, thus transforming the desired possessions into owned objects. Similarly, he was only comfortable in college districts—colleges, where talent and style supposedly overwhelm social origins, where a shared student style obliterates differential "breeding." That undoubtedly accounted for the worshipful manner in which he always considered college districts and their inhabitants: "College students are beautiful people. Good-looking people. Healthy people. Exciting people." He confirmed this by spending not only his salad days in Seattle's university district, but by considering only other college districts as possible places to live, even when he was on the run from the law. He consciously embraced politics because, through them, one could rise regardless of one's social origins; and this too was clearly what accounted for his interest in the law. Even his sport—skiing—while class-conscious enough, permitted this enterprising thief to equip himself for it with a few deft shoplifting tours. Through the classlessness of the colleges, the political game, and the ski slopes, he tried his best to jostle among the right sort.[56]

Bundy the Rebel

Bundy reached first for an establishment image. The Young Republican was described by his colleagues as "a believer in the system," and it was this "believer" who attacked the student protesters with words and club. But when it became apparent to him that his psyche could not make the transition from Tacoma bungalows to California socialites, when he abandoned the closest thing to love he ever experienced, he radically altered his ideological stance, and became Bundy the rebel. This metamorphosis is evident in every confrontation he would now have with the authorities—a rebellion that was usually misinterpreted by observers as a kind of psychotic self-destructiveness. From the moment of his first arrest in Utah, he treated the police with a dangerous contempt more consistent with a radical than a Republican: "I thought I had a bunch of klutzes who were going to fuck me around," he said of his interrogating officers. He first offered them a bogus alibi, which fell apart after the merest scrutiny, and essentially complained that his interrogation gave him no room to *perform*: "I thought there might be some time for song and dance. I didn't even get much dance in." Subsequently, as Michaud and Aynesworth noted, "By his actions, Ted invited the detective to pursue him, apparently expecting to tease and humiliate the opposition." Why should he chart such a treacherous course for himself? In this rebellious spirit, Bundy would photograph police who were stalking him, leave them notes, or playfully confront them: these were not the actions of a confident middle-class person faced with a serious charge. Later, a psychiatrist wrote that "in a certain sense, Mr. Bundy is a producer of a play which attempts to show that various authority figures can be manipulated," which is most insightful, but he concluded that "Mr. Bundy does not have the capacity to recognize that the price for this thriller might be his own life." Surely he is in error about Bundy's "capacity": The true rebel is contemptuous of both his life and the consequences of his performance, not incapable of perceiving them.[57]

It was while awaiting trial in Utah that he first began to taunt the press. "I was trying to project an image," he said of his dealings with the media. "I was feeling proud of myself. That's when I started to be pleased about fucking with the press. From then on, it was a lot of fun." Bundy the rebel was finding his feet. Out on bail in Seattle, he strutted about with law books, commenting loudly and sarcastically on the remarkable opportunity he had been given to participate in the legal system. At his trial in Utah, when the prosecutor asked him why he carried a crowbar in his Volkswagen, he replied with an air of mocking civility, "Well, it's a useful tool. What can I say, Dave?" And when the prosecutor asked him to estimate how many miles he could expect from a tank of gasoline in his Volkswagen, he merely responded: "Oh, I'm not really thinking about it, Dave. I thought you made your own conclusion. I'm not here to do mathematical problems." These were not the words of someone who was trying to fight his conviction; rather, he was trying to fight something quite different. But what?[58]

For the Utah trial he had waived his right to a jury; but this had provided him with an insufficiently appreciative audience for his performance as rebel. For his trials in Florida, he would steel himself to play before a jury and, through the television and press coverage, to the entire nation. He described the FBI as himself, calling them "Fornicators, Bastards and Imposters"; issued "Statements to the Media" in which he compared his position to that of the Soviet dissidents; and fought constantly with his attorneys, frequently firing them. Always, he would paint himself as the persecuted rebel, flamboyantly carrying a copy of *The Gulag Archipelago*. He was, he said, unjustifiably attacked by a malicious judicial system; he was the dissenting intellectual paying the price of his independence. It was a bizarre posture, perhaps, but no one can deny that he lived it.[59]

Bundy the Bastard

Theodore Robert Bundy was born on November 24, 1946, in the Elizabeth Lund Home for Unwed Mothers in Burlington, Vermont, the result of a brief liaison between his twenty-two-year-old mother and a man she described as "a sailor," although there were hints that this sailor came from a monied family. Had Louise Bundy been truly proletarian, the event might have been brushed off as one of no significance, but she was not: She was from a deeply religious lower-middle-class Philadelphia family, and she was made to feel her "shame." Too many knew the story of Ted's paternity in Philadelphia, so at the age of four, son and mother moved to Tacoma, Washington, where the secretary Louise soon met the army cook Johnnie Bundy. They were married on May 19, 1951, when Ted was not yet five. This provoked a corollary shame in Ted, for they were not wealthy. So much was this the case that Ted and his stepfather would spend hours laboring in the fields of the market gardens near Tacoma to supplement their slender income, sweating and bending for a few dollars a day while the cars of the wealthy wafted past. This would mean little to someone whose sense of self was secure, but a great deal to someone cracking under the weight of the hierarchy.

Perhaps the ultimate responsibility of the social order is to implant in each individual his or her sense of identity. Few have had such a fearful absence of a crisp identity as Ted Bundy. The man was forever disguising himself, and not just to avoid capture. He wore a false mustache when working for the Republican Party, studied the arts of make-up in theater school, frequently altered his hair or his weight to change his appearance dramatically, and used false casts and false facial hair as basic props in his theft of the idealized women. Yet he did this not in some deranged or delusional semiconsciousness, for he was very much aware that much of his life was "a Walter Mitty kind of thing. I'm disguised as an attorney today," he told the judge in Florida, revealing more about his inner self than he was prone to do.[60]

The social stain of illegitimacy, infinitely more intense in the 1950s than it is today, sunk deep into Bundy's soul. He felt intensely that this illegitimacy deprived him of a past and that, as Winn and Merrill remarked, "without a past it was impossible to have a 'meaningful relationship.'" In his public and "Republican" statements, he would always claim to have risen above any anxiety on this matter: "One thing I had come to terms with long ago was the circumstances of my birth." Yet in any personal relationships he had, he always took pains to emphasize the agony his illegitimacy caused him. A childhood friend recalled the day Bundy told him he was illegitimate: "I think I said I thought it was no big deal. But he said something to the effect that for him it made a big difference. This was important to him. It wasn't just something to be swept under the rug. When I made light of his situation he said, 'Well, it's not you that's a bastard.' He was bitter when he said it." As an adult, in a conversation with his friend Rule, she remembered him saying words to the effect that: "You know, I only found out who I really am a year or so ago. I mean, I always knew, but I had to prove it to myself. . . . I'm illegitimate. When I was born, my mother couldn't say that I was her baby."[61]

Bundy has given contradictory accounts of how he discovered his illegitimacy, and of whether his mother admitted her relationship to him (sometimes he claimed she said she was his sister); but the revelation seemed to bring his social development to an abrupt halt. "In junior high everything was fine," he later recalled, "but I got to high school and I didn't make any progress. I felt alienated from my old friends. They just seemed to move on and I didn't. I don't know why and I don't know if there's an explanation. Maybe it's something that was programmed by some kind of genetic thing. In my early schooling, it seemed like there was no problem in learning what the appropriate social behaviors were. It just seemed like I hit a wall in high school. I didn't think anything was wrong, necessarily. I wasn't sure what was wrong and what was right. All I knew was that I felt a bit different." This new alienated and confused Bundy was not popular with his schoolmates, and he had only one date during high school. He felt comfortable only in the social niches—the classroom and the ski slopes—which offered avenues for social mobility. "I spoke up in class. It's a formalized setting and the ground rules are fairly strict. Your performance is measured by different rules than what happens when everybody's peeling off into little cliques down the hallway."

Thus the social order literally deprived him of his identity and acted upon him as a kind of disordering and unbalancing hallucinogen. He tried to fight back by constructing his own identity, but inevitably it was an artificial and alienating process—what Michaud and Aynesworth described as being "like an alien life form acquiring appropriate behavior through mimicry and artifice." "I didn't know what made things tick," Bundy said. "I didn't know what made people want to be friends. I didn't know what made people attractive to one another. I didn't know what underlay social interactions." Society would pay dearly for its malfunction.[62]

Bundy the Lover

Bundy as lover was Bundy as failure. Indeed, his off-and-on affair with the only woman he has convincingly claimed to have loved, functions as source, symbol, and metaphor for his meteoric passage through the social hierarchy. He made his bid for social advancement at college: driving the classless car and living in the classless university district, he eschewed the fraternity social life which, with its intense class consciousness, by definition declassed him. "I didn't feel socially adept enough. I didn't feel I knew how to function with those people. I felt terribly uncomfortable." Instead, he set about fabricating a middle-class identity, the fullest expression of which was his love for the California socialite. He courted her in the second year of college and then followed her to California for the summer, enrolling in a summer college program. Soon he found himself falling behind the other students: "I found myself thinking about standards of success that I just didn't seem to be living up to," referring ambiguously to both his courses and his lover. Sensing inadequacy and a "loser," the socialite dropped him, and what remained of 1967 was "absolutely the pits for me—the lowest time ever." He returned to Seattle for the following academic year, but was barely able to attend class and finally withdrew from school. Utterly demoralized, he traveled across the country, searching for his roots among his eastern relatives. He returned to Seattle for the ultimate trauma to his fragile ego, to find himself proletarianized, working as a busboy in a hotel dining-room and as a night stocker in a Safeway store. "I absorbed all this uncertainty and all this confusion about why I was doing what I was doing, wondering where I was going, all by myself. . . . I'm not the kind of person who socialized a lot, there was no way to let off steam." Soon he was letting off steam and descending into the lumpen proletariat by becoming a thief and shoplifting everything he wanted—stealing, among many other things, a television set, his clothing, a stereo, art, home furnishings, even a large ornamental tree.[63]

As he touched bottom, his fortunes suddenly improved. A casual encounter with an acquaintance led to his employment with a black politician contending for the Republican nomination for lieutenant governor. "I just pitched right in. Oh boy! Here we go again. I hadn't had a social life for some time. It just felt good to belong again, to instantly be part of something. . . . The reason I loved politics was because here was something that allowed me to use my talents and assertiveness. You know, the guy who'd raise his hand in class and speak up. And the social life came with it. You were accepted. You went out to dinner with people. They invited you to dinner. I didn't have the money or the tennis-club membership or whatever it takes to really have the inside track. So politics was perfect. You can move among the various strata of society. You can talk to people to whom otherwise you'd have no access."[64]

His candidate lost, and he formed a relationship with Elizabeth Kendall, the daughter of a prosperous Utah professional. By this time, however, he was avidly reading violent pornography and peeping into women's windows. Moreover, the mounting rage inside him converted into deep cyclical depressions: "It wasn't dictated by the cycle of the moon, or anything else," he told Michaud and Aynesworth. "Not mood swings, just changes. It's goddamn hard for me to describe it. All I wanted to do was just lay around, just consume huge volumes of time without doing a thing." Still, he had not given up yet. He returned to the University of Washington in the summer of 1970 and completed his degree in psychology in 1972 while working part-time for a medical supply company and the Seattle Crisis Clinic. His applications to several law schools were rejected. By now he was fantasizing in earnest, scouting his future killing grounds in endless drives through the countryside, studying the terrain.[65]

What remained of 1972 and 1973 would be the years of decision for him: He would start to kill in January of 1974. Meanwhile, however, his star continued to rise. The election of 1972 enabled him to re-enter the political system, and he worked as a volunteer for the incumbent Republican governor. After the election, a strong letter of support from the re-elected governor gained Bundy admission to the University of Utah's College of Law for the fall of 1973. He waited, busying himself with government contracts and positions. Persuaded by a colleague that Washington's University of Puget Sound would be a more appropriate school for someone wanting a career in the state, he enrolled there, telling the Utah faculty that he had been injured in an automobile accident.

Now, flushed with success, he revived his moribund affair with the California socialite. He flew to San Francisco to see her, this time as a man of some substance, his Young Republican image complete. He seemed different to her now, more desirable, no longer a loser, her "erstwhile wishy-washy beau transformed into a Man of Action." They met frequently and by Christmas of 1973, she thought they were engaged to be married. For his part, however, he had already abandoned his plan to rise with her in the hierarchy: Either he had rehearsed his lines so often that they had become ashes in his mouth, or he felt unable to maintain the facade of Royal Consort. In either case, it was this crisis that foreclosed his conventional career. Neither did he like what he saw when he went to class at his new law school: an anonymous office building in downtown Tacoma, and not the ivied campus he had expected. According to Michaud and Aynesworth, "the perceived taint of attending a *déclassé* law school was every bit as demeaning to him in his mid-twenties as Johnnie and Louise's boxy Ramblers were to him as a child." He seemed to have made no effort to do well at school and quickly began to fail. Clearly, the hour of decision had come: He decided to commit himself to another career. He never contacted his "loved one" again, and when she called him a month later in a rage, to terminate the engagement, he had already begun to kill. "Why the hell haven't you written or called?" Bundy remembered her shouting at him. "Well, far out, you know," he thought he told her through his alcoholic haze, relieved merely to be rid of her and the unshoulderable burden of aspirations she represented.[66]

Having failed at *social* mobility, through either a brilliant career or a fashionable marriage, he turned his attention to another kind of mobility. "Another factor that is almost indispensable to this kind of behavior," he said later in his discussion of the killings, "is the mobility of contemporary American life. Living in large centers of population and living with lots of people, you can get used to dealing with strangers. It's the anonymity factor." Having made the fateful commitment of the remainder of his life, he would now deal exclusively with strangers.[67]

The Thief in the Night

"I want to master life and death."

Ted Bundy[68]

Why did Bundy kill? He has told us much, but has done so in his own fashion, which is to say that he contradicted himself ten times over. Sometimes he blamed it all on a bad seed, a warp in his genetic structure. At other times, he blamed the prevailing anomic culture of strangers, which permits or even encourages the dehumanization of others. Alternatively, he claimed he killed as a matter of judicial convenience, eliminating the problem of having a witness to his rape: "Self protection," he said, "required that the girl be killed." He also claimed he raped and murdered for the sheer sexual pleasure it gave the "entity" within him; but he also said he did it in order to possess a female person. At times he stated that the tensions and stresses in his life generated the murderous rage, while at other times he claimed the need to kill was self-generating and self-sustaining, a kind of force that existed on its own. Yet after a nonviolent sexual encounter with a young woman hitchhiker, he considered killing her, only to find that "the justifications were not there." What justifications?[69]

Whom he killed at least is clear. He murdered only one type of person, over and over again—the young, beautiful, long-haired and upper-middle-class (at least in appearance) "idealized woman." *When* did he begin to kill? He did so when he formed the opinion that he was incapable of sustaining the rise in the social hierarchy he so devoutly desired. Finally, there is a studied sameness as to how he killed. He would entice the otherwise unenticeable through a ruse, most commonly in a feigned need for help (a broken arm or leg). Through stealth or force he would get them in his car and there gain "control" over them, either by handcuffing them or by crushing their skulls with a heavy instrument. Then he would spirit them away to a private place and abuse them sexually for as long as he felt secure. Sometimes his victims were conscious and terrified, but more often they were battered unconscious—and sometimes they were dead. If he felt uncommonly safe, he might keep them (dead or alive) for days, pausing even to adjust their make-up or shampoo their hair. When he was finished with them, if they were not already dead, he would strangle them and dump their bodies in a burial ground. If it were not for bird hunters combing the thickets, many of the bodies might never have been found: many more, it seems certain, remain undiscovered.

Initially then, it seems clear that his task took a purely homicidal form—to avenge himself, in a sexually satisfying way, on the segment of society that had excluded him (by humiliating him to the point where he could not even accept their acceptance of him).

Yet the task underwent a metamorphosis, and his struggle with the authorities became the culmination of the task—and how appropriate, for were the authorities not the controllers of the society that had invalidated him? He first tested this during the events surrounding his trial in Utah. There, his bizarre posturing with the police and the court gave him immense satisfaction. Transferred to the Colorado prisons, he devoted his days to comprehending the metamorphosis. As he wrote to his mistress, "It is time to rethink this awful experience because the stimulus of standing alone in the face of great odds is not satisfying any more. It is time to re-evaluate the value of living without being alive. . . . I want to look around me now. I want to master life and death." He had much to rethink, for it was only a few months earlier, during his trial in Utah, that he had "felt a deep sense of fulfillment. I felt relaxed but emphatic; controlled, but sincere and filled with emotion. It didn't matter who was listening, although I desired each word to strike the judge as forcefully as possible. Briefly, all too briefly, I was myself again, amongst free people, using all the skill I could muster, fighting the only way I know how: with words and logic. And all too briefly, I was testing the dream of being an attorney." Now it all came together. Carrying copies of the works of Aleksandr Solzhenitsyn, and flirting with Mormonism (he said he thought he was "like the brothers of Amulek, being persecuted for our beliefs"), he found his ultimate *persona*: the persecuted dissident, publicly struggling for his belief in freedom. The trials now became the vehicle for the expression of his task—to confound the authorities and, in doing so, become their equal.[70]

His escape from prison gave him the opportunity to resign from his task, but it was absurd to even think of doing that, for the killing and the escaping and the defending had now become the essence of his life and being. Hence his choice of the sorority house and his final murder of the little girl: Having understood that he was incapable of abandoning his task, he completed it in a manner designed to be the most shocking possible, giving substance to French scholars Peter and Favret's proposition that "only to those who are excluded from the social nexus comes the idea of raising the question about the limits of human nature."[71]

Yet these murders exhausted him. Instead of escaping, he drifted erratically through Florida until he was captured by the police in Pensacola. Within hours, he was in the hospital emergency room, with ample opportunity to escape, but he did not seize upon it. He claimed not to understand why: "I just can't seem to get up on my own two feet and go for it"—but he must have known that to escape would merely have delayed the discharge of his most awesome responsibility, the trial. During his formal interrogation shortly thereafter, he saw the event theatrically and clearly as a task now almost complete: "They made their solemn commitment to me. We all sat around the room, and the tension mounted. I thought it was really quite dramatic. Maybe I overstate the event, but to me it was the end of the road, you know, right there." He made his confession to a priest, possibly a full one (we can never know). The violence was over.[72]

He struggled to give a confession to the interrogating police, but seemed unable to do so. "I can't talk about it, I'd be a fool. . . . I tried to help you understand me. . . . I tried to help you understand me a little bit more." When the police suggested that he was merely afraid to confess, he replied: "I'm not afraid to die." Then an insightful detective added, "You're afraid you're going to go before your story gets told. Sure," replied Ted. "That's right," said the detective, "and Ted

Bundy will have lived for nothing." It was at that time that Bundy told his jailer: "I realize I will never function in society again. I don't want to escape, but if I get the chance, I will. I want you to be professional enough to see that I never get the chance."[73]

In the trial that was to come, in the blaze of lights from daily national television coverage, he consummated his dream of becoming an attorney. Throughout the trial, he gave the impression to all that being his own attorney was the fullest expression of his life. As he put it: "The state prosecutor, with all his skill and training . . . a guy with a year and a half of law school can let the air out of his tires."[74]

An Adieu

His Republican employer had called him "a believer in the system," and so he was. He opposed all radical causes until he realized he was annulled himself—pronounced by himself unable to climb the hierarchy. Only then did he embark upon his radical crimes, crimes possible only for those so disenfranchised that they can reverse all social values and thereby act as gods. His world had spun apart twice; first, when he had discovered his illegitimacy and thereby lost his identity and purpose, and second, when he had discovered his inability to live with the creature he had fabricated in order to win the socialite. Many others before him had endured such humiliations, but had gone on to reconstruct their lives in a spirit of defiance, or of humility. But Bundy could not take that course. He wanted revenge "for what the system has done to me"; and just as the impoverished materialist Bundy had become a common thief, so the socially annulled climber resolved to steal the ultimate object. Killing those who were at once the object of his desire, the symbol of his annulment, and the now closed avenue for his escape, became the purpose of his existence.[75]

Once he had glimpsed his attainable future as "common," he could not endure it. It was necessary for him to seize control of events and to immortalize himself and his achievements in the process, catapulting himself on to the nation's center stage. He would not accept a verdict of insanity, even though that might have saved his life, for to have done so would have invalidated his rebellion, just as the bastardly verdict had invalidated his person. There was thus a rational reason why he appeared to behave irrationally in court: What Tanay and the other observers thought was the manifestation of Bundy's mental disease—his "inability" to recognize the weight of the evidence against him—was in fact a reflection of his alternate purpose. His innocence or guilt was irrelevant to his purpose, which was simply to confront and confound the authorities by attacking the quality of their case—thus fulfilling his "dream" of becoming an attorney. Ultimately, through the cleverness of his apparently insane maneuverings ("insane" because they denied him life), he was declared sane. Thus society acted against itself to legitimize his deeds. The earlier, Young Republican Bundy had, according to his biographers Winn and Merrill, "a visionary personal cast" to his political ideology. "Ted Bundy wanted to do something about America." And so he had. Alas, however, like all our multiple murderers, he had punished the innocent—which is to say he repaid ten thousandfold the original crime of society.[76]

Today, only the families of his victims remain to mourn, for like all our murderers, he felt no remorse. Awaiting execution in a Florida prison, he studied "Oriental philosophy—Buddhism, Taoism, and spiritual-physical traditions of the East," and found them "much in tune with the way I have become. I find that the pressures on me have actually permitted me to enter into a period of growth," he told his biographers. No matter how we tried to exact revenge, we could not, for his serene face revealed his fulfillment and contentment: "Anybody matures, I'm sure," he once said, "no matter where they are. But so many times in these past couple of years I felt like I was looking down from a mountain and seeing so many things I never saw before. I feel much more confident about myself. It's really marvelous! I feel not powerful, but in control of things." Such serenity was little wonder, for the man had mastered life and death.[77]

Bundy devoutly maintained his innocence for a decade, marrying one of his admirers during his trial and impregnating her behind a visitors' room water cooler. Toward the end, he finally admitted his guilt, but deployed a variety of excuses for what he had done: pornography, he claimed, had perverted his good character; drugs had desensitized and maddened him; and an allegedly sexually abusive grandfather had damaged him. Despite these attempts to exonerate himself, he was executed in a Florida prison in 1989.

5 Putting Something Over on High-Class People

ALBERT DeSALVO*

"I didn't mean to hurt nobody, I never wanted to hurt nobody."

Albert DeSalvo[1]

M ore widely known as the "Boston Strangler," Albert DeSalvo is one of the least understood of all modern multiple murderers. He is also one of the best publicized. He was the subject of a film and many books following his deadly rampage through the city of Boston. The murders seemed to be the work of a frenzied madman: He usually strangled his victims with their own stockings in their own apartments. It was widely believed that he was simply a "psychotic" with a maniacal sexual deviation—and there was certainly no doubt that he claimed to have had a formidable sexual drive that demanded release five or six times each day. This construction worker's career in sexual assault began first with molestation and then rape. He would pose as a scout for a modeling agency, flattering and cajoling (or forcing when necessary) hundreds of women into bed with him.

---

* DeSalvo's confessions are extensive and are available in a number of publications. The most reliable study of the man is Gerold Frank's *The Boston Strangler,* but I also found much of use in George W. Rae's *Confessions of the Boston Strangler,* and some in Harold K. Banks' *The Strangler!* and James A. Brussel's *Casebook of a Crime Psychiatrist.* Frank's book is both pioneering and scholarly.

Recent charges suggest DeSalvo may not have been responsible for *all* the crimes attributed to him, but the evidence remains inconclusive.

Then, suddenly, with no apparent conscious preparation, his task surfaced and he began to kill. He murdered thirteen women and then, just as suddenly, the task was completed. He was not an intelligent man, and he only dimly perceived his own motivations—which had to be teased out of him by police and psychiatric interrogators. Yet he was not caught by the police for the stranglings: He only came under suspicion for the murders because of his repeated pleas for help from his mental hospital cell (where he had been detained only for the rapes). As it began to dawn on the judicial and psychiatric authorities that DeSalvo the rapist might in fact be who he claimed to be—the Boston Strangler—they entered into a joint venture aimed at unraveling the motives for the bizarre series of murders. DeSalvo cooperated with the inquiry in every way, but the results were impoverished both by his own bewilderment at what he had done, and by his tendency to revel in his center-stage position in what he called "the biggest story of the century."[2]

In more ways than one, he was right. Raised in intolerable hunger and cold in the Boston slums, his violent and alcoholic father subjected him and his mother to savage beatings (he watched him break his mother's fingers one by one). We can only guess at the humiliation he endured after his father sold him and his sister as slaves to a farmer (an enslavement that lasted for months); but we can posit that his thefts during adolescence were an attempt to recoup his situation. We know that the rigid lower-middle-class German woman he met, adored, and married while serving with the U.S. Army in Europe became the focus of his attempt to enter the world of lower-middle-class gentility. When his beloved utterly rejected his physical, emotional, and status needs, he felt excluded from the social class whose membership he so deeply coveted. Thus, as he could rationalize within the context of violence-justifying male culture, his war on lower-middle-class women was legitimate. The stage was set for his purple explosion.

The Killing Time

His first attempt to kill was a failure. It was marred by the indecision and self-consciousness of the novice. In early June of 1962, he tried to strangle a Scandinavian woman in her Boston apartment. Her long dark hair had reminded him of his wife's, but the urgency of his task had not yet obliterated his compunctions. He was immensely strong, but she fought him until, he later recalled, "I looked in a mirror in the bedroom and there was me—strangling somebody! 'Oh God, what am I doing? I'm a married man. I'm the father of two children. Oh God, help me!'" Unable to complete the murder, "I got out of there fast. It wasn't like it was me—it was like it was someone else I was watching. I just took off." It took a week for him to pull himself together and steel himself to his mission.[3]

He made his first kill on June 14, 1962. Telling his wife that he was going fishing, he drove into Boston and selected an apartment building that suited his needs. He wandered through the corridors until he knocked on the door of Anna Slesers, a fifty-five-year-old Latvian immigrant. When she answered the knock, he told her that he had been "sent to do some work in your apartment." As she led him to the bathroom to show him the work that in fact had to be done, "I hit her on the head with the lead weight. She bled a lot, terrible," he remembered, " . . . after I put the belt around her neck, I ripped open her robe and I played with her and I pulled her legs apart, like this, and I had intercourse. . . . I think she was still alive when I had intercourse with her."*

"Then I look around and I'm angry and I don't know why and I don't really know what I'm looking for, you understand me?" He then "washed up in the bathroom," walked into the living room and turned off the record player, put on a raincoat that was hanging in a cabinet, and left. He disposed of his bloody clothes by throwing them into the ocean. Slesers' son later discovered her body and called the police: They

---

* DeSalvo used the word "intercourse" as a kind of euphemism for any form of sexual activity that resulted in orgasm.

found her lying on her back, nude under the housecoat which had been spread apart, with the housecoat's cord, DeSalvo's biographer, Gerold Frank, noted, "knotted tightly about her neck, its ends turned up so that it might have been a bow, tied little-girl fashion under her chin." Subsequent medical investigation showed no evidence of rape.[4]

Two weeks later, on June 28, 1962, he made his second kill. He knocked on the door of eighty-five-year-old Mary Mullen and told her that "I got to do some work in the apartment." She accepted his imposture as a maintenance man and let him into the apartment. When her back was turned to him, he remembered: "She was talking nice—and I don't know what happened. All I know is my arm went around her neck. I didn't even squeeze her . . . and she went straight down. I tried to hold her; I didn't want her to fall on the floor. . . . She died in my arms, this woman." He picked up her body and placed it on the couch, correctly assuming that police would think her death was from natural causes. "I didn't touch her. I didn't do anything to her—she went, just like that. She passed out. If I close my eyes, as I do now, it's just like being there. I picked her up and put her on the couch and I left."[5]

Two days later, on June 30, 1962, he killed twice. Selecting an apartment building at random and then an apartment, he knocked on the door of Helen Blake, a sixty-five-year-old retired practical nurse. As it was morning, Blake answered the door in her pajamas. Since she had previously asked the apartment supervisor to do some repairs in her apartment, she welcomed DeSalvo with the comment: "Well, it's about time." As he remembered, "We had some conversation. She was telling me about her niece, a very nice woman, you know, talking about her niece." He suggested they inspect the bedroom to determine if it needed any repairs, and he moved behind her as she pointed to a window that required adjustment. "While she was pointing I grabbed my hand right behind her neck; she was a heavy-set, big-breasted woman. She went down right away—she fainted, passed right out." He then "picked her up, took off her pajamas—the buttons popped—I took everything clean off. She was unconscious. I got on top, I had intercourse." He bit into her body, wrapped a brassiere around her neck, and then a nylon stocking over that. Then he went out into the kitchen and began what would become one of his trademarks—a major ransacking of the apartment, for no apparent purpose (nothing, for example, was stolen). He tried to pry open a chest under her bed, but the knife he was using snapped. "I just dropped the handle then and took off. I left her about 10:20 A.M." Her body lay undiscovered for two days until concerned neighbors called the police. They found Blake lying face down on her bed, the tops of her pajamas shoved over her shoulders. Her brassiere had been tied in a bow under her chin. The apartment had been torn apart: Bureau drawers had been left open, and the drawer of the living room's desk "had been placed on the floor, as if the killer had crouched there and carefully examined what it held; letters, stationery, rubber bands, a religious medal, and curiously enough, one of a pair of dice." Medical examination revealed that she had been sexually assaulted, but that sexual intercourse had apparently not taken place.[6]

He spent the next few hours "just riding around," in a kind of daze, "like in the middle of the world," until he turned into the parking lot of a still-fashionable apartment building. He pushed the buzzers until one tenant responded, Nina Nichols, a sixty-eight-year-old retired physiotherapist and widow. She was wary at her door when DeSalvo gave his usual "maintenance man" story, but when he said she could call the building supervisor to check on him, she relented. "I felt funny," DeSalvo recalled. "I just didn't want it to happen. But I went in and I proceeded from one room to another. When we got to the bedroom I looked at the windows. . . . she was turned away—that's when it happened. Because I grabbed her and she fell back with me on the bed, on top of me." He wrapped a belt around her neck and tried to strangle her with it, but the belt snapped. Finally, he choked her with one of her own silk stockings. He claimed to have had "intercourse" with her. When he finished, he inserted a wine bottle in her vagina: "For what reason I don't know, I stuck the bottle in her." Then he began his now-customary aimless ransacking of the apartment, not knowing what he was searching for, but sensing that he was not looking for something to steal. "I didn't have in my mind the idea of taking anything." When the telephone rang, he left. Nichols' body was discovered within hours. The apartment looked as if it had been burglarized. Bureau drawers were hanging open and her possessions were strewn about the floor. Nichols lay on the bedroom floor, her legs spread, her housecoat shoved up to her waist. The ends of the stockings which had cut into her flesh and strangled her were "arranged on the floor so they turned up on either side like a grotesque bow," Frank recorded.[7]

He then waited six weeks until August 19, 1962, before he made his fifth kill. Ida Irga was a seventy-five-year-old widow living quietly in a once-fashionable Boston neighborhood. Following his customary procedure, he randomly pressed the buzzers on her apartment building until someone responded: "When I get to the top of the stairs, she's on the landing, looking down over the iron railing, waiting for me. I told her I was going to do some work in the apartment." She was suspicious, but he allayed her fears by insisting that "If you don't want it done, forget it. I'll just tell them you told me you don't want it done." She relented, and as soon as he stood behind her in the bedroom, his arm went around her neck. "She passed out fast. I saw purplish-dark blood, it came out of her right ear . . . just enough for me to see. I saw it more clearly when I put the pillowcase around her neck, but I strangled her first with my arm, then the pillowcase. I think I had intercourse." When police entered her apartment two days later, they found Irga lying on her back in a torn nightdress. "Her legs," the police officer wrote, "were spread approximately four to five feet from heel to heel and her feet were propped up on individual chairs and a standard bed pillow, less the cover, was placed under her buttocks," leaving her in what Frank called "this grotesque parody of the obstetrical position." Why did DeSalvo now begin to add extra humiliation to the corpse and extra pain to the families of the victims? Irga had been sexually assaulted and her apartment ransacked, but her valuables had not been stolen.[8]

The following day, August 20, 1962, he killed Jane Sullivan, a sixty-seven-year-old nurse who lived alone. He entered her building in his usual manner and found her in the midst of moving in to her new apartment. She mistook him for one of the movers and led him to the closet to show him something. "That's where it happened," DeSalvo remembered. "I'm behind her. . . . I put my right arm around her, we both fell back on the floor. She struggled and struggled, she was so big there was nothing to grip hold of—she finally stopped struggling. It took about a minute and a half." He could not remember if he had raped her. Her body was not found for ten days—ten days of disintegration in the August heat. She was discovered grossly exposed, kneeling face down in the bathtub, her housecoat and girdle shoved above her waist, her underwear around her ankles. She had been strangled with two of her own stockings. The condition of her body made it impossible to determine if she had been raped; but her apartment had been ransacked.[9]

Then the pattern appeared to change abruptly: from now on, he would usually kill young women, and his sexual assaults would be more explicit. On December 5, 1962, he made his seventh successful assault, killing twenty-year-old Sophie Clark, a student at the Carnegie Institute of Medical Technology. He had driven aimlessly until he found a suitable building. He then knocked on the apartment door of one woman, who frightened him away by pretending her husband was in the bedroom. In another wing of the same building, he knocked on Sophie Clark's door: "A Negro girl, really beautiful, with beautiful long hair. . . . it was very appealing, the way she was dressed." He first told her he was there to do repair work on the apartment, but then returned to an earlier stratagem. "I gave her fast talk. I told her I'd set her up in modeling. I'd give her from twenty to thirty dollars an hour." He asked her to "turn around, let me see how you're built," and when she did so, "That was it. I grabbed her around the neck with my right arm, she was very tall, because she fell on top of me on the settee, my legs went around her legs—she didn't give me any struggle at all." He had intercourse with her as she lay there unconscious, and when she began to awaken, "To keep her from screaming, I grabbed two nylons out of a drawer. She was the one I had to tie really tight. She started to fight. I made it so tight, I couldn't see it. . . . I ripped her clothes off her, ripped off her slip, and put it around her neck, then the stockings. . . . Too deep. . . . Whew! . . . So tight." Curiously, DeSalvo remembered that "Afterwards I looked through some magazines there." Clark's roommate discovered her body a few hours later: She was on her back, her bathrobe spread open, a gag in her mouth, her legs spread apart. As always, bureau drawers had been ransacked and their contents thrown about the room. A classical record collection, magazines, and Clark's photograph album had been disturbed, as if someone had leafed through them, searching for something.[10]

He made his eighth kill within a few weeks, stealing the life of a twenty-three-year-old Boston secretary, Patricia Bissette, on December 30. He forced her lock that Sunday morning and found her standing in front of him with a blanket wrapped around her, demanding to know who he was. "I gave her the fast talk," he remembered. "I said I was one of the fellows living upstairs and where was her girl friend?—there were three names on the door, and I named one of them." She responded that they were out, but invited DeSalvo in for a cup of coffee, and put on a Christmas record. "I was looking at her and getting worked up. I went over to her, I was on my knees. . . . She said, 'Take it easy.' I said, 'Nobody's here, nobody can hear you. I can do what I want to you.'" This angered her and she asked him to leave, but as she stood up, she turned her back to him. "Next thing, before she knew it, I had my arm around her neck, she fell back on top of me, and she passed out." He ripped off her pajamas: "I picked her up. I remember seeing her on the floor stripped naked." He raped and strangled her.

Curiously, and reminiscent of Aiko Koo for Edmund Kemper, he felt remorse at killing her. "She was so different," he remembered ruefully. "I didn't want to see her like that, naked and. . . . She talked to me like a man, she treated me like a man." We will return to this particular case, for when the killer feels ambivalence, he is pointing toward his motive for the murders. Still, it saved none of their lives. Bissette's body was found the following day, lying on her back on the bed, a sheet tucking her in. The medical examiner removed the sheet and found her strangled with her own stockings. Her pajamas had been pushed up to her shoulders and there was evidence of recent sexual intercourse. Her apartment had been ransacked.[11]

His next attempt occurred six weeks later, on February 18, 1963. He entered the apartment of a twenty-nine-year-old German-born (like his wife) waitress and, when she turned her back to him, he grabbed her under his arm and kicked her to the floor. She fought back, kicking and biting; she bit his finger so hard that he momentarily loosened his hold, and then she screamed. As she remembered it, a workman then appeared at the edge of the roof, and DeSalvo fled. DeSalvo remembered it differently. "She was in the position, she was ready to go, she was good as gone. I had both arms around her from behind—but I couldn't do it. I don't know why. She grabbed my finger in her mouth, she was biting it down to the bone—I had a knife, I could have ripped her open . . . and I didn't. . . . I couldn't hit her. I could see her brown hair . . . and when I turned and saw her face, I couldn't put my hand to hit her. I said, 'I'm going to let you go,' and I started to give up, but she still had my finger in her mouth and I was doing everything to get her to open her mouth and she wouldn't. I could've laid, I could've hit her with my fist and knocked her out—I don't know what held me back."[12]

Three weeks later, on March 9, 1963, he was successful once more, beating and stabbing to death sixty-nine-year-old Mary Brown. He entered her building, picked up a piece of pipe lying on the floor, knocked on her door, and told her he had been ordered to paint the kitchen. "As she walked from the kitchen, her back to me, I hit her right on the back of the head with the pipe. She went down. . . . Her things were ripped open, her busts were exposed. I got a sheet from a chair and covered her. I kept hitting her and hitting her. . . . This is terrible . . . because her head felt—it felt like it was all gone." He took a fork from the kitchen: "I remember stabbing her in the bust, the right one . . . and leaving it in her. . . . It was bloody. . . . Oh, wasn't it, my God!" The autopsy report concluded that Brown had died from a skull fracture and manual strangulation, and also found evidence of a sexual attack.[13]

His tenth victim was murdered on May 6, 1963. Twenty-three-year-old Beverly Samans was a graduate student in rehabilitation counseling at Boston University. DeSalvo felt great difficulty in describing this murder because he thought it was "shocking" in some way that the others hadn't been. He entered her apartment in his usual way and, brandishing a knife, forced her into the bedroom. She was terrified of getting pregnant and DeSalvo remembered her pleading with him: "Promise me you won't get me pregnant, you won't rape me." He promised her he would not, laid her down on the bed and tied her wrists behind her, placing a gag in her mouth and a blind over her eyes. "Then I was going to have intercourse with her, anyway, and she began talking, 'You promised, you said you wouldn't do it to me, don't, don't, I'll get pregnant.' The words kept coming and coming. . . . I can still hear her saying, 'Don't do it—don't do that to me.' . . . She made me feel so unclean, the way she talked to me. . . . No matter what I did, she didn't like it. . . . She started to get loud. . . . She kept yelling or trying to yell . . . and I stabbed her. Once I did it once . . . I couldn't stop. . . . I reached over, got the knife . . . and I stabbed her in the throat. She kept saying something. I grabbed the knife in my left hand and held the tip of the breast and I went down, two times, hard. . . . She moved, and the next thing you know, blood all over the place . . . I kept hitting her and hitting her with that damn knife . . . I stabbed her two times in the breast, too. I hit her and hit her and hit her. Why? That's what I'm trying to tell you. . . . It was just like my . . . Irmgard [DeSalvo's wife]." Samans's nude body was found two days later, her wrists bound behind her with a sequined silk scarf, a nylon stocking tied around her neck. She had been stabbed twenty-two times.[14]

Something in him seemed to have been temporarily satisfied by Samans's murder, because he waited four months before he killed again. On September 8, 1963, he killed fifty-eight-year-old Evelyn Corbin, a youthful divorcée who worked on an assembly line. He entered her apartment as the maintenance man, but found her wary. "How do I know you're not the Boston Strangler?" he remembered her asking him. He "won her confidence" by volunteering to leave. In the bathroom, he threatened her with the knife and she began to cry, saying, 'I can't do anything—I'm under doctor's orders.' I was going to do it to her anyway, but she was all in tears; she said she'd do it the other way." When it was finished and she turned her back to him to replace the pillow, he grabbed her and tied her hands in front. "I got on top of her, sitting on her hands. I put the pillow on top of her face so I couldn't look at her face. . . . I strangled her manually. She did try to bounce me off. She couldn't do it, and then she didn't breathe any more." A neighbor discovered Corbin's body within hours of her death. Her housecoat had been ripped open and pushed up and her legs spread apart. Her underpants had been stuffed into her mouth as a gag, and she had been strangled with her nylon stockings. One stocking was tied in the form of an elaborate bow around the ankle of her left foot. Her apartment appeared to have been searched: Bureau drawers were open, a jewelry tray had been set on the floor, and the contents of her purse dumped on a couch.[15]

His task was now nearing its completion, but it was another three months before he killed again. On November 23, 1963, feeling awkward because President Kennedy had just been assassinated (and wondering if a killing was appropriate on this day), he murdered for the twelfth time: twenty-three-year-old Joann Graff, an industrial designer and Sunday School teacher. His usual stratagem brought him into her apartment, but—interestingly—he was appalled by the shabby condition of her rooms. "It was a very cheap apartment with really cheap furniture—even the Salvation Army wouldn't take it. Just like she was living out of a suitcase. The kitchen was terrible, the flooring was very bad." Still, he proceeded despite his qualms about her substance. He threatened her with a knife and forced her into the bedroom. "I put my hand right around her neck and pulled her backwards on the bed, and we fell on the bed, she was on top of me . . . and she passed out. . . . I took off her clothes. . . . Her busts were large. . . . I know I possibly may have bitten her. . . . I just had intercourse with her, and that was

it. It was very fast—all over within a matter of probably ten minutes."
He remembered strangling her with her own leotards. After he was finished, he left hurriedly and drove home for supper. "I had supper,
washed up, played with the kids, watched TV." The medical examiner
later determined that she had been strangled with two nylon stockings
intertwined with her leotards, tied around her neck in a flamboyant
bow. She lay on her bed, her blouse shoved up above her shoulders, her
legs spread. There were tooth marks on her left breast, and the apartment had been ransacked. Nothing had been taken.[16]

The thirteenth and final murder took place six weeks later, on January 4, 1964, when he killed nineteen-year-old Mary Sullivan, a nurse's
aide who had recently moved to Boston. She answered the door, holding in her hand a knife that she had been using to peel potatoes. She did
not think to use her own knife when he threatened her with his. He
forced her into the bedroom, where he tied and gagged her: "I got on
top of her so she could not be in any position, you know, to reach up
and scratch me. . . . She was still alive when I had intercourse with her,
she was alive, she allowed me to do it to her." He had intercourse with
her with her sweater pulled over her head "so I could not see her face."
Then he strangled her, cut the ascot from her wrists, and flushed it
down the toilet. He carried her body to another bed, removed her
sweater and straddled her, masturbating so that the semen struck her
face. Then, he admitted, he "done something" with a broom. "I feel I
did not insert it, at least I hope I didn't, to hurt her insides. You might
say, 'What do you mean, hurt her insides? She's dead anyhow.' But it
still—it's—it's to me a vicious thing. . . . Mary Sullivan was the last one.
I never did it again. I never killed anyone after that. I only tied them
up, I didn't hurt them." Her body was discovered a few hours later by
her roommates. The manner in which her body had been left seemed
to be the Strangler's ultimate insult. The police report recorded that her
body was "on bed in propped position, buttocks on pillow, back
against headboard, head on right shoulder, knees up, eyes closed, vis-
cous liquid (seminal?) dripping from mouth to right breast, breast and
lower extremities exposed, broomstick handle inserted in vagina, steak

knife on bed . . . seminal stains on blanket." A pink scarf had been tied
with a huge bow under her chin, and a gaily colored card placed against
her left foot. The card read: "HAPPY NEW YEAR."[17]

The Explaining Time

> "There is got to be some kind of explanation as to why this has all
> happened."
>
> *Albert DeSalvo*[18]

Despite a childhood poisoned by unspeakable physical abuse—including being sold as a "slave"—he did not begin to kill until he felt that his
social aspirations, such as they were, had become unreachable. Once
incarcerated, he tried to cooperate fully with the authorities and tell
them everything he knew about the murders. But since he barely
understood his own motives, he could only explain the mechanics of
how it had been done, and dwell on the grisly details of violation and
the act of destroying a life. Still, although at first he confessed only to
bewilderment and mystification at his own behavior, like Kemper,
Bundy, and Berkowitz, he did ultimately offer a number of alternative
explanations. However, unlike Kemper, who offered many explanations in order to mystify his audience, DeSalvo did so only because he
himself groped half-blind toward a conclusion. But in the end, he did
tell us enough.

   Why did he confess? When the police had announced on the radio
that the Strangler, once caught, would be sent to a mental institution,
he had considered turning himself in while he was still killing. But
shortly thereafter, he remembered that the governor had hinted that he
would press for capital punishment in this case, and DeSalvo had abandoned his thoughts of surrender. He seems to have made the decision
to confess when the police telephoned him to come to the station on
molesting charges. "I looked at my wife," he remembered. "She was
crying, sitting near me and the telephone. I knew she was crying and

vomiting all day, ever since the call came that morning. I couldn't see her cry any more. She was crying her eyes out, all red—she said, 'Al, are you in trouble again?' I held my hand over the mouthpiece. 'Don't you worry,' I said. 'I'll take care of it.' . . . I knew I couldn't go on any longer. I told the detective, 'Look, I'm coming down tonight.' I says, 'I'm going to come down now. Tomorrow might be too late. I want to get it all cleared up.' He didn't know what I meant, but I knew. I knew deep down this was the way it must end, I think I knew it from the very beginning."[19]

Yet he did not confess all at once. At first, he denied any involvement in the stranglings, and only hinted to detectives and fellow prisoners that he might be implicated in much more than simple molestation and rape. He told one detective, whom he especially liked, "If you knew the whole story you wouldn't believe it." But when the detective demanded that he explain himself, he merely replied vaguely, "It'll all come out, Leo. You'll find out." Once incarcerated in Bridgewater State Hospital, he boasted constantly about his sexual assaults, even during group therapy. He ambiguously asked one fellow inmate: "What would happen if a guy was sent up for robbing one bank when there were really thirteen banks robbed?" More overtly, he asked his attorney: "What would you do if someone gave you the biggest story of the century? Bigger than the Brinks robbery. It only happens once in maybe two million times. Like Jack the Ripper. I've been known as the Cat Man—the Green Man—the Phantom Burglar—and now the Boston 'S' Man." When an old friend visited him in the hospital and told him he would get life imprisonment for the rapes, DeSalvo replied, "Eddie, I could get life fifty times and they couldn't pay me back for what I done. My family would have to change their name." Again, he told a fellow inmate awaiting trial for the murder of his young wife: "Hell, what you did was nothing. When you find out what I did—I've killed a couple of girls." A few months later, he told his attorney that he had murdered thirteen women and sexually assaulted nearly 2,000, which in fact seems a likely estimate.[20]

Then he changed his mind about confessing. He had spoken to his wife on the telephone and, according to Frank, she had become hysterical and had threatened to kill herself and the children if he admitted he was the Strangler. The following day, during an interview with a Bridgewater psychologist, DeSalvo refused to submit to a routine test. He did express an interest, however, in what people were thinking "about all the excitement." When the psychologist told him that she did not wish to discuss the stranglings, he replied, "I understand that. Besides, I never confessed to being the Strangler. My name's never been in the papers in connection with those things. [The Strangler] should be studied, not buried."[21]

A few weeks later, his attorney arranged for him to be examined by a California hypnoanalyst, and DeSalvo agreed to undergo this eerie experience. In a deep hypnotic trance, punctuated by shattering screams from DeSalvo whenever he came to the brink of recalling the actual killings, he would speak only of the events leading up to the murders. The hypnoanalyst then left him with a post-hypnotic suggestion that he would write down any dream he had that night. The following day, DeSalvo presented him with a dream that edged closer to a confession, detailing the sexual assault and binding—but not the killing—of one of his victims. Unfortunately, this promising development was derailed when the hypnoanalyst insisted on exploring a Freudian theme in which DeSalvo, in attacking the women, was in reality attacking his own crippled daughter. In a deep hypnotic state, DeSalvo wept and denied it, then cried out, "You're a liar!" as his hands shot out at the hypnotist's throat. The hypnotism sessions went no further. The police, meanwhile, had been frustrated in their search for the Strangler because none of the survivors of his attacks could positively identify him.[22]

It was not until the spring of 1965, with the manhunt for the Strangler now in its third year, that the mental patient Albert DeSalvo confessed to police that he was the Strangler. But this information did not pour out until he had established a relationship of deep trust with an official. He prefaced his confessions with an explanation of why the murders had occurred most often on weekends (a fact the police had always taken as significant): "I could always get out of the house Saturday by telling my wife I had to work," he said. "You got to realize this. . . . I just drove in and out of streets and ended up wherever I ended up. I never knew where I was going, I never knew what I was doing—that's why you never nailed me, because you never knew where I was going to strike and I didn't either. So we were both baffled. . . . I didn't know so how could you know?" Through the summer and autumn of 1965, in endless sessions, he recited his homicidal *mémoire,* telling everything to the authorities because he wished to understand himself.[23]

DeSalvo Mystified

The recurring theme in his revelations was his mystification at his own behavior. Like so many multiple murderers, DeSalvo usually spoke of his killings in a distancing third person—a linguistic means of removing oneself from full responsibility—as if the murders had been done by someone else and he had only observed them ("I looked in a mirror in the bedroom and there was me—strangling somebody!"). With DeSalvo, however, the distance seemed to have been created not just to spare himself embarrassment, but to express his bewilderment. Still, he insisted that "I am doing my utmost to give you the clearest picture I can without giving you false details."

He seemed to feel overwhelmed by a kind of compulsion that he could neither control nor understand. When Nina Nichols had let him into her apartment, urging him to be quick because she had to go out, he remembered: "But I already know that she ain't going nowhere after I close that door behind me even though I fight it all the way. It's funny. I didn't want to go in there in the first place. I just didn't want it to happen." Nor could he understand why he searched and ransacked the apartments of his victims. When asked what he was looking for, he could only reply: "I didn't know at that time—probably anything. . . . To be honest with you, I never took anything from that apartment, from any of the apartments. . . . I wasn't up there for money, for stealing. . . . That's what I'm trying to find out myself. I done these things, I know, I went through them. . . . Yes—why didn't I take it?

That's what I'd like to know, too. I understand she had a diamond, too. Why didn't I take that? . . . I don't think I was actually looking for anything to steal." He did venture the suggestion that "I might have searched to make it look that way that something was being taken," but later admitted that he did not know if that was correct.[24]

When he was asked why he seemed reluctant to discuss certain details of the murders, such as the insertion of bottles into vaginas, his interrogators suggested this reluctance might stem from his lack of understanding. "That's part of it," he agreed. "And because it's so unbelievable to me that it was really done by me. Why I done it I don't really understand, but I know at this moment that to do it—well, I wouldn't. . . . I can remember doing those things. As for the reason why I did them, I at this time can give you no answer." Had he been thinking of anything when he killed? "No, I just did it." Still, he always knew what he had to do: At Jane Sullivan's, "as soon as I saw her, I had a quick look at the room. I knew what I was there for. Whatever it came to, that was it." Nor did he understand the symbolic content of his acts. "There was nothing about Anna Slesers to interest any man—why did I do it? She was getting ready for a bath. Why didn't I put her in a tub when I put Mrs. Sullivan in a tub? Just like why did I leave a broom and a bottle? I don't understand it."[25]

He seemed to regret especially the killings of the young women. About Sophie Clark, he said: "There was no need for it to happen." He denied suggestions he had killed her to possess her: "It wasn't the reason for having her. This is where the whole thing is messed up. There was no reason to be there, period. There was no reason for her to die. Nothing was taken away from her, no money, no nothing. How can I explain it to you? I'd sit there, looking to find something, looking through photographs like I was looking for someone." About Patricia Bissette, he said: "She talked to me like a man, she treated me like a man. I don't know why I did it. She did me no harm—and yet I did it. Do you follow me? Why did I do it to her? Why did I do it?" About the Joann Graff murder, during the traumatic days of the Kennedy assassination, he said: "I cried . . . when people started talking about

how the president was shot—then, that he was dead. I just stood there
and cried. Could the president be killed that day and I went out and
still did something? Could I have shot out that way toward Lawrence
that day, that afternoon? I heard someone say later it wasn't bad
enough the president died but someone had to strangle somebody. . . .
That Graff thing—it was so senseless that it makes sense, you know?
To me, it's so unrealistic as to why these things occur."[26]

Yet he fully knew that he was doing the killings. "I knew it was me.
I didn't want to believe it. It's so difficult to explain to you. I knew it
was me who did it, but why I did it and everything else—I don't know
why. I was not excited, I didn't think about it; I sat down to dinner and
didn't think about it at all. It was all the same thing, always the same
feeling. You was there, these things were going on and the feeling after
I got out of that apartment was as if it never happened. I got out and
downstairs, and you could've said you saw me upstairs and as far as I
was concerned, it wasn't me. I can't explain it to you any other way. It's
just so unreal. . . . I was there, it was done, and yet if you talked to me
an hour later, or half hour later, it didn't mean nothing, it just didn't
mean nothing. I'm realizing that these things are true and that these
things that I did do, that I have read in books about, that other people
do, that I didn't think or realize I would ever do these things. It's true,
God knows it's all true. I wish it wasn't. I don't want to be the person
who did these things. There's no rhyme or reason to it. I'm not a man
who can hurt anyone—I can't do it. I'm very emotional. I break up at
the least thing. I can't hurt anyone and here I'm doing the things I
did. . . . Thank God they had no loved ones, no children—all single
women. I can be very thankful for that. . . . But, still and all, a life is a
life. It's not a dream any more—it's true—and all these things happened. . . . I have a daughter, and I have a son and a wife, but when my
children grow older, I want them to get an understanding of me. . . .
I never really wanted to hurt anybody. Why didn't I do this before,
and why didn't I do it after? What drove me to do these? There's got
to be reason. I don't think I was born like this. Why did I start? Why
did I stop?"[27]

The Assignation of Blame

"I think there's a lot more involved in this than just being a rape artist."

Albert DeSalvo[28]

He seemed genuinely to have been bewildered by the cause of his crimes. Yet as the interviews extended through the summer and autumn, he offered several explanations, even—quite untypically for multiple murderers—at one point blaming himself. Astonishingly, the most vehemently expressed blame was directed toward his wife, Irmgard, as if her coolness toward him somehow justified his grotesque massacre of the innocents. As he wrote to her from the mental institution, "You will admit that if you treated me different like you told me all those years we lost, the love I had been searching for, that we first had when we were married. Yes, Irm, I stole them. *But why.* What happened when Judy was born and we found out she may never walk. How you cried Al please no more babies. Irm from that day on you changed. All your love went to Judy. You were frigid and cold to me, and you can't denie [sic] this. That's why we were always fighting about sex, because you was afraid to have a baby. Because you thought it would be born abnormal. Irm I even asked doctors what was wrong with our sex life and they all said—until you have another baby, and it is born normal will you then be free to love again. . . . Irm I'm not saying this is all your fault. Because I am the one who did wrong. But I had reason I loved you. After I came out of jail—despite everything I tried to do—you denied me my rights as a husband you constantly told me I had to prove myself and in short you tried to make my life a hell whether you knew it or not." Later, when police asked if he had ever been afraid he would hurt his wife, he continued his theme: "In her own way she was hurting me more than anything. If she'd given me the proper sex I wanted, at least treated me like a person and not degraded me all these times, I wouldn't be going out to find out if I was a man or not. . . . 'I used my sex to hurt you,' she told me. I couldn't understand why she, who I loved, treated me like dirt. She'd say, 'Don't go out at night'—for two, three years, I didn't. I stopped bowling. She once said, 'Don't ever leave me—you're the only one I know in this country.' I did everything for her. Why didn't I ask for help? I wanted to—and I talked it over with Irmgard, but, as I have said, she did not think it was 'nice' to have to admit things about yourself like that."[29]

To support this dubious and self-serving proposition that it was his rage against Irmgard that had driven him to kill, he claimed that the reason he had killed Beverly Samans with such savagery—repeatedly driving a knife into her—was because, when she had demanded that they not have intercourse, she had reminded him of his wife. "It was just like my . . . It was Irmgard. I grabbed her [Irmgard] right by the throat, she made me feel so low, as if I was asking for something I shouldn't have, that I wanted something dirty. I wanted to kill her that night! Asking her to make love was asking a dead log to move. It was always 'Do it quick, do it fast, get it over with'—she treated me lower than an animal. . . . I loved her so much, yet I hated her. I was burning up. How many nights I would lie next to her, so hot, so wanting to be loved and to love her—and she would not—*She* [Samans] reminded me of her. 'Don't do it, don't do it!' "[30]

This explanation may have seemed plausible enough, at least in the context of a brutal and self-absorbed male culture, but it contained significant contradictions. First, the two women whom he had released from his assaults were those who—in their ethnicity, their manner of speech, and their physical appearance—most closely resembled his wife. Why did he let them go? As well, if it seemed logical enough that he, both loving and hating his wife, might have displaced his rage upon another to save his frenzied love for his wife, it is also true that many people both love and hate their spouses without feeling driven to launch a sustained campaign of murder. Why then did he not merely find a new and loving wife? Thus we must conclude that DeSalvo's appalling relationship with his wife was neither necessary nor sufficient cause for murder. Few of our multiple murderers were so encumbered, and we must search for commonalities if we are to comprehend this social phenomenon.

A second, and infinitely more plausible, explanation for the generation of DeSalvo's rage was his extraordinary childhood, which reads like some Dickensian nightmare. His memories of this period were independently confirmed by accounts from family friends and social workers. "My father would come home drunk a lot and bring these prostitutes with him right up into the house and strike my mother in front of them and make me ashamed to have him for a father who could do things like that to a good woman like my mother. One of my first memories is him beating my mother. I guess I was less than five years old but I remember it. He knocked her over the couch and they fought and he hurt her hand so bad that I can still hear her screaming with the pain and all us kids screamed with her and the old man went around like a crazy man hitting us until some cop or somebody came and put him in his place, the man who came wasn't big, but it was different with my father when he had to fight with a man, you understand me? We didn't have to do anything to get beaten, just be around when the old man was ready to hand out the beatings. I saw my father knock my mother's teeth out and then break every one of her fingers. I must have been seven. Ma was laid out under the sink—I watched it. He knocked all her teeth out. Pa was a plumber, he smashed me once across the back with a pipe. I just didn't move fast enough. He once sold me and my two sisters for nine dollars, sold us to some farmer in Maine. No one knew what happened to us.* For six months Ma hunted for us and couldn't find us.[31]

"But we would take off over to Eastie, Noddle Island, and hide out under the piers and he would be afraid to come looking for us there because the other kids living there would've helped us kill him just for the couple of bucks they might get off his body. The Eastie piers . . . was a kind of second home for me and my brothers. You know, that was a dangerous place. They was kids there with no home at all. That was where they lived—under the piers and in the old warehouses and wharves. They was wharf rats, that's what people called them and they

---

* DeSalvo never elaborated on this period of his life, so we can only speculate on what he and his sisters endured during their captivity.

was just like rats—and they was a million real rats there, too, big ones that wasn't afraid of you—those kids, those wharf rats, I saw them roll a drunk one night, landing on him the way the real rats would land on one of their own kind who was sick or hurt all in a big dirty, wiggling pile, ripping and tearing until the thing they were on was dead and eaten to bones. Them kids was small, some of them wasn't more than ten, eleven, but they was a lot of them and they got that drunk down, just like the real rats, and they practically tore him to pieces then dumped his body into the water. Nothing happened to them, bodies was always being fished out of the harbor all beat up and fish-eaten. But I say this to tell you about the kind of vicious kids them wharf rats were and that is where I spent a lot of time when I was a kid—not that I was vicious. I was too shy and scared. I didn't like to fight and didn't think I could and was very much surprised to find out that I could fight pretty good when the time came. That was later.[32]

"Other things I remember about when I was a kid in Chelsea are always being too cold in the winter—the house was heated by a coal fire in the kitchen stove and we never had enough coal because of what we got came from the welfare and sometimes the old man would work out a deal for money with the coal man instead of coal. And I remember never having enough to eat, that is another thing I remember. It wasn't that we were hungry and starving, it was just that we didn't get enough, we could always have used more. Even now I can feel that uncomfortable feeling I used to get when I was a little kid, wanting more food so bad and not being able to get it. They was kids over there ate the plaster off the tenement walls and that is a fact. I think a kid growing up that way always has, down underneath, the need to go for all he can get, no matter how, because he is a person who never quite got enough of a full belly.[33]

"I can't remember a time when I wasn't learning something I'd've been better off not knowing. My father took me down to the five and ten cent stores in Boston, Chelsea, Eastie, and showed me how to cop stuff off the counters. I was five years old when he began teaching me this. . . . Now I look back on all that I could see it getting worse all the

time. The stealing got worse. It went from shoplifting to purse snatch-
ing and then to B and E [breaking and entering] and then to robbery.
And now, at this late date, I can see that it went from robbery to rape
to murder. All this was before I was twelve because by then I'd had two
arrests—one for larçeny from the person and the other my first B and
E . . . and I was twelve when I was sent to Lyman School for delinquent
boys. At Lyman School I really began to learn things. Now Lyman
School is supposed to be a place where bad boys are taught how to be
good. That is a laugh, ain't it? That is not the case at Lyman School at
all. You can learn just about every form of sexual perversion there. You
can learn a lot about how to steal. They is nothing criminal that you
can't learn there. . . . When you get out of Lyman School you know
how a criminal thinks and you are a boy who knows a lot about sexual perversion."[34]

Paroled from Lyman School, he immediately began breaking and
entering on a truly gargantuan scale, for he was an ambitious boy, anxious to better his lot. During this period, his family's lawyer, Sheinfeld,
was his primary support, professionally and personally. "He was a
very good man, Mr. Sheinfeld, to me. I do not blame him for anything,
only blame myself, and what Mr. Sheinfeld said was true. I was taking
awful risks and I was certain to bring disgrace on myself and more misery to my family. But I didn't know. I couldn't see it as clear as some
people who have had a better life. Mr. Sheinfeld, although he was a very
good man, was the same as the guys from the Probation and Parole
Office," observed DeSalvo, displaying a remarkable class consciousness. "He was on the inside of something I'd been on the outside of all
my life. Oh, I know that guys who have come from bad homes have
made good, it's not that, it's just my own personal reaction to what my
bad home was like—and it's this thing, this urge, that I had."[35]

This catalog of horrors from DeSalvo's childhood—this child slave
sold to a farmer; this witness to fantastic assaults upon drunks, and
upon his mother; this boy with the frozen body in winter and the
burning half-empty belly all through the year—was sufficiently
provocative, it would seem, to have spawned a multiple murderer. Yet

only the killers Lucas and Panzram shared such squalid childhoods; and one can speculate on many other criminal careers which might seem more appropriate for someone from such a stunted background (for example, a career in *professional* murder). Why then should this background have driven him to kill in such bizarre fashion, without profit, and at a time in his life when he had finally escaped from his lumpen-proletarian background, when he had "made good" as a devoted husband and father, with a steady job and an admiring employer, a home and car of his own? In his own terms, he had moved inside of something he had been outside of all his life. What manner of revenge could he have been pursuing on his bloody trail? Yet another element in DeSalvo's assignation of blame was his terrible sexual drive, which received a great deal of attention from his analysts. His remarkable sexual capacity was soon appreciated in his neighborhood, and it rewarded him with "a lot of sex on the side from the girls and queers around the neighborhood. Some of them was amazed at how I could come and then five minutes later come again. The queers loved that and they would pay for it, too, which was all right with me since I needed the dough and there was some relief from the urge that was pushing me to sex all the time, but it really was Woman that I wanted—not any special one, just Woman with what a woman has, not just to come, but to have the breasts and body to play with, to bite and kiss, then to go into. . . . I didn't even care so much what She looked like, or how old She was. . . . it was Woman and not a pretty woman, or any special woman, but Woman that I wanted, even then." Early on, too, his mind began to associate sexuality with breaking and entering, a fact that Freudian psychologists made some use of. "I didn't like rolling drunks. I was a B and E man, mostly. There was something exciting, thrilling, about going into somebody's home. . . . I think now, too, that it had something to do with going into bedrooms where women had been sleeping, or were sleeping and there was times when I would get a rail on just standing there outside the bedroom door listening to some woman breathe. . . . so you see what urge was all part of this and it was only a matter of time before I would feel strong and tough enough to go into the bedroom when the woman was there and make her let me do what I wanted with her."[36]

In this light, was it possible for him to have forged a marriage more *unsuitable* than that which he forged with his beloved Irmgard? About Irmgard, the repressed and puritanical immigrant, who could not bring herself to relieve his demanding urges, he said: "She was very innocent and scared of sex. I think they taught her to be scared of sex, her family, and she never got over that. . . . but, to be honest, I think, too, that she was a cold woman which is really bad for a guy like me who is so much in need of sex all the time, you understand me? I was in love with her . . . and I found myself wanting her after we was married, morning, noon and night I wanted her over and over. . . . I would sit there looking at her and wanting her, or I would lie in bed and want her so badly and right after I would have her, I'd want her again. . . . She didn't like it. . . . I've told you that I need a lot of sex, five or six times a day don't mean much to me. . . . I can come back minutes after intercourse. . . . The terrible urge never leaves me. . . . I used to say to myself: 'What's wrong with me?'"[37]

Even before he confessed to the murders, he had described much of his frenzied sexuality in a letter to his lawyer: "How could I tell my wife I am oversexed and have a drive and urge I cannot control," he wrote. "Even you Mr. Sheinfeld, when you had my case in 1961 in Cambridge involving all them women, you asked me if I got a thrill or feeling when I touched them, and I lyed [sic] to you and said no, because I was ashamed to admit it of my sex drive. But now its got out of hand. . . . I was trying with all my heart to be good but my drive got so bad I found myself relieving myself at least four or five times a day. It was so bad. But when I went out and did what I did that I am in here for it was so strange because it was like I was burning up inside and the feelings I was getting put me like a daze it would be like a dream I would not no [sic] where I was going but I was thinking and seeing a woman in my vision in front of me wondering what kind of a body she would have and so on. Sometime before I even got anywhere I found myself sitting in the car while driving, already releaved [sic]. But in five min it came back again. I was all ready again." Indeed, during his non-homicidal assaults, he often ejaculated before he touched his victims: "They even said some of the women that they felt when I just got nexted [sic] to them, they had a feeling that I had just releaved [sic] myself because after that I just tied them up and left without even doing anything to them. Its true I just put my hand on and I was finished. And then realized again what I had done. In almost all the cases the women said more than half I didn't even touched them but tie them up and run whitch [sic] took only 3–5 min—so you see I was so build up by the time I found a woman I just got near her and I was releaved [sic]."[38]

DeSalvo's sexual explanation is a compelling one. Yet he frequently failed to engage in anything resembling sex with his victims. As importantly, the purely sexual desire had already been sated by the rapes (if it is possible to think of rape as a sexual act in any sense) and assaults that both preceded and followed the string of murders. There seemed in fact to be no explicitly *sexual* reason as to why he was driven to kill: at no time did he admit to any particularly sexual response derived from the killing. For once in his life, during his confessions, he tried very hard to be scrupulously honest, and to transcend his lower-middle-class notions of what was "nice" to talk about and what was "shameful." Indeed, at times he was very astute, most especially when describing the murder of Patricia Bissette: "Now I say that I had intercourse with her while she was unconscious, but still alive. . . . all the time when I was doing this, I was thinking about how nice she had been to me and it was making me feel bad. She had treated me right and here I was doing this thing to her which she didn't want me to do. . . . I am sorry about that one, really sorry, but she shouldn't've asked me to stay and then they was the thing I felt. . . . What I mean by that is that a thing pushes a man. . . . *I don't know if I done this for a sex act or for hatred or for what reason.* I think I did this not as a sex act but out of hate for her—not her in particular, but for a woman. I don't think that a sex act is anything to do. It is what everybody does, from the top to the bottom of the world, but that is not what I mean. It is one thing to do it when a woman wants you to do it and another when she don't, you understand me? If women do not want you to do what is right and natural then it is dirty if they don't. You are really an animal if you do it just the same, is what I mean, you see? But all I can say is that when I saw her body the sex act came in. I did not enjoy the sexual relations with this woman. I was thinking too much about that she would not have wanted me to do it. There was no thrill at all." Precisely. His sexuality was an obvious and explicit part of the assault, but it was as much an afterthought as a motivating force. Even as afterthought, it frequently yielded little pleasure. Why then did he sustain such dangerous and unrewarding assaults? Why too would he claim to feel hatred for "women" in general when the only loving people in his entire life had been his mother, his wife, and his beloved crippled daughter?[39]

A fourth theme running through his lexicon of blame was the notion that he was from time to time overwhelmed by an almost "mental," certainly uncontrollable, compulsion to kill. He explicitly linked this to his behavior as a child when he had tortured cats. "I liked horses, but I didn't like cats. Or maybe it wasn't that I didn't like cats but just that I didn't think of them the way I did of horses. I used to shoot cats . . . with a bow and arrow, put it right through their bellies and sometimes they'd run away with the arrow right through them, yowling, and I don't recall being too upset by that even though I'm an emotional guy and can be upset easily. . . . sometimes when I would see them, before the shot, I'd get such a feeling of anger that I think I could've torn those cats apart with my bare hands. I don't understand this, but just then I hated them and they hadn't done nothing to me . . . then sometimes when I see them with the arrow through them, dying, I get mad, too, and none of it makes any sense to me . . . especially since I don't usually hate cats or like them, either, for that matter, you understand me?"[40]

He thought of this compulsion as a kind of mental disorder that would periodically seize hold of him. "I was a very good provider and took very good care of my family. I would like to say that if it was not for my sickness, which had not been given the help it needed to make it better, I was making something out of my life . . . trying to bring out the best in me. . . . It is true that my sickness was always with me. It made me go out and do things I knew was wrong. But it was a very immediate thing and I had to do what I did." This "sickness" developed a kind of inflating pressure inside him screaming for release, he thought. When he was alone with a woman in her apartment, "I was all hot, just like you're going to blow your head off—like pressure right on you, right away—I—I—to explain it or to express it, as soon as I saw the back of her head, right?—everything built up inside of me. Before you know it I had put my arm around her and that was it. By that time, it has gotten beyond my ability to control. There is nothing I can do about it by that time."[41]

Strangely, however, the "compulsion" to kill disappeared just as suddenly and completely as it had appeared. After the murder of Mary Sullivan—the tying of that most flamboyant bow and the writing of that insulting message HAPPY NEW YEAR—he returned to simple sexual assault. "Mary Sullivan was the last one. I never did it again. I never killed anyone after that. I only tied them up, I didn't hurt them. . . . Once in Cambridge I was in three places in a row after that and I started to cry and I said, 'I'm sorry, I don't know why I'm here,' and I took off." Moreover, he maintained a kind of consistency in his insistence upon a theory of compulsion. Unlike many multiple murderers, who resist the plea of insanity because it would annul their task, DeSalvo (who barely understood the nature of his mission) wanted to be found insane by the courts, for it would have relieved him of any responsibility for his crimes. Moreover, it would hold out to him the possibility that he might be "cured," and even eventually be released.[42]

However, the compulsion "explanation" is refuted by the calm and pragmatic terms in which he explained the cessation of the homicidal assaults. "My wife was treating me better," he offered, explaining himself now in social and economic terms. "I was building up, you might say, my better self, the better side of me, I was very good at my job, they liked me, I got two raises." He understood the personal deprivations that had generated his hatred, but the inarticulate nature of his rebellion—half-conscious and but dimly perceived—could not justify his behavior to himself. He could only cope with what he had done by claiming that a form of insanity had provoked the works he had wrought.[43]

Our portrait of his confessed motivation remains quite incomplete, however, without an explication of his curious but sustained social critique—a kind of personal and primitive *class war*, to which he frequently alluded. Admitting that he was the infamous Measuring Man, who, on the pretext that he could offer modeling jobs, took women's measurements in their apartments while feeling their sexual parts (few complained until no modelling jobs were offered), he told police: "I want to tell you all about it. I been a poor boy all my life, I come from a bad home, you know all that, why should I kid you? Look, I don't know anything about modeling or cameras. . . . I'm not educated and these girls was all college graduates, understand me? *I made fools of them*. . . . I made them do what I wanted and accept me and listen to me. That was why I was around measuring them. . . . I give it to you—I wanted to build myself up. They were all college kids," he told the probation officers, "and I never had anything in my life and I outsmarted them. I felt they were better than me because they were college people."[44]

This fascination with the niceties of social class, not pure chance, determined the neighborhoods he would select for his assaults and killings. "So I go and at first I'm kidding myself that I'm going to take a shot out toward Swampscott. . . . Now Swampscott . . . is a fancy place with big houses and lots of them smart and educated broads like I used to fool over around Harvard Square but they grew up and got married and now they got kids—girls—like they used to be and you wonder do these girls go to the bathroom and smell and do they play with themselves—excuse me for being vulgar, but I'm trying to tell you what I thought and what I even think now, you know they is an expression around Boston: 'She thinks her shit don't stink.' And that means she thinks she's too good for what a woman is made to do—sleep with a man when he wants and needs her and to let him do what he wants with her even if she thinks it ain't nice. . . . And anyway I don't go to Swampscott because I don't like the way they make me feel like an animal, those kinds of broads, and that is why I always put something over their faces and eyes so that they can't look at me."[45]

Incarcerated at Bridgewater, but before he had admitted to being the Strangler, he told a psychologist that the Strangler "should be studied, not buried." According to Frank, DeSalvo also insisted that it was only the poor who were punished, that "rich people could do all kinds of sex things and get away with it. They just bought their way out. I want to say here, too," DeSalvo later said, "about the Measuring Man kick that it give me an idea about how you can talk women into things. When you hear about it, it don't sound like it would work with a kid—all it takes a few sharp questions and a little ordinary sense to see through it, but very few of them did. They was married women who should've known that they didn't have the shapes to be models. But they was flattered, it raised their egos, and they fell for it. Some of them that called the cops did so because they was disappointed that I didn't send anybody [to take photographs]. . . . they wanted to know why I hadn't. Mostly, I got a big kick out of those girls around Harvard. I'm not good-looking, I'm not educated, but I was able to put something over on high-class people. I know that they look down on people who come from my background. They think they are better than me. They was all college kids and I never had anything in my life but I out-smarted them. I was supposed to feel that they was better than me because they was college people. . . . when I told them they could be models that was like saying the same thing: You are better than me, you are better than anybody, you can be a model. . . . Anybody with any sense could've found out. They never asked me for proof."[46]

"They was times when I was doing that Measuring Man thing," he admitted in a most provocative fashion, "that *I hated them girls* for being so stupid and I wanted to do something to them . . . something that would make them think, even for a little while . . . that would let them know that I was as good as they was, maybe better and smarter too. Now they was a lot of them girls. I want to say that they was at

least five hundred and some of them was so excited by what I was saying that they let me measure them without any clothes on at all. They
was some of those girls just needed a little push to get into bed with.
All this time, I was still afraid to try to force any of these women. If
they said the least thing, I would get out as fast as I could. It wasn't
until later that I come to the point of being able to force them. I think
I am right in saying that at the time I was the Measuring Man it all
could've been stopped. After I got out of the Middlesex County House
of Correction [for the Measuring Man offenses] there was no stopping
it. That is the way it seems to me."[47]

In a similar vein, DeSalvo remarked to an interrogating attorney,
"You are a man, you know what I mean, sure you have been to them
high-class colleges and you got all them big excuses, but you have had
that thing in your pants too—I think this is one of the troubles, sir, that
guys like you, who have played with yourselves, who have looked
with real lust on women, some of them far too young, away out of
your range of possibility with a great deal of lust are afraid to admit it
because somehow it takes you down from the goddamn pedestal on
which society places you—but you are only a man." Taking umbrage
at the expression on the face of this interrogator, he commented: "Let
me say this, sir, to you who sits across the table from me with such a
shocked face, just let me say this. . . . I ain't got nothing to lose no more,
you know, and I couldn't give less of a goddamn for your world which
is a nice society for you as long as you have money. . . . Have you ever
thought of what it would be like for your ass if you didn't have dough?
. . . I bet you ain't."[48]

His wife's behavior toward him exacerbated his sense of social
humiliation, he thought, even though it is clear that *he* provoked her
behavior. "If she at least treated me like a person and not degraded me
at all these times. . . . My own mother said that I was too good to my
wife, doing housework for her, cleaning the floors, that I treat her so
good that she don't have no respect for a man who does all those
things for her." Nowhere was his social awareness better encapsulated
than in his snobbish disappointment when he saw Joann Graff's apart-

ment: "It was a very cheap apartment with really cheap furniture—even the Salvation Army wouldn't take it." What sensibility was being violated here? Why should it matter to him that the homes of his victims be unambiguously middle class in style and furnishings? Earlier, he had told his probation officer, "Boy, it makes me feel powerful when I can make those girls do what I want—make them submit to me. I'm nothing in this life. . . . But I want to be something." When his probation officer had asked him if he wished to be caught, he had replied, "Yeah, I'd be somebody then. I'd get publicity in the papers." And when he ultimately made his full confession, he did so in the defiant rhetoric of a rebel: "If you're going to die for telling the truth, to hell with it. You only live once. What good am I alive? If the rich people live and the poor people die, then I die. There'll be other people coming along." To do what?[49]

Finally, as I have mentioned previously, DeSalvo also blamed himself, although it is by no means clear whether he took this unusual step as a means of castigating himself, or as a way of subtly justifying and glorifying his own role. "For a long time, I've known that I needed help. I done nothing about it. I should have, but I didn't. They was no one to push me to do it. Later, when it was real bad and I was married to Irmgard, it wasn't her fault that she didn't understand that it was help and not hell that I needed. Now I am not blaming Lyman School for the way I am. I'm not blaming anybody but myself. Them psychiatrists say I can blame other things . . . yes, to some extent as you have just said, society . . . but I am not doing that. A man does what he does and he has to take the blame himself. That is how I feel about it. . . . I often think about who is to blame and I find that it is myself because I could've done other things. I could've tried to get help. Even when I was older and working and supporting myself and my family I could've done something, but I didn't."[50]

Encounter with Psychiatry

> "I went to one [a psychiatrist] in 1961. It was the hardest thing to
> go look for help. I told him about the drive I had and he told me
> it's up to me."
>
> *Albert DeSalvo*[51]

DeSalvo was exposed to a number of psychiatrists during his life, but
he was not able to convince them that his problems were severe until
he confessed to the sexual assaults. He was first examined when, at the
age of thirteen, he was in the "reform" school. The psychiatrist found
that he had an IQ of ninety-three, and wrote: "This boy needs adequate social supervision and redirection of his interests into super-
vised groups such as the Boy Scouts and the YMCA." He received no
further attention until sixteen years later, when he was arrested for his
first run of sexual assaults. "That was the first time as an adult I talked
with a psychiatrist," DeSalvo remembered. "I come very close to getting some help there, but Bridgewater is not the place to get much help,
I can tell you. . . . This psychiatrist said that I needed help, he said that
I had a long time disturbance and that he recommended a psychological study. . . . He said I had psychopathic tendencies—I know what
that means—that I should not just be put in jail. But they didn't help
me . . . they sent me to jail. I came out in April, 1962. . . . By then it was
too late to save any of those women." DeSalvo had warmed to his
Bridgewater psychiatrist: "He was a very understanding man and I
think he was right in what he said about me about the psychopathic
tendencies—and he agreed with me that I needed help." In fact, the
psychiatrist had written with insight about DeSalvo: "The picture is
that of a long-disturbed personality with polymorphous perverse incli-
nations involving fantasies of grandeur and omnipotence," and he had
recommended a detailed examination to determine "the directions of
the psychopathic tendencies." His recommendations were ignored,
and DeSalvo served a conventional prison sentence.[52]

After DeSalvo was released from prison, and the Strangler was at large, police turned to psychiatry in their search for a profile of the killer. No intellectual tool is as cruel and unfair as hindsight, but one cannot help commenting that the profiles were not always accurate. One psychiatrist suggested that the killer was a "psychotic sex pervert suffering from the most malignant form of schizophrenia" and living in a fantasy world. Another wondered if the Strangler's victims were unconsciously signaling to the killer, through some subtle process of nonverbal communication, a sexual personality that the Strangler was seeking. This psychiatrist went on to speculate that in ransacking the victims' apartments, the killer was searching for a phallic symbol. A third psychiatrist suggested that the Strangler was a man searching for his own sexual potency, and was killing his own mother again and again in an effort to find this potency. As the hunt intensified and the public clamor increased, other and more mystical forms of intellectual inquiry were embraced: A Dutch "psychic detective" was interviewed at length for his perceptions, and an advertising copywriter, who claimed he had extrasensory perception, spoke to the police at length, in a trance.[53]

Prominent Boston psychiatrists formed a committee to examine the killings. They concluded that the murders were probably the work of two men, one of whom killed the older women; and they speculated that the killer(s) of the young women were "unstable members of the homosexual community," while the killer of the older women was a passive heterosexual who had been dominated by his mother, "a sweet, orderly, neat, compulsive, seductive, punitive, overwhelming woman [who] might go about half-exposed in their apartment, but punish him severely for any sexual curiosity." Consequently, they argued, "the boy grew up to feel that women were a fearful mystery. He was inhibited heterosexually but the overwhelming respectability of his background probably kept him from much overt homosexuality." They might have fared better had they concentrated on the social, instead of the sexual, characteristics of the victims, and the killer. Still, at least one of their number was more insightful when called upon to explain why the Strangler had not killed since the murder of Mary Sullivan. On hearing the details of her death, psychiatrist James Brussel commented that "I would not be a bit surprised if you did not hear from this man again. I think he has had it." Brussel had deduced that if the killings were the Strangler's search for potency, he had ended his search and been "cured," judging from the spectacular signs of potency on the body of Mary Sullivan.[54]

When DeSalvo was arrested for sexual assault, the police wondered if he was the Strangler, but rejected the idea because he did not fit the psychiatric profile. As Frank put it, nothing fit: "no consuming rage toward his mother, no Oedipus complex, surely no problems of potency—rather, fear and contempt for his father, and shame for the way his father had treated his mother." In Bridgewater, the psychiatric staff examined DeSalvo and concluded that he suffered from "a sociopathic personality disorder, marked by sexual deviation, with prominent schizoid features and depressive trends," which is to say a "diagnosis" entirely in keeping with their knowledge that he was a rapist and molester. They thought he was a borderline psychotic, but competent to stand trial. When the court ordered DeSalvo returned to Bridgewater for a second evaluation, he began to babble incoherently in his cell: This time, the staff found him psychotic, "potentially suicidal and quite clearly overtly schizophrenic." It would be months before anyone believed his persistent claims that he was the Strangler.[55]

Further disagreement between the psychiatrists was provoked at hearings which were held to determine DeSalvo's competence to stand trial for the sexual assaults. Dr. Robert Mezer testified that DeSalvo suffered from "chronic undifferentiated schizophrenia" which "would make it difficult for him to accept the world of reality as most people know it." Dr. Samuel Tartakoff essentially agreed, but characterized DeSalvo as a "sociopath with dangerous tendencies, an individual who from early life has shown deviations from what are usually considered normal patterns of behavior, thinking, and emotional reactions." Dr. Ames Robey argued quite differently. He thought DeSalvo was a victim of "schizophrenic reaction, chronic undifferentiated type," and concluded that "My opinion is that I cannot—repeat—cannot consider him competent to stand trial." He had watched DeSalvo in the hospital, vacillating "back and forth, sometimes appearing strictly sociopathic; at other times almost like an acute anxiety hysteric; at other times appearing much more obsessive and compulsive; again appearing very close to wild overt psychosis." At times, he thought, "he appeared to be almost very much what we refer to as in a homosexual panic, or sexual panic of some sort." Robey felt that DeSalvo "has a real need, because of his underlying illness, to prove to himself and to others his own importance," although he did not speculate on why DeSalvo should have such an intense need.[56]

An Interpretation

"Many people have died for a good cause. I think these people may not have died in vain."

Albert DeSalvo[57]

What are we to make of this supposed "mother-hater" who loved his mother most tenderly and protectively and was her favorite child; this "raging animal" who killed only women, but worshiped his wife and was devoted to his crippled daughter; this man "in search of his potency" who could leave his semen on bodies and clothes a half dozen times a day and still feel unsatisfied; this "psychotic" who spoke freely and openly to us in a language we could all understand, but who thought that his victims "died for a good cause"? We are tempted, as were Peter and Favret when writing of a nineteenth-century killer, to close such an ugly dossier and remain silent—but if we did so, we would have failed to "discharge our debt to these corpses."[58]

One might have little difficulty in understanding why someone condemned to a life of vile and empty suffering could explode in some fantastical homicidal adventure, marking in a lurid pen his otherwise anonymous passage through time. But DeSalvo, like so many of our multiple murderers, had *escaped* his ugly proletarian origins; he had been freed from "enduring the unlivable, day in and day out." It is true that his childhood was enough to break a lesser man—enduring endless beatings from his father; watching his father break his mother's fingers and drag prostitutes into the house for his public enjoyment; staring at the abandoned urchins on the docks as they killed a drunk for his wallet; feeling the caresses of pedophilic homosexuals in return for a paltry fee; and, with his sister, being sold into slavery. Yet these assaults upon his body and his spirit did not destroy him.[59]

Even before he had left the world of tenement and school, a fiercely ambitious core within him initiated what must have been for him a dizzying and precipitous rise in the social order. If he hated reform school, his behavior was exemplary in public school: There, he capitalized on what qualities he had, especially his humility. "I never got good marks, but the teachers liked me—I was a kind of teacher's pet, running errands, buying sandwiches for them—so I got by." He would use these same qualities during his years in the army, where he prospered as a spit-and-polish soldier, attentive to rank and rule: "always the sharpest uniform, best-dressed, shoes polished, best-kept vehicles ... I made Colonel's Orderly twenty-seven times." As a child in a violent world he had lacked the confidence to fight, but in the army he discovered he had special gifts, and for two years he held the title of the U.S. Army's European Middleweight boxing champion.[60]

His marriage to the intensely petite bourgeoise, Irmgard, both reflected and enhanced his social rise: He worshiped her, and why should he not, for she came from stock of such refinement that "no one in her family ever even saw the inside of a jail." In forging such a cross-class marriage, he had repeated the pattern of his detestable father—a lumpen proletarian of the most violent sort, with convictions for larceny, non-support, assault and battery, breaking and entering, common brawling, wife-beating, and assault with a deadly weapon—who had married the homely daughter of a respectable family (whose father was an officer in Boston's Fire Department). Indeed, when DeSalvo's case came to light, it was examined by a court justice who remembered her: "I liked his mother," he recalled. "Came from a fine Yankee family." Thus a curious social fact emerges: that DeSalvo was forged in a crucible whose primary activity appeared to be a kind of class war, in which the proletarian husband assaulted the bourgeois wife with unspeakable brutality. DeSalvo was determined not to duplicate this calamity, and while he married "up" to improve his position, he treated his wife with the utmost respect, nay servility. She would insult him in front of his friends, "make me feel like nothing . . . she gave me an inferiority complex," he complained, and she wounded him most deeply when she insulted his family. To make matters impossible, the sexual drives of these partners could rarely have been so mismatched. Soon he would be seducing and assaulting women all over Germany (where he was stationed), although he was never charged with these activities. When he returned to America and left the army, he resumed his pattern of sexual molestation, and eventually was arrested as the Measuring Man in 1961, and was committed to a state hospital for one year.[61]

In the hospital, full of enthusiastic love, and excited to be reunited with his wife, he told the psychiatrist of his slavish relationship: "I can hardly wait to get out so I can be with her and treat her the way a wife should be treated, even if it means washing her feet." But when he was released, she rejected him utterly, and his world spun, for he concluded that his exclusion from the class he coveted was for all time. "I come out of jail after one year, all alone for one year in one room, and Irmgard tells me, 'I wasted a year of my life.' She puts me on probation. I must learn to control my sex wants, she told me. . . . She would say I was dirty and sickening and called me an animal. I felt less than a man in bed with her." Shortly after his release, he put what he had read in prison ("Detective books—I read a lot of sexy stuff") to the test, and his career in multiple murder was launched. But what had happened to him? Why was it now, in his words, "too late to save any of those women"? His molesting and rape during his years as the Measuring Man might have been enough to relieve his sexual drive and release his still-smouldering anger; but such activities were insufficient to protest his total exclusion from the social niche he desired so slavishly. He claimed that many of the women he molested actually enjoyed it—misperceiving fear, he even bragged that one victim gave him a hundred dollars and begged him to return. Certainly he fantasized that many saw his molestation as admiration, not insult. But now he required an unambiguous method of convincing them and society of his avenging and insulting intent: He would kill, mutilate their bodies, and leave humiliating messages (dumping them in bathtubs, leaving them in obscene positions, or scrawling offensive notes). Thus was born his task: As half-conscious and unarticulated as it was, it would serve his need to protest his exclusion, reverse his degradation, and reinstate him as a man.[62]

After he began to kill, the psychiatrists who monitored the case made many false assumptions, based upon their dogma that the unconscious expression of sexuality is the prime force in human behavior. But dogma makes its practitioners contemptuous of facts; and so they did not examine the killings, or ascertain the distinct elements, replete with social symbolism, that were repeated in each murder. The first, the significance of which was ignored by all the commentators, was the striking *social homogeneity* of the lace-curtain neighborhoods he assaulted. DeSalvo would not, the reader will recall, hunt in upper-class Swampscott because its confident and sneering women intimidated him—which is to say they emphasized too much the status barriers he had been unable to climb. Neither did he prey upon the teeming tenements, whose denizens interested him not at all (how could it be otherwise, for they were not the class who excluded him). Rather, his killings were all in bourgeois areas—once fashionable, but often now in genteel decline—which provided him with lower-middle-class targets. They were middle-class enough to provoke his retribution, yet not so elevated from him as to render him tongue-tied and incapable of action, disarmed by status anxiety. As with all our multiple murderers, he attacked a very specific social category, a narrow band in a stratified society—the segment that represented all those who oppressed, excluded, and annulled him. Small wonder then that he was outraged and disdainful of Graff's "cheap" apartment, for it threatened to violate his purpose.

A second element in our comprehension of his acts was the means by which he *gained entry* to the apartments of his victims. The method he chose for both the earlier molestations and the later killings was the ruse. At times, it might have been easier (and certainly less risky, for the method he chose courted discovery) for him to have forced his way into the apartments (perhaps slipping a lock?). Yet to do so would have negated the meaning of his assaults, which was to put "something over on high-class people." The ruse, then, was essential to his purpose, which was both to outwit and then humiliate his betters, thus proclaiming his superiority. The public and the professionals paid a great deal of attention to this matter, but only to guess how he was able to gain entrance so easily to these apartments: They did not wonder why, in a world of easily jimmied doors and windows, he did not use force.

A third component to his enterprise was the sex, but this has been much misinterpreted. The psychiatrists noted the alteration in his sexual behavior as he progressed through the series of killings. At first, they found no signs at all of semen on the bodies, only seed spilled upon the floor. Evidence of actual intercourse did not appear until the later murders of young and attractive women. They deduced from this that he had "decided" to stop preying impotently on elderly women because his potency had now grown to the point where he could rape nubile younger ones. But we know that in fact the women were picked entirely at random by the simple expedient of whoever answered a buzzer and opened a door. He raped them if he found them attractive: Otherwise, the sheer intoxicating excitement of the violence drove him to ejaculate in his clothing or to masturbate in front of the corpse. It was small wonder that he could do either since his sexual drive was so strong: He sometimes ejaculated involuntarily while performing tasks as mundane as driving to work. What was important about the sex was that he was attacking (like Kemper, Bundy, and Berkowitz) an idealized Woman—but not the fresh middle-class university students of these other killers, not women of a certain appearance, but women of a certain class—the solid lower-middle class. The sexual release, when it was there at all, was not a prime motive; rather, it was an extra benefit to his task.

Finally, having selected a lower-middle-class victim, having duped her through a ruse, having killed her and violated the corpse with obscene decoration or arrangement, he turned to the last unvarying element, the *ransacking* of the apartment, searching for he knew not what: "I never took anything. I never wanted anything." At first, the police assumed he hunted for valuables, until they realized he left them all behind. The psychiatrists assumed he searched for some Freudian instrument. What is the reality? "I'm angry and I don't know why and I don't really know what I'm looking for," he had said. He rifled purses, went through bureau and desk drawers, thumbed through magazine and record collections, all in a kind of daze, and angry because he did not know what he was looking for, angry because he had not found it. Poring through photograph albums and record collections, hunting through accounts in bankbooks, he looked for some key to what he was doing and who he was. He found it, finally, in the apartment of his last victim, and that is why he did not need to kill any more. What he searched for materialized as the Happy New Year card, which enabled him to hurl at society the ultimate insult: Thus his task was the insult, his enraged answer to his exclusion, and the insult was epitomized in the card. When he placed it upon her foot, he came consciously to know why he had killed—to degrade, humiliate, and subordinate human beings. Thus he was released from his task, for he had fulfilled its objectives.[63]

His task was now discharged. He had put things over on high-class people, outwitting them and stealing their most precious possessions, their lives, and in the process had gained additional relief for his sexual drive. He had claimed his manhood, and as if in recognition of this, Irmgard now warmed to him once more, and gave him "so much loving." Perhaps too he allowed himself the luxury of half-believing he might fall heir to the life of which he dreamed. But he was soon arrested for the earlier rapes. Moreover, the need to confess was growing, for no one seemed to know what he had done or why. It was necessary for him to let the world know that his victims had died not in vain, but for a good cause. Besides, he now believed that Irmgard's love for him was false: "Our last two months together you made me feel for the first time like a man," he told her. "You gave me love I never dreamed you had to give. But why—only because you had just about everything you dreamed of . . . everything you wanted, house fixed up, all the money coming in." Amazingly, the rapist and murderer who had betrayed the love of both his wife and children felt that he himself had been betrayed: Now, in his volunteered confession to the authorities, he would avenge this alleged offense.[64]

An Adieu

Having fulfilled his need to explain and tell, having come to understand at least a measure of what he had done, he begged for absolution by being declared insane. He was deeply depressed when the courts refused this forgiveness, for he was only a sometime rebel, too timid to take the responsibility for what he had wrought. Like so many rebels before him, the cause had lost all its luster. He tried to make a kind of recompense by reverting to his proletarian self, abasing himself by playing body-servant to the elderly prisoners: "Right now I shave all the old men, I wash them up—I could help these people, give them a better life. Even if I may never be released, I'll be doing something for them. . . . I think I have a fairly decent attitude toward this whole thing. I still think I can make a contribution. Many people have died for a good cause. I think these people may not have died in vain." Like many of our multiple murderers, this conservative functionary felt ill at ease in understanding that the good cause on whose behalf he had killed so wantonly had been the cheapest form of vengeance. In any case, like so many other men, he seemed content to blame his wife for his own failings. He may well have been relieved when, less than a decade after his conviction, he was stabbed to death in a prison brawl.[65]

6 The Demons Were Turning Me into a Soldier

DAVID RICHARD BERKOWITZ*

"You are hereby ordered to unleash your terror upon the people.
'Destroy all good and ruin people's lives.'"

David Berkowitz[1]

This illegitimate, adopted son called himself the Son of Sam in his many and various taunting *communiqués* to the police and to his public. His clever manipulation of the press made him a great celebrity long before he was captured. He is significant to us not only as an additional illustration of our theme, but also as one of the few to offer detailed evidence that he might actually be deranged. In claiming to have been tormented by howling demons of the night, he appeared to be "insane," and this gave his public much comfort. Unfortunately, there is abundant evidence that his thoughts and behavior were not in any sense directed by demon forces—as he originally claimed—or even uncontrolled; and a close examination of his person forces us to revoke his proffered madman credentials. Because he is both a creature of his time and a special test of the utility of the notion of mental ill-

* Berkowitz's confessions, letters, and prison diary are available in a variety of published sources. His early pieces tend toward hysteria and fabrication, although they contain much of interest; but his later confessions have the ring of literal truth to them. The most scholarly and thoughtful studies of the man are Lawrence Klausner's *Son of Sam* and David Abrahamsen's *Confessions of Son of Sam*. In addition, I found George Carpozi Jr.'s *Son of Sam* and Charles Willeford's *Off the Wall* to be of some use.

Recent journalistic attempts to abridge—or even deny—Berkowitz's guilt have lacked all credibility.

ness, at least in a forensic context, his case demands close scrutiny. What we know is that his sense of social identity was dizzyingly kaleidoscopic—this Jewish convert to evangelical Christianity; this sometime auxiliary police officer with a succession of dead-end jobs; this gun worshiper who refused to carry a gun while serving with the U.S. Army in Korea; this illegitimate child who did not kill until he discovered that his social father was one man, his natural father a second man, and his stepfather a third. He could not launch his career as an international celebrity, nor construct a tolerable social identity, until he became the avenging Son of Sam.

The Killing Time

"I am the demon from the bottomless pit here on earth to create havoc and terror. I am War, I am death. I am destruction!"

David Berkowitz[2]

According to his prison diary, the demon he claimed he was and the demons who were to direct him first took shape early in his childhood. "There is no doubt in my mind," he wrote, "that a demon has been living in me since birth. All my life I've been wild, violent, temporal, mean, cruel, sadistic, acting with irrational anger and destructive. When I was a child I often had very real and quite severe nightmares. . . . I saw monsters often and I heard them, which often caused me to go screaming hysterically into my parents' room. . . . Now I know that they were real—just like now. I've been tormented all my life by them—never having peace or quite [sic]." During his childhood and adolescence, this demonic behavior took the form of setting fires in empty lots. When he was twenty-one, he began recording the location of his fires: between September of 1974 and December of 1975, he recorded 1,488 fires and fire alarms, a handful of which led to serious damage. As his anger built toward its culmination, he shot several neighborhood dogs, and began to send threatening letters to neighbors.[3]

During November of 1975, when he was twenty-two, he made serious preparations for his vendetta. He took a month off from his work as a security guard and locked himself in his small apartment in working-class Yonkers. He nailed blankets over the windows to keep out the daylight, slept on a bare mattress, and left the apartment only to buy the cheap food which, along with masturbation, was his only pleasure. He began to write messages on the living-room walls: "In this hole lives the Wicked King." "Kill for my Master." "I turn children into Killers."[4]

His first attempt to kill ended in failure. On Christmas Eve, 1975, armed with a hunting knife and a feeling that the time had come to act, he left his apartment and drove toward Co-op City, the middle-income high-rise community in which he had lived with his father. Parking his car, he spotted his first victim, and walked toward her with the demon voices, he later claimed, murmuring in his ear. "She has to be sacrificed," they said, as they wished to "drink her blood." He was conscious of his mission's importance: "I had a job to do, and I was doing it." Yet after his hunting knife arched into her back, the results disappointed, even terrified, him. "I stabbed her, and she didn't do anything. She just turned and looked at me. It was terrible. She was screaming pitifully and I didn't know what the hell to do. It wasn't like the movies. In the movies you sneak up on someone and they fall down quietly. Dead. It wasn't like that. She was staring at my knife and screaming. She wasn't dying." Panicked by the screams, he broke off the assault and fled. Later, he told a psychiatrist that he had been mystified by the woman's fear: "I wasn't going to rob her, or touch her, or rape her. I just wanted to kill her." The identity of this woman was never discovered: Presumably her heavy winter coat absorbed the knife blows.[5]

As he ran past the apartment block in which he had lived with his father, he saw fifteen-year-old Michelle Forman approaching. "I didn't know how to kill," he later told his psychiatrist, David Abrahamsen. "I stabbed her; she looked at me. I stabbed her again. It was terrible." His biographer, Lawrence Klausner, recorded that Forman was struck three times in the upper body, then twice in her face, before she fell screaming, blood spurting from her. "I never heard anyone scream like that," Berkowitz remembered. "The way she screamed constantly, I kept stabbing and nothing would happen. She kept fighting harder and screaming more. I didn't know. . . . I just ran off." She was taken to the hospital suffering from six stab wounds to the head and body, and a collapsed lung, but she survived the assault. Berkowitz celebrated his first "victory" at a cheap restaurant.[6]

It was six months before the voices urged him to act again, he said. On the evening of July 6, 1976, he put his Charter Arms .44 Special Bulldog pistol in a paper bag and began cruising the streets, waiting for "some kind of signal to use the gun." When he saw a car stopped at an intersection with two girls in the front seat, the voices called to him to "get them!" He followed their car as they pulled into a driveway, but by the time he had parked his own car and moved toward them in the dark, they had disappeared.

Soon after, he quit his job. He spent his days searching for work and his evenings cruising, "looking for a victim, waiting for a signal." He found a position installing air-conditioning in new buildings. Soon his hunt would meet with success.[7]

On the night of July 28, 1976, carrying his pistol once more in a paper bag, with the voices shrieking at him for "blood," he set out to hunt, looking for women to slake the demons' thirst. In the Bronx, he passed a parked Oldsmobile with two young women chatting to each other in the front seat; Donna Lauria was an eighteen-year-old medical technician, and her nineteen-year-old friend, Jody Valenti, was a student nurse. "I knew I had to get them," Berkowitz remembered. "Those were my orders. I never saw them until moments before the shooting." He parked his car around the corner and strode confidently toward the Oldsmobile, determined to make the kill "as a kind of joke." As he reached the car window, he opened fire, emptying five cartridges into the women in the car. The first bullet burst the window and struck Lauria in the neck, while the second bullet hit Valenti in the thigh. Writhing in pain, Valenti fell forward, sounding the horn. "I just started to shoot at the window," Berkowitz recalled. "And I just saw the glass come in. My eyes were transfixed to the glass. Thousands of little pieces—you could see them. . . . I emptied the gun and I was still pulling the trigger and it was clicking, but I didn't know it. . . . I went straight home and went to bed."[8]

At home, he sank into a deep and untroubled sleep. He awoke with a sense of fulfillment, to discover in the newspaper that he had killed Lauria: "I never thought I killed her; I couldn't believe it. I just fired the gun, you know, at the car, at the windshield. I never knew she was shot." He was, he said, "elated" when he went to work at the taxi company: "I was at work promptly at 6:45 A.M. That day I made out better than usual in both tips and fares." As the killer Edmund Kemper had done with his first victim, Berkowitz imagined himself to be in love with Lauria: At one point, he even claimed that the demons had arranged a form of marriage between him and her spirit.[9]

A few weeks of contentment passed, but by mid-September, the demons were tormenting him again and he began to cruise the streets, hunting. The howling of the demons disturbed his rest on the night of October 23, 1976, and at 1:45 A.M., he stuffed his pistol in his belt and drove into Queens. He pulled up behind a parked Volkswagen owned by Rosemary Keenan, the eighteen-year-old daughter of a city police detective.* Twenty-year-old Carl Denaro, whose shoulder-length hair made it impossible for Berkowitz to tell if he was male or female, was in the passenger seat. Berkowitz emptied his .44 into the car. "I was more frightened than they were," said Berkowitz. "Only one bullet struck the young man, and he really wasn't the intended target. I had fired with one hand, and wildly. Boy, did I mess up. But really, I was very nervous. I stayed a couple of minutes watching," then "I ran to my car and drove off quickly to a White Castle [restaurant]." Denaro had been shot in the back of the head, but he recovered after two months of treatment during which a metal plate was placed in his skull. Keenan was unhurt. Berkowitz studied the tabloids the following day to confirm that he had indeed shot a man.[10]

---

* This is another of the peculiar coincidences that litter these cases. Just as Seattle Police Chief Swindler's daughter had been a friend of Bundy, so Keenan's father would soon be working on the Berkowitz case.

The evening of November 26, 1976, found him cruising again. He drove aimlessly through the killing ground until just before midnight when he saw Donna DeMasi, sixteen, and Joanne Lomino, eighteen, returning to their homes after an evening at the movies. Donna noticed a figure standing behind a lamp post and said, "Joanne, there's a guy watching us over there. He's kind of scary. Let's walk faster." As they did so, he followed them. Berkowitz recalled: "By the time I was able to get back and hide behind the lamp post, they started to walk. I followed. They saw me and walked faster. By the time I'd crossed the street and got to them, they'd gotten to one of the girl's houses. They knew I was behind them and they tried to get in the door." As the girl fumbled nervously for her house key, "I started across the grass to them. Everything was going right. They were right in front of me. I didn't want to get them frightened, so I began to ask them for directions. All the while I was getting closer. They turned back to the door for an instant, but it stayed locked. Then they turned their heads to me. I had the gun out and pointed it in their direction. Then I shot twice. They both were hit and they fell on either side of the stoop. It was just like it should be. You shot them, and they fell. It was as simple as that." In a state of exultation, he emptied his .44, firing two shots through the front window of the Lomino home and one into the sky. DeMasi had been shot in the neck: The bullet had shattered her collarbone, but she would recover. The bullet which struck Lomino had crushed her spine; she would be a paraplegic.[11]

Berkowitz had now served his apprenticeship in serial murder. He had lacked confidence during the first three shootings: "I realized I was doing something that was not only illegal but also dangerous," he later told Abrahamsen. "I, too, could have been killed or wounded. Perhaps the man in the car would pull out a gun and chase me. I didn't know what would happen. The possibility of an off-duty police officer or a patrol car passing through the vicinity when the shots were fired was also taken into consideration by me. So I guess I had a lot to fear." Now he would comport himself as a professional: calm and entirely controlled, without fear.[12]

Five weeks after the maiming of Lomino and DeMasi, on the night of January 29, 1977, he found once more that he could not sleep. He tucked his .44 in his waistband and began hunting through Queens, his killing ground. Something made him park his car and begin to walk. Just past midnight, he noticed a couple walking toward him. "We just passed each other. We almost touched shoulders," but the voices commanded him, he said, to "get her, get her and kill her." Christine Freund, twenty-six, entered the car of her lover, John Diel, thirty, and they embraced. Berkowitz watched them, and wanted "just to kill her. I wasn't told to kill him. I aimed for her head, you know, quick and efficient. I guess practice makes perfect. I was able to control the gun, physically. After walking up, I stood in front of the window, crouched slightly. I brought the gun up with two hands. I opened fire. Three shots were all I had to use. The glass flew into the car and I hit her. I just wanted to kill her, nothing more. I only used three of the five shells in the gun. There really wasn't any reason to use them all. I knew I had hit her. I had to save my ammunition. After I shot her I began to run. I ran to my car. . . . I think I heard the car's horn blowing, and I think I heard the man get out. He began to scream. But by that time I was far away." Diel remembered kissing Freund as the window exploded; and he heard her scream as two bullets struck her right temple and neck. The third bored into the dashboard. He stumbled from the car and tried to flag down passing cars, but none would stop. Someone called the police, and an ambulance took Freund to the hospital, where she died at 4 A.M. Berkowitz said that he had known right away that he had killed Freund because "the voices stopped. I satisfied the demons' lust."[13]

While no evidence yet conclusively linked the different shootings to one another, intuitive police officers were beginning to sense that a single killer was hunting in Queens—in what only seemed to be unrelated incidents. In the meantime, Berkowitz, who had grown bored with construction and security work as well as taxi-driving, scored well on a civil service examination: In March of 1976, he began work with the post office as a letter sorter at the highest salary he would ever earn, $13,000 per year.[14]

On March 8, 1977, his day off, he was hunting in Queens once again, walking through the middle-class area of Forest Hills. Virginia Voskerichian, twenty-one, a Russian language major at Barnard College, was walking home from school, carrying her textbooks. When they were barely a step apart, he pulled the pistol from his pocket. "She was pretty, slender, and dressed nicely. Without really looking about, because my eyes were focused directly on her only, I just pulled out my revolver from a plastic bag and I shot her once in the face. I don't know why I chose her. I could hardly make out her facial features in the darkness." Voskerichian tumbled into the bushes that bordered the sidewalk and died instantly. As Berkowitz ran back to his car, he passed the first witness to see him leaving the scene of a murder: "Hi, mister," Berkowitz said to him. Walking toward his car, police in a passing patrol car thought he looked suspicious and pulled over to question him; but as they were about to do so, a call came over their radio reporting that a woman had been shot, and they left the scene. Berkowitz returned to his apartment. The single bullet he had fired had cut through the textbooks Voskerichian had raised in front of her face to protect herself, passed through her upper lip, shattering several of her teeth before crashing through her head and lodging in the skull near the spinal cord. However, police were now able to compare ballistic information on the spent bullets: On March 10, they were able to announce that at least three of the Queens attacks had been by the same man firing the same gun. A warrant was issued, using a vague description from witnesses and survivors.[15]

His awareness that he was on a mission intensified. He was pursuing a "conspiracy of evil": In his early confessions, he claimed the conspiracy was that of the demons. Later, he was silent on the matter. Still, on April Fool's Day, he began to compose a letter to the head of the homicide task force that was hunting him. On April 17, he stuck his pistol inside his waistband and went hunting in Queens; this time he had decided to kill both a man and a woman. Valentina Suriani, eighteen, a student of acting at Lehman College, and Alexander Esau, twenty, a helper on a tow truck, parked their car some time after mid-

night and began to embrace. At 3 A.M., still hunting, Berkowitz noticed
them and parked his car a block away. He walked toward the couple,
and fired four times. "It was my best job," he told Abrahamsen,
"because it resulted in two deaths. Plus, I left my first carefully con-
cocted note on the scene. My shooting pattern improved greatly due to
my fearlessness, which slowly developed, and my two-handed shooting method. Four shots were fired. Three hit the victims out of four
fired." He ran back to his car feeling, he said, "flushed with power,"
and drove past the apartment of Donna Lauria (for whom he felt reverence), stopping only at a cheap restaurant to gorge on hamburgers
and chocolate malts. Suriani was already dead, but Esau did not die for
another eighteen hours.[16]

He was contented for more than two months, until June 25, 1977,
when his mind began to wander again to the girls of Queens. "The
demons wanted girls. Sugar and spice and everything nice." He left his
apartment at 10 P.M., carrying his .44 in a paper bag, and began cruising through Queens. He parked his car and began to walk until he saw
a young couple in a car. "I saw her long hair. I looked about. The
street was deserted. I then began to approach the car from the rear,
keeping just behind the right rear fender. . . . I could see them clearly
in the front seat. The window was closed. They weren't looking in my
direction. I crouched down to bring myself level with the girl, and I
fired." Judy Placido, a recent high school graduate, and Sal Lupo were
talking when "all of a sudden," Placido remembered, "I heard echoing
in the car. There wasn't any pain, just ringing in my ears. I look at Sal,
and his eyes were open wide, just like his mouth. There were no
screams. I don't know why I didn't scream; I'll never know why, I just
didn't." Lupo had been hit in the right forearm, Placido in the head,
neck and shoulder. After the shooting, Berkowitz was disappointed: "I
was angry. I don't see how that girl lived. The window deflected the
bullet. It wouldn't go through the window right. I mean, I tried." He
ran back to his car, but he was unafraid, for "the demons were protecting me. I had nothing to fear from the police."[17]

His last kill was in Gravesend Bay, a middle-class section of Brooklyn. Stacy Moskowitz, a twenty-year-old telex machine operator, and Robert Violante, a twenty-year-old clothing salesman, met in a restaurant on the night of July 30. Berkowitz had begun to stalk one couple in a Corvette, but the car drove off before he could reach it. Violante's Buick pulled into the newly vacated space. "They kissed and embraced," said Berkowitz. "I had an erection. I had my gun out, aimed at the middle of Stacy's head, and fired. One bullet struck her head and another nicked her. I didn't even know she was shot, because she didn't say anything. Nor did she moan. Then I got in my car and drove off." Violante remembered that "I heard like a humming sound. A humming. A vibrating. First I thought I heard glass break. Then a humming. Then I didn't hear Stacy any more. I didn't feel anything, but I saw her fall away from me." Violante had been shot twice in the face and was blinded for life. Moskowitz had been shot once in the head and died thirty-eight hours later. A mile away, Berkowitz, a man at peace with himself, parked his car and bought a newspaper. He sat on a bench in a park: "I sat on it for a long time. I sat there for the rest of the night. When the sun rose, I read the news."[18]

Berkowitz slept late on the morning of August 10. He had failed to carry out a plan to open fire on crowds in the upper-class Hamptons, and now had formed a plan to wreak similar havoc in a nightclub in Riverdale. The duffel bag in the back of his car contained his extra tools: a semi-automatic rifle with four loaded magazines, an Ithaca 12-gauge shotgun, and two .22 rifles. But it was not to be. The police had painstakingly put together the circumstantial evidence linking Berkowitz to the Son of Sam (the final piece being a traffic summons he had received near the site of one of the killings). When they checked his car this time, they discovered his arsenal. At 6 P.M., they surrounded his apartment. At precisely 10 P.M., Berkowitz emerged from the apartment block and began walking toward his car, carrying a triangular-shaped paper bag. As he started the car, the detectives approached him from behind—as he had approached so many parked cars. One detective rapped his gun against the window and shouted, "Freeze, police!" According to the arresting officer, "The guy turned around and smiled

at us. He had that stupid smile on his face, like it was all a kid's game."
Berkowitz's hand remained clearly visible on the steering wheel. They
eased him out of the car and spread-eagled him. "Now that I've got
you," the detective asked, "what have I got?"

"You know," Berkowitz replied.

"No, I don't. You tell me."

"I'm Sam," said Berkowitz, smiling.[19]

The Confessions

"And huge drops of lead
Poured down upon her head
Until she was dead
Yet, the cats still come out
At night to mate
And the sparrows still
Sing in the morning."*

David Berkowitz[20]

The world already regarded Berkowitz as quite mad; as insane in every
possible sense of the word—medically, legally, and morally. The letters
he had sent to the press and the police during his killing spree provided
what seemed to be strong evidence supporting this belief, as did his
behavior in court and in the hospital. Most telling of all seemed to be
his prison diary, published in 1981 as an appendix to Klausner's
thoughtful book. The *persona* Berkowitz presented to the public, and
the documents he produced, were his attempt both to explain and to
disguise (perhaps from himself as well as from others) his enterprise's
inner meaning. At any rate, he felt that it was difficult for others to
understand him.

---

* This poem, written by Berkowitz, was found in his pocket after his capture.

The Demonology

"Questioned, he told his inquisitors he had killed at the behest of voices. 'Demons' had made him do it. 'Sam,' a 6,000-year-old man, had passed on these instructions to kill—through his dog."
David Abrahamsen[21]

"People feel a certain eeriness about me," Berkowitz wrote in his non-descript handwriting in his prison diary, "something cold, inhuman, monsterous [sic]. This is the power and personality of the demon's. This is the spell used by "Them" to turn people away from me and create a situation of isolation, lonliness [sic], and personal frustration, as part of their Master Plan. I've been tormented all my life by them [the demons]—never having any peace or quite [sic]. In fact, last week I went 'beserk' [sic] because they slapped me in the head and made terrible noises." While his homicidal spree was running its course, his neighbors and their dogs appeared to him as demons. Many nights they screamed at him, for they hid in the walls of his apartment. One night, Berkowitz remembered, "I kicked in the wall. I jumped and kicked. I tried to kick his face in. Nothing happened. It just didn't have any effect. I could hear deep in the wall a lot of sounds. Voices, thousands of them. Screams. Funny sounds. Music. Like drums. . . . I tried to do what they said, but they were never satisfied. Sometimes I argued with them, asking why they were making me do these things. But they never answered. They just laughed at me. I wasn't a bad person, but they were making me do bad things. I didn't want to. I did everything they said to do, and still they weren't satisfied." Were these "legitimate" delusions, or the constructions of a not terribly intelligent young man who was trying to divest himself of responsibility for his actions?[22]

Let us return to his prison diary, which opens with calm reflection on his own life and that of others. "When I look at all the prisoners in Kings County Hospital I cannot help but feel sorry for them. Their [sic] like lost souls; many in and out of institutions for all of their lives; little hope, no family, no friends. I think people only want peace and comfort in life but apparently few know how to find it. It seems like the only savior these patients have is thorazine but they really need Jesus. I never thought my life would turn out like this—what a mess. If it wasn't for my family and their love, and my lawyers and their supportive help I don't believe I would survive this ordeal. Some, I guess, are more fortunate than others. Love and companionship and a closeness to God are all that is necessary to challenge the adversary, Satan (Sam). Yes, the demons are real. I saw them, I felt their presence, and I heard them." But there is no more insanity here than that routinely dispensed at any evangelical gathering. The blandness continues: "I only wish they would let me read the newspapers here. Especially when its [sic] about me. I feel I just have to know what people are saying about me. The judge (Mr. Starkie) hates me I'm certain. He must think I'm some type of woman hater. But I thought the newspapers had done away with that theory when I was apprehended. If a girl had recently jilted me as the judge suspects then I would like to know who she was myself. Who could this mystery woman be?"

Then without warning, the demons surface. Berkowitz's handwriting shrinks and sprawls as he tries to communicate the "fact" that he is possessed once more. "I am a gladitor [sic] against the forces of darkness! I am come into these circumstances so that I might save many lives. I am willing to die to be at peace, to obtain it. I am willing to go to jail so I might be free. My life must be dedicated to the people on earth. Might it be possible to convince the world about the dark spirit forces that live on earth? I will die for this cause! Oh, death, you are victory."

Again he alters, becoming almost academic in his scholarly self-analysis. "After reading the book *Hostage to the Devil* by Malachi Martin I now have no doubt that I am a person who had been visited by an alien force or being. The evidence is overwhelming. Especially since my life fits in so well with the pattern of a person possessed by an intelligent force. The best evidence is a letter to my father dated long before to [sic] shootings began. This letter stated a devine [sic] mission that I felt was intended for me—one of importance although now that

I look back at it the whole mission makes no sense. Page 523 of H. to the D. the last paragraph—'It always alienated them from their surroundings and from those nearest to them.' There were even times after my arrest in which I doubted the reality of the demons, thinking of myself to be a person hallucinating or living a delusion but now, after reading Mr. Martin's work, I am convinced beyond my own self doubt about demons."

He combines a purported sense of social responsibility with his demonology, even drawing up the blueprints for new social institutions to cope with the demons. "Now I must go about to correct the wrongs of Son of Sam although they were good works when you look at them from distorted 'alien' eyes and from an 'evil' intelligence point of view. I need to have more personal freedoms such as keeping a pen in my cell, being able to go out, under guard and mail letters, go to the post office, and have a hotline telephone in my cell that leads directly to Chief of Detectives Keenan's office. I know that if the police set up a "Demon Task Force" then a tremendous step would be taken. It would be a monumental step in the annals of justice and historical law. Also, society needs to erect a "Demon Hospital" in which suspected cases of demon possession could be treated and alenniated [sic]. There is no telling how many crimes may have been committed by the possessed or how desperately they too need help.

"The demons have an amazing way of leaving you feeling like an empty vacum [sic]—leaving your life void of many things. However, the unclean spirits will fill the very same void which they so subtly created with evil light (darkness) and evil knowledge. "The void has been filled," I told Mr. Breslin; however, it was replaced with a dark foul substance that resulted in death and destruction. It is this distorted view that makes everything good look bad and everything evil appear right. So I gave up my personal freedom thinking it bad, only to obtain a type of freedom equivalent to that of a dog on a long chain. I can work but I can't have freedom. I can be loved but I cannot love. I could feel and admire good yet, have no good in me.

"There is, no doubt, a deep hidden array of forces behind the Son of Sam killings. This is not a trial simply to be put into black and white. This trial has far greater significance and far greater depth than one could imagine. The S.O.S. shootings probe hidden motives and expose spirits and forces that never before surfaced in an open courtroom. Good and Evil, God and Lucifer, yet, while every seat in the courtroom is taken, likewise, every corner space at the ceiling will be taken by those of the spirit world. There is no doubt in my mind that the outcome of this trial would affect all of God's angels and all of Satan's demons. . . . I have a fear now that I to [sic] will become a demon or, I may be a demon right now. Sometimes the need to kill becomes so overwhelming that I fear myself. However, I know that this is not me. I'm certain there is someone inside me, an alien presense [sic] whose need to obtain blood and kill is in relation to his rebellion to God. This belief of an alien presence is not an escape of responsibility because I am looking forward to a jail cell as opposed to having an apartment filled with demons. Furthermore, I, David Berkowitz, do not wish to kill anymore but live my life in peace and with a positive purpose. I wrestle with the evil one daily and silently. I know that if I were home alone I would be busting up my household possessions or punching myself in the head and arguing with the demons who ran amok in my apartment." But what is there about incarceration that would stop the demons from tormenting him?

"My apartment is what I called it even though I always felt that I didn't own it. I mean I paid the rent but I hated that apartment so much because of the demons that dwelled in it—I was even thinking of setting fire to it. I paid the rent; I signed the lease, I moved in it seeking quiet and rest only to find noise and terror. No, this isn't my apartment. It was reserved for me in the hopes of trapping me, leaving me near broke and unable to escape from the final foe—'Sam Carr' who is but isn't. Sam, who is dead but alive and who torments the earth. . . . What can I do? How can I make people understand? I am worried and with good reason that I may, one day, evolve into a humanoid or demon in a more complete state. I fear that with the loss of my humaness [sic] I will become like a zombie. As a matter of note, some people thought I was void of emotions when they examined me. This is exactly what happens to those possessed. I want my soul back! I want what was taken from me! I have a right to be human." But who had stolen his soul, and precisely what was taken from him?

The calm tone of the diary then changes abruptly, as if the demon spirit had entered his soul once more. The handwriting alters too: "I am Abaddon the Destroyer. I take the lives of those unwilling to give them up. I obtain their blood for Sam and the demons. . . . There were so many things that I wanted to do, so many places I wanted to visit. However, I couldn't. I had no rights as a person. I just couldn't enjoy myself when I had time off—my mission was all I lived for and I hated it. I hated my life as SON OF SAM. But what could I do? Even when I went to Florida I couldn't even stop to sightsee—I had no peace or rest. You could tell by the way I drove down there non-stop, then to Texas non-stop, that I did in fact, have a supernatural power and a special satanic mission.

"I am the demon from the bottomless pit here on earth to create havoc and terror. I am War, I am death, I am destruction! I know who has whored and pimped. I know who has committed grevous [sic] sins and who has spit on their mother and father. Where is the great one who can cast me away into darkness? Where is his coming? I suppose that he likes me at my temporary place—in David the shit the filth. I am the filth and the come. I am the wretch the filth the vomit! I am he the Son of Sam who fears nothing I destroy! I kill and stomp to pieces the people of earth in the name of that wretched. I am kind I am hell I am death. Meysa [victim Stacy Moskowitz's mother] the whore the harlot shall not escape Gods curse her children shall die all three for she whored her body and sold her flesh for a mere penance [sic]. Who is like the great whore the harlot of cum who sells herself. Who is like the Son of Sam, me, a fallen angel who has come to kill and to establish the kingdom of terror and misery—me, Son of Sam the killer who fears neither death nor hell. Who is Stacy who sells her soul for a penis? Let us make war with civilization and destroy and cause terror. . . . No peace comes to earth through the gun of kings. Who is sly and cunning? Who can outwit the president? Son of Sam and legion of us destroy and vomit uncontrollably."

Once again, he returns to his mundane "self"—in his terms, the spirit might temporarily let loose the bonds of possession and allow the "real" David Berkowitz to emerge. "The hours pass by so slowly its [sic] hard to make them pass. I guess I have to take the hours piece by piece and not take the day on a whole. Next to the demons, the worse [sic] thing is boredom. . . . What is death that a person should fear it? Perhaps one really fears having to lose ones [sic] possessions, loved one's [sic] or maybe the person fears having to meet God and be shown all of their sins. . . . I miss the freedom of travel—New Patty, Bear Mountain, Ferry Point park. It was a glorious experience to just get in my car and travel."

Berkowitz concludes with a bogus-sounding commitment to society and a modest bleat of self-pity. "I owe society a chance to make myself good and repay them for all the troubles I caused as a result of my illness. Someday, people will see a new David Berkowitz and the end of Son of Sam [indeed, it would only be a matter of months]. Son of Sam can be dead forever if the courts, doctors, and me are willing to work together. I am. I owe my freedom to Jesus Christ the Son of God. 'I and the Father are one,' says Jesus. I have made myself a promise not to remain locked up behind bars forever. I have a debut [sic] to pay to society and one day I will be free to repay it. I must repay society and now that I am a Christian I will work to help other people find true freedom and eternal life. In this hospital I found Jesus Christ and it is Him who I am obligated to. I must tell society about the truth and hope." He closes his diary with sad drawings of his face, next to which he wrote, "I am never happy. Rather I am sad. Very often I cry when alone in my cell. I am very nervous. I never never rest or relax. I am going to have a nervous breakdown. I am possessed! I sleep restlestly [sic]. I feel like screaming. I must be put to death. Demons torment me. I am not going to make it." Buried in a creation halfway between a doodle and a drawing, are two words: "HELP ME."

The Revised Version

"I must slay a woman for revenge purposes to get back on them for all the suffering they caused me."

David Berkowitz[23]

In February of 1979, less than a year after he had been sentenced to several hundred years in prison, Berkowitz confirmed his celebrity status by calling a press conference, announcing that his story of Sam Carr, demons, and spirit possession had been an invention. A few weeks later, he wrote to his former psychiatrist, David Abrahamsen, and confessed that the entire demonic story had been a well-planned, carefully coordinated hoax. "I did know why I pulled the trigger," he now admitted. "It would be a good idea if we talked." In the spring of 1979, Abrahamsen began making trips to Attica prison to visit Berkowitz because the latter had "expressed a desire to have a book written, a book that would deal not only with his crimes but also with his emotions."[24]

Berkowitz said matter-of-factly that he had bought the .44 pistol when he realized how much more difficult it was to kill someone with a knife. And he knew precisely what he intended to do with the pistol when he bought it. "I knew I was going to have to do something with it. I think it was going to be shooting people, you know." He described at some length the elaborate and carefully made plans he developed for the killings. "I used to visit my sister, and when I did, my gun, maps, extra ammunition, and other related paraphernalia were always carefully stored in my car for quick use. I did travel in the vicinity of Glen Oaks Village and Floral Park as well as many other places. Yes, Queens was special to me—very special. This I can't explain. Shooting someone in Queens was an obsession. When I got my bad urges about family, knowing that my gun was so close . . . I'd just go take a long walk to release any mental tensions I had for the moment. Walking for me has always been very therapeutic." The sheer professionalism that he displayed expressed itself not only in his planning, but also in the wary manner with which he conducted his operations. "I was angry when I did [miss], because I went to so much trouble to succeed and I took such huge risks. I familiarized myself with the streets and possible escape routes from those central areas. Also I managed to learn all the streets by repeated trips into the area. I mean, there were nights in which I traveled all through a certain area but it turned unproductive. Toward the end of my spree I developed a keen perception of police tactics. After a while, I was able to spot an unmarked car regardless of its disguise. Some were taxicabs, some were beat-up old rattletraps, but they were police cars just the same, and I 'made' them. Unmarked police vans were also a frequent sight."[25]

He conceded that he had experienced some ambivalence about the killings, but it had never been enough to stop him. At worst, it had made his earlier performances nervous and amateurish: "There were times I was troubled over my sudden urges after the shootings began," he told Abrahamsen. "I wanted to take a life, yet I wanted to spare a life. I felt I had to kill someone. . . . I wanted to and I didn't want to . . . [but] I was determined and in full agreement with myself that I must slay a woman for revenge purposes to get back on them for all the suffering they caused me. Of course you would disagree extensively with my immoral view. I don't blame you. Because I, too, realize that this was a poor excuse for all I've done. However, at the time I sincerely believed that I was justified. I believed that I had every moral right to slay a chosen victim. As gross and perverted as this sounds, it was my belief." Nevertheless, his ambivalence emerged merely as a kind of uncertainty or, as he put it (parroting the perspectives of the court psychiatrists), "I guess that shooting with one hand, which I did unconsciously, was a result of my inner conscience speaking to me, and that secretly I wished I had missed."[26]

More disturbingly, his growing confidence was bolstered by the extraordinary coverage the media were giving his activities—a coverage which, not without insight, he interpreted as a form of encouragement. "At this point [the Freund/Diel shootings] I imagine I didn't care much anymore, for I finally had convinced myself that it was good to do it, necessary to do it, and that the public wanted me to do it. The latter part I believe until this day. I believe that many were rooting for me. This was the point at which the papers began to pick up vibes and information that something big was happening out in the streets. Real big!" Later, in a spirit reminiscent of the reluctance with which a satiated lover contemplates yet another amorous bout, he would say: "Now that I look back on this, none of it makes any sense."[27]

Berkowitz was at pains to underline that he had abandoned his earlier religious ideals and now hated God (and all authority). "I hate God," he told Abrahamsen, "and I don't like him because of all the things he did. I blame him for taking my mother. I hate him for making me, my life. . . . But I think he is a liar. He has disappointed me. I fear God, his power, his ability to kill, hell, a personal terror. God has a grip on me and many others via fear."[28]

Still, he tried to leave us with the impression that his primary rage stemmed from, and was directed toward, his disappointing relationships with women. "When I returned home from the army, I tried to go out with some of the girls in Co-op City. They didn't find me attractive. I began to hate girls. I always hated them." When Abrahamsen tried to explore the symbolism of shooting women in parked cars, Berkowitz first responded with an intense and self-justifying puritanism. "I'm trying to remember if Esau and Suriani were having sex [something that, given his almost photographic recall of the killings, he would surely have no trouble doing]. I know they were embracing, but I can't remember if they had their clothes off or not. If they did have their clothing off, and were engaged in sex, then I would be somewhat justified in killing them. Sex outside of marriage is a heinous sin."[29]

Abrahamsen struggled to link the killings in parked cars to the possibility that Berkowitz was himself conceived in a parked car, in an illicit relationship, and was avenging himself for this reality. It was a suggestion that merely puzzled Berkowitz. "Betty [Betty Falco, his natural mother]," Berkowitz wrote, "never told me that she ever sat in a car or that she was impregnated in a car. But it is true that many unwanted children are brought into this world as a result of careless sexual encounters in automobiles. As for those parked cars, I cannot say what drew me to them. Maybe you could take an educated, professional guess. I'm at a loss to explain the hidden motivations. Maybe it was just a question of opportunity—a chance to catch them off guard and with their pants down, to catch them unawares, so to speak." We will return again to his "hidden motivations."[30]

Encounter with Psychiatry

> "Please dad I need you now. I've reached an agreement with the
> doctors that I am not well. I'm sure that you must realize that I'm
> no cold blooded killer. Rather, there is a problem with my mind."
>   *David Berkowitz*[31]

How did the psychiatric authorities interpret Berkowitz's life? Was he a victim of a mental disease and not a cold-blooded killer? Perhaps. The story of the development of Berkowitz's "mental illness" is a controversial and provocative one. According to Abrahamsen, he had been told of his adoption when he was three years old, and from early childhood had fantasized about death. Certainly he was a troubled child: Abrahamsen wrote that "he was unhappy, lonely, obsessed by rejection and neglect. He became antisocial and destructive. He was caught up in fantasies of self-aggrandizement, but he never developed any genuine self-esteem." Nevertheless, as Klausner noted, Berkowitz passed through the elementary and high school system without providing grounds for intervention, and he slipped through the army's psychological testing program, such as it was. Similarly, none of his post-army employers found any pathological cues to interdict.[32]

It was only when he began to kill that an amazing variety of experts turned their attention to him, although they knew him only as the Son of Sam. Klausner noted that the Omega homicide task force hunting him consulted biorhythm specialists, exorcists, astrologers, handwriting analysts, numerologists, hypnotists, psychologists, and psychiatrists in their frustrated attempts to find patterns in the killer's behavior. The psychiatrists were sometimes no less eccentric than the exorcists, no more prescient than the astrologers. One psychiatrist told police that paranoid schizophrenics such as the Son of Sam unconsciously killed at locations that invariably formed a triangle, a theory that drew some attention until another psychiatrist pointed out that any three points make a triangle. Similarly, nothing more useful than laughter was obtained from the comment of a German psychiatric consultant who announced to an audience of policemen and psychiatrists: "Gentlemen. Every time he shoots his gun, he's ejaculating!"[33]

In May of 1977, the police commissioner released an insightful psychiatric profile that diagnosed the killer *in absentia* as "neurotic, schizophrenic and paranoid," and possibly obsessed with demonic possession. More useful, however, were the police's own notions about Sam—that he led a double life and did not always appear to be insane. "He's the kind of guy," said Commissioner Tim Dowd, "who probably goes to work every day. Maybe he does something with statistics. An accountant or a clerk. He just kind of melts into the city scene. He doesn't *look* crazy." Still, no one had much to go on: Berkowitz saw to that.[34]

After his arrest, the task of the psychiatrist became the determination of whether Berkowitz was "insane, to determine if Mr. Berkowitz is suffering from any mental disease or defect that would preclude a trial." As always, the legally relevant issues were whether Berkowitz could understand the nature of the offense with which he was charged, and whether he was able to assist his attorneys in the preparation of his defense. On August 29, the psychiatric team, headed by Dr. Daniel W. Schwartz, director of forensic psychiatry at Downstate Medical Center in Brooklyn, submitted its report, based on a total of eleven hours of interviews with Berkowitz spread over six days. "It is the opinion of each of us," the report concluded, "that the defendant is an incapacitated person, as a result of mental disease or defect, lacks capacity to understand the proceeding against him or to assist in his own defense." Their diagnosis was "paranoia," and their prognosis was "guarded."[35]

It was at this point, when the prosecution felt it needed its own psychiatrist, that the court appointed Dr. David Abrahamsen to conduct an additional examination. Abrahamsen's report denied the incompetence conclusion from the defense psychiatrists, and instead found Berkowitz competent to stand trial and to assist in his own defense. "David feels that his distorted beliefs are of such importance," Abrahamsen added, "that all other topics should be relegated to the sidelines. Thus the defendant's main excuse for committing the crimes is his delusions. . . . It is also noteworthy that the delusions the defendant states he has, seem to be more transitory and situational, rather than constant. They may, in fact, be exaggerated by him." Abrahamsen ably concluded that "while the defendant shows paranoid traits, they do not interfere with his fitness to stand trial."[36]

This provoked intense conflict within the court. The prosecution moved that the state-appointed psychiatrists re-examine Berkowitz, while the defense asked for a new competency hearing. After the re-examination was performed, Schwartz's colleague Weidenbacher reversed his earlier decision and found Berkowitz to be competent, doing so on the peculiar and remarkably non-psychiatric grounds that Berkowitz had become a Christian and was espousing *bona fide* Baptist doctrines (and presumably could not therefore be insane). However, this time Dr. Schwartz now felt unable to draw a firm conclusion—reflecting, presumably, the intense political pressure within the courtroom. The newly appointed defense psychiatrist, Dr. Martin Lubin, found Berkowitz incompetent. Abrahamsen seemed to be the only one to see Berkowitz and his delusion for what they were: "Your Honor," he told the judge, "the defendant is as normal as anyone else. Maybe a little neurotic." Berkowitz's counsel changed their plea to guilty, and he was sentenced to a total of 365 years in prison.[37]

After the Trial

Abrahamsen was the only psychiatrist to appreciate the element of exaggeration and embroidery implicit in Berkowitz's demonology; strangely, this insight seemed to have drawn the two together. After the trial, when the Son of Sam denounced his demonology, he wrote to Abrahamsen and expressed a desire to have a book written about him "that would deal not only with his crimes but also with his emotions. To understand the psychological makeup of Berkowitz," Abrahamsen later wrote, "would be a challenge to any psychoanalyst. He was not a mindless, psychotic killer, but rather a complex human being, inexorably driven to destroy himself and others."[38]

However, Abrahamsen's subsequent preliminary analysis in a popular magazine produced a hodgepodge of unintegrated insights.* The analysis began with a narrow focus on the family: "The circumstances of his upbringing remind us how much we are a product of our formative years. By tracing Berkowitz's feelings, thoughts, and deeds, one can see where tenderness fought rage, where love battled hate, where reality and fantasy lived side by side." He made much of Berkowitz's "desperate search for his biological mother," and suggested even that "to an extent his crimes are the horrifying consequences of his finding her." This paradoxical notion that Berkowitz's warm and loving reception by his natural mother and sister should create a murderer was mediated, for Abrahamsen, through the notion that although he was warmly received by them, their reality overwhelmed him. "Meeting his biological mother, Betty Falco, proved to be the ultimate frustration." Berkowitz had "fantasized a complete family, a blissful reunion. After finding Betty, he learned that his real name was Richard Falco. But then he learned that his mother's former husband, Tony Falco, had left her years before he was born. His real father, she told him was her lover of years' standing, a married man, Joseph Kleinman, who had died several years earlier. Berkowitz was staggered. Even the name on his birth certificate was a hoax. 'I was an accident, unwanted,' he said. 'My birth . . . was either out of spite or accident.' By the time he learned this," Abrahamsen concluded, "there had been too many psychological traumas. Despair and rage had settled in. His feelings of murderous rage toward women, which he so far had been able to keep in check, were ready to be unleashed." So for Abrahamsen, the discovery of the true

* His complete analysis later appeared in book form.

shape of his genealogy "was one of the precipitating events that brought into action Berkowitz's murderous, sadistic impulses." No one would deny the unsettling effect this would have upon him, but the notion that this might have provoked many murders of women needs much clarification.[39]

A second and inevitable theme was Berkowitz's warped sexuality, which Abrahamsen saw as a kind of prime cause. "Berkowitz's sexual feelings played a significant role in his mass killings, yet for a long time he minimized, even denied, that sexual emotions had anything to do with his murders." Yet was this denial a function of Berkowitz's disordered sexuality (as Abrahamsen charged), or simply a true denial? We know that Berkowitz was sexually aroused during his crimes, but it may not have been his primary motive. "During my first interview with him," Abrahamsen continued, "as I questioned him about his relationship with women, he began to talk about the demons who had wanted so much from him." When Abrahamsen asked what it was that the demons had demanded, Berkowitz replied: "The demons wanted my penis." But this was at the time when Berkowitz was still fabricating his demonology—justifying his own activities and trying to save himself from both responsibility and prison—an interpretation that the Freudian Abrahamsen ignored because Berkowitz was expressing a sexual (and therefore true) version of events. "By then he felt he already had said too much, and he absolutely refused to go on. He wasn't ready; he had entered a mine field of explosive feelings, from which he hurriedly retreated." Or, alternatively, his imagination had run out.[40]

A year later, Abrahamsen raised the subject once again: "Now I wanted an answer to a question: Why did he kill? There were several topics Berkowitz and I touched upon for the first time that day in Attica, but one remark in particular struck me. 'I joined the army,' he declared, 'in order to lose my virginity.'" Abrahamsen recalled that Berkowitz had first boasted to him of losing his virginity at sixteen when in reality, "Berkowitz's first sexual experience, as he later admitted, was in Korea when he was about nineteen years old. At Attica he told me that in Korea, if you wanted 'to have oral sex, you went to one town, and if you had to have sex naturally, then you went to a different town. I was most satisfied when I did it to them, when I sucked them.'" This is interesting material, but Abrahamsen deduced from this preference for oral rather than genital sex not only that Berkowitz had a kind of sexual immaturity, but that this immaturity explained his murders. "His preoccupation with oral sexuality to the exclusion of genital intercourse, both in fantasy and in reality, suggests his immature sexual development. He preferred petting and fondling to adult genital intercourse." Abrahamsen left aside the possibility that such a preference might be dismissed as merely individual taste rather than pathological flaw. He then deduced that "another sign of Berkowitz's undeveloped sexuality was his use of masturbation as a substitute for sexual intercourse. At the time Berkowitz went into the army, he masturbated compulsively several times a day, every day. Even when he raved against sex as a sin and was actively enrolled in every available church program, he couldn't wait to go back to his room in the barracks and masturbate. When he masturbated, he always fantasized he had a girl. And, he said, 'When I did it, most often my fantasy involved oral sex between heterosexual couples . . . I always fantasized about girls. Now I cannot go to sleep unless I masturbate first.'" This might seem to have some significance, unless one realized how frequent masturbation must be in an alien environment where vigorous young men had few opportunities for conventional relationships other than frequent trips to brothels. Still, Abrahamsen concluded, "More and more in his sex life, fantasy had become his reality." But is this not true for a pathetically large proportion of humanity? "While his neurotic shyness induced him to masturbate rather than approach a girl sexually, he never learned that a girl was capable of giving him better and greater pleasure. His sexual fantasies about women were almost constant, but he did little to realize them in real life. He was a loner. In fact, he was afraid. Afraid of being impotent, he blamed women for his own shyness. . . . 'I began to hate girls. I always hated them.' Almost every waking moment, he once told me, he found himself fantasizing, and he was greatly troubled by his fantasies. They were almost all either sexual or violent. 'I'm really quite perverted,' he confessed."[41]

Abrahamsen argued that Berkowitz's sexual inadequacy "was rooted in the circumstances of his childhood. He knew from a very early age that he was an adopted child, and lived with the fear of being deprived of basic physical and emotional gratification. Having lost one mother, his biological mother, he feared he might also lose his second, adoptive one. That is, in fact, what happened. Pearl died of cancer when David was fourteen. This loss caused him so much anxiety and grief that it overwhelmed his feelings of love, inhibiting their natural expression." Yet what kind of an explanation is this? Many people suffer the tragedy of the loss of a parent, even an adoptive one, in their childhood, yet it does not render future love impossible. Indeed, one might argue the opposite case just as effectively, that such experiences can make the individual even more dependent upon loving relationships. In either case, it makes no sense to proffer this as an explanation for multiple murder.[42]

A third theme centered on authority, which Abrahamsen explored in terms of Berkowitz's unresolved Oedipal conflict, and in his purported witnessing of the "primal scene. Berkowitz also associated physical affection with competition and antagonism [and what person does not on occasion?]. He told me, 'He [his adoptive father] made me leave the room when they wanted to be alone. I resented it. I felt deprived. It was my father who took me out of the room. I asked him, 'What are you going to do, kiss?' Here we see the classical psychological confrontation of childhood," Abrahamsen argued, "in which the young boy battles the father for the affection of the mother. The beginning of self-determination is the child's way of coming to terms with this struggle, if he is to grow successfully into adolescence. But Berkowitz's ego was not secure enough for him to assimilate and transcend this experience. He could only turn toward his own fantasies to find an outlet for sexual desires." Drawing the thread still further, Abrahamsen linked Berkowitz's hostility toward his father with what he felt toward God. "If Berkowitz's sexuality was affected at this time by this unresolved Oedipal conflict, so also was his attitude toward authority figures. At one point during our initial conversation at Attica, having just discussed sexual matters, he launched into a diatribe against God. . . . His fear of God was the same fear he had of his father when he challenged him for his mother's attention. He had to be his mother's favorite."[43]

Brushing aside the question of how jealousy for the mother might lead to multiple murder, Abrahamsen pursued the primal scene theory without corroborating evidence of any kind. "It is probable," he speculated, "that as a child he had seen his adoptive parents making love and had since repressed that primal scene. In 1977 he was to be a witness to another love scene as he stalked Stacy Moskowitz and Robert Violante. . . . in observing the young couples, he felt he participated in the lovemaking, and to an intense degree he was also a voyeur, which he greatly enjoyed. In a twisted way he had become both a voyeur and a participant. He too wanted to partake in the act. When he shot his victims he was transfixed, continuing to pull the trigger as if he were both emotionally and sexually engaged." Unfortunately, the evidence from anthropology makes it clear that the "primal scene" is a cultural invention: There are many societies in which it is normal for the young to watch their parents having intercourse, and that observing this scene provokes nothing more than rude giggles or guffaws. It seems most likely that it was only our repressed Victorian ancestors, fascinated and horrified by human sexuality, who could concoct a theory attributing mental disorder to such a glimpse.[44]

When Berkowitz invited Abrahamsen to "take an educated, professional guess" about whether there was a relationship between the killings in parked cars and his own possible conception (which Berkowitz knew nothing about) in a car, Abrahamsen wrote: "My educated guess is that he was indeed trying to 'catch them off guard and with their pants down'—literally. His reunion with Betty Falco was enough to send him off on his murderous expeditions, enough to make him want to catch a woman with her pants down and to punish her— he was that furious and that disappointed with his newfound mother."

But Berkowitz was disappointed with the complexity of his conception and his genitors, not with his natural mother, who had smothered him with love![45]

Nevertheless, Abrahamsen was Berkowitz's Boswell, and we must follow him to his conclusions. His position essentially was that this man with a crippled sexuality, this voyeur, this victim of the primal scene and of unresolved Oedipal conflict, took out his rage for his natural mother on his victims. "Within our sexual fantasies themselves, violence often plays a part. In the disturbed (though not necessarily psychotic) mind, however, these feelings literally fuse together, and the person may act accordingly. Such was the case of sexuality and violence in the life of David Berkowitz. Violence took over his sexually colored aggression. He confessed to me that he 'had fantasized about shooting women for a long time.' Although he had nobody in particular in mind, he knew it would be pretty women. He fantasized about shooting women, and he fantasized about having sex with them. His hostile feelings toward women made him sometimes want to 'cause bodily harm, but not while having sex.' But despite this assertion, it is clear from the link he makes between the two that his sexual and murderous fantasies were very much closer to each other than he realized."[46]

But did Berkowitz simply fail to "realize" something, in that special way that psychiatrists so routinely deny their patients any insight into their own conditions? Or was Berkowitz trying to tell Abrahamsen something he could not comprehend? Indeed, Berkowitz explicitly denied everything Abrahamsen had so patiently constructed when he emphasized the *non-sexual* motive behind the killings. After murdering Donna Lauria, "I was literally singing to myself on the way home. . . . The tension, the desire to kill a woman, had built up in me to such explosive proportions that when I finally pulled the trigger, all the pressures, all the tensions, hatred, had just vanished, dissipated, but only for a short time. *I had no sexual feelings. It was only hostile aggression.* I knew when I did it, it was wrong to do it. *I wanted to destroy her because of what she represented. I never knew her personally. I knew what she represented.*" What can this remarkable denial mean? Why did Abrahamsen so studiously ignore it? Who and what did his victims represent, and what was the source of this "hostile aggression"? To answer this, we must turn to a social interpretation of his life.[47]

The Metamorphoses of a Serial Murderer

> "I hate rebels but I love revolutionaries."
>
> *David Berkowitz*[48]

The person who was Richard Falco and then David Berkowitz was, like all of us, constructed of many parts, any one of which he might choose to bring to the surface. Unlike many of us, his self-absorption and superficiality enabled him to pass from one social *persona* to another almost without comment, as if they did not contradict each other. If we are to understand him, we cannot pass over each transformation with his facile manner. The man who was to make his life's work the killing of pretty women in Queens shed many skins, as would a snake, before settling on his coherent identity as the Son of Sam.

The Brat

Multiple murderers do not have quite the kind of childhoods we would expect: Expert opinion varies, but by no means all appear to have been "abused" in the conventional sense (which is to say reared in the turmoil of sexual or physical assault). Certainly there was no evidence whatever of any form of brutality in the dull, lower-middle-class Jewish home in which Berkowitz was raised. Nor did he reveal any maniacal urges in childhood. He merely demonstrated that complex of behaviors which has been recently dignified with the euphemism "hyperactive," which is to say that he was widely regarded as a spoiled and uncontrollable brat. As one neighbor recalled: "His parents had a difficult time with him. Kids would complain that he hit them without reason. [But] his parents were nice and they gave him the kinds of toys any child would cherish. More for sure than any kid in the neighborhood."[49]

He seemed strange to some, but no more so than would any other willful, spoiled little bully. The neighbor whose account has the most convincing ring of truth to it thought the young Berkowitz was "a handful. His mother was taking him to psychiatrists. He did a lot of very strange things. He would push people. He always had a vivid imagination, but what he would say was a little beyond what the average child would say. His mother would laugh and smile." A music teacher, charged with trying to explain the rudiments of the saxophone to Berkowitz, remembered that "he was terrible. But the music was the least of it. One time I went into the house and he was throwing a tantrum. Tearing curtains off the wall, throwing pictures, screaming, and kicking. I said I'd come back later. He used to make his mother cry terribly. The tantrums, his arrogance was something else. He was the most erratic kid I've ever known." This is interesting, but all it offers us is one variation of a type of child with which every neighborhood is cursed: here exploiting the early knowledge of his adoption through endless tantrums with his bewildered adoptive mother.[50]

Super Patriot

The willful child embraced his true persona early on—although he would reject it for several years—as he evolved into an arch-conservative patriot. As he emerged into manhood during the dying months of the Vietnam War, and still troubled by the death of his adoptive mother and his father's remarriage, it made sense for this pseudo-John Wayne to join the army. "I wanted to serve the country and get an education through the Army," he explained. Moreover, he was suitably enraged when a radical stepsister, who lived in a California commune, sent him an anti-war collage to protest his enlistment. "It really got him mad," his childhood friend, Iris Gerhardt, recalled. "It was an anti-war type of thing with photographs and her own drawings that said American soldiers were killers and that Dave shouldn't do it too. He really resented that. He showed it to us and said, 'How'd you like to get something like this if you were going into the Army?'"[51]

Explaining his patriotism at a time when such a stance was profoundly out of step with his generation, he admitted: "I sort of lived like behind the times. I wanted to see some action, prove something to myself. It was rebellion then against parents, country and stuff. Kids were hippies and into drugs. I guess, then, I was very patriotic. Nobody else, except a couple of people, were." He was transferred to Korea, not Vietnam, after basic training, and he arrived flaunting his new persona. "I got there in the unit and I was really, you know, just out of training. I was really gung-ho, super straight." Then Berkowitz the super patriot would temporarily disappear, for like everyone else in the army in Korea, he recalled, he changed. "Wow! When we got exposed to everything, everyone changed. Almost everybody went crazy." This persona would resurface through his life (when he took a job as a security guard or served as an auxiliary policeman), but for now he was about to experience his second great transformation.[52]

The Rebel

He was ideologically conservative but, like most of our multiple murderers, his interaction with his social environment produced a fuzzy rebellion. For Berkowitz, this would be expressed as a 1960s-style anti-establishmentarianism which periodically blended with radical religion. Not long after his arrival in Korea, he was self-importantly writing his friends in the U.S., urging them to "keep the movement moving on the home front and I'll keep it moving here." On January 21, 1972, he wrote his friend Gerhardt, formally announcing what must have been a puzzling ideological shift. "I don't play anymore conservative patriot scenes. I woke up. The world is all fucked up (thanks Nixon). We've got to have some peace. The only thing on my mind is Drugs, Music, Pollution, Poverty, Peace and Love . . . I despise religion, hate prejustice [sic], greed, etc. That's all the world is. A cold mass of hell. It sucks. We're all doomed to the grave."[53]

Despising religion, he changed his mind and converted to evangelical Christianity. In his typically bogus style, he wrote: "One day me
and Jesus talked ya know, the usual story. Anyhow, we got to some big
thinking. So I decided to do what I wanted to do in this particular situation." Appropriately, he began zealously to proselytize his fellow
soldiers on the base. One remembered him "telling the guys they
shouldn't be drinking and swearing and running around with women.
But as an individual, I didn't think he was bad. He was a little off
sometimes, but so were a few other guys who seemed just as strange."[54]

His newfound Christianity would periodically backslide, but his
half-baked radicalism would not. Soon he refused to carry his rifle on
duty and was placed on court-martial. On February 2, he wrote to his
friend Gerhardt explaining the incident: "I have finally proven that I'm
not going to play with there [sic] guns anymore. I made myself promise that I was not to carry any weapons while my unit was on the field.
So that day while I was in the chowline, a major and a captain walked
up to me and said, "Private, where is your gun?" And I said, I didn't
bring it to the field and I refuse to bring it to the field. Well, all hell
broke out after that. They just can't tell me when to carry a gun. I
explained to them but they didn't do much good. I also explained it to
the chaplain. And guess what? He's with me all the way. He never carried a gun in his life. He is trully [sic] a man of God, and so am I and
he knows it. Of course, I'm for a court martial but I'll win. I'll have to
prove that I'm a conscientious objector, which I am. It's going to be a
ruff [sic] fight but I have one thing going for me. That is God. He's on
my side. There is one thing you must admit about me. That is, when
have you ever known me to say things about love, Peace, God, etc. I
mean, can you ever remember me talking about all this back in the
world. . . . These feelings have been deep inside . . . now don't think I'm
going insane or anything like that because I'm not . . . yes it's the real
me . . . they come out with a little help from my friends. I must truly
thank my friends for helping me. Because now I'm an individual again.
Free from the war pigs and there [sic] evil ways."[55]

Thus were sown the seeds of the Son of Sam. For all our multiple murderers, the *content* of their ideas matters not at all. This explains how easily they can shift from one extreme to another, since the only important thing is that they take some form of rebellious stance—a Baptist hippie rebelling against the military establishment one day, a super patriot rebelling against his parents and his generation the day before. In this ideological flux, too, Berkowitz must have first caught the scent of how he could establish an identity, and call the world's attention to the affairs of David Berkowitz.

By mid-March, this tentative new identity had been forged, and he wrote to Gerhardt: "Since I got here all I've been doing is fighting the establishment. It gets pretty hard to keep fighting all the time but I and a few others know where [sic] right. I'm just to [sic] anxious to see this great new world develop. But I get down sometimes when I see and think that I'll be dead before I can ever see this change take place. I don't feel like fighting. When I say fighting I don't mean with any violence. When do you think people will see the light. . . . It gets really bad when I get the impression that I have no support from anybody and I'm fighting a losing battle. I often feel this way so I get the urge to escape for awhile. In other words I just take my mind out of the rat race and get into deep meditation. When I do it gives me a chance to think and plan my next move." One can only marvel at the superficiality of motivation that permitted his rebellion to tire within a few weeks. Similarly, we should note how his lack of support (for which we should read applause) weakened his commitment. Still, by his standards he held fast. In May of 1972, he would formally announce his refusal "to learn how to kill my fellow man. . . . There ain't nobody gonna get rich over my dead body. Nobody is gonna send me to a war so they can make some money by having me use their products like guns, bullets, bombs, etc." And in June, he saw "the Army as nothing more than a tool of the government to use against another nation. It's just a game of politics. I cannot see why man would wage war on another man. We're all supposed to love each other but we don't. . . . I want to promote love and brotherhood. We don't have much love here on earth. . . . War never did a person any good. . . . I want to be free. . . .

I will be pretty soon. There is something I must do first. Give me about 50 days for planning. I sure would like mankind to be free. Hey love, tell me how to be free, tell me how to find peace. I haven't found any answers yet." What was this "next move" that would take "50 days" to plan and might yield him peace?[56]

Soon he would find his peace through killing the representatives of the group he felt had betrayed him. For the moment, however, he could only hint at his long-term intentions. "They taught me how to fight. They taught me about many weapons, demolition, riot control and self defense. All of these courses will come in handy one day. I plan to use them and it's not going to be the way the lifers want me to use them. I will use these tactics to destroy them the way they destroyed millions of people through the wars they started. One day there will be a better world. After a few heads from the heads of state are removed . . . the poor man is not lazy like the rich man. . . . I am displeased with it and I will try to change it. . . . I will make it my resolution to find out what is in the heads of our fearless leaders. I will find out what is in their heads even if I have to crack them wide open. . . . I hate rebels but I love revolutionaries." He would soon break open many heads in pursuit of his rebellion but, like all our multiple murderers, he did not have the wherewithal to challenge the ruling elite he felt oppressed him: Like all his fellow killers, his impotent rebellion would steal the lives of those innocents who were available to him.[57]

The Demons

Still, something was missing before he could put his plans into action, some ideological mediator that would resolve his fear and ambivalence of killing. After he left the army and returned to America, his lot was a succession of dead-end jobs, punctuated by the trauma of his father's move to Florida and the discovery of his complex parentage. Alone in both his world and his apartment, he found his mediator in the demons who began to visit him. Consciously or otherwise, he constructed a host of spirit forces—arrayed in ranks and hierarchies— who instructed him to do what he wished to do. His demonology has been widely reprinted, but it is central to his homicidal career and must be reviewed briefly here.

He first made his demons public in the letter he wrote to police Captain Joseph Borrelli, one of the senior officers hunting the Son of Sam. "I am deeply hurt by your calling me a wemon [sic] hater," read his four-page letter, left near the bodies of Suriani and Esau. "I am not. But I am a monster. I am the 'Son of Sam.' I am a little brat. When father Sam gets drunk he gets mean. He beats his family. Sometimes he ties me up to the back of the house. Other times he locks me in the garage. Sam loves to drink blood. 'Go out and kill,' commands father Sam. Behind our house some rest. Mostly young—raped and slaughtered—their blood drained—just bones now . . . I feel like an outsider. I am on a different wavelength than everybody else—programmed too [sic] kill." The letter served the dual purpose of announcing the existence of his demons and taunting the police. "Attention all police: Shoot me first—shoot to kill or else keep out of my way or you will die! . . . Police: Let me haunt you with these words; I'll be back! I'll be back! To be interrpreted [sic] as bang bang bang, bank [sic], bank—ugh!! Yours in murder Mr. Monster."[58]

A few months later, he wrote to the *New York Daily News*, developing the theme that he was under the control of Sam and therefore was not responsible for the killings. "Mr. Breslin, sir," he wrote to a columnist, "I don't think that because you haven't heard from [me] for a while that I went to sleep. No, rather, I am still here. Like a spirit roaming the night. Thirsty, hungry, seldom stopping to rest; anxious to please Sam. I love my work. Now, the void has been filled." To underline this point, he signed himself, "Sam's creation—.44."[59]

During the course of his killings he added new characters to the demonology. One was a neighbor, Craig Glassman, whom Berkowitz claimed was a spirit who had the "power to go into my mind. . . . Someone constantly yelled and howled in that apartment. The noise was deafening. The house, my room, shook, trembling." He began to write messages on his apartment walls, allowing his delusions to take him where they would. "As long as Craig Glassman is in the world, there will never be any peace, but there will be plenty of murders. . . . Craig Glassman worships the devil and has power over me. . . . My name is Craig Glassman and I shall never let a soul rest." In mid-June, he sent anonymous threatening letters to Glassman, referring to demons and Satan and "the streets running red with blood at the judgment." In the letters, he described himself as "the slave," while Glassman was "the master" who "drove me into the night to do your bidding." Later, in his prison diary, he developed his demonology still further, but what was the significance of all this literary creativity? What role did the demons play in the formation of his enterprise?[60]

The Synthesis

> "I love my work. Now the void has been filled."
>
> *David Berkowitz*[61]

What was this "void" that had opened in the life of David Berkowitz? What was there in the act of multiple murder that filled this void so completely and left him in such enviable states of ecstasy and fulfilment? To understand the man, we must focus on the enduring social realities in his life and on the social category of his victims, for only then can we decipher the hidden messages in his acts and public communications.

When he began to kill is especially informative. He did not do so during his late adolescence in New York when his imagination was already aflame with violence. He did not do so during his military service in Korea, when he went to great lengths to parade his superficial notions of non-violence before his fellows. He did not do so immediately upon his return to America when, ironically, he found himself guarding the gold of the rich in Fort Knox; or when he went through a series of unstable jobs, passing from one to another in unpredictable bursts. Rather, he did so when he was living in his own apartment and was the holder of a lifetime position in the post office. This was no lashing out of the dispossessed.

Abrahamsen was quite correct in pointing to the discovery of his illegitimacy as Berkowitz's primary crisis. "He was unhappy, lonely, obsessed by rejection and neglect," Abrahamsen wrote. "Meeting his biological mother, Betty Falco, proved to be the ultimate frustration." The effect of this discovery that "My birth . . . was either out of spite or accident" was not to provoke some mental disease, but to invalidate his credentials as a social person, to challenge the very basis of his identity and existence. Like Ted Bundy, who was presented with a similar challenge, Berkowitz crumbled. To rebuild himself would require an entirely new and powerful redefinition of the world. To reconstruct this view, to allow himself to act (and in doing so, regain his humanity), he drew into himself the month before the killings began. At that time, he wrote to his father and revealed some of the dark thoughts that now obsessed him: "Dad, the world is getting dark now. I can feel it more and more. The people, they are developing a hatred for me. You wouldn't believe how much some people hate me. . . . Most of them are young. I walk down the street and they spit and kick at me. The girls call me ugly and they bother me the most. The guys just laugh." The focus of his anger was already clear.[62]

Yet he was tormented by the problem of overcoming his reluctance to kill: "I wanted to take a life, yet I wanted to spare a life. I felt I had to kill someone. . . . I wanted to and I didn't want to." He found the solution in the demons. Berkowitz spoke a form of truth when he claimed it was the demons who had turned him into a soldier. In his cramped apartment, alone for twenty-eight days, his mind in neutral, he began to fabricate (a form of lying to oneself with which we are all familiar), and so construct his demonology. Drawing material from somewhere in his consciousness, he scrawled messages with a Magic Marker on his apartment walls: "In this hole lives the Wicked King, Kill for my Master," and "I turn children into Killers." In the months that were to come, he would flesh out his vision of a spirit order to which he was bound in slavery. It was a simple way of dealing with the ambivalence that, by the third killing, would disappear entirely. His analysts had observed, but failed to explain, the fundamental significance of the fact that "what is common to all of Berkowitz's murders is that his mind raised obstacles to killing." Once he had examined his life and found it unendurable, the demons were the mechanism that could orchestrate his rage. "I believed that I had every moral right to slay a chosen victim," he said, and in his own terms he was right—for the act would fill the void in his life.[63]

The Women of Queens

> "The wemon of Queens are prettyist of all. I must be the water they drink. . . . To the People of Queens, I love you."
> *David Berkowitz*[64]

He began to kill in order to give meaning and excitement to his life. But *whom* did he kill? He killed the attractive young women of one borough, Queens. "Queens was special to me—very special. . . . Shooting someone in Queens was an obsession." Why Queens? What was there about the borough that distinguished it from other residential areas? Why did he hunt the streets of Queens, looking for a release of what he called his "hostile aggression," wanting "to destroy her because of what she represented"? Queens is the ultimate lower-middle-class family borough. To one who tottered on the edge of the middle class, to one who was utterly destabilized by the complexity of his illegitimacy, Queens must have been the epitome of everything solid and desirable from which he felt excluded. It was entirely natural then that, living in industrial blue-collar Yonkers, he would (as do many serial murderers) prey on one class segment above him in the social hierarchy. When he wrote to the public during his killings, he abased himself in a sense by addressing them "from the cracks in the sidewalks of New York City and from the ants that dwell in these cracks and feed on the dried blood of the dead that has settled into these cracks . . . from the gutters of New York City, which are filled with dog manure, vomit, stale wine, urine and blood." Waging his private war, he would raise himself from the vomit in the gutter by destroying the most vulnerable and beautiful possessions of those who betrayed and excluded him.[65]

Late in his killings (as did Starkweather), he tried to raise his class focus and kill further up the social ladder. He prowled through middle-class suburban Huntington, but it was too neat and did not "feel right" for his killings. He even planned a massive assault upon the stately mansions of Southampton, and went heavily armed to this "final assignment," in which "I'd have to kill as many as I could, as quickly as possible. That would give the demons meat for a long spell." Yet he called it off, explaining vaguely that it had begun to rain: "They wanted me to kill, but there had to be a nice day for it. Since the day had turned bad, they called the whole thing off." Was it the rain, or was it precisely the same reaction of intimidation that had stopped DeSalvo from preying on the mansions of the upper class? Intimidated by the very social standards his rebellion was protesting, he could only function near his own social niche. The essence of the process was encapsulated in Klausner's description of the killing of Virginia Voskerichian: "Looking into the houses, David thought they were privileged and secure. He remembers thinking he would like to have grown up in this community. . . . Then he saw a slight, attractive young woman walking toward him."[66]

As he had anticipated, his first kill left him with a profound sense of personal fulfillment. "You just felt very good after you did it. It just happens to be satisfying, to get the source of the blood. I felt that 'Sam' was relieved. I came through." Sam had allowed him to overcome his ambivalence and wreak revenge on the society that had nullified him. His only concern was his growing lack of empathy. "I no longer had any sympathy whatsoever for anybody. It's very strange. That's what worried me the most. I said, 'Well, I just shot some girl to death and yet I don't feel.'" Yet his mission was too important for him to quibble so: "The demons were turning me into a soldier. A soldier can't stop every time he shoots someone and weep. He simply shoots the enemy. They were people I had to kill. I can't stop and weep over them. You have to be strong and . . . you have to survive." The rebel was now at war. "You're a soldier in both cases," he explained. "In the United States Army you can't stop to feel grief. You desensitize yourself."[67]

We are a strange species, *Homo sapiens,* for we are often the very

things we hate: as Bundy the disguised and illegitimate sex murderer
lambasted the FBI as "bastards, fornicators and imposters," so
Berkowitz the empty rebel raged that "I hate rebels." He had struggled
in former social incarnations to be different persons. He had worn
coats of many clashing ideological colors: He had been the super
patriot and the spit-and-polish soldier, the anti-violence Bohemian
and the peace-loving Christian. Yet none of these persona could
address themselves to the yawning chasm in his life. His soul could not
rest nor his identity coalesce until the demons helped to unleash his terror upon the people, to "destroy all good and ruin people's lives." He
would assault the warmth and security he coveted for himself and "get
back on them for all the suffering."[68]

During the killings, much of his spoken and written rage was
directed toward the parents—putative and otherwise—of himself ("son
of the Evil One, Sam"), the grieving mother of Stacy Moskowitz ("the
whore, the harlot"), the mother of the bewildered neighbor Glassman
("I curse your mother's grave. I am pissing on her, Craig, urinating on
her head"). But it was not mere mother rage that catapulted him into
multiple murder: Rather, mothers stood as symbol and source of
his relationship to the social order. In making war upon them and
their daughters, he was merely reversing what he saw as their ancient
privileges: "Some pretty girls at eighteen lived three times over, with all
the attention they got. If a pretty girl dies, what the hell, she had a
good time."[69]

Small wonder then that he had a smirk upon his face when he was
led to jail. The photographers captured that infuriating expression for
all time and distributed it around the world, for he was now a figure of
renown. His smirk was not that of one who despised his audience (as
many journalists have since charged); rather, it was the smug and self-
satisfied response of someone who was very shy, but who has been discovered to have done something marvelous, or to possess something
wonderfully rare. Despite his claims of insanity, he was no different
from any of our other multiple murderers: He killed for the same reasons as had all the others. The unwanted accident had claimed his

identity in the process of taking his revenge. "It was only hostile aggression," he said. Looked at in terms of the central propositions of his culture, it made a certain sense to achieve fame and dignity through violent display. Now he would be a celebrity for all time, propelled by his acts from the suffocating anonymity of an illegitimate and friendless postal clerk living in a small apartment in a working-class neighborhood. "I had a job to do, and I was doing it," he had said manfully. For the price of incarceration—a trifling sum for one who has no social bonds—he had exacted his manhood and achieved a kind of immortality. Such an accomplishment surely buoys his spirits as he lives out his days in prison, holding court with his several biographers.[70]

7 The Modern Mass Murderer

"I know your character," he said to me. "His name is Herostratus. He wanted to become famous and he couldn't find anything better to do than to burn down the Temple of Ephesus, one of the Seven Wonders of the World."

"And what was the name of the man who **built** the Temple? I don't remember," he confessed. "I don't believe anybody knows his name."

"Really? But you remember the name of Herostratus? You see, he didn't figure out things too badly."

Jean-Paul Sartre, "Herostratus"

Motives

They usually wrap themselves in ideological cloaks, these mass killers, seeing themselves as the heroes of their own stories: Thus they avenge the school ground bullying and perceived disdain at Columbine through a carefully prepared massacre; or they claim recompense for the government's clumsy and brutal folly with Waco's Davidian cult by bombing the federal building in Oklahoma City; or they perpetrate a workplace mass murder to compensate for their loss of a coveted promotion or job; or they fight racist discrimination by opening fire on white passengers in a commuter train; or otherwise release their hatred upon a race, religion, gender or community. Whatever they may claim, it is ever *personalized and non-political revenge*. They claim to be righting real or imaginary wrongs when in fact they are acting entirely for themselves, not others, and often for the most superficial slights. In a culture still intoxicated with ancient notions of manly private vengeance, with ready access to the instruments of mass death, no provocation is too trivial to trigger a homicide, no insult too ambiguous to form the foundation of a mass murder. We are emotional creatures, we *Homo sapiens*, and if we are insufficiently controlled, we can be dangerous indeed.

To illustrate this instantaneous response: As I write, seventeen-year-old Cedric Archer lies dead in Brooklyn after the kind of spontaneous "righteous slaughter" (for which all the Americas are justly famed) following a brief argument with a dozen men regarding which sports utility vehicle is "the best." It seems that Archer was passing the men who were sitting in front of their homes in their Flatlands neighborhood and comparing the respective merits of the Cadillac Escalade and the Lincoln Navigator, neither of which any of them owned. Archer overheard the conversation and ventured his own forthright opinion, an argument immediately ensued, the *New York Times* reported. Archer drew his .45 caliber pistol to reinforce his point, and a shootout began with the group (who seem to have previously armed themselves in order to sit upon their front steps). Archer was shot four times and killed, while a second man was hit in the leg. There are hundreds of such homicides each year in America, inevitably so in a culture that has both the violent sensibility and the physical equipment to hand when a minor provocation occurs. Perhaps the dominant cultural and social institutions were unindicted co-conspirators in this random event; as they might also have been when Timothy McVeigh, allegedly acting entirely alone, mixed nine parts fertilizer and one part fuel oil to create the explosion which laid waste the Federal building and killed 168 people.

The workplace is especially provocative of mass murders in America. Indeed, *workplace homicide is a leading cause* of occupational fatalities in the United States, with 860 workplace killings committed in a recent year. Psychological experts struggle to find "tests" that will tell them which employee will go berserk and stage a mass murder, rather than devote their energies to a rather more fruitful enterprise—trying to determine the cultural and social factors that might explain why America is the only western developed nation that routinely produces such killers and killings.

Mass killers do not, as is popularly believed, suddenly "snap" and explode into a murderous uncontrollable rage that compels them to do what they are doing. It is quite clear that such killers "generally act with calm deliberation, often planning their assault days, if not months, in advance"; and "they aim to kill those individuals they are convinced are responsible for their miseries, frequently [but not necessarily] ignoring anyone not implicated in the plot against them."[1]

Unlike serial killers, who avoid firearms whenever possible because they are such an impersonal way to kill, mass killers prefer weapons of mass destruction—rapid-firing firearms or bombs. Mass murderers are similar to serial killers in that their acts are also personalized social protest, and in that they are neither revolutionary nor deranged; but they are also quite *different*. Mass killers are much more likely to come from relatively stable families. Moreover, they do not wish to use their killings as a catapult into international celebrity. Rather, they wish to avenge themselves in one sustained burst, and then *die*. During the course of their development, in one manner or another, they become intensely aware of the impossibility of bettering their condition. The D.C. Snipers and Starkweather experienced poverty and perceived stigmatization throughout their lives; Essex did not experience it until he left the warmth of his family and community for the racist embrace of the U.S. Navy.

Regardless, their confrontation with the social abyss renders their lives unbearable. Invariably, they choose to die in an explosion of violence directed at a group they feel oppresses, threatens, or excludes them. Thus in the engineering school in Montreal, Lepin murdered the hated women students who had usurped his position; Huberty murdered the Hispanics who had risen to his ambitions; Starkweather murdered the middle classes whom he felt despised him as "garbage"; and Essex murdered the whites who oppressed him. Because Essex was black in a white-dominated and racist world, he touched a sensitive chord in the American psyche, and became a kind of revolutionary hero. Still, his protest was merely personal and racist, not progressive. When he shot the young white woman kneeling at his feet as she cradled her young dead husband in her arms, he no more killed whites to help his fellow blacks than Lepin killed women on behalf of men. In fact, it seems likely that Essex made his final commitment to the killings not for lofty ideological reasons, but because he could not come to terms with the degraded status inherent in the only career offered to him—the repairman of vending machines.

Whether mass killers subsequently become "heroes" depends not on the internal motivation or coherence of what they do, but on whether their personal protest is congruent with fashionable themes in the culture. In the two detailed case studies in this volume, Essex's anti-white assault was congruent with mainstream liberal thought, and it was therefore applauded, at least in radical circles. Starkweather's anti-middle-class assault, however, was incongruent with fashionable notions, even threatening to the white liberal class: his killings were therefore dismissed as warped and senseless.

Data

Love Spurned

Joseph Ferguson was only twenty years old, but he was already a supervisor at Burns Security in Sacramento. We know relatively little about his early years, except to note that his family life was very strange indeed. He lived with his father, his mother was absent, and in fact in jail, where she had been sent for molesting Joseph and his siblings. As a security worker, he naturally had no criminal record; but after the killings, the police would find a Nazi flag and white supremacist literature in his room, along with two assault rifles.

All this was taking place in a city that was already mystified by the family annihilation perpetrated by a Ukranian immigrant, *Nikolay Soltys*, an unemployed shoemaker living on welfare and frustrated because he could neither learn English nor qualify for a career in chiropractic. Soltys, twenty-seven, had seized the attention of Sacramento and the admiration of Ferguson when he slashed to death his young and pregnant wife, and his three-year-old son, whose body was found face down in a bloody cardboard box. Soltys then traveled to the home of his uncle, aunt and two cousins and murdered them. His wife had previously complained that Nikolay would beat her head against the wall until she lost consciousness, then revive her and begin beating her again. Those who knew the couple said that he had never cared much for his son. He disappeared after the killings, leading police on a ten-day nationwide manhunt: Police placed him on the FBI's "Most Wanted" list and posted a $70,000 reward for information leading to his apprehension. He was finally captured in his mother's back yard, hiding under a desk. Although several psychiatrists had asserted that Soltys was not a suicide risk, he hanged himself in his cell six months later.

But Soltys's suicide took place months after Ferguson was already dead. At the time of Ferguson's mass murders, Soltys was very much alive and a marvelous *inspiration* to him, a kind of role model. Indeed, during his rampage, Ferguson had made several calls on his cell phone, saying he wanted to kill more people and do so more spectacularly than Soltys had been able to do: "He was going to outdo Soltys," said a police spokesman.

What had happened was that Joseph's conventional life had spun apart. First his girlfriend, fellow Burns guard Nina Susu, had ended their romance; and then in a fit of spite he had vandalized her car. When Susu reported this to their employer, Joseph was suspended from his job. Burns officials had notified the FBI that he might be dangerous because he had made threats after the suspension, but the FBI check had revealed no history of violence and nothing had been done. Ferguson began killing one week later. He first shot Nina Susu and a colleague, Marsha Jackson, a thirty-two-year-old single mother of three, while they were both working at a city maintenance yard. Then he drove to a city-run marina, where he shot and killed another Burns guard, George Bernardino, forty-eight, and John Glimstad, a nineteen-year-old worker at the marina who happened to be there at the scene. Shortly after, he handcuffed another former colleague to a tree at the Sacramento Zoo and fled in his car, but he did not kill her because, police said, "he thought she was just a nice person."

Police began evacuating selected Burns employees from their homes and escorting them to safe houses. Unfortunately, Ferguson had already made it to the home of a Burns supervisor. He held the supervisor and his wife captive for twelve hours while he made a curious videotape, showing just how clearly he understood his impact on his firm, his city, and the media. In the tape, he boasted that "I giveth and I taketh away, that's how it goes in fucking life." Wearing a black bulletproof vest, fingerless gloves and brandishing a 9mm semi-automatic pistol, the self-aware killer told the camera: "I put on a hell of a show. I've taken four victims, this should be good enough to last about a week on the news. It's time to feed the news media." He added that he would soon kill himself. He then killed the supervisor, his fifth victim, and fled in the family car as the supervisor's wife called the police.

Police soon spotted him and chased his car. Ferguson fired more than 200 rounds at the pursuing officers before his car swerved into a light pole. When police caught up to his car, he was sprawled on the seat: The sheriff's sniper noted that Ferguson was not moving, and when police approached the vehicle, they found that he had shot himself.

Difficulties in School

Robert S. Flores Jr., forty-one, was a licensed practical nurse who worked part-time in a hospital run by the Southern Arizona Veterans Administration in Tucson, Arizona. But Flores was an ambitious man: He had previously served in the military, and was now studying for an advanced nursing degree at the University of Arizona. There were, however, tensions in his life; he had recently been divorced, and he had experienced financial problems in meeting his child support payments. Moreover, he was not doing well at school: College officials said he was failing his course work; fellow students described him as "belligerent and potentially dangerous"; and a school staff member had earlier "raised an alarm about him" and suggested he was "depressed and capable of violence," although no action had been taken in response to this.[2]

Flores entered the nursing school at 8:30 in the morning of October 28, 2002, and found his victims, three female nursing instructors, and shot them dead. The first victim, Robin E. Rogers, fifty, a retired Air Force nurse who, her husband later recalled, "enjoyed teaching," was killed in her office on the nursing school's second floor. The second, Barbara Monroe, was shot in front of twenty students while giving a class on critical care. His third victim, Cheryl McGaffic, forty-four, was also killed in the classroom: She had previously complained to her husband that she found Flores "very, very intimidating" and had "felt threatened by him," and when her husband had asked her to report Flores to the school officials, she had replied: "That won't do any good." Students fondly remembered McGaffic as the admired faculty member who taught the course on "Death and Dying," and who had been known to be especially sympathetic to those who had experienced a personal loss. "It's just so sad that this was the way she went," said nursing student Jessica Odom. "If it hadn't been her, she would be counseling us right now on how to cope with this whole situation."

Flores, speaking to two students he knew, told all of them to flee, and then shot himself, falling on his backpack, which police thought might contain explosives. They locked down the medical complex, but the bomb squad found nothing. Police later blew out the back window of Flores's Jeep while looking for explosives in the vehicle and searched Flores's apartment with a bomb-sniffing dog, but once again found no explosives.

Another nursing student remembered Flores as "an obnoxious jerk—belligerent, angry and rude. He would tell the teachers off if he didn't get the grade he wanted: He would blow up and call them names in class." She said that earlier in the year, Flores had bragged about receiving a permit to carry a concealed weapon: "He was real happy about it."

The Montreal Massacre

On what would become the infamous sixth of December, 1989, "*Marc Lepine*" (real name, Gamil Gharbi), the product of a tortured marriage between an Algerian immigrant and his Québecois bride, perpetrated Canada's most appalling mass murder. Armed with a Ruger .223 semi-automatic carbine, Lepine entered the University of Montreal's engineering school, the Ecole Polytechnique. Walking through the school's classrooms and hallways while screaming "I hate feminists," he ordered the men out of the rooms and shot dead fourteen innocent young women before turning the rifle on himself. In perpetual honor of the fallen women, December 6 became a national day of mourning in all the places of worship across Canada.

Thirteen of the victims had been engineering students. One was a university secretary. Most of the women were in their twenties. To honor them here, we offer this roll call: Genevieve Bergeron, Helene Colgan, Nathalie Croteau, Barbara Daigneault, Anne-Marie Edward, Maud Haviernick, Maryse Laganiere, Maryse Leclair, Anne-Marie Lemay, Sonia Pelletier, Michele Richard, Annie St. Arneault, Annie Turcotte, and Barbara Maria Klueznick.

In the wake of the massacre, many rival ideological and political groups seized upon the tragic events to advance their own agendas. Thus the government-funded anti-gun coalition proclaimed the killings had been possible because rifles were not legally registered in Canada; while the radical rump of the pro-gun coalition argued that if the students had all been armed, they would have been able to return fire and thus abort Lepine's murderous spree. Similarly, radical feminists argued that these murders not only revealed the true brutal inherent nature of males, but also were only the opening salvo in a planned series of suicidal mass executions, a "war on women" that was part of a "worldwide conspiracy for the mass extermination of women." If each ideological group espoused its share of the truth, they all ignored the larger reality: How can a civilization create such monsters, or condone such abuse and assault for so long, without knowledge and without intervention?

To struggle to understand a killer is neither to forgive him nor to justify his actions. Nor is it possible to grant redemption to those who created him. Yet it is important to grasp his perceived motives, and balance them against the reality of his life. In the killer's suicide note (made public one year later by journalist Francine Pelletier), Lepine had written that he intended to commit suicide for purely "political" reasons. "Even if the media label me as a mad killer," he had written, "I consider myself a rational erudite person. I have decided to send the feminists, who have always ruined my life, to their maker." His note named an additional fifteen prominent Quebec women, among them Pelletier, whom he had also hoped to kill.

We know almost nothing about the childhoods of those who become mass killers: typically, they commit suicide at the end of their rampage, as did Lepine, or they are shot dead by police. Most commonly they have had little or nothing to say about their crimes. That is what makes the unique court document below of such special interest, for here is Lepine's childhood. Here is his mother testifying in court at her application for divorce from Mr. Gharbi, when the incubating mass murderer was still a child. Here the texture of Lepine's childhood begins to show. As we glimpse the brutality of the father (who refused to speak to the public about his son), let us remind ourselves that no brutality justifies the acts of the son.

Testifying at her divorce hearings, Mrs. Gharbi said that her "main motivations in asking for a divorce from my husband are that I haven't lived with him for five years, [and] I was always afraid for the children and myself. He was a very cruel man who did not seem to be able to control his emotions and who used his hands against me and the children at the most insignificant things, sometimes making their nose bleed and preventing me from consoling them, preventing me from taking them in my arms. It became intolerable."

> Q: Did he mistreat you personally?
> A: He hit me many times, yes.

Q: Could you please be more explicit; what exactly and when? *A:* When I lived with my husband he did not allow me to work outside the home. I remember that at the time he didn't have a secretary and I couldn't type, I was a two-finger typist. In any case, he forced me to work at all hours and every time I did a typo, he would hit me on the nape of the neck. It sometimes made me dizzy and at times happened late at night. It was whenever he felt like it. Another thing also is that I couldn't depend on my husband to cooperate, for example, in our children's education or whatever. I felt a little like a servant in my own home. My husband wouldn't even get himself a glass of water. As far as the children are concerned, I remember one time going out to do some errands. The children were still very, very little and I had asked him to look after them for a little while, the time it would take me to do the errands. When I returned home, he had put the children in a room, still in their snowsuits. He hadn't even removed their snowsuits. The lord and master was in bed, in his pajamas, reading, the little one in a wet diaper, dirty and they were still wearing their boots and snowsuits. He really didn't look after them at all, at all, at all, at all, at all."

After Mrs. Gharbi had legally separated from her husband, she moved to a cottage the court had provided for her. Despite the court's ban on her husband visiting her, she remembered:

My husband, in spite of the court's judgment, came to Ste-Adele when all my family was there and created a scene, like those he often created. He wanted everyone to leave even though it was the house he had "let" me have. He wanted my family to leave. They were there visiting me. He took the pot of potatoes which were cooking and threw it out into the snow—the pot, the potatoes and the entire supper I had prepared. He attacked me personally and . . . he grabbed my arm and shook me by the two arms like this, and I fell in the snow. I wasn't dressed for that and

I almost broke my, I almost hit my head on some rocks. My brother-in-law came to help me and he tried to calm my husband down and let's say that there was a fight between the two up to the point of tearing off each other's clothes. The shirts came off and so on. In any case he was uncontrollable, uncontrollable. I had a lot of bruises all over my body, and a psychological shock followed.

I was afraid of my husband; I was afraid to approach him. My son [Marc Lepine] was so afraid of seeing his father, that he hit the steering wheel [while I was driving] and I almost had an accident that day. When I had told him we were going to see his father, he became violent, he didn't at all want to see his father. The children are very afraid of their father.

Q: Let's come back to the children. Can you tell us about any events when your husband would have assaulted the children?

A: My husband would come home at strange hours without even letting me know whether or not he would be home for dinner. I often made dinner needlessly. Anyway, in the mornings, my children would awake at a normal time, 6:30, 7:00 and they were in a good mood, singing. My children have a happy disposition. Since they sang too loud because my husband wanted to sleep, or if the children didn't go and say good morning to him every day, he hit them, especially the boy. The little girl was still quite young. Hit my son in the face which would sometimes leave week-long marks. His hands were strong and he didn't control his force. . . .

Let's say that at Christmas '69-'70 my family was at the house and again it's a question of food. Perhaps I served my guests too well. Anyway, my husband violently hit me in the face. I was bruised and it prevented me from returning to my guests. I spent four hours in the basement, not daring to go upstairs because I was crying and could not stop. He had hit me so hard that I felt ill. No one dared to come down because when my husband was violent no one went near him.

I didn't want to be killed. I wanted to live, look after my children and lead a balanced life."

Q: Can you tell the court how your husband behaved when you went out with him?

A: Before we had a car, we took the bus and there were often "misunderstandings." I don't know. My husband seemed to be a masturbator by profession. In the bus instead of acting like everyone else and sitting with his wife wherever there was room, he would fondle his penis at the back of the bus where there were women. He always chose a place where there were a lot of women and use his hands to try and fondle himself. It happened at other times when we would go out and I used to dread those occasions because I would always lose one or two friends. He made advances to other women and he rubbed himself against them when they danced. It was so obvious.

I remember one time when he had danced with my friends and they told me afterwards that they didn't want to see me again because of my husband. They didn't mince their words. I remember one time I asked him to please try and control himself in my presence. He replied, what should it matter if he masturbated because I benefited from it. That's the kind of answer I received. From that time on [my] sexual desire for my husband gradually faded and I didn't even want to be near him.

Q: I understand there were fights in your home because you went out with other men?

A: That was never correct. I remember an argument one night. I was going to night school taking a personal development course because I wanted to occupy my mind with something positive, and it was graduation. Several women went out together. I had the car, took a few people home and came in around 2:00 in the morning. It was probably one of the very few times I went out alone until that time and when I returned home he was waiting. He turned on the light, I think he threw a drink in my face and told me that as long as my name was Mrs. Gharbi, I would come home at a reasonable hour. I stood up for myself and asked him if I questioned him when he came home at 4:00 most mornings. He let me know clearly that a woman was not equal to a man. A woman was a man's servant. I preferred not to talk any further because I knew it wouldn't do any good. As a defense mechanism, I kept quiet. Things calmed down.

Q: You said, Mrs. Gharbi, that you don't object to your husband taking out the children. . . .

A: I would object to the children being alone with him, yes. I would be afraid especially since I've now spoken with the children and they're still afraid of their father. I mean it's subject to my psychiatrist assuring me that it would not emotionally hurt my children and if there was proof that my husband, because there are still fears that he would beat them . . . I would probably still be very afraid of leaving them with him because I don't want to have emotionally unbalanced children, they're still afraid of him and they remember. I would certainly be very afraid of leaving them alone with him.

The children had to adapt to my changing life for five years and I had a lot of [difficulties]; I had to be separated temporarily from my children during the week, make arrangements for them to live with a family because my main concern has always been their emotional well-being. I had to study, work, security guard every two days so I preferred for a while to leave them with a family. The children have been back with me full-time since June '75 and due to circumstances, last year I went to Ste Justine Hospital because my daughter developed "énurésie." It wasn't normal at her age to wet the bed. I had her checked to see if there were any physical problems. There was nothing and a psychologist at Ste Justine advised me to undergo family therapy so that we could re-examine the need to love and love together because it seemed that we had problems in expressing our need to love and be loved because the separation had been somewhat difficult. That was a year ago. All three of us underwent therapy at Ste Justine for a year to re-establish this emotional balance that the children [were missing]; there were a few problems and now everything's good. The three of us are building a life and I would probably hesitate. I would prefer to consult my psychiatrist to see if it would be beneficial for the children or if it would upset them.

Mrs. Gharbi's sister, Mrs. George, confirmed this account, and added that she had seen her sister with a black eye after being beaten. She also complained that "Mr. Gharbi has made advances to me and he's very vulgar toward women. He rubs himself in such a way, I don't know how to say it. . . . well, he rubs his penis against you in a very vulgar manner, publicly, even in his wife's presence."

Mr. Gharbi was countersuing for divorce at the same proceeding. He admitted knowing nothing about the whereabouts of his children during his separation from his wife: "The only thing I know is that the children were going from sitter to sitter, house to house, and that she left them at the drop of a hat with her sister, her mother, and others." When asked by the court why he was suing for divorce, he replied: I am absolutely against divorce in moral principle, in all principles. There has never been a divorce in my family. We've always been against divorce." But, he said, he had discovered "what kind of a person I had married," and he was "asking for this divorce on the grounds of Mrs. Gharbi's multiple adultery, harassment, physical and moral cruelty, for having estranged my children and trying to turn them against their father."

Q. This morning, Mr. Gharbi, your wife testified that you hit her. Can you explain to the court exactly what happened?

A: In all marriages it's understandable that difficulties exist, pressure especially when there are financial problems, a decrease in the standard of living. It's well known that these difficulties can create friction between individuals. Mrs. Gharbi had been used to a pretty high standard of living, did not deal well with a diminished one, and she looked for reasons at the drop of a hat. I can't deny there were problems between us, discussions, I can't deny it. However this morning's character assassination is false, completely false because I never hit, pushed, whatever. It's always easy to make the husband the monster. What happened this morning is a very good character assassination.

Q: So you never hit your wife?

A: I never hit my wife.

Q: You never hit your children?

A: Never. It's well known that a father must discipline his children and my practice was to put them in a corner. That was the punishment when I was young. I draw your attention on the fact that every time I went away, the first thing the petitioner would tell me when I returned home was that the children had done this, had done that. She was too lazy to punish them and she always wanted the father to do it. She derived great pleasure in not punishing them.

Q: What do you mean by saying you made your children stand in the corner?

A: It means that as punishment the children stand in a corner for ten, fifteen minutes or whatever so that they realize what they did was wrong.

Q: So how long did you make them stay in the corner?

A: Ten, fifteen minutes; it was proportionate to the act, no more than that.

Q: During this time where were the children's hands?

A: The children's hands were hanging on their side; sometimes so that they would understand better they placed them on their heads for a few minutes, a form of physical exercise.

Placing his hands on his head in the universal gesture of surrender, the son capitulated to the dominant sensibility. The character capable of mass murder was now being fire-formed. We thus move closer to an understanding of his rationalizations. But why did he kill women, when it was his father who abused him so and gave him such unhap-

piness? The father taught him that brutality against women was appropriate and acceptable, even manly, and that women were unworthy servants of men. By acquiescing for so long to these insults, the tortured
mother unintentionally left the child with the feeling that she concurred with this brutal and sexist behavior. In a significant sense, then,
she unknowingly legitimized that mentality (or, in the killer's words,
"ruined" his life by exposing him to this grief). Small wonder then that
his rage against his idiot father might be displaced upon his mother or
that he might misperceive the desire of any woman to be a complete
person as an insult to the natural order of things. No wonder he
attacked the only gender that had ever shown kindness to him.

Theory

Typologies
There are some like myself (and the late Professor Sir Edmund Leach)
who regard the classification of "types" as a murky form of butterfly
collecting, but many more scholars relish the task. Levin and Fox clas-
sify mass killers and agree with most current commentators that the
motive behind the majority of mass killings is revenge—"either against
specific individuals, particular categories or groups of individuals or
society at large." The largest single category of these revenge massacres includes husbands who murder their estranged wives and children; and alienated employees who avenge themselves on their boss or
fellow employees. In the 1986 murder of fourteen postal employees in
Oklahoma by a disgruntled fellow worker, for example, Levin and
Fox argue that the killer was "in a sense trying 'to kill the post office,'
much like the estranged husband or father might attempt 'to kill the
family.'" The victims in such massacres are often strangers, but are not
entirely randomly selected: They are chosen because they are members
of a category of person—racial, familial, economic, or communal—
who the killer feels are responsible for his unhappiness. "He seeks to
get even, not with specific people whom he knows, but with anyone

who fits his single criterion for hate." Nevertheless, some mass murders are motivated purely by profit, as in the gangland robbery and
execution of thirteen guests at the Wah Mee Club in Seattle in 1983.[3]

The Frequency of Mass Murder

A senior FBI agent once told me that the FBI Academy did not spend
much time analyzing mass killers because such killers made little or no
attempt to hide themselves, and were therefore "not a police problem."
Mass murder is also less "sensational" than serial killing, and thus it is
only recently that we have had any notion of the numbers of mass
murderers. Levin and Fox examined 329 such massacres (defined as
having four or more victims, including familicides)[4] that had occurred
in the United States between 1976 and 1989. The mass killings were
perpetrated by more than 400 offenders, and claimed almost 1,500 victims. "Although hardly of epidemic proportions," an average of two
mass murders took place every month in the U.S., producing an annual
total of over 100 victims. The killers are also older than "normal"
homicides, averaging thirty-eight, and 93 percent are males.

Nor did they find evidence of any recent increase in the rates of
these offenses, and noted that unlike single-victim crimes (which tend
to have an urban character), "mass murders do not tend to cluster in
large cities." The most striking differences are regional ones: The
southern states, known for their high overall murder rates, "witness
very few mass killings"; while states with high transient populations—
especially Texas, Florida, Alaska and California—"have had more than
their share."

8 Hate White People—
Beast of the Earth

Mark James Robert Essex*

"The quest for freedom is death—then by death I shall escape to freedom."

Mark Essex[1]

The mental life of mass murderers is not so difficult to decipher once we have uncovered the social messages that constitute the ciphering key. Many such killers do contrive to leave a kind of enigmatic wake behind them, because the date at which they are stopped is when they are riddled with police bullets (as was the case, for example, with Charles Whitman's shootings from the University of Texas tower in 1966). Yet it is a grievous error to believe that dead men tell no tales, and Essex is perhaps the finest illustration of this point. It is an equally monumental error to dismiss Essex, as so many have done, as a kind of deranged "sniper," and hope to leave it at that. He was much more.

During his killing spree, Essex seemed to address himself to some fundamental issues in American life. His "sniping" was an integral part of a coherent campaign. Moreover, he tried to "explain" it in his

---

* Essex did not leave us much, but what is available is reprinted in Peter Hernon's splendid study, *A Terrible Thunder*, which is not only a spellbinding account of the case but also contains extended conversations with Essex, memories of friends and relatives and written statements. Ronald Tobias' *They Shoot To Kill* is very much a secondary, and occasionally inaccurate, source. I am grateful to Harriet and Elliot Liebow who, in introducing me to the slums of Washington, D.C., gave me some sense of the black experience in urban America.

earlier comments to his friends and family, in his writings on his apartment walls and ceilings, and in his shouted remarks as well as his homicidal actions during the actual assault. His central rebellion, despite the wretched and racist form it ultimately took, was an interesting one, aimed directly at what he perceived to be the racist white establishment in America. Appropriately then, he tried to kill its most visible and powerful representatives, those uniformed, generally white, agents of social control—the police (although he did not shrink from murdering civilians, so long as they were white). He conducted his explosion of radical creativity with considerable style and finesse: He challenged the entire police and military forces of the great city of New Orleans. The ensuing gunfight came close to destroying an entire city block, and he escaped to freedom in death, leaving behind him ten dead, twenty-two wounded, and millions of dollars' worth of property in ruins. More important to his purpose, he created many admirers for himself in the radical community—and left in his wake an air of imminent insurrection felt so intensely by both the public and the authorities that something might almost have come of it. In his own terms, it was both an exit with panache and an achievement of which few young persons dared dream.

Kill Pig Devil

His first kill was on New Year's Eve of 1974. He hid across the street from the New Orleans' police department's Central Lockup and opened fire with his Ruger .44 magnum semi-automatic carbine. His first four shots were fired in rapid succession and narrowly missed the head of police cadet Weatherford, blasting cement chips off the wall around him. After the briefest pause during which cadet Weatherford took cover, cadet Al Harrell, one of the few young blacks in the New Orleans police, came into view. Essex unleashed a volley of shots at the nineteen-year-old. The third shot struck Harrell in the chest, passing through "the anterior thorax causing severe lacerations to the heart," as the death certificate later read. The .44 magnum bullet was not yet spent, and after it passed through Harrell's body, it struck Lieutenant Horace Perez in the ankle. Perez blacked out. Observing the assault, a detective called both for an emergency ambulance and for all available police to rush to the Lockup. Within seconds, they were swarming over the area with shotguns and revolvers ready, fanning out into the area from which the shots had been fired. Their assailant had disappeared.[2]

A few moments later, police officers Edwin Hosli and Harold Blappert were investigating a ringing alarm in a company office a few blocks from the Lockup. Carrying flashlights, and unaware of the recent shooting, they prepared to check out the building. Essex was hiding inside the office. His first shot struck Hosli in the abdomen, ripped through one kidney, collapsed a lung and perforated the bowels, spilling fecal matter through the body cavity. It would take Hosli two months to die. A second shot shattered the squad car's windshield, and a third ricocheted off the hood and penetrated the windshield, while a fourth struck the building behind the officers.[3]

Within minutes, more than thirty police surrounded the office: Six men fired shotguns with heavy loads at the door, disintegrating it, and then sent in a dog. A subsequent search of the premises revealed that the assailant had entered the hemp factory by shooting the lock off the door. Blood stains on the window glass through which Essex had left the office indicated that he had been wounded, and bloody handprints on the window sill suggested that he had tried to dry the blood. Among the items he left behind was a brown leather purse with a black owl painted on its side containing fifty .38 caliber bullets.[4]

Apparently anxious to ensure that police knew where he was going, and to draw them into an ambush, Essex left a trail of bullets—two together always pointing in the same direction—at periodic intervals along his path of retreat from the hemp factory to the front of the First New St. Mark Baptist Church. There he waited. Incredibly, as police arrived in front of the church and found the cartridges, they were pulled out of the neighborhood by a police administrator who was concerned with the high level of tension in this black area. During the "cool-off" period that the administrator wanted, the assailant disappeared from the church.[5]

Although he would not kill for another week, he did not remain inactive. During the afternoon of January 1, 1975, he seems to have set two fires in nearby warehouses in the heart of the city; the fires smouldered for five days, and 200 firefighters were called in to douse the flames. He seems to have returned periodically to the church over several days: On the evening of January 3, police received a complaint that a man was hiding in the church. When they searched the church, one policeman recalled, "the evidence our man had been there was unbelievable. Hidden in the ladies' bathroom, we found a cloth sack filled with .38 caliber rounds. We also found blood stains on several doors and window sills."[6]

On the morning of January 7, he walked into a grocery store managed by Joseph Perniciaro, who had reported seeing him to the police (it was not determined how Essex had received this information). He entered the store carrying a rifle and called to the manager, "You, you're the one I want," and shot him in the chest. Essex ran for several blocks, then stuck his rifle through the window of an idling car and told the driver, who was black, to get out. "I don't want to kill you," the driver remembered him saying, "but I'll kill you too." Essex drove off, heading toward the downtown Howard Johnson's Hotel, which would be the scene of his ultimate demonstration to the authorities.[7]

He parked his car, and climbed the hotel's outer staircase to the eighth floor—but was refused entry by the hotel staff. On the ninth floor, he rapped on the outer door and asked a maid: "Let me in, sis, I got something to do," she remembered him asking. She refused, and he climbed the outer staircase once more. He finally gained entrance on the eighteenth floor where, carrying his rifle, he brushed past three black employees with the remark, "Don't worry, I'm not going to hurt you black people, I want the whites." A twenty-seven-year-old white doctor of medicine, Robert Steagall, stepped into the corridor as Essex passed his room. They struggled with one another until Essex shot him in the arm and chest. When Steagall's wife, Betty Steagall, rushed at them screaming, and knelt next to her husband, Essex shot her through the head. He then entered the Steagalls's room, set fire to the drapes, and ran down the hall back to the staircase. The fires began to spread, smoke billowing from the rooms.[8]

Frank Schneider, the front-office manager, and Donald Roberts, a bellman, were on their way up to investigate the sounds and smoke. As they stepped out of the elevator on the eleventh floor, they saw Essex standing a few yards away. Schneider and Roberts ran for the nearest exit. "We heard one shot and that was the one that went over my head as I was running low," Roberts said later. "Then the second shot apparently got Frank, who was running behind me; and I kept running." Schneider had been shot in the head and killed.[9]

Walter Collins, the hotel's general manager, and Luciano Llovett, a maintenance man, went up to investigate the reports of a man in the hotel with a rifle. On the tenth floor, Collins saw a youth with a gun and started to run. The bullet hit him in the back and he collapsed to the floor. When he heard Essex leave the corridor, he began crawling on his elbows and knees toward the landing.[10]

Patrolmen Michael Burl and Robert Childress were the first policemen to reach the hotel. As they ascended the hotel's elevator, the first fire engines began to arrive outside the building. Fire Department Lieutenant Tim Ursin was climbing a ladder up the side of the building when Essex appeared on one of the balconies and fired at him: The bullet struck Ursin in the left arm, scoring a wound so severe that his left forearm later required amputation. Essex continued firing when any policemen or firemen showed themselves.[11]

A chaotic scene soon developed (although it was nothing compared to what was to come): Explosions from Essex's .44 carbine mingling with sporadic return fire from police, screams from the hotel guests trapped in their rooms, and billowing smoke from the burning floors. The chaos deepened as police began firing at random at the hotel's upper floors—in contravention of all notions of fire control. For his part, Essex continued to prefer uniformed targets; so much so that he even allowed a detective, who appeared to be a civilian, to pass unscathed through the killing ground. By 11:00 that morning, 100 policemen had surrounded the hotel. That number would swell to over 600 policemen from Louisiana, Texas, and Mississippi, as well as FBI, Treasury, and other federal agents (totaling twenty-six state, local, and federal law enforcement agencies), before the affair was finished.

Patrolman Charles Arnold climbed to the tenth floor of an office building across the street from the hotel. When he pushed open the window, Essex fired a shot which shattered on Arnold's shotgun and tore into his jaw, knocking him to the floor. Arnold later told Essex's biographer, Peter Hernon, that as he spat out pieces of jawbone, teeth, and blood, someone had looked at him and said, "Good Christ! He blew your whole face off." As the firing continued, Robert Beamish, a forty-three-year-old broadcasting executive, tried to sneak past the swimming pool out of the hotel, but Essex spotted him and shot him in the stomach, blowing out his belly button. Beamish jumped or fell into the pool, where he remained for two hours. Inexplicably, Essex continued to pass up some targets, whimsically allowing some to pass unscathed.[12]

Now he raced through the upper floors of the hotel, shooting, and setting fires in as many rooms as he could manage. Firemen who were trying to fight the fires found themselves exposed to increasingly uncontrolled shooting from the police. The absence of police and fire control severely exacerbated the danger to the growing number of tourists who had begun to gather around the hotel to witness the event—some of them, presumably radicalized blacks, shouted, "Right on!" each time the sniper fired.[13]

Patrolman Kenneth Solis was using a loudspeaker to direct the tourists to take cover when Essex shot him in the right shoulder and under the rib cage, shattering the shoulder and exposing splintered bone. Another bullet hit Sergeant Emanuel Palmisano as he ran across the plaza to help Solis: The bullet fractured Palmisano's left arm, entered his body under the armpit, traveling down his back and grazing his spine. Patrolman Philip Coleman responded to the cries for help from the wounded by driving his squad car across the plaza, sunk low in the driver's seat. Patrolman Paul Persigo died instantly from a shot through the mouth as he stood gazing at the hotel's upper floors. An unidentified man in a civil defense helmet was shot in the right arm as he walked along the street; and when ambulance driver Chris Caton ran out to rescue him, another bullet hit Caton in the back, crushing his shoulder blade, collapsing one lung, and exiting under the armpit. Civilians armed with rifles, some clad in ill-fitting military uniforms, were beginning to show up near the hotel and began to join in the attack on Essex—adding to the air of farce enveloping the scene.[14]

A crowd of several hundred young blacks was now on the street. They acted as a kind of cheering section for Essex: Each time he fired, the crowd moved forward a few paces, chanting, "Kill the pigs, kill the pigs," and, as Hernon wrote: "As the tempo of the gunfire increased, these chants became louder, fiercer. Several empty bottles were thrown. . . . Many of the blacks were drinking wine from bottles in brown sacks. 'Hang on, baby,' one of them shouted. 'When it gets dark, we gonna help you.'"[15]

Deputy Superintendent Louis Sirgo of the New Orleans police led a small assault team up to the top floors of the hotel. On the stairs above the sixteenth-floor landing, a shot from Essex's carbine fractured Sirgo's spinal cord, breaking the vertebral column and perforating his left lung, liver, and right kidney. He died within minutes. Essex continued firing as he ran from floor to floor, lighting more fires (most often by igniting each suite's telephone book and placing it under a curtain or mattress), while nervous and utterly uncoordinated police barely managed to avoid shooting at each other.[16]

When Officer Larry Arthur of the tactical squad smashed through the locked door opening onto the hotel roof, Essex shot him in the abdomen and shouted, "Free Africa! Come on up, pigs!" Essex would not leave the roof alive. For the rest of the siege, he would pop in and out of the concrete cubicles that protected the doorways to the roof, jumping out from them to fire at different angles and then taking shelter again as the torrent of inaccurate and uncoordinated fire from the police bracketed his position. During a lull in the firing, Essex was heard to scream, "Happy New Year's, pigs! I've killed four of you motherfuckers. Come on up and I'll kill four more." At mid-afternoon, police fired a dozen tear-gas cannisters at the roof. The gas settled on the roof and then dispersed without effect. To taunt them, Essex shouted, "I'm still here, pigs!" Meanwhile, elected officials were beginning to panic. They thought Essex's attack might not be just one individual's idiosyncratic action: "The thing that worried us the most," said one councilman, "was the question, what if this was the beginning of something much bigger? We wondered whether a revolution was coming, whether other blacks would come to the sniper's assistance." Essex would have been pleased.[17]

When a small and unarmored police helicopter circled near the hotel, a volley of shots from Essex drove it off. Soon after, however, a U.S. Marine Air Reserve CH-46 ex-Vietnam armored helicopter, carrying two Marine sharpshooters armed with M-14 .308s and three policemen with AR-15 .223s, flew to the scene through rain and fog. For what remained of the day, the helicopter would make a total of forty-eight passes over the hotel, and do so in the midst of undisciplined fire from police and civilians. On one swoop, police in the helicopter mistakenly opened fire on a stairwell in which police officers were hiding. "The rounds just poured in on us," one of the policemen later said. "They riddled the door, the hole, everything. Plaster and concrete went flying from the walls and we went tumbling down those stairs. It was amazing no one was killed."[18]

As the gunners on the helicopter poured magazine after magazine into the cubicles, a radio station disc jockey broadcasted a "request" from police for citizens with large-caliber rifles to come to their aid. This fabricated request produced a "large number of morons, marginal types, all of them armed to the teeth" at the hotel, all offering to "get the sniper." The police evicted the vigilantes, but the following morning, another group was discovered approaching the hotel by stealth. Incredibly, according to police, one woman telephoned them to offer blankets for the sniper, whom she thought was "probably freezing up on that roof." Their response to the offer has not been recorded. At no

point during this operation did any police strategist apparently consider the obvious way to conclude the assault (which would have prevented all police and civilian casualties): to simply clear the area of all
human targets, and wait out the sniper.[19]

Meanwhile, Essex continued to address his fire and his abuse at the
police. "Come on up, you honky pigs!" he shouted. "You afraid to fight
like a black man?" The police responded in kind, shouting, "Fuck you!
Fuck you. Fuck you. Fuck you." Once again, the helicopter swooped
down on the wrong stairwell and opened fire on the police crouching
there. A black policeman briefly tried to talk Essex into surrendering,
but Essex merely shouted, "Fuck you. Power to the people!"[20]

The last moments of Mark Essex came at just before nine that night.
As the helicopter dove at him once more, he ran out of a cubicle and
fired, then ran back inside; at that point he seems to have been hit. As
the helicopter pilot remembered it: "I guess the guy figured it was
over. They were pouring a lot of lead in there, and he ran out firing."
He was met by the full-automatic fire from the helicopter, as well as the
heavy rifles (including .375 and .458 "elephant guns") from the hundreds of police on adjoining roofs. One of the gunners in the helicopter, firing on full automatic, said Essex "came out, running toward the
helicopter, firing as he came. He was looking straight at us, holding the
gun at the waist and firing. He took two or three steps before we
opened up. I hit him a whole clip from the thighs to the neck. He was
running at full tilt and his momentum carried him another five or ten
feet. Then the bullets caught him and held him up, sort of like when
you shoot at a pie plate and keep it rolling." Firing his high-velocity
Weatherby rifle from the roof of the Bank of New Orleans, another
officer said: "The guy came out and turned around to shoot. . . . that's
when I fired. I hit him in the buttock, and he tumbled forward and
dropped his rifle. Then some guys with the big stuff, the .375s and .458
elephant guns, opened up. One of those shells hit his leg. It looked to
me like it blew it off." The officers with perhaps the best view of
Essex's last stand said: "I think what happened is that some tracers
burned up after hitting the walls of the cubicle. Whatever it was, he

came out running and screaming and his left arm was up, the fist clenched. It looked like he was running on a charcoal grill. With all that shooting, there was a ring of red fire around him. The bullets actually held him up, twisting him around. Then he went down on his back about twenty feet from the cubicle. Everyone kept shooting."[21]

The heavy fire from the helicopter and the adjoining roofs shattered a water pipe on the roof, unleashing a four-foot wall of water which roared down the stairwell in which the police were watching and swept them off their feet in a wave of weapons, bandoliers, clothing, and police. Moreover, the officers believed there might be a second sniper on the roof, and they continued to "see, hear," and shoot at the "second sniper." As Hernon described the scene: "Long into the night, police yelled insults from the Rault Center and other buildings as they tried to bait the gunmen into revealing their positions. 'Where does it hurt, Leroy?' they shouted, their voices lost in the darkness. 'Hurts all over, don't it.' No one answered from the roof. 'Power to the people, nigger.'" Reports then came in that another sniper had definitely been spotted on the roof. The police opened fire once more, their spotters observing the flashes of the bullets hitting the building, but interpreting them as muzzle flashes from a second sniper returning their fire. The noise of the police shooting was so intense that it was impossible to tell from whence it came, and thus to disconfirm any notions of a second sniper. In the rising crescendo of police fire, nevertheless, there could still be heard the distinctive sound of a Thompson .45-caliber submachine gun firing on full automatic, and the steady boom of a .375 Holland and Holland big game rifle.[22]

To compound this farce, late that night, the police sent in the K-9 corps. The dogs climbed to the roof, but one of them was so sickened by the tear gas that it simply curled up on its side. A second dog's trainer refused to let it go out alone on the roof, frightened that "they'll kill my dog." A third dog's trainer agreed to send in his dog, but the dog would not oblige. At 5 A.M., the helicopter made another strafing run in the gathering light, pouring fire into the cubicles, but succeeding only in awakening the five policemen who had fallen asleep in the stairwell. Then began the inevitable process in which the police began to shoot at each other. When one officer gingerly stuck his helmet on a stick and climbed slowly out on the roof, police without radios opened fire on him, mistaking him for the sniper. When a police team stormed the roof a little before two in the afternoon, police from City Hall opened fire on them. Soon the assault team was joined by thirty other zealous officers, standing shoulder to shoulder in a semi-circle around the boiler room: They opened fire together and the ricochets careered around the roof, wounding nine of them, three seriously. Essex would have loved it.[23]

His body lay twisted on the roof. One leg was virtually severed from his body; the torso was a crushed pulp; the face had been almost shot away; but the left hand was still clenched in a fist. Officers in the morgue later counted at least 200 bullet holes in Essex's body and noted that the gall bladder was the only organ not destroyed by the small arms fire. All that remained in his pockets were two bullets and one firecracker. An inquiry later determined that he had fired between 100 and 150 rounds to kill nine persons and seriously wound another ten during the hotel assault. Police found his stolen car parked within a block of the Central Lockup. In the glove compartment was printed material from the state's Department of Employment on discrimination in hiring practices. In the trunk, police found a duffel bag on which the word WARRIOR had been printed by hand in black ink.[24]

A Curiously Happy Childhood

The conscious mental life of our civilization, conditioned as it is by notions that it is primarily childhood that produces the man, makes us assume that we will find something bizarre in Essex's family or community to explain his murderous behavior. It would be most satisfactory if we could demonstrate that he had come from a brutalizing family, or a community discolored by ugly racism—and that these experiences had established subconscious drives to manufacture a manhood crushed in childhood. Yet we search in vain for such evidence. Indeed, the evidence from both family and community points resolutely in another direction.

Essex was a young African-American raised in a thoughtful, progressive, and gentle home, in a community that was insulated from all the vilest excesses of urban or southern racism. We do not know the precise details of the ideological atmosphere in which he was raised, although we can state with little fear of contradiction that it was nonviolent. What we can be certain of is that the gentility of his family and community failed to prepare him to accept numbly with suitable meekness the racism he would encounter later on in the navy, or prepare him for the limitations to his chances in life that he would confront in the outside world. What is the process whereby a gentle and non-racist youth is transformed into a violent racist—one who hates with such ferocity that he can kill not only the uniformed white authority figures, but also shoot in the head a young woman kneeling dazed beside her husband's body? To comprehend this transformation, we must follow Essex through his brief and tortured life. To do so, we must examine the artifacts of his life through the prism of the system of social class and race in American life. We will make no progress if we dwell merely on the superficial elements that have engaged some commentators (such as Essex's tiny stature) who have argued that his actions stemmed from his personal inadequacies. It takes more than diminished height, or the reputed sharp tongue of a mother, to finance an explosion of mass murder.

To reach below the surface of Essex's life is to marvel at the uncommon happiness of his childhood. He was a cub scout and well regarded by most, if not all. He spent many hours fishing for perch and catfish in the waters near the town; and a teacher described him as a "crack shot on rabbits and squirrels." He attended a neighborhood primary school and a high school in the downtown business district. As only twenty-nine of the school's one thousand students were black, his minority status constituted no threat to the established white order of Emporia, Kansas. Certainly his relations with other white youngsters were good, for they were his playmates in childhood and his dates during adolescence. The family home was no ghetto slum: It was a detached single-story house in a faded suburb, with a large playground across the street.[25]

His family's social-class affiliation is critical. Essex's father was no unemployed slum-dweller conditioned to accept his station in life. His father was a foreman, not a worker, in a small, family-owned firm in Emporia, and they could well afford their lower-middle-class style of living. Ironically and more destructively, he grew up with the deadly misapprehension that his race might not matter very much in the larger scheme of things—or even not at all. His family obviously discussed the racist evils of the society at large; but his own experience of it was once or twice removed. Even when his brothers and sisters left Emporia, they went to other places where the racism was subtle and subdued—a brother found a measure of peace in Cedar Rapids, as did sisters in Los Angeles and Waterloo, Iowa. Most critically, as the son of a foreman who owned his own respectable home, he must have felt that it was possible for him to make a life as a man in his society—a belief that no slum-dwelling urban black could sustain beyond puberty—and even form dangerous ambitions (whether or not they were beyond his personal gifts). Thus the crisis that must hit many blacks in adolescence did not hit Essex until he was an adult and in the navy—a far more difficult time for an individual to absorb the social message that he or she is worthless, especially a young man reared on self-respect. If a class or race is to be easily subordinated, its self-respect must be looted systematically in childhood: In this special sense, the system failed.

Neither was there any agency in the community adequate to decode that social message. Emporia's factories and slaughterhouses did not deny a place to blacks: Only one black owned his own business, but

many labored in the factories and slaughterhouses. The community's
roots in the anti-slavery movement were deep. The town had sent a
144-man regiment to fight the Confederacy during the Civil War, and
the ruins of John Brown's log cabin remain as a monument only a few
miles to the east. The majority of the community were of Welsh and
English stock, shaping a milieu that was deeply religious, prosperous,
and puritanical (Emporia was the first "dry" community in the Mid-
west). Less than two percent of its 28,000 people were black; and if the
black and Hispanic families lived in the shabbier eastern end of town,
the system that kept them there was subtle and without violence. A
further safety-valve was that the community exported its most aggressive and ambitious blacks, who searched elsewhere for their dreams,
for they were not content with Emporia's mediocre horizons. This
was not at all the stuff of the destruction of the spirit and the body that
Elliot Liebow described in *Tally's Corner,* his classic study of the black
slums in Washington, D.C.[26]

Essex was an average student in school—and it was this essential
mediocrity, combined with his inappropriate ambition, which were to
doom him to his fate. He had a special aptitude for technical subjects,
and his teachers and schoolmates remembered him as a "smiling,
friendly boy who was always laughing and joking," who dated both
black and white girls, and whose ambition was to be a minister. A former girlfriend said: "He really didn't talk about wanting to be anything
else. I know his mother was really happy about him wanting to become
a minister." He spent one unsatisfactory semester at Kansas State College, after graduating from high school, and then enlisted in the navy
in 1969, partly to avoid the draft and certain assignation to Vietnam.
He scored in the top 25 percent in the navy's entrance examination—
which emphasized technical matters—and, impressed with the navy's
programs, he signed up for four years. Hernon said Essex was "elated"
when he discovered he was to be sent to San Diego. That elation would
soon disappear, for he was about to be exposed to a hurricane.[27]

The Manufacture of Despair

"There is no place in this white man's navy for a self-respecting
black man."

Mark Essex[28]

The metamorphosis of Essex from a cheerful young Midwestern black
into a deeply embittered and increasingly committed young pseudo-
revolutionary was accomplished within a few months in the U.S. Navy.
He enlisted on January 13, 1969, and arrived in San Diego in early February for three months at the Naval Training Center. By April, Hernon
wrote, Essex "had finished boot camp with an outstanding performance rating and was encouraged to take advanced training in a
specialty." His superiors encouraged his essentially middle-class aspirations and assumptions, and advised him to enroll in the Naval Dental Center. After completing their three-month course in X-ray
procedures and oral surgery, he was rated outstanding and assigned to
the Dental Clinic at the Naval Air Station at Imperial Beach in July.
There he established a solid working relationship with the young dentist to whom he was assigned, and who would later describe Essex as
"a pretty good athlete. . . . He was a good team man, sort of an all-
American boy. In those days he was just the nicest person in the world.
He was concerned about everybody around him, concerned about
learning his job. . . . He was the kind of person I liked to have around,
a happy-go-lucky kid who was very hard to get rattled. I'm very
demanding, especially when it concerns dentistry. I demanded a lot out
of him and he delivered. His folks flew out to visit him early in his tour.
They were just fine people. I really liked them. They were nice, down-
home people who really enjoyed living and loved their son." A co-
worker described Essex in similar terms: "He was an easygoing guy.
He would sing to himself and be real friendly with everyone. I remember when I first got to the clinic he took time out and helped me. He
showed me how to work with the doctors."[29]

Despite his positive attitudes and sunny personality, an epidemic of racial harassment on the Imperial Beach base began to trouble him. He wrote to his parents to complain that the navy "is not like I thought it would be, not like in Emporia. Blacks have trouble getting along here." When Essex discussed the problem with his black friends on the base, they advised him to adjust to the reality, to work hard enough to receive promotion, and thus be removed from contact with the worst racists. Essex took the advice to heart and was promoted from recruit to seaman in less than a year; but the harassment continued, and as Hernon observed, "It was increasingly clear that blacks were second-class citizens in the Navy, and it was hard for him to understand why no one seemed willing to change things."[30]

Nurtured in the blandness of Emporia, his assumptions about himself as a full citizen and human being were being bombarded, and he had no ready defense for such an assault. When he took an extra job as bartender at the enlisted men's club, he found that while white bartenders could go anywhere without permission, he could not enter certain rooms without first asking a white sailor. The car he bought to celebrate his twenty-first birthday was halted by security guards each time he entered or left the base: Invariably he had to produce his license, registration, and insurance as if they did not know him. Frequently, he was ordered out of the car as the guards searched its every seam, elaborately unscrewing even the door panels to make their racist point. When he began to date a Mexican woman and took her to the enlisted men's club, "conversation stopped, heads turned, and it wasn't long before the half-whispered [racist slurs and] comments began to circulate."[31]

The rebellion first surfaced when Essex and his three black bunk mates were put on report for "excessive noise in the barracks." They were accused of playing a stereo late into the night, and forced to face a disciplinary hearing. They were convinced that they were being discriminated against, since whites played their stereos just as loudly and without punishment. Essex and his friends decided to fight the charge and demanded a summary court-martial, which would allow them to argue their case. Essex's patron and boss, the dentist, conducted his own private investigation into the affair and was convinced the matter was a clear case of racial discrimination. The sailor who filed the complaint, he said, "was a guy who was obviously just a prejudiced individual. He didn't like blacks in general. . . . He told me that he walked into Essex's room and here was 'all this nigger shit.'" The dentist told the commanding officer about his findings and the court-martial proceedings were halted. But Essex was not satisfied, for he and his friends were then separated and assigned to different barracks. It was vindication, not compromise, that he sought.[32]

Essex felt that he and his friends had been "sold out," and thought that once they had been isolated in their new barracks, "it was really going to hit the fan." As Hernon wrote, "His prediction proved accurate. The riding continued unabated. He was a pariah who lived in virtual silence. No one openly called him 'nigger.' They didn't have to, for he was subjected to every petty indignity imaginable—endless bed checks, extra guard-duty tours, and constant admonitions to turn down his stereo even when the volume was so low he could barely hear it. There were even laughs when he combed his low-riding bush haircut, which he kept well trimmed for fear of being put on report for violating grooming regulations." At the enlisted men's club, the once-muted racial tension escalated into louder and more vicious racial slurs; and the same slurs hounded him into the mess hall or gymnasium until his work at the dental clinic began to suffer and he was forced to take sedatives.[33]

Two black friends of Essex during that period later told the *New York Times* that "all the young blacks around the base were being hassled. Essex felt that he was getting a particularly rough deal and that he wasn't going to take it lying down. White sailors in the enlisted men's club came down hard on Essex, regarding him as a 'cocky nigger'. . . . But what really burned Essex up was the riding he got from petty officers and other officers. They would write him up for the smallest infraction and usually he would get a Captain's Mast while the white got off scot-free. We all had that sort of experience." Another friend commented that "Essex came into the Navy expecting to be treated in the same decent way he always had been treated back in Emporia, and he found it wasn't like that at all."[34]

The first explosion of violence from Essex took a remarkably long time to emerge; but in August of 1970, a racial slur triggered a fistfight. As the incident was reconstructed, a white petty officer had remarked to Essex about black "smilin' and shufflin'," and prolonged the taunting until Essex jumped on the man's chest and began flailing at him with his fists. The fight was interrupted by a passing officer, but the chain of thought it had provoked was not. As Hernon noted of this release from the colonial mentality: "For the first time in his life he had struck a white man, a fact so unbelievably startling that its significance was only now beginning to ring in his brain. The blow had seemed as natural as a thunderstorm in summer and as he thought about it, recreating the fight in his imagination, savoring it, he realized that what he had done was more than justifiable; it was heroic." But Essex paid a heavy price for that blow: Everywhere on the base, he was now a marked man, a black who had struck a white NCO. A friend remembered him concluding that "if a black sailor can't get a fair shake when he's in the right, then to hell with the whole United States Navy."[35]

In increasing despair, Essex went absent without leave on the morning of October 19, 1970, one month after the base commander had halted his court-martial. Even with the sleeping pills, he had been unable to sleep, lying awake and dreading another day of racial harassment and denial of self. Sitting in the bus depot waiting for a bus to Emporia, he decided it was necessary for him, purely as a matter of self-preservation, to get out of the navy. He telephoned his parents and told them, "I'm coming home. I've just got to have some time to think." He spent his days in Emporia thinking "about what a black man has to do to survive." According to Hernon, "The intensity of his bitterness at first surprised, then worried his parents, but when they gently tried to caution him about the dangers of hatred, his head would jerk up as if pulled by strings. 'What else is there?' he would say. 'They take everything from you, everything. Your dignity, your pride. What can you do but hate them?' He vowed that he was unwilling to wait any longer to be treated 'like a man.'"[36]

Mrs. Essex later recalled for Hernon that her son "told us he didn't see how he could go back to the Navy and start it all over again." While she cautioned moderation, he replied that he was not being treated with "moderation," but "like a nigger." The distraught parents asked their minister to intervene: "He told me," the minister recalled, "how badly the navy had treated him and how fed up he was. We talked a lot about discrimination and I remember him telling me how he had seen 'the whole picture' in the navy. He was very, very bitter. I'll tell you, I was worried about the boy after we talked. So were his parents." Eventually, however, their counsel prevailed, and Mark returned voluntarily to the navy after a month's absence without leave. "He had had his time to think," Hernon wrote. "He had had his chance, as he would say later at his court-martial, 'to talk to some black people.'" Essex reported to his base's military police and awaited his court-martial.[37]

The Trial

> "I have two years left and when I get out I want to become a dentist."
>
> *Mark Essex*[38]

Before the trial, Essex—not yet utterly alienated from white society—explained his dilemma to his patron, the dentist Hatcher. "I just couldn't hack it any more, and I felt like everybody was out to get me," Hatcher remembered him saying. "I really had to go home to get my head straight, and my mom and dad told me that I had to do it this way. So here I am. You do whatever you have to do and then, that's it. I'm getting out." When Hatcher tried to argue that Essex should not run away from the problem, Essex replied, perhaps with greater wisdom: "Nothing is going to change, doctor. The same old hassles will go on, and me and all the other blacks will keep on coming out on the bottom." Clearly, he had already made his dual decision to leave the navy and to conclude that nothing could be changed—at least not by conventional action.[39]

The trial was appropriately Kafkaesque. Essex's lawyer based his defense on the prejudice issue and used the dentist Hatcher as his primary witness. Hatcher, Essex's superior officer on the base, testified that Essex was "by far . . . the best [assistant] that I have worked with. He is outstanding in his professional performance and duties [and] . . . in my relationship with him he has proven to be a very personable, very warm person. He is sincerely worried about other people, about their needs, about their problems [and] . . . he constantly volunteers his services because he wants to help people." Hatcher further testified that the story behind Essex's absence without leave could be traced to his being put on charge for excessive noise in the barracks: "The men felt that they were being unjustly accused because of their color, and . . . my investigation showed that the man who made the original complaint was a very biased individual, and very obviously racially prejudiced. He had very possibly, to my way of thinking, influenced the other witnesses . . . so that the picture given to the court-martial was a very biased one. The captain, after hearing this, talked to the man who made the original complaint . . . and decided that the whole case was a matter of injustice.[40]

"He [the captain] at this time ordered that the court-martial be stopped," Hatcher's testimony continued, "and brought the four men before him and made what I think he felt was an honest attempt to get at the problem [but] . . . I think that the feeling from all four of them was that it was just another whitewash of the situation, that, in fact, the captain was not going to be able to do anything. . . . I think that Essex, in this case being the most sensitive and the most responsible of the four, felt that he had been sold out, and he was very despondent over it. Immediately after the initial complaint was lodged and was brought to the XO's mast, they [the four sailors] were separated. . . . They put Essex in a room with totally incompatible people and the harassment started almost immediately, and he was again forced into a situation, this was before the court-martial even came about, that was nothing but a constant hassle, and this in his living spaces, the only place . . . he could go to relax. The harassment occurred in the mess hall lines, recreation areas, and so forth. So all put together, he was a very upset person during this time. . . ." The remarkable Hatcher continued with a denunciation of the harassment that Essex had experienced, and of his own doomed attempts to abridge it.[41]

When it came time for Essex to testify, he essentially concurred with Hatcher. "I am the accused," he said chillingly. "I believe that Dr. Hatcher explained most of everything as to the reason that I went UA. When we asked for a court-martial, the four black people felt that it was a case of discrimination. We had certain things happen to us before we went to trial. . . . I went UA because I just needed time to think. . . . I had to talk to some black people because I had begun to hate all white people. I was tired of going to white people and telling them my problems and not getting anything done about it. I am twenty-one years old. Almost every time I drove on the base they would search my car. I had a fight in front of the chow hall. Some friends of mine were going back to the barracks, and I was going to chow and they asked me to bring back some chicken for them, and I asked them what color the chicken was to be, and they said that it should be black. Well, someone said to me, "Why does it have to be black, what is wrong with white?" and I jumped on his chest. . . . I have two years left and when I get out I want to become a dentist."[42]

For the crime of fleeing from racist abuse, Essex was sentenced to forfeit ninety dollars of his pay each month for two months, was restricted "to the limits of the Naval Air Station . . . for a period of 30 days," and was "reduced to the pay grade of E-2." The presiding judge could only say that "the prejudice issues that were raised by the defense, while not excusing your offense, do materially explain your actions." Essex left the room with an emotionless expression and the conviction that the system had failed and excluded him. Several weeks later, Essex was asked to sign a document acknowledging that he had been considered "for an administrative discharge for reason of unsuitability due to a character beha*vior disorder." Shortly after this ultimate degradation, the station's commanding officer recommended that Essex be "separated from the naval service . . . [as his] further retention in the service would not be in the best interests of the navy. Essex con-

tinues to display flagrant disregard for military authority, despite frequent counseling at the departmental and command level. Essex's
impulsive behavior, and inability to accept the responsibilities of military service have rendered him a severe liability to this command."
Thus the system vindicated itself in this extraordinary document, and
"explained" Essex's reaction to intolerable racist abuse as a "behavior
disorder." Therein lay the intolerable affront that Essex would redress
by carefully planned behavior in which he would accept the responsibilities of quite another form of military service.[43]

The Creation of an Ideologue

"It's a revolution!"

Mark Essex[44]

The emotional preconditions for his task were created in the profound
contradictions embedded in the social order. These were transmitted
with the utmost rigor to young Essex. It now remained for him to
explore whatever ideological alternatives were available to him in order
to reconstruct his damaged sense of self. He appeared to find it in the
burgeoning black radicalism of the time. However, like all our multiple murderers, as a true ideological conservative he would not join a
revolutionary movement. He would only absorb its rhetoric and style
in order to carry out a personal vendetta, an individualized protest
against the exclusion of this marginal middle-class black from his own
aspirations. It should come as no surprise that his rebellion took such
a racist form, for the spirit of the times gave ideological—even divine—
sanction to racist excess. All this must have been intoxicating for a
maturing martyr and rebel.*

* For popular accounts of the extreme form these radical black offshoots took, see
Clark Howard's *Zebra* and Robert Tannenbaum and Philip Rosenberg's *Badge of the
Assassin.*

It is not clear exactly what Essex's movements and contacts were during his post-navy career. The journalist Tobias thought that "there was scattered evidence to suggest that Essex had connections with black militant groups," but admitted that "it was not clear." Still, Tobias concluded that since there was an abundance of black revolutionary literature in Essex's apartment, there "seemed little doubt that Essex was intimately connected with black extremist factions." There was insufficient evidence for such a conclusion. Tobias noted that Essex spent "most of the time" between his discharge from the navy in February 1970 and April of 1972 with his parents in Emporia, but added that "he took mysterious trips to New York and New Orleans supposedly to 'visit old Navy friends.'" Whatever the actual contacts with militant groups may have been, "Essex left Emporia somewhat abruptly and went to New Orleans where he joined a militant Black Muslim friend from the navy." One police report commented that "during this entire investigation into the background of Mark Essex, no firm physical evidence was found which would link him to any of the known subversive or militant groups, although his possible involvement with several such groups was hinted by more than one source interviewed. There can be no doubt that Essex was well trained both in firearms and urban guerrilla tactics . . . and while the investigation failed to develop the sources of and scope of any such training, there is some evidence to indicate that he did undergo a period of training shortly after his release from the Navy." Despite the paucity of the evidence, there was no doubt in the police investigators' minds that Essex's behavior had been a coordinated and well-considered campaign, part of a group's terrorist strategy. As one detective remarked, "This was expert, well planned, well executed, and demonstrated the techniques of urban modern guerrilla warfare."[45]

We will never know the precise details of whether he was involved in personal encounters with revolutionary groups; but it matters not, for the important thing is that in his post-navy maturation, he was exposed to the writings and thoughts of black revolutionary intellectuals, and that his state of mind was such that he was willing to kill and die for such notions. Since no action followed his death, it is unlikely that his terrorism was anything other than an individual communiqué. The origin of his ability to make such a social statement lay in the shock of his sudden exposure to white racism. An ugly or lame child may grow accustomed to such stigmatization: it is the beauty whose face is suddenly destroyed or the athlete whose body is crippled by accident who experiences the sharpest pain—a shame requiring terrible expiation.

Essex cannot have been exposed to radical thought during his adolescence in Emporia—or if he was, it made no impact upon him. He would only have felt the intense and Christian sense of injustice which his mother articulated in her no-nonsense way. It was in the navy, Hernon wrote, "that Essex began to read about the black movement, something he had rarely done in Emporia. With interest he followed in the newspapers the legal battles of Huey Newton and Bobby Seale, who had founded the Black Panther Party in 1967 . . . [and of a] five-hour gun battle in Los Angeles between police and eleven Panthers, including three women." At this time, too, he formed new associations. What the sociologists call "the significant other," the influential friend, was to be Rodney Frank, a New Orleans black with an extensive arrest record who was in the navy at Imperial Beach with Essex. It was Frank who would interpret Essex's experience for him. According to the police report, "Fellow sailors and superior officers reported that Essex began to have a change of attitude as he became more closely associated with Rodney Frank. Frank, who was described as being militant and antagonistic, later became a Black Muslim, and his attitude toward the white population may have influenced Mark Essex's thinking." A later FBI report noted that Essex, while in the navy, also "associated with and received black militant literature from a member of the Black Panther Party," and Hernon said that Essex "mingled off-base with other tough-talking blacks in the San Diego area. These individuals . . . undoubtedly felt their relationship with Essex was one of student-teacher: The naive black from backwoods America needed to be informed what it was like to be beaten down by the system. What influence they had on Essex is not known; whatever it was, it became increasingly clear to Dr. Hatcher and others that the young sailor had changed."[46]

Hatcher even dated the change to Essex's twenty-first birthday on August 12, 1970. "The change was very sudden," he remembered. "It seemed to come in a matter of weeks. . . . I have a feeling that he got in with a group of blacks who really felt they were being put down. . . . Several times he talked about going downtown and meeting with some guys who were putting out an underground newspaper. . . . Once the harassment started, after the fight and after he started getting into trouble, the conversations we had were very terse. He was almost a defeatist at that point. He was really down on the system. And as I said, it really came overnight. It was very quick, and I couldn't understand it. . . . During that first year all our conversations had been happy ones. But then they became very short. He was kind of defensive, belligerent sometimes." Essex's torment was profound: As his sister later put it, he was in the midst of the process in which "the navy became his own private hell."[47]

Hernon correctly noted that Essex was "a casualty of history," and reminds us of the prevailing mood of protest within the armed forces at the time, in which black sailors also began to rebel. "Fights swept U.S. military bases and naval stations. In Vietnam, black GIs drafted to fight in a war in which they didn't believe were accused of blowing up—fragging—white officers. Morale disintegrated. . . . Resistance organized, and groups with names like "Black Liberation Front of the Armed Forces" were established. Sabotage increased. In May of 1970, for example, nuts, bolts, and chains were dumped down the main gear shaft of the *U.S.S. Anderson* while she was in San Diego. Other ships were similarly damaged. The revolt of Seaman Essex was the revolt of every black in uniform."[48]

According to the New York City police's Intelligence Division, Essex went to New York in February, shortly after his discharge from

the navy, and established contact there with the most militant wing of
the Black Panthers. "At that time," the black undercover detective
recalled, "that was the headquarters for the Eldridge Cleaver faction of
the Panther Party. He must have gotten the revolutionary rhetoric hot
and heavy." He spent three months there, at a time when the Panther
Party was in such serious financial trouble, due to a severe drop in
membership, that Stokely Carmichael, an early hero of the party, had
remarked that "the Panthers are practically finished." Out of fashion,
the Panthers were divided by the inevitable ideological disputes and
had split into two rival factions. The dispute was so divisive that soon
after Essex arrived in New York, a shooting war broke out between the
two factions and several members were killed.[49]

   Still, there was no need to be a member, or a part, of any revolutionary party when the monthly publication of the Cleaver wing, *Right
On*, contained the ideology and instructions for the developing urban
guerrilla. "There were, for instance, discussions of revolutionary tactics; 'how-to' techniques for killing 'pigs,' including where to shoot
them (in the head) and what kinds of weapons to use . . . diversionary
tactics, how to manufacture bombs and incendiary devices; first aid;
and propaganda." The fashionable revolutionary texts were Chairman
Mao's *Red Book*, Che Guevara's *Guerrilla Warfare*, and Carlos
Marighella's *Mini-Manual of the Urban Guerrilla*. Marighella stresses
that the "perfection of the art of shooting makes him a special type of
urban guerrilla—that is, a sniper." Similarly, reference was often made
to a "Vanguard Party, capable of leading the black masses into an open,
violent revolt to overturn the 'racist capitalistic superstructure,'" and
to a "Black Messiah" who would carry a rifle, not a cross. In this mael-
strom, Essex's adult identity was forged. He had little choice by then,
for as one undercover officer remarked: "Essex probably peddled the
paper, and I'd be surprised if he didn't pick up a lot just by reading it.
It's all part of the indoctrination. You read about revolution and killing
pigs; you talk about it constantly until it's almost a kind of narcotic."[50]

   Hernon speculated quite reasonably that Essex must have become
"disillusioned" by his time in New York. "The Panthers were weak,

hopelessly divided—instead of shooting 'pigs' they were shooting one another—and for a young, increasingly angry black, polarized by violent rhetoric and conceivably interested in armed revolution, it must have been a serious disappointment to see his heroes in such disarray." He left New York just before militant blacks attacked four city policemen, killing two of them. At home he read and reread *Black Rage*: "As a sapling bent low stores energy for a violent backswing, blacks bent double by oppression have stored energy which will be released in the form of rage—black rage, apocalyptic and final." Not long after one thousand state troopers opened fire on rioting Attica prisoners, killing twenty-eight prisoners (mostly black), Essex purchased the recommended Ruger .44 magnum carbine and began to practice using the weapon. Late that summer, he decided to move to New Orleans. He left quietly, without telling his parents, for he was certain they would not approve of such a move. With him went his Ruger carbine and his .38-caliber Colt revolver.[51]

In New Orleans, he joined his navy friend, Rodney Frank. While Frank joined the Black Muslim Mosque and sold its newspaper, *Muhammad Speaks*, Essex made one final attempt to grasp a tolerable social status and proscribe his coming suicide. He enrolled in a government training program for underprivileged persons, studying vending-machine repair with pay. This was no easy way of simply obtaining funds, and Essex's instructors reported that he was an enthusiastic and dedicated student. Still, his anxiety reflected itself in his mindless watching of television hour after hour. As well, he was now studying his "heritage," reading books on Africa and learning words from Zulu and Swahili, even dropping them into conversations and adopting the Swahili word for "bow" as his nickname. In late October, he returned to Emporia for a brief visit, and appeared to be in good spirits.[52]

When he returned to New Orleans, his inner contradictions tortured him with headaches and night sweats. "Thrust up to the edge of an abyss, he could see no way to cross. More and more he stayed to himself, withdrawing to his apartment to watch television or to read." Soon he would grasp fully the insufficiency of his attempt to embrace

the identity of a repairer of vending machines. The incident that ultimately committed Essex to his radical course was the police shooting
of two black college students at a campus demonstration in Baton
Rouge on November 16. With that, Essex committed himself to
becoming a god. Late in December, he sent his declaration to a television station: "Africa greets you . . . on Dec 31 1974 appt 11 the Downtown New Orleans Police Dept will be attack . . . Reason—many. But
the deaths of two innocent brothers will be avenged. And many others . . . P.S. Tell Pig Gurusso [the police chief] the felony action squad
ain't shit." The letter was signed with his Swahili nickname, "Mata"
(bow). He attended his final vending-machine repair class, then wrote
his parents a letter vowing total war against whites. "Africa, this is it
mom," he wrote. "It's even bigger than you and I, even bigger than
god. I have now decided that the white man is my enemy. I will fight
to gain my manhood or die trying." Having committed the remainder
of his destiny, like a Kamikaze warrior, he distributed his most prized
possessions among friends—although he did not, apparently, inform
them of his intent.[53]

During that period, it would seem, he daubed the walls and ceilings
of his apartment with slogans of his hate and rebellion. "The largest
wall was practically covered with the word 'AFRICA,' which was
painted in wavy letters three feet high and bordered with a black margin. Beneath it, in red, was written, 'My destiny lies in the bloody
death of racist pigs.' The words 'destiny' and 'death' were underlined.
In some places the paint had run in streaks. Next to the slogan 'Revolutionary justice is black justice' was the word 'blood,' and above that
the letters 'KKK.' Also painted in red, 'Blond hair, blue eyes.' The
words 'hate' and 'kill' were splashed everywhere, seemingly at random.
Next to the word 'Africa' was scrawled, 'Hate white people—beast of
the earth.' Inside the giant C of 'AFRICA' Essex had carefully penciled
in, 'The quest for freedom is death—then by death I shall escape to
freedom.' Near the ceiling was spelled out, 'The Third World—Kill Pig
Nixon and all his running dogs.' No inch of wall space was spared."
There were also many words, many of them garbled and misspelled,

from Swahili. Essex had left his last will and testament, and done so with an uncharacteristic trace of humor; for when the detectives entered the apartment and looked up at the ceiling, they read his painted insult to them: "Only a pig would read shit on the ceiling."[54]

The Authorities Respond

> "Essex was caught between two worlds which retarded the maturation of his self-identity."
>
> *Ronald Tobias*[55]

Hard upon his actions there followed an inevitable deluge of self-serving responses from the authorities, both judicial and intellectual. Leftist ideologues established the legitimacy of his grievance and linked it to the obvious form of society but, typically, ignored the sufferings of his victims. For their part, the rightist ideologues devoted their efforts in equally predictable fashion to exonerate society of all blame and lodge responsibility for the crime in some flaw (such as the retardation of the maturation of his self-identity) in Essex. "He was overwhelmed by the sudden insistence of black survival in a hostile environment where the whites controlling it were less permissive than they had been in Emporia," said Tobias. This unreasonable insistence that blacks should survive, this non-permissive navy attitude toward blacks, seemed to have been at the root of Essex's retarded maturity, thought the spokesmen of the right.

Yet it was not simply journalists who drew such flaccid conclusions. During Essex's first psychiatric examination, when he was in trouble in the navy in early February of 1971, the navy psychiatrist had admitted that there was "no clinical evidence of delusion, hallucinations, inappropriate affect, impaired reality testing, thought disorder, or organic brain disease," but found Essex's judgment to be "poor, impulsive, and immature." The doctor concluded that Essex had an "immature personality" and represented "a liability to himself and to the United States Navy." Then, in a prophetic observation, he wrote: "The patient gives a history of no previous suicidal gestures which were done to manipulate those about him or his environment. At this time, he denies that he wishes to kill himself. However, he alludes to the fact that he 'might do something' if he doesn't get what he wants."[56]

After the shooting, the state's attorney general told newsmen that he was "now convinced that there is an underground, national, suicidal group bent on creating terror in America. Their purpose is to cause the people to be dissatisfied, to bring race against race, black against white, young against old, to cause internal national chaos." This sentiment was echoed by the U.S. attorney general, who promised that "the full force of the Department of Justice would be behind a national investigation" to uncover the conspiracy. Louisiana Governor Edwin Edwards told reporters that "he would consider state laws to reinstate capital punishment for certain 'heinous crimes.'" He also said that he had "no information whatsoever on a nationwide conspiracy to kill policemen."[57]

More analytically, a black assistant to the mayor commented: "This event will be what we make of it. There are lessons to be learned. The police will learn tactical lessons. Hopefully, by the same manner, I think people all around this country will learn . . . there are real hard problems to deal with. [Many young blacks] were drawing a link to that man on the roof and blacks pursuing their legitimate grievances." In a similar vein, a black activist told Hernon that "A lot of white people have written Mark Essex off as just a crazy nigger, an extremist. They forget what Malcolm had to say about extremists. He said, 'You show me a black man who isn't an extremist and I'll show you one who needs psychiatric attention.' . . . He was a man who was terribly frustrated and decided to fight. Most blacks deal with frustration in other ways, or if we are violent, we've been brainwashed to the point where we channel our violence against one another. It was different with Essex. And as I watched the shooting at the hotel that Sunday, I kept thinking, why doesn't that happen more often? I don't think Essex believed that he was going to kick off a revolution as some have suggested. I think he just wanted to act. He didn't give a damn any more about what would happen; he wasn't looking at the result. . . . The system had fucked him over. The only thing he thought he could do to the system was to try to destroy it, and if he died trying, he died."[58]

More traditionally, Louisiana psychiatrist Dr. William Bloom depoliticized and diminished Essex's rebellion by analysing him in terms of a short and impotent person. "He was very short," he told a journalist, "and yet he had a very big gun. . . . There's not a great deal of difference between his drawing of a sword and the image of him striking death with his .44 magnum carbine. The gun probably helped him compensate for feelings of powerlessness. If he saw himself as a crusader, striking back, he would not have to feel disenfranchised. His concept of self-esteem is very important. By acting in the spirit of a black revolutionary, he may well have been acting against injustices which he perceived to have been done against him. The slogans which he sprayed across the walls of his dingy apartment certainly indicated he hated the police as symbols of the white power structure. By killing them, he would assert his manhood and gain esteem from some elements of the black community. And by gaining esteem, he could defend his fragile identity, which probably was the biggest fight. . . . After looking at his apartment and seeing all of those racist slogans painted on the walls, I would say that Essex had no clarity of concept; the slogans from various revolutionaries were mixed together." Bloom admitted that "we can't seem to build any case that Essex was neurologically defective or psychotic. As far as I know, there were no signs of mental illness in his family." Still, he concluded that "I do think, however, that there were indications he was suicidal."[59]

The most important document in the intervention of the state in this case was undoubtedly that prepared by police Superintendent Giarrusso, who moved to exonerate the state. "For his [Essex's] acts," Giarrusso wrote, "he paid with his life and, thus, inflicted pain and suffering on his own family." Drawing attention to the fact that one of Essex's victims had been black, another had been a woman, and that a third one was younger than Essex, he concluded: "They all shared the commonality of membership in a society, a society that Mark Essex had rejected because, in his opinion, it had failed to meet its expectations." Giarrusso cautioned that "an attempt may be made to explain Essex's violent acts against his fellow human beings by the presentation of evidence carefully selected to support the premise that society was the compelling contributor to those acts and, if not responsible therefore, at least to blame." For Giarrusso, this notion seemed easy to refute: "In not accepting that premise, I reject the selected evidence offered in its support. To do otherwise, in my opinion, would fix upon society, instead of individuals, the blame for all criminal acts."

Yet where did he find the idea that both cannot be blamed; or that in blaming one, the other was therefore exonerated? It mattered not, for his task was not to understand a phenomenon, but merely to blame the actor. "Mark Essex's footnote in history should state clearly that he murdered and executed, without justifiable cause or purpose; that society did not fail him, but that he failed society; that if society inflicted any indignities upon him, such indignities were minuscule by comparison."[60]

In the final analysis, it was two sociologists who asked the important questions. The social scientist, William Swanson, commented that Essex's apparently suicidal behavior could be linked to other phenomena: "I do think that Essex was suicidal. I think that he was suicidal in the sense that he did think he could start something, that he might begin a revolution . . . start something that was big. I think that he thought that when he went up on the roof of that hotel that he wasn't coming down. He was suicidal in the sense that he was willing to sacrifice himself for the cause. That may not have been realistic but not delusional in that he thought he was a Black Messiah, the chosen one. There are many examples of this kind of suicide through history. It's called altruistic suicide, and one of the best examples is the Kamikaze pilot of the Second World War." More profoundly, sociologist Daniel Thompson pierced the heart of the issue when he observed: "The problem for society to ponder out of all this is a fundamental one. How is it to deal with such supreme alienation? It doesn't matter whether the individual be black or white, although in Essex's case it's obvious that his blackness precipitated his action. The question is, what do you do with the man who is alone, cut off, willing to die?"[61]

Internment

> "Man seems to take justice into his own hands when god or secular authorities fail. It is as if in his passion for vengeance he elevates himself to the role of god, and of the angels of vengeance."
>
> *Erich Fromm*[62]

If we rely on conventional explanations for such outrageous behavior, we are inevitably left perplexed. Essex was no troubled victim of an abusing family, displacing hatred of father on an innocent society. Neither was he a deranged individual suffering from some mental disease, for even his inquisitors cleared him of any serious charges of this nature. Yet this pleasant young man from a prosperous and loving home killed and wounded several dozen of his fellow human beings—including one of his own race—and came close to obliterating an entire city block. In passing, he exposed the incompetence of the city's security forces (as he had said he would do in his *communiqué* to the media).

Essex shares the self-absorption and simple-mindedness of all our multiple murderers, but he is the only one of their number whose protest *seems* to be more than entirely personal, the only one who appeared to act politically, which is to say on behalf of others besides himself. Indeed, this won him much sympathy in certain circles, for he seemed to represent the needs and aspirations of the disenfranchised black masses. Yet the only difference between Essex's rebellion and that of our other multiple murderers is that many people could identify with, even approve, his outrage at his particular exclusion (in a way they could not, for example, with the failed entrance to the lower-middle classes that haunted DeSalvo). In fact, however, his protest proceeded from precisely the same individual reasons as that of all the others in this book. He had no revolutionary social theory other than a racist hatred, no concept of organized response beyond the .44 magnum.

One is led inexorably to the conclusion that if he had remained in Emporia and perhaps risen to be a junior executive in a meat-packing plant (instead of venturing into the racist trap of the U.S. Navy) he would have remained forever the gentle and delicate young man he was when he walked through the gates of the San Diego naval yard for the first time. One suspects that if he had been able to fulfill his earlier dream of becoming a dentist, or even if he had been able to come to terms with his considered career in vending-machine repair, he and his victims would have survived. Thus the killing stemmed entirely from his personal crisis: that he could not tolerate the lowly achievement that his society and his limited personal talents would make available to him.

His final hours were theatrical and entirely in keeping with the fashionably violent codes of his culture. John Wayne would have understood his explosion into purple ceremony. He had decided that only through monstrous acts could he feel that he addressed himself to what historians of crime Peter and Favret call "the rule of lies and the foul machine at whose whim his fellows, the disinherited of the earth, are and have always been crushed, each day, each life." But the act that was a discourse fell hard on perpetrator and victim alike, along with all their intimates. No repayment, despite the many millions of dollars in lawsuits against the city, could return what had been stolen. The victims were buried during *days* of funerals: Among the first was Patrolman Paul Persigo, at thirty-three, the youngest accredited Rose Show Judge in the United States. He did not deserve to die; and neither did the others who followed him into their graves.[63]

Essex was too proud to face a life he perceived as "devoid of all future, deprived of all prospects," or to thereby endure "the unlivable, day in and day out." In Emporia, his parents gave a hint of the moral rectitude that provided the ideological basis for their son's decision, the means by which a young man described by a lifelong friend as "sort of a soft kid, a delicate sort of man," was transformed into a heartless killer. "Young blacks are not going to accept the white racist society," his mother told a reporter. "It's a clear signal, a clear signal for white America to get off the seat of its pants and do something. I don't want my son to have died in vain. If this terrible thing will awaken white America to the injustices that blacks suffer, then some good will have come of it." His sister added that after "Jimmy went into the navy, he really saw what life, the world was all about. He saw that white people control the world, and blacks were being oppressed by the white man. He didn't like society the way it is. He wanted to change things. The navy to Jimmy was his own private hell." Undoubtedly it was, alas, but he changed nothing: however, it mattered not, for his goal had been merely to release his own personal anger, to stage his private rebellion.[64]

The warrior with 200 bullet holes in his body was buried in an unmarked grave in Emporia. A few days after the funerals, one of the policemen who had been in the Marine helicopter that had attacked Essex shot a slum black who had tried to kill him. As attendants placed the youth in the back of the ambulance, a woman's voice rose over the darkened New Orleans slum: "Sniper comin' back. Sniper comin' back to get you all." As if to confirm this—and to deny the reality that many died for nothing—young blacks sometimes search for Essex's unmarked grave and, finding it, stand beside it in silence.[65]

9 Dead People Are All on the Same Level

CHARLES STARKWEATHER*

The Killing Time

"Shooting people was, I guess, a kind of thrill. It brought out something."

Charles Starkweather[1]

Painfully, he passed through his impoverished childhood, morbidly sensitive to his family's low estate, his entire being acutely attuned to every real or fancied social slight that came his way. By the time he reached adolescence, he was embittered and enraged—emotions which were only exacerbated by his degrading social position as garbageman (in which he felt perpetually imprisoned)—caring for the refuse of the rich, with no hope of escape. A brief but spectacular vendetta offered more to his spirit than an eternity of submission.

---

* Portions of Starkweather's autobiography were printed as a magazine article, "Rebellion," and much more was reproduced in James M. Reinhardt's *The Murderous Trail of Charles Starkweather.* William Allen's thoughtful *Starkweather: The Story of a Mass Murderer* was also most useful, as was *Caril*, by Ninette Beaver, B.K. Ripley and Patrick Trese.

Starkweather killed first in a robbery. Soon after, he embarked upon his spree: a week-long burst of destruction during which he murdered ten more people. He was nineteen. His personal style mirrored rebellious adolescents' heroes of the day so successfully (especially the cult figure James Dean, who appeared in the film *Rebel Without a Cause*) that it lent his crimes an ominous air of impending insurrection. To neutralize this potential social threat, the media strove to invalidate him, dismissing him as merely "warped" and immature, a kind of meaningless adolescent fantasy. Thus the significance of his homicidal rage remained largely unexamined, as the authorities repudiated his message merely by refusing to decipher it.

His first kill took place during a routine gas station hold-up, and it seemed to be an entirely pragmatic operation in which an inconvenient witness was silenced. Starkweather had known most of those who worked at the gas station, and he had memorized their routines. He also guessed that the new attendant would not recognize him with a bandanna around his face. At 3 A.M. on December 1, 1957, carrying a twelve-gauge shotgun, he forced twenty-one-year-old Robert Colvert to hand over the money, a total of $108, then shoved him into his car and drove to a remote location outside their city of Lincoln, Nebraska. As they left the car, Colvert tried to grab the gun: "I got into a helluva fight and shooting gallery," Starkweather later recalled. "He shot himself the first time. He had ahold of the gun from the front, and I cocked it and we was messing around and he jerked it and the thing went off." As Colvert tried to stand up, Starkweather pressed the muzzle against the back of Colvert's head and pulled the trigger. "He didn't get up any more." The killing filled Starkweather with sensations of serenity that he had not experienced since childhood; and left him with the feeling that he was now sufficiently powerful to violate the laws of man.[2]

He did not kill again immediately. He spent the next six weeks with his fourteen-year-old girlfriend, Caril Fugate, practicing knife-throwing and shooting, while the shape of his task crystalized in his mind. On the morning of January 21, 1958, carrying a cheap single-shot .22 bolt-action rifle, he visited Caril's home. An argument ensued, in the course of which Caril's mother, Velda Bartlett, told him she no longer wanted him to see Caril. At the height of the argument, according to Starkweather, "She didn't say nothing. She just got up and slammed the shit out of me . . . in the face." He left the shabby house, but returned a few minutes later to find Caril's stepfather, Marion Bartlett, waiting for him in the kitchen: "The old man started chewing me out. I said to hell with him and was going to walk out through the front door, and he helped me out. Kicked me right in the ass. My tail hurt for three days." He returned to the Bartlett home that afternoon to find Caril and her mother "yelling their heads off." Caril's mother turned to him and accused him of impregnating Caril, and then, according to Starkweather, "she got up and slapped the shit out of me again . . . in the head . . . both sides. I hauled off and hit her one back . . . in the head. . . . My hand wasn't closed . . . it knocked her back a couple of steps. She let out a cry, a war cry or something, and the old man came flying in. He picked me up . . . by the neck . . . and started carrying me to the front door. I kicked him somewhere and he put me down. We started wrestling around in the front room. . . . Then he took off for the other room. I knew what he was heading for [a weapon] so I thought I'd head for the same thing."[3]

As Starkweather hurriedly slipped a cartridge in the .22, Marion Bartlett ran at him with a claw hammer: The bullet struck him in the head and he collapsed. Velda Bartlett entered the room carrying a large kitchen knife. As Starkweather remembered the events: "The old lady Bartlett said she was going to chop my head off, and I loaded the gun again. . . . The old lady started to take a few steps toward me . . . and Caril jerked the gun away and said she'd blow her to hell. . . . The old lady got mad and knocked her down. . . . I grabbed the gun from Caril. . . . I just turned around and shot her in the face. She went on by, heading for the little girl [Caril's two-and-a-half-year-old half-sister, Betty Jean Bartlett]. . . . She just stopped, and I thought she was going to pick up the girl, but she never, she just turned around and looked at me again . . . and I hit her with the butt of the gun. . . . She fell down, but she wasn't quite all the way down, so I hit her again. . . . She just laid there. . . . After I hit the old lady, I just came up with the butt of the gun and hit the little girl. . . . She fell down against the table . . . stood there screaming. . . . Caril was yelling at her to shut up."[4]

According to Starkweather, Caril then informed him that her step-father was still alive in the bedroom. "I picked up the knife that the old lady had . . . and started to walk in there, in the bedroom . . . and the little girl kept yelling, and I told her to shut up, and I started to walk again, and just turned around and threw the kitchen knife I had at her. . . . They said it hit her in the throat, but I thought it hit her in the chest. I went on into the bedroom. Mr. Bartlett was moving around quite a bit, so I tried to stab him in the throat, but the knife wouldn't go in [so] I just hit the top part of it with my hand, and it went in." He stabbed Mr. Bartlett several more times in the throat and waited to make sure he was dead. Then he reloaded the gun and sat down to watch television—"I don't even remember what was on. I just wanted some noise," he later told police. "It was too quiet." Later, they wrapped the bodies in rugs and bedclothes, stuffed Caril's mother down the outhouse seat, left the baby's body on the seat, and then dragged the stepfather's body into the chicken coop.[5]

The young couple did a cursory cleaning of the house, removing some of the blood and mess. They then remained in the house as lovers for six days. "To Charlie," his biographer, William Allen, observed, "the best week in his life was under way. The criminologist James Rein-hardt quoted him as saying that they lived like kings, that he had never had a more wonderful time, that at last there was nobody to order them around. He felt no guilt because of what he had done." For six days, they fended off various callers with excuses. Concerned relatives con-tinued to call the police, but the police did not enter the house when they arrived there: They were mollified by the polite reception they received, and by the sign on the door that read, "Stay a way Every Body is sick with the Flue." When it finally appeared to the couple that they might be discovered, they left Lincoln in Starkweather's car: The bodies were found a few hours later, and the police issued an alert.[6]

Charles Starkweather and Caril Fugate drove to the farm of seventy-year-old August Meyer, an old friend of the Starkweather family: They had broken bread together many times, as Starkweather had often hunted on Meyer's property, making a gift to Meyer of half of what he had shot. However, Meyer's lane was mired in mud and melting snow, and the car soon got stuck. Later, Starkweather claimed that was why he had decided to kill Meyer: "Caril got pissed off because we got stuck. She said we ought to go up and blast the shit out of him because he didn't shovel his lane. I said it, too." After several attempts failed to free the car, they walked to the farm. In reconstructing the murder, Starkweather claimed—as he would with all the murders he committed—that it had been "self defense." As he remembered it, he had asked Meyer for a horse to pull the car out of the mud; but, inexplicably, he said, "I got into a helluva argument with Meyer. He couldn't understand why I got stuck there. He thought we should have gotten stuck up closer to his house."[7]

After a heated discussion, according to Starkweather, Meyer said he was going into the house to get his coat, but appeared instead on the porch with a rifle and fired at him. "I felt the bullet go by my head," but Meyer's rifle jammed after the first shot. "Meyer started running back in the house, and I shot him . . . at almost point-blank range with the sawed-off .410 [shotgun]." He dragged Meyer's body to the wash-house and covered it with a blanket. When Meyer's dog approached them, he shot the dog. He then ransacked the house, eating Jello and cookies, and stealing what cash he could find (less than $100), along with socks, gloves, a shirt, a straw hat, and a .22 pump-action repeating rifle. They took a brief nap before making another attempt to extricate their car. They soon realized that their frantic digging with a single shovel was in vain. Eventually, they were freed by a passing farmer who tied his truck to the car and pulled it out of the mud. Curiously, Starkweather insisted that the farmer take two dollars for the job, and let him go with profuse thanks. Within moments, the car was mired once more.[8]

Carrying Meyer's .22 rifle and Bartlett's sawed-off .410 shotgun, they abandoned the car and walked down the road until they were offered a lift by two popular and conservative local high school students, seventeen-year-old Robert Jensen and his fiancée, Carol King. Starkweather later claimed that at this point he had toyed with the idea of telephoning a policeman he knew and turning himself in; but, he said, he did not relish the idea of being "captured" by the chubby young Jensen, thereby making Jensen into a kind of hero. After a few moments' ambivalence, he threatened Jensen with his gun, took his money, and ordered him to drive to a nearby abandoned school. As Jensen walked down the steps of the school's storm cellar, Starkweather shot him from behind. He later claimed that Jensen had tried to grab his gun, but, regardless, Jensen was shot six times in the left ear. He gave several conflicting statements regarding how he had then killed King; but he was alone with her in the cellar for some fifteen minutes. He originally said that he had shot her when she began to scream, but later claimed that Caril had shot her.[9]

Their bodies were not found until the following day. Jensen was fully clothed and was lying on his stomach in a pool of blood at the bottom of the stairs. King was partly nude and was lying on top of Jensen. Her coat had been pulled over her head, her jeans and panties pulled down around her ankles, and her lower body was streaked with blood and mud. Several stab wounds had been directed at her groin, one of them extending through the wall of the cervix into the rectum. An autopsy found internal damage to the vagina, the cervix, and the rectum, caused by an undetermined sharp instrument, but the examiners found no indication of sexual attack and no presence of sperm. Starkweather later admitted that he had been "tempted" to rape King, and that he had "pulled her jeans down," but he was reluctant to admit that he had been involved in her mutilation and insisted that Caril had done it out of jealousy.[10]

He later claimed that after they left the murder scene, he decided to abandon the spree and turn himself in to the police. "She kept trying to talk me out of it," he insisted. "We was going down shooting on the highway. I told her I was going to give myself up and she said no I wasn't. I said yes I was and she said no I wasn't." Undoubtedly, however, the reality was that he was merely airing his misgivings and anxieties, for there was no one to stop him had he truly wished to quit. Fascinated by their own accomplishments, they continued to argue about whether to go and live with Starkweather's brother in the state of Washington. Then ("incredibly," according to the commentators), after driving for three hours in the direction of Washington, they turned the car around and headed back to Lincoln. Allen wrote that Starkweather tried to explain this decision with facile claims "that he had been too tired to go on, he had to get some rest [and] the car wasn't running well either, and he thought it would be easier to pick up another one in Lincoln," but these claims make no sense: Both rest and alternate automobiles would have been obtained more safely elsewhere. The fact of the matter seems to be that they wished to view their exploits and to complete the pillaging of their community. They drove past Caril's house to see if the police had discovered the bodies of her family, and accelerated away quickly when they saw the police gathered around the house. From there, they drove to a section of Lincoln that had special meaning to Starkweather, and would play an important role in the fulfillment of his task—"the wealthy country club section of town." It was not yet dawn. They fell asleep in their parked car.[11]

Ostensibly, their plan was to spend the day in one of the mansions, then steal a car, and leave by stealth at nightfall. Starkweather would not be moving in a strange environment, for he knew it well from his job on the garbage route. Although he had not collected garbage from the house they ultimately selected, he had often done so from the same area's estates (or performed odd jobs in them), and he knew the names and occupations of many of the inhabitants. As they drove through the neighborhood, he pointed out several possibilities to Caril before settling on a mansion belonging to forty-seven-year-old industrialist C. Lauer Ward, president of bridge-building and steel companies, and a well-known and highly regarded Lincoln business figure. His wife, Clara, forty-six, was a graduate of the University of Nebraska and, like Ward, was active in community affairs. Lillian Fencl, fifty-one, had been the Wards' maid for twenty-six years.[12]

Mr. Ward was out at work, but Mrs. Ward was upstairs when, brandishing their weapons, Starkweather and Caril forced the maid, Fencl, to admit them to the house. When Mrs. Ward came downstairs, she was ordered to sit at the table. The women soon asked if they could do housework while they waited, and Starkweather grew bored with watching them. He spent several hours wandering through the mansion's elegant rooms, fascinated by the opulence. Before noon, he ordered Mrs. Ward, *not* the maid, to serve him pancakes in the library, and then petulantly changed his order to waffles. "They was real nice to us," he told Reinhardt. "And I took it while I had it. I knowed it couldn't last long." In the early afternoon, Mrs. Ward asked if she might go upstairs, and when Starkweather went to check on her a few moments later, he said, "She took a shot at me. . . . She just stepped out of the boy's room and she took a shot at me with the .22. . . . She started going for the top of the steps. . . . I had the knife. . . . I threw the knife at her. . . . It stuck to her back. . . . She was moaning and groaning. . . . I dragged her into her bedroom. . . . I laid her on her bed and just left her there." When the Wards' dog began to pester him, he broke its neck with a blow from his rifle butt. He then made certain that Mrs. Ward was secure: "I put the rope around her, or I took a sheet and cut the sheet and put a piece of sheet around her mouth and hands. . . . After that I bound her feet and hands and covered her up."[13]

That afternoon, he telephoned his father and, without giving away his location, asked him to deliver a message to his estranged friend, Robert Von Busch, that he (Starkweather) intended to kill him for trying to come between him and Caril. He also wrote a letter, styled as if it had been written from both Caril and himself, addressed to "the law only," and offering a measure of explanation. "Then ne and chuck live with each other and nonday the day the bodys were found, we were going to kill our selves but BOB VON BRUCK and everybody would not stay a way . . . and [I] hate my older sister and bob for what they are they all ways wanted ne to stop going with chuck snow that sone Kid bob Kwen [knew] would go with ne . . . i feel sorry for Bar, and have a ask [ass] like bob. I and Caril are sorry for what has happen, cause I have hurt every body cause of it and so has caril. but i'n saying one thing every body that cane out there was luckie there not *dead* even caril's sister [sic]."[14]

When Mr. Ward returned to his home at 6 P.M., he was confronted at the door by Starkweather: Ward grabbed the gun and tried to wrest it from him, but Starkweather managed to push him down the basement steps. He raced down behind Ward to retrieve the .22 rifle which had also fallen into the basement, and as he did so, Ward tried to run back up the stairs. Starkweather shot him in the back. Despite his wounds, Ward continued running through the kitchen and living room, and had opened the front door when Starkweather shot him again. "It probably struck him in the head," he later recalled. "I was standing about five feet from him, maybe less. . . . I asked him if he was all right and he didn't answer." After this, he forced the maid, Fencl, upstairs and tied her up, stealing ten dollars from her and seven dollars from Mrs. Ward. He denied any involvement in killing Fencl, but Caril later insisted that he had tied her legs and hands to the bed and "started stabbing her, and she started screaming and hollering. . . . He put a pillow over her face. . . . Every time he stabbed her she moaned. . . . He said he didn't think she was ever going to die . . . and he cut the strips holding her legs and covered her over [with] a blanket that laid on the bed."[15]

The bodies were discovered the following morning when a concerned business associate stopped by the home to ask why Ward had not appeared at the office. He found Lauer Ward inside the front door, with bullet wounds in his temple and back, and a stab wound in the neck. Clara Ward, clad only in a nightgown, was lying on the floor in one of the bedrooms, with multiple stab wounds to her neck, chest, and back. Lillian Fencl's body was tied to a bed in another bedroom, her chest, stomach, hands, arms, and legs covered with many stab wounds.[16]

Now there were nine known dead. The surrounding population responded with fearful alacrity: The governor called out the National Guard, whose members began cruising the streets in jeeps armed with mounted machine guns: "False tips, weird and fantastic rumors added to the situation. People began to fly apart. Work and school ground to a halt. The panic and confusion spread," Allen recorded.[17]

Now piloting Ward's black Packard limousine, Starkweather and
Caril turned west once more, heading for the state of Washington.
Starkweather later stated that, as they drove, they threw notes out of
the car, informing the world of what they had done. They drove
through the night, not stopping until they reached a small town near
the Wyoming border. There they filled the Packard with gas and themselves with candy bars and nine bottles of Pepsi-Cola before continuing their journey. Worried that the police might be looking for their
conspicuous limousine, Starkweather began looking for a replacement.
He found it when he saw a Buick parked off the highway, with thirty-
seven-year-old salesman, Merle Collison, asleep on the front seat. He
awakened Collison and demanded that the two of them trade cars.
When Collison refused, Starkweather opened fire with the .22. The
results of the autopsy later showed that the salesman had been shot in
the nose, cheek, neck, chest, left arm, right wrist, and left leg. Starkweather's own account of the killing was especially contradictory, perhaps because, as Reinhardt suggested, he felt embarrassed by the
murder, since its "cold-bloodedness" made it difficult for him to
rationalize his usual "self-defense" plea. According to Reinhardt, he
thought that he would be considered cowardly because of the way in
which the salesman had been murdered; and his solution to the problem was to settle finally on a story that implicated Caril in the killing.[18]

In the meantime, Collison's corpse had slumped forward and
jammed in the front seat. As Starkweather tried to shove the body out
of the car, another car drove by. "I thought they had had an accident,"
the driver, a geologist, later testified, "so I turned my car around and
came back. . . . Then I asked, 'Can I help you?' He straightened up with
a rifle he had behind him and said, 'Raise your hands. Help me release
the emergency brake or I'll kill you.' It was then I noticed the dead
man behind the wheel. As I approached him, I grabbed at the gun and
we fought for it in the middle of the highway. I knew that if he won I
would be dead, so I managed to wrestle it from him." As the two of
them struggled for the gun, a Wyoming deputy sheriff drove past and
stopped his car. Caril immediately ran toward his cruiser and jumped

in, telling the sheriff, "He's killed a man." Starkweather freed himself
from the geologist and, seeing the danger, drove off quickly in the
Packard, heading back east toward the town of Douglas, Wyoming.
The sheriff called ahead for a roadblock and started off in pursuit;
soon he was joined by other cruisers, all pursuing Starkweather into
Douglas at a hundred miles per hour. The entire chase clogged in the
town's traffic until police began shooting at the Packard's tires and the
traffic quickly dispersed. They then cleared the town at speeds rising
to 120 miles per hour, and continued until police bullets finally
smashed the Packard's rear window. Within seconds of the window's
disintegration, Starkweather stopped suddenly in the middle of the
highway. He seemed to have thought he had been shot, since he was
bleeding copiously from one ear; in fact, he had merely been cut by a
piece of flying glass. He left the car and, despite the fact that police
were shooting at the ground in front of him, he insisted curiously on
carefully adjusting his shirttails before he lay face down on the road
and surrendered. The arresting officer later told reporters that Starkweather was meek once he was captured: "He thought he was bleeding to death. That's why he stopped. That's the kind of yellow son of
a bitch he is." He made no comment on Starkweather's fastidiousness
with his shirt.[19]

His murderous spree was over, but his task was only beginning to
flower. Allen described his *performance* as the officers escorted this
mad-dog killer to Nebraska's State Penitentiary. The party was met by
a "crowd of newsmen, photographers, and movie cameramen. Caril,
her head covered by a scarf, smiled tightly into the lenses. Charlie pretended to ignore the attention, but nevertheless was the better subject.
Bloodied, in chains, shabby-haired, a cigarette dangling from his lips,
wearing his black leather motorcycle jacket, tight black denim pants,
blue and white cowboy boots with a butterfly design on the toes—he
was a perfect-looking young rebel-killer."[20]

The Killer As Autobiographer

"Why did it have to happen to me? It is not fair. . . . It is not
right. . . . Why was the world against me?"

Charles Starkweather[21]

It is clear that this embittered and impoverished garbageman thought
of his killing spree as an organized retributive task, governed by the
rules that regulate warfare. He expressed some regret that he had shot
the sleeping salesman, "but I had to shoot quick. It was the end, I
guess. People will remember that last shot. I hope they'll read my
story. They'll know why then. They'll know that the salesman just
happened to be in there. I didn't put him there and he didn't know I
was coming. . . . When soldiers have to take a place or do something
they don't ask if there's any children and old people, women, or is anybody asleep?" Like a soldier, he was only following the dictates of a
higher plan. It made sense then that these "things didn't bother me. . . .
How could I be particular about people I had to kill?" What does he
mean when he says he *"had"* to kill?

Curiously, his recounting of the killings changed over time, and were
issued in radically different versions—so much so that, according to the
journalist N. Beaver and her colleagues, "Before his trial began, Starkweather had made seven statements of record, all of which conflicted or
contradicted each other in at least one respect." Each successive version
was more detailed, and seemed to implicate Caril more, but the reader
is left wondering whether his motive was accuracy or revenge.[22]

His lengthy autobiography makes it clear that there were only two
dimensions of the universe that moved him deeply, his hatred for
humanity and his love of nature. Even the house in which he grew up
was tainted by its association with humanity, for it was a construction
of human beings, designed to illustrate their mean hierarchical
motives—"the house was [a] shabby white one-story structure," he
said. But when he left the works of mankind and tuned in to those of
nature, he waxed as poetical as can be expected from a virtually illiter-

ate young man. "I was raised in this house through most of my child-hood, the place to me looked like a [sic] enchanted forest, with its large trees surrounding the house, and at times in the evenings when the sun was setting in its tender glory, with its beautiful colors in the western sky, and the birds singing in their melodies that came softly from the trees—everything was nice and pretty, so peaceful, and tran-quil—it was as though time itself was standing still. I fell in love with this adventurous land in my earlier days, and the flames still burns [sic] deep down inside of me for the love of that enchanted forest."[23]

My Fighting Reputation

If his entire being is discolored with hatred, if all his memories are filled with the terrible insults that generated his rage, they seem trivial indeed when examined closely. The slights and humiliations he remembered were surely the lot of a major portion of humanity: He was, for exam-ple, always the last boy to be picked for teams, but what artist and intellectual in this century has not whined about the same experience? He was always teased about his red hair and bowed legs, but who passes through childhood without having his or her physical peculiarities sin-gled out and giggled over? These are sadnesses, to be sure, for children are as cruel to one another as adults; but they are not what any analyst can easily accept as justification or explanation for mass murder.

Still, there can be no doubt that he hurt intensely, nor any doubt that he reacted to those wounds with sullen rage. "My rebellion against the world started that first day in school," he wrote, "and from that first day I became rebellious. I had stayed in my rebellious mood even to this day. Why had I become rebellious against the world and its human race?—'cause that first day in school I was being made fun at, picked on, laughed at. Why were they making fun of me? My speech for one thing and the other was my legs, I was a little bowleged [sic]. In those younger years of my life I haded builded [sic] up a hate that was as hard as iron and when people tease, make fun of and laugh at a little young-ster in hers [sic] or his early childhood, that little youngster is not going to forget it. I wouldn't deny I was like a hound prowling for fights, quarreling, and doing wild things and placing everyone among my enemies. Kids picking on me and not having a thing to do with me caused me to have black moods, at least that is what I call them, 'cause most of the time, I would just sit in one place and stay motionless in a gloomy manner and it was obvious that there was no reasoning with me when in one of my black mood [sic] and boys and girls that I knew didn't bother me while I was in my motionless and gloomy manner, they would just let me be and stay in my black mood and even to this day I still have them [sic] melancholy moods."[24]

In his memory, the entire pattern of his life was encapsulated in the first day at school. "School that first morning we didn't go to much, Mrs. Mott let everyone play and do what they wanted, I didn't get along that day in school with the others, they made me a little mad but more upset than anything else, they didn't seem to want to have anothing [sic] to do with me, not let me play with them or anything else and that's the reason I played in the sandbox by myself that first morning, everybody left when I came over to play with them in the sandbox, they'd left went off among some other girls and boys talking about me, because out of corner [sic] of my eye, I glanced at them, the girls giggling and boys giving off their snickers, then they wented [sic] off occupying them selves to some other simple tasks." Was this some form of paranoiac madness? Did he seriously expect us to believe that a sad incident in a sandbox created a multiple murderer? He swore we should. Could a child that young be so class conscious? "I said to myself that some day I'd pay them all back, and a overwhelming sense of outrage grew, it roused itself in my mind for a wild thirsting revenge, I wanted in general revenge upon the world and its human race, my mind and heart became black with hatred as it builded [sic] up in me, a drawn veil of a dilatory cloud seem [sic] to come before my face, the tribute was gratifying, I could not anglyze nor recoqnice [sic] my emotions as I broked [sic] down into tears. . . . I had the whole sandbox to myself." Is this ludicrous self-pity, or super-sensitivity?[25]

If he overstated the significance of the first day of school, there can be no doubt that he accurately described a growing conviction which formed early enough in life for his rampage to start at the age of nineteen. "The hate that became strong inside of me when I was a youngster by those who were making fun and always teasing me are the ones that started me to fight. I would beat them down and if I had to I would beat them down again until they knew that I wasn't going to take it from them. At times and with the right emphasis my attitude was merely a sporadic outburst, but at other times as I realized now was something thronie [sic], when I was fighting those who picked on me, I fought fast and a little furiously like a mamiac [sic] in rage and fury and as I fought sense of outrage grew to striving, to throw, to bend, to hurt and most of all to beat those who teased me, but as I fought the general opinion of school kids became particularly that I had a reputation for meanness or generosity and that word REPUTATION. . . . As many other kids know is a hard thing to stand up to at times, when they say that your [sic] a fighter and have the reputation for doing nothing but fighting and then there's going to be a few kids like yourself that are going to fight and try to take that reputation away from the other fellow.[26]

"My fighting repretation [sic] stayed with me throughout my school years and even after I had stopped going to school that repetation [sic] stayed with me, but my rebellion started against the world and the human race when I was being maded [sic] fun at and that being made fun at is what cause my fights when I was a youngster, but I assure you that's not the reason for fighting when I gew [sic] up but the hatred I had builded [sic] up inside of me stayed with me and it made [me] hate everybody other than my family, but with that strong hatred, a person wouldn't look at me cross eye without getting into a fist fight. My speech and bowllegs [sic] were my main cause for being made fun at as I grew older my speech defect was over come and I can now prononuce [sic] words with a defined and correct pronunciation as well as anyone else and for my bowllegs [sic], their [sic] just as crokked [sic] as before, I have never been able to grow out of them and if I have to say so myself, I believe a pig could run between them without touching the sides." In this vein, he described his childhood as a succession of cruel humiliations, as, for example, when a gang of boys took one of his paintings. They "all gathered around the boy that had my painting and right away they started making wise cracks about it. . . . The boy with my picture . . . said, "This is a piece of junk, besides being a red head, bowlleged [sic], wood pecker—you can't even draw," and at that, tore it in half and as the laughter and giggling began he glanced around at them and finished ripping it into little pieces. . . . Then one of the girls yelled searcastily [sic] he's going to cry—hes [sic] a cry baby then they started in the red headed bowlleged [sic] wood pecker is a cry baby."[27]

An important problem here is that while Starkweather remembered a childhood of rage and fighting, no one else remembered him in this way. A neighbor told Reinhardt that "Charles was a pretty quiet sort of boy most of the time"; his parents thought that he was "a normal boy"; and Reinhardt "could find no evidence in Charles' school record that Charles' citizenship was adjudged 'bad' by any teacher. In fact, his 'citizenship' record was rather consistently above average. There were no differences of opinion among his former teachers as to whether he could be considered a behavior problem; though I found none who apparently thought that his outward show of pugnacity, his explosive temper, and withdrawal tendencies were signs of deep-seated disturbances." The school's psychologist had reported that "many students lack his special insight, but his difficulty was in actually dealing with what he saw, and how to appropriate it. Here he showed inadequacy." Similarly, a school counselor concluded that "he did not have as many fights as he claimed he had," and a teacher suggested: "He is inclined to be timid, doesn't associate too easily but gets along well enough with boys; not so well with girls. Doesn't like to participate in games with other children, either indoors or out." Another thought that "he seems especially fond of two of his brothers and fond of his mother. . . . Often refers to the attention and care that his mother has given him."[28]

What is the significance of the great disparity between Starkweather's autobiography and the memories of those who observed him? It is not necessary, I think, to deduce from this that one or the other lied, or was misled: Likely the fights were real enough in Starkweather's tormented imagination. More important, what are we to make of the warmth and pride that characterized his relationship with his family, especially his mother? Should not our killers come from ruthlessly abusive families in order to fit our preconceptions?

Something Worth Killing For

His alienation from the world was intensified by his reaction to the women he pursued. Before he met Caril, he later wrote, "Yes, I went out with girls, some were mild dates with nice Christian girls, but most of the girls I went out with, were either the gibberty-gibbet type, that used too much make-up, and dressed in expensive clothes, or they were the harlot type, that weren't hard to get a date with, and easy to get along with. I had my fights that seem to happen every other day, and like almost everybody, I had my dreams of things I wanted. But of all the dreams, fights, and women to me none of then [sic] ever seen [sic] to fit in this world. I guess that's what I meant when I said, 'I don't know life, or what it was good for,' and the reason I didn't know, I just didn't take time to fine [sic] out. When I was younger, I always said to myself that I was going to have the knowledge of what life was good for in this world, but as I grew older, the more I didn't care to fine [sic] out, and that's the reason why I didn't have time."[29]

His adolescent fantasy-woman was revealed in his response to a drawing Reinhardt showed him of a well-dressed and clearly middle-class woman standing in front of a garden wall and surrounded by modern patio furniture: She was "the kind of girl I used to think I'd like to have . . . [but] that kind a girl would look like hell in my kind a surrounding. . . . You got a give the right kind a place to be in," he told Reinhardt. But the reality was that before he met Caril, "nobody could ever ask me how I was getting along with my girl friend. Until I met Caril I never had the kind a kid gets along with. I had a nice girl once, but she got to upsetting my death deal and I had to drop her. . . . Nobody cared about me and my girl friends anyhow. . . . One thing sure I never give nobody much a chance to be dirty to me if I didn't have to." Previous women, then, were either unsuitable in terms of social class, or would interfere with his already rapidly coalescing "death deal."[30]

When he met Caril, everything seemed to slip into place. The liaison spawned no fantasies of conventional marriage and family; and it could not be expected to since its purpose was to provide a romantic and sexual adjunct to his task. Once contracted, the relationship grew obsessive, so much so that he quit his job in order to be free to meet Caril when she walked home from school, perhaps afraid that she might turn to another. Now his identity was fully formed, his task clarifying: "Having Caril with me doing the things we was doing together as the end was coming on was different from anything I'd ever had before. It didn't seem real somehow." He knew that he did not have "much future with Caril," but "whatever it was, was for the both of us." With Caril beside him, his purpose gained in meaning: "One time I was afraid to die, I used to want to shoot up the world for no reason, I used to want to throw garbage in somebody's face, I was mad at the world. Then Caril made things clear; then everything had a reason. I knowed the end was coming, but it had a reason too." Through his relationship with her, it was possible for him to understand why he "hated the world. I was something to her. She never cared what I looked like. I looked good to her and she liked me because I lived in a shack and she thought whatever I done was good, and if I didn't do no drawing or drive no hot rods that was good too. She meant something that nothing else had ever meant. . . . I knowed that without her it was going right back to the hated world I was trying to leave. . . . I started a new kind of thinking after I met her, and it all ended me right here [sic]. It was something to live for, something to live with. How long? It didn't matter. We had to be together," he told Reinhardt. "That's the way it looked then . . . to live with Caril and die with Caril. Anyways I wanted her to see me go down shooting it out and knowing it was for her, for us; I guess for all this hateful world had made us for."[31]

Yet, this great love would not survive trial and imprisonment. If the first words he had blurted out to the arresting officer had been that his beloved had had nothing whatever to do with the murders, his position soon wavered, then reversed itself. Once he was incarcerated, he began to implicate Caril in the killings, and his emotions for her changed rapidly, and without apparent provocation, from love to hate. "My feelings toward Caril are of great regret for ever knowing her," Starkweather wrote, sitting at his table in his cell in the Nebraska State Penitentiary. "Our love in the beginning was very ardent and passionate. But as time went along our love tapered off to emotional passion and then began to fade out. Today my love for Caril is completely dead." If within hours of his capture he had written his parents denying Caril's involvement in the murders—"But dad i'm not real sorry for what i did cause for the first time me and Caril have more fun, she help me a lot, but if she comes back don't hate her she had *not* a thing to do with the killing all we wanted to do is get out of town"—within days he was insisting that Caril had killed two of the women victims. How appropriate this conclusion was, for the relationship had served its purpose both in hardening his resolve and adding sexual excitement to his task. She no longer played a meaningful role in his life and she now could take her place with the rest of humanity as the enemy. A few months later, he was willing to testify against her in court, and it was this testimony that was one of the prime factors that ensured her conviction.[32]

Death's Pursuit

> "The world is lifeless anyhow, like the people I killed."
>
> *Charles Starkweather*[33]

He looked at life through curiously deadened eyes: Little wonder then that all he saw seemed "lifeless." Paradoxically, the only thing that gave meaning to this universe of death-in-life was his adolescent fascination with death. Reinhardt noted that by the time Starkweather was seventeen, two years before the killings erupted, he had become "obsessed with a recurring delusion that Death had him 'marked,' and he took a 'strange bewildering delight'" in the thought. This delusion came to him in almost corporeal form when he was seventeen. "She comed [sic] in a dream," Starkweather remembered of Death's first appearance to him. "She tolded [sic] me . . . don't be in no hurry. I won't let you forget. One time Death comed [sic] to me with a coffin and tolded [sic] me to get in . . . then the coffin sailed away with me in it till it comed [sic] to a big fire. . . . The coffin sort of melted, I guess, I was down there on a street with great flames of fire on each side of me. But it wasn't hot like I'd always thought hell would be. . . . It was more like beautiful flames of gold . . . then I woke up."[34]

Similarly, Reinhardt observed that "Charles had other Death dreams when no word was spoken. These he believed were sent to remind him that 'earth-time' was running out." Starkweather explained this closing tryst with Death: "For always after one of those dreams I had a accident just like the one in the dream, only it wasn't so bad. . . . Oh, but it was not just in dreams [that Death came]. She comed [sic] when I was awake, too." Most often, Death came to his bedroom window just before dawn when he was still asleep. "I don't know how it was," he remembered, "but I would always wake up and see her standing there in the window . . . and all I could see would be the part from the waist up. It was a kind of half human and half bear . . . only it didn't have no neck. It just tapered off from a big chest to a small pointed head. . . . It didn't have no arms and no ears." These mystical visitations were sometimes accompanied by "mournful" whistling sounds: "It was close and loud at first, but it got further and further away and the sound became mournful and sad until I couldn't hear it no more. . . . For about a minute or two, I couldn't move my legs or arms." Yet Death instilled no fear in him: "The world on the other side couldn't be as bad as this one. . . . Besides, nobody has to tell me what a mean world this is. . . . I knowed that Death was coming, but I never thought it would be coming like this," he told Reinhardt. "Eleven people dead who wasn't expecting her and me here waiting." This mingled contempt and fascination for Death explained his love of fast and dangerous cars, for they assured him that "death was close by." He had even considered helping Death by crashing the car: "But, I guess if she had wanted any help she'd a tolded [sic] me."[35]

In a fundamental sense, Death became what he pursued, as it pursued him. He dreamt of "snarling faces, dreams of wishing death would come soon. Then I got so Death was a friend." With Caril beside him, he would pursue Death in the grand manner, making his mark upon the universe in a way no garbageman could, leaving messages that "couldn't rub out, like tracks cut in a rock." With Caril, "something worth killing for had come. The thought of dying was old to me. Something to live for, before dying, was new. . . . Why run away from Caril, why run from death, why go back to the hate and shame and hiding, when all that I wanted, all that was left was mine until the clock run down." He understood that his destiny had become "to live with Caril and die with Caril. Anyways I wanted her to see me go down shooting it out and knowing it was for her, for us; I guess for all this hateful world have [sic] made us for. . . . Sometimes I thought about murdering the whole human race. I never thought much about killing individuals."[36]

As he waited for death in his prison cell one night, his victims came to him "in a dream," he told Reinhardt. They gazed at him through the bars in the same way that Death had stared at him through his bedroom window. The ghost of the farmer August Meyer spoke to him: "You can't get out this way," Starkweather remembered him saying, "you'll have to go another way." When he recounted the dream, he concluded that "it makes everything even. . . . It evens what I done and what everybody is [sic] done. . . . These people were in my way." He even abandoned his fate to God, most forcefully when he was asked if he thought his sentence might be commuted: "Not if the old man upstairs is satisfied with me the way I am. What do I mean? Well, I'll tell you. . . . If He thinks I've suffered enough He'll let me go to the chair, [but if He does not], well, the old man wouldn't have nothing else to do but give me life. The old man upstairs wouldn't double-cross Death."[37]

Without regret, he would leave the universe that to his deadened eyes appeared as little more than a barren moonscape. "The world is lifeless anyhow, like the people I killed. It is just a hell of a world. It ain't worthy going back to anyhow." "[When] I go to the chair, I'll be no more dead than the people I killed. They was buried and their rel-

atives grieved. Only my mother would grieve for me. But millions
will read about me, I guess, and talk about me, don't you think?" It was
satisfaction enough that he would leave this sign of his passage.[38]

Class Consciousness

"They had me numbered for the bottom."

Charles Starkweather[39]

His loathing of the social system and its infinite gradations was matched
in intensity only by his romantic and sentimentalized view of nature. As
he wrote: "I found the beauty of the countryside, in forest and woods
of so many times while camping or hunting. At times instead of hunting I would set down against a large tree, and enjoy the scenery that
made me delightfully full of satisfaction. . . . My neck would be bent back
as I gazed above and between the jagged limbs, and branches of green-
ish, brown, and yellowish foliage, into the sky of miles, and miles, of
undiscover, unknown previously [sic] existence, and the more I sat and
gaze [sic] into the far miles of the sky a wave of something would come
over me, something like directness, and frankness, in a fascinating world
away from that of non-committed civilization." Yet if he loved nature
for its own qualities, it was clear that its prime attribute for him was as
a counterpoint to civilization and humanity. Inevitably, humanity
would intrude and spoil his reverie—"Sometimes the dreams . . . would
disappear with a quick flash at hearing the snap of a twig, or the sound
of a voice," and when the spell was broken, an "irresistible, and irre-
sponsible feeling would sweep over my soul." In the night, occasional
horrifying dreams would awaken him with a start, and only the shaft of
moonlight across his bed could calm him. "Sometimes," he told Reinhardt, "it took me away from the things I hated. . . . It made me forget."
The moonlight's glow would help him to forget his poverty temporarily, to forget the worn curtains and the broken furniture, and perhaps
even hint at mitigation: "I knowed [sic] better, but that I imagined, I
guess, it was what I wanted to imagine."[40]

None of our multiple murderers had quite such an anguished awareness of his position at the bottom of the social hierarchy, and only the
killer Mark Essex seemed to have felt such enraged despair. In the
midst of this, Starkweather sympathetically recognized the impotence
of his own slum-dwelling family. "My dad ain't to blame. . . . I just got
fed up with having nothing and being nobody. . . . Poverty gives you
nothing. People who are poor take what they can get." Marriage and
a conventional career were pointless, for "it would be the same thing
all over again." One of Caril's prime attractions was that she "never
cared what I looked like. . . . When we would go together there would
be no 'uppity' kids from big houses whose old man was a doctor or
president of a bank. We'd make people the way we wanted to make
them." He recognized and felt profoundly the hidden injuries of class:
"What did not make this world a good place to live in was that nobody
cared about me for what I could do. They hated me because of the way
I looked, and because I was poor and had to live in a goddamned
shack; it didn't matter what we all loved each other; that my mother
worked hard away from home to help support us children, and washed
our clothes and cooked and got us off to school. All these goddamn
kids cared about was: 'What kind of a job does your old man have?
What kind of a house do you live in? What do your legs look like? Are
you taller than any girl in school?'"[41]

His flesh crawled when he considered the clothes he wore, for he
could afford only to buy them in a second-hand store. As Reinhardt
observed, he was forced "to cover his nakedness with the clothes that
people who hated him had worn and thrown away." Starkweather felt
that "it was like wearing the skin of a dead man" to wear those clothes,
"only these people whose clothes covered [me] were not dead." He
would have to "see about that." He often wondered what it would be
like to "sleep in a big hotel, to eat in a fine restaurant, and ride in a pull-
man train. I used to stand outside the Cornhusker [an expensive restau-
rant] and watch the people eating inside. It filled me with hate; not the
people in there eating. I just hated the world that made me what I was.
They say this is a wonderful world to live in, but I don't believe I ever

did really live in a wonderful world. I haven't ever eaten in a high-class restaurant, never seen the New York Yankees play, or been to Los Angeles or New York City, or other places that books and magazines say are wonderful places to be at, there haven't [sic] been a chance for me to have the opportunity, or privilege, for the best things in life." He knew the folk sayings that "a man makes his own world," and must pay "for his mistakes"; but he knew also that "people who say such things wear nice clothes, eat in fine restaurants and know what to say to the girls." They were the sort who received the credit that was due them. "I got no credit for nothing, I got blamed for everything that somebody don't like." Like many before him, he decided that "I'll make my own world, I decided, I'll start today. Caril and me will have the kind of world we want."[42]

Searching for a career, he took his first job at the Newspaper Union, but "the people was always watching me. They had me numbered for the bottom. . . . I tried to do work good as anybody, even done things by myself that two of us should a done. . . . I used to think: now, no more hating, no more fighting. . . . I've done what is right . . . then something would happen to take it all out of me. I used to wonder why 'no goods' like some I knowed was getting praised for doing what they done. Guess it's 'cause they talked better 'n I did; 'cause they had better places to sleep in at night." It was here, at the bottom of the hierarchy, that the frustrated rebel emerged: "They made me hate. They couldn't a made me like them without their changing and they wasn't going to change." He turned for guidance to his family, but they could not understand his refusal to accept his position: "I am not blaming my old man. . . . Guess he didn't make me this trouble and I don't remember anything about my home life that wasn't better than what I had away from home. It's just that he was not much for understanding things, I guess. I mean things like a kid thinks about when nothing ain't going right."[43]

To ensure that he would see Caril every day when she came home from school, and perhaps to escape the visible and therefore punishing hierarchy of the Newspaper Union, he left his position and took another that symbolized his detested bottom-feeding role: He joined his brother on a garbage truck. "Throwing garbage" was a job he hated, and he internalized society's contempt for the task. His entrapment in it enraged him further: "A girl deserves better than a garbage hauler [and only] nincompoops . . . would do this dirty work. . . . A kid ain't no good without money." At daybreak, his brother's voice calling him to work made him want to "throw garbage in somebody's face." Now reduced to handling the offal of his betters, his sullen rage for his tormentors intensified: "Nobody knowed better than to say nothing to me when is a heaving their goddamn garbage [sic]." Now it began to dawn on him that only "dead people are all on the same level."[44]

Only the knowledge of his task, and his impending death, sustained him: "I knowed the end was coming, but it had a reason." The price he had had to pay in order to live was too high for his slim emotional pocketbook. "Misery, fear, hate . . . I guess I was frustrated. . . . Anyhow I got fed up being everybody's nobody . . . being unresponsible . . . that's what they was saying. . . . Well I got responsible didn't I? Can't anybody be a man if he pays for it? I was paying plenty for being a nobody. . . . Sure I had fun killing squirrels, rabbits and pheasants. They ain't responsible. They don't make their rules as you say. I never hated rabbits. Rabbits ain't never done me no harm. They didn't hate me. Now I said to myself, I guess it's time to be responsible, time to get mixed in something."[45]

Suddenly the task was both defined and imminent. He awoke one morning feeling "like a new man," with a new and strange sense of purpose: "Something like I never felt before. The cost will be payed [sic] and nobody can't never say he was cheated," he remembered resolving. The night before his first murder, he thought: "These braggarts and good people are not laughing at a stupid garbage type. . . . They'll have something real interesting to say after tomorrow. . . . I am not going to die like a rabbit. . . . I am going to have something worth dying about . . . and I'm not going to be the first one to die neither." Others before him, he thought, had murdered people with infinitely less justification: "They murdered people who never done them no harm. The people I murdered had murdered me. They murdered me slow like. I was better to them. I killed them in a hurry."⁴⁶

In the past, "sometimes the hate was so real I could feel it coming to life like something kind of dead or asleep and beginning to wake up and stir around. Then I always wanted to do something . . . maybe go out and rob a bank or throw garbage in some old bitch's face." But now that the tiger had been unleashed, he no longer felt the overwhelming frustrated hatred. "That isn't the way I felt when I killed them people. I killed Caril's parents because they tried to break us up. The kid was crying and there wasn't nothing to do with it. Them others, well, it was each that way out. Dead people don't talk. Besides they can't fight for nothing." What then was his ultimate aim? "I must get her away. I'll let her see that I'll kill for her." It would be a monumental gesture: "Soon, I'll be buried with the dead days. Better to be left to rot on some high hill behind a rock, and be remembered, than to be buried alive in some stinking place, and go to bed smelly like a garbage can every night." Still, the gesture was not to be an empty one, for not only was it a romantic declaration of love and hate, but it would also release him from the "stinking place. What kind of future do you think I'd have throwing garbage and picking up a whore . . . how long do you think I'd a lived? Forty years? . . . too long . . . ten years? . . . too long . . . better a week with the one who loved me for what I was."⁴⁷

He was that most dangerous of men, the one who has nothing to lose. "The world is lifeless anyhow," he said, "like the people I killed. It is just a hell of a world. It ain't worth going back to anyhow." He had no wish to return to a stigmatizing universe of "rich men's children, vulgar streetwalkers," and "crazy bosses. The more I looked at people the more I hated them because I knowed they wasn't any place for me with the kind of people I knowed [sic]. I used to wonder why they was here anyhow? A bunch of goddamn sons of bitches looking for somebody to make fun of . . . some poor fellow who ain't done nothing but feed chickens." It was time to make his move: "Everything was closing in on us fast like a trap-door that starts falling when the animal moves toward it. There was only one way of escape and that was toward the trap-door. The faster we moved the faster it seemed to fall."[48]

Toward the end of his killing spree, when he might have escaped had he headed resolutely west to Washington state, he turned back to Lincoln and drove straight to the upper-class district. Now he would spend his remaining "earth-time" marauding among his betters. But he did more than kill: Reinhardt asked him how he passed the time in the Ward home. "You don't think I just sit around in that mansion on my ass, do you?" He spent the day examining the furniture, lying on the beds and couches, absorbing the texture of upper-class life through its expensive springs and silken slip covers. Perhaps most important, the garbageman savored the sadistic revenge of ordering the mansion-dweller, Mrs. Ward, to serve him pancakes in the library. "Then," he said, "I decided I wanted a waffle." Mrs. Ward brought it to him, her penultimate act in life a servile one. "Ah yes," Starkweather reminisced, "they was nice to us." Later, in the quiet of his prison cell, he wished for nothing more than that his life's story would be read by millions: "Then I would go with my dreams fulfilled. . . . Only my story will live." Now fulfilled on death row, his headaches disappeared, and he slept deeply.[49]

The Ideological Authorities

"Nobody remembers a crazy man."

Charles Starkweather[50]

If it was important to Starkweather that he not be declared insane (as it was for so many other of our multiple murderers), for such a designation would invalidate both him and his mission, it was equally important to society that he *be* found "insane." Try as they might, however, the authorities could not do so. The press made a sustained attempt to diminish him, singling out in him (as mankind has done since time immemorial) the shared iniquities of the generation they had created. "If Charles Starkweather were a case apart," read an editorial in Omaha's *World-Herald*, "a biological accident, a monstrous freak of nature, then today all Americans could take a deep breath of relief and give thanks that his mad career of murder had been brought to an end. But although his crimes were of a violence beyond precedent, nevertheless there was a certain flavor to the Starkweather story which brought back to mind a thousand others which have been told in recent years to an unbelieving America. The sideburns, the tight blue jeans, the black leather jacket—these have become almost the uniform of juvenile hoodlums. And the snarling contempt for discipline, the blazing hate for restraint, have become a familiar refrain in police stations and juvenile courts throughout the land. To a greater degree than ever before, influences are pulling some youngsters away from the orbit of the home, the school, and the church, and into the asphalt jungle. That is the problem." They were quite right, of course, and it was appropriate that they should single out Starkweather for what they saw as not his insanity, but his terrifying *normality*. The authorities and the public were moved: They correctly sensed the beginning of a fracture line that might shatter all the traditional structures; and in this process, they saw the rebel Starkweather playing a significant symbolic role that must be crushed. At that late stage, all they could hope to do was to use his impending execution as a warning to all rebellious youth. To underline their point, they circulated his maudlin capitulation—his article, "Rebellion"—in popular magazines, abridging his autobiography to show only its truncated remorse.[51]

The medical and psychiatric examinations were apposite illustrations of the curious tendency for psychiatric diagnosis to accord with the needs of the "side" (prosecution or defense) which has hired the psychiatrist. This revealed itself even in something as relatively "objective" as IQ testing. The prosecution, who wished Starkweather to be found culpable (which required that he be declared "sane"), measured his IQ some thirteen points higher than the defense, who wished him to be found insane and not responsible—although Allen suggested here that this disparity may have been less a function of test subjectivity than of Starkweather's own active cooperation with the prosecution: "He simply hadn't tried as hard for the defense." He may have been right, but certainly his lawyer stretched the truth when he insisted that Starkweather's IQ was "only a point or two above an idiot," a remark that Starkweather was profoundly displeased to hear.[52]

The diagnostic differences were even apparent in their analyses of his physical condition. The defense lawyer, Allen, wrote: "made an unsubstantiated claim that he could have a brain tumor or 'pressure on the brain.'" Attempts to "find" some legally useful disorder were frustrated by Starkweather himself, who hindered defense lawyers at every opportunity. He refused to allow the defense's doctors to administer an electroencephalogram to test for brain damage, or to explore his perforated eardrum, which the enthusiastic defense suggested could indicate an infection near the brain, and raise the possibility of organic brain damage. Ultimately, the defense medical team's physical examination could only draw attention to the unremarkable facts that Starkweather was "a short, stocky young fellow with breasts somewhat large but muscularly developed, with tenderness in the spot where we usually expect it to be if a peptic ulcer is present, with a hole in his left eardrum, which apparently has been there quite a long time, with decreased deep tendon reflexes." On the other hand, the prosecution psychiatrists insisted that their examination disclosed no evidence whatever of brain damage or disease.[53]

The prosecution's psychiatric witnesses—two psychiatrists and a psychologist—all testified that they had examined Starkweather and found him to be sane, with no evidence of psychosis: They concluded that he suffered from a minor personality disorder. They agreed that this disorder was insufficiently debilitating to warrant committal to an institution, and reminded the court that if he were committed, he would inevitably be found sane and then released. Their specific diagnosis was "that Charles had a personality disorder characterized by emotional instability, considerable emotional insecurity and impulsiveness, [and] that this would fit into a category under the antisocial personality disorder." One of the psychiatrists felt certain that Stark-

weather knew the "enormity of his acts" and that he "seemed to recognize the nature and consequences of the acts he had committed." The
two state psychiatrists agreed that "Starkweather's comprehension"
was "adequate" or "good," and one of them commented on his "very
fine memory ability," concluding that he was "neither medically nor
legally insane."[54]

The defense psychiatrists agreed with each other that Starkweather
was suffering from a diseased mind. One stated that, "my observations
lead me to the opinion that Charles Starkweather is suffering from a
severe mental disease or illness of such a kind as to influence his acts
and has prevented him from using the knowledge of right and wrong
at the time of commission of such an act. A number of important facts
were found. One of the very important things which I found was that
he is suffering from a severe warping of the emotional faculties; that is,
he is unable to experience feelings that other people do. People don't
mean anything to him. They are no more than a stick or a piece of
wood to this boy." He thought that if Starkweather had been examined
before the murder spree, his disturbance would certainly have been
detected, and concluded that "this person is dangerously sick and has
to be put under maximum security because he is dangerous." He
thought Starkweather's perceptions were "distorted. He will pick out
things which are not important because of his particular way of looking at things. The act of killing meant to him no more than stepping on
a bug. You can take a creature out of a jungle and tame him and maybe
develop a surface crust of being domesticated . . . but . . . when such a
creature tastes blood it breaks through and a wild rampage occurs in
which a primitive impulse comes back." Following this fanciful diagnosis, this psychiatrist refused to give a name to Starkweather's mysterious "disease," saying only that he did not believe in conventional
psychological terminology.[55]

A second defense psychiatrist commented on how easy it had been
to fluster Starkweather, and found him deficient in his performance
under stress, from which he was able to conclude: "If things would
come at him one at a time, slowly as in a routine job, he would be able

to handle these things, but if things began to flood in on him such as
the work not going right, the sprinkler in the ceiling coming on, or
somebody yelling and a whistle going all at once, I don't think he
could function. . . . He would be like a frightened animal." Starkweather
was in this confused state during the murder spree, the psychiatrist
believed. He concluded that Starkweather had never developed into an
adult human being: "Yes, he walks around in the body of a human
being, but the thoughts and the feelings are not there like they are in
an ordinary person, who has learned by being around others and has
feelings for them, and in relation to them. This is the way we learn to
be people. I don't think he has ever learned to be a person."[56]

A third defense psychiatrist testified that Starkweather had a kind of
stunted emotional repertoire: "I would say that his range of emotions
is limited, that he feels perhaps two that we are familiar with: anger and
fear, or anxiety. The other shadings of emotions—pity, sympathy, the
feeling of attachment for another individual (for the entire person and
not just a quality or an attribute of them) is something I think he is
striving for but actually only has a dim recognition of. . . . When I
asked him what happened and how he felt through this when he committed these acts, he has always come back with the same thing: 'Self-
defense.'" He thought that Starkweather's cheerful behavior during
and after the murders "would indicate a diseased mind. A person who
had committed the act of killing three people including a young child
and then returned to friends and family and appeared to be normal and
cheerful was not able to feel things the way other people [did]." Still,
the defense medical team admitted that his condition could not be
regarded as legal insanity, but declined to give a label to Starkweather's
condition.[57]

For their part, neither Starkweather nor his family wanted him to be
declared insane, although their motives were surely quite different.
The family did not wish the "taint" of insanity to stain their family tree;
and, on occasion, Starkweather himself pretended that it was to save
them embarrassment that he resisted such a categorization. "I have
always loved my mother, I am sorry about causing her so much trou-

ble. . . . When she cried at the court house . . . she was crying for something already dead. How could she know that I was going [to] the chair for her—for her and my sister and every one of my family. . . . I could of give them the 'taunt' [sic] of insanity just to save my life. It wouldn't a done no good no how 'cause I was already dead, or same as dead. . . . nobody ever gets back hisself [sic] again. Wouldn't it be better for me to be dead than having my family taunted with insanity? [sic]" Yet it should be clear that this pseudo-heroic pretense was at best something that reinforced, not caused, his rigid stance on the insanity question. He was terrified that "they might try to prove insane," not because of any altruistic concern for his family, but because "nobody remembers a crazy man." Indeed, he resisted every attempt to thus invalidate him and his mission, ultimately cooperating fully with the prosecution and resisting his own defense team. He sat through the jury selection with a "half-smirk" on his face, "seeming either scornful or bored with the proceedings," but "clutched the corner of the counsel table and glared" when his lawyer placed his IQ near that of an idiot. The jury took less than twenty-four hours to find him guilty of murder in the first degree, and to specify the death penalty.[58]

Buried Alive

"Better to be left to rot on some high hill behind a rock, and be remembered, than to be buried alive in some stinking place."

Charles Starkweather[59]

The last months of his life were spent, for the most part, in the elaboration and justification of his rebellious image. In the photographs taken of him at the time, as he was led in chains by heavily armed policemen, an expression of sheer vindictive delight dominated his face. Alone in his cell, the photographs revealed only the distant aloofness of the spy who had come in from the cold, or the soldier who had bravely completed his mission. So consistent was this personal stance, this maintenance of image, that Reinhardt was moved to complain that "in approximately thirty hours of interviewing I never witnessed a sign of genuine remorse in this killer." How could it have been otherwise, when to show remorse would be to capitulate utterly, to render meaningless his sacrifices?[60]

The Killings

What were the origin and meaning of Starkweather's apparently meaningless spree? It is natural to believe—and certainly he himself encouraged that belief—that he had merely gone on a kind of uncoordinated rampage, murdering in "self-defense" anyone who got in his way. But he did not go at random: He chose specific places and types of persons (as did all our multiple murderers) because they were in actual or symbolic relation to the forces that denied him what he wished from life.

His first victim was the gas station attendant, a clean-cut and apparently decent young man with, judging from his photographs, the conservative air of someone who had in fact just been discharged from the armed forces. Allen has told us that "whether Colvert lived or died depended if he recognized Charlie through the disguise," but there is much doubt as to whether this was the case. He had already angered Starkweather the day before when he had refused the latter credit to purchase a stuffed toy dog as a Christmas gift. Further, if there had been no clear intent to kill, there would have been no late-night drive into the countryside (since Colvert had not recognized him, or resisted, until he was shoved from the car on the lonely road). To punish the innocent is the fundamental outrage committed by all our multiple murderers, but from Starkweather's perspective, Colvert's "flaunted" respectability and links to those who controlled wealth were sufficient condemnation. Soon, he would work more closely toward what he thought were his real enemies.[61]

The second set of kills, the three members of the Bartlett family, was central to his mission. They *might* have lived had they not tried so spiritedly to deny him the companion and witness he needed for the proper discharge of his mission, but that is unlikely. They stood in exact relation to what he wanted (Caril) but would be denied for all time. Their verbal and physical assaults upon him did not, as he claimed, require homicide to terminate them: He could in fact have simply taken Caril and left. But he chose not to do so, and for reasons that make perfect sense when viewed from within the logic of the spree. Its purpose was to strike a blow at those "lifeless" ones who denied him his own life: Who better then to annihilate than the Bartletts? How better could he express his disdain for his victims than by living in their home close by their rotting bodies, fornicating with their daughter, and eating their food?

The killing of the old family friend, the farmer August Meyer, seems especially cruel and inexplicable, for had they not broken bread together many times before? Having shared his hunting trophies with Meyer, he must have known that the spoils from an attack on Meyer could yield little more than a few dollars, and a gun or two. Certainly his "explanation" that he decided to kill him because he had left his farm's entry lane uncleared makes no sense at all. Neither does his claim of an unprovoked attack by Meyer. This murder cannot be understood until it is compared to its opposite: to the sparing of the life of the passing farmer who had helped extricate their stranded car from the mud. Rather than killing him, Starkweather insisted on paying him for the service. The answer surely lies then in each one's perceived relationship to treasure he coveted. Meyer, whatever his own slim resources, was a landowner, and one to whom Starkweather had often been forced to pay tribute, as "serf," in the form of shared game; whereas the passing farmer seemed to be a pure proletarian like himself, demanding no tithes and offering only kindness. In this sense, he was slowly killing his way up the social ladder.[62]

Still, Jensen and King, the young couple who were next to die, also offered only kindness—a lift and good will—and they received their own execution as recompense. If to us they must seem the least likely candidates for execution, to Starkweather and Caril Fugate they must have seemed virtually the *most* likely. If Jensen and King were not wealthy, they certainly bore all the marks of happy and conventional middle-class America, which is to say they stood as perfect symbols of that which the spree was designed to assault. They were two unexceptional young people who, according to Allen, "saw nothing wrong with the world, nothing major to rebel against." Every fiber of their being must have radiated the fact that they "had never been alienated from anything," and it was thus entirely appropriate, given the logic of Starkweather's scheme, to strike down these wholesome representatives of the established order. It was not clear if it was he who had mutilated King (for he later claimed that Caril had done so in a fit of jealousy), but it would be in no way inconsistent with his task.[63]

Still, the young couple was merely middle-class. With each killing he had worked his way closer to the apex, up the social hierarchy from gas station attendant to working-class family to small landowner to middle-class persons. Now it was time to go directly to the source. It was for this reason that his otherwise inexplicable decision—to turn away from escape to Washington state and drive back to Lincoln's country club district—can now appear as entirely rational. The mission would not have been properly discharged without a direct assault on those at the top of the social pyramid. Who better to select than a family from the wealthy area in which he had daily humiliated himself, handling their waste and offal, and performing their menial chores? His behavior inside the Ward home is especially revealing: in his savoring of the material culture of the rich and his insistence that the lady of the house, not the maid, wait upon him. The maid was no landed aristocrat, but she was clearly part of the mansion and the established order—reason enough to destroy her too. Starkweather claimed that Caril had dispatched the maid; but it matters not, for either way the mission was clearly defined and responsibly completed.

The only murder which later troubled Starkweather was his last: the salesman Collison—who did not fit the hierarchical climb, and who was killed for purely utilitarian reasons. Reinhardt thought Starkweather's compunctions about this murder must have been because he could not "rationalize self-defense. . . . He thought people would think him cowardly because of the way the salesman died." But viewed from our perspective, no such rationalization is necessary: In fact, Collison was killed because he stood in the way, pure and simple. He was only a marginal member, at best, of the oppressive class. In killing him, Starkweather felt the same awkwardness that Edmund Kemper had felt upon killing young Aiko Koo, whose middle-class credentials he suspected to be marginal.[64]

The Meaning

Those who perceive themselves to be among the truly dispossessed—including the killers Starkweather, Panzram, and Essex—all share the notion that the bottom of the social order is the only niche they will be allowed to occupy. Too ambitious and self-regarding to accept this position, too cynical to sustain any hope of escape from it (or too acute to be comforted by idle dreams), their lives are rendered hopeless. Only a spectacular adventure, like a killing spree, can give meaning to one whose despair is so extravagant: Only in this way can they leave their mark upon the world. It is thus entirely consistent with their perceived position that they formulate their homicidal sprees, and do so with a remarkable sense of class consciousness. Starkweather castigated other murderers who "murdered people who never done them no harm." To him, his own were justified, despite the fact that he had never known half of them, because in terms of their relation to the established order, they were "the people [who] . . . had murdered me . . . slow like."[65]

A rigidly stratified society maintains itself not just through force of arms, but by keeping its lower denizens oblivious to their fate. As the French scholars Peter and Favret observe, "Enduring the unlivable, day in and day out," wading through lives "devoid of all future, deprived of all prospects," they become problematic only if they perceive their conundrum and abandon all hope: "Should one of them perceive it even for a moment, his whole world falls apart." Such a man was Starkweather: He knew his fate and dismissed it as without value. Such men are dangerous, for they can proceed to carve their mark and exact their revenge with neither scruple nor remorse. Starkweather's biographer,

Reinhardt, insisted that "the answer must surely be found in the warped values this boy read into life. His ego was empty and defeated; he imagined himself rejected by society, as symbolized by social position and power. These things—position and power—he could not hope to attain and hold by honest toil. Without them, as he had come to believe, life was worthless." But Reinhardt was a simple criminologist, whose unwarped values were formed during his own success in life. Surely there was little "warped" about Starkweather's perception of his inevitable fate; and certainly he *was* "rejected," and would continue to be so unless he accepted the lowly position his life offered him. As a guardian of the social order, Reinhardt spoke for many when he demanded that Starkweather adjust to his position, and carry the garbage without complaint.[66]

However, Starkweather saw all too clearly that "a kid ain't no good without money," that only "nincompoops" haul garbage and accept the social stigma that goes with the act. His almost frenzied sensitivity to his low estate turned early to pseudo-radical protest, which took the form of his rebellion. His "sense of outrage grew to striving, to throw, to bend, to hurt and most of all to beat those who teased me," and to turn his boiling hatred on "everybody other than my family," who shared his position and nursed some of his wounds. Killing those who possessed what he wanted, who stood in relation to him as overlord (in reality or as symbol), "makes everything even. . . . It evens what I done and what every body is done [sic]." Without hope of escape, death for him was no obstacle or dilemma, for "the world on the other side couldn't be as bad as this one," could not exceed "the mean world this is." The alternative future he saw so clearly for himself—of "throwing garbage and picking up a whore"—offered insufficient recompense for his humiliation. His relationship with Caril had made him understand fully why he so hated the world: It was because he would not be able to keep her, for "poverty gives you nothing." For a brief time he would create his own world, a world in which he kept what he wanted. Then he would depart in a blaze of snarling glory. "I started a new kind of thinking after I met her. . . . Something worth killing for had come.

It was supposed to be my way out, the last fling before the ending. Guess it's better than just going out like a light with no flicker."[67]

Capitulation

If Starkweather displayed no remorse whatever to Reinhardt, his 200-page autobiography did incorporate a few pages of pseudo-remorse, which were published in a popular magazine under the title "Rebellion," to draw a suitable moral. Those few pages were seized upon by a popular press anxious to suppress the story of his true motivation and to promulgate a kind of morality play in which the consequences of rebellion were clearly outlined. We cannot know if his claims were "sincere" in any sense at all; but even if they were not, it would be by no means inconsistent with the spirit of most multiple murderers finally to acquiesce in this way, to accept the morality of the dominant class. After all, they were never revolutionaries, only rebels angered at their own lowly estate. Having made their radical protest, their anger is dispersed and their headaches and sleepless nights abated. They can now make a separate peace. It should come as small surprise then to see the photograph of the killer with his autobiographer during his last weeks, looking bookish and now smoking a pipe—the 1950s badge of college status.

In his widely distributed capitulation/autobiography, which resurrected all the moralistic clichés of some small-town fundamentalist preacher, Starkweather wrote: "Around eleven o'clock the night Caril Fugate and I were apprehended, it was very quiet in the Douglas, Wyoming, jail. I was lying upon the top bunk and was feeling low and hopeless. Then a clear perception of truth came to me of the villainous and outraging [sic] acts committed, and I thought I would vomit. It all seem like a fantastic dream, but it was no dream, and I knew it. Exhausted as I was, I couldn't sleep. I simply laid there, staring at a couple names that had been scratched into the steel wall, and was lost in my own thoughts. I said to myself, why? Why, why, had everything had to happen to me? . . . I determined then that I would write these thoughts and remembrances down. For I wanted to do something for my parents. I had caused them enough trouble. And I wanted to warn other boys so they wouldn't take the road I took." [68]

"Today," he continued, in what must stand as one of the least convincing documents in the annals of multiple murder, "my feelings are of great sorrow and remorse for the people I killed. And for the heartache and sorrow and grief caused people who lost their loved ones. I pray that God will be forgiving of what has been done. . . . Today I know that this was wrong. . . . Today, after a year of imprisonment, I can count my life in hours. I have had a great deal of time for thought and to retrace back over my life. I hold no fear for the electric chair, it is the price I am paying for taking the lives of others. . . . Now I feel no rebellion toward anything or anyone, only love and peace. I received this love and peace through the Bible. And if I could talk to young people today I would tell them to go to school, to go to Sunday school, to go to church and receive the Lord Jesus Christ as your own personal Savior. Our God is a kind God. . . . And I would say to them to obey their parents or guardians, and stay away from bad influences, and never undertake anything that you don't understand, and if in doubt don't do it. And most of all don't ever let your intentions and emotions overpower you. If I had followed these simple little rules, as I was advised to do many times, I would not be where I am today." Whatever his motives may have been in composing this hymn to the republic—and we can only speculate—he was neither the first nor the last rebel to have his mind wonderfully concentrated by his impending execution and the heavenly events that might transpire shortly thereafter.[69]

In any case, by the day he died he had reverted to the persona of the swaggering soldier of fortune. Those who watched his execution and what preceded it commented unfavorably on the "stiffness" with which he gave his mother a last embrace, the quick and abstracted handshake he gave his father, and the correct cult-figure style with which he rammed his hands in his pockets and walked boldly ahead of the guard. Reinhardt and the other observers were incensed that he showed neither remorse nor a fear of death, for it invalidated their punishment. No one seemed impressed that he remained in character to the end, striding briskly into the death chamber, and advising his executioners to tighten the straps that bound his arms and chest to the electric chair. When asked if he had any last words, he "pressed his lips together and emphatically said no." The switch which sent 2200 volts coursing through his body was pulled three times: The first shock stunned him, the second rendered him unconscious, and the third "stopped his heart."[70]

10 A Historical Overview

> "Other sinnes onley speake; Murther shreikes
> out."
>
> *The Duchess of Malfi*

This book has explicated the texts left by a half-dozen killers of our time. It has not focused on these murderers because their thoughts or acts are of any merit, but because it is only through a detailed examination of their careers that we can hope to understand the origin and meaning of their activities. We have taken as our starting point the observation of Robert Darnton that it is precisely "when we run into something that seems unthinkable to us [that] we may have hit upon a valid point of entry into an alien mentality." Having done this, we will now try to marry the great historical and anthropological enterprises. In doing so, we will "have puzzled through to the native's point of view" and mounted an explanation of the inexplicable. So far we have tried to reveal the immediate motives behind the killers' acts: Now our task is to transcend the immediate, to suggest that these motives are neither insane nor random but buried deeply in the social order, part of a continuously evolving social process.[1]

The murderer of strangers has probably always been among us. However much we may wish to dismiss him as a freak, an aberration, or an accident, his tastes and desires are part of the human repertoire, the human experience, and the human capability. Nor must we dismiss him and his behavior as meaningless, for mankind is a gregarious and social species, and anything its members do has some social meaning. But wherein lies the origin of the social process we have now described, that sequence of events which so deforms a man that he comes to think of himself as a kind of automaton, a "robot" going through the motions of social life without any hope that future events might make his life endurable? The killers customarily explain themselves in conventional ideas borrowed from the wider culture, as did the torturer and multiple murderer, *Joseph Kallinger*, in his autobiographical poem, "The Unicorn in the Garden."[2]

When I was a little boy,
My adoptive parents,
Anna and Stephen,
Killed the unicorn in my garden

Exiled from the street,
Isolated from other children,
I lived among shoes and knives and hammers.
Unknown, unwanted, unloved,
I learned to shape soles, replace heels, drive nails.
My own soul was hidden from me by the shop's
Dead world.
A robot to their will,
I died with the unicorn in my garden.

Yet this self-pitying interpretation leaves unanswered so many questions. If his own adoptive parents were so insensitive to his needs, why was he dramatically more so when he tortured and murdered his own small son? If his childhood was so difficult, was his adulthood (he had a bearable occupation, in which he was very highly regarded, and a loving wife and family, who seemed devoted to him) provocative of anything resembling his gruesome acts? I think not. It is therefore incumbent upon us to look much more deeply into the historical process and its impact upon the lives of individuals, if we are ever to have anything resembling a clear understanding of these men.

Before we do so, let us be clear about the manner of beast we have been discussing, and how he stands in relation to other "criminal" species. He is not quite like the majority, whose thefts of *property* garner a combination of financial profit and "the intoxicating pleasure of intense activity." Such property offenses attract bank robbers, political commissars, and corporate executives, not the men of whom we speak (who reap neither wealth nor security from their crimes). Neither is the multiple murderer quite like those who commit crimes against the *person* (be it rape, assault, or even homicide), for these offenses tend to be little more than a demonstration of individual power and a cathartic release of rage. Our multiple murderers transcend mere catharsis and temporary gratification: Their aim is a more ambitious one, a kind of sustained sub-political campaign directed toward "the timelessness of oppression and the order of power." But their protest is not on behalf of others, only themselves; their anguish is trivial, not profound; and they punish the innocent, not the guilty. It is thus only an extreme version of other nihilistic crimes, in which the killer typically reverses all social values as his only way of making "a demonstration to the authorities" in a manner so forceful that they must consider it. Since all he is protesting is his lack of a crisp identity and his refusal to tolerate the position society has allocated him, it is less than tragic—even ironic, but intellectually unacceptable—that what Peter and Favret call a "clumsy psychiatry" tries to declare him insane and suggest that:

> . . . the natives speech had no weight, was not even an effect of monstrosity; such criminals were only disturbed children who played with corpses as they played with words. The resentment they displayed had no reason for its existence; it was merely a product of their imagination.[3]

There is one problem that remains undiscussed and it is central to any biographical enterprise: If we can speak for the mass of humanity in sociological terms, how can we hope to do so for any individual? According to the late historical sociologist Philip Abrams, "The problem of accounting sociologically for the individual in particular is really only a more precise version of the problem of accounting for individuals in general." Analyzed in historical terms, "Lenin and Luther, the Sun King and Shakespeare no more elude or defy sociological explanation than do Russian proletarians in 1900." Abrams insists, and our data force us largely to concur, that "becoming a deviant is not a matter of personal or social pathology, social disorganization, deprivation, broken homes, viciousness, bad company or chance but of *a negotiated passage to a possible identity*" in which the individual can only be understood as "creatively seizing opportunities for personal self-definition"—as did all our multiple murderers.

Individuals are their biographies. And insofar as a biography is fully and honestly recorded what it reveals is some historically located history of self-construction—a moral career in fact. The setting of the biography is this or that historically given system of probabilities or life chances. The biography realizes some life chances within that system and perforce abandons others.

The point then is that to understand an exceptional individual, we must observe "the meshing of life-history and social history in a singular fate"; which is to say that we must look at the social system's matrix of choices and opportunities, rewards and punishments, in terms of which each individual calculates his future. Later in this chapter, we will suggest that nowhere more than in modern America is an individual likely to negotiate the identity of a multiple murderer.[4]

Yet the problem remains that while many people are subject to the same tainted origins and thwarted ambitions, only a tiny minority of them become killers. Why then do most of them refuse to do so? There are no data that would allow us to address the problem in any scientific fashion, no control group of biographies of individuals who have been diverted from the formative process at different stages. Yet it seems most likely that such people (the vast majority) are touched, however superficially, by some person or institution that renders their lives bearable—offering the common life of "quiet desperation" in place of the massive refusal of self and life that characterizes our killers. We can only posit that somewhere in the journey from institutionalized or illegitimate child to lofty but thwarted ambition, some family member, a lover, a job, or group membership (or the hope of any of these) offers most people a taste of fulfillment and interrupts their passage to murderous identities.

The Literature

> "For crimes against persons (murder, rape, assault) we have no theory as to the value of such offenses, and hence no theory as to what would affect the returns from such crimes."
>
> *Ralph Andreano and John Siegfried*[5]

Homicide

The poverty of conventional explanation is nowhere better represented than in the above quotation from a group of economists who confess to being bewildered by a crime which offers no economic return. The other social sciences have fared rather better in their attempts to deal with homicide, at least in its "normal" manifestations. We have already demonstrated that, at least in theory, single and multiple murder are quite different phenomena, with profoundly different characteristics. The psychiatrist Lunde has made it clear that "the most important single contrast between mass murderers and murderers of a single person is a difference in their relationships to the victims," the former killing strangers, the latter killing intimates. This curious phenomenon of the murder of strangers is extremely rare in so-called "primitive" societies, a fact which social scientist Stuart Palmer corroborates with anthropological data showing that "in the vast majority of non-literate societies analyzed, 41 out of 44, homicidal victims and offenders are rarely if ever strangers." Nevertheless, it is in modern, industrializing societies that multiple "recreational" murder becomes a major homicidal theme. In criminologist Wolfgang's classic study of 550 homicides in 1958 in Philadelphia, 12.2 percent of the killings were between strangers; and the FBI report that 15.5 percent of the 22,516 murders committed in the U.S. in 1981 were between strangers.[6]

The perpetrators of the types of murder are also profoundly different. Virtually all social analysts agree that single murder is the province of the truly disenfranchised. "It is the oppressed who are the homicidal," writes Palmer. "The poor, the uneducated, those without legitimate opportunities, respond to their institutionalized oppression with outward explosions of aggression." This notion of exactly who the oppressed are has been much refined in the current debate on whether it is absolute poverty or relative inequality (or subcultural variation) which actually accounts for homicides. Nevertheless, Williams' tentative conclusion in the sociological journals remains that "racial economic inequality is a major source of criminal violence in the United States," and that "poverty, in addition to racial inequality, also provides 'fertile soil for criminal violence.'" It is obvious that our multiple murderers are drawn from very different social niches, for they are rarely from the ranks of the truly oppressed; they are rarely women or black. Indeed, they are generally white and gainfully employed, and, sometimes, have reasonable expectations of "brilliant" futures. They are not at all the same men who kill an intimate in a moment of rage or venality, and whose generally spontaneous acts are not part of any organized and meaningful campaign. Lunde was quite right then to berate the scholars of homicide for their "tendency to assume that the single fact of having committed a murder is a sufficient basis for identifying a class of people, murderers" who are essentially the same, for nothing could be further from the truth.[7]

There are perspectives on homicide other than the purely sociological, but they tend to be mired in irrelevancy or based on mechanisms that do not exist. Perhaps the most popular of these has been the *pseudo-biological* school, which has held a certain sway since the nine-

teenth-century criminologist Lombroso began measuring the fore-
heads of Italian criminals and the twentieth-century criminologists, the
Gluecks, assessed the testicles of American delinquents—all searching
for the "criminal physical type." This tradition tends to fixate on such
unfathomable matters as the purported brain temperatures of murderers, and has long ago been revealed as ideology masquerading as science. The "discovery" of the XYY chromosomes is perhaps the best
known example of this nonsense: Many unsubstantiated claims have
been made that the possession of this chromosome inclines the victim
toward violence (including falsely attributing such XYY chromosomes
to Richard Speck, the Chicago nurse-murderer). These notions persist
in the popular culture despite the fact that later studies have established
that only a small proportion of violent offenders actually have XYY
chromosomes. Furthermore, the imprisoned offenders who did have
the XYY chromosomes were actually *less* likely to have committed violent crimes than those with "normal" chromosomes. Indeed, the only
reasonable conclusion that has so far come out of the biological
approach is sociobiologist Edward O. Wilson's observation that there
is no evidence whatever for any universal aggressive instinct (as had
been posited by ethologists such as Lorenz and Ardrey), and that
human "behavior patterns do not conform to any general innate
restrictions." Sadly for the scientific enterprise, most "sociobiolo-
gists"—even ones as literate as Melvin Konner—simply ignore the
reality that human evolution's super-development of the cortex (or
thinking, conscious part of the brain) has overridden any instinctive or
genetically coded behaviors among humans. Similarly, they ignore the
reality that if human behavior were genetically determined, it would be
everywhere the same instead of ranging from the gentility of the
"primitive" Fore peoples of New Guinea to the violence of South
America's Yanomamo.[8]

The *psychological* tradition also looks for the cause of aggression
within the individual, but finds it buried in the psyche rather than in
the chromosome. Here, the assumption which runs throughout the literature is that anyone who murders must be suffering from some form

of psychopathology, a dubious assumption indeed when working-class culture so obviously venerates violent display as an intrinsic manifestation of manhood. The psychologists and psychiatrists differ as to where they find the cause of this disorder. The psychiatrist Abrahamsen points to "persistent internal conflict between the environment around them and the world within them—the world of infantile sexual and life-preserving drives," a conflict which is caused by some traumatic experience in early childhood (before the child is two!). The psychologist Megargee hypothesizes that the violent criminal virtually always "has" one of two types of personalities, either "undercontrolled" or "overcontrolled," which leaves the critic marveling at how many walk the tightrope between the two. Still, two of America's most gifted psychiatrists refute their profession's stance. Lunde notes that "the incidence of psychosis among murderers is no greater than the incidence of psychosis in the total population"; and Willard Gaylin readily admits that psychiatry occupies a "primitive position" regarding "the nature of the cause of the disease." My criticism here is not that psychology and psychiatry have nothing to contribute to the study of murder, for they certainly do; but rather that they, no more than a pseudo-biology, cannot account for variations in homicide rates over time or between societies. Their special gift in fact is not at all to account for cause—for that lies within tensions generated in the social order—but to analyze the process in which the individual psyche accommodates itself to its environment.[9]

Multiple Murder

If the literature on homicide has a certain richness about it, curiously, no such assessment can be made about the subject of our inquiry. Multiple murder has attracted very little specialized attention and should the reader glance through a dozen books, he will have mastered the number which have devoted themselves exclusively to the phenomenon. The first is still the best; but it (criminologist Bolitho's *Murder for Profit*) concerns itself only with the mendacious economic form that we ignore here—killing for profit. However, Bolitho's comments, now almost eighty years old, repay close examination. He noted then what those who followed him overlooked, that the killers were no "deranged automata" and that they were "the worst men, not madmen."

> If they very commonly construct for themselves a life—
> romance, a personal myth in which they are the maltreated hero,
> which secret is the key of their life, in such comforting day-
> dreams many an honest man has drugged himself against despair.

He observed that many of them thought of themselves as being in a kind of "social war, in which his hand is against society, and all is fair," but he understood that this is a common way of thinking among any "men in an unsheltered corner of this competitive world." He concluded with a remarkably sophisticated recognition of the complicity of the modern nation-state in the creation of these multiple murderers, remarking of the Fritz Haarmann case in Germany between the wars that: "The State had used all its best tools upon him: church, prison, army, school, family, asylum—it can hardly disclaim direct responsibility from the result."[10]

What might have been the beginning of a rich tradition of inquiry soon dissolved. In 1928, two years after the publication of Bolitho's book, criminologist Guy Logan published his *Masters of Crime*, which purported to be a study of multiple murder. In fact, however, it was merely unanalyzed case material, and the subject lay unstudied for another thirty years. Then two books appeared in 1958. Criminologist Grierson Dickson's *Murder by Numbers* focused on what today we would call serial murderers, and argued that their motives were either "profit" or "perversion." Regrettably, his work is purely descriptive, and he has no explanation for the phenomenon, merely noting in passing the "unfortunate origins" of the killers and that "parental influence was either absent or hostile." He did however observe one of the striking qualities of the killers, the fact that "lack of economic security does not seem a factor to be considered, as few of our subjects came from really poverty-stricken homes"; and he registered the conclusion that "not one of our perverts could have had that feeling, so comforting to a youngster, that he was a normal boy among other normal boys . . . [for] all of our perverts felt themselves to be set apart from their fellows, mostly by a sense of shame or inferiority." Still, he does not tell us *why* this should be so.[11]

In that same year, crime writer Philip Lindsay published *The Mainspring of Murder,* which again rehashed the classical cases without venturing into much explanation. Yet Lindsay came the closest, despite the fact that he devoted only a few paragraphs in his attempt. "Mass Murder," Lindsay wrote, "is largely a modern phenomenon."

> It begins its great career in the late eighteenth century, growing stronger during the nineteenth century until it arrives in full real horror in the twentieth century. Why? One point which cannot be avoided is its link with industrialism. With the dying of a pastoral England and the growth of industry with wretched communities gathered in towns and cities, the spirit of hatred grew to fury and the lost ones struck at a world they distrusted and feared.

Having glimpsed the key to the puzzle, he passes on, whining evermore about the advance of socialism and the collapse of individuality in modern society. Still, he also noted the strange paradox that it did not seem to be economic insecurity (which had always been with us), but personal and spiritual insecurity that formed the breeding ground for the modern multiple murderer.[12]

Until the late 1980s, when the subject became academically respectable, the only modern authority was Donald Lunde, whose *Murder and Madness* largely concerns itself with multiple murderers who are, in contrast to single murderers, "almost always *insane.*" To Lunde, the killers are either victims of a paranoid schizophrenia—"a psychosis characterized by hallucinations ('hearing voices' in most cases), delusions of grandiosity or persecution, bizarre religious ideas (often highly personalized), and a suspicious, hostile, aggressive manner"—or they arc victims of sexual sadism, "a deviation characterized by torture and/or killing and mutilation of other persons in order to achieve sexual gratification." Regrettably for this theory, however, none of our multiple murderers in this volume was reliably diagnosed as a victim of *any* serious mental disorder.[13]

Lunde's second point, which also is contradicted by all our data, is that while "we do not *know* the precise causes of these psychotic mentalities," we do know that they "are *not a product of the times*. Other countries and other centuries have produced sex murderers similar to those I have described from recent U.S. history." Lunde takes great pains to lodge the cause of these behaviors in the psyches of the killers, arguing that for "rare individuals, for reasons that are not well understood, sexual and violent aggressive impulses merge early in the child's development, ultimately finding expression in violent sexual assault." Very much in a Freudian vein, he dwells on the sexual pleasure the killers sometimes receive from the murder and mutilation of their victims, reflecting on their rich fantasy lives in which "they imagine sadistic scenes and derive great pleasure from this activity." Lunde's gifts are considerable, but his imprisonment within traditional psychiatry makes it difficult for him to transcend the non-explanation and mere categorization of his art. For an explanation, we must turn to the forces that create, shape, and deform individuals in a modern stratified society.*[14]

---

* If there was virtually no social theory of multiple murderers, there was a great deal of purely descriptive case material. See, for example, Hilda Bruch, "Mass Murder: The Wagner Case"; Robert Hazelwood and John Douglas, "The Lust Murderer"; Robert Brittain, "The Sadistic Murderer"; Allen Bartholomew, K.L. Milte, and F. Galbally, "Sexual Murder: Psychopathology and Psychiatric Jurisprudential Considerations"; James Calvin and John MacDonald, "Psychiatric Study of a Mass Murderer"; Marvin Kahn, "Psychological Test Study of a Mass Murderer"; as well as M. Foucault, *I, Pierre Rivere . . .* ; and Donald Lunde and Jefferson Morgan, *The Die Song*.

The Historical Metamorphoses

"We are encountering more and more . . . [of those who] have
turned the life instinct on its head: Meaning for them can only
come from acts of destruction."

Roger Kramer and Ira Weiner[15]

Multiple murderers are not "insane" and they are very much products
of their time. Far from being a randomly occurring freakish event, the
arrival of the multiple murderer is dictated by specific stresses and
alterations in the human community. Moreover, far from being
deluded, he is in many senses an embodiment of the central themes in
his civilization as well as a reflection of that civilization's critical tensions. He is thus a creature and a creation of his age. As such, we
would expect him to change his character over time, and all the evidence suggests that that is precisely what he does. In what follows, I
shall show that the pre-industrial multiple killer was an aristocrat who
preyed on his peasants; that the industrial era produced a new kind of
killer, most commonly a new bourgeois who preyed upon prostitutes,
homeless boys, and housemaids; and that in the mature industrial era,
he is most often a faded bourgeois who stalks middle class victims as
well as vulnerables. Thus for each historical epoch, both the social origins of the killers and the social characteristics of their victims are
highly predictable: They are thus very much men of their time.

The Pre-Industrial Multiple Murderer

Our evidence is not what we might wish, but we must take what is
available, and the overwhelming weight of that makes it clear that individual murder for its own sake was very rare in the archaic order of the
pre-industrial era. Indeed, the famous multiple murderers of that era
killed for profit—as was the case with Sawney Bean in fifteenth-century Scotland who murdered to steal the possessions of passersby and
eat their bodies; so too with Madame de Brinvilliers in seventeenth-
century France who murdered her family to inherit their wealth; and

with Catherine Montvoisin, also in seventeenth-century France, who arranged (for payment) the elimination of hundreds of infants.

The only names that emerge from this era as indisputably our subjects of inquiry are aristocrats of great wealth and achievement.[16] The Countess Erzebet Bathory was a fifteenth-century Hungarian/ Romanian pedophile who reportedly tortured and murdered dozens of little girls, the daughters of "her" peasants. The Baron Gilles de Rais was born in 1404 into one of the greatest fortunes of France. According to contemporary court documents, during the last eight years of his life, retired to his great estates, he murdered somewhere between 141 and 800 children, mostly boys. He would take the local children to his castle and, after raping them in one manner or another, would torture and kill them. His accomplice Griart told the court in 1440 that "the said Gilles, the accused, exercised his lust once or twice on the children. That done, the said Gilles killed them sometimes with his own hand or had them killed." As to the manner in which the children were killed, Griart remembered that "sometimes they were decapitated, and dismembered; sometimes he [Gilles] cut their throats, leaving the head attached to the body; sometimes he broke their necks with a stick; sometimes he cut a vein in their throats or some other part of their necks, so that the blood of the said children flowed. As the children were dying," wrote his biographer, Leonard Wolf, "Gilles, the artist of terror, the skilled Latinist who read Saint Augustine; Gilles, the devoted companion of Jeanne d'Arc, squatted on the bellies of the children, studying their languishing faces, breathing in their dying sighs."[17]

When the court interrogators asked him who had induced him to do his crimes and taught him how to do the killings, the Baron replied: "I did and perpetrated them following [the dictates] of my imagination and my thought, without the advice of anyone, and according to my own judgment and entirely for my own pleasure and physical delight, and for no other intention or end." Under threat of being put to the torture, he confessed that "for my ardor and my sensual delectation I took and caused to be taken a great number of children—how many I cannot say precisely, children whom I killed and caused to be killed;

with them, I committed the vice and the sin of sodomy . . . and . . . I emitted spermatic semen in the most culpable fashion on the belly of . . . the children, as well before as after their deaths, and also while they were dying. I, alone, or with the help of my accomplices, Gilles de Sillé, Roger de Bricqueville, Henriet [Griart], Etienne Corrilaut [Poitou], Rossignol and Petit Robin, have inflicted various kinds and manners of torture on these children. Sometimes I beheaded them with daggers, with poignards, with knives; sometimes I beat them violently on the head with a stick or with other contusive instruments. . . . Sometimes I suspended them in my room from a pole or by a hook and cords and strangled them; and when they were languishing, I committed with them the vice of sodomy. . . . When the children were dead, I embraced them, and I gazed at those which had the most beautiful heads and the loveliest members, and I caused their bodies to be cruelly opened and took delight in viewing their interior organs; and very often, as the children were dying, I sat on their bellies and was delighted to see them dying in that fashion and laughed about it with . . . Corrilaut and Henriet, after which I caused [the children] to be burned and converted their cadavers into dust."[18]

In a manner that will be unfamiliar only to those who have not read the other confessions in this book, the Baron interrupted his homicidal memoir to lecture the grieving parents on how to raise children. But first, during the reading in open court of his crimes, surrounded by the families of his victims (peasants all), he allowed himself to express outrage at the lowly estate of those who were acting as his judges. Hearing the bishop and the vicar of the inquisition name his acts in front of the peasant parents, he shouted: "Simoniacs, ribalds, I'd rather be hanged by the neck than reply to the likes of such clerics and such judges. It is not to be borne . . . to appear before such as you." Turning to the Bishop Malestroit, he sneered, "I'll do nothing for you as Bishop of Nantes."[19]

Following threats of excommunication and torture, he capitulated. "From the time of my youth I have committed many great crimes," he told the court, "against God and the Ten Commandments, crimes still worse than those of which I stand accused. And I have offended our Savior as a consequence of bad upbringing in childhood, when I was left uncontrolled to do whatever I pleased [and especially] to take pleasure in illicit acts." Once more reminiscent of the killers of later centuries, he begged his judges to publish his confessions, and do so in "the vulgar tongue" so that the peasants would know of what he had done. What was the moral he wished to point out to his audience? "When I was a child, I had always a delicate nature, and did for my own pleasure and according to my own will whatever evil I pleased. To all [of you who are] fathers and mothers, friends and relatives of young people and children, lovingly I beg and pray you to train them in good morals, [teach] them to follow good examples and good doctrines; and instruct them and punish them, lest they fall into the same trap in which I myself have fallen." The Baron was hanged and burned on October 26, 1440.[20]

Why should the classic cases of pre-industrial multiple murder be wealthy and powerful aristocrats? And why has this class vanished from participation in modern multiple murder? What was happening in the second quarter of the fifteenth century to put special stress upon the ancient landed aristocracy? The world into which de Rais and Bathory were born had existed for centuries: It was essentially a two-class social universe, a vast mass of peasants and a tiny collection of "noble" overlords, who expropriated the surplus of the former. These were hard times for humanity—and especially the peasants—for plague, famine, and war were frequent and devastating. There were, however, some compensations. The peasants' transfer of their surplus to their rulers was balanced by the provision of minimal security for the cultivators, who were given rights of use of the land in perpetuity. A social correlate of this relative economic security was the humanizing personalization of social relationships. The historian Peter Laslett has written that although exploitation was endemic to the system, "everyone belonged to a group, a family group," and "everyone had his or her circle of affection: every relationship could be seen as a love-relationship." This is not to say that "love" was the rule, or even the norm, in human encounters; but rather that human relationships were personalized and on a human scale: Whether the relationship was full of warmth or riddled with conflict, it was a relationship between human beings. Institutional relationships and life were virtually unknown, and if groups of men and women occasionally worked together in rural life, they did so as households cooperating with one another for mutual goals. This personal world of the peasant did not encourage the growth of our multiple murderers.[21]

What was happening to the landed aristocracy? It was in a state of *crisis*, assaulted on all sides by peasantry and merchants. For historian Immanuel Wallerstein, the crisis of feudalism began between the thirteenth and fifteenth centuries. What provoked this crisis was that "the optimal degree of productivity has been passed" in the archaic feudal system, and "the economic squeeze was leading to a generalized seignior-peasant class war, as well as ruinous fights within the seigniorial classes." Moreover, the peasantry had begun to protest its condition, and peasant revolts became "widespread in western Europe from the thirteenth century to the fifteenth century"; peasant republics were declared in Frisia in the twelfth and thirteenth centuries and in Switzerland in the thirteenth century; French peasants rebelled in 1358 as they did in Italy and Flanders at the turn of the fourteenth century.[22]

Critical to our purpose, the fifteenth century—the time of the Baron Gilles de Rais and the Countess Erzebet Bathory—was the era in which the established order strove to reassert itself, often through the savage repression of political and religious peasant rebellions. This was the century, Wallerstein wrote, that "saw the advent of the great restorers of internal order in western Europe: Louis XI in France, Henry VII in England, and Ferdinand of Aragon and Isabella of Castile in Spain. The major mechanisms at their disposal in this task, as for their less successful predecessors, were financial: by means of the arduous creation of a bureaucracy (civil and armed) strong enough to tax and thus to finance a still stronger bureaucratic structure." It can be no coincidence that the only pre-industrial multiple murderers who killed purely for its own sake and of whom we have reliable record, were members of that threatened established order. Neither does it require an impossible stretch of the imagination to comprehend that the manner in which the aristocrats (consumed with class-based anxiety and accustomed to giving free rein to all their emotional impulses) tortured and killed the children of the peasantry was a personalized expression of the sweeping repressive thrust of their class, and a sexual metaphor in which they tested and enforced their terrible powers. Thus their indulgence of their violent sexual fantasy was an embroidery upon the central political event of their era—the subordination of the rebellious peasantry and the restoration of the absolute powers of the old nobility. What better way to deal with this threatened domination than through the idle torture and murder—as if they were nothing—of the class which dared stake a claim to equality? Three centuries later, with the bourgeoisie ascendant, another noble, the Marquis de Sade, would be relegated to harmless fantasizing and scribbling—for his class was already redundant: de Rais and his *confrères* had lost their struggle.[23]

The Industrial Era

Toward the end of the eighteenth century, there began that profound upheaval of all economic and social relations that we call the industrial revolution. It created entirely new social classes, raising some to prominence and dominance, and displacing others. "The key figure of the eighteenth century," the gifted historian Robert Darnton wrote, was "the owner of the modes of production, a certain variety of Economic man with his own way of life and his own ideology." This new man was the bourgeois; he "acquired class consciousness and revolted [against the old aristocracy], leading a popular front of peasants and artisans." The political culture necessary for the fusion of "this striking force" was designed to allow the bourgeoisie "to saturate the common people with its own ideas of liberty (especially free trade) and equality (especially the destruction of aristocratic privilege)." By the nineteenth century, the series of mechanical inventions made possible a new economic order dominated by machine production. The new bourgeoisie which owned this machinery gained control of the emerging industrial states and relegated the old aristocracy to the sidelines of history (or joined with them through marriage). But it was neither from the ranks of the old aristocracy, nor from the triumphant new bourgeoisie that the leaders of the *homicidal revolution* would be drawn: there are no Wedgewoods or Rockefellers among the multiple murderers of the time. This should not be surprising, for unthreatened classes do not produce them.

Throughout the industrializing world, traditional communal life and activity were snuffed out. In Laslett's terms,

> ... the removal of the economic functions from the patriarchal family at the point of industrialization created a mass society. It turned the people who worked into a mass of undifferentiated equals, working in a factory or scattered between the factories, the mines and the offices, bereft forever of the feeling that work was a family affair, done within the household.

The new industrial order, Wolf wrote, "cut through the integument of custom, severing people from their accustomed social matrix in order to transform them into economic actors, independent of prior social commitments to kin and neighbors."

> This liberation from accustomed social ties and the separation which it entailed constituted the historical experience which Karl Marx would describe in terms of "alienation." The alienation of men ... from themselves to the extent to which they now had to look upon their own capabilities as marketable commodities; their alienation from their fellow men who had become actual or potential competitors in the market.

The capitalism of the late eighteenth and nineteenth centuries was thus an extraordinarily *radical* force, and its capture of the emerging industrial system left the new worker naked and exposed. At the same time, Europe and America altered their living arrangements in order to supply the workers for the new factory system; vast and anonymous cities were created. Wolf provides British data to illustrate this clustering of populations in urban areas. In 1600, only 1.6 percent of the population in England and Wales lived in cities of 100,000 or more; but the figures through the nineteenth century document the flight from the land. By 1801, one-tenth of the population was living in cities, a proportion which doubled by 1840 and doubled again by the end of the century. By 1900, Britain was an urban society. To this depersonalized new world— in which the worker lost even that tattered blanket of protection of kin and community, and instead toiled in vast factories and took rooms in anonymous boarding houses—was added a further humiliation. The new bourgeois ideology penalized the losers, the unemployed or the under-employed, for the new cultural system transmuted "the distinction between the classes into distinctions of virtue and merit."[24]

Such conditions of poverty and humiliation, insecurity and inequality, entailed many social costs, among the most notable of which was the creation of new types of murderers. Wilson complains that murder in the pre-industrial era had been essentially dull, springing generally "out of poverty and misery": Such murders "do not really involve much human choice—much good or evil." The nineteenth and early twentieth centuries would be much more obliging, for "with a few interesting exceptions, all the 'great' murder cases of the nineteenth century—Lizzie Borden, Charles Bravo, Dr. Pritchard, Professor Webster—concerned the socially comfortable classes. Not the extremely rich or the aristocracy . . . but the middle classes." Indeed, one is driven to note the number of professional, especially medical, titles attached to their names—Dr. William Palmer, Dr. Thomas Cream, Dr. Marcel Petiot, and many others.[25]

Of those multiple murderers who were killing apparently for its own sake, two homicidal themes emerged. The major theme was one in which middle-class functionaries—doctors, teachers, professors, civil servants, who belonged to the class created to serve the new triumphant bourgeoisie—preyed on members of the lower orders, especially prostitutes and housemaids. If the prevailing "need" of the era's economic formations was to discipline the lower orders into accepting the timetable of the machine and industrial employment, then this form of homicide can be usefully seen as the means by which these new members of a new middle class took the prevailing ethos to its logical conclusion. In killing the failures and the unruly renegades from the system—those whose very existence must have seemed an affront to the lofty status and high morality of the new class—and doing so with such obvious pleasure, they tested their power and enforced the new moral order. We will never know the identity of "Jack the Ripper," who terrorized the prostitutes of London by disemboweling them with surgical precision; but we do know that Dr. Thomas Cream began to poison prostitutes in London in 1891, offering them drinks from his toxic bottle, and sending taunting letters to the police.

By the third quarter of the nineteenth century, they began to appear everywhere in the western world, but most especially in the advanced industrializing nations of England, France, Germany, and the United States. By the early twentieth century, it had become a common art form. Few cases have left us with much detail to analyze, although we do have their gory crimes and brief confessions. Between 1920 and 1925, Grossman, Denke, Haarmann, and Kurten were all killing in Germany. In Hungary in 1931, *Sylvestre Matuschka* blew up a train, killing twenty-five and maiming 120 others. At first he explained that, "I wrecked trains because I like to see people die. I like to hear them scream. I like to see them suffer"; but later he struck a curiously modern note by blaming his action on a demon spirit named Leo. In France, during the 1860s, *Joseph Philippe* strangled and cut the throats of prostitutes; and many more followed his path. In the 1920s, Earle Nelson raped and killed at least twenty boarding-house landladies, strangling in an arc from San Francisco to Winnipeg. In Chicago, *Herman Mudgett* (alias Dr. H. H. Holmes), a medical student who had abandoned his studies when he had run out of funds, killed dozens of young women in his "castle." Among his last words before he was hanged in 1896 was a curious confession: "I have commenced to assume the form and features of the Evil One himself." *Hamilton Fish,* the son of a Potomac River boat captain and a deeply religious man

who wished to be a minister, began a serial murder career that spanned
decades, torturing and murdering at least a dozen children, primarily
from the working classes. His last child-victim was young Grace Budd:
after he killed her, he wrote to her mother: "On Sunday June the 3—
1928 I called on you at 406 W 15th St. Brought you pot cheese—
strawberries. We had lunch. Grace sat in my lap and kissed me. I made
up my mind to eat her. On the pretense of taking her to a party. You
said Yes she could go. I took her to an empty house in Westchester I
had already picked out. . . . How she did kick—bite and scratch. I
choked her to death, then cut her in small pieces so I could take my
meat to my rooms, Cook and eat it. How sweet and tender her little ass
was roasted in the oven. It took me 9 days to eat her entire body. I did
not fuck her tho I could of had I wished. She died a *virgin*."[26]

The Major Theme: Petit Bourgeois Sensibilities

The major homicidal theme of this era was one in which newly middle-class persons (with all the insecurities such *arriviste* status entails)
disciplined the lower orders who threatened their morbid sensitivity to
their class position, or who behaved without the appropriate "refinement" required by the new era. Perhaps the best illustration of these
points was contained in the *Wagner case* of 1913. He was one of ten
children of an alcoholic and braggart peasant father who died when he
(Wagner) was two years old, leaving drinking debts of such magnitude
that the homestead had to be sold. His mother's second marriage ended
in divorce when he was seven, reportedly because of her promiscuity.
Even as a child, "he was known in the village as 'the widow's boy,'" the
psychiatrist Bruch recorded, "and suffered from depressions, suicidal
thoughts, and nightmares." Somehow Wagner obtained an education
and qualified as a school teacher; but he never recovered from the
hypersensitivity that such a rapid rise in the social hierarchy can create.

During the night of September 4, 1913, the citizens of
Muehlhausen . . . were awakened by several large fires. As they
ran into the street, they were met by a man, his face covered by

a black veil, who was armed with two pistols. He shot with great accuracy and killed eight men and one girl immediately; 12 more were severely injured. Then his two pistols ran out of ammunition, and he was overpowered and beaten down with such violence that he was left for dead; however, he was only unconscious. He had 198 more bullets in his possession. The innkeeper identified the murderer as his 39-year-old brother-in-law, who had been a schoolteacher in this village more than ten years earlier.

Wagner confessed that during the preceding night he had quietly killed his wife and four children. . . . He also confessed that he had come to Muehlhausen to take revenge on the male inhabitants for their scorn and disdain for him. However, even while lying severely wounded and exposed to the hatred of the attacked people, he noticed that no one employed the term of abuse that would refer to his sexual sins, which he felt had been the cause of all the persecution, ridicule, and condemnation.

Wagner's life was spared when it was recognized, during the pretrial examination, that he was mentally ill. He was committed to an insane asylum, where he spent the rest of his life, 25 years.

During the preceding week [before the killings] he had written a series of letters which were not mailed until September 4 . . . one which contained a complete confession of all his crimes. It was addressed to the largest newspaper in Stuttgart and was to be used as an editorial. . . . Wagner had planned to return to his brother's house the following night with the intent of killing him and his family and of burning down his house as well as the house in which he had been born. As a final step he had planned to proceed to the royal castle in Ludwigsburg, overpower the guards, set fire to the castle, and die in the flames or jump off its walls, thereby terminating his own life.

He was vituperative in expressing his hatred against Professor Gaupp, in whom he had confided the motives for his deed and who had then expressed the opinion that he was mentally sick and therefore not responsible. . . . "If I am insane, then a madman has been teaching all these years."

[Former associates] described him as an admirable citizen, dignified, somewhat quiet. . . . Only a few had noted a certain amount of standoffishness and affectation. All commented on the fact that in a region in which a heavy dialect was spoken by educated and uneducated alike, he insisted on using high German, even in his private life.

This fateful chain of events had its beginning, according to his self-accusation, with one or more sodomistic acts in the late summer of 1901, when he was 27 years old. . . . Of decisive importance was the fact that his sexual urges and acts stood in irreconcilable contrast to his high moral standards and ethical concepts. His deep sense of guilt never diminished . . . he soon began to make certain "observations" and to "hear" certain slanderous remarks, which led to the unshakable conviction that his "crime" was known. He felt himself continuously observed, mocked, and ridiculed, and lived in constant dread of arrest. He was determined not to suffer this public shame and humiliation, and therefore he always carried a loaded pistol. . . . He began an affair with the innkeeper's daughter. . . . His future wife gave birth to a girl in the summer of 1903 and he married her (with many inner misgivings) in December 1903. He felt that he no longer loved her and that she was intellectually not his equal; he considered her more a servant than a wife. . . . She objected to his spending money and time on his literary interests. There were five children. . . . He was unhappy about the birth of each child and felt confined by the financial hardship of a large family subsisting on the meager income of a village schoolteacher.

Gradually he began also to make "observations" in Radelstetten [the village in which he had taken a new position] and felt convinced that the people of Muehlhausen had communicated their "knowledge" to the people at his new location. He could notice it because of certain insinuations and the occasional arrogance which some allegedly showed against him. He felt caught in the old dilemma: There was never a direct statement, but he "heard" pointed remarks containing hints. He knew if he reacted he would be publicly humiliated. . . . Gradually the conviction ripened that there was only one way out. He must kill himself and his children, out of pity to save them from a future of being the target of contempt and evil slander and to take revenge on the people of Muehlhausen who had forced him to this horrible deed. . . . Since the men of Muehlhausen had started and spread the slander, they had to die. In a life that as a whole had been a series of depressing and frustrating disappointments, he was grateful that it had been given to him to avenge his terrible torture and suffering. He was disappointed to learn that he had killed only nine people [plus his own family].

Even in 1938, when he knew that death from advanced tuberculosis was imminent, he still felt that he had been justified in his action—that even if he had killed all of them it would not have balanced the suffering that had been inflicted on him. . . . The people of Muehlhausen had made it impossible for him to lead a decent life of work and orderliness and to gain recognition as a literary figure and great dramatist. . . . Since his student days literature had been his great love and avocation. He craved literary success, not only during the frugal days. . . . His profession of schoolteacher was not satisfactory to him. He considered himself in all seriousness as one of the greatest dramatists of his time and spoke with condescension of those whose works were performed.*

I have quoted Bruch at great length because in many important respects the Wagner case can be treated as *the* text for the purple explosion of middle-class multiple murder in the nineteenth and early twentieth centuries. What were the central themes in the memoir of

* "Mass Murder: The Wagner Case," by Hilda Bruch, Vol 124. pp. 693–698. 1967. Copyright 1967, the American Psychiatric Association. Reprinted by permission.

this tormented man? Were his delusions of persecution merely bizarre psychic accident, or did they reflect some of the central fractures in the social order of his time? Let us re-examine his life and his confessions. The son of a drunken peasant and a promiscuous mother, his childhood must have been cursed with the demeaning insults of his fellows. Yet he rose from this crushing poverty and abasement to a modest position in the marginal middle classes as the village schoolteacher. But his ambitions were loftier still, for he regarded himself as a literary genius and he hungered for the recognition such status would bring. Being young, he contracted a sexual relationship with the innkeeper's daughter and impregnated her. The rigid demands of his time and his class meant that he had to marry her. This threatened his hard-won status, for an innkeeper's daughter was socially beneath him: Moreover, she did not understand his middle-class (which is to say literary) pretensions or the expenses they entailed. Soon he had ceased to "love" her, and began treating her as "more a servant than a wife."[27]

The new industrial order created a host of new "professions," marginal middle-class occupations with a certain status which the clever sons of peasants might fill. Yet few things are so corrosive to the individual as rapid social mobility: He is no longer in the world that he knows; he does not know quite how to behave, nor how much leeway the public will allow him in the performance of his role. All he knows is that the penalty for failure is disgrace and an unceremonious return to the ugly status from which he has escaped; hence the common quality of a defensive status hysteria—which manifests itself as a kind of extreme personal insecurity—that is found so often among those who have risen or fallen dramatically in the social hierarchy. For Wagner, this fearful hysteria focused on the possibility that his brief pre-marital homosexual affair might be discovered: It was not his "high moral standards" that made it impossible for him to cope with this memory, but his high social aspirations which would all collapse if he were unmasked as a sodomist. More and more his fear expressed itself in odd ways—most especially in his strange affectations of speaking and dressing over-formally and inappropriately (inappropriately to whom?

To those who understand precisely the demands of middle-class status). Might the neighbors know of his shame? He must watch their every gesture and hear their every word, looking for signs that they would unmask him. His morbid sensibility—only an intense version of the compulsive rigidity of his new class—began to dwell upon, then became obsessed with, this fear of exposure until he was interpreting all the behavior of his fellow villagers in these terms. They knew, they sensed, they felt. Real or fancied insults and slights were converted immediately into "knowledge" of his guilt. Yet he could not react: He could not charge them with tormenting him for if he did so, "he would be publicly humiliated." Therein lay the seed of his terrible crimes: The only way to avoid the impossible abasement of himself and his family, and claim revenge, was to kill them all.

But why burn down his house and that of the royal family? Nothing could have been more appropriate; for in this double and incendiary act he would destroy all evidence of his humble origins and erase his lowly past, while obliterating the seat and symbol of the entire social order—the royal castle—that orchestrated his anguish. This was not so much delusional madness as the response of a sensitive person driven by an unrelenting fear: he knew that its origins lay in the social order, and he sensed that only such a murderous campaign could justify his existence and bury his shame. Small wonder then that he was so affronted when the psychiatrists and court declared him insane, for he knew he was struggling with something that was very real. "If I am insane, then a madman has been teaching all these years," he cried. He knew that he had spared himself any further torment and avenged himself on his oppressors; and ensured that they understood his mission by announcing it to the public in an editorial in the largest newspaper in Stuttgart. No case better represents the timorous nature of the new petit bourgeoisie than Wagner, disciplining the social inferiors who threatened his position.

The Minor Theme: Proletarian Rebellion

The second major homicidal theme that emerged in the burgeoning industrial era was one in which the lower orders engaged in a kind of sub-political rebellion that expressed their rage at their exclusion from the social order. Their confessions remain scanty so we must piece together what we can; still, there is enough to suggest a great deal. If the killer Panzram gives us chapter and verse, his contemporary, *Peter Kurten*, from the Germany of the 1920s raises many questions. Kurten murdered two boys when he himself was only nine years old; then as an adult, he murdered several dozen men and women, boys and girls, by knifing, by strangling, and by hammering. When he was finally captured, the forty-seven-year-old married factory laborer (whose father had been jailed for abusing him and raping his sister) insisted that, "I derived no sexual satisfaction from what I did. My motives were principally to arouse excitement and indignation in the population. Through setting fire to the body I thought I would increase the rage." But why did he desire to so antagonize his fellows? The authorities rooted through his past and discovered that as a youth he had spent much time in the Chamber of Horrors, a waxwork exhibition in Kölnerstrasse. A childhood friend recalled that he always gravitated toward the wax figures of murderers. Kurten once said to him, "I am going to be somebody famous like those men one of these days." After his arrest, he spoke of his younger days in prison for the murder of the two children: "In prison, I began to think about revenging myself on society. I did myself a great deal of damage through reading blood-and-thunder stories, for instance I read the tale of 'Jack the Ripper' several times. When I came to think over what I had read, when I was in prison, I thought what pleasure it would give me to do things of that kind once I got out again." But why should he need such terrible revenge, and why take it out on the innocent?[28]

For a full explanation of this metaphor we must turn to the American *Carl Panzram*,* one of a small proportion of our murderers who

---

* See Gaddis and Long's *Killer* for Panzram's journal.

come from anything resembling a truly oppressed segment of society. He was imprisoned first in 1903, when he was eleven, for breaking into a neighbor's home; for that he was subjected to the sexual and physical brutality of a reform school staff. He did not begin his twenty-year career in multiple murder until he had experienced years of unspeakable torture (which he documented and catalogued in his journal) and sexual assault in the nation's prison system. He raped and murdered sailors, "natives," little boys, whomever he could get his hands on; he destroyed property wherever and whenever he could; and he hatched far more ambitious schemes, which came to naught: poisoning a town, blowing up a passenger train and, he hoped, staging a political incident that might spark a war between Britain and the United States. "In my lifetime," Panzram wrote as he sat in prison *eagerly awaiting his execution,* "I have murdered 21 human beings, I have committed thousands of burglaries, robberies, larcenies, arsons and last but not least I have committed sodomy on more than 1,000 male human beings. For all of these things I am not the least bit sorry. I have no conscience so that does not worry me. I don't believe in man, God nor Devil. I hate the whole damned race including myself." He concluded that, "We do each other as we are done by. I have done as I was taught to do. I am no different from any other. You taught me how to live my life, and I have lived as you taught me. I have no desire whatever to reform myself. My only desire is to reform people who try to reform me. And I believe that the only way to reform people is to kill 'em." He wrote his journal/manifesto, he said, "so that I can explain my side of it even though no one ever hears or reads of it except one man. But one man or a million makes no difference to me. When I am through I am all through, and that settles it with me. . . . If you or anyone else will take the trouble and have the intelligence or patience to follow and examine every one of my crimes, you will find that I have consistently followed one idea through all of my life. I preyed upon the weak, the harmless and the unsuspecting. This lesson I was taught by others: Might makes right."[29]

Panzram traced the origin of his commitment to revenge against all humanity to the torture sessions he endured in the "reform school. At that time I was just learning to think for myself. Everything I seemed to do was wrong. I first began to think that I was being unjustly imposed upon. Then I began to hate those who abused me. Then I began to think that I would have my revenge just as soon and as often as I could injure someone else. Anyone at all would do. If I couldn't injure those who injured me, then I would injure someone else. When I got out of there I knew all about Jesus and the Bible—so much so that I knew it was all a lot of hot air. But that wasn't all I knew. I had been taught by Christians how to be a hypocrite and I had learned more about stealing, lying, hating, burning and killing. I had learned that a boy's penis could be used for something besides to urinate with and that a rectum could be used for other purposes than crepitating. Oh yes, I had learned a hell of a lot from my expert instructors furnished to me free of charge by society in general and the State of Minnesota in particular. From the treatment I received while there and the lessons I learned from it, I had fully decided when I left there just how I would live my life. I made up my mind that I would rob, burn, destroy, and kill everywhere I went and everybody I could as long as I lived. That's the way I was reformed in the Minnesota State Training School. That's the reason why."[30]

Despite his protestations, his resolution did not harden completely until he had been tortured beyond all endurance at the various penitentiaries—for the crime of refusing to bow to authority. Yet once his philosophy had been formed and his life committed to it, there was no turning back until he sickened of life entirely and capitulated to the authorities, demanding his own execution. In his final days in prison, he was well-treated: "If in the beginning," he wrote, "I had been treated as I am now, then there wouldn't have been quite so many people in this world that have been robbed, raped, and killed, and perhaps also very probably I wouldn't be where I am today. Why am I what I am? I'll tell you why. I did not make myself what I am. Others had the making of me." Still, he rejected all thoughts of "rehabilitation. I could not reform if I wanted to. It has taken me all my life so far, 38 years of it, for me to reach my present state of mind. . . . My philosophy of life is such that very few people ever get, and it is so deeply ingrained and burned into me that I don't believe I could ever change my beliefs. The things I have had done to me by others and the things I have done to them can never be forgotten or forgiven either by me or others. I can't forget and I won't forgive. I couldn't if I wanted to. The law is in the same fix. . . . If the law won't kill me, I shall kill myself. I fully realize that I am not fit to live among people in a civilized community. I have no desire to do so."[31]

When anti-capital punishment groups tried to block his execution, Panzram entered into a kind of conspiracy with federal officials to obtain his own death. Musing alone in his cell, he wrote: "Wherever I go, there is sure to be bad luck and hard times for somebody and sometimes for everybody. I am old bad-luck himself. . . . I had a lot of different people ask me at different times who I was and what good I was. My answers were all the same. 'I am the fellow who goes around doing people good." Asked what good I had ever done anyone: Again my answers were the same to all. 'I put people out of their misery.' They didn't know that I was telling them the truth. I have put a lot of people out of their misery and now I am looking for someone to put me out of mine. I am too damned mean to live. I intend to leave this world as I have lived in it. I expect to be a rebel right up to my last moment on earth. With my last breath I intend to curse the world and all mankind. I intend to spit in the warden's eye or whoever places the rope around my neck when I am standing on the scaffold. . . . That will be all the thanks they'll get from me."[32]

The day before his execution, he promised visiting journalists that he would "prance up those thirteen steps like a blooded stallion," and he asked the guard to ensure that the scaffold was "strong enough to hold me." Robert Stroud, later to become famous as the "birdman of Alcatraz," was in an adjoining cell during Panzram's last night of life: "All night long that last night," Stroud remembered, "he walked the floor of his cell, singing a pornographic little song that he had composed himself. . . . The principal theme was 'Oh, how I love my round-eye!'" When Panzram's cell door opened just before six A.M. and he saw two men in clerical garb, he roared: "Are there any Bible-backed cocksuckers in here? Get 'em out. I don't mind being hanged, but I don't need any Bible-backed hypocrites around me. Run 'em out, Warden." When Panzram finally emerged from his cell, his biographers Gaddis and Long recorded, he "was almost running ahead, half dragging his taller escorts." Panzram stared straight ahead at the rope, pausing only at the foot of the gallows to notice his audience. He paused for a moment and spat, then returned his gaze to the rope. "Everyone's nostrils inhaled the sweet smell of new oak and hemp. He hurried up the gallows, as toward a gate."[33]

The Modern Era

> "This is the American Dream. . . . In America, anything is possible if you work for it."
> *Vice-Presidential candidate, 1984*

Culture

No quality of American culture is more jarring than the *culture of violence*. Its continued assertion (sometimes subliminal, sometimes blatant) of the nobility of violence is propagated with excitement and craft in all popular cultural forms, including films, television, print and the Internet. This cultural predilection must have been immeasurably enhanced by the daily television coverage of the Vietnam War, which for the first time brought real bloodletting into every American living room and rendered death sacred no more. Subtly encouraged thus to act out their fantasies, our killers would find that their murderous acts would both validate and relieve their grievances. Whether in the media or at the level of the street, the glowing mythology often surrounding violence creates a situation in which the most trivial provocation can result in a savage explosion. Moreover, such vulnerables are primed for their purple displays by a *culture of fear* in which people are "taught" to be fearful of one another, ever poised for the onset of sexual and physical assault.

In *Seductions of Crime*, Katz's marvelous study of the "moral and sensual attractions in doing evil" in modern American culture, Katz shows how homicide is commonly conceived and expressed as "righteous slaughter" (which is to say that it is both ethically correct and emotionally conditioned); and how remorse and regret are largely removed from the equation. Here then we can find an armed street culture in which "dissing" one another—showing disrespect in matters as insignificant as maintaining eye contact for too long, or bumping into another, or "stealing" a lover or a parking place—can be perceived and felt as legitimate provocation for a homicide, or even a mass murder.

Across the nation, as many as one half of American homicides are provoked by such "trivial altercation." Moreover, the culture permits the "impassioned killers" to see themselves as somehow fundamentally moral, "defending both the morality of the social system and a personal claim of moral worth," even "upholding the respected social statuses of husband, mother, wife, father, property owner, virile male, deserving poor/self-improving welfare mother, and responsible debtor." It is precisely here—in condoning an atmosphere tolerant of physical confrontation—that American civilization unwittingly encourages those at the bottom to cross the line to homicidal assault. It is precisely here, at the level of "deep culture," that the dominant ethos desensitizes its population to murder.

Why should trivial altercations provoke so many killings? Gottfredson and Hirschi conclude that the under-socialized members of *any* civilization "will tend to be impulsive, insensitive, physical, risk-taking, short-sighted, and nonverbal" and are therefore most likely to risk criminal acts. In such under-controlled persons, outbursts of violence can be sparked by mere "momentary irritation," because "people with low self-control tend to have minimal tolerance for frustration and little ability to respond to conflict through verbal rather than physical means." Thus the noisome "irritation caused by a crying child [or a noisy neighbor] is often the stimulus for physical abuse," and the disrespect from "a taunting stranger in a bar is often the stimulus for aggravated assault." Those who exercise such limited control are more

commonly found among the working classes, and those who have the
least to lose are always more prone to violent display. But in a culture
that validates and conditions these beliefs and behaviors, the responses
are found with greater frequency and throughout the social order.[34]

This, then, is the cultural milieu which has for two centuries glorified violence as an appropriate and manly response to frustration. *The
History of Violence in America* documented the public response to a
bank robbery in which a young girl was shot in the leg: The Kansas City
Times reiterated the dominant cultural theme by describing the robbery as "so diabolically daring and so utterly in contempt of fear that
we are bound to admire it and revere its perpetrators." A few days later,
the same newspaper underlined this when it commented that

> It was as though three bandits had come to us from storied
> Odedwald, with the halo of medieval chivalry upon their gar-
> ments and shown us how the things were done that the poets sing
> of. Nowhere else in the United States or in the civilized world,
> probably, could this thing have been done.[35]

Social Structure

If the culture thus underwrites an explosive response to low levels of
frustration, and if it has evolved over the centuries to separate its peoples from one another through fear, then changes in the social structure
that add to the levels of frustration escalate still further the risk of
multiple murder.

In the immediate aftermath of the Second World War, the industrial
economies moved into an era of unprecedented expansion and prosperity. With the growth of the industrial sector came a parallel development of all government and social service agencies—running the
gamut from education to medicine to welfare. This remarkable growth
in both the corporate and social sectors created two postwar decades
in which individuals with even the most marginal of qualifications and
abilities could enter occupations which offered a real measure of dignity and recompense. These were quiet years for homicide in general

and multiple murder in particular as the population scrambled to better itself. The increase in the rate of production of these most modern of killers began again in the mid-1960s and has continued ever since: This directly paralleled, and may well have owed its initial impetus to the *closure* that was taking place in the American economy. From the mid-1960s onwards, the myriad of middle-class positions that had been created since the Second World War began to be filled, or reduced in number and "downsized." Inexorably, more and more socially ambitious but untalented (or unconnected) young men and women must have found it difficult to achieve their goals of "successful" careers and crisp identities. A proportion of these people—we can never know precisely how many—began to fantasize about revenge. A tiny but increasing percentage of them began to react to the frustration of their blocked social mobility by transforming their fantasies into a vengeful reality.

Thus the *character* of both killers and victims underwent a further transformation. The social origins of the killers continued to fall: Gone were the aristocrats of the fifteenth century, and the doctors and teachers of the nineteenth century. Now the killers were drawn from the ranks of the working and lower-middle classes; for the most part they were security guards, computer operators, postal clerks and construction workers. Conversely, the social origins of the victims pursued an opposite path: Where they had been peasants in the fifteenth century; housemaids, homeless boys and prostitutes in the nineteenth century, now they were as likely to be drawn from the middle-class neighborhoods: university students, aspiring models, and shoppers in middle-class malls. Both killer and victim had altered their form because the nature of the homicidal protest had changed radically. It was no longer the threatened aristocrat testing the limits of his power; no longer the morbidly insecure new bourgeois tasting the limits of his hard-won power. Now it was an excluded individual wreaking vengeance on the symbol and source of his excommunication.

Was this increase a consequence only of the predatory nature of capitalism? The evidence does not warrant such a conclusion. The structures of humiliation and deprivation coalesce around *any* hierarchical industrial system, whether it be capitalist or communist; and neither system appears to hold any monopoly on alienation and exclusion, dehumanization and depersonalization. We would thus have expected the communist bloc states also to produce multiple murderers—but in varying numbers, according to the degree with which their respective cultures glorify and venerate violence. Unfortunately, we cannot confirm these speculations since communist bloc states restricted the flow of information to their citizens; but the Soviet-era "Vampire of Silesia," whose diary is reprinted in Chapter Two, is an interesting illustration of what we might expect, as was the well-known case of the prolific killer, Andrei Chikatilo. Valery Chalidze's review of Soviet crime made it clear that multiple murder was common enough in the former USSR. In the early 1960s, Chalidze wrote, one man "became well known to the Moscow public" for murdering children in their own apartments: Curiously, the official explanation given for his behavior was precisely the same as any Western psychiatrist or court might offer—"his crimes appeared to be the acts of a maniac, and the general belief was that his motives were sexual." Since the collapse of the Soviet Union, indigenous homicide and multiple murder rates appear to have escalated radically, but a full understanding of this awaits further analysis.[36]

The simple fact of human social life is that in order for individuals to behave "normally," they must grow up feeling that they have some place in the social order—which is to say a coherent and socially constructed identity. Unfortunately, individuals who bear these social characteristics often come to feel excluded from the social order—a separation I have often heard in "reform schools," where juveniles refer to civilians as "humans"—and such exclusion can exact a fearful price. But many people who bear these social characteristics grow into a mature and balanced adulthood. Why should some fail to do so? Several other factors are necessary in the biography before a multiple murderer can be produced. He must also be inculcated with an ambition—or a "dream"—which either circumstances rob from him (as when DeSalvo's wife Irmgard refused him admission to the lower-middle class), or which he cannot feel at ease in living (as when Bundy spurned his long-sought socialite fiancée). He is never Durkheim's contented man, who:

> vaguely realizes the extreme limit set to his ambitions and aspires to nothing beyond. . . . He feels that it is not well to ask more. Thus, an end and goal are set to the passions. . . . This relative limitation and the moderation it involves, make men contented with their lot while stimulating them moderately to improve it; and this average contentment causes the feeling of calm, active happiness, the pleasure in existing and living which characterizes health for societies as well as for individuals.

It is in this light that we must interpret and understand the fierce social ambition of so many of our multiple murderers—and the feeling of being a robot that torments so many of them as they pursue their goals.[37]

Finally, for the production of multiple murderers to reach the unprecedented levels that it has in the America of the early twenty-first century, we require the existence of cultural forms that can mediate between killer and victim in a special sense—ridding the potential victims of any humanity, and the potential killer of any responsibility. Both sociologists Christopher Lasch and Barbara Ehrenreich have argued most persuasively that we have developed these forms with little refinement. Lasch devoted a volume to delineating the nature of this "culture of competitive individualism" which carries "the logic of individualism to the extreme of a war of all against all, the pursuit of happiness to the dead end of a narcissistic preoccupation with the self." Ehrenreich dwelt upon the sources of this ideology which so encouraged the severing of responsibility between people. She saw its roots in the developing post-war male culture of "escape—literal escape from the bondage of breadwinning." Here, men were urged to take part in the superficial excitement of "the nightmare anomie of the pop psychologists' vision: a world where other people are objects of consumption, or the chance encounters of a 'self' propelled by impulse alone."[38]

Thus the freedom for which mankind had struggled over the centuries proved to be a two-edged sword. The freedom from the suffocation of family and community, the freedom from systems of religious thought, the freedom to explore one's self, all entailed heavy penalties to society—not the least of which was the rate of multiple murder. Whether the industrial system was socialist or capitalist, its members were forced to look upon themselves and others as marketable commodities. It can hardly be surprising then that some fevered souls, feeling like automatons, might choose to coalesce their fuzzy identity in a series of fearful acts. Their ambitions crushed, some would lash out in protest at objects (most often sexual) which they had been taught to see as essentially insignificant. Now the question asked by the killer Bundy seems less inappropriate: "What's one less person on the face of the earth, anyway?"

Each of our case studies reveals that at a certain point in his life, the future killer experiences a kind of *internal* social crisis, when he realizes that he cannot be what he wishes to be—cannot live his version of the American dream. When these killers reach that existential divide, the seed is planted for a vengeance spree. Sometimes their motives are entirely conscious (as with the D.C. Snipers, Essex, Bundy, and Panzram); while with others (like Berkowitz and DeSalvo), they are only dimly understood. In either case, it is unrealizable ambition that motivates them, as they launch a kind of sub-political and personal assault on society, aiming always at the class or group they feel oppresses or excludes them. Some require minimal justification for their acts, obtaining temporary relief from their rage through the killings and then "forgetting" or compartmentalizing their memories, as when DeSalvo remarked: "I was there, it was done, and yet if you talked to me an hour later, or half hour later, it didn't mean nothing." Still others construct elaborate intellectual (Panzram) or spiritual (Berkowitz's demons) rationalizations to explain and justify their killings. Only a few (such as Joseph Kallinger, and California's Herbert Mullins, who murdered to "stop earthquakes") detach themselves so much from conventional reality that they construct their own universes, thereby entering that state the psychiatrists call madness.

Yet what they are *all* orchestrating is a kind of social leveling, in which they rewrite the universe to incorporate themselves: No one expressed this more clearly than Starkweather when he said that "dead people are all on the same level." They are all engaged in the same process, claiming their "manhood" by punishing the innocent; in doing so they recreate the dehumanized industrial system in a form that gives themselves a central position. One hundred eyes for an eye: It is by no means the first time in human history that retaliating men have grossly exceeded the degree of the original insult. Neither do they form their missions in a private vacuum, bereft of all advice, for the larger culture encodes in them a respect for violent display—an especially central theme in the media messages beamed at the working class—and the ready availability of stimulating materials in books and magazines, films, videotapes, and the Internet, teaches them to link their lust with violence. If we were charged with the responsibility for designing a society in which all structural and cultural mechanisms leaned toward the creation of the killers of strangers, we could do no better than to present the purchaser with the shape of modern America.

The Negotiation of Murderous Identity

The twilight of the human race on this planet may well have been the thirty or forty thousand years our ancestors dwelt in relatively egalitarian (one assumes) hunting and gathering societies. In such non-stratified societies, there was little specialization of labor, little production of surplus, and few opportunities for aggressive and ambitious individuals to overcome the reluctance of their fellows to submit to any expropriation of the social commodities for which human beings compete—power, prestige, and wealth. However, something like 10,000 years ago all our ancestors began to make the shift from hunting and gathering to agriculture and pastoralism—new forms of economy that captured a larger amount of energy for each hour of work. When eight could thus do the work to feed ten, the stage was set for the production of a surplus and the expropriation of that surplus by an emerging class of elites. And so the form and structure of society was entirely rewritten: Now rank and hierarchy, not mutual obligation, began to emerge as *the* organizing principles of human society. That development provided the framework for the growth over the millennia of social classes: clusters of individuals with mutual interests who stood in opposition to individuals of other social classes. Over time, new classes emerged and struggled for ascendancy, as did the bourgeoisie in the nineteenth century. Thus some groups are more threatened than others in different periods of history. It is precisely at the point in time when a single class is most threatened (when its rights are challenged by another class, its legitimacy questioned by a discontented proletariat, or its newfound status imprecisely defined) that we can expect to find some members of that class beginning to fantasize about killing members of another class.

Thus the multiple murderer does not appear at random through history. He appears at special points in social evolution, during periods of particular tension. Durkheim's thoughts on destruction (although he was concerned with self-destruction) are central here. Despite the glories of humanity, it remains a fragile species. Its equilibrium is in such a delicate state of balance that any crisis (financial, industrial, or social) in the larger system disorients the individuals in that system. It matters not whether they are crises of prosperity or of poverty: It merely matters that individuals' expectations are profoundly shaken.

> Every disturbance of equilibrium, even though it achieves greater comfort and a heightening of general vitality, is an impulse to voluntary death. Whenever serious readjustments take place in the social order, whether or not due to a sudden growth or to an unexpected catastrophe, men are more inclined to self-destruction.

In the archaic, pre-industrial period, it was the old and "noble" landed aristocracy which was most threatened by the rebellious peasantry and the rising mercantile classes. It makes a certain terrible sense that it was among this threatened class that fantasies of disordered self-indulgent sexuality might turn to the torture and murder of the lower orders. During the industrial revolution of the late eighteenth and nineteenth centuries, while the aristocracy retired to its estates to lick its wounds and the rising bourgeoisie reveled in its ascendancy, it was the new marginal middle classes—men like Wagner and Dr. Cream—who, insecure in their unaccustomed roles, would grow obsessed with a sense of possible exposure and failure. During that period, it would primarily be doctors, government clerks, and school teachers who might discipline those of the lower orders—who perhaps whispered about past errors or who flaunted their indifference.[39]

In the early twentieth century, a new homicidal theme emerged. Proletarian revolt became a minor expression, in which those (like Panzram) who glimpsed their utter exclusion, who felt their torture at the hands of the bourgeois institutions constructed for their "rehabilitation," wreaked a similar havoc. These proletarians would continue into the modern era, as with the D.C. Snipers, but they would be a minor theme: Their class would find alternative forms of protest, either in direct political action, or in smothering their claims in drugs and alcohol, or just as commonly in theft. Murder for its own sake had relatively little appeal to a class with such immediate problems.

The major homicidal form of the modern era is the man who straddles the border between the upper-working class and the lower-middle class. Often, as with Robert Hansen in Alaska or cousins Kenneth Bianchi and Angelo Buono in Los Angeles (The "Hillside Stranglers"), they continue a metaphor from the earlier era and discipline unruly prostitutes and runaways. Commonly, too, they punish those above them in the system—preying on unambiguously middle-class figures such as university women. In any case, they are all justifying their behavior and drawing their ideas from a *dehumanizing mass culture* that glorifies and legitimizes violence as an appropriate—even "manly"—response to the disappointments that are a normal part of life. In such a cultural milieu, self-control remains untaught, even stigmatized as submission and cowardice.

All class-based industrial nation-states, regardless of their professed ideologies, transform their members into either winners or losers. By the mid-1960s, however, the increasing closure of middle-class positions meant there would be many more losers, many more who were alienated and despairing. Moreover, as these positions were closing, other social forces within society continued their transformation of neighbors into strangers: The constriction of the extended family, the expansion of the anonymous city and suburb, the geographic mobility of individual familial units, and the disintegration of marriage and parenthood all made it progressively easier for the potential killer to overcome his scruples. The murder and mutilation of such enemy-strangers is but the abuse of a commodity. Thus we find the source of our new multiple murderer primarily among the ambitious who failed—or who believed they would fail—and who seek another form of success in the universal celebrity and attention they will receive through their extravagant homicides. In the performance of this task they are aided immensely by the extraordinary tolerance the social system offers their activities, providing only paltry resources for the monitoring and apprehension of potential killers.

Whether they kill all at once in a bloody hour or day, or whether they kill over an extended period, whether their motives appear to be economic, "sexual," or "psychotic," the objects of our study are all much of a kind. They all decide independently to construct a program of killing many strangers. On the surface of things they appear to be doing it for the thrill of sexual excitement or the intoxication of conquest; but the truth is they do it to relieve a burning grudge engendered by their failed ambition. Some are so finished with life that they wish to die when they have discharged their brief task: They come to be called "mass murderers," and they leave it up to a bewildered public to decipher their message. Others wish to live and tell their stories and bask in their fame: They usually come to be called "serial murderers."

"The tragedy and irony is that what has produced this abomination is the achievement of the freedom for which mankind has struggled for centuries—freedom to explore one's self without reference to rigid systems of thought. That freedom exacts a terrible price, for it releases humans too much from their social contract. Under such conditions, those whose ambitions are denied (and there are more of these each year since the 1960s when closure first occurred), in a culture which so glamorizes and rewards violence, find a solution to all their problems in that purple explosion. As many more come to feel excluded in this time of industrial and social crisis, we can expect many more to follow the path of the University of Chicago undergraduate, William Heirens, who searched for something—he knew not what—in the dissected entrails of a kidnapped child, and wrote in lipstick upon the walls of another victim's apartment: 'FOR HEAVEN'S SAKE CATCH ME BEFORE I KILL MORE I CANNOT CONTROL MYSELF.'"[40]

Punishment of Multiple Murderers

There is a widespread public anxiety that such notorious killers might one day be released from prison. This fear is fanned by the fact that in many jurisdictions—in the U.S., Canada, and elsewhere—the law requires that all convicted murderers be automatically *considered* for parole after serving a specified period of time in prison. Thus each time this usually perfunctory and legally mandated process is to be performed with notorious killers—say, with Myra Hindley in Britain, with Charles Manson in the U.S., or with Clifford Olson in Canada—there is almost universal media and public hysteria that these killers might actually be paroled.

However, the facts do not justify this concern. It is true that Mary Bell who, as a preadolescent, murdered two small boys in England, was released and given a new identity after serving several decades in prison. Inexplicably, so was Denis Lortie—who murdered several people in Quebec's government buildings—after serving less than a decade. Caril Fugate, who was convicted at fourteen of being an accomplice to Charles Starkweather's murderous rampage across Nebraska, was paroled after eighteen years in prison and given a new identity.

Yet these are rare exceptions, and multiple murderers do not normally receive parole. It is true that single murderers are usually released, and so many of them should be since their recidivism rate is very low (well below one percent in Canada). However, most courts implicitly recognize that multiple murderers have constructed their entire identities on the basis of their killings and that they therefore pose a continuing threat to society. Most politicians understand that to release such killers would be to corrode all sense of popular justice and irrevocably weaken their own chances of reelection. Most states in America specifically prohibit the release of serial and mass murderers and employ either the death sentence or life imprisonment without parole to deal with such cases. In Hickey's U.S. sample of 157 male serial killers, one-fifth had been executed, another fourteen percent were awaiting execution, a few had committed suicide or been killed in prison, and the remainder will be incarcerated for the rest of their lives.[41]

Justice and the Death Penalty

Is justice done in such cases? What would be an appropriate punishment for those who have utterly abandoned their own humanity and that of their victims? Are multiple murderers the only people who deserve to die, as some states stipulate? What about those who savagely rape and kill a child or a woman? What about those who kill a 7/Eleven clerk simply to eliminate a witness to their robbery or to vent their frustration? What about those who do not kill at all, yet perpetrate crimes of such barbarity that they clearly do not deserve to live? I am thinking, for example, of one man in California who kidnapped a fourteen-year-old girl, held her captive in his basement while he repeatedly raped her, then cut off both her arms and left her to bleed to death. In fact, this amazing young woman somehow escaped from the basement, was rushed to hospital, and lived to accuse her attacker. Did he "deserve" to live?

What do we say to the unrepentant killers and, more surprisingly, the dozens of well-meaning people who gather around them to worry about their "rights"? The British *Guardian* recently reported that the family of twelve-year-old *Polly Klaas*, kidnapped from her home and then raped and murdered, had been forced to start a campaign to stop her loathsome killer from "seeking young pen pals via a prisoners'

charity web site, the Canadian Coalition Against the Death Penalty."
Marc Klaas, her father, told the press: "This guy killed my daughter,
and there he is, smiling and asking for pen pals. . . . I'd hack the [web
site of the] son-of-a-bitch if I could." But "managers of the site, which
has web pages and pen pal requests for more than 1,000 condemned
prisoners, were defiant." What is the sensibility of these "defiant"
defenders of the rights of child killers? Why is it so disconnected from
the feelings of the victims' families?

According to the United Nations, one-half of the countries in the
world, virtually all undeveloped Third World nations, still execute and
torture prisoners. There are firing squads in Liberia; amputations in
Sudan; beheadings and amputations in Saudi Arabia. In Iran, men are
flogged in public for crimes like blasphemy or disturbing the peace;
some are even starved to death. Communist China is the world's leading executioner: Those who are about to die are first gruesomely
paraded in open trucks through the streets to their execution. The death
penalty is invoked for murder, bank robbery, and political corruption
in China, often with a bullet in the head, and tens of thousands of Chinese criminals have been executed in the past twenty years. In a recent
year when the U.S. executed sixty-six people, China put to death at least
3,000, perhaps ten times as many per capita as the American rate.

But America is the *only* modern developed nation that still deploys
the death penalty. Most modern societies find an ethical path that allows
them to distinguish between what the offenders deserve and what society is willing to allow to be perpetrated in its name. By comparison, the
U.S. is ruthless, even vindictive, in its treatment of criminals: Despite all
its executions, however, America still has the highest murder rate in the
western developed world—and by a very large margin.*

Is the death penalty a deterrent to other would-be killers as so many
"law and order" politicians proclaim? It seems such a plausible idea
that the worse the punishment for a crime, the more that punishment
will deter persons contemplating a homicide from committing such

* America is also one of the world's largest jailers, with more prisoners in California
alone than in most of Western Europe combined.

crimes. But plausible ideas do not always withstand close scrutiny, and nothing better represents this flaw in common sense than the death penalty for murder. The fact is that the vast majority of homicides in any country are committed in a moment of uncontrolled passion; and the killers are acting according to deeply emotional cultural notions of manliness and righteousness, not calculating the possible punishments for their deeds.

Do homicide rates skyrocket when the threat of death is removed? Fortunately, it is no longer necessary for us to speculate on the effectiveness of the death penalty as a deterrent to further crime. In their brilliant study of this phenomenon, *Violence and Crime in Cross-National Perspective*, Rosemary Gartner and Dane Archer have provided conclusive international evidence that it is not. Assembling data from 110 nations that had abolished the death penalty during the last century, they found that in some nations, homicide rates rose after abolition while in others the homicide rates fell. This means that the rates *are immune to the death penalty*. It is other factors that cause fluctuations in homicide rates, and *the death penalty has no measurable deterrent value.*

Nation	Percentage Change After Abolition*
Austria	–1%
England & Wales	–3%
Finland	–31%
Israel	–57%
Italy	–3%
Sweden	–65%
Switzerland	–21%
Canada	+38%
Denmark	+5%
New Zealand	+100%
Norway	+11%

* Adapted from Archer and Gartner 1984:133

Thus our common sense expectations are confounded when subjected to scientific evidence. "If capital punishment is a more effective deterrent" than any of the alternatives, then "its abolition ought to be followed by homicide rate increases." But this was not the case at all, and in fact more often than not, abolition was followed "by absolute *decreases* in homicide rates." This does not of course mean that the abolition of the death penalty *causes* a decline in homicide, but rather that despite our assumptions and prejudices, there is no apparent connection between punishment and the likelihood that the crime will occur. In fact, homicide rates are caused by much more complex factors—by social and economic turmoil, and by deeply embedded cultural notions of the legitimacy of violence.[42]

Thus we can no longer speak about the death penalty as a deterrent against homicides: It is a personal and philosophical principle, not a scientific one. Supporting the notion of the death penalty is a moral and philosophical position, inextricably linked with personal notions of justice and vengeance, *not* a statement with any scientific foundation. What *should be done* with such killers now that we can no longer delude ourselves that execution is an effective deterrent? The maximum that can be tolerated by those who feel there has already been too much killing is to ensure that life imprisonment is truly for life and that such killers are utterly sealed off from the rest of humanity for the remainder of their lives. If we fear the cost of guarding, feeding, housing, and clothing them, let us empty our prisons of the tens of thousands of prisoners who are the victims of the mindless and ineffective "War on Drugs" (which is little more than a war on poor blacks and Hispanics), a war that only benefits organized crime (by keeping the street prices of illegal drugs unnaturally high) and government justice programs (by funding the endless proliferation of enforcement and legal personnel).

Reducing Violence

Every civilization occasionally produces individuals with a personality many psychologists and psychiatrists gloss as "psychopathic." By this they refer to those who have little or no feeling for others, low levels of impulse control, no remorse or guilt for what they might do, and whose primary pleasure lies in the sadistic abuse and manipulation or even obliteration of others. If modern societies are remarkably similar to one another, they nevertheless vary enormously in the proportion of their psychopathic population that goes on to commit rape, torture, and murder. Indeed, we suspect that in most societies the majority of "psychopaths" go on to live relatively normal lives, perhaps rising in politics, university administration, government, or the corporate world. In others they are more likely to act upon their illegal sexual fantasies. Why this difference?

America is one of the world's great civilizations. Its contributions to art, literature, theater, film, music, medicine, science and technology are unparalleled, as are its veneration of personal freedom, its industrial capacity and its military prowess. But its crime problem is also without parallel: Americans are five to ten times more likely to be murdered than western Europeans, and three to four times more likely than Canadians—all this despite the nation's harsh treatment of its criminals. How can they escape from this trap?

America's pattern of bullyboy politics and pugnacious personalities was established long before Teddy Roosevelt instructed his minions to "carry a big stick," a reiteration of a much older American cultural principle which seems to revere aggressivity. "In America," wrote Clancy Sigal, "murderers are more valued, certainly more admired, than their victims." No wonder Lewis Lapham thundered that by the 1980s, America's film heroes "had become paramilitary figures . . . paranoid and enraged—angry at anybody and everybody to whom they could assign the fault for the world's evil."[6]

Sadly, there is nothing unique in the world about a man (and occasionally a woman) who goes on a killing rampage. But these atrocities happen far more often in modern America than anywhere else. Where did they learn the script they are acting out? A civilization pays a tragic price if it encodes in its citizens any of the following notions:

. . . That violence has an intoxicating beauty and nobility

. . . That a man must personally avenge his dishonor

... That it is acceptable to demean or abuse any vulnerable class, gender, or ethnic group

... That wealth, power and prestige are everything that matters

... That winning is glorious and losing is shameful

... That the suffering of others is their fault, not ours.

Some scholars have argued that the cause of all this lies buried in the institutionalized oppression at the bottom of the hierarchy, released as child abuse by the disordered family toiling at the bottom of society and avenged later in life as a (often sexualized) killing spree; but perhaps a more significant element in the formation of murderous personalities is *cultural*, the set of ideas implanted in the maturing child about the righteousness of slaughter, the cultural codes that "teach" young persons—especially males—that violence is appropriate in a variety of social situations beyond self-defense. Moreover, a nation that does not bend its energies to ameliorating the deprivation and alienation of those on the bottom pays a heavy price in murder. It is no coincidence that the nations of western Europe—England, France, the Netherlands, Germany, Austria, and the Scandinavian nations—with their generous welfare and educational systems are the ones that (along with Japan) produce the lowest homicide rates in the world. America would do well to remove its ideological blinkers and examine its friends more closely.

The Integration of Theory

How much further can we expect to advance in our understanding of the wellsprings of human aggression? Alas, not much further so long as we maintain the present fratricidal structure of modern science—in which the disciplines compete with one another, like the cheapest politicians, for funding and dominance. This is an intellectual disaster, choking the hope of all scientific advance and dooming the field to stagnation.

In his magisterial work, *Europe and the People without History*, Eric Wolf remarked that the primary intellectual achievement of the twentieth century was also its greatest weakness. Science had divided human behavior and experience into manageable "bits" such as history, biology, economy, psychology, society, and so on; but then, lost in these arbitrary distinctions, made no comparable attempt to reassemble what had been so artificially dismembered. Indeed, we are only at the beginning of our understanding of human behavior (healthy or otherwise), and a true and deepened comprehension of pathological aggression is unlikely to emerge until the insights from each discipline are integrated in a meaningful and balanced way.

The basic dilemmas remain unchanged: The social sciences have charted the cultural and structural pressures that ultimately create pathological behavior; yet they are unable to explain why the majority of people exposed to these social pressures do not kill. The psychological sciences have dissected a portion of the psychological and biological vulnerability to aggressive behavior in any individual; yet they are unable to explain why there are such massive differences between societies (and genders and social classes) in their levels of violence. Everywhere in the world, physical violence is overwhelmingly a male domain; yet radical feminist analysis is rarely able to transcend mere sexism in its analysis of the cause of differences between men and women.

One of the most intriguing possibilities is the proper integration of the levels of understanding offered by these various academic disciplines. Thus the social and economic forces that create so many violent and "dysfunctional" families could be analyzed, together with the psychological mechanisms that severely abused children develop to cope with their obliteration. In turn, these socioeconomic and psychological factors would, in cases of individuals with biological/chemical deficits that mitigate against impulse control, create individuals "programmed" to revel in the display of vengeful savagery. Such a balanced and integrated enterprise awaits its polymathic leader.

Notes

N.B. In the interests of readability and to avoid notation clutter, the numbering of sources has been limited to one numeral per paragraph or section. References to sources noted below each number are listed in their order of appearance within each respective section of the text.

Chapter One

1 Lucas, in Rone Tempest, *Los Angeles Times,* Oct. 30, 1983; and Lucas, on ABC Television News' *20/20,* July 1984
2 Lucas, ibid
3 *Maclean's* magazine, July 30, 1984
4 Etna Huberty, in ibid
5 *Associated Press,* April 16, 1984; *People* magazine, April 30, 1984; and *Time,* April 16, 1984
6 Based on dispatches from: Fox Butterfield, N.R. Kleinfield and Erica Goode, David M. Halbfinger, Sarah Kershaw, Blaine Harden, Tim Golden, David Gonzales, Nick Madigan, Francis X. Clines, Christopher Drew, and Charlie LeDuff, all writing in the *New York Times;* from Serge F. Kovaleski and Mary Beth Sheridan in the *Washington Post;* Bob Orr in *CBS News;* and items in CBS *News online, The Associated Press,* and the *Guardian* (UK).
7 Peter J. Wilson 1974: 138
8 Amnesty International 1983: 36
9 On PBS TV's *Frontline,* May 1984
10 Widely published press reports
11 Nilsen in Lisners 1983: 178–180
12 Unpublished correspondence

13 Gaylin 1983: 249
14 Hickey 1991: 20
15 Ratner 1996: 128–129

Chapter Two

1   Holmes & De Burger (1988), 48–59
2   Fox 1971: 63–65
3   Leyton, M. et al. 1997: 17
4   Lunde 1979: 48–56
5   Hare n.d.: 95–96
6   Giannangelo 1996: 19, 48, 53
7   Meloy 1998: 6; Egger 1998: 28
8   Cameron & Frazer 1987: 166–168
9   Hickey 1991: 107, 124, 56, 111–112, 107, 143
10 Jenkins 1994: 156–157; Cluff 1997: 293, 305–306
11 Egger 1990: 29; Jenkins 1994: 40, 49, 33
12 See Hickey 1991; Ratner 1996; 125–127

Chapter Three

1   Kemper, in Cheney 1976: 140
2   Lunde 1979: 54
3   Cheney 1976: 9; and Dr. Joel Fort, in ibid, 183
4   Lunde 1979: 54–55; and West 1974: 187
5   Cheney 1976: 14, 10
6   Ibid, 15; and Lunde 1979: 54
7   Mrs. Clarnell Kemper, quoted in Cheney 1976: 18; Lunde 1979: 55; Cheney 1976: 21; and Lunde 1979: 55
8   Kemper, in Cheney 1976: 22; quoted in Cheney 1976: 23; and Lunde 1979: 55
9   Cheney 1976: 41–42
10 Kemper, in ibid, 87, 90
11 Kemper, in ibid, 89–91
12 Kemper, in ibid, 95; Cheney 1976: 96–97; and Kemper, in ibid, 97–98
13 Ibid, 53, 104, 105
14 Kemper, in ibid, 105; and Cheney 1976: 108
15 Kemper, in ibid, 113; and Cheney 1976: 113–114
16 Kemper, in ibid, 123, 125
17 Kemper, in ibid, 127; and Cheney 1976: 129

18 Kemper, in ibid, 140
19 Kemper, in ibid, 132
20 Kemper, in ibid, 133; and Cheney 1976: 133
21 Kemper, in ibid, 134
22 Cheney 1976: 135–137, 138–139
23 West 1974: 200; Kemper, in ibid, 200; and Cheney 1976: 148
24 Kemper, in ibid, 169
25 Kemper, in ibid, 154
26 Cheney 1976: 142
27 Ibid, 142
28 Kemper, in West 1974: 196; Kemper, in Cheney 1976: 127, 195
29 Kemper, in ibid, 166
30 Kemper, in ibid, 194, 166
31 Kemper, in ibid, 128
32 Cheney 1976: 167
33 Kemper, in Cheney 1976: 140, 143
34 Kemper, in ibid, 86, 152
35 Kemper, in ibid, 152
36 Kemper, in ibid, 87, 141
37 Kemper, in ibid, 145, 86
38 Kemper, in West 1974: 187, 163; and Kemper, in Lunde 1979: 55
39 Kemper, in Cheney 1976: 88; Kemper, in West 1974: 164; Kemper, in Cheney 1976: 90; and Kemper, in West 1974: 167
40 Kemper, in ibid, 199
41 Kemper, in Cheney 1976: 146, 147
42 Kemper, in ibid, 108
43 Kemper, in ibid, 171; and Kemper, in West 1974: 200
44 Kemper, in Lunde 1979: 55; and Kemper, in West 1974: 193
45 Kemper, in ibid, 199
46 Kemper, in Cheney 1976: 147
47 Cheney 1976: xiii
48 Kemper, in West 1974: 188
49 Mrs. Clarnell Kemper, in Cheney 1976: 8; Mrs. Clarnell Kemper, in West 1974: 194; Kemper's father, in West 1974: 194–195; and West 1974: 195
50 Kemper, in Cheney 1976: 11–12; and Lunde 1979: 54
51 Kemper, in West 1974: 189–190
52 Kemper, in ibid, 186
53 West 1974: 16–17; and Kemper, paraphrased by a neighbor, in West 1974: 17–18
54 Kemper, in ibid, 192

55 Kemper, in ibid, 163–164; West 1974: 83; and Kemper, in ibid, 198
56 Kemper, in Lunde 1979: 198; and Kemper, in Cheney 1976: 69
57 Kemper in West 1974: 192, 160; and Kemper, in Cheney 1976: 153
58 Kemper, in ibid, 32
59 Kemper, in ibid, 144
60 Kemper, in ibid, 140
61 Kemper, in ibid, 147, 148
62 Kemper, in ibid, 151; Kemper, in West 1974: 197, 193–194
63 Kemper, in Cheney 1976: 128; and Kemper, in West 1974: 198
64 Kemper, in Cheney 1976: 39–40, 143
65 Kemper, in ibid, 88
66 Kemper, in ibid, 99; and Kemper, in West 1974: 163
67 Kemper, in Cheney 1976: 106–107, 109
68 Kemper, in ibid, 172
69 Quoted in Cheney 1976: 194
70 Quoted in ibid, 23
71 Quoted in ibid, 23
72 Quoted in ibid, 30
73 Quoted in Lunde 1979: 89–90
74 Quoted in Cheney 1976: 3
75 Dr. Joel Fort, in Cheney 1976: 175
76 Dr. Joel Fort, in ibid, 176–177
77 Dr. Joel Fort, in ibid, 179, 181
78 Lunde 1979: 35, 53
79 Kemper, in Cheney 1976: 152
80 Kemper, in ibid, 152
81 Kemper, in ibid, 129, 151–152, 154
82 Kemper, in ibid, 154
83 Kemper, in ibid, 152, 155
84 Kemper, in Lunde 1979: 89

Chapter Four

1 Bundy, in Michaud and Aynesworth 1983: 324
2 Larsen 1980: 100; Kendall, in Larsen 1980: 102; and Michaud and Aynesworth 1983; 120, 121
3 Ibid, 30–31
4 Ibid, 31–32; and Bundy, in ibid, 127
5 Ibid, 32–33; quoted in ibid, 34–35; and ibid, 36–37, and 56

6   Rule 1980: 64; and Bundy, in Michaud and Aynesworth 1983: 131,132–133, 136
7   Bundy, in ibid, 137–138
8   Rule 1980: 68; and Michaud and Aynesworth 1983: 40
9   Ibid, 40; Bundy, in ibid, 140–143; and Kendall 1981: 52
10 Michaud and Aynesworth 1983: 54
11 Ibid, 91–92
12 Ibid, 108–110, 104
13 Ibid, 113
14 Ibid, 229
15 Ibid, 260–261
16 Bundy, in Winn and Merrill 1980: 314
17 Quoted in ibid, 110; and quoted in Larsen 1980: 94
18 Winn and Merrill 1980: 28–29
19 Quoted in Michaud and Aynesworth 1983: 319; quoted in Winn and Merrill 1980: 154; and Daryl Ondrak, in ibid, 86
20 Quoted in Michaud and Aynesworth 1983: 319, 320
21 Quoted in Winn and Merrill 1980: 163
22 Quoted in ibid, 164; and quoted in Larsen 1980: 159
23 Bundy, in Rule 1980: 203–204, 208
24 Bundy, in ibid, 207
25 Winn and Merrill 1980: 296; and Emanuel Tanay, in Michaud and Aynesworth 1983: 264
26 Bundy, in ibid, 313
27 Bundy, in Rule 1980: 218; and Bundy, in Larsen 1980: 182
28 Bundy, in Rule 1980: 312, 322
29 Bundy, in Winn and Merrill 1980: 302, 309
30 Bundy, in ibid, 309–310, 311
31 Bundy, in ibid, 313, 314, 315
32 Bundy, in Michaud and Aynesworth 1983: 24; and Bundy in Winn and Merrill 1980: 358
33 Bundy, in ibid, 119
34 Cathy Swindler, in Larsen 1980: 5–6; and quoted in Larsen 1980: 154
35 Louise Bundy, in Winn and Merrill 1980: 354–355
36 Bundy, in Larsen 1980: 297, 156–157
37 Bundy, in ibid, 232; and Bundy, in Winn and Merrill 1980: 109
38 Rule 1980: 21; Winn and Merrill 1980: 113; and Bundy, in ibid, 110
39 Rule 1980: 31
40 Bundy, in Winn and Merrill 1980: 104, 280
41 Ibid, 22

42 Bundy, in ibid, 116
43 Ibid, 23; and Bundy, in ibid, 116–117
44 Bundy, in ibid, 118
45 Bundy, in ibid, 119–120, 121–122
46 Bundy, in ibid, 123
47 Bundy, in ibid, 123
48 Bundy, in ibid, 130, 141
49 Bundy, in ibid, 219
50 Ibid, 220, 232, 307
51 Bundy, in Rule 1980: 221
52 Michaud and Aynesworth 1983: 59–61
53 Bundy, in Rule 1980: 201; Kendall 1981: 14; and Bundy, in Michaud and Aynesworth 1983: 23
54 Larsen 1980: 96; in Rule 1980: 167; and Bundy, in Larsen 1980: 157
55 Bundy, in Winn and Merrill 1980: 107
56 Bundy, in Larsen 1980: 232
57 Bundy, in Michaud and Aynesworth 1983: 113, 150; and unidentified psychiatrist, in ibid, 152
58 Bundy, in ibid, 163, 180, 181
59 Bundy, in ibid, 265, 267
60 Bundy, in Winn and Merrill 1980: 321, 289
61 Ibid, 257, 104; Terry Storwick, in Michaud and Aynesworth 1983: 65; and Bundy, in Rule 1980: 27
62 Bundy, in Michaud and Aynesworth 1983: 65–67, 68
63 Bundy, in ibid, 69, 70–72
64 Bundy, in ibid, 72–73
65 Bundy, in ibid, 76, 78–79
66 Ibid, 82, 83, 84
67 Bundy, in ibid, 324
68 Bundy, in Kendall 1981: 164
69 Bundy, in Michaud and Aynesworth 1983: 133, 144
70 Bundy, in Kendall 1981: 164; Bundy, in Rule 1980: 207; Bundy, in Winn and Merrill 1980: 172
71 Peter and Favret 1975: 188
72 Bundy, in ibid, 251, 254
73 Bundy, in ibid, 318, 317, 319
74 Bundy, in ibid, 321
75 In ibid, 113, 169
76 Ibid, 107

77 Bundy, in Michaud and Aynesworth 1983: 312, 307.

Chapter Five

1   DeSalvo, in Frank 1967: 352
2   DeSalvo, in ibid, 251
3   DeSalvo, in ibid, 313
4   DeSalvo, in ibid, 288; DeSalvo, in Rae 1967: 9; and Frank 1967: 288–289, 20
5   DeSalvo, in Frank 1967: 351–352
6   DeSalvo, in ibid, 291–293; and Frank 1967: 28
7   DeSalvo, in ibid, 293, 294, 296; and Frank 1967: 25
8   DeSalvo, in ibid, 299–300; and Sgt. James McDonald, in ibid, 39
9   DeSalvo, in ibid, 301, 43
10 DeSalvo, in ibid, 302–303
11 DeSalvo, in ibid, 304–306, 56
12 Ibid, 155, 309–310
13 DeSalvo, in ibid, 312; DeSalvo, in Rae 1967: 123; and Autopsy report, quoted in Rae 1967: 123
14 DeSalvo, in Frank 1967: 355–357, 65
15 DeSalvo, in ibid, 316–317, 83–84
16 DeSalvo, in ibid, 314–315, 85
17 DeSalvo, in ibid, 320–323; and Police report, in ibid, 87–88
18 DeSalvo, in ibid, 335
19 DeSalvo, in ibid, 325
20 DeSalvo, in ibid, 243–244, 250–251; and quoted by Edward Kearney, in Frank 1967: 252, 253, 254
21 DeSalvo, in ibid, 265
22 Ibid, 273–274
23 DeSalvo, in ibid, 288 and 309
24 DeSalvo, in ibid, 313, 293; DeSalvo, in Rae 1967: 31; and DeSalvo, in Frank 1967: 295–296
25 DeSalvo, in ibid, 296–297, 300–301
26 DeSalvo, in ibid, 303–304, 306, 316
27 DeSalvo, in ibid, 315, 320–321, 330, 352–353
28 DeSalvo, in Brussel 1968: 193
29 DeSalvo, in Frank 1967: 275–276, 326–327; and DeSalvo, in Rae 1967: 97
30 DeSalvo, in Frank 1967: 357
31 DeSalvo, in Rae 1967: 27; and DeSalvo, in Frank 1967: 329

32　DeSalvo, in Rae 1967: 27–28
33　DeSalvo, in ibid, 27–28
34　DeSalvo, in ibid, 39–40, 29
35　DeSalvo, in ibid, 47
36　DeSalvo, in ibid, 48
37　DeSalvo, in ibid, 73–74
38　DeSalvo, in Frank 1967: 334–336
39　DeSalvo, in Rae 1967: 109–110
40　DeSalvo, in ibid, 61–62
41　DeSalvo, in ibid, 97; DeSalvo, in Frank 1967: 296–297; and DeSalvo, in Rae 1967: 108
42　DeSalvo, in Frank 1967: 323, 380
43　DeSalvo, in ibid, 323
44　DeSalvo, in Rae 1967: 82–83; and DeSalvo, in Frank 1967: 240
45　DeSalvo, in Rae 1967: 22
46　DeSalvo, in Frank 1967: 265; and DeSalvo, in Rae 1967: 85
47　DeSalvo, in ibid, 86
48　DeSalvo, in ibid, 130, 133
49　DeSalvo, in ibid, 143–144; and DeSalvo, in Frank 1967: 314, 338–339, 330
50　DeSalvo, in Rae 1967: 40–41
51　DeSalvo, in Frank 1967: 325
52　Dr. Doris Sidwell, quoted in Frank 1967: 342; and DeSalvo, in Rae 1967: 78, 84, 87
53　Dr. Philip Solomon, quoted in Frank 1967: 48; Dr. Ames Robey, quoted in ibid, 138; and R. James A. Brussel, quoted in ibid, 142
54　Quoted in ibid, 165–166, 168; Dr. James A. Brussel, quoted in Rae 1967: 142; and Dr. James A. Brussel, quoted in Frank 1967: 172
55　Ibid, 244; and quoted in ibid, 245
56　Dr. Robert Mezer and Dr. Samuel Tartakoff, quoted in ibid, 371–372; and Dr. Ames Robey, quoted in ibid, 372
57　DeSalvo, in ibid, 331
58　Peter and Favret 1975: 175
59　Ibid, 175
60　DeSalvo, in Frank 1967: 364, 365
61　DeSalvo, in ibid, 366; Rae 1967: 26; Justice John MacLeod, quoted in Frank 1967: 342; and DeSalvo, in ibid, 366
62　DeSalvo, in ibid, 366–367, 321
63　DeSalvo, in Rae 1967: 9
64　DeSalvo, in Frank 1967: 367, 277

65 DeSalvo, in ibid, 331

Chapter Six

1 Berkowitz, in Willeford 1980: 71
2 Berkowitz 1981: n.p.
3 Berkowitz 1981: n.p.; and Klausner 1981: 265–266
4 Berkowitz, in ibid, 13
5 Berkowitz, in ibid, 15–16
6 There is a discrepancy here between two accounts: Abrahamsen says there was only one knife assault, while Klausner describes two. It is not a significant matter. Berkowitz, in Abrahamsen 1983: 62; Klausner 1981: 17; and Berkowitz, in ibid, 18
7 Berkowitz, in ibid, 56–57
8 Berkowitz, in ibid, 58, 60; and Berkowitz, in Abrahamsen 1983: 63
9 Berkowitz, in Klausner 1981: 62–63; and Berkowitz, in Abrahamsen 1983: 63
10 Berkowitz, in ibid, 190; Berkowitz, in Klausner 1981: 88; Berkowitz, in Abrahamsen 1983: 190; and Klausner 1981: 89
11 Donna DeMasi, in Klausner 1981: 95–96; Berkowitz, in ibid, 98–99; Klausner 1981: 99; and Carpozi 1977: 50
12 Berkowitz, in Abrahamsen 1983: 190
13 Berkowitz, in Klausner 1981: 106–107
14 Klausner 1981: 115–116
15 Berkowitz, in Abrahamsen 1983: 190–192; Berkowitz, in Klausner 1981: 120–121; Carpozi 1977: 83; and Klausner 1981: 126–127
16 Berkowitz, in Abrahamsen 1983: 192; Klausner 1981: 134; and Carpozi 1977: 109
17 Berkowitz, in Klausner 1981: 179, 185; Judy Placido, in Klausner 1981: 185; Berkowitz, in Abrahamsen 1983: 192; and Berkowitz, in Klausner 1981: 187–188
18 Berkowitz, in Abrahamsen 1983: 194; Robert Violante, in Klausner 1981: 226; and Berkowitz, in Klausner 1981: 234
19 Detective John Falotico, in Klausner 1981: 350–351
20 Berkowitz, in Willeford 1980: 272
21 Abrahamsen 1983: 62
22 Berkowitz 1981: n.p. All quotations in this section are from his prison diary, unless otherwise noted; and Berkowitz, in Klausner 1981: 195–196
23 Berkowitz, in Abrahamsen 1983: 63

24 Abrahamsen 1983: 62; and Berkowitz, in ibid, 62
25 Berkowitz, in ibid, 63
26 Berkowitz, in ibid, 63
27 Berkowitz, in ibid, 190, 192
28 Berkowitz, in ibid, 194
29 Berkowitz, in ibid, 193–194
30 Berkowitz, in ibid, 195
31 Berkowitz 1981: n.p.
32 Abrahamsen 1983: 62
33 Klausner 1981: 162; Dr. Edwin Wind in Klausner 1981: 291; and quoted in ibid, 140
34 Police Commissioner Tim Dowd, in ibid, 163
35 Judge R. A. Brown, in ibid, 369; and Dr. Daniel W. Schwartz, in ibid, 373–374
36 Dr. David Abrahamsen, in ibid, 374
37 Klausner 1981: 374–375; and Abrahamsen, in Klausner 1981: 375
38 Abrahamsen 1983: 62
39 Ibid, 62–63
40 Ibid, 192; and Berkowitz, in ibid, 193
41 Ibid, 193, 194
42 Ibid, 194
43 Ibid, 194
44 Ibid, 194
45 Berkowitz, in ibid, 195
46 Ibid, 194
47 Berkowitz, in ibid, 195 (my italics)
48 Berkowitz, letter to Iris Gerhardt, in Carpozi 1977: 281
49 Mrs. Lillian Goldstein, in ibid, 241
50 Goldstein, in ibid, 241; and David Margolies, in ibid, 245–246
51 Gerhardt, in ibid, 257
52 Berkowitz, in Klausner 1981: 69–70
53 Berkowitz, in Carpozi 1977: 259, 268–269
54 Berkowitz, to ibid, 259; and Davi Zammit, in Carpozi 1977: 260
55 Berkowitz, in ibid, 270–271
56 Berkowitz, in ibid, 275, 278–280
57 Berkowitz, in ibid, 280–281
58 Berkowitz, in Klausner 1981: 141–142
59 Berkowitz, in Carpozi 1977: 134
60 Berkowitz, in Klausner 1981: 177–178
61 Berkowitz, in Carpozi 1977: 134

62 Abrahamsen 1983: 62; and Berkowitz, in Klausner 1981: 12
63 Berkowitz, in Abrahamsen 1983: 63; Berkowitz in Klausner 1981: 13; and Abrahamsen 1983: 192, 63
64 Berkowitz, in Klausner 1981: 141–142
65 Berkowitz, in Abrahamsen 1983: 63, 195; and Berkowitz, in Klausner 1981: 168
66 Berkowitz, in ibid, 313, 315; and Klausner 1981: 119
67 Berkowitz, in ibid, 63
68 Berkowitz, in Willeford 1980: 71
69 Berkowitz, in ibid, 68; and Berkowitz, in Klausner 1981: 41
70 Berkowitz, in ibid, 16

Chapter Seven

1 James Alan Fox and Jack Levin, 2001. *The Will to Kill: Making Sense of Senseless Murder.* Boston: Allyn & Bacon. See also their earlier work, *Mass Murder.*
2 From an article in the *New York Times* by John M. Broder
3 Levin & Fox 1996: 65–68
4 Forty percent of this total are familicides, usually by a distraught or depressed parent.

Chapter Eight

1 Essex, in Hernon 1978: 255
2 Hernon 1978: 47, 19–22
3 Ibid, 49
4 Ibid, 55–56
5 Ibid, 68
6 Ibid, 93; and anonymous policeman, in ibid, 95–96
7 Ibid, 110–111
8 Ibid, 112–114
9 Donald Roberts, in ibid, 116
10 Ibid, 117–118
11 Ibid, 123
12 Ibid, 126–129
13 Ibid, 134–138
14 Ibid, 140–154
15 Ibid, 156
16 Ibid, 161–163, 172–174

17 Essex, in Hernon 1978: 176–178, 180–182; and Councilman Peter Beer, in ibid, 184
18 Detective L. J. Delsa, in ibid, 198
19 Councilman Peter Beer, in ibid, 203; and Hernon 1978: 200–203
20 Ibid, 204, 210
21 Sgt. Saacks, in ibid, 211; Alex Vega, in ibid, 212; and Officer Thomas Casey, in ibid, 213
22 Hernon 1978: 223, 226–231
23 Ibid, 232–234, 243–244
24 Ibid, 246–253
25 Rev. Mr. Chambers, in ibid, 52
26 Ibid, 50–52
27 Ibid, 52–53; Renee Greene, in ibid, 53; and Hernon 1978: 22–23
28 Essex, in ibid, 66
29 Hernon 1978: 23, 24; Lt. Robert Hatcher, in ibid, 24; and Paul Valdez, in ibid, 24–25
30 Essex, in ibid, 25
31 Hernon 1978: 25
32 Hatcher, in ibid, 38
33 Hernon 1978: 38
34 C. B. Wilson, in ibid, 39–40; and Fred Allen, in ibid, 40
35 Ibid, 18–19; and Essex, in ibid, 19
36 Essex, in ibid, 46, 52, 53
37 Mrs. Essex, in ibid, 53–54; and Rev. Mr. Chambers, in ibid, 54
38 Essex, in ibid, 63
39 Essex, in ibid, 58
40 Hatcher, in ibid, 59–60
41 Hatcher, in ibid, 60
42 Essex, in ibid, 62–63
43 Hernon 1978: 63–64; and Naval Station Commanding Officer, in ibid, 64
44 Essex, in ibid, 146
45 Tobias 1981: 81–82, 87–88; police report, in ibid, 89; and anonymous detective, in ibid, 107
46 Hernon 1978: 25–26; police report, in ibid, 26; FBI, in ibid, 26; and Hernon 1978: 26–27
47 Ibid, 36–37; and Penny Fox, in ibid, 38
48 Hernon 1978: 53–54, 64–65
49 Detective Edwin Cooper, in ibid, 71; and Hernon 1978: 71–72
50 Carlos Marighella, quoted in Hernon 1978: 73; and Detective Edwin Cooper, in ibid, 74

51 Hernon 1978: 74; and Grier and Cobbs 1968, quoted in ibid, 81
52 Hernon 1978: 87, 90–91
53 Ibid, 98–99; and Essex, in ibid, 101–102
54 Hernon 1978: 256
55 Tobias 1981: 112
56 Hernon 1978: 281
57 Louisiana Attorney-General William Guste, in Hernon 1978: 240; U.S. Attorney-General Richard Kleindienst, in Hernon 1978: 240; and Louisiana Governor Edwin Edwards, in Hernon, 239–240
58 New Orleans' Exec. Asst. to the Mayor, Robert Tucker, in Hernon 1978: 260–261; and Larry Jones, St Bernard Neighborhood Development Center, in Hernon 1978: 277
59 Dr. William Bloom, in Hernon 1978: 279–280
60 New Orleans Police Supt. Clarence Giarrusso, in ibid, 278–279
61 Dr. William Swanson, in ibid, 280–281; and Dr. Daniel Thompson, in ibid, 216
62 Erich Fromm 1975, quoted in ibid, 101
63 Hernon 1978: 177
64 Peter and Favret 1975: 175; Rex Williams, in Hernon. 1978: 264; Mrs. Essex, in ibid, 266; and Penny Fox, in ibid, 266–267
65 Quoted in Hernon 1978: 283

Chapter Nine

1   Starkweather, in Reinhardt 1960: 78
2   Starkweather, in Allen 1976: 35–36, 40
3   Starkweather, in ibid, 48–49,
4   Starkweather, in ibid, 50–51
5   Starkweather, in ibid, 51, 55–56
6   Allen 1976: 59, 65–68
7   Ibid, 73; and Starkweather, in Allen 1976: 77–78
8   Starkweather, in ibid, 78–79; and Allen 1976: 81–82
9   Ibid, 88, 90
10 Ibid, 91–92
11 Starkweather, in Allen 1976: 93; and Allen 1976: 94, 95
12 Ibid, 95–96
13 Starkweather, in Allen 1976: 98, 99, 100
14 Starkweather, in ibid, 102–103
15 Starkweather, in ibid, 108; and Caril Fugate, in Allen 1976: 111–112
16 Allen 1976: 113

17 Ibid, 118
18 Ibid, 120, 123
19 Joseph Sprinkle, in Allen 1976: 124; Caril Fugate, in ibid, 124; Allen 1976: 126; and Sheriff Earl Heflin, in Allen 1976: 127
20 Allen 1976: 135
21 Starkweather, in Reinhardt 1960: 22
22 Starkweather, in ibid, 82–83; and Beaver et al 1974: 91
23 Starkweather, in Reinhardt 1960: 52
24 Starkweather, in ibid, 27–28
25 Starkweather, in ibid, 28–29, 46
26 Starkweather, in ibid, 28
27 Starkweather, in ibid, 95–96
28 Quoted in Reinhardt 1960: 9, 10
29 Starkweather, in Reinhardt 1960: 23
30 Starkweather, in ibid, 14b [sic], 48
31 Starkweather, in ibid, 49, 54, 60, 61, 74, 75, 78
32 Starkweather, in Beaver et al 1974: 198; and Starkweather, in Allen 1976: 128
33 Starkweather, in Reinhardt 1960: 90
34 Reinhardt 1960: 32
35 Reinhardt 1960: 32; Starkweather, in Reinhardt 1960: 32–35
36 Starkweather, in ibid, 74–75, 78
37 Starkweather, in ibid, 19, 34
38 Starkweather, in ibid, 90, 94
39 Starkweather, in ibid, 48
40 Starkweather, in ibid, 58–59, 65
41 Starkweather, in ibid, 67, 75, 101. This passage is what Reinhardt calls a "free" or rough quotation.
42 Reinhardt 1960: 81; and Starkweather, in Reinhardt 1960: 81–82, 77, 22–23, 65
43 Starkweather, in ibid 48–49
44 Starkweather, in ibid, 13, 54, 56
45 Starkweather, in ibid, 60, 104
46 Starkweather, in ibid, 104–105, 49–50
47 Starkweather, in ibid, 50, 51, 53
48 Starkweather, in ibid, 90, 99, 100, A "free" quotation
49 Starkweather, in ibid, 93, 90
50 Starkweather, in ibid, 32
51 Quoted in Allen 1976: 137–138

52 Allen 1976: 153; and quoted in Allen 1976: 144
53 Allen 1976: 148, 139; Dr. John O'Hearne, quoted in ibid, 148; and Reinhardt 1960: 11
54 Dr. Robert Stein, quoted in Allen 1976: 153; and quoted in Reinhardt 1960: 11
55 Dr. Nathan Greenbaum, quoted in Allen 1976: 148–149
56 Dr. John O'Hearne, quoted in ibid, 150
57 Dr. John Steinman, quoted in ibid, 151–152; and Allen 1976: 153
58 Starkweather, in Reinhardt 1960: 98, 32; and Allen 1976: 144
59 Starkweather, in Reinhardt 1960: 51
60 Reinhardt 1960: 16
61 Allen 1976: 33
62 Howard Genuchi, in Allen 1976: 82
63 Allen 1976: 86
64 Quoted in ibid, 123
65 Starkweather, in Reinhardt 1960: 50
66 Peter and Favret 1975: 175–176; and Reinhardt 1960: 3
67 Starkweather, in Reinhardt 1960: 13, 28, 19, 34, 53, 67, 74–75, 99
68 Starkweather 1959: 10
69 Starkweather 1959: 13
70 Allen 1976: 178

Chapter Ten

1 Darnton 1984: 262
2 Joseph Kallinger, in F.R. Schreiber 1983: 410–411
3 Cusson 1983: 47; and Peter and Favret 1975: 186, 198
4 Abrams 1982: 267, 273–274 (my italics), 280, 297
5 Andreano and Siegfried 1980: 14
6 Lunde 1979: 48; Palmer 1972: 40; Wolfgang 1975: 207; and FBI 1982: 11
7 Palmer 1972: 40; cf. Williams 1984, Blau and Blau 1982, Flango and Sherbenou 1976, Gastil 1971, Loftin and Hill 1974, Messner 1982, 1983, Smith and Parker 1980, who are among the major contributors to the debate; Williams 1984: 288–289; cf. Rule 1980; Stark 1984; and Lunde 1979: 98
8 Cf. Calvert-Boyanowsky and Boyanowsky 1981; for a fascinating discussion of this, see Fox 1971. A solid if polemical critique of sociobiology can be found in Lewontin, Rose and Kamin 1984. Wilson, Edward 1980; Konner 1982; and Montagu 1978

9   Abrahamsen 1973: 9–10; Megargee 1966; Lunde 1979: 93; and Gaylin 1983: 274

10   Bolitho 1926: 7, 8, 274, 294

11   Dickson 1958: 203–204

12   Lindsay 1958: 194

13   Lunde 1979: 48

14   Ibid, 49, 59, 53

15   Kramer and Weiner 1983: 73

16   Wilson (Colin) 1969: 29ff. See also Dickson 1958

17   Griart, in Wolf (Leonard) 1980: 145

18   de Rais, in ibid, 202, 205

19   de Rais, in ibid, 194

20   de Rais, in ibid, 204–205

21   Wolf (Eric) 1969: 279; and Laslett 1984: 5, 7ff

22   Ibid, 24

23   Ibid, 29

24   Darnton 1984: 109–110; Laslett 1984: 18; Wolf (Eric) 1969: 279–280; and Wolf (Eric) 1982: 360, 389–390

25   Wilson (Colin) 1969: 89–90

26   Quoted in Lucas 1974: 5–6; Logan 1928: 66ff; quoted in Miller 1978: 156; and Hamilton Fish, quoted in Angelella 1979: 150

27   Bruch 1967: 697, 693–697

28   Peter Kurten, in Dickson 1958: 135, 137

29   Carl Panzram, in Gaddis and Long 1970: 11–12

30   Panzram, in ibid, 28, 31–32

31   Panzram, in ibid, 238, 165, 251–252

32   Panzram, in ibid, 213–214, 30t–309

33   Panzram, in ibid, 323; quoted in ibid, 325; Panzram, in ibid, 325–326; and Gaddis and Long 1970: 326–327

34   Katz 1988: 19–44; Gottfredson and Hirschi 1990: 90

35   Frantz, in Graham and Gurr (eds) 1969

36   Chalidze 1977: 107

37   Durkheim 1961: 919

38   Lasch 1979: 21; and Ehrenreich 1983: 51, 182

39   Durkheim 1961: 918

40   Heirens, in Freeman 1955

41   Levin and Fox 1985: 194–195; Hickey 1991: 154–155

42   Archer and Gartner 1984: 136

43   Clancy Sigal, *Guardian Weekly*, Sept. 1993; Lewis Lapham, *Harper's*, Apr. 1994

References

Abrahamsen, David. 1973. *The Murdering Mind.* New York: Harper & Row.
——— 1983. "Confessions of Son of Sam." *Penthouse* 15: 58-194
——— 1985. *Confessions of Son of Sam.* New York: Columbia University Press
Abrams, Philip. 1982. *Historical Sociology.* Ithaca: Cornell Univ. Press
Allen, William. 1976. *Starkweather: The Story of a Mass Murderer.* Boston: Houghton Mifflin.
Altman, Jack and Marvin Ziporyn. 1967. *Born to Raise Hell: The Untold Story of Richard Speck.* New York: Grove Press.
Amnesty International. 1983. *Political Killings by Governments.* London: Amnesty International Publications.
Angelella, Michael. 1979. *Trail of Blood: A True Story.* New York: New American Library.
Andreano, Ralph and John J. Siegfried (eds.). 1980. *The Economics of Crime.* New York: John Wiley.
Archer, Dane and Rosemary Gartner. 1984. *Violence and Crime in Cross-National Perspective.* New Haven: Yale University Press.
Banks, Harold K. 1967. *The Strangler! The Story of the Terror in Boston.* New York: Avon.

385

Bartholomew, Allen A., K.L. Milte and E. Galbally. 1975. "Sexual murder: psychopathology and psychiatric jurisprudential considerations." *Australian and New Zealand Journal of Criminology* 8: 143-152.

Beaver, Ninette, B.K. Ripley and Patrick Trese. 1974. *Caril.* New York: J.B. Lippincott.

Berkowitz, David. 1981. "Prison diary." In Klausner 1981.

Blau, Judith R. and Peter M. Blau. 1982. "The cost of inequality: metropolitan structure and violent crime." *American Sociological Review* 47: 114-129.

Bolitho, William. 1926. *Murder For Profit.* New York: Garden City.

Brittain, Robert P. 1970. "The sadistic murderer." *Medicine, Science and the Law* 10: 198-207.

Bruch, Hilde. 1967. "Mass murder: the Wagner case." *American Journal of Psychiatry* 124: 693-698.

Brussel, James A. 1968. *Casebook of a Crime Psychiatrist.* New York: Dell.

Buchanan, Edna. 1979. *Carr: Five Years of Rape and Murder.* New York: E.P. Dutton.

Calvert-Boyanowsky, Jocelyn, Ehor O. Boyanowsky, et al. 1981. "Patterns of passion: temperature and human emotion." In D. Krebs (ed.), *Readings in Social Psychology: Contemporary Perspectives.* New York: Harper & Row.

Canter, David. 1994. *Criminal Shadows: Inside the Mind of the Serial Killer.* London: HarperCollins.

Cameron, Deborah and Elizabeth Frazer. 1987. *The Lust to Kill: A Feminist Investigation of Sexual Murder.* New York: New York University Press.

Capote, Truman. 1965. *In Cold Blood.* New York: New American Library.

Carpozi, George Jr. 1977. *Son of Sam: The .44 Caliber Killer.* New York: Manor.

Chalidze, Valery. 1977. *Criminal Russia: Essays on Crime in the Soviet Union.* New York: Random House.

Cheney, Margaret. 1976. *The Co-Ed Killer.* New York: Walker.

Cluff, Julie, Allison Hunter and Ronald Hinch. 1997. "Feminist perspectives on serial murder: a critical analysis." *Homicide Studies* Vol. 1, No. 3: 291-308.

Cusson, Maurice. 1983. *Why Delinquency?* Toronto: University of Toronto Press.

Damore, Leo. 1981. *In His Garden: The Anatomy of a Murderer.* New York: Arbor House.

Darnton, Robert. 1984. *The Great Cat Massacre: And Other Episodes in French Cultural History*. New York: Basic Books.

Dickson, Grierson. 1958. *Murder by Numbers*. London: Robert Hale.

Durkheim, Emile. 1961. "Anomic Suicide," In Talcott Parsons, Edward Shils, Kasper Naegele and Jesse R. Pitts (eds.), *Theories of Society: Foundations Of Modern Sociological Theory*. New York: Free Press.

Egger, Steven A. (ed). 1990. *Serial Murder: An Elusive Phenomenon*. New York: Praeger.

———— 1998. *The Killers Among Us: An Examination of Serial Murder and Its Investigation*. Upper Saddle River, N.J.: Prentice Hall.

Ehrenreich, Barbara. 1983. *The Hearts of Men: American Dreams and the Flight From Commitment*. New York: Anchor.

Federal Bureau of Investigation. 1982. *Crime in the United States*. Uniform Crime Reports. Washington DC: U.S. Government Printing Office.

Flango, Victor E. and Edgar L. Sherbenou. 1976. "Poverty, urbanization, and crime." *Criminology* 14: 331-346.

Foucault, Michel (ed.). 1975. *I, Pierre Riviere, having slaughtered my mother, my sister, and my brother: A Case of Parricide in the 19th Century*. New York: Pantheon.

Fox, James Alan, and Jack Levin. 2001. *The Will To Kill*. Boston: Allyn & Bacon.

Fox, Richard G. 1971. "The XYY offender: a modern myth?" *Journal of Criminal Law, Criminology and Police Science* 62 (1): 59-73.

Frank, Gerold. 1967. *The Boston Strangler*. New York: New American Library.

Freeman, Lucy. 1955. *"Before I Kill More..."*. New York: Crown.

Fromm, Erich. 1975. *The Anatomy of Human Destructiveness*. New York: Harper & Row.

Gaddis, Thomas E. and James O. Long. 1970. *Killer: A Journal of Murder*. New York: Macmillan.

Galvin, James A.V. and John M. MacDonald. 1959. "Psychiatric study of a mass murderer." *American Journal of Psychiatry* 115: 1057-1061.

Garelik, Glenn and Gina Maranto. 1984. "Multiple murderers." *Discover* 5: 26-29.

Gastil, R.P. 1971. "Homicide and a regional culture of violence." *American Sociological Review* 36: 412-427.

Gaylin, Willard. 1983. *The Killing of Bonnie Garland: A Question of Justice*. New York: Penguin.

Giannangelo, Stephen J. 1996. *The Psychopathology of Serial Murder: A Theory of Violence*. Westport, CT: Praeger.

Gottfredson, Michael R. and Travis Hirschi. 1990. *A General Theory of Crime*. Stanford: Stanford University Press.

Glueck, Sheldon and Eleanor Glueck. 1956. *Physique and Delinquency*. New York: Harper.

Godwin, John. 1979. *Murder U.S.A.: The Ways We Kill Each Other*. New York: Ballantine.

Gradon, Kacper. 2003. Translation of "The "Diary" of Z. Marchwicki." In Jozef Gurgul (ed.). 1981. "*Anna*". Warsaw, Poland: Ministry of Internal Affairs (3 vols).

Graham, H.D., and T.R. Gurr (eds.). 1969. *The History of Violence in America: Historical and Comparative Perspectives*. New York: Praeger.

Gresswell, David M. and Clive R. Hollin. 1994. "Multiple murder: a review." *British Journal of Criminology* 34: 1-14.

Grier, William and Price Cobbs. 1968. *Black Rage*. New York: Basic Books.

Hare, Robert D. n.d. "Psychopathy and crime." In Laura Otten (ed.), *Colloquium on the Correlates of Crime and the Determinants of Criminal Behavior*. Mitre.

Hazelwood, R.R. and J.E. Douglas. 1980. "The lust murderer." *FBI Law Enforcement Bulletin* April: 1-5.

Hernon, Peter. 1978. *A Terrible Thunder: The Story of the New Orleans Sniper*. New York: Doubleday.

Hickey, Eric W. 1991. *Serial Murderers and Their Victims*. Pacific Grove, CA: Brooks/Cole.

Holmes, Ronald M. and James De Burger. 1988. *Serial Murder*. Beverly Hills, CA: Sage.

Hobsbawm, E.J. 1969. *Bandits*. Harmondsworth, UK: Penguin.

Howard, Clark. 1980. *Zebra*. New York: Berkley.

Jenkins, Philip. 1992. *Intimate Enemies: Moral Panics in Contemporary Great Britain*. Hawthorne, N.Y.: Aldine de Gruyter.

———— 1994. *Using Murder: The Social Construction of Serial Homicide*. New York: Aldine de Gruyter.

Kahan, Marvin W. 1960. "Psychological test study of a mass murderer." *Journal of Projective Techniques* 24: 147-160.

Katz, Jack. 1988. *Seductions of Crime: Moral and Sensual Attractions in Doing Evil*. New York: Basic Books.

Kendall, Elizabeth. 1981. *The Phantom Prince: My Life With Ted Bundy*. Seattle: Madrona.

Kennedy, Foster, Harry R. Hoffman and William H. Haines. 1947. "A study of William Heirens." *American Journal of Psychiatry* 104.

Keyes, Daniel. 1981. *The Minds of Billy Milligan.* New York: Random House.

Keyes, Edward. 1976. *The Michigan Murders.* New York: Pocket Books.

Kiger, Kenna. 1990. "The Darker Figure of Crime: The Serial Murder Enigma", in Steven A. Egger (ed) 1990.

Klausner, Lawrence D. 1981. *Son of Sam.* New York: McGraw-Hill.

Konner, Melvin. 1982. *The Tangled Wing: Biological Constraints on the Human Spirit.* New York: Holt, Rinehart and Winston.

Kramer, Roger and Ira Weiner. 1983. "Psychiatry on the borderline." *Psychology Today* 17: 70-73.

Kraus, R.T. 1995. "An enigmatic personality: case report of a serial killer." *Journal of Orthomolecular Medicine* 10(1): 11-24.

Larsen, Richard W. 1980. *Bundy: The Deliberate Stranger.* Englewood Cliffs: Prentice-Hall.

Lasch, Christopher. 1979. *The Culture of Narcissism: American Life in an Age of Diminishing Expectations.* New York: Warner.

Laslett, Peter. 1984. *The World We Have Lost: England Before the Industrial Age.* New York: Charles Scribner's.

Levin, Jack and James Alan Fox. 1985. *Mass Murder: America's Growing Menace.* New York: Plenum.

—— 1996. "A Psycho-Social Analysis of Mass Murder", in T. O'Reilly-Fleming (ed).

Levine, Richard. 1982. *Bad Blood: A Family Murder in Marin County.* New York: Random House.

Lewontin, R.C., Steven Rose and Leon J. Kamin. 1984. *Not In Our Genes: Biology, Ideology, and Human Nature.* New York: Pantheon.

Leyton, Elliott. 1986. *Compulsive Killers: The Story of Modern Multiple Murder.* New York: New York University Press. Published simultaneously in Canada as *Hunting Humans: The Rise of the Modern Multiple Murderer.* Toronto: McClelland and Stewart.

—— 1991. *Sole Survivor: Children Who Murder Their Families.* London: Penguin (reprinted 2001, London: John Blake).

—— 1996. *Men of Blood: Murder in Modern England.* London: Constable. Published simultaneously in Canada, Toronto: McClelland and Stewart (reprinted 2001, London: John Blake).

—— 1999. "Serial and mass murderers", in Lester Kurtz (ed.), *Encyclopedia of Violence, Peace and Conflict* (3 vols). New York: Academic Press.

—— 2000. (ed.) *Serial Murder: Modern Scientific Perspectives.* Aldershot, UK: Dartmouth/Ashgate Press.

Leyton, Marco, M. Diksic, S.N. Young, H. Okazawa, S. Nishizawa, J. Paris, S. Mzengeza, and C. Benkelfat. 1997. "PET study of brain 5HT synthesis in borderline personality Disorder." *Biological Psychiatry* (Abstract) Vol 41(7S): 17.

Lindsay, Philip. 1958. *The Mainspring of Murder.* London: John Long.

Lisners, John. 1983. *House of Horrors.* London: Corgi.

Loftin, Colin and Robert H. Hill. 1974. "Regional subculture and homicide." *American Sociology Review* 39: 714-724.

Logan, Guy B.H. 1928. *Masters of Crime: Studies of Multiple Murderers.* London: Stanley Paul.

Lucas, Norman. 1974. *The Sex Killers.* London: W.H. Allen.

Lunde, Donald T. 1979. *Murder and Madness.* New York: W.W. Norton.

Lunde, Donald T. and Jefferson Morgan. 1980. *The Die Song: A Journey Into The Mind of a Mass Murderer.* New York: W.W. Norton.

Mailer, Norman. 1980. *The Executioner's Song.* New York: Warner.

Meloy, J. Reid. 1988. *The Psychopathic Mind: Origins, Dynamics, and Treatment.* Northvale, NJ: Jason Aronson.

Megargee, E.I. 1966. "Uncontrolled and overcontrolled personality types in extreme and social aggression." *Psychological Monographs* 80.

Messner, Steven F. 1982. "Poverty, inequality, and the urban homicide rate." *Criminology* 20: 103-114.

———— 1983. "Regional and racial effects on the urban homicide rate: the subculture of violence revisited." *American Journal of Sociology* 88: 997-1007.

Michaud, Stephen C. and Hugh Aynesworth. 1983. *The Only Living Witness.* New York: Simon and Schuster.

Miller, Orlo. 1978. *Twenty Mortal Murders.* Toronto: Macmillan.

Montagu, Ashley (ed.). 1978. *Learning Non-Aggression: The Experience of Non-Literate Societies.* Oxford: Oxford University Press.

Olsen, Jack. 1974. *The Man With The Candy: The Story of The Houston Mass Murders.* New York: Simon and Schuster.

O'Reilly-Fleming, Thomas (ed.). 1996. *Serial and Mass Murder: Theory, Research and Policy.* Toronto: Canadian Scholars' Press.

Palmer, Stuart. 1972. *The Violent Society.* New Haven: College & University Press.

Panzram, Carl. 1970. "Journal". In Gaddis and Long 1970.

Parkin, Frank. 1979. *Marxism and Class Theory: A Bourgeois Critique.* New York: Columbia University Press.

Peter, Jean-Pierre and Jeanne Favret. 1975. "The animal, the madman, and death." In M. Foucault (ed.) 1975.

Rae, George W. 1967. *Confessions of the Boston Strangler.* New York: Pyramid.

Ratner, R.S. 1996. "Ideological homicide." In T. O'Reilly-Fleming (ed.).

Reinhardt, James M. 1960. *The Murderous Trail of Charles Starkweather.* Sringfield, Ill: C.C. Thomas.

Ressler, R.K., Ann W. Burgess and John E. Douglas. 1988. *Sexual Homicide: Patterns and Motives.* Lexington, KY: Lexington Books.

Rule, Ann. 1980. *The Stranger Beside Me.* New York: New American Library.

Sartre, Jean-Paul. 1941. "Herostratus". *Decision* Nov-Dec: 60-73.

Schreiber, F.R. 1983. *The Shoemaker: The Anatomy of a Psychotic.* New York: Simon and Schuster.

Schwartz, Ted. 1981. *The Hillside Strangler: A Murderer's Mind.* New York: Doubleday.

Smith, M. Dwayne and Robert Nash Parker. 1980. "Types of homicide and variation in regional rates." *Social Forces* 59: 136-147.

Stack, Andy. 1983a. *Lust Killer.* New York: New American Library.

——— 1983b. *The Want-Ad Killer.* New York: New American Library.

——— 1984. *The I-5 Killer.* New York: New American Library.

Starkweather, Charles. 1959. "Rebellion." *Parade* 4: 10-14.

Tanay, Emanuel. 1976. *The Murderers.* Indianapolis: Bobbs-Merrill.

Tanenbaum, Robert and Philip Rosenberg. 1979. *Badge of the Assassin.* New York: Fawcett Crest.

Thompson, Thomas. 1979. *Serpentine.* New York: Dell.

Tobias, Ronald. 1981. *They Shoot To Kill: A Psycho-survey of Criminal Sniping.* Boulder: Paladin.

Wallerstein, Immanuel. 1974. *The Modern World System I: Capitalist Agriculture and the Origins of the European World Economy in the Sixteenth Century.* New York: Academic Press.

West, Donald. 1974. *Sacrifice Unto Me.* New York: Pyramid.

Williams, Kirk R. 1984. "Economic sources of homicide: re-estimating the effects of poverty and inequality." *American Sociological Review* 49: 283-289.

Wilson, Colin. 1969. *A Casebook of Murder.* London: Leslie Frewin.

Wilson, Edward O. 1980. *Sociobiology.* Cambridge, Mass: Harvard University Press.

Wilson, Peter J. 1974. *Oscar: An Inquiry Into the Nature of Sanity.* New York: Random House.

Willeford, Charles. 1980. *Off The Wall.* Montclair, N.J.: Pegasus Rex.

Winn, Steven and David Merrill. 1980. *Ted Bundy: The Killer Next Door.* New York: Bantam.

Wolf, Eric. 1973. *Peasant Wars of the Twentieth Century.* New York: Harper.

———— 1982. *Europe and the People Without History.* Berkeley: University of California Press.

Wolf, Leonard. 1980. *Bluebeard: The Life and Crimes of Gilles de Rais.* New York: Potter.

Wolfgang, Marvin E. 1975. *Patterns in Criminal Homicide.* Montclair, N.J.: Patterson Smith.

Acknowledgments

I owe the reader a garland of apologies and explanations, all arising from the presumptuousness I display in writing a book about people I have never met, who live in a nation I have hardly ever visited. These deficiencies are not merely a function of the difficulty encountered by any non-police person who wishes to make contact with a large number of prison inmates. Equally important is the fact that I have reached that time of life when an anthropologist may tire of the rigors of fieldwork—of the tacky huts we perch in, the chilblains and amoebic flukes we accumulate, the unctuous smiles we sustain as we make a virtue of the necessity of getting along with our informants, and the manipulative relationships of which we are both perpetrators and victims. I have done my duty during twenty years of the non-judgmental obsequiousness we both dignify and obscure with the phrase "participant-observation." I have completed major field stints among the *nouveau riche* business people of British Columbia; among fishermen in an Irish village nestling in the shadows of the Mountains of Mourne; with dying miners and widows on the foggy south coast of Newfoundland; among the sophisticated bureaucrats of the Workmen's Compensation Board in old St. John's; and most debilitating of all, with the memorably exploitative juvenile delinquents and their families in an Atlantic community. Thus I have truly had enough; and I see no breach of responsibility in planning a series of books that would save me from the nightmare of enforced sociability.

If the reader feels no sympathy, let me ask what category of person it could possibly be more sensible to avoid than multiple murderers? I have never knowingly met a murderer, multiple or otherwise, and I am more than content to keep things as they are. In asserting this, I go no further than did the early anthropologist Sir James Frazer, whose brilliant work, *The Golden Bough,* was one of the very first books to record the study of "primitive" peoples. When Frazer was asked by a suspicious reader if he had ever actually met a primitive, he is reported to have replied with considerable *hauteur.* "Certainly not!" A similar archness would inform my own response to such a query. Still, I had little choice, for it is only the police who have anything resembling free passage in the scattered penal institutions which house my informants. If I have never met any of the persons I study, I have corresponded at length with some of them, although many more refused to answer my letters (for they are celebrities . . . and their thoughts are much in demand), and so many, of course, are now dead. Thus, it should be emphasized that this book contains no new data of any kind: It is simply a revision of the classic texts, from which I have taken for my data the acts and words of the killers as they are recorded in such published literature, and reinterpreted them in terms of modern social analysis. The book is therefore a search for meaning in those acts and words of multiple murderers that hitherto have been dismissed as bizarre or merely "psychotic."

I am also largely a stranger to America, the nation in which the book's events occur. However, I do not feel that this lack of personal exposure damages my analysis beyond repair since in the modern world it is hardly necessary to go to America: If you merely stand still, America will come to you, via its formidable cultural apparatus. America's scholars, films, television, books, magazines, newspapers, records, and videotapes have kept me tolerably well-informed. At any rate, if Carl Sagan can talk about outer space without having been there, then I can venture to discuss the intimate lives of strangers without having met them or lived in their country. My method has been simply to depend on the vast *corpus* that is American scholarship for my understanding of the society. In order to come to "know" the multiple murderers, I have relied upon the splendid, literate, and scholarly accounts of their lives that have been published by gifted journalists and other talented writers. They have provided me with an enormous amount of material, including the diaries and confessions of the killers, as well as the writers' painstaking attempts to reconstruct the sequence of events, the prevailing mood, and the cluster of imponderables that inevitably surround both the killer and the killings. In this manner, a number of eminent authors have been transformed into my personal research assistants; and I must express my gratitude to Norman Mailer, Lawrence Klausner, Gerold Frank, Thomas Gaddis, Leonard Wolf, Richard Levine, Donald Lunde, and Truman Capote who, among many others, have labored so mightily on my behalf. They have been superb and undemanding research assistants indeed. They have interviewed the killers at great length, collected their confessions and their psychiatric interviews, and offered them to me as a gift. Criminologists customarily disregard their work, but they make a grievous error in doing so, for in recording every thought and movement of the modern multiple murderer, the writers have made possible the illumination of many dark corners of the human spirit.

This project has gone on for what seems an interminable time, and a number of good souls have participated in it as my actual assistants. Mr. David Bartlett acted as my official university research assistant, thanks to a generous grant from Memorial University, and he did yeoman work on my behalf in hunting sources and negotiating with libraries. He also suggested the title. Ms. Jeannie Kinsella Devereaux acted as my honorary assistant, rooting through magazines and newspapers for long-lost journalistic accounts. A tenured professor should not admit that he knows little of libraries, but I have spent my professional life interviewing the living, not squatting in library carrels interviewing the dead. That era ended with this book, and I am especially grateful to librarians Bernadine Conran, Ronald Crawley, and Joy Tillotson for introducing me to the intricacies of the world's library system. It was also necessary for me to establish relationships with international second-hand book dealers who could provide me with the bloodthirsty titles I sought: Oxford's Blackwell's were, as always, especially helpful, as was New York's Howard Frisch. Finally, I must thank the platoon of friends and relatives who functioned as my honorary clipping service: My mother, Mrs. Lilyan Levson in Los Angeles, my brother, Dr. Bryan Leyton in Seattle, Dr. Richard Nelson in Alaska, Professor Volker Meja in Germany, and Dr. Thomas Nemec in Newfoundland all kept me up to my ears in fresh magazine and newspaper material.

Many of my professorial colleagues took me to be quite mad when I set my hand to this task. Still, I must record my debt to those colleagues at the university whose conversations over the past twenty years have immeasurably enriched my understanding of *Homo sapiens:* Douglas Hay, Juan Corradi, Ronald Schwartz, Volker Meja, Victor Zaslavsky, Rex Clark, Judith Adler,

Frederick Johnstone, George Story, and the late David Alexander have all been especially provocative.

It is not customary for anthropologists to deal with the police unless, as the British say, they are assisting the police with their inquiries, but my subject has demanded that my contacts with them be frequent. Fortunately, the major police forces around the world have been extraordinarily helpful, and I must acknowledge my debt to a number of individuals for their helpful suggestions and kind encouragement—especially the late Rick Holden, as well as Stuart Kirby and Rupert Heritage of the British police; Dale Henry and Jack Lavers of the Royal Canadian Mounted Police; John House of the Royal Newfoundland Constabulary; Roy Hazelwood, Robert Ressler and John Douglas of the Federal Bureau of Investigation; and Kacper Gradon of the Polish National Police.

I am also indebted, as always, to Bonnie Leyton, my wife and friend for one half a century; to Philip Jenkins for an unending stream of generously volunteered insights and data; to the late Professors George Story and David Alexander, who always reminded me of scholarly duties when my commitment flagged; to the Social Sciences and Humanities Research Council of Canada for providing me with the wherewithal to purchase eighteen months of quiet in my study; to Ann Rule, Dr. Willard Gaylin, Dr. Donald Lunde, and Dr. David Abrahamsen, whose paths I followed with their encouragement and forbearance; and to my publishers around the world, especially Jonathan Webb at McClelland and Stewart in Toronto, Jon Riley at Faber in London, and Philip Turner at Carroll & Graf in New York, whose warm ministrations kept this volume alive.

Index

NATURAL
WONDERFOODS

NATURAL
WONDERFOODS

100 AMAZING FOODS FOR
· HEALING · IMMUNE-BOOSTING ·
· FITNESS-ENHANCING · ANTI-AGING ·

DUNCAN BAIRD PUBLISHERS
LONDON

Natural Wonderfoods
Paula Bartimeus, Charlotte Haigh, Sarah Merson, Sarah Owen, and Janet Wright

Distributed in the USA and Canada by
Sterling Publishing Co., Inc.
387 Park Avenue South
New York, NY 10016-8810

This edition first published in the UK and USA in 2011 by
Duncan Baird Publishers Ltd
Sixth Floor, Castle House
75–76 Wells Street
London W1T 3QH

Managing Editor: Grace Cheetham
Editor: Ingrid Court-Jones
Managing Designer: Manisha Patel
Designer: Rachel Cross
Photographs by: Simon Scott, Simon Smith and Toby Scott, and William Lingwood

Library of Congress Cataloging-in-Publication Data available

ISBN: 978-1-84483-970-4

10 9 8 7 6 5 4 3 2

Typeset in Warnock Pro
Color reproduction by Colourscan, Singapore
Printed in Malaysia for Imago

For information about custom editions, special sales, premium and corporate purchases, please contact Sterling Special Sales Department at 800-805-5489 or specialsales@sterlingpub.com.

Publisher's note: The information in this book is not intended as a substitute for professional medical advice and treatment. If you are pregnant or breastfeeding or have any special dietary requirements or medical conditions, it is recommended that you consult a medical professional before following any of the information or recipes contained in this book. Duncan Baird Publishers, or any other persons who have been involved in working on this publication, cannot accept responsibility for any errors or omissions, inadvertent or not, that might be found in the recipes or text, nor for any problems that might arise as a result of preparing one of these recipes or following the advice contained in this work.

Notes on the recipes
Unless otherwise stated:
• All recipes serve 4
• Use large eggs, and medium fruits and vegetables
• Use fresh ingredients, including herbs and chilies
• 1 tsp. = 5ml
• 1 tbsp. = 15ml
• 1 cup = 240ml

contents

Key to symbols

ANTIBACTERIAL

ANTIVIRAL

ANTIOXIDANT

ANTI-INFLAMMATORY

ANTIAGING

ANTICANCER

DETOXIFYING

BLOOD-SUGAR BALANCING

ENERGY-BOOSTING

GOOD FOR THE BRAIN

GOOD FOR HAIR, TEETH, AND NAILS

GOOD FOR THE SKIN

GOOD FOR THE EYES

GOOD FOR THE HEART

GOOD FOR THE IMMUNE SYSTEM

GOOD FOR THE MUSCULOSKELETAL SYSTEM

GOOD FOR THE DIGESTIVE SYSTEM

GOOD FOR THE HORMONAL SYSTEM

Introduction

Our ancestors knew well the healing power of natural foods and turned to them to combat all manner of maladies. It's only now, centuries later, that research has begun to confirm the therapeutic benefits of these foods can be scientifically proven. In fact, some wonderfoods have been found to work even better than drugs—and without the adverse side effects.

Most experts now agree eating a diet rich in natural, health-giving foods can help us to ward off common complaints, such as colds, coughs, and infections, as well as to protect ourselves against chronic degenerative diseases, including cancer, heart disease, and arthritis. So, next time you're feeling below par, instead of turning to the medicine cabinet turn to your own refrigerator or kitchen cupboard where, with the help of this great book, you're likely to find a remedy.

It really is possible to eat your way to good health and improve the way you feel and look. *Natural Wonderfoods* includes 100 delicious and nutritious foods you can easily introduce into your diet for maximum impact on your health. The food entries offer practical and reliable information, as well as recipes for tasty dishes, beauty treatments, and home remedies (the latter two marked ✳ and ✦ for easy reference), a nutrient list, and at-a-glance symbols highlighting each food's health-enhancing properties.

Most fruit and vegetables, especially, have wide-ranging benefits. Many health conditions stem from nutrient deficiencies, so they can be alleviated—and often cured—by eating better. Base your diet on a wide range of vegetables and fruits, backed by wholegrain cereals and organic meat and dairy products, with as little processed food as possible.

Let's take a closer look at the food groups and their nutrients.

FRUITS

Generally fruits contain more vitamins than vegetables, whereas vegetables rate higher in the mineral stakes. Most fruits are exceptionally cleansing and alkalizing, helping to eliminate toxins from the body and to regulate the digestive system by stimulating movement of the digestive tract and improving the body's ability to absorb nutrients. Fruits are also a fantastic source of enzymes, natural sugars, and cell-protective phytochemicals.

As the body digests fruits relatively quickly (within 30 minutes), they are best eaten on their own, separately from other foods that take longer to digest. This prevents them from fermenting in the digestive tract. Between meals is probably a good time to fit them in, unless you opt for an all-fruit breakfast, for example.

Both fresh and dried fruits are nutrient-rich, with dried fruits also being an excellent source of minerals. While freshly pressed fruit juices are good for you, it's advisable to dilute them with water to reduce their fruit-sugar content. This will help to curb blood-sugar fluctuations and lower the calorie count, which can add up when fruits are juiced, as well as reduce the risk of dental cavities.

VEGETABLES

If there's one food group we can never eat too much of, it has to be veg-etables. Abundant in vitamins, minerals, fiber, and water, vegetables help to cleanse and alkalize the body, neutralizing acidity and reducing the toxic load. They are also low in fat and calories (with the exception of starchy vegetables, such as potatoes, winter squash, and yams) and are one of the best sources of phytochemicals—potent plant compounds that help to protect the body against disease.

Scientific research suggests that phytochemicals slow down the aging process and reduce the risk of diseases, including cancer, heart disease, high blood pressure, osteoporosis, and arthritis. Most of them function as antioxidants, helping to counteract the hazardous effects of free radicals—unstable molecules that damage body's cells. In fact, free-radical damage is thought to be one of the main causes of aging. Phytochemicals exert various other properties, such as stimulating the immune system, regulating hormones, and providing antibacterial and antiviral activity. The great news is that all vegetables are full of these nat-ural plant components, of which hundreds have now been identified.

Try to make vegetables a central feature of main meals and find new ways of incorporating them into your diet, so you eat generous amounts every day. When preparing salads, instead of sticking to basic ingredients, such as lettuce, cucumber, and tomatoes, use them only as a base, and add a variety of other colorful ingredients, such as celery, red bell pepper, radicchio, beet, fennel, watercress, and carrots. Cooked vegetables are good, too, especially in the winter. To preserve fragile nutrients such as vitamin C, steam, stir-fry, or bake them rather than boil them, or add them to soups and stews. Juicing is another great way of reaping the goodness from vegetables in a more concentrated form.

MEAT AND DAIRY

Protein is vital for strong immunity and building strong bones and muscles, as well as essential for repairing the body's tissues, and meat and dairy products abound in it.

This vital component is required to manufacture all cells, including the immune system's antibodies and enzymes. It is made up of amino acids, which play a key role in immune health—for example, the amino acid glutathione is an important antioxidant and detoxifier. Many people are deficient in protein, so we have included protein-rich foods, such as chicken, lamb, eggs, and live yogurt.

FISH

As well as being a great source of protein, fish, such as sardines, salmon, and fresh tuna, are a superb source of the essential fatty acids (EFAs) that play such a vital role in helping us to feel and to look fantastic. Not only do EFAs play a central role in keeping the brain active, the mind agile, and the nervous system healthy, but they are also fundamental to the preservation of the elasticity of the skin and to keeping the hair glossy and healthy, and to improving our fitness.

Seafood, such as shrimp and oysters, are also loaded with useful minerals, such as iodine, which regulates the thyroid gland, and zinc and selenium, powerful antioxidants that boost immunity and help to fight off infections.

NUTS, SEEDS, AND OILS

All these foods provide protein, minerals, and vitamin E, which are very important for the skin, reproductive organs, and circulatory system. They are also packed with the healthy fats associated with lowering high cholesterol, balancing hormones, and reducing inflammation.

The high fat content of nuts and seeds means they are calorie-laden, so eat them in moderation. They are ideal sprinkled on salads, cereals, and desserts, or as snacks. Also, nut and seed butters make flavorsome spreads on toast or crackers.

GRAINS, LEGUMES, AND BEANS

Grains are the primary source of energy for many people throughout the world. Unrefined grains are rich in slow-releasing carbohydrates that help sustain and fuel the body. They are also rich in fiber to aid digestion. There are two main types of fiber—soluble and insoluble. Soluble fiber helps to stabilize blood sugar levels and to lower high cholesterol, while insoluble fiber regulates bowel movements. Grains contain both types.

Some grains, such as quinoa, provide the body with complete protein; other grains need to be combined with beans, legumes, or seeds to make their protein more usable by the body. This can easily be achieved and we often do it when preparing meals in traditional combinations—for example, in baked beans on toast, rice and dhal, and so on.

Like fruit and vegetables, grains supply many healing vitamins, minerals, and phytochemicals. Most grains supply B-vitamins, which are needed for normal metabolism and a healthy nervous system, along with calcium and magnesium and various trace elements. If you are allergic or intolerant to gluten (a sticky protein found in wheat, rye, and oats), there are plenty of grains that are gluten-free, such as rice, millet, buckwheat, and quinoa.

Collectively known as legumes, dried beans and the edible seeds of certain plants are an excellent source of protein, especially when combined with grains, as well as soluble and insoluble fiber and complex carbohydrates. This makes them ideal energy foods for balanced blood sugar. They also contain a broad spectrum of minerals and a brain nutrient called lecithin. If legumes cause you to bloat, their gassy effects can be avoided by adding a few bay leaves or a strip of kombu seaweed during the cooking process.

HERBS, SPICES, AND OTHERS

Besides adding taste and aroma, herbs and spices boost the nutrient content in all kinds of meals. Some, such as garlic and ginger, are particularly versatile in their culinary uses, while giving fantastic healing and health-enhancing benefits.

To preserve the nutrients of both fresh and dried herbs, add them to dishes toward the end of the cooking time. They also make fabulous substitutes for salt and some aid digestion. It is best, however, to add spices earlier to allow their flavor to develop fully. Herbs and spices can be made into medicinal teas to help to relieve various health problems.

There are some foods that do not fit into any of the categories mentioned so far, but without which no book on wonderfoods would be complete. These include condiments, such as apple cider vinegar, which has long been valued as a curative; the natural sweetener, honey, which also has amazing healing properties; and tofu, which is a low-fat food jam-packed with nutrients, often used in Oriental cuisines.

STORING FOOD

Fresh fruit and vegetables lose much of their vitamin content in storage. So shop where you know food is fresh, keep it in a refrigerator or a cool place, and eat as soon as possible. Fresh meat should be placed on a plate on the bottom shelf of the refrigerator, where it can't drip onto anything. Fresh herbs can be kept in a sealed jar with a pinch of salt, covered with olive oil, or for a few days in the refrigerator, wrapped in damp paper.

SUPPLEMENTS

It's always better to get your nutrients from a balanced diet than by taking supplements. No one knows exactly how it works—only that the whole fruit or vegetable seems to provide a full range of nutrients in the right balance. Beta carotene, for example, is so good for the lungs that smokers who get plenty of it in their diet reduce their risk of lung cancer. Yet, taking beta carotene supplements seems to increase their cancer risk. It's almost impossible to overdose on nutrients from fruit and vegetables, but it's easy to unbalance your levels of vitamins, and especially minerals, if you take them in the large quantities supplied by supplements. The only exception is vitamin B12. Vegans who can't get enough of this from their diet should take this as part of a vitamin-B-complex supplement.

EAT ORGANIC

Organic foods are produced in much the same way food was grown for thousands of years, until the twentieth century. Organic farmers don't use synthetic chemicals or sewage sludge. Their animals are given medicines only when they're unwell, not to make them put on weight faster or as a way of counteracting the unhealthy conditions of factory farms. It's worth paying a little extra to eat organic, although the price difference is narrowing all the time. Not all scientific studies have found that organic foods are more nutritious, but many have—and none has found them less healthy!

SWEET, SOUR, TANGY, OR JUICY, FRUIT IS NOT ONLY DELICIOUS, IT'S PACKED WITH VITAL NUTRIENTS THAT HELP YOUR BODY TO FUNCTION AT ITS BEST

01 | wonder FRUITS

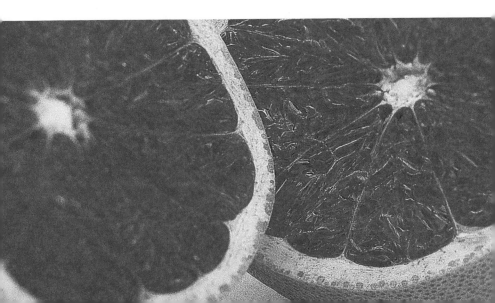

Lemon

VITAMINS B3, B5, B6, C, E, BETA-CAROTENE, BIOTIN, FOLIC ACID; CALCIUM, COPPER, IODINE, IRON, MAGNESIUM, MANGANESE, PHOSPHORUS, POTASSIUM, SELENIUM, ZINC; LIMONENE; FLAVONOIDS; FIBER; CARBOHYDRATE

Arguably the most versatile of all fruits, the lemon contains a wealth of health-enhancing properties. Used originally by the Romans to sweeten the breath, the lemon is packed full of nutrients and is used today to treat a number of ailments.

Like other citrus fruits, lemons are powerhouses of antioxidant vitamin C, which helps to boost the immune system, assist the healing of wounds, and strengthen the walls of blood capillaries. The high level of vitamin C in lemons also means they are vital for healthy skin and gums. They are a good source of flavonoids, such as quercetin, which boost the effects of vitamin C, and are particularly important for the health of blood vessels and to prevent varicose veins.

Lemons contain limonene, a chemical that has been shown to slow the rate of cancer growth. Limonene also has antiseptic qualities to help to kill germs—one of the reasons lemons are traditionally used as a gargle for sore throats and to treat infections of the respiratory tract. Lemons also have powerful antifungal properties. They are a popular ingredient in beauty products, such as skin cleansers and hair conditioners, because, when used in treatments, lemon juice inhibits bacterial growth and is astringent, strengthening, and toning. The fruit's dissolving and extracting qualities can also help in the topical treatment of skin infections, such as boils and abscesses.

As lemons are a liver stimulant, they can be used for detoxification purposes. Despite the sourness of lemon juice, it is a popular drink when diluted in water, with a cleansing taste few other fruits can match. During a brief detox fast, it quells the appetite and freshens breath. Being one of the most concentrated food sources of vitamin C also makes it the ideal addition to a glass of water to help soothe a postexercise dry throat. Or, try diluting freshly squeezed lemon juice with warm water and drinking it on an empty stomach first thing in the morning to give your metabolism a kick-start. (Take care, however, not to drink the juice too often as it can have a detrimental effect on tooth enamel.)

Lemons stimulate the gallbladder, which, in turn, aids liver and digestive functions. Citric acid, which encourages healthy digestion, makes up 7 to 8 percent of a lemon, the highest concentration found in any fruit. Used in a marinade or salad dressing, lemon juice breaks down some of the tough components of meat. Its calming effect on the stomach relieves bloating and heartburn. Lemons also have a slightly antibacterial effect, reducing the risk of discomfort in the intestines.

The health-giving properties of lemons can be utilized in many ways. The fruits make a great flavoring agent in drinks and foods, from baked goods to sauces. Lemon juice can be sprinkled onto peeled fruit, such as apples and bananas, to stop them browning, and the fruit's zest and pith can be added to stews and soups to give the dish extra nutrients.

ZESTY LEMON DRESSING *serves 2*

4 tbsp. lemon juice
¾ cup tomato juice
1 garlic clove, crushed
1 tsp. wholegrain mustard
grated zest of 1 lemon

Add all the ingredients, apart from the lemon zest, to a jar with a screw top and shake well. Pour into a bowl and add the zest, blending in with a fork. Drizzle immediately over a salad.

✦LEMON POULTICE *for boils & abscesses*

1 lemon, sliced
gauze bandage

Use the bandage to tie a slice of lemon against the boil or abscess. A hot-water bottle can be used to apply heat, if desired. Leave for about 10 minutes, then discard. Repeat 2 or 3 times a day until the boil opens and drains.

✦LEMON TONER *to treat thread veins*

4 tsp. vegetable glycerin
juice of 1 lemon
1 drop neroli essential oil
1 drop rose essential oil

Mix the vegetable glycerin with the lemon juice and add the essential oils. Apply twice daily to thread veins. Keeps in a sealed jar up to 3 months.

TANGY FISH

4 skinless tuna or other fish fillets
juice and grated zest of 1 lemon
juice and grated zest of 1 lime
2 tbsp. olive oil
2 tsp. finely chopped chives
1 tsp. ground black pepper

Preheat the broiler and place the fish on a foil-lined broiler pan. Mix the zests with the oil and coat each fish fillet. Broil 8 to 10 minutes until the fish is cooked through, turning once. Mix together the juices, chives, and pepper. Pour the mixture over the fish and serve immediately.

SUGAR-FREE LEMONADE

3 cups carbonated water
2½ cups white grape juice
juice of 3 lemons
1 tbsp. agave syrup

Put all the ingredients in a glass pitcher and stir. Serve chilled with plenty of ice.

LEMONY STUFFING BALLS *makes 10 balls*

1 small onion, quartered
1 egg, beaten
1 tbsp. chopped rosemary
1½ cups fresh white breadcrumbs
juice and grated zest of 1 lemon

Whiz the onion, egg, and rosemary in a blender until smooth. Mix the breadcrumbs with the lemon juice and zest in a bowl, then add the onion mixture and beat together. Form into 10 balls. Place on a baking sheet and bake in a preheated oven at 350°F 25 minutes, or until golden brown. Serve as an accompaniment.

Orange

VITAMINS A, B1, B3, B5, C, E, K, BETA-CAROTENE, FOLIC ACID; BETA-SITOSTEROL; CALCIUM, IODINE, IRON, MAGNESIUM, PHOSPHORUS, POTASSIUM, SELENIUM, ZINC; LIMONENE, HESPERIDIN; FIBER

Native to Asia, oranges are high in vitamin C and fiber, and rich in natural sugars for quick energy. Highly popular, they contain many disease-fighting compounds.

Oranges are one of the top sources of vitamin C, which is crucial for strong immunity, helping to fight viruses and produce disease-fighting cells to battle bacteria. A medium-size orange provides more than the average daily requirement of vitamin C, which can also help to reduce postexercise muscle soreness. Particularly effective against colds, flu, and other respiratory ailments, including asthma, oranges have also been found to reduce the risk of stomach ulcers and kidney stones.

They contain beta-sitosterol, a plant sterol that helps to prevent tumor formation. In addition, oranges are rich in vitamin B5, which helps to stimulate the body's immune response, and are loaded with fiber, needed for a healthy heart and digestive system. High in the antioxidant hesperidin, oranges are said to protect the heart farther by raising healthy HDL cholesterol and lowering "bad" LDL cholesterol, and to stop harmful free radicals from clogging up the arteries—a key risk factor for heart disease.

The wealth of vitamins and minerals found in oranges help to maintain healthy, youthful skin, and prevent eye problems. The fruits also contain limonene, a compound that has anticarcinogenic properties. Their natural sugars help diabetics to maintain their blood-glucose levels. Oranges are even reputed to reduce cellulite.

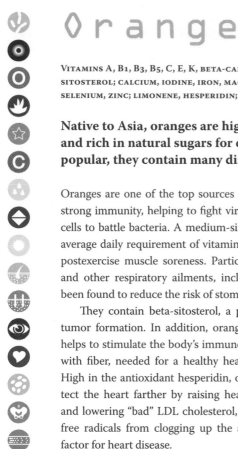

TANGY PANCAKES

1 egg
⅔ cup skim milk
½ cup all-purpose flour
grated zest of 1 orange
2 oranges
1 tbsp. sugar
1 tbsp. unsalted butter
4 tbsp. plain yogurt, to serve

Beat together the egg and milk, then fold in the flour and orange zest. Peel both the oranges, and divide them into segments. Put the orange segments in a saucepan. Add the sugar and cook over low heat 2 minutes. Melt a little butter in a skillet, then add one-quarter of the batter mixture for each pancake, turning once and cooking until golden brown. Serve with the oranges and the yogurt.

ORANGE-YOGURT SUNDAES

4 tbsp. plain yogurt
grated zest of ½ orange
2 oranges, peeled and sliced
1 banana, sliced
1 tbsp. berries of your choice
¼ tsp. cinnamon

Mix together the yogurt and the zest and chill for an hour. In a separate bowl, mix together the fruit and cinnamon, then chill. Divide the fruit salad into bowls and spoon the yogurt over. Serve immediately.

CHOCOLATE ORANGES

3½ oz. semisweet chocolate, grated
1 tbsp. golden syrup
grated zest of 1 orange
4 tbsp. light cream
4 oranges, peeled

Put the grated chocolate and syrup in a heatproof bowl and melt slowly over a pan of simmering water. Once they have melted, turn off the heat and stir in the zest and cream. Divide the oranges into segments and arrange them on plates. Drizzle the sauce over and serve.

Grapefruit

VITAMIN B3, B5, C, E, BETA-CAROTENE, BIOTIN, FOLIC ACID, LYCOPENE;
CALCIUM, IODINE, IRON, MAGNESIUM, PHOSPHORUS, POTASSIUM; FLAVONOIDS;
LIMINOIDS; FIBER; CARBOHYDRATE

The perfect breakfast food, grapefruit is loaded with antioxidants and is a powerful detoxifier.

The grapefruit is thought to have originated in the Caribbean island of Jamaica, before reaching the rest of the world in the eighteenth century. There are several different varieties, including yellow, pink, and ruby-red types. The pink and red varieties are colored by lycopene, a carotenoid with heart-protective and anticancer properties. These are also sweeter in taste and are, therefore, the best option for anyone who dislikes the more tangy flavor of the white variety. The fruit is delicious cut in half so the flesh can be scooped out, and simply eaten on its own, or drizzled with a little honey. It also works well juiced, either alone or in combination with other fruit, such as apple or raspberries, although juicing removes the benefits offered by its fiber content.

The high vitamin-C content of grapefruit enhances immunity, helping to reduce and relieve colds, heal cuts, and reduce bruising, and it also has antiaging properties. The pink variety, in particular, is a good source of potassium and bioflavonoids, both of which are important for the heart and circulation, as well as the skin and immunity. Bioflavonoids also strengthen blood capillaries. The fruit's seeds contain an antiparasite, antifungal compound which, although not edible whole, can be taken in supplement form (grapefruit seed extract). Grapefruit is also rich in alpha hydroxy acids (AHAs), which make it an effective toner when used topically.

Every part of a grapefruit is a powerful detoxifier. Its flesh and zest are thought to contain compounds that help to inhibit cancer development. The pulp is high in pectin, a soluble fiber that binds with excess cholesterol to remove it from the body, and helps to eliminate toxins.

Consuming a grapefruit first thing in the morning can kick-start the digestive system and relieve constipation, while starting a meal with grapefruit is an old diet trick that does seem to work. In a study, in 2006, scientists found this simple action helped some very overweight volunteers to lose weight. Their blood sugar levels were healthier than usual afterward, too. Other evidence suggests that eating grapefruit can steady insulin levels. So, these nutrient-rich fruits might help to prevent the vicious cycle in which gaining weight leads to diabetes, and diabetes makes people put on even more weight.

STUFFED GRAPEFRUIT

2 grapefruit, halved, flesh removed and
  chopped
1 avocado, pitted, peeled, and cubed
1-inch piece gingerroot, chopped
1 pear, peeled, cored, and cubed
1 green bell pepper, seeded and chopped
2 black olives, pitted and halved
2 tbsp. lemon balm, finely chopped

Mix the grapefruit flesh with the avocado, ginger, pear, and bell pepper, then divide the filling among the 4 halves. Garnish with the olives and lemon balm and serve.

GRAPEFRUIT AND CHICKEN SALAD

grated zest of 2 grapefruit
4 tbsp. honey vinaigrette (see p.271)
2 cups shredded cooked chicken
2 grapefruit, peeled and sliced
4 sweet bell peppers, seeded and cut
  into rings

Add the grapefruit zest to the vinaigrette. Pour it over the chicken pieces. Put the grapefruit slices and the pepper rings into a dish and pile the chicken on top.

*GRAPEFRUIT BEAUTY MASK *to tone the skin*

1 small grapefruit, peeled and broken
   into segments
¾ cup plain yogurt

Remove the pith and seeds from the grapefruit segments and put the with the yogurt in a blender. Whiz to make a paste. Put the mixture in a bowl, cover, and leave in the refrigerator 1 hour. Apply to your face and leave about 10 minutes. Gently remove with cool water.

CITRUS FRUIT SALAD

3 large handfuls mixed salad leaves
2 tbsp. chopped parsley leaves
1 tbsp. chopped cilantro leaves
1 tbsp. sunflower seeds
½ pink grapefruit
1 tbsp. olive oil
1 tbsp. lemon juice
1 tbsp. orange juice

Put the salad leaves, parsley, cilantro, and sunflower seeds in a large bowl. Cut the grapefruit into segments and add them to the bowl. Drizzle the olive oil and citrus juices over the salad, then toss gently and serve immediately.

HONEY-MARINATED GRAPEFRUIT

4 ruby grapefruit
2 tbsp. honey
1 tbsp. chopped fresh mint

Squeeze the juice of 1 grapefruit and grate 1 teaspoon of the zest; set aside. Warm the honey in a pan. Add the juice and zest and mix well. Peel the 3 remaining grapefruit and segment. Arrange on a plate and cover with the marinade; leave to stand 15 minutes. Sprinkle with the mint.

Banana

VITAMINS B2, B3, B5, B6, C, K, BETA-CAROTENE, BIOTIN, FOLIC ACID; CALCIUM, COPPER, IODINE, IRON, MAGNESIUM, MANGANESE, PHOSPHORUS, POTASSIUM, SELENIUM, ZINC; FIBER; CARBOHYDRATE; TRYPTOPHAN

The ultimate fast food, bananas provide a potent mix of vitamins, minerals, and carbohydrates.

A banana is often a favorite fruit of babies and children and in adult life can trigger feelings of being safe and nurtured. Rich in healthy carbohydrates, bananas are ideal when you crave comfort foods, as they feel enjoyably self-indulgent and they're stuffed with nutrients that soothe and lift your mood. They contain tryptophan, which the body converts to serotonin to ease depression and promote peaceful sleep.

Bananas contain high levels of B-vitamins, which the body needs to produce energy. These include vitamin B5, which aids the formation of the immune system's killer cells, and B6, which improves the body's ability to clear away waste matter and reduces fatigue and premenstrual symptoms. Bananas are also a good source of immunity-enhancing vitamin C, and contain manganese, which works with this vitamin to produce the virus-fighting substance interferon. In addition, they are high in potassium, which regulates body fluids and nerve function.

As well as maintaining healthy nerve and muscle function, bananas lower blood pressure and protect against heart disease by maintaining fluid balance and preventing plaque from sticking to artery walls. They are also rich in fiber, and are, therefore, highly beneficial to the digestive tract, soothing and helping to restore normal function after constipation or diarrhea. Bananas contain fructooligosaccharides, which help to feed "good" bacteria in the gut and to aid digestion, and they act as antacids, useful for heartburn or ulcers.

Ripe bananas contain the ideal carbohydrate combination to replace muscle glycogen before or during exercise, making them a valuable food for athletes. Glucose, the most easily digested sugar, is immediately absorbed into the bloodstream for instant energy, while the fructose in bananas is absorbed more slowly, providing a steady supply of fuel over time. Banana skins can soften corns and calluses.

BROILED BANANAS WITH LIME SYRUP
serves 2

heaping ½ cup sugar

juice and grated zest of 2 limes

7 tbsp. water

4 bananas, sliced into chunks

Put half the sugar in a saucepan with the lime juice and zest and the water. Bring to a boil, reduce the heat, and simmer 10 minutes, or until thick. Place the bananas on some foil, sprinkle with the remaining sugar, and broil, turning occasionally, until golden and soft. Drizzle with the lime syrup and serve.

✦BANANA SKIN POULTICE *for corns & calluses*

2 small, unripe banana skins

strip of cloth

Using the cloth, bandage a piece of unripe banana skin, gummy-side down, onto the corn or callus. Leave overnight and discard in the morning; repeat the following night. After 2 days, soak your feet in hot water, then scrape away the softened corn with a pumice stone; repeat as necessary.

*BANANA CONDITIONER *to moisturize dry hair*

1 ripe banana
2 tsp. grapeseed oil

Mash the banana with a fork, then mix with the oil to make a thick paste. Massage into the hair and scalp, then cover with plastic wrap and leave 30 minutes. Wash out the conditioner using a mild shampoo.

SPICED BANANAS

4 bananas, peeled
4 tsp. lemon juice
2 tsp. ground cinnamon
2 tbsp. slivered almonds

Cut the bananas in half lengthwise and place on a greased baking sheet. Sprinkle with the lemon juice and cinnamon and place under a hot broiler until the bananas brown. Scatter the almonds over and serve.

BREAKFAST SMOOTHIE *serves 2*

2 ripe bananas
20 raspberries
20 blueberries
2 cups plain yogurt
½ tsp. ground ginger

Whiz together the bananas, berries, and yogurt in a blender until smooth. Pour into 2 glasses, sprinkle the ginger over and serve immediately.

BANANA MILKSHAKE

2 bananas, chopped
2 cups soy milk or milk of your choice
1 tbsp. maple syrup
1 tbsp. natural vanilla extract
1 tsp. ground nutmeg

Put the bananas, milk, maple syrup, and vanilla extract in a blender and whiz until smooth. Serve chilled, sprinkled with the nutmeg.

Apple

Vitamins B3, C, E, K, beta-carotene, biotin, folic acid; calcium, chromium, iron, magnesium, manganese, phosphorus, potassium, zinc; malic acid, quercetin; flavonoids; fiber; carbohydrate

Over the course of centuries, apple has acquired the reputation as a healthful fruit and remedy, so confirming the old adage, "an apple a day keeps the doctor away."

Apples have a huge number of health benefits, and scientists are only just starting to identify their numerous life-enhancing nutrients, but the apple's superstar role is in digestion and detoxification. Eating an apple aids a detox by helping you feel full sooner and for longer, and can alleviate even chronic constipation, a widespread problem often caused by poor nutrition. Constipation prevents the body getting rid of toxins and can lead to more serious conditions, from hemorrhoids to colon cancer.

Apples are rich in soluble and insoluble fiber, both of which help food to progress at a healthy pace through the digestive system. These fibers pick up toxic waste, such as heavy metals, along the way, as well as cholesterol, which is one reason why apples are also good for the arteries. The toxins and cholesterol can then be safely excreted, with the help of the soluble fiber, pectin. It forms a gel-like substance that softens the body's waste and helps it to leave the body naturally. Pectin has a regulating effect on the speed of digestion, slowing it down as well as speeding it up when necessary. It can also help to alleviate diarrhea, for example, which removes food from the system too quickly for vital nutrients to be absorbed and can lead to dangerous levels of dehydration.

Apples also contain malic acid, which

neutralizes acid by-products and helps the body to use energy efficiently. They slow the rise of blood sugar and help to control diabetes. Studies have found that eating apples can even help to improve lung function.

According to some studies, apples can reduce the risk of several common cancers, as well as protect the brain from the damage that causes conditions, such as Alzheimer's and Parkinson's diseases. Antioxidant compounds in the skin of apples—in particular quercetin, epicatechin, and procyanidin—are thought to be responsible for this protective action. Quercetin is also an anti-inflammatory, making apples useful in the treatment of arthritis and allergic reactions, and reducing the risk of sun damage to skin. The vitamin C content of apples boosts immunity, while their high water content rehydrates the body.

BAKED APPLES *serves 2*

4 tbsp. unsalted butter

4 tsp. dried currants

4 tsp. sugar

4 tsp. slivered almonds

1 tsp. cinnamon

1 tsp. ground nutmeg

2 cooking apples, peeled and cored

2 tbsp. crème fraîche, to serve

Preheat the oven to 350°F. Combine all the ingredients, except the apples, in a bowl. Divide the mixture in half and stuff it into each apple. Wrap the apples individually in foil, then bake 20 minutes. Serve topped with crème fraîche.

✦AGE-OLD APPLE AND LICORICE INFUSION
for gastric, kidney & pulmonary conditions

4½ lb. apples, unpeeled
   and thinly sliced into circles

1 quart water

2 small pieces licorice root

Place the apples in a saucepan and cover with the water. Add the licorice root and boil 15 minutes, then strain and discard the apple and licorice. Drink throughout the day.

APPLE, PEAR, AND MINT JUICE

8 apples, cored
8 pears, cored
12 stems mint

Wash all the fruit, then cut it into chunks, leaving the skin on. Feed through a juicer with the mint. Pour into large glasses and drink immediately.

APPLE CHARLOTTE

2 lb. 4 oz. cooking apples, peeled, cored,
 and sliced
2 tbsp. honey
½ tsp. cinnamon
pinch of ground nutmeg
8 slices of bread, buttered on both sides

Preheat the oven to 375°F. Heat the apples with 2 tablespoons water in a pan, stirring until the mixture forms a thick purée. Stir in the honey, cinnamon, and nutmeg. Line the side and bottom of a greased, deep cake pan with half the bread, spoon the purée in, and top with the other half of the bread. Bake 30 minutes, or until golden brown. Serve hot.

APPLE AND APRICOT CRUMBLE

¾ cup plus 2 tbsp. apple juice
6 apples, peeled, cored, and chopped
heaping ¾ cup apricot jam
4 tbsp. unhydrogenated margarine
1 cup oatmeal
3 tbsp. oat bran

Put the apple juice in a pan and bring to a boil. Add the apples and simmer, covered, until the liquid evaporates. Mash the apples, then add the jam and spread in a baking dish. Work the margarine into the oats and oat bran to form a crumble topping. Spoon it over the fruit and bake at 350°F 30 minutes.

Pear

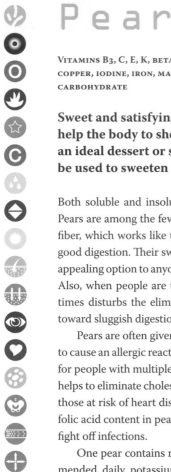

VITAMINS B3, C, E, K, BETA-CAROTENE, BIOTIN, FOLIC ACID; CALCIUM,
COPPER, IODINE, IRON, MAGNESIUM, PHOSPHORUS, POTASSIUM, ZINC; FIBER;
CARBOHYDRATE

**Sweet and satisfying, pears are rich in fiber, which can
help the body to shed excess weight. Besides making
an ideal dessert or snack, pears and pear juice can
be used to sweeten cakes and cereals instead of sugar.**

Both soluble and insoluble fiber help to fill you up in a healthy way.
Pears are among the few fruits that contain a high quantity of insoluble
fiber, which works like tiny scrubbing brushes in the colon to promote
good digestion. Their sweet taste and refreshing juiciness make them an
appealing option to anyone who has given up sugary treats to lose weight.
Also, when people are trying to lose weight, the change in diet sometimes disturbs the eliminatory system. Pears counteract any tendency
toward sluggish digestion if you're eating less than usual.

Pears are often given as a baby's first fruit, as they are the least likely
to cause an allergic reaction. This also makes them one of the best fruits
for people with multiple food allergies. The insoluble fiber in pears
helps to eliminate cholesterol from the body, which is useful for
those at risk of heart disease. The antioxidant vitamin C and
folic acid content in pears also boost immunity and help to
fight off infections.

One pear contains roughly one-tenth of the recommended daily potassium intake for most adults—a
mineral lost through perspiration. This means that
pears make great snacks
for exercisers, as
they counteract
the low potas-
sium levels
that can lead
to fatigue and
muscle cramps.

BROILED PEARS

4 pears, halved and cored

2 tbsp. dried currants

4 tbsp. apple juice

Broil the pears under low heat
5 minutes, turning once. Sprinkle
the currants on top and pour the
apple juice over. Serve immediately.

PEARS IN CAROB

1¼ cups white grape juice

6 pears, peeled, cored, and cut in half
    lengthwise

10 oz. silken tofu

3 tbsp. brown rice syrup

2 tbsp. hazelnut butter

1 tsp. carob powder

1 tsp. grain coffee substitute

2 tbsp. sunflower oil

Put two-thirds of the grape juice
in a pan and bring to a boil. Add the
pears, reduce the heat and simmer,
covered, 8 minutes until the liquid
evaporates. Divide into four dessert
bowls. Put the remaining juice and
ingredients in a food processor and
whiz until creamy. Serve with the
cooked pears.

POACHED PEARS

4 pears, peeled

¼ cup honey

½ cup apple juice

1 tsp. ground ginger

Place the pears, honey, juice, and
1 cup plus 2 tablespoons water in a
pan. Sprinkle with the ginger and
bring to a boil. Reduce the heat
and simmer, covered,
20 minutes. Leave to
cool in the syrup.

Fig

VITAMINS B3, B5, B6, C, BETA-CAROTENE, BIOTIN, FOLIC ACID; CALCIUM, COPPER, IODINE, IRON, MAGNESIUM, MANGANESE, PHOSPHORUS, POTASSIUM, ZINC; FIBER; CARBOHYDRATE

Nature's own laxative, figs are indigenous to Iran, Syria, and other parts of Asia, and are generously high in health-enhancing compounds.

Figs contain active ingredients that stimulate the intestinal action necessary for bowel movement, relieving constipation, which is often a problem in later life. They also contain more fiber than any other dried or fresh fruit, aiding satiety by promoting a feeling of fullness in the stomach and helping to balance blood sugar levels. In addition, their high fiber content provides an additional laxative effect.

Two of the minerals found in figs help to protect the skeletal system: calcium, vital for bone growth in children and bone density in adults, and potassium, which also helps to control the blood pressure and water balance in the body.

Calcium is particularly important for female athletes who train at high intensity. This is because they can experience low estrogen levels and amenorrhea, which can increase bone loss and the need for calcium. Most of us eat too much sodium (mainly from salt) and not enough potassium, which balances some of sodium's effects. While excess sodium causes the body to excrete calcium, potassium helps to reduce this loss. It also counteracts sodium's harmful effects on blood pressure and lowers the risk of developing heart conditions. Figs are also rich in iron, needed to stave off anemia, making them an excellent food for pregnant women and convalescents.

Dried figs offer a concentrated burst of simple carbohydrate for instant energy—Spartan athletes in ancient Greece were said to eat figs to boost their performance—while fresh figs provide a unique, sweet taste and crunchy texture, and a higher dose of the vital antioxidant vitamin C. Figs also provide useful amounts of vitamin B6, without which we can suffer from a poor memory and increased stress levels. Used topically, they are good at drawing out poisons.

✦FIG SYRUP *for constipation*

⅓ cup dried figs
⅓ cup prunes
2 cups water
1 tbsp. dark molasses

Put the figs, prunes, and water
in a saucepan and set aside to soak
8 hours. Bring to a boil, then reduce
heat and simmer until the fruit is soft
and the excess liquid reduces. Stir
in the molasses, then cool and whiz
in a food processor. Transfer to a jar,
and store in the refrigerator. Drink
4 teaspoons of the syrup as needed.

FIGS STUFFED WITH ORANGE-ANISE CREAM

16 figs
½ cup cream cheese,
  at room temperature
1 tbsp. fresh orange juice
2 tsp. grated orange zest
1½ tsp. honey
½ tsp. aniseed, crushed

Trim and discard the stems from
the figs. Cut an "X" down through
the stem ends and gently push each
fig open. In a bowl, combine the
cream cheese, orange juice, orange
zest, honey, and aniseed. Beat until
creamy. Spoon a dollop of mixture
into each fig. Store in the refrigerator
up to 2 hours.

Grape

VITAMINS B1, B3, B6, C, K, BETA-CAROTENE, BIOTIN, FOLIC ACID; CALCIUM, COPPER, IODINE, IRON, MAGNESIUM, MANGANESE, PHOSPHORUS, POTASSIUM, SELENIUM, ZINC; ANTHOCYANINS, ELLAGIC ACID, FLAVONOIDS, QUERCETIN; FIBER; CARBOHYDRATE

These sweet and juicy vine fruits are nature's cleansers and make excellent detoxifiers. A great source of instant energy, succulent grapes provide all-around protection.

Grapes contain an enormous number of compounds that are uniquely nourishing, thus giving them a reputation as a food for convalescents. This aromatic fruit can prevent and help to treat any number of age-related conditions, from anemia and fatigue to arthritis, varicose veins, and rheumatism.

Since the earliest times, grapes have been dried to make raisins. Dynamos of concentrated nutrients, raisins are full of fiber and are an exceptionally high-energy food. They are also rich in the minerals iron, potassium, selenium, and zinc. Selenium, in particular, is a very important antiaging nutrient, offering protection from heart disease and boosting the immune system. In addition, selenium is good for the skin and is thought to help keep fine lines and wrinkles at bay.

In folk medicine, grapes were used to purify the blood, clean the digestive system, and counter liver and kidney disorders. Their high vitamin C content means they are helpful for mopping up harmful free radicals, and being high in both water and fiber, grapes are a great aid for detoxifying the skin, gut, kidneys, and the liver.

Full of powerful antioxidants, including astringent tannins, flavonids, and anthocyanins, grapes help to prevent "bad" LDL cholesterol from oxidizing and blood from clotting, and strengthen capillaries, so protecting the heart and the circulatory system. Black grapes also contain quercetin, which helps to minimize inflammation, aiding the cardiovascular system farther, as well as promoting healthy digestion.

Grapes can help to stabilize immune response by moderating allergic reactions. They also contain cancer-preventing ellagic acid, as well as resveratrol, which is found specifically in red grapes. This compound, together with pterostilbene and saponins, aids heart health by reducing the risk of blood clots and relaxing blood vessels.

When fitting in food before exercise is a problem, grapes provide a refreshing solution. Grapes make an ideal preworkout snack, as they are light, rich in quick-energy carbohydrate, and easily digestible, and they replenish some of the fluid and minerals you'll lose as you sweat. It helps if you can keep them in your pocket and nibble them as you go along.

GRAPE CLEANSER *serves 1 or 2*

20 seedless grapes
6 celery stalks
handful watercress

Press the ingredients through a juicer, alternating the grapes, celery, and watercress. Mix well and drink immediately.

GRAPE JUICE

6 lb. black grapes
piece of cheesecloth

Place the grapes in a large stockpot. Mash them so the juice flows, then cover with water and bring to a boil. Reduce the heat and simmer 10 minutes. Mash them again, breaking up as many grapes as possible. Secure the cheesecloth over another pan and pour the juice through it. Leave the juice to stand overnight. Remove the cloth and drink.

Pineapple

VITAMINS B1, B2, B3, B5, B6, C, E, K, BETA-CAROTENE, BIOTIN, FOLIC ACID; COPPER, IRON, MAGNESIUM, MANGANESE, PHOSPHORUS, POTASSIUM, ZINC; BROMELAIN, FIBER

Not only a delicious exotic fruit, pineapple also has a special health asset in the form of bromelain, an enzyme that helps in the digestion of protein and can reduce inflammation and swelling throughout the body.

In ancient Asian medicine, pineapples were thought to act as a uterine tonic, but today they are best known for their anti-inflammatory action. The enzyme bromelain found in fresh pineapple is a protein-digesting enzyme that aids the digestive system and inhibits the action of a number of inflammatory agents, thereby easing inflammatory conditions, such as sinusitis, rheumatoid arthritis, and gout; speeding recovery from injuries and surgery; helping to alleviate fluid retention; and preventing blood clots and conditions, such as arteriosclerosis. Bromelain can also help the gut to operate efficiently and effectively, and is, therefore, a useful remedy for digestive problems.

Pineapple is an excellent source of manganesean—an essential cofactor in a number of enzymes important for antioxidant defenses and energy production and needed for skin, bone, and cartilage formation. In addition, pineapple is rich in antioxidant vitamin C, which supports the immune system and defends against damaging free radicals, which can cause premature aging. Vitamin C, along with manganese, also helps to make bone-protecting collagen. Used topically, pineapple can help to soften and remove dead skin through the action of its enzyme bromelain.

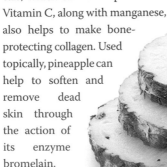

PINEAPPLE AND CUCUMBER SALAD

2½ cups peeled and thinly sliced
   cucumber
a pinch of salt
heaping 1¾ cups peeled, cored, and
   chopped pineapple
2 tbsp. mayonnaise mixed with
   lemon juice, to taste
mint leaves, to serve

Put the cucumber in a colander,
sprinkle with salt and leave
20 minutes. Rinse off the salt and
squeeze out the water. Mix the
cucumber and pineapple in a bowl.
Cover and chill 2 hours, then add the
mayonnaise and toss well. Garnish
with mint leaves to serve.

PINEAPPLE AND HONEY MARINADE
for salmon or chicken

1¼ cups peeled, cored, and finely
   chopped pineapple
2 garlic cloves, crushed
1 to 2 tbsp. honey
1 tsp. ground allspice
1 tsp. ground nutmeg
1 tsp. cinnamon
1 tsp. ground cloves
a pinch of salt

Mix together all the ingredients and
leave to stand 15 minutes. Pour it
over the salmon or chicken and leave
to marinate 2 hours before cooking.

PINEAPPLE AND MANGO SALSA

1 large mango, peeled, pitted, and
   chopped
½ pineapple, peeled, cored, and chopped
¼ red onion, chopped
½-inch piece gingerroot, peeled and grated
1 garlic clove, crushed
½ red chili, seeded and finely sliced
handful cilantro leaves, roughly chopped
juice of 2 limes
1 tsp. sesame oil

Put the mango and pineapple
in a nonreactive bowl with the onion,
ginger, garlic, chili, and cilantro, then
toss together. Drizzle the lime juice
and sesame oil over the mixture and
toss again. Cover and chill until
required. Serve with broiled or
grilled fish or chicken, or as a dip.

Kiwifruit

VITAMINS B3, B5, B6, C, E, BETA-CAROTENE, BIOTIN, FOLIC ACID; LUTEIN;
CALCIUM, COPPER, IODINE, IRON, MAGNESIUM, MANGANESE, PHOSPHORUS,
POTASSIUM, SELENIUM, ZINC; FIBER; CARBOHYDRATE

Named after an indigenous New Zealand bird, kiwifruit is a top immunity booster containing more vitamin C than oranges.

The immunity-enhancing abilities of the kiwifruit lie mainly in its super-dose of vitamin C. Just one fruit contains around 120 percent of an average adult's daily recommended intake, and unlike many other fruits, the nutrients remain intact long after harvesting, with 90 percent of its vitamin C content still present after six months' storage. And although vitamin C is well known for warding off colds, its effects go much farther than that. It protects the body from all kinds of infections and inflammation, and is particularly effective against respiratory diseases. Scientists have found that it helps to reduce coughing, wheezing, and rhinitis. In addition, people who eat kiwifruit are less likely than others to suffer from asthma attacks. However, the fruit shouldn't be given to very small children as it can sometimes cause allergies.

Kiwifruit are loaded with lutein, a carotene, which, together with vitamins C and E, helps to reduce blood clotting as well as blood fats. Their high levels of vitamins C and E are particularly good for preserving youthful skin and protecting vision, and being potassium-rich, kiwis can prevent many age-related conditions from high blood pressure to insomnia and exhaustion.

A good source of fiber, kiwifruit have mild laxative qualities, which help to promote an efficient digestive system. In helping to eliminate toxins from the body, kiwis also help to lower cholesterol levels, which enhances heart health. Phytonutrients in kiwis have been found to have an antithrombotic effect, which is good news for people who are at high risk of heart disease and stroke. According to research, blood clotting was significantly reduced in those consuming two to three kiwifruit a day. With farther studies, this fruit could possibly become a natural alternative to aspirin as a blood-thinning agent.

KIWIFRUIT AND AVOCADO SALAD

3 kiwifruit, peeled and sliced

2 avocados, pitted, peeled, and sliced

1 apple, cored and sliced

2 tsp. lemon juice

3 tbsp. olive oil

1 tbsp. wine vinegar

2½ cups shredded lettuce

Place 2 of the kiwifruit, the avocados, apple, and lemon juice in a bowl and mix together. Crush the remaining kiwifruit, then blend with the olive oil and vinegar. Pour the mixture over the fruit and toss again. Serve on a bed of shredded lettuce.

KIWIFRUIT ICE

4 kiwifruit, peeled and chopped

2 cups unsweetened apple juice

1 tbsp. lemon juice

½ tsp. grated orange zest

Combine the kiwifruit, apple juice, and lemon juice in a blender and whiz until smooth. Stir in the orange zest. Pour mixture into an 8-inch freezerproof tray and freeze until almost firm. Spoon the frozen mixture into a bowl and beat until fluffy. Return the mixture to the tray and freeze again until firm. Leave at room temperature about 10 minutes to soften before serving.

Mango

VITAMINS B3, C, E, BETA-CAROTENE; POTASSIUM; FIBER

Regarded by many as the most delicious tropical fruit of all, mango is also offers many health benefits. It is perfect in fruit salads and desserts, but it works equally well in savory dishes.

An average-size mango contains almost the total recommended daily allowance of the antioxidant vitamin C for most adults, which produces collagen—a protein central to healthy skin and connective tissue. It also helps the body to heal faster from aches, pains, bumps, and bruises.

Mango is one of the few fruit sources of vitamin E, an important antioxidant that helps to fight damaging free radicals in the body, as well as boosting the action of disease-battling antibodies and also speeding up postexercise recovery rates. Together with vitamin C, the vitamin E in mango protects the brain from memory loss. With bright orange-yellow flesh, mangoes are high in beta-carotene, the precursor to antiviral vitamin A, which is needed for clear skin, healthy lungs, a strong heart, and excellent overall immunity.

A powerful detoxifier, mango is a useful source of potassium, important for maintaining normal blood pressure. The fruit is full of fiber, which is vital for a well-functioning digestive system.

MANGO SMOOTHIE *serves 2*

1 mango, peeled, pitted, and sliced
½ pineapple, peeled, cored,
  and chopped
10 strawberries, hulled
⅓ cup pineapple juice
⅓ cup plain yogurt

Place all the ingredients in a blender and whiz until smooth and creamy. Serve immediately.

MANGO LASSI

2 cups plus 2 tbsp. plain yogurt
1½ mangoes, peeled, stoned, and sliced
¼ cup sugar
8 ice cubes
4 pistachios, cut into slivers
4 almonds, cut into slivers
a pinch of saffron threads

Blend the yogurt, mango, sugar, and ice until frothy in a blender. Pour the lassi into glasses and garnish with the nuts and saffron threads.

TROPICAL FRUIT SALAD

1 mango, peeled, stoned, and cubed
4 kiwifruits, peeled and sliced
1 papaya, peeled, seeded, and sliced
8 lychees, peeled, seeeded, and halved
1 pineapple, peeled, cored, and cubed
pulp of 4 passion fruit

Combine all the ingredients together in a large bowl. Leave for 1 hour for the juices to mingle, then serve.

Papaya

VITAMINS B3, B5, C, BETA-CAROTENE, BIOTIN, FOLIC ACID; CALCIUM, IODINE, IRON, MAGNESIUM, MANGANESE, PHOSPHORUS, POTASSIUM, SELENIUM, ZINC; PAPAIN, FIBER; CARBOHYDRATE

First used in Mayan medicine, papayas have beautiful yellow-orange flesh and are packed with carotenoids, helpful for many diseases. Also known as pawpaw, papaya can be eaten ripe as a succulent fresh fruit or cooked in curries and stews in its unripe green state.

Papaya comes out on top in the antioxidant stakes, with half an average fruit providing a whopping 38 milligrams of powerful carotenoids. It can, thus, help to protect against cancer and cardiovascular disease, and to treat skin irritations. Papaya contains protease enzymes, such as papain, which are similar to those present in the stomach, therefore, favoring healthy digestion. The enzymes also reduce inflammation in the body, so they are beneficial in easing joint pain from conditions such as arthritis and sports injuries. Used topically, papain literally digests dead skin cells and acts as a mild exfoliant. It is also said to aid the healing of skin sores.

The fruit is a mild diuretic, and is particularly useful in treating children's urinary and digestive ailments, while its edible seeds have been used to treat stomach aches and fungal infections. Papaya is an excellent source of vitamin C. As well as supporting the immune system, this antioxidant prevents the build-up of plaque in blood-vessels. Papaya is rich in fiber, which lowers cholesterol levels and helps to prevent colon cancer by binding with toxins.

*PAPAYA EXFOLIATING LOTION

to brighten and rejuvenate the skin

1 large fresh papaya
piece of cheesecloth
1 cup chamomile infusion, cooled

Peel the papaya, remove the seeds, and purée the flesh in a blender. Press the purée through a piece of cheesecloth to extract all the juice. Mix the juice with an equal amount of chamomile infusion and stir well. Using cotton balls, apply the lotion to your face and neck, avoiding contact with your eyes. Leave about 10 minutes, then rinse off with cold water. This keeps in the refrigerator up to 2 days.

THAI-STYLE SALAD

2 papayas, peeled and seeded
1 red bell pepper, seeded
8 scallions, trimmed and chopped
3½ oz. bean sprouts
a large handful mint leaves, chopped
1 tbsp. sugar
1 tbsp. lime juice
1 tbsp. fish sauce

Dice the papaya and the bell pepper into ½-inch cubes. Put them in a large bowl with the scallions, bean sprouts, mint leaves, sugar, lime juice, and fish sauce and mix well, then serve.

Blueberry

VITAMINS B2, B3, B5, C, E, K, BETA-CAROTENE, FOLIC ACID; CALCIUM, IRON, MAGNESIUM, MANGANESE, PHOSPHORUS, POTASSIUM, SELENIUM, ZINC; FLAVONOIDS, ELLAGIC ACID, TANNINS; FIBER, CARBOHYDRATE

Blueberries are the number one fruit for helping to protect cells from free radical damage and aging, containing great youth-preserving antioxidants, which boost immunity and stave off many conditions. Historically a resource for herbalists and physicians, this sometimes tart, scented fruit prevents the growth of "unfriendly" bacteria to keep the gut clean and healthy.

According to research, one average serving of blueberries provides as many antioxidants as five average servings of broccoli, apples, or carrots, and this superfood ranks top in antioxidant activity compared to 40 other fresh fruits and vegetables. Eat blueberries three or four times a week for full immunity-boosting benefits. They can be eaten raw as a snack, with plain yogurt and nuts for a light breakfast, or combined with other berries and a little cream for a delicious dessert.

The berries get their beautiful blue color from anthocyanins—potent antioxidants that combat cell damage, improve circulation, and help to protect against heart problems, stroke, cancer, and gum disease, and to enhance eyesight. Ellagic acid, another antioxidant found in blueberries, and the compound resveratrol, are also thought to help to prevent the development of cancer.

The proanthocyanidins (a type of flavonoids) contained in blueberries increase the potency of its vitamin-C content, so supporting collagen, which helps to keep the skin elastic. They also protect the eyes and blood vessels. Another useful compound in blueberries is pterostilbene, which has antidiabetic and cholesterol-lowering properties and might reduce cognitive decline.

Blueberries are a fine source of agents lethal to bacteria, especially *E.coli*, and are a common folk remedy for diarrhea and stomach upsets. They are rich in tannins, which have an anti-inflammatory effect on the body's tissues, and are said to kill microbes and fight the bacteria that cause urinary tract infections. In addition they are a traditional remedy for the treatment of coughs and colds.

These "wonderberries" might also aid in the reversal of neurodegenerative symptoms, such as loss of balance and coordination. They help to improve brain function and have been found to protect against dementia, and to preserve memory and learning ability in old age.

Used topically, blueberries' fruit acid content helps them to act as a gentle astringent and peeling agent.

BLUEBERRY SMOOTHIE *serves 2 to 3*

1⅔ cups blueberries
1 cup raspberries or other
summer berries
½ cup plain yogurt

Whiz the blueberries, raspberries, and yogurt in a blender, then serve. When temperatures are sizzling, add 4 ice cubes to the blender before blending to make a cooling drink.

✦BLUEBERRY TEA *for coughs*

2 tbsp. chopped blueberry leaves
1 cup water, just boiled
honey, to taste

Place the leaves in the water and leave to infuse 5 minutes, then strain. Sweeten with honey to taste. Drink 1 cup every 4 hours.

BLUEBERRY SAUCE

1⅔ cups blueberries
⅓ cup sugar
1 tbsp. lemon juice
a pinch of salt
½ tsp. vanilla extract

Wash the blueberries and crush them in a bowl. Add the sugar, lemon juice, and salt and mix well. In a saucepan, heat the mixture, stirring, then boil 1 minute. Stir in the vanilla extract. Serve with cake, pudding, or ice cream. This keeps in the refrigerator up to 5 days.

BLUEBERRY AND PEAR CRUMBLE

6 tbsp. butter, diced
⅔ cup all-purpose flour
½ cup oatmeal
4 tbsp. brown sugar
2 large pears, cored and sliced
½ cup blueberries

Preheat the oven to 350°F. Rub the butter into the flour in a mixing bowl until the mixture is like breadcrumbs. Stir in the oatmeal and brown sugar. Mix together the pears and blueberries in a lightly greased baking dish. Sprinkle the crumble topping over the top, put the dish on a baking sheet and bake 40 to 45 minutes until brown on top.

BLUEBERRY FOOL

1 lb. 2 oz. silken tofu
¾ cup plus 2 tbsp. apple juice
1⅔ cups blueberries, plus extra to serve
1¼ cups agave syrup
7 tbsp. unrefined sunflower oil
1 tsp. vanilla extract

Put the tofu and apple juice in a food processor and whiz until smooth. Add the blueberries, agave syrup, sunflower oil, and vanilla and continue to blend until thick and creamy. Spoon into dessert glasses or bowls and serve chilled, decorated with a few blueberries on the top.

Cherry

VITAMINS B3, B5, C; BETA-CAROTENE, BIOTIN, FOLIC ACID; BORON, CALCIUM, IRON, MAGNESIUM, MANGANESE, PHOSPHORUS, POTASSIUM, SELENIUM; QUERCETIN, FLAVONOIDS, ELLAGIC ACID; FIBER; CARBOHYDRATE

These sweet summer treats are potent detoxifiers and are packed with antioxidants, making them excellent immunity boosters.

Cherries are rich in flavonoids, such as anthocyanins, antioxidant substances that the body uses to help to make disease-fighting chemicals. Aching joints and fragile bones are an unwelcome symptom of aging, but cherries can do a lot to protect them. They supply the mineral boron, which can help to prevent the steady loss of bone density with advancing age. And their rich anthocyanin content acts as a powerful anti-inflammatory, combating pain in joints and muscles, as well as fibromyalgia—pain in the fibrous tissues of the body, such as the muscles, tendons, and ligaments. These antioxidants can also strengthen blood vessels and slow down the aging process of the skin. And it is also the anthocyanins in cherries that give them the same heart-protective effects as red wine. These benefits, in turn, help people to stay active, which promotes general good health, as well as better bone strength and increased physical coordination.

Cherries are a rich source of quercetin, another strong anti-inflammatory substance, which helps to relieve painful conditions such as rheumatoid arthritis, and gout – a form of arthritis that occurs when uric acid crystals accumulate in joints, leading to pain and inflammation. In studies, cherries have been found to significantly decrease uric acid levels, thus limiting the formation of the gout-inducing crystals.

Like many other berries, cherries contain the phytochemical ellagic acid—a powerful compound that blocks an enzyme cancer cells need to develop. They also contain selenium, a mineral with powerful immunity-boosting properties, and antioxidant vitamin C, which destroys free radicals in the body, aiding the fight against viruses and bacteria. In addition, vitamin C strengthens collagen, maintains healthy-looking skin and hair, and helps to protect against eye disease.

Other antioxidants in cherries include superoxide dismutase (useful in joint, respiratory, and gastrointestinal health) and melatonin—one of the most potent known free-radical scavengers, which is important for the immune system. Low melatonin levels have been associated with sleep problems, so cherries might be useful to aid sleep. Melatonin is also commonly used to combat jetlag.

Cherry stems can be made into an infusion that is a traditional remedy for cystitis and bladder infections.

CHOCO-CHERRIES *serves 1 to 2*

scant 1½ cups cherries, stems left on
3½ oz. good-quality semisweet chocolate, melted

Dip each of the cherries into the chocolate. Place on a greased plate and chill until set.

CHERRY PARFAIT

heaping 2 cups cherries, pitted
2 cups plain yogurt
*   or soy yogurt*
1¼ cups crunchy granola cereal
2 tbsp. shredded coconut, plus extra
*   to serve*
1 tbsp. cherry jam (optional)

Put all the ingredients in a food processor and blend until creamy. Serve chilled, sprinkled with extra coconut.

CHERRY AND RHUBARB COMPÔTE

heaping 2¾ cups cherries, pitted
3 rhubarb stalks, chopped
3 tbsp. apple juice
2 tbsp. fruit sugar
plain yogurt, to serve

Put all the ingredients in a pan. Bring to a boil, reduce the heat, and simmer, covered, about 8 minutes, stirring occasionally. Serve with plain yogurt.

C r a n b e r r y

VITAMINS B5, C, K, BETA-CAROTENE, FOLIC ACID; CALCIUM, IRON, MAGNESIUM, MANGANESE; PHOSPHORUS, POTASSIUM, SELENIUM; ELLAGIC ACID, FLAVONOIDS, TANNINS; FIBER; CARBOHYDRATE

These tart, tangy berries are high in antioxidant vitamin C, making them great immunity-boosters.

Native North Americans first introduced Europeans to cranberries to help them to combat scurvy, and it became recognized that the acidity of cranberries increases the natural acidity of urine, thus preventing bacteria from thriving. One of the natural-health success stories of the past few years, cranberries have proved their value in preventing urinary tract infections, such as cystitis. The powerful ingredient is a flavonoid called proanthocyanidins, which is more abundant in cranberries than in most other fruits. Proanthocyanidins prevent bacteria sticking to the urinary tract wall, and prevent infections of the stomach in the same way. Other compounds in this berry have been found to inhibit plaque-causing bacteria in the mouth, which causes tooth decay and gum disease. Cranberries can also combat kidney stone formation.

A valuable source of antioxidant vitamin C, cranberries are also rich in beta-carotene and folic acid, enabling them to help to ward off colds, flu, and many other diseases, including some cancers. Many people now eat cranberries every day, as a first line of defense.

If you have difficulty finding the fresh berries, buy dried cranberries, juice, or extract instead. For maximum benefit, drink a glass of unsweetened cranberry juice or take 800mg of cranberry extract daily.

CRANBERRY AND BANANA SMOOTHIE

1¼ cups unsweetened cranberry juice
1¼ cups white grape juice
2 bananas, chopped
10 strawberries, hulled
1¾ cups plain yogurt
 or soy yogurt
3 tbsp. honey

Put all the ingredients in a blender and whiz until smooth. Drink immediately.

CRANBERRY-ORANGE RELISH

2 cups cranberries, fresh
 or frozen
1 orange, unpeeled, cut into eighths and
 seeded
1 apple, unpeeled, cut into eighths and
 cored
⅓ cup sugar
1 tsp. ground ginger

Blend the fruit in a food processor. Stir in the sugar and ginger, then transfer to a jar. Cover with a lid and refrigerate at least 4 hours. Use as required.

CRANBERRY SAUCE

½ cup dried cranberries
1 cup plus 2 tbsp. cranberry
 or orange juice
1-inch piece gingerroot, peeled and finely
 chopped
1 tbsp. red wine (optional)
2 tbsp. honey

Place the cranberries and juice in a sauce pan and soak 30 minutes. Bring to a boil, then add the ginger and wine, if using, reduce the heat and simmer 10 minutes, stirring. Mix in the honey and serve with roast turkey, meat, or a nut roast.

Strawberry

Vitamins B2, B3, B5, B6, C, K, folic acid; copper, iron, magnesium, manganese, iodine, potassium; flavonoids; fiber; omega-3 fatty acids; ellagic acid

These favorite berries have been popular throughout the ages and were prized for their therapeutic properties in ancient Rome. Strawberries enhance liver and gallbladder functions, and are a traditional remedy for treating gout, arthritis, and kidney stones.

One of the delights of summer, strawberries are full of disease-fighting and age-defying nutrients. Packed with vitamin C, an average one cup serving of strawberries gives 50 percent more than the recommended daily average adult intake of this immunity-boosting vitamin. Try fresh strawberries with a pinch of pepper for a novel taste with a sharp edge. The vitamin C in strawberries is essential for the manufacture of collagen—a protein that helps to maintain the structure of the skin, keeping it elastic and young looking. Vitamin C also plays an important role in healing wounds and can ward off gingivitis, the gum disease that affects three out of four adults. It can also help to dissolve tartarous incrustations on the teeth.

Strawberries contain ellagic acid, a phytochemical shown to help fight cancer and destroy some of the toxins in cigarette smoke and polluted air. Their B-vitamin content makes them useful for supporting the nervous system and fighting stress-related conditions, as well as building resistance to disease, while their high iron content makes them therapeutic for anemia and fatigue.

These colorful berries are also rich in fiber for a healthy heart and digestive system. They are a mild laxative and help regenerate intestinal flora.

STRAWBERRY AND RICOTTA SPREAD

1 cup strawberries, hulled
2 limes
2 tsp. confectioners' sugar
7 tbsp. ricotta cheese
cinnamon bagels, to serve

Mash the strawberries with a fork and grate the zest of the limes. Add the confectioners' sugar and the lime zest and stir well into the ricotta cheese to form a smooth mixture. Spread over toasted cinnamon bagels for a delicious breakfast treat.

STRAWBERRY SMOOTHIE *serves 2*

1 cup strawberries, hulled
1 banana, chopped
⅔ cup plain yogurt
scant ⅔ cup unsweetened
*   soy milk*
mint leaves, to decorate

Place all the ingredients, except the mint leaves, in a blender and whiz until smooth. Serve in tall glasses topped with mint leaves.

BROILED FRUIT KEBABS

3 kiwifruit, peeled
½ pineapple, peeled and cored
3 bananas
16 strawberries
6 tbsp. pineapple juice
2 tbsp. agave syrup or honey

Soak wooden skewers in cold water at least 30 minutes, then drain. Cut the kiwis, pineapple, and bananas into 1-inch cubes. Thread alternate pieces of the strawberries and cut-up fruit onto the skewers. Combine the pineapple juice and syrup and brush over the kebabs. Broil about 6 minutes, turning frequently.

Raspberry

Vitamins B2, B3, B5, C, E, K, beta-carotene, biotin, folic acid; calcium, copper, iodine, iron, magnesium, manganese, phosphorus, potassium, selenium, zinc; ellagic acid; flavonoids; fiber

These jewellike, soft berries are packed with health-enhancing antioxidants and other protective nutrients that are powerful fighters of infections and diseases, including cancers and heart problems.

One of the top fruit sources of fiber, raspberries are helpful for keeping cholesterol low and improving digestion, as well as detoxifying the body and keeping blood sugar levels steady. Raspberries are naturally astringent and can, therefore, help to treat upset stomachs and diarrhea. They have antimicrobial effects that can prevent the proliferation of bacteria and fungi in the digestive system. One of these, *Candida albicans*, causes the irritating vaginal infection called thrush and has also been linked with digestive disorders such as irritable bowel syndrome. Raspberries are also said to protect against allergies.

Like other berries, raspberries are high in anthocyanins, powerful antioxidants that help the body to produce cells to fight off unwanted invaders. The anthocyanins in raspberries have anti-inflammatory properties, thus protecting from conditions such as arthritis.

The fruits also contain ellagic acid, which is anticarcinogenic and prevents adverse cellular changes and might be especially useful for preventing cancers of the mouth, throat, and colon. It is also thought to promote the healing of wounds.

Raspberries contain high levels of infection-fighting vitamin C, which boosts immunity and can help to prevent everything from heart disease to eye problems. They are packed with a host of absorbable minerals, including calcium, potassium, iron, and magnesium, all of which are essential to general good health. Raspberries are also particularly helpful to those suffering from heart problems, fatigue, and depression, as well as convalescents.

Traditionally, an infusion made from raspberry leaves can facilitate labor by acting as a uterine relaxant and a tonic.

RASPBERRY BRULÉE

3¼ cups raspberries
1 tsp. vanilla extract
1¼ cups plain yogurt
2 tbsp. sugar

Place the raspberries in 4 ramekins or flameproof dishes. Combine the vanilla extract and yogurt, and spoon the mixture over the fruit. Cover the surface of each ramekin with the sugar, then caramelize under a very hot broiler 2 minutes, or until crisp. Leave to cool, then serve.

RASPBERRY COULIS

3½ cups raspberries
1 tbsp. fruit sugar
1 tsp. lemon juice

Put all the ingredients in a food processor and blend. Strain the mixture through a fine nylon sieve into a bowl, pressing on the solids. Serve the sauce on top of ice cream or other desserts.

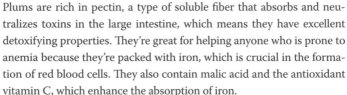

Plum and prune

VITAMINS A, B2, B3, B5, B6, C, BETA-CAROTENE, FOLIC ACID; CALCIUM, COPPER, IODINE, IRON, MAGNESIUM, MANGANESE, PHOSPHORUS, POTASSIUM, SELENIUM, ZINC; MALIC ACD; CARBOHYDRATE; FIBER

This versatile fruit can be eaten fresh or dried and is a useful source of immunity-boosting antioxidants

Plums are rich in pectin, a type of soluble fiber that absorbs and neutralizes toxins in the large intestine, which means they have excellent detoxifying properties. They're great for helping anyone who is prone to anemia because they're packed with iron, which is crucial in the formation of red blood cells. They also contain malic acid and the antioxidant vitamin C, which enhance the absorption of iron.

Prunes are dried plums, both of which have made headlines in relation to their rich phytochemical content, namely neochlorogenic and chlorogenic acids. These antioxidant compounds help to neutralize hazardous free radicals in the body, protecting cells from damage and slowing down the aging process.

Containing many of the same nutrients as fresh plums, prunes also have a very beneficial effect on the digestive system. They have long been used as the most-effective, yet gentle, natural remedy for constipation. Prunes contain a natural laxative called diphenylisatin, which is why they are so useful for keeping the bowel regular. Their fiber-rich bulk softens food waste that has dried out during an excessive delay in the colon, and helps it move painlessly on and out of the body. Yet, they can also slow the movement of food from the stomach if it is emptying too quickly, causing indigestion or wind. Prunes are known to lower cholesterol by helping the body to excrete fats, and feeding the good bacteria in the intestine, helping to prevent harmful bacteria breeding.

While prunes have long been regarded as a rich source of fiber, it is perhaps less well-known that, weight for weight, they are the most potent of all antioxidant foods. Eating prunes is also a sweet way of increasing beta-carotene and potassium intake. Their high level of potassium keeps blood pressure in check, while their vitamin B6 protects the heart and boosts brain power. Like plums, prunes are also full of iron, which provides energy and prevents fatigue, making them an ideal snack for anyone who exercises strenuously. Their combination of iron and vitamin A is especially good for stimulating hair growth, while vitamin A itself maintains youthful skin and protects the eyes.

AROMATIC STEWED PRUNES *serves 2*

1 cup soft pitted prunes
juice of 2 oranges
a pinch of cinnamon
plain yogurt, to serve

Put the prunes in a pan with the orange juice and cinnamon, and bring to a boil. Reduce the heat, then simmer, covered, about 15 minutes. Serve hot or cool with yogurt.

PLUM COMPÔTE *serves 2*

16 ripe but firm plums
2 tsp. ground allspice
2 tbsp. dark brown sugar
1 cup plus 2 tbsp. orange juice
grated zest of ½ orange
plain yogurt, to serve

Place the plums in a large baking dish. Add the allspice, sugar, and orange juice and zest. Place the dish in a preheated 350°F oven and bake 30 minutes. Serve with the yogurt alongside for spooning over.

A p r i c o t

VITAMINS A, B2, B3, B5, C; BETA-CAROTENE, LYCOPENE; CALCIUM, IRON, POTASSIUM; ZINC; FIBER; TRYPTOPHAN

As their bright orange color indicates, apricots are rich in beta-carotene. They have been prominent in Indian and Chinese folklore for 2,000 years. These fragrant stone fruits are bursting with nutrients, and are delicious eaten fresh or dried.

Apricots are thought to have originated in ancient Armenia, although they have a long history throughout Asia and the near East.

These flavorsome fruits have high levels of beta-carotene, which the body turns into antiviral and anticarcinogenic vitamin A. It is the most abundant antioxidant found in apricots, helping to protect the skin and lungs from oxidation damage and supporting the immune system. It also prevents free radicals from damaging the eyes. Eating fresh apricots can be helpful to those suffering from infections, particularly those of the respiratory tract. Dried apricots supply iron and produce hemoglobin, beneficial to anyone suffering from anemia. They also have a balancing effect on the nervous system, treating mental fatigue, mild anxiety, and insomnia, and yield an oil that is highly nourishing for the skin.

An excellent source of vitamin B5, which is crucial for the production of antibodies, apricots are also high in vitamin C, which is essential for all immune functions. In addition, apricots contain lycopene, which is one of the most powerful antioxidants. Lycopene is known for its ability to prevent the build-up of fatty deposits in the arteries and it also has strong anticarcinogenic properties.

Apricots are rich in the amino acid tryptophan, which the body converts to the feel-good chemical serotonin. This brain chemical lifts your mood, making you feel more optimistic, improving self-esteem, and even helping to control impulsive behavior. And it helps you sleep well, too. Some of the tryptophan is also converted to niacin, or vitamin B3, if necessary. A shortage of this nutrient can cause lethargy, so eating apricots can keep energy levels high.

APRICOT CRUMBLE

5¾ cups peeled, pitted and roughly
chopped apricots
⅓ cup sugar
⅔ cup wholewheat flour
¼ cup oatmeal
2 tbsp. demerara sugar
4 tbsp. unsalted butter, cut into
small pieces
crème fraîche or sour cream, to serve
(optional)

Preheat the oven to 375°F. Place the apricots in a baking dish and sprinkle with ¼ cup of the sugar. In another bowl, combine the remaining ingredients and rub together until the mixture resembles breadcrumbs. Cover the apricots with the crumble mixture and bake 40 minutes until bubbling and golden. Serve with crème fraîche, if desired.

*APRICOT MASSAGE OIL
for dry, sensitive skins

9 oz. apricot seeds
3 cups carrier (base) oil, such as
almond or olive
piece of cheesecloth

With a mortar and pestle, grind the seeds to release the oils, then place them in a clear glass jar. Pour the carrier oil onto the seeds, secure, and shake. Place in a sunny spot and leave 2 to 6 weeks. Pour the oil through a cheesecloth-lined sieve into a pitcher, then pour into dark glass bottles. Store up to a year. Apply liberally to the skin when needed.

Pomegranate

VITAMINS B1, B2, B3, B5, B6, C, E, BETA-CAROTENE, BIOTIN, FOLIC ACID; CALCIUM, COPPER, IRON, MAGNESIUM, PHOSPHORUS, POTASSIUM, SELENIUM, ZINC; ELLAGIC ACID; FIBER; CARBOHYDRATE

Steeped in symbolism since ancient times, pomegranate now has superfood status, thanks to recent research into its amazing healing attributes.

Drinking a glass of pomegranate juice a day could help to protect you against three major problems of old age: heart disease, cancer, and osteoarthritis. According to studies, a medium-size glass of pomegranate juice contains almost three times as many antioxidants as the same amount of red wine, green tea, or orange juice. Removing the edible seed clusters from the fruit can seem tricky, but you can do this easily by tapping on the outside with a wooden spoon until they fall out.

Pomegranate is abundant in antioxidants called punicalagins, which have been shown to prevent several forms of cancer by protecting the body against free radicals, which can harm cells. They also keep the skin youthful and protect it from sun damage.

In men who already have prostate cancer, pomegranate has been found to slow the rate of tumor growth. It might also reduce the risk of developing various cancers because of its extremely high ellagic acid content, which has anticarcinogenic and anti-heart disease properties. The pomegranate's polyphenols work as powerful antioxidants, preventing heart damage and the build-up of plaque in the arteries. They not only lower high blood pressure, but also help to fight LDL "bad" cholesterol, which is linked to heart attacks and strokes.

Pomegranate eases the pain and disability of osteoarthritis by slowing the deterioration of cartilage and preventing inflammation. It contains plenty of healing vitamins, including B1, which helps the body to convert food into energy, and B2, which helps to tame free radicals and is also central to memory function. Its vitamin C content also offers protection against cardiovascular disease, cancer, and eye problems. Pomegranate might also have antiviral and antibacterial properties, and has been shown to discourage the formation of dental plaque.

FRUIT SALAD WITH POMEGRANATE

1 pomegranate
1 bunch white seedless grapes, removed
*   from the stems*
1 cup strawberries, hulled and chopped
1 banana, chopped
1 peach, pitted and chopped
⅔ cup blueberries
4 tbsp. fruit juice of choice
1 tbsp. lemon juice
1 tbsp. honey
a pinch of ground nutmeg, to serve

Cut the pomegranate in half horizontally and, using a wooden spoon, bash until the seeds fall out. Put them in a bowl with the other fruits. Combine the fruit juice, lemon juice, and honey, then pour it over the fruit and mix gently. Serve sprinkled with the nutmeg.

POMEGRANATE CUP

¾ cup plus 2 tbsp. plain yogurt
2 tsp. honey
4 pomegranates
4 mint sprigs, to serve

Place the yogurt in a small bowl and stir in the honey until well combined. Cut each pomegranate in half horizontally and, using a wooden spoon, bash until the seeds fall out. Mix the pomegranate seeds with the yogurt and honey mixture, garnish with mint, and serve.

Cantaloupe melon

VITAMINS A, B3, B6, C, BETA-CAROTENE, FOLIC ACID; POTASSIUM; FIBER

These succulent summer fruits offer a mouthwatering slice of nutritional goodness bursting with antioxidants to fight aging free radicals.

Cantaloupe melon is also known as rock or musk melon. Just one average slice provides more beta-carotene and vitamin C than your body can use in a whole day. Cantaloupe melon is one of the richest sources of beta-carotene, which the body converts to vitamin A, an antioxidant that is crucial for the production of disease-fighting lymphocyte cells. This fruit is also rich in vitamin C, which we need for all immune functions and to protect us against colds, cancers, and heart disease. Both vitamin C and beta-carotene are naturally antiaging and aid cell repair and growth, as well as supporting the circulatory system.

Cantaloupe also contains potassium, which can lower high blood pressure and "bad" LDL cholesterol. Its high water content gives it a mildly diuretic action, helping to detoxify the body. Its B-vitamins enhance the production of energy and help to stabilize blood sugar.

The dense texture of this fragrant melon makes it a satisfying replacement for any foods you're limiting, just as their sweetness meets the need that might otherwise be filled by empty-calorie snacks.

RED MELON SALAD

1 pink grapefruit, peeled
2 cantaloupe melons, peeled, seeded, and
  cubed
10 raspberries
1-inch piece gingerroot, peeled and grated

Divide the grapefruit into segments
and combine with the melon in a
large bowl, then set aside 30 minutes
to let the juices mingle. Spoon into
four serving bowls and decorate with
the raspberries and the ginger.

*MELON LOTION
to cool and hydrate the skin

¼ cantaloupe melon
a piece of cheesecloth
½ lemon
1 tbsp. olive oil

Whiz the melon in a blender, then
strain the juice through cheesecloth.
Squeeze 1 teaspoon lemon juice.
Combine the melon juice, lemon
juice, and olive oil in a container, then
cover and store in the refrigerator.
Apply twice daily to the face and neck
with cotton balls. This keeps in the
refrigerator up to 2 days.

MELON AND GINGER

2 small cantaloupe melons
2 tsp. lime juice
1-inch piece gingerroot, finely chopped
2 tsp. cinnamon
4 tbsp. cherries (optional)

Quarter the melons and cut away the
skin. Scoop out and discard the seeds.
Cut the flesh into wedges or scoop
into balls. Add the lime juice and
ginger and mix together well. Dust
with cinnamon, top with cherries, if
using, and serve.

A v o c a d o

VITAMINS B1, B2, B3, B5, B6, C, E, K, BIOTIN, CAROTENOIDS, FOLIC ACID; CALCIUM, COPPER, IODINE, IRON, MAGNESIUM, MANGANESE, PHOSPHORUS, POTASSIUM, ZINC; BETA-SITOSTEROL, GLUTATHIONE; OMEGA-3, -6 AND -9 FATTY ACIDS; TRYPTOPHAN; LECITHIN; FIBER

One of the few fruits that contains fat, avocado boasts a wealth of health-boosting properties

Strictly speaking, avocado is a type of pear, so, therefore, a fruit, although it is typically used in savory dishes. It is native to Central America, and was discovered by Spanish invaders in the sixteenth century. It is now popular throughout the world and grown in various tropical regions. With a smooth, buttery texture and mild, creamy taste, avocados are best eaten when ripe. As they are normally picked before they are ripe, avocados take about a week to ripen at room temperature, although storing them in a paper bag with a banana can speed the process.

Scientists have found that people are more relaxed after a higher-fat meal, and even feel less pain. (No wonder people eat junk foods when they're feeling low!) Avocados are the healthier alternative: instead of saturated fat, they provide healthy monounsaturated fat, which raises levels of "good" cholesterol while slightly lowering fatty triglycerides. Another type of fat in this delicious, creamy food is lecithin, which plays a role in improving brain function. Some fat is also necessary for the body to absorb nutrients that can improve your mood, such as avocado's vitamin E, which is also an antioxidant that neutralizes the damaging effect of toxins in the body, boosts resistance to infection, and has an antiaging effect.

The high content of vitamins C and E in avocados is excellent for keeping the skin soft, supple, and healthy, and for maintaining glossy hair. They have high levels of the antioxidant lutein, which studies have shown helps to protect against eye problems and cardiovascular disease. Avocados are rich in tryptophan, along with vitamin B6 and folic acid, which help the body turn tryptophan into the feel-good chemical serotonin. Just one avocado provides a good amount of the average adult's recommended daily intake of vitamin B6—essential for helping the body release energy from food.

Avocados are rich in potassium, which staves off fatigue, depression, heart disease, and strokes and is essential for healthy blood pressure and muscle contraction. They are said to have a unique antibacterial and antifungal substance in the pulp, as well as to harmonizing the liver and soothing the nervous system.

Loaded with fiber, avocados are also a source of linoleic acid (known as omega-6 fatty acid), which the body converts to gamma-linolenic acid (GLA), a substance that helps to thin the blood, soothe inflammation, and improve blood sugar balance. They are high in omega-3 fatty acids, helping to prevent wrinkles, enhance brain power, and treat arthritis. They also contain oleic acid, the building block for omega-9 fatty acids, which are excellent for the skin and have anti-inflammatory properties.

Avocado's range of B-vitamins help the immune cells to destroy harmful invaders, as does glutathione, a powerful substance that boosts the action of the body's natural killer cells. In addition, they contain the plant chemical beta-sitosterol, which lowers "bad" cholesterol and is particularly beneficial to the prostate gland.

Shunned by dieters because of their high calorie count, avocados might aid weight loss by satisfying hunger and improving metabolism. With 20 vitamins, minerals, and phytonutrients, avocados are one of nature's superfoods for anyone aiming to get fit. They contain more protein than any other fruit, making them ideal for strength and endurance.

✳ A V O C A D O   F A C E · P A C K   *to rejuvenate tired skin*

1 avocado, pitted and peeled
1 tsp. honey
1 tsp. lemon juice
1 tsp. plain yogurt

Mash all the ingredients into a paste, then leave in the refrigerator 30 minutes. Apply the pack to your face and leave 10 minutes before removing with cool water.

AVOCADO AND BABY SPINACH SALAD

juice of 2 limes
2 tsp. honey
a pinch of salt
2 avocados, pitted, peeled, and cubed
16 cherry tomatoes, halved
2 handfuls baby spinach, washed and torn
  into pieces

Make the dressing by combining the lime juice, honey, and salt in a jar, then seal and shake well. Put all the remaining ingredients in a bowl and coat with the dressing. Mix gently and serve immediately.

GUACAMOLE *makes 1 large bowl*

2 avocados, pitted and peeled
juice of 1 lime
2 garlic cloves, crushed
1 onion, finely chopped
2 tomatoes, peeled and chopped
1 small red chili, seeded and finely
  chopped
1 tbsp. cilantro leaves, finely chopped

For a chunky dip, mash the avocados by hand with the lime juice until smooth, then add the remaining ingredients and combine thoroughly. For a smoother texture, blend the ingredients in a food processor. Serve as a dip for crudités.

TANGY SUMMER SALAD

3 tbsp. olive oil
1 tsp. honey
1 red onion, grated
1 tsp. Dijon mustard
4 avocados, pitted, peeled, and sliced
1 pink grapefruit, peeled and broken into
  segments
a large handful arugula leaves

Beat the oil, honey, onion, and mustard together in a bowl. Add the avocados, grapefruit, and arugula, toss well in the dressing, and serve.

Tomato

VITAMINS A, B3, B5, B6, C, E, K, BETA-CAROTENE, BIOTIN, FOLIC ACID, LYCOPENE; CALCIUM, CHROMIUM, COPPER, IODINE, IRON, MAGNESIUM, MANGANESE, MOLYBDENUM, PHOSPHORUS, POTASSIUM, ZINC; FIBER

A favorite ingredient in many dishes, this juicy, sumptuous fruit was discovered by the Aztecs of Central America, and its 7,000-plus varieties are all packed with health-enhancing nutrients.

A tomato is full of vitamins and minerals, but it is most renowned for the life-saving properties of a versatile caretenoid called lycopene, which gives tomatoes their vivid red color and helps to prevent cancer, particularly cancer of the prostate, breast, lung, and endometrium. Lycopene neutralizes free radicals before they can cause damage, therefore staving off everything from wrinkles and sun-damage to heart attacks. Studies indicate that lycopene might have twice the anticarcinogenic punch of beta-carotene. Unusually, lycopene is unharmed by food processing and cooking, which means tomato-based products, such as sauces, offer many of the same benefits as the fresh fruit.

Tomatoes are filled with the antioxidant vitamins C and E, as well as beta-carotene. Together they can help to prevent everything from cataracts to heart disease and cancer. Vitamin C is powerfully antiviral and crucial for all functions of the immune system and it also supports connective tissue in the body and boosts immunity. In addition, tomatoes contain a little iron, which is easily absorbed when accompanied by vitamin C, and prevents anemia and fatigue.

The high levels of beta-carotene in tomatoes are necessary for the production of vitamin A. This helps to maintain a healthy thymus gland, which plays a vital role in immune response. Tomatoes are also rich in potassium, which regulates fluid balance.

A bottle of tomato juice keeps minerals at a safe level when you're running. Most of us get too much sodium in our diet, but a long run can dangerously reduce the body's levels of minerals, particularly sodium—especially if you've drunk a lot of water. A drink of bought tomato juice replenishes fluid and sodium.

GAZPACHO

6 ripe tomatoes, chopped
½ onion, finely chopped
½ cucumber, peeled and diced
1 green bell pepper, seeded and diced
juice of 1 lemon
3 garlic cloves, chopped
3 tbsp. parsley leaves, chopped
2 tsp. vegetable bouillon powder

Place all the ingredients in a blender and whiz until smooth. Divide into four bowls. Chill 30 minutes, then serve with an ice cube floating in each bowl, if desired.

SUN-DRIED TOMATO PESTO

24 sun-dried tomatoes in oil
½ cup macadamia nuts, chopped
5 cups basil leaves
3 garlic cloves, crushed
1½ tsp. tomato paste
1 tbsp. balsamic vinegar
1 tbsp. lemon juice
1 cup tomato juice
4 tbsp. olive oil
salt and ground black pepper

Blend all the ingredients together in a food processor until smooth. Transfer to a bowl and season to taste. Store up to 5 days in a covered container in the refrigerator.

SPICY GARDEN COCKTAIL

8 celery ribs, with leaves
4 tomatoes, cut into chunks
4 small cucumbers, cut into strips
celery salt, optional
hot chili sauce, to taste
ice cubes

Remove the celery tops from the ribs, reserving 4 to garnish. Feed the tomatoes, cucumbers, and celery ribs through a juicer. Coat the rims of 4 tall glasses with celery salt, if using, and pour the juice into the glasses. Add the chili sauce to taste and several ice cubes. Stir well. Garnish with the celery tops and serve immediately.

CHILLED TOMATO SOUP

8 tomatoes, peeled, seeded, and chopped
2 cucumbers, diced
4 cups tomato juice
2 red bell peppers, seeded
    and diced
2 garlic cloves, crushed
1 tbsp. red wine vinegar
1 tbsp. olive oil

Blend half the tomatoes, half the cucumber, the juice, bell peppers, garlic, and vinegar in a blender. Stir in the oil and remaining tomatoes and cucumber. Chill at least 30 minutes before serving.

TOMATO RAITA

30 cherry tomatoes
1¾ cups plain yogurt
1 scallion, trimmed and finely chopped
1 tbsp. finely chopped cilantro leaves
1 tbsp. finely chopped mint leaves
½ tsp. roasted ground cumin
salt, to taste

Cut the tomatoes into quarters, place them in a flameproof dish and broil until slightly soft. Leave to cool, then transfer to a bowl. Add the yogurt, scallion, cilantro, mint, cumin, and salt. Mix well and serve as a dip.

Olive and olive oil

VITAMINS E, K, BETA-CAROTENE; CALCIUM, COPPER, IODINE, IRON, MAGNESIUM, MANGANESE, PHOSPHORUS, POTASSIUM, SELENIUM, ZINC; POLYPHENOLS; OMEGA-9 FATTY ACIDS; FIBER

The regular consumption of olives and olive oil in Mediterranean countries might explain the robust health enjoyed by many people who live there.

There are hundreds of olive varieties. In general, black varieties are moist and full flavored, while green have a milder taste. One recent scientific study suggests that eating olives on a regular basis can play an important role in protecting bones against osteoporosis and is associated with a lower risk of colon cancer, which becomes more common in later age.

Olives also contain a substance called squalene, which has heart-protecting properties, and the phytochemicals oleoeuropein, which lowers high blood pressure, and oleocanthal, which relieves inflammation.

Olive oil is a monounsaturated fat that is believed to have anti-carcinogenic properties, and help to lower high blood pressure and prevent diabetes. It lowers levels of harmful LDL cholesterol while leaving the beneficial HDL cholesterol alone. Research into the effectiveness of olive oil against clogging of the arteries reveals that the olives' monounsaturated fats prevent the oxidation of cholesterol, and, therefore, stop it from sticking to artery walls and causing heart attacks.

Other studies suggest olive oil also contains hefty concentrations of antioxidants, including chlorophyll, carotenoids, and polyphenolic compounds—all of which not only fight age-accelerating free radicals, but also protect the olives' important vitamin E content. Their rich supply of polyphenols, known to have anti-inflammatory and anticoagulant actions, are also thought to help stave off conditions such as osteoporosis and arthritis.

Olive oil is high in oleic acid, an omega-9 fatty acid, which demonstrates anti-inflammatory properties to calm and soothe the skin. In addition, the essential fatty acids in olives have been shown to boost the body's ability to remove unwanted stored fat in the cells. Rich in vitamin E, which helps to keep skin wrinkle-free and hair glossy, it also stimulates the secretion of bile, helping to soften and expel gallstones. The vitamin E content can also reduce the severity of hot flashes.

Used topically, olive oil makes an excellent skin moisturizer and hair conditioner, and can also soften wax inside the ears.

TAPENADE

1 ¼ cups olives, pitted and chopped
4 tbsp. capers, drained and chopped
4 tbsp. anchovies, chopped (optional)
juice of 1 lemon
1 tsp. ground black pepper
2 tsp. olive oil

Place all the ingredients in a bowl. Mix well, or briefly blend in a blender for a smooth texture. Serve on fresh bread or as a dip with crudités.

✦OLIVE OIL AND LEMON DRINK
to soothe inflammation

2 tbsp. extra virgin olive oil
juice of ½ lemon

In a cup, combine the olive oil and the lemon juice and stir. Drink on an empty stomach every morning and wait at least 30 minutes before having breakfast. Repeat for at least 3 weeks to notice an improvement.

*HOT OIL TREATMENT
to treat a dry scalp and hair

½ cup olive oil

½ cup boiling water

Pour the olive oil and boiling water into a large, heatproof glass bottle or a jar with a lid. Shake well until the oil emulsifies. When the mixture cools slightly, massage it into your hair, taking care not to burn your scalp. Put a shower cap or plastic bag over your hair and wrap it in a hot towel that has been soaked in hot water and then wrung out. Leave about 30 minutes, then shampoo your hair as usual.

GREEK PASTA SALAD

3⅓ cups wholewheat pasta
3 tomatoes, chopped
½ cucumber, peeled and chopped
1 scallion, trimmed and chopped
½ cup pitted black olives
⅓ cup cubed feta cheese
5 tbsp. chopped parsley leaves
3 tbsp. olive oil
salt and ground black pepper

Cook the pasta in boiling salted water until *al dente*, then drain. Transfer to a large bowl and add all the other ingredients, mix well and serve.

OLIVE AND NUT DIP

2 cups pitted green olives
1 cup shelled walnuts
⅓ cup pine nuts
2 tbsp. grated Romano cheese
1 tbsp. olive oil
breadsticks, to serve

Whiz the olives, walnuts, and pine nuts in a blender until smooth. Mix in the grated cheese and olive oil. Serve with breadsticks.

MINI KEBABS *makes 24*

24 black olives, pitted and halved
24 cherry tomatoes, halved
48 basil leaves
24 cubes feta cheese
ground black pepper

Spear 2 olive halves, 2 tomato halves, 2 basil leaves, and a cube of feta onto each of 24 cocktail sticks, alternating ingredients. Season, arrange on a serving dish, and serve.

NATURE PAINTED
VEGETABLES IN A
RAINBOW OF COLORS,
RICH IN A SPECTRUM OF
VITAMINS AND MINERALS
TO BOOST YOUR HEALTH

02 | wonder
VEGETABLES

Asparagus

VITAMINS A, B1, B3, B5, C, E, K, BETA-CAROTENE, BIOTIN, FOLIC ACID; CALCIUM, COPPER, IRON, MAGNESIUM, MANGANESE, PHOSPHORUS, POTASSIUM, SELENIUM, ZINC; ASPARAGIN; GLUTATHIONE; FLAVONOIDS; FIBER; PROTEIN

In mythology, asparagus has been renowned since ancient times both as an aphrodisiac and medicinally, for its healing properties. High in nutrients, low in calories, and rich in flavor, asparagus has a wealth of health-enhancing benefits to offer.

Asparagus is a natural diuretic, encouraging the body to flush out toxins. With its active compound asparagin stimulating the kidneys, bladder, and liver, asparagus is a powerful detoxifier. Its cleansing, anti-inflammatory properties make it useful for easing indigestion, irritable bowel syndrome, and rheumatoid arthritis. It is also rich in the flavonoid rutin, which we need to maintain a healthy circulation.

According to folklore, asparagus is considered to be a tonic for the reproductive system. It is a fantastic source of folic acid, which is believed to prevent damage to the arteries that supply blood to the heart and the brain. Folic acid has also demonstrated powerful anti-carcinogenic properties and is said to prevent birth defects. A one-cup portion of asparagus provides more than two-thirds of the daily amount of folic acid recommended for most adults.

Asparagus is a rich source of beta-carotene, vitamin C, and the anti-oxidant glutathione, which all lower the risk of heart disease and cancer. The vegetable is also high in antioxidant vitamin E, which fights wrinkles and premature aging, protects the heart, and keeps the brain young.

Eating asparagus is said to give a natural high. The spears not only taste delicious, but also supply numerous minerals and vitamins, including many of the B-vitamins, which play a central role in supporting brain function and the nervous system. If any of these are in short supply, you can be tired, depressed, anxious, or constantly on edge. This can happen quite easily if you're not eating a wide range of healthy foods. B-vitamins work best together, rather than individually, keeping energy levels high and supporting mental and emotional health.

ASPARAGUS WITH HONEY AND GARLIC

1 lb. asparagus spears, trimmed
1 tsp. mustard
2 tbsp. honey
2 garlic cloves, crushed
½ tsp. chopped thyme

Steam the asparagus 5 minutes until just tender. Drain well, then arrange on a plate. Mix together the mustard, honey, garlic, and thyme, and pour the dressing over the asparagus. Serve immediately.

BALSAMIC-ROASTED ASPARAGUS

1 lb. 2 oz. large asparagus spears, trimmed
2 tbsp. extra virgin olive oil
salt and freshly ground pepper
2 tbsp. balsamic vinegar
grated lemon zest, to garnish

Preheat the oven to 200°C. Coat the asparagus spears in the olive oil and season with salt and pepper. Roast on foil on a baking sheet 20 to 25 minutes, turning them 2 or 3 times. Drizzle with balsamic vinegar. Garnish with lemon zest.

✦ ASPARAGUS TINCTURE
for inflammatory conditions

10 young asparagus spears, trimmed
2 cups vodka

Chop the asparagus and place in a glass jar. Cover in vodka and seal the jar tightly. Stand in a dark, cool place 10 days, then discard the asparagus. Take 8 to 10 drops with 1 tablespoon water 3 times a day, as needed.

Globe artichoke

VITAMINS B1, B2, B3, B5, B6, C, E, K, BETA-CAROTENE, BIOTIN, FOLIC ACID; CALCIUM, COPPER, IRON, MAGNESIUM, MANGANESE, PHOSPHORUS, POTASSIUM, SELENIUM, ZINC; CYNARIN; FLAVONOIDS; FIBER

This attractive and sophisticated vegetable is a form of thistle and a member of the daisy family. Recognized mostly for its detoxifying effects, globe artichoke protects the liver and supports the gallbladder, making it a useful vegetable for many traditional remedies.

Originating in the Mediterranean, artichokes are the unopened flower buds of a perennial plant. Each bud consists of several parts: outer leaves that are tough and inedible at the tip but fleshy and tender at the base; an inedible choke, or thistle, which is enclosed within a light-colored cone of immature leaves; and a round, firm-fleshed base, known as the heart. Both the leaves and heart have a long history of therapeutic use.

Globe artichokes have traditionally been used as a hangover remedy and have detoxifying qualities. They are also valuable as a diuretic, helping to relieve water retention and high blood pressure. This makes them a useful addition to the diet of people suffering from conditions such as gout, arthritis, and rheumatism. They have been used to lower blood sugar and to help to lower high cholesterol levels by inhibiting the production of more cholesterol. The antioxidant flavonoids they contain also help to keep the arteries healthy.

The ancient Greeks and Romans saw globe artichokes as a valuable digestive aid, and modern research has shown that their compound cynarin encourages the breakdown of fat, as well as increasing the flow of bile and improving liver function. The hearts are particularly good for combating indigestion if eaten at the beginning of a meal. Cynarin also reduces the risk of gallstones and eases irritable bowel syndrome.

The high levels of B-vitamins in artichokes are beneficial for boosting energy and mental alertness, and together with their vitamin C, play an important role in strengthening the immune system.

ARTICHOKE SALAD

8 artichokes

4 large tomatoes, cut into wedges

1 red onion, finely sliced

½ green bell pepper, seeded and chopped

½ cup green olives

1 garlic clove, crushed

6 tbsp. olive oil

4 tbsp. lemon juice

1 tsp. Dijon mustard

salt and ground black pepper

If using fresh artichokes, break off the outer leaves and cut away the inner leaves. Scrape out the chokes and boil the hearts about 20 minutes until tender. Rinse and combine in a large bowl with the tomatoes, onion, bell pepper, and olives. Beat the remaining ingredients together to make the dressing, then drizzle it over the vegetables, and serve.

HOT ARTICHOKE DIP WITH PITA BREAD

8 pita breads

1 cup cream cheese

12 oz. mozzarella cheese

scant 1 cup mayonnaise

1 cup grated Parmesan cheese

1 onion, finely chopped

2 garlic cloves, crushed

2½ cups marinated artichoke hearts,
   drained

Preheat the oven to 350°F. Cut the pita breads into small triangles, and bake on a tray about 10 minutes. Combine the other ingredients in a food processor and whiz. Put the mixture in a baking dish and bake 30 minutes. Serve hot with the pita dippers.

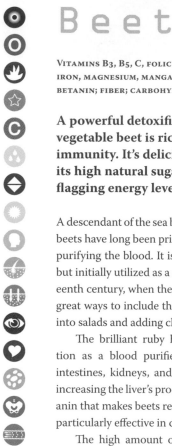

Beet

VITAMINS B3, B5, C, FOLIC ACID, BETA-CAROTENE; CALCIUM, COPPER, IODINE, IRON, MAGNESIUM, MANGANESE, PHOSPHORUS, POTASSIUM, SILICA, ZINC; BETANIN; FIBER; CARBOHYDRATE

A powerful detoxifier and blood purifier, the root vegetable beet is rich in many nutrients crucial for immunity. It's deliciously sweet yet low in calories, and its high natural sugar content is excellent for reviving flagging energy levels.

A descendant of the sea beet that grows around the Mediterranean coast, beets have long been prized for their medicinal qualities, particularly for purifying the blood. It is thought beets were first used in Roman times but initially utilized as a cooking ingredient by French chefs in the eighteenth century, when they introduced it in dishes. Today, there are many great ways to include this vegetable in the diet, including grating it raw into salads and adding chunks to slow-cooking soups and stews.

The brilliant ruby hue of beets gives them a traditional reputation as a blood purifier and great cleanser, especially of the liver, intestines, kidneys, and gallbladder. It certainly aids cell cleansing by increasing the liver's production of detoxifying enzymes, and the betacyanin that makes beets red has antiviral and antioxidant properties and is particularly effective in combating cancerous changes, too.

The high amount of fiber contained in beets improves digestive health, aiding the absorption of food and helping to regulate bodily processes—two key factors in successful weight loss. It also stimulates the circulatory system, speeding up metabolism.

A rich source of natural sugars, beets provides easily digestible carbohydrates. Its dietary fiber slows down the absorption of these carbohydrates into the blood, which means the body is supplied with a steady stream of energy. Betacyanin also boosts the activity of natural antioxidant enzymes in the body, which protect cells against the dangers of free radical damage.

Beets are naturally high in assimilable iron, and can help conditions such as anemia, heart problems, constipation, and liver toxicity, as well as restlessness and anxiety. The iron in beets enhances the production of disease-fighting antibodies, white blood cells (including phagocytes). It also stimulates red blood cells and improves the supply of oxygen to cells. Beets also contains manganese, which is needed for the formation of interferon, a powerful anticancer substance. In addition, it contains silica, which is vital for healthy skin, hair, fingernails, ligaments, tendons, and bones.

As effective cooked as it is raw, fresh beets can be juiced, used in salads, or made into soups. Beets are a popular component of juice fasts, when mixed with a sweeter juice, such as apple, to dilute the taste. Scientists have found that the juice combats the effects of nitrates—chemical preservatives in processed meats that can cause colon cancer. This nutrient-rich vegetable also makes an excellent detox juice, especially when mixed with carrot, spinach, and cabbage.

GINGERED BEETS

4 raw beets (with tops), scrubbed
  and chopped
2 tsp. sesame seeds
1 tbsp. light soy sauce
1 tbsp. extra virgin olive oil
1 tbsp. finely chopped gingerroot
¾ cup grated carrots

Steam the beets over high heat 30 to 40 minutes until tender. Steam the tops 3 to 4 minutes until they wilt. Toast the sesame seeds in a dry pan until brown. Then, in a bowl, whisk together the soy sauce, olive oil, and ginger, add all the other ingredients, and toss well. Serve warm, or as a salad dish.

RAINBOW ROOT SALAD

2 large cooked beets, peeled and grated

3 carrots, peeled and grated

1 parsnip, peeled and grated

1 red onion, grated

juice of 1 lemon

1 tbsp. olive oil

Mix the grated vegetables together in a large bowl. Drizzle the lemon juice and oil over, then serve.

ROASTED BEETS

4 beets, washed (unpeeled)
1 tbsp. olive oil
1 tsp. salt

Preheat the oven to 350°F. Brush the beets with a little olive oil, sprinkle with salt, and roast about 1 hour (depending on size): when cooked, a skewer or knife tip will easily slice into the flesh. The roasted beets will serve 4 as an accompaniment or 2 when sliced over a green salad.

BEET SOUP

2 tbsp. olive oil
1 onion, chopped
2 garlic cloves, crushed
4 large beets, peeled and chopped
2 carrots, peeled and chopped
4 cups vegetable or chicken stock
4 tbsp. plain yogurt

Heat the oil in a large pan and fry the onion 2 to 3 minutes, then add the garlic and cook another minute. Add the beets, carrots, and stock and bring to a boil. Cover and simmer 45 minutes, or until cooked. Purée, then divide into bowls and top with the yogurt.

RAW BEET SALAD

2 beets
½ celery root
1 carrot
2 tbsp. sunflower seeds
1 tbsp. chopped parsley leaves
2 tbsp. chopped chives
4 tbsp. plain yogurt
1 tbsp. olive oil
1 tbsp. lemon juice
salt and ground black pepper

Peel and grate the beets, celery root, and carrot. Put them in a large bowl with the sunflower seeds and herbs. Mix together, using your hands, then add the remaining ingredients and mix well.

Carrot

VITAMINS: B1, B3, B5, B6, C, E, K, ALPHA-CAROTENE, BETA-CAROTENE, BIOTIN, FOLIC ACID, LYCOPENE; CALCIUM, CHROMIUM, IODINE, IRON, MAGNESIUM, MANGANESE, PHOSPHORUS, POTASSIUM, SELENIUM, SILICA, ZINC; BIOFLAVONOIDS; LIMONIN; FIBER

Carrots are packed with nutrients, which are particularly beneficial for eye health and vision. Known for their ability to aid night vision, these versatile root vegetables can be used in both sweet and savory dishes or pressed into a delicious, sweet juice.

Carrots were planted by the early English settlers in Jamestown. The bright orange vegetables have become well known for their cleansing effect on the blood and liver, and for their ability to boost eyesight.

Carrots are among the richest sources of beta-carotene, which is converted by the body into the antioxidant vitamin A to help to prevent heart disease and speed up postexercise recovery time. Besides giving carrots their reputation for aiding vision, beta-carotene promotes healthy digestion and protects against cancer. It's also of great benefit to the skin, and helps to strengthen cells against viruses and infections such as colds and bronchitis. Carrots are also full of the antioxidant vitamins C and E, which are crucial for supporting immunity and fighting the damaging and aging effects of free radicals.

Carrots contain vitamin K, which we use for bloodclotting and the healing of wounds, while their fiber content aids digestion and keeps the heart healthy. The chromium found in carrots helps to stabilize blood sugar levels, making them useful for controlling diabetes and sugar cravings, and the highly concentrated sugars in carrots are easily absorbed for on-the-spot energy. The silica content of carrots is valuable for keeping the skin youthful. The vegetables are also loaded with fiber and water, which cleanse the liver, boost detoxification, and plump out the skin to stave off wrinkles. They are also recommended for increasing red blood cells and are said to be useful in treating jaundice and eczema.

Carrots are fibrous root vegetables, which have tough cell walls that do not give up their nutrients easily, so to get the full nutritional value from them, carrots should be juiced or cooked rather than eaten raw. Try grating them into cakes, chopping them into stews, soups, and stir-fries—cooking them in oil allows the body to use more beta-carotene. Nibbling on raw carrot sticks and drinking the juice, however, also have benefits, as eating just two raw carrots a day appears to reduce high cholesterol levels. This is likely to be due to calcium pectate, a type of soluble fiber that provides them with their characteristic crunchiness.

CARROT CAKE

½ cup butter, plus extra for greasing
⅓ cup honey
½ cup brown sugar
1⅔ cups wholewheat flour
1 tsp. baking powder
1⅓ cups peeled and grated carrots
1 tsp. cinnamon

Grease an 8-inch cake pan. Beat the butter, honey, and sugar together in a bowl. Fold in the remaining ingredients, then spoon into the pan. Bake in a preheated oven at 350°F 1 hour until firm. Remove from the oven and leave to cool, then turn out onto a wire rack to finish cooling.

CARROTS IN ORANGE

3 cups carrots cut into batons
1 tbsp. olive oil
1½ cups chopped onions
1 tsp. caraway seeds
4 tbsp. orange juice

Parboil the carrots 5 minutes, then drain. Heat the oil in a pan and fry the onion 3 minutes, then add the caraway seeds and fry 2 minutes. Add the carrots and orange juice and turn up the heat until the juice boils. Reduce the heat and simmer 5 minutes, or until most of the fluid evaporates. Serve immediately.

Potato

VITAMINS B1, B3, B5, B6, C, K, BIOTIN, FOLIC ACID; CALCIUM, COPPER, IODINE, IRON, MAGNESIUM, MANGANESE, PHOSPHORUS, POTASSIUM, SELENIUM, ZINC; CHLOROGENIC ACID; FIBER; PROTEIN, CARBOHYDRATE

Simple yet immensely versatile, the potato is the world's number one vegetable crop and has long been used as a folk remedy. This staple food is packed with vitamins and many other health-giving nutrients.

Potatoes are one of the cheapest and most readily available sources of vitamin C—a nutrient that is vital for keeping the immune system healthy by fighting off damaging free radicals. It also fends off viruses that cause common ailments, such as colds, coughs, and flu. New potatoes are richer in this important antioxidant than old ones. Most of the fiber, which aids digestion and lowers cholesterol, is found in the skin. Their potassium content means they can help to control high blood pressure.

Don't overlook the value of potatoes if you're aiming to get fit. They're rich in vitamin B6, which—among many other essential services —is needed to mobilize the body's glycogen stores. Vitamin B6 is also needed by phagocytes to mop up waste matter from cells and to make the immunity-boosting amino acids crucial for good health.

Potatoes are packed with complex carbohydrates, the best form of energy food. Complex carbs play two roles, both essential to fitness. By providing slow-burning fuel, they give you enough energy to complete your workout or game without flagging halfway through. And they help the body to maintain the muscle it has built.

Potato peel also contains a substance called chlorogenic acid, which is an anti-carcinogenic compound. In fact, peeling removes many nutrients, so try to eat potatoes in their skins.

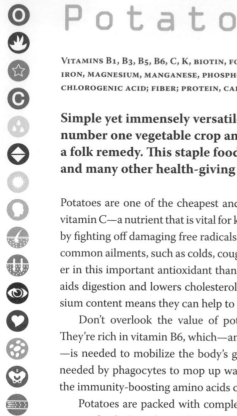

GARLIC MASHED POTATOES

6 potatoes, peeled and diced
5 garlic cloves
1¼ cups milk or soy milk
4 tbsp. olive oil
1 tsp. salt
a pinch of ground black pepper
1 tsp. ground nutmeg

In a heavy-based saucepan, boil the potatoes and garlic in the milk until tender, topping up with enough water to cover them. Drain well. Add the olive oil, salt, pepper and nutmeg, then mash until smooth. Serve as a side dish.

✦ POTATO JUICE *for healthy digestion*

9 oz. potatoes
lemon juice, to taste

Scrub and peel the potatoes, then chop into bite-size pieces before blending in a blender to a fine purée. Add lemon juice to taste. Drink 2 tablespoons before each meal. Do not take for longer than 24 hours.

TUNISIAN POTATOES WITH EGGS

4 eggs
3 cups diced potatoes
juice of 1 lemon
2 tbsp. ground cumin
2 tbsp. olive oil
½ tsp. harissa

Boil the eggs 10 minutes. Set aside to cool, then peel and chop. Boil the potatoes 5 to 10 minutes until tender, and drain. Mix together the remaining ingredients and pour over the potatoes. Place on top of the eggs and serve.

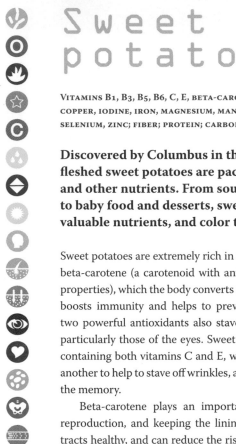

Sweet potato

VITAMINS B1, B3, B5, B6, C, E, BETA-CAROTENE, BIOTIN, FOLIC ACID; CALCIUM, COPPER, IODINE, IRON, MAGNESIUM, MANGANESE, PHOSPHORUS, POTASSIUM, SELENIUM, ZINC; FIBER; PROTEIN; CARBOHYDRATE

Discovered by Columbus in the West Indies, orange-fleshed sweet potatoes are packed full of beta-carotene and other nutrients. From soups, casseroles, and salads to baby food and desserts, sweet potatoes add taste, valuable nutrients, and color to any meal.

Sweet potatoes are extremely rich in antioxidants. They are rich in both beta-carotene (a carotenoid with antiviral, anticancer, and antioxidant properties), which the body converts to vitamin A, and vitamin C, which boosts immunity and helps to prevent cardiovascular disease. These two powerful antioxidants also stave off some age-related conditions, particularly those of the eyes. Sweet potatoes are one of the few foods containing both vitamins C and E, which work synergistically with one another to help to stave off wrinkles, and to protect the eyes and preserve the memory.

Beta-carotene plays an important role in vision, bone growth, reproduction, and keeping the lining of the digestive and respiratory tracts healthy, and can reduce the risk of cancer, especially endometrial cancer. For those with respiratory problems, antioxidant vitamin C acts on the lining of the lungs and makes breathing easier. Vitamin E is vital for healthy skin.

Full of fiber, especially the skin, this vegetable can help to lower cholesterol and enhance digestive function. Sweet potatoes are a complex carbohydrate and despite the name "sweet," they contain blood-sugar-regulating properties, which makes them a useful food for diabetics.

So, how can something that provides all the comfort of sweetness and carbohydrates be good for you? This cheery tuber is packed with folic acid, which helps to raise your spirits. It is rich in iron and vitamin B6, so can offset any deficiency, especially for women during their

periods. This vital vitamin alleviates premenstrual syndrome and food cravings, as well as helping to relieve depression. It also helps to prevent mood swings, boost the memory, and protect the heart.

Sweet potatoes are low in fat and loaded with potassium, which helps to maintain fluid balance in cells, making them a useful food for dieters. An oven-baked sweet potato is the perfect light meal for anyone heading off to the gym for a workout. Always buy orange sweet potatoes—the ones with red skins—as the white variety contain far less beta-carotene.

MASHED SWEET POTATOES

4 sweet potatoes, peeled and chopped

3 carrots, peeled and chopped

1 cup frozen peas

2 tbsp. butter

salt and ground black pepper

Steam the sweet potatoes, carrots, and peas 20 to 25 minutes until soft. Transfer to a bowl, add the butter and salt and pepper, and mash until creamy. Serve instead of mashed white potatoes.

SWEET POTATO SUMMER SALAD

3 sweet potatoes, baked in their skins, then peeled and diced

4 scallions, trimmed and sliced

2 celery ribs, trimmed and sliced

½ cup walnut halves, chopped

1 green bell pepper, seeded and sliced

scant 1 cup crème fraiche or sour cream

2 tbsp. white wine vinegar

Place all the ingredients in a large salad bowl and mix together thoroughly. Serve as a side dish.

Yam

VITAMINS B1, B3, B5, B6, C, E, BETA-CAROTENE, BIOTIN, FOLIC ACID; CALCIUM, IODINE, IRON, MAGNESIUM, MANGANESE, PHOSPHORUS, POTASSIUM, SELENIUM, ZINC; FIBER; CARBOHYDRATE

This starchy root vegetable has been a staple food in many parts of the world for centuries. Packed with fiber to aid digestion, it is an excellent power food and a delicious and sustaining form of slow-releasing carbohydrate.

Yams come in yellow, white, and purple varieties, with the yellow one being very rich in beta-carotene. This is needed by the body to produce vitamin A, which, in turn, is vital for strengthening cell membranes, keeping out viruses, preventing cancer, and assisting the body in dealing with stress and pollution. Its vitamin B1 is useful for boosting energy levels, and for easing depression and stress, both of which can suppress the immune system. It is also a good source of manganese, a trace mineral that helps the body with the metabolism of carbohydrates.

Full of fiber and used in a similar way to potatoes, yams have a lower glycemic index, so they provide a more sustained form of energy. This makes them a good source of carbohydrate for diabetics and weight-watchers. They also contain vitamin C, a powerful antioxidant that fights harmful free radicals and boosts immunity, and vitamin B6, which relieves prementrual symptoms.

High in potassium and low in sodium, yams help to regulate the fluid balance exercise so easily depletes through perspiration. Discoretine, a chemical in yams, is useful for athletes, as it reduces blood sugar and increases blood flow through the kidneys. This helps the excretion of excess salt, which, in turn, reduces high blood pressure.

MASHED YAM AND SPINACH

3 cups peeled and diced yams
10 oz. spinach
3 tbsp. olive oil
1 onion, sliced
salt and ground black pepper

In a pan, boil the yams 20 minutes until tender, then mash and set aside. In another pan, place the spinach in hot water and leave to wilt. Heat the oil in a skillet and fry the onion until soft. Add the yam and spinach, combining them well. Season and serve as a side dish.

CITRUS YAMS

2 yams, peeled and chopped into
    1-inch chunks
4 tbsp. olive oil
1 tbsp. chopped parsley leaves
1 tbsp. chopped cilantro
juice and grated zest of 1 orange
juice and grated zest of 1 lime

In a steamer or a saucepan, steam the yam 20 minutes until tender. In a bowl, whisk together the oil, parsley, and cilantro, then add the juice and zest of the orange and lime. Add the cooked yam into the dressing. Serve as a first course, side-dish or a snack.

YAM DUMPLINGS ROLLED IN POPPY SEEDS

1 yam, peeled and chopped into 1-inch
    chunks
3 egg yolks
½ tsp. cayenne pepper
1 tsp. cornstarch
3 tbsp. self-rising flour
4 tbsp. poppy seeds

In a pan, boil the yam 20 minutes until tender. Drain and leave to cool, then purée in a blender or food processor. Put in a bowl and mix in the egg yolks, cayenne, cornstarch, and flour. Form into balls and roll in the poppy seeds. Line a steamer with foil and place over simmering water. Add the dumplings and steam 10 minutes, then serve.

Broccoli

VITAMINS A, B1, B3, B5, B6, C, E, K, FOLIC ACID, BETA-CAROTENE, BIOTIN; CALCIUM, IODINE, IRON, MAGNESIUM, MANGANESE, PHOSPHORUS, POTASSIUM, ZINC; LUTEIN, ZEAXANTHIN; SULFORAPHANE; INDOLES; FIBER

A member of the cabbage family (Cruciferae), broccoli has ancient beginnings, dating back to Roman times. It has been shown to aid many conditions, packing a more powerful nutrient punch than any other vegetable.

Broccoli is a powerhouse of antioxidant vitamin C, which is crucial for immune response. It's also full of fiber, vital for a healthy digestive system, and has detoxifying properties to help to cleanse the liver. It is rich in iron and, therefore, helps to treat anemia. Broccoli contains calcium and magnesium, which stave off osteoporosis and are vital for bone health, and lutein and zeaxanthin, which reduce the risk of eye disease.

Broccoli contains a number of chemical compounds, including indoles, carotenoids, and the vitamin A precursor, beta-carotene, known to inhibit the activation of cancer cells, and which has been associated with lower rates of both heart and eye disease. As broccoli can increase vitamin A in the body, it also helps to improve various skin conditions. It is also a rich source of carotenoids, which are important for the thymus gland, which regulates the immune system, and is packed with B-vitamins, needed for good immune and nervous system health.

As well as aiding the body's detoxification processes, broccoli is rich in sulforaphane, which strengthens cells to resist damage and fights the development of tumors. Sulforaphane works with another compound, diindolylmethane, to inhibit cancer growth and promote antiviral and antibacterial activity. It has been found to improve digestion by fighting the tough bacterium *Helicobacter pylori*, which eats away at the stomach lining and can create ulcers. Broccoli counteracts these painful effects, and might even reduce the amount of harmful bacteria in the stomach.

Packed with nutrients, broccoli is also a brilliant energy-reviver. Its zinc enhances mental alertness, vitamin B5 helps the body to metabolize fats into energy, and the folic acid encourages the production of serotonin, a mood-lifting chemical in the brain.

BROCCOLI STIR-FRY *serves 2*

2 tbsp. sesame oil

2-inch piece gingerroot, peeled and grated

1 broccoli head, chopped

1 garlic clove, crushed

Heat the oil in a skillet or wok, then add the ginger and broccoli. Stir-fry 3 minutes, before adding the garlic. Contine stir-frying another 2 minutes. Serve immediately, as a side dish.

WARM BROCCOLI AND SESAME SALAD

1 broccoli head, separated into florets

2 tbsp. olive oil

4 tbsp. soy sauce

4 tbsp. rice wine vinegar

2 tbsp. sesame oil

4 tbsp. toasted sesame seeds

Preheat the oven to 375°F. Blanch the broccoli 1 minute. Drain, spread on a baking sheet, coat with olive oil, and roast 10 minutes. Transfer to a bowl. Whisk the soy sauce, vinegar, and sesame oil. Stir in 3 tablespoons sesame seeds. Pour over the broccoli, then sprinkle with the remaining seeds.

CHINESE-STYLE BROCCOLI

1 lb. 5 oz. broccoli

½ cup sliced canned and drained water chestnuts

2 tbsp. sunflower oil

a small piece gingerroot, peeled and grated

a pinch of grated lemon zest

1 tsp. soy sauce

½ cup water

1 chicken bouillion cube

Cut the broccoli into florets. Put the water chestnuts, oil, ginger, and lemon zest in a saucepan. Heat, add the broccoli, and toss 1 minute. Add the rest of the ingredients. Bring to a boil, then cover and simmer 5 minutes. Serve immediately.

BROCCOLI WITH ALMONDS

1 lb. broccoli florets
1 tsp. olive oil
⅔ cup slivered almonds
juice of 1 lemon
2 tbsp. broccoli sprouts (optional)

Put the broccoli florets in a steamer and steam 5 to 10 minutes until they are just tender. Meanwhile, heat the olive oil in a pan over low heat and fry the slivered almonds until golden brown. Mix together the broccoli and almonds in a serving dish and sprinkle with lemon juice. Top the dish with broccoli sprouts, if using.

THICK BROCCOLI SOUP

1 tbsp. olive oil
2 shallots, finely chopped
1 garlic clove, crushed
1 sweet potato, peeled and diced
1 tomato, chopped
3 cups vegetable stock
heaping 1 cup chopped broccoli
croutons, to serve

Heat the oil in a saucepan and slowly fry the shallots, garlic, sweet potato, and tomato 2 to 3 minutes until brown. Add the stock and broccoli and bring to a boil, then reduce the heat to low and simmer, covered, 20 minutes. Pour the mixture into a blender and whiz until smooth. Return to the pan and heat through. Ladle into bowls and serve with croutons sprinkled over the top.

SPICY BROCCOLI

2 broccoli heads, broken into florets
1 onion, finely chopped
2 tbsp. sunflower oil
1 tbsp. curry powder
½ tsp. cayenne pepper
1 cup light cream
⅔ cup slivered almonds

Steam the broccoli 6 to 8 minutes until tender. In another pan, fry the *no.* onion in the oil until soft. Add the broccoli, spices, and cream, and simmer 5 minutes. Sprinkle with the almonds. Serve as a side dish.

Kale

VITAMINS B2, B3, B6, B12, C, E, K, BETA-CAROTENE, FOLIC ACID, LUTEIN;
CALCIUM, COPPER, IRON, MAGNESIUM, MANGANESE, POTASSIUM, SILICA, ZINC;
FLAVONOIDS, GLUCOSINOLATES, FIBER;

This leafy winter superfood will help to keep you healthy through the coldest time of the year. Bursting with vitamins and phytochemicals, kale is one of the top vegetable immunity-boosters.

Curly kale is thought to have originated in the Mediterranean region. Like cabbage and Brussels sprouts, it is a member of the Cruciferous family, sharing with these vegetables the ability to retain high levels of water and nutrients in its leaves, which makes it a very beneficial food. Curly kale can be eaten raw, steamed and served as a side dish, or lightly stir-fried. As it is in season in winter, it makes a nutritious addition to the diet during the colder months.

Kale is rich in everything from carotenoids and B-vitamins to a host of antiaging and beautifying trace minerals. It is exceptionally high in beta-carotene, which the body turns into vitamin A. If you're a smoker, or a passive smoker, kale can help to protect your lungs from damage. A compound in cigarette smoke has been found to cause vitamin A deficiency, which can lead to lung diseases, including emphysema and cancer. But foods rich in beta-carotene can counteract these effects. Kale is also one of the best sources of lutein and zeaxanthin, carotenoids that help prevent eye disease. And the vitamins B6 and B12 in kale help boost brain power and prevent memory loss, improve energy, and bolster the immune system's ability to mop up invader cells.

A valuable source of calcium for the bones, kale also contains silica for the skin, hair, teeth, and nails. Kale has high levels of glucosinolates— natural plant chemicals that block cancer-causing substances, stimulate detoxifying, and repair enzymes in

the body and suppress cancer cell division. It also contains flavonoids, needed for healthy circulation and to stimulate immune response, and plant sterols, important for keeping cholesterol levels low. It has high levels of antioxidant vitamin C, making it a potent defender against colds and viruses. Its anti-inflammatory effects also reduce the risk of asthma attacks and joint pains. It contains vitamin K, which promotes blood clotting and healing, and good amounts of immunity-boosting minerals, including iron and zinc.

Kale is a good source of fiber, which aids digestion and keeps blood sugar levels steady. And all this comes for less than 40 calories a portion. Meanwhile, its long-term benefits as an antioxidant, cleansing free radicals and reducing the risk of cancer, are stacked up in your favor, too.

SESAME KALE

1 tbsp. sesame oil

2 garlic cloves, crushed

scant 6½ cups roughly chopped kale

1 tsp. soy sauce

1 tbsp. toasted sesame seeds

Heat the oil in a saucepan and sauté the garlic 30 seconds over medium heat. Add the kale leaves and 2 tablespoons water and increase the heat, stirring frequently until the water evaporates. Stir in the soy sauce and the sesame seeds just before serving.

KALE WITH GARLIC AND RED PEPPERCORNS

2 cups water

scant 6½ cups roughly chopped kale

2 tbsp. extra virgin olive oil

½ small onion, finely chopped

2 garlic cloves, crushed

½ tsp. salt

½ tsp. ground black pepper

¼ tsp. crushed red peppercorns

Put the water in a saucepan and bring to a boil. Add the kale and cook 2 minutes, then drain and press until barely moist. Put the oil in a large pan and sauté the onion and garlic over low heat 4 to 5 minutes. Stir in the kale, salt, pepper, and peppercorns and cook over medium heat 3 to 4 minutes. Serve immediately.

Spinach

VITAMINS B2, B3, B5, B6, C, E, K, BETA-CAROTENE, BIOTIN, FOLIC ACID; CALCIUM, CHROMIUM, COPPER, IODINE, IRON, MAGNESIUM, MANGANESE, PHOSPHORUS, POTASSIUM, SELENIUM, SODIUM, ZINC; LIPOIC ACID; OMEGA-3 ESSENTIAL FATTY ACIDS; PROTEIN; TRYPTOPHAN; FIBER

As every admirer of Popeye knows, spinach is nature's own source of iron. This popular type of greens contains a powerhouse of nutrients that protect the body from numerous degenerative diseases.

The great health benefits offered by spinach reside in its large number of nutrients working together. Its high iron content makes it good for combating anemia and is also effective at preventing premature hair loss, while its high plant "blood," chlorophyll, benefits those suffering from fatigue and is thought to help to fight cancer.

Spinach is loaded with carotenoids, which the body converts to antioxidant vitamin A to help to trigger immune response to fight infections. It also helps to prevent lung, breast, and cervical cancers, as well as to fight heart disease. Its vitamin C content keeps skin, hair, and mucous membranes healthy, while its B-vitamins improve energy and nervous-system conditions and the lipoic acid helps to maintain the memory.

Containing a wealth of minerals, spinach is rich in zinc, required to boost immunity, and calcium and magnesium, which work together with vitamin K to stave off osteoporosis. Just 2 tablespoons of cooked spinach contain more than the daily requirement of vitamin K and most of the beta-carotene the average adult needs. It's a myth that the oxalate content of spinach prevents the body from absorbing calcium—it contains far more calcium than the oxalates can bind. Magnesium also relaxes and dilates blood vessels and helps to keep the muscles flexible.

Spinach is an anti-inflammatory and a diuretic, and can also be used to ease constipation and night blindness. Containing at least 13 flavonoid antioxidants, it might reduce the risk of heart disease and stroke. It is also rich in lutein, which guards against age-related eye diseases.

Used topically, spinach has emollient properties, helping to soften the skin and surface tissues.

SPINACH RISOTTO

1 tbsp. olive oil
4 tbsp. unsalted butter
2 onions, finely chopped
1¼ cups Arborio rice
1 small glass white wine
3½ cups vegetable stock
4 good handfuls spinach
1 cup freshly grated Parmesan cheese

Heat the oil and butter in a pan and fry the onions until golden. Add the rice, stirring 1 minute, then add the wine and leave until absorbed. Add enough stock to cover, leave to be absorbed, and keep adding until all the stock is used and the rice is tender. Stir in the spinach and cook until it wilts. Remove from heat and sprinkle with Parmesan, then serve.

◆ SPINACH POULTICE *for calluses and heel spurs*

1 cup spinach leaves, crushed
gauze bandage

Wrap the spinach leaves in the bandage and tie to the affected area. Leave 20 minutes, then discard. Repeat as necessary to soften and soothe inflamed or hardened tissue.

CHEESE AND SPINACH MELT

1 onion, chopped
1 tbsp. olive oil
2 garlic cloves, crushed
⅓ cup pine nuts
10 oz. baby spinach leaves
heaping 2 cups grated cheddar cheese

Slowly fry the onion in the oil, then add the garlic and pine nuts and stir in the spinach until it wilts. Drain off any excess liquid, then add the cheese, stirring until it melts. Use the mixture in crêpes, on toast, or to stuff vegetables.

Brussels sprout

VITAMINS B1, B2, B5, B6, C, E, K, FOLIC ACID, BETA-CAROTENE; CALCIUM, COPPER, IRON, MAGNESIUM, MANGANESE, PHOSPHORUS, POTASSIUM; GLUCOSINOLATES; FIBER; OMEGA-3 ESSENTIAL FATTY ACIDS; PROTEIN

A small but powerful defender of the immune system, this crunchy vegetable easily punches above its weight in nutrients thanks to its high levels of antioxidants.

Brussels sprouts are crammed with phytonutrients, such as sulforaphane, a glucosinolate that triggers the release of detoxifying and anti-carcinogenic enzymes. The vegetables are a good source of vitamin B5, an immune stimulant that triggers the production of antibodies, and they contain lots of immunity-building vitamin C, which keeps us youthful by preventing eye disease and protecting the memory. Sprouts are also a good source of folic acid, which plays an important role in reproductive-health and fights heart disease.

Dense in fiber, Brussels sprouts keep the digestive system working efficiently and cholesterol low. They are good for the skin, too, giving it a healthy, lustrous glow.

With their high vitamin and mineral content, Brussels sprouts are especially effective in supporting the immune system during the winter months when infections are most likely to strike.

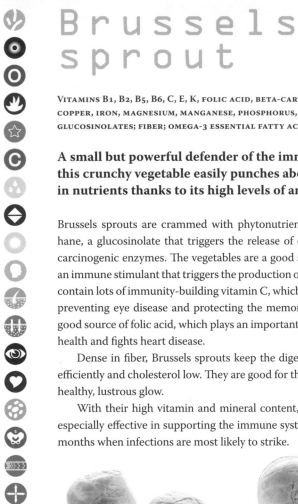

NUTTY SPROUT STIR-FRY

2 onions, sliced

1 cup blanched almonds

4 tbsp. olive oil

6½ cups trimmed and sliced Brussels
  sprouts

ground black pepper

Fry the onions and almonds in the oil until the onions are soft. Blanch the sprouts 1 minute in a pan of lightly salted boiling water, then drain and add to the pan with the onions and almonds, stirring gently until the sprouts are tender. Season to taste with black pepper and serve.

BRUSSELS SPROUTS WITH BACON

1 lb. Brussels sprouts, trimmed

4 oz. Canadian bacon, diced

¼ cup roasted, salted pistachio nuts,
  shelled

4 tbsp. balsamic vinegars

salt and ground black pepper

Steam the sprouts 5 to 10 minutes, until almost tender. In a skillet, cook the bacon until crisp. Remove the bacon and set aside. Add the sprouts to the pan and stir-fry 1 to 2 minutes. Add the pistachios and vinegar and cook 1 to 2 minutes until the vinegar glazes the sprouts and nuts. Return the bacon to the pan, season, mix well, and serve immediately.

BRUSSELS SPROUTS WITH CHESTNUTS

4 bacon slices (optional)

14 oz. Brussels sprouts, trimmed

14 oz. chestnuts, cooked or vacuum-
  packed

2 tbsp. butter

salt and ground black pepper

Broil the bacon, if using, then cut into strips. Steam or boil the sprouts 5 minutes, or until cooked but still crunchy. Drain the sprouts, then add the chestnuts, butter, and the bacon strips, if using. Season and serve immediately.

Cabbage

VITAMINS A, B1, B2, B3, B5, B6, C, E, K, U, BETA-CAROTENE, BIOTIN, FOLIC
ACID; CALCIUM, IODINE, IRON, MAGNESIUM, MANGANESE, PHOSPHORUS,
POTASSIUM, SELENIUM, SULPHUR, ZINC; FIBER; OMEGA-3 OILS;
GLUCOSINOLATES; INDOLES, PROTEIN

**Packed with antioxidants and cancer-fighting
compounds, cabbages were used in therapeutic rituals
in ancient Greek and Roman times.**

A member of the cruciferous food family, cabbage contains powerful
anticarcinogenic compounds, namely indoles and glucosinolates. Studies have shown that people who eat at least three servings of cruciferous vegetables each week have a lowered risk of prostate, colorectal, and
lung cancer. Indoles also help to deactivate estrone, a dangerous form of
estrogen that is associated with breast cancer.

Cabbages are rich in antioxidant nutrients, such as vitamin C, which
mops up free radicals and protects the cardiovascular system. It also promotes healthy skin and glossy hair, and boosts immunity. A cabbage's
beta-carotene enhances the immune system, reduces blood pressure,
and fights heart disease. Cabbages provide folic acid, and might, therefore, reduce birth defects. Their phytonutrients help the liver to remove
toxins and they also combat arthritis and eye disease. Red cabbage is
richest in vitamin C and and can help to ward off Alzheimer's disease.

A substance unique to raw cabbage known as vitamin U, or S-
methylmethionine, has had remarkable success in healing stomach and
duodenal ulcers within as little as
four days. And cabbage can
be a useful aid for general
gastro-intestinal health
—the German ferm-
ented cabbage dish
sauerkraut supports
the digestive tract by
promoting the growth of
friendly bacteria in the gut.

Cabbage leaves can be used placed over leg ulcers and wounds to help to heal them. Mastitis or breast inflammation, often experienced by breast-feeding mothers, might also be relieved in this way.

It is a good idea to let cruciferous vegetables stand for a few minutes after chopping them, as this creates many healthy compounds.

STIR-FRIED CABBAGE WITH FENNEL SEEDS

1 green cabbage
2 tbsp. balsamic vinegar
1 tsp. fennel seeds
a pinch of cayenne pepper
salt and ground black pepper

Wash the cabbage and shred it into thin strips. Put the balsamic vinegar in a wok and heat until sizzling. Add the cabbage, fennel seeds, cayenne pepper, and salt and pepper. Cook until the cabbage is softened and slightly brown.

CABBAGE AND APPLE SALAD *good*

1½ cups shredded red cabbage
1½ cups shredded green cabbage
2 tbsp. olive oil
1 tbsp. lemon juice
1 garlic clove, crushed
4 apples, chopped

Mix together the shredded cabbages, olive oil, lemon juice, and garlic in a large bowl. Refrigerate at least 2 hours until ready to serve. Add the apples, season, if desired, toss well, and serve immediately.

✦RAW CABBAGE POULTICE
for inflammation, such as arthritis and mastitis

5 inside cabbage leaves
3 tbsp. hot chamomile tea
soft cotton cloth

Chop the cabbage leaves into small pieces and place in a bowl. Add the chamomile tea and combine. Roll mixture in the cloth, apply to the inflamed area, and leave 5 minutes. Repeat as required.

Cauliflower

VITAMINS B3, B5, B6, C, FOLIC ACID; CALCIUM, MANGANESE, POTASSIUM, ZINC; GLUCOSINOLATES; INDOLES; OMEGA-3 ESSENTIAL FATTY ACIDS; FIBER

Thought to have originated from China, cauliflower is a great source of health-giving phytochemicals.

Among the many health-giving attributes of cauliflower is its ability to aid cell detoxification. Processed food is full of manufactured chemicals and even "healthy" food can contain elements that have harmful side effects. The liver works hard to filter out these toxins, which can cause cell damage leading to cancer and other diseases, and is helped by cauliflower, which is rich in antioxidants. But cauliflower's most powerful effects come from compounds, such as glucosinolates, which fuel and strengthen the liver during all stages of detoxification. The glucosinolate sulforaphane steps up the production of enzymes that sweep toxins out of the body, while Indole-3-carbinol reduces levels of harmful estrogens that can foster tumor growth, particularly in the breast, prostate, lung, stomach, and colon.

Cauliflower is high in vitamin C, folic acid, and zinc, all known for boosting immunity. Vitamin C has antiviral properties, while folic acid is vital for reproductive health, and zinc aids the healing of wounds. A large serving of cauliflower provides all the vitamin C most adults need in a day.

The most important nutrients for energy production and supporting the adrenal glands are the B-vitamins that cauliflower has in large supply. Cauliflower also has antiallergenic properties that can help to ease asthma and skin allergies.

INDIAN-STYLE CAULIFLOWER

no

1 onion, finely chopped
1 tbsp. olive oil
1 garlic clove, crushed
1 tsp. ground ginger
1 tsp. ground coriander
1 tsp. ground turmeric
1 head cauliflower, cut into
   small florets
2 tbsp. water

In a skillet, gently fry the onion in the oil 5 minutes. Add the garlic, spices, cauliflower, and water. Cover and simmer, stirring occasionally, until the cauliflower is tender. Continue to cook, stirring, until the cauliflower is dry. Serve as a side dish.

CAULIFLOWER WITH PARSLEY AND HOT RED PEPPER

1 head cauliflower
¼ cup water
5 black olives, pitted and finely chopped
1 tbsp. finely chopped parsley leaves
1 tsp. red wine vinegar
a pinch of crushed red pepper flakes

Put the cauliflower and water in a saucepan. Cover the pan and bring to a boil. Reduce the heat and cook 4 to 5 minutes until the cauliflower starts to soften. Stir in the olives, parsley, vinegar, and pepper flakes. Cook 1 minute, or until heated through thoroughly. Serve hot or cool.

CAULIFLOWER PROVENÇALE

1 tbsp. olive oil
1 large onion, chopped
2 garlic cloves, crushed
2 small zucchini, diced
14 oz. canned tomatoes
1 large head cauliflower, cut
   into florets

no

Heat the oil and fry the onion 2 to 3 minutes. Stir in the garlic, add the zucchini and tomatoes, and simmer 5 to 10 minutes. Meanwhile, steam the cauliflower 5 to 10 minutes until tender, then place in a hot serving dish. Pour the sauce over it and serve immediately.

Onion

VITAMINS B1, B6, C, FOLIC ACID; CHROMIUM, COPPER, MANGANESE, MOLYBDE-NUM, PHOSPHORUS, POTASSIUM, SELENIUM; SULFUR COMPOUNDS; QUERCETIN, FLAVONOIDS; FIBER

A member of the Allium family, the onion has long played a central role in folk medicine and has a wealth of health-giving properties. As strong in healing power as it is in taste, this vegetable keeps disease at a safe distance.

The powerful anti-inflammatory effects of onions make them a vital ingredient in nourishing winter dishes. They are full of nutrients that counteract respiratory problems at all levels, from the nasal congestion caused by a cold to the wheezing of asthma. Their antibacterial action combats all kinds of infectious disease and they protect the digestive system, reducing the risk of intestinal growths that can lead to cancer. The same compounds cause the onion's smell and its healing effects, so the more pungent the onion, the more good it will do you.

Protectors of the circulatory system, onions contain many compounds that help to lower cholesterol, thin the blood, and prevent the formation of clots and the hardening of arteries. They might halt the progression of cancerous tumors in the gut. Containing sulfur, an important constituent of the building blocks of skin, nails, and hair, onions help to keep us looking our best. Another attribute of sulfur is that it also inhibits the body's inflammatory response, thus treating everything from insect bites to allergies.

Onions have an exceptionally high level of the flavonoid quercetin, a strong antioxidant that can block the formation of cancer cells. Quercetin is anti-inflammatory, antibiotic, and antiviral and, like beta-carotene, not destroyed in cooking. These nutrient-dense vegetables are also thought to suppress the activity of the *Helicobacter pylori* bacterium, which causes stomach ulcers and food poisoning.

A good source of antioxidant Vitamin C, which fights off harmful free radicals and supports the immune system, onions are also loaded with selenium, another powerful immunity-booster that also cleanses the liver and staves off wrinkles and sun damage.

For anyone aiming to reach peak physical fitness, onions can offer several minerals, including chromium, manganese, and potassium, which help to break down fat deposits and speed up the metabolism. Onions' quercetin has been shown to reduce muscle fatigue. Studies suggest onions can help maintain healthy bones by inhibiting the activity of osteoclasts—the cells that break down bone.

FRENCH ONION SOUP

4 tbsp. olive oil
scant 4 cups thinly sliced onions
2 garlic cloves, crushed
2 tbsp. apple juice
4 cups beef stock
1 ¼ cups dry white wine
salt and ground black pepper

In a heavy saucepan, heat the oil. Add the onions, garlic, and apple juice, and cook 5 to 6 minutes, stirring constantly. Turn down the heat and cook about 20 minutes. Pour in the stock and wine and season with salt and pepper. Bring to a simmer, then cook, uncovered, 1 hour. Pour into bowls and serve immediately.

✦ ONION COMPRESS
for inflamed wounds, headaches & earaches

4 onions, finely chopped
white cheesecloth or linen bag

Lightly steam the onions and wrap in the white cheesecloth or linen bag. Apply to the inflamed area or aching parts. Once the compress cools down, replace it with another. Repeat up to 4 times in succession, or until the symptoms are alleviated.

Celery

VITAMINS B1, B2, B3, B5, B6, C, E, K, BETA CAROTENE, BIOTIN, FOLIC ACID; CALCIUM, IODINE, IRON, MAGNESIUM, MANGANESE, MOLYBDENUM, PHOSPHORUS, POTASSIUM, SELENIUM, SODIUM, ZINC; FIBER

A member of the parsley family, celery can stimulate the kidneys and help to flush out the system. Just five celery sticks make up one of the recommended daily portions of fruits and vegetables for most adults.

Thought to have its origins in southern Europe and North Africa, celery was known as a medicine by the ancient Greeks, while its culinary uses were first explored in Europe in the Middle Ages.

Full of B-vitamins for energy and immunity-boosting Vitamin C, celery is good at aiding the elimination of waste via the urine, thus acting as a detoxifying agent, and cleansing the liver, which helps to keep skin looking youthful. It is an anti-inflammatory, clearing uric acid from painful joints, and is well known as a remedy for gout and rheumatism. Celery is a useful antiseptic in the urinary tract and might help to lower blood pressure and prevent cancer. Celery seeds are more potent than other parts of the plant.

It is believed that we burn more calories chewing, swallowing, and digesting celery than we get from eating it, making the vegetable popular with dieters. Its high water content acts as a diuretic helping to eliminate puffy hands, ankles, and feet.

A stick of celery is the athlete's secret weapon because it's rich in a string of nutrients that keep energy levels high. Its vitamin C content aids recovery from sports injuries by strengthening cell walls. And being higher in sodium than most vegetables (although nowhere near a harmful level), celery can prevent the dangerous mineral imbalance that results from drinking too much water during an energetic workout. Vital minerals can be lost in the sweat following vigorous exercise or during a fever. Celery juice, with its high concentration of water, potassium, and naturally occurring sodium, can help to replace this loss by hydrating the body and restoring electrolyte balance. As celery juice has a strong flavor, most people prefer it mixed with other juices, such as carrot.

Celery contains a rich spectrum of other health-enhancing minerals, including calcium, iron, magnesium, and selenium, which work together to normalize the body's acid–alkaline balance. An acidic state caused by stress or eating harmful foods can lead to numerous health problems. Celery seems to counteract this acidity, thereby improving conditions such as fatigue, rheumatism, and joint pain.

CLASSIC WALDORF SALAD

5 celery ribs, trimmed and chopped

2 apples, chopped

a bunch white seedless grapes

1 scallion, trimmed and chopped

handful chopped walnuts

2 tbsp. mayonnaise

2 tbsp. plain yogurt

½ tsp. celery seeds

ground black pepper

Put the celery, apples, grapes, scallion, and walnuts in a large bowl. Put the remaining ingredients in a separate small bowl and stir well to make a dressing. Tip the dressing onto the salad and mix well. Serve immediately.

✦CELERY-SEED TEA
for rheumatism & urinary infections

heaping 1 tsp. celery seeds

2 cups water

Place the seeds and water in a stainless-steel saucepan. Bring to a boil, then remove from the heat and leave to infuse 10 minutes. Strain and drink up to 3 times a day depending on the severity of symptoms.

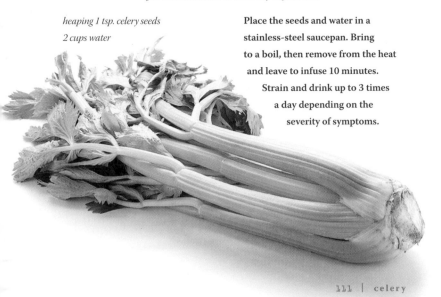

Bell pepper

VITAMINS B3, B6, C, E, K, BETA-CAROTENE, BIOTIN, FOLIC ACID, LYCOPENE; CALCIUM, IODINE, IRON, MAGNESIUM, MANGANESE, PHOSPHORUS, POTASSIUM, ZINC; FIBER

The wide range of vitamins and minerals in this colorful vegetable makes it a great all-around immunity-booster. Whether eaten raw as a crunchy crudité or softened in a stir-fry or roasting dish, bell peppers pack a powerful nutritional punch.

Sweet bell peppers come in several colors: red, green, orange, yellow, and even purple. The green and purple varieties have a slightly bitter taste, while the red, yellow, and orange peppers have a sweeter flavor.

Whatever their color, however, they provide a healthy serving of immunity-boosting nutrients, including two antioxidants that work well together: beta-carotene and vitamin C. Together, these offer protection against cell-damaging free radicals and protect the lungs from winter infections, asthma, and even the ravages of second-hand smoke. The body turns the beta-carotene into antiviral, immunity-boosting vitamin A, while vitamin C is said to protect against memory problems and eye disease, and to combat stress. Peppers also contain flavonoids, thought to enhance vitamin C's antioxidant action by strengthening its ability to protect the body against disease. An average serving of bell peppers contains the more than the daily needs of these vitamins for most adults.

Red bell peppers are especially high in cancer-fighting lycopene, which in conjunction with the vitamin C and carotenoids, farther protects vision and reduces the risk of eye diseases. Lycopene also helps to fight almost every aspect of the aging process, including deterioration of the skin structure and damage to the arteries.

With a high water content, which helps to flush out toxins from the body, bell peppers also contain fiber, which is important for digestive health and for preventing the build up of cholesterol in the blood that can cause heart attacks and strokes. The B-vitamins in peppers also help to ward off atherosclerosis and heart disease by reducing levels of homocysteine, a substance that damages blood vessels.

STUFFED BELL PEPPERS

3 tbsp. olive oil

7 oz. cherry tomatoes

2 garlic cloves, finely chopped

1 red onion, finely chopped

1 bunch basil, shredded

1 cup diced mozzarella cheese

1 cup grated Parmesan cheese

4 red bell peppers, tops cut off and
   reserved and bodies seeded

ground black pepper

Preheat the oven to 425°F. Spoon 2 tablespoons of the olive oil into a baking dish and place in the oven. Meanwhile, combine all the ingredients, except the peppers, in a bowl with the remaining olive oil. Fill each pepper with equal amounts of the mixture, then replace the tops. Place in the dish and cook 20 minutes. Serve immediately.

ROASTED BELL PEPPER DIP

1 large red bell pepper

7 tbsp. milk

½ tsp. paprika

½ tsp. salt

2 tsp. extra virgin olive oil

2 tsp. apple cider vinegar

1 tbsp. chopped basil

Preheat the oven to 400°F. Put the whole pepper on a baking sheet in the center of the oven and roast 20 to 30 minutes until the skin blackens. Remove from the oven and leave to cool. Peel off the skin, seed and core, and save any juice. Blend all the ingredients, including the pepper and its juice, in a food processor to a smooth creamy texture. Serve either chilled as a dip or warm as a sauce.

BROILED BELL PEPPER SALAD

4 bell peppers, seeded and cut
   into strips
handful walnut halves
2 tbsp. olive oil
1 tsp. vinegar
1 head lettuce, roughly torn
salt, to taste

Broil the peppers under a hot broiler until the skin is black and blistered. When cool enough to handle, peel off the skin and discard. Heat the walnuts slowly in 1 teaspoon of the oil in a skillet until crisp. Mix together the remaining oil, vinegar, and salt. Place the lettuce in a serving bowl with the peppers and walnuts on top. Pour the dressing over and serve while still warm.

RED BELL PEPPER SAUCE

2 red bell peppers, seeded and chopped
1⅔ cups cashew nuts
1 tsp. dried dill
1 garlic clove
1 tbsp. chopped onion
pinch of ground black pepper

Put all the ingredients in a food processor and blend until creamy. Serve over rice or couscous, or steamed vegetables, or use as a sandwich spread.

RED BELL PEPPER SALSA

1½ red bell peppers, seeded and chopped
2 large, juicy tomatoes, finely diced
small red chili pepper, seeded
1 small cucumber, seeded and finely diced
4 tbsp. chopped cilantro leaves
juice and grated zest of ½ lime

Mix all the ingredients together in a nonmetallic bowl. Serve as a dip or a sauce.

Squash

Vitamins B1, B3, B5, B6, C, E, K, beta carotene, folic acid; calcium, copper, iron, magnesium, manganese, phosphorus, potassium, selenium, zinc; fiber; omega-3 fatty acids; protein; complex carbohydrate

Squash is a nutritional winner and is delicious in soups and stews and with other roasted vegetables. A bright orange "superveg," it gives a powerful boost to the body's immune defenses.

The solid flesh of squash, such as butternut and pumpkin, provides a healthy dose of age-defying nutrients. Extracts from squash have been found to help ease the swelling of the prostate gland, which bedevils many older men. Eating squash regularly might help to prevent it developing. Their rich array of nutrients, including beta-cryptoxanthin, counteract the cell damage that leads to cancer and heart disease. And they have anti-inflammatory properties that can relieve the pain of many age-related conditions, such as arthritis.

Like all orange fruits and vegetables, the butternut squash is a great source of beta-carotene, which the body converts to vitamin A, needed

for maintaining a healthy immune system, as well as for good digestion and respiratory-tract function.

A great provider of energy-sustaining carbohydrates, squash contains high levels of the minerals potassium and magnesium, which help to maintain efficient energy production. A lack of these minerals can lead to fatigue, muscle cramps, and an increased risk of high cholesterol, high blood pressure, and heart problems.

ROASTED BUTTERNUT SQUASH WITH CHEESE AND WALNUTS

4 tbsp. olive oil

2 garlic cloves, crushed

2 butternut squash, halved and seeded

1½ cups diced cheese, such as cheddar

1 cup walnut halves

Preheat the oven to 375°F. Place the oil and garlic in the hollow of each squash. Roast the squash 1 hour, or until tender. Scoop out most of the flesh, leaving enough to keep the shape. Mix together the flesh with the cheese and walnuts. Return this mixture to the squash halves and cook a few minutes until the cheese is soft. Serve immediately.

SPICY ROASTED VEGETABLES

3 tbsp. sunflower seeds

1 tsp. cayenne pepper

1 tsp. cumin seeds

1 tsp. ground coriander

1 tsp. ground ginger

1 butternut squash, peeled and seeded

2 zucchini, chopped

1 red bell pepper, seeded and sliced

3 cups button mushrooms

3 tbsp. olive oil

1 tbsp. balsamic vinegar

Toast the sunflower seeds and spices in a skillet over low heat 3 minutes. Chop the squash into 2-inch chunks. Place the squash and other vegetables in a baking dish. Add the oil, balsamic vinegar, seeds, and spices and mix well together. Bake in a preheated oven at 375°F 1 hour, stirring occasionally, then serve.

Eggplant

VITAMINS B1, B3, B6, C, K, BETA-CAROTENE, BIOTIN, FOLIC ACID; CALCIUM, COPPER, IODINE, IRON, MAGNESIUM, MANGANESE, PHOSPHORUS, POTASSIUM, SELENIUM, ZINC; CHLOROGENIC ACID; ANTHOCYANINS; FIBER

Thanks to its high number of healing compounds, eggplant helps to ward off many illnesses. The polished purple skin of this plant has very powerful qualities.

Well known as a main ingredient in the Greek dish moussaka, eggplants contain many beneficial substances. Some people need more iron in their diet, but too much iron isn't a good thing—it increases the body's production of free radicals, by-products of metabolic processes that damage the cells. Eggplants contain a host of phytonutrients that mop up harmful free radicals. One of them is chlorogenic acid, a powerful antioxidant that lowers levels of harmful cholesterol and has antibacterial and antiviral properties. Another is nasunin, an anthocyanin found to protect fats in brain cells, which might help slow down the aging process of this vital organ and which also helps the body excrete excess iron. This reduces the risk of conditions such as cancer, heart disease, and arthritis.

A member of the nightshade family, eggplants should be avoided by osteoarthritis sufferers, as they can increase inflammation in the joints.

BABA GANNOUSH

2 large eggplants
6 garlic cloves, crushed
4 tbsp. tahini
4 tbsp. lemon juice
1 tbsp. olive oil
a bunch parsley
bread and crudités, to serve

Preheat the oven to 375°F. Bake the eggplants on a baking sheet 30 minutes. Slice in half, scoop out the flesh, and chop, then drain in a colander at least 10 minutes. In a bowl, mash the garlic, tahini, and lemon juice with the eggplant to form a smooth paste. Add the oil and sprinkle with parsley. Serve with bread and crudités.

EGGPLANT GRATIN

2 eggplants
3 tbsp. olive oil
1 cup grated cheddar cheese or dairy-free
    alternative

Preheat the oven to 425°F. Cut the eggplant into slices and brush the sides with the oil. Arrange in a baking dish in overlapping slices, cover with foil, and cook 25 minutes. Meanwhile, preheat the broiler. Uncover and cook 10 minutes longer. Remove the dish from the oven, sprinkle with the cheese and place under the broiler until melted.

EGGPLANT AND RICOTTA ROLLS

1 large eggplant, trimmed
3 tbsp. olive oil
juice and grated zest of 1 lemon
scant 1 cup ricotta cheese
4 sun-dried tomatoes in oil, drained and
    chopped
ground black pepper

Cut the eggplant lengthwise into ¼-inch-thick slices. Cover with the oil and lemon juice and zest. Place on a baking sheet and broil each side 3 minutes. Put some ricotta, tomato, and black pepper on each slice. Roll and secure with a wooden toothpick. Broil 2 minutes, then serve.

Mushroom

Vitamins B1, B2, B3, B5, B6, B12, C, E, folic acid; calcium, chromium, copper, iron, magnesium, manganese, phosphorous, potassium, selenium, zinc; lentinan; L-ergothioneine; eritadenine; beta-glucan; protein; omega-6 essential fatty acids

These highly prized fungi have been revered and valued by ancient peoples for thousands of years, both as a tasty food and a potent medicine. They supply key nutrients to prevent high cholesterol and stimulate the immune system with their powerful disease-fighting capabilities.

There are many species of mushroom available today in supermarkets. Among the more common ones are button, cremini, and portobello mushrooms, but all species are packed with health-giving nutrients. Made up of between 80 and 90 percent water, they are very low in calories and are, therefore, a useful food for dieters.

Mushrooms are one of the richest sources of a powerful antioxidant called L-ergothioneine, which combats cell damage. Research is being done into their cancer-fighting properties, including reducing the risk of breast cancer. And their minerals might ease the pain of arthritis. Mushrooms might also help to slow down age-related muscle loss, as they provide protein in a form the body can easily use.

All mushrooms are high in B-vitamins, particularly vitamin B3, which might slow the onset of age-related dementias. They are a rich source of potassium, which helps to regulate blood pressure—an average portobello mushroom contains more potassium than a banana. Mushrooms are also an important source of vitamin B12 for vegetarians, which is vital for maintaining healthy energy levels and combating arthritis.

Brimming with the antiaging antioxidants vitamin E and selenium, mushrooms help to maintain healthy skin and hair, and protect against heart disease. The fungi are a slow-release energy food, thanks to their high content of vegetable protein. They're also especially rich in chromium, which helps to stabilize blood sugar levels and, in turn, helps to control sugar cravings. The older you are, the less likely you are to be taking in enough chromium.

Shiitake mushroom: Native to China, Japan, and Korea, shiitake mushrooms have been used in those countries for thousands of years to prevent and treat illness. In ancient China they were prescribed by physicians to help to beat a range of conditions, from colds and flu to gastrointestinal problems. Recently, these mushrooms have been the subject of several studies that are researching their pro-immunity and healing powers.

These fungi contain lentinan, a compound that has been shown to help lower cholesterol. Lentinan has also been isolated and licensed as an anticancer drug in Japan because of its ability to stimulate the immune system to deactivate malignant cells. In addition, lentinan is understood to trigger the production of the antiviral and antibacterial substance interferon, which might help inhibit the progress of the HIV virus, as well as treat cancer, diabetes, chronic fatigue syndrome, and fibrocystic breast disease. The mushrooms are also rich in the amino acids that enhance general immune function. They contain eritadenine, a digestive enzyme that is thought to lower cholesterol, while their tyrosinase lowers blood pressure. They are also rich in iron, which staves off anemia.

Although shiitake mushrooms are more expensive than many other varieties, a small amount gives great health benefits and satisfies the appetite. They can be bought fresh, pickled, or dried, and can be used in dishes in the same way as ordinary field mushrooms.

Maitake mushroom: Another type of fungus from the Far East with excellent healing powers is the maitake mushroom. Maitake mushrooms contain beta-glucan, which stops the HIV virus from killing white blood cells, possibly preventing AIDS. Beta-glucan is known to be highly effective in shrinking cancerous tumors. Maitake mushrooms are also used to treat high blood pressure and liver disease.

Reishi mushroom: This fungus is used in extract or essence form as a treatment for liver disorders, hypertension, and arthritis. Studies have shown that it has antiviral, antibacterial, antioxidant antiallergic, and anti-inflammatory properties, and scentists believe it helps fight tumors. In addition, the reishi mushroom is used to combat high blood pressure and asthma.

GLAZED SHIITAKE MUSHROOMS

1 lb. shiitake mushrooms
1 tsp. canola oil
5 tbsp. chicken stock
1 tsp. cornstarch
2 tsp. soy sauce
1 tbsp. dry sherry

Discard the shiitake stems and slice the mushroom caps. In a large pan, heat the oil, add the mushrooms and 2 tablespoons of the stock and cook, stirring, 5 to 6 minutes. In a small bowl, dissolve the cornstarch in the remaining stock. Stir in the soy sauce and sherry. Add the mixture to the pan and cook 2 minutes, or until the mushrooms are glazed.

MUSHROOM PÂTÉ

5⅓ cups chopped cremini mushrooms
2 tbsp. olive oil
1 tbsp. soy sauce
scant 1 cup mascarpone cheese
2 tbsp. chopped tarragon

In a skillet, fry the mushrooms in the oil 2 minutes. Add 4 tablespoons water and simmer 10 minutes. Leave to cool, then drain and purée in a blender. Stir in the remaining ingredients. Refrigerate at least 1 hour, then serve.

SHIITAKE NOODLES

9 oz. thick egg noodles

3 tbsp. soy sauce

1 tbsp. oyster sauce

1 tsp. brown sugar

1 tbsp. sesame oil

2 small red chilies, seeded and sliced

7 oz. firm tofu, drained and diced

2-inch piece gingerroot, peeled and grated

2 garlic cloves, crushed

2 cups sliced shiitake mushrooms

6 scallions, trimmed and chopped

Cover the noodles in boiling water and leave to soften 5 minutes, then drain. In a bowl, mix together the soy sauce, oyster sauce, and sugar. Heat the oil in a wok. Stir-fry the chilies, tofu, ginger, and garlic 2 minutes, then add the noodles, mushrooms, sauce mixture, and scallions. Toss together well and serve immediately.

FRIED SHIITAKE MUSHROOM SALAD

3 large handfuls mixed salad leaves

a bunch watercress, trimmed

4 tbsp. olive oil

1 lb. shiitake mushrooms, stems removed
    and caps sliced

8 garlic cloves, crushed

ground black pepper

Put the salad leaves and watercress in a bowl. Heat 3 tablespoons of the oil in a pan and sauté the mushrooms and garlic until tender. Add the contents of the pan to the salad with the remaining oil. Toss well, season with black pepper, and serve.

STUFFED MUSHROOMS

4 large mushrooms, such as portobellos

4 tbsp. olive oil

4 scallions, trimmed and chopped

1 red bell pepper, seeded and chopped

2 small zucchini, chopped

8 green olives, pitted and chopped

2 tbsp. oatmeal

1 tbsp. chopped basil leaves

1 tbsp. soy sauce

mixed salad leaves, to serve

Preheat the oven to 350°F. Remove the mushrooms' stems. Heat the oil in a skillet and slowly fry the scallions, pepper, zucchinis, olives, and oatmeal 3 minutes. Stir in the basil and soy sauce. Place the mushrooms on a baking sheet and spoon the mixture over. Bake 15 to 20 minutes. Serve on a bed of salad leaves.

Fennel

VITAMINS B1, B3, B5, B6, C, E, BETA-CAROTENE, BIOTIN, FOLIC ACID; CALCIUM, COPPER, IRON, MAGNESIUM, PHOSPHORUS, POTASSIUM, SELENIUM, ZINC; ELLAGIC ACID; ANETHOLE, QUERCETIN, RUTIN; CARBOHYDRATE; FIBER

Part of the parsley family, the fennel plant and seeds have ancient healing properties and are also popular culinary ingredients. Used particularly in French and Italian cuisine, fennel boasts a host of antiaging properties.

Fennel is well known for its antispasmodic, analgesic, and diuretic properties. It can be used to ease digestive problems, combat fluid retention, and reduce intestinal spasms. Because it aids the elimination of toxins through the urine, it is also a useful remedy for arthritis and gout. Its volatile oils have an antiseptic effect, and are considered particularly useful for combating urinary infections.

Rich in phytonutrients, including rutin, quercetin, and anethole, fennel has been shown to reduce inflammatory conditions, such as arthritis. Rutin strengthens blood capillaries, thereby improving poor circulation, while quercetin inhibits inflammatory conditions, such as asthma. Anethole is antispasmodic, preventing the intestinal spasms often experienced by people with irritable bowel syndrome.

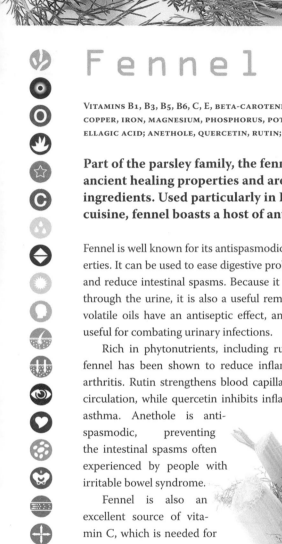

Fennel is also an excellent source of vitamin C, which is needed for the proper functioning of the immune system, to protect the brain, and to avoid aging of the arteries. Fennel is fiber-rich and might help to reduce elevated cholesterol levels. In addition, it's a good source of folic acid, a vitamin that lowers the risk of heart disease.

SAUTÉED FENNEL

1 tbsp. olive oil
2 fennel bulbs, trimmed and finely sliced
8 garlic cloves, crushed
ground black pepper
wholegrain bread and cheese, to serve

Heat the oil in a saucepan. Add the fennel and garlic and sauté until slightly soft, then season with pepper. Serve as an accompaniment or with bread and cheese as a light meal.

✦FENNEL MOUTHWASH *to protect teeth & gums*

½ tsp. fennel seeds
½ tsp. ground cloves
2 tbsp. pure grain alcohol or good-quality vodka
1 cup plus 2 tbsp. distilled water
paper coffee filter

In a bowl, mix the spices into the alcohol. Cover with a clean dish towel and set aside 3 days, then strain through the coffee filter placed in a strainer. Add the water. Store in a sealed bottle 6 weeks. Gargle with 1 tablespoon at a time.

✳FENNEL-SEED INFUSION
to cleanse & tone the skin

2 tsp. fennel seeds, crushed
2 thyme sprigs, crumbled, or ½ tsp. dried thyme
½ cup boiling water
juice of ½ lemon

In an heatproof bowl, combine the fennel seeds and thyme and cover with the boiling water. Add the lemon juice and leave to steep 15 minutes. Strain, and when cold, store, covered, in a jar in the refrigerator. Dab evenly on the face and neck every morning with a cotton ball, then rinse off with warm water.

Lettuce

Vitamins B1, B2, B3, B5, C, E, K, beta-carotene, biotin, folic acid; calcium, chromium, copper, iodine, iron, magnesium, manganese, molybdenum, phosphorus, potassium, selenium, silica, zinc; fiber; protein; tryptophan; lactucarium

A salad staple, lettuce helps to cleanse the blood, relax the nerves, and eliminate excess fluid as well as providing vital nutrients for helping the body to make energy.

It looks insubstantial, but a lettuce leaf could be a powerful protector against one of the most frequent accidents that disable older people. Scientists have found that older women who eat lettuce every day have half as many hip fractures as those who eat it less than once a week. It's the vitamin K content that does so much good. Any kind of lettuce helps, but, as with other leafy foods, the darker the color of the leaves, the more nutritional value the lettuce contains.

With its high potassium content, lettuce is also a mild diuretic, while its chlorophyll helps to detoxify the blood and liver. Other nutrients in lettuce include folic acid, important for preventing birth defects, and beta-carotene and vitamin C, two antioxidant vitamins, which help to bolster the immune system.

This leafy vegetable contains many minerals, including iron, calcium, magnesium, and zinc, all of which help to generate energy. Equally important is the folic acid content—this B-vitamin protects the heart by converting a harmful chemical called homocysteine into benign substances. If not converted, homocysteine can directly damage blood vessels, greatly increasing the risk of heart attack and stroke.

Lettuce also contains a natural sedative that relaxes the nervous system and induces sleep.

PEAS AND LETTUCE

4 tbsp. butter
2¼ cups shelled peas
8 large romaine lettuce leaves,
    cut into strips
4 tbsp. stock or water
1 tsp. ground black pepper

Melt the butter over low heat and add the peas and lettuce. Add the stock or water and bring to a boil, then simmer, covered, 5 minutes, or until the peas are tender. Season with pepper and serve.

GREEN SALAD SUPREME

3 large handfuls mixed lettuce leaves
½ cucumber, sliced
⅔ cup cubed feta cheese
1 avocado, pitted, peeled, and chopped
2 tbsp. salad cress
2 tbsp. chopped chives
2 tbsp. olive oil
1 tbsp. apple cider vinegar
salt and ground black pepper to taste

Put all the ingredients in a large bowl, toss well, and serve immediately.

CHEESY BROILED LETTUCE

1 romaine lettuce
1 tbsp. olive oil
7 oz. Camembert cheese, thinly sliced
2 tsp. balsamic vinegar

Preheat oven at 425°F. Cut the lettuce lengthwise into quarters, brush with the oil, and broil 2 minutes on each side. Arrange in a shallow baking dish, top with thin slices of Camembert, and drizzle with the vinegar. Bake 5 minutes, or until the cheese is bubbling, then serve.

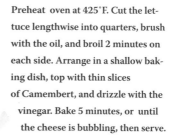

Cucumber

VITAMINS A, B3, B5, C, K, BETA-CAROTENE, BIOTIN, C, FOLIC ACID; CALCIUM, IODINE, IRON, MAGNESIUM, MANGANESE; MOLYBDENUM, PHOSPHORUS, POTASSIUM, SILICA, SULFUR, ZINC; CAFFEIC ACID; EREPSIN; FIBER

Laden with water, this popular salad vegetable is well known for its skin-healing properties. Packed with mineral-rich fluid, it aids digestion by keeping the body well hydrated.

Appreciated both as a food and as a skin-healer by the ancient Egyptians, Greeks, and Romans, cucumbers are one of the best diuretic foods thanks to their high water and balanced mineral content. By promoting the flow of urine, and "flushing" it through the kidneys, cucumber helps the body to eliminate toxins, thereby aiding detoxification.

Cucumber can be used topically to relieve various skin afflictions, including puffy eyes and sunburn. Its vitamin C and caffeic acid, which relieve inflammation and water retention, might explain why it is so effective for the skin. Popular in beauty products, cucumber helps to maintain a youthful appearance, thanks to its hydrating and anti-inflammatory properties.

The rich fiber content of cucumbers keeps the digestive system moving and, unlike some other high-fiber foods, comes balanced with its own supply of fluid. Eating cucumbers can ease or prevent constipation, which is often exacerbated by not drinking enough water. It's helpful, too, if you've had diarrhea, because as well as rehydrating, it replaces vital minerals. Cucumber is also a source of erepsin, an enzyme that helps the body to digest protein. Fresh cucumber juice can alleviate acid reflux and indigestion and is also useful for treating gum disease.

The minerals in cucumbers are clustered in the peel. The magnesium and potassium help to keep blood pressure in check. Cucumbers are a rich source of silica, needed for healthy skin, bone, and connective tissue, and together with sulfur, this mineral promotes the growth of healthy hair and strong nails. Silica also plays a major role in preventing cardiovascular disease and osteoporosis.

GARDEN SALAD

4 oz. baby spinach leaves
1 cucumber, chopped
8 radishes, trimmed and thinly sliced
2 carrots, peeled and thinly sliced
1 scallion, trimmed and chopped
2 tbsp. chopped parsley leaves
1 tbsp. olive oil
juice of ½ lime

Combine the vegetables and parsley in a large bowl. Pour the olive oil and lime juice over and toss well. Serve immediately.

CUCUMBER AND MINT SALAD

4 tbsp. chopped mint leaves, plus
   a few leaves, to serve
1 large cucumber, chopped
2 celery ribs, trimmed and chopped
2 tsp. white wine vinegar
½ cup plain yogurt

Mix together the chopped mint, cucumber, and celery in a serving bowl. In a separate bowl, whisk the vinegar into the yogurt. Pour the dressing over the salad, add the mint leaves, and serve.

*CUCUMBER LOTION *to cleanse the skin*

½ small cucumber
5 mint leaves
4 tbsp. milk
2 drops grapefruit seed extract

Peel and chop the cucumber. Remove the mint leaves from their stems and chop. Put both in a food processor with the milk and whiz until smooth. Pour the mixture into a saucepan and bring to a boil. Reduce the heat and simmer 2 minutes, then leave to cool. Pour into a clean bottle and add the grapefruit seed extract. Store in the refrigerator and use within a week.

Alfalfa

VITAMINS A, B3, B5, C, D, E, K, BETA-CAROTENE, FOLIC ACID; CALCIUM, IRON,
MAGNESIUM, MANGANESE, PHOSPHORUS, POTASSIUM, SILICA, SODIUM, ZINC;
CHLOROPHYLL; SAPONINS; PROTEIN; FIBER; ENZYMES

**Highly digestible and containing huge amounts
of antioxidants, alfalfa can be sprinkled onto any
salad or added to any sandwich to boost your nutrient
intake—and at virtually no calorie cost.**

Long popular among health-food enthusiasts, alfalfa sprouts are packed
with enzymes and easily digestible nutrients, which are unleashed during the sprouting process. Besides being a storehouse of amino acids,
vitamins, and minerals, alfalfa contains several phytochemicals that can
protect against disease. Canavanine, an amino acid analogue, exerts anticarcinogenic activity, while the plant estrogens found in this food help
to balance hormones. Other compounds abundant in alfalfa sprouts
include saponins, which reduce cholesterol by binding to it so that
the body can excrete it, and chlorophyll, a powerful blood-builder and
detoxifying agent.

These sprouted seeds provide abundant amounts of vitamin A for
the eyes, B-vitamins for the nervous system and brain power, vitamin C
for immunity and eye health, and vitamin E for the skin and the heart.
They are also high in calcium and phosphorus for the bones, iron to prevent anemia, magnesium and potassium to lower the risk of heart disease, zinc to prevent premature hair loss, and silica to promote glowing
skin, strong nails, and glossy hair.

Alfalfa is one of the few sprouted seeds that is readily available in
supermarkets. It will also significantly boost zinc intake, particularly
when combined with Belgian endive, to improve both liver and hormone
function, as well as promoting cellular growth and renewal.

Packed with nutrients, sprouts provide a burst of energy to see you
through any form of exercise. Alfalfa contains a compound that inhibits
fungal growth, an occasional by-product of sweaty environments. Rich
in enzymes and fiber, alfalfa sprouts are easy to digest and contain very
few calories, so they are useful for anyone trying to lose weight, too.

TOFU, AVOCADO, AND ALFALFA PITA POCKETS

7 oz. smoked tofu, sliced

4 wholewheat pita breads

2 large handfuls alfalfa sprouts

2 avocados, pitted, peeled, and sliced

2 tomatoes, sliced

12 pitted black olives, chopped

2 tbsp. tahini

Preheat the broiler to high. Broil the tofu slices on both sides. Warm the pita breads briefly in an oven, then cut them along the top and stuff with the tofu, alfalfa, avocados, tomatoes, and olives. Put the tahini and 6 tablespoons water in a bowl and mix well. Spoon this mixture over the filling and serve.

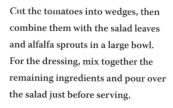

ALFALFA SALAD

4 large tomatoes

8 oz. mixed salad leaves, such as lettuce, watercress, and spinach

2 cups alfalfa sprouts

1 tsp. white wine vinegar

2 tsp. olive oil

1 scallion, trimmed and chopped

1 garlic clove, crushed

salt and ground black pepper, to taste

Cut the tomatoes into wedges, then combine them with the salad leaves and alfalfa sprouts in a large bowl. For the dressing, mix together the remaining ingredients and pour over the salad just before serving.

Watercress

VITAMINS B1, B3, B5, B6, C, E, K, BETA-CAROTENE, BIOTIN, FOLIC ACID;
CALCIUM, IODINE, IRON, MAGNESIUM, MANGANESE, PHOSPHORUS, POTASSIUM,
ZINC; GLUCOSINOLATES; FIBER; PROTEIN

Packed with more than 15 vitamins and minerals, watercress has long enjoyed superfood status. This robustly flavored salad leaf is a powerful immune-system stimulant.

Weight for weight, watercress contains more calcium than milk, more iron than spinach, and as much vitamin C as oranges, making it an excellent food for the bones, blood, and immune system. It is also a fabulous source of lutein and zeaxanthin—types of carotenoids that reduce the risk of eye disease. Watercress also possesses a unique compound called PEITC, which has not only been found to inhibit the growth of cancer, but is thought to kill existing cancerous cells as well. It also contains phenethyl isothiocyanate, a compound that helps the liver to detoxify and is particularly potent against lung cancer and bronchitis.

Watercress is rich in glucosinolates—plant chemicals that boost the activity of cancer-preventing enzymes. It contains the key antioxidant vitamins needed for a fully functioning immune system, along with vitamin B6, which enhances the action of phagocytes, white blood cells responsible for cleaning up waste matter. Watercress helps the release of bile from the gallbladder, which is important for the digestion of fat, and it also prevents memory loss.

A diuretic, watercress has expectorant and depurative properties, therefore easing inflammation, ulcers, and boils and improving skin quality. It is also a good source of the mineral manganese, and iron, both of which help the body resist infections. Watercress is also a useful source of iodine, which is essential for the proper functioning of the thyroid.

STIR-FRIED WATERCRESS WITH ALMONDS AND GINGER

4 tbsp. slivered almonds

2 tbsp. sesame oil

1 lb. watercress, chopped

2-inch piece gingerroot, finely chopped

4 tbsp. miso

4 tbsp. rice vinegar

Heat a wok or pan and briefly dry-fry the almonds until lightly toasted, then immediately tip out of the pan and set aside. Add the oil to the wok and stir-fry the watercress and ginger 3 minutes. Add the miso, rice vinegar, and the almonds and stir well. Serve.

CREAMY WATERCRESS SOUP

4 tbsp. butter

2 bunches watercress, chopped

1 onion, diced

¼ cup all-purpose flour

2¼ cups milk

2 cups vegetable stock

6 tbsp. light cream

Melt the butter in a pan and slowly fry the watercress and onion 3 minutes. Stir in the flour and cook 1 minute. Slowly add the milk and then the stock, stirring constantly. Bring to a boil and stir until thick. Cover and simmer 30 minutes. Whiz the soup in a blender, then add the cream and reheat without boiling. Serve.

WATERCRESS, ENDIVE, AND ORANGE SALAD

4 Belgian endives

juice of 1 lemon

7 oz. watercress, stems discarded

4 oranges, peeled

2 carrots, peeled and grated

⅔ cup apple juice

salt and ground black pepper, to taste

Slice the endives, place in a large salad bowl, and squeeze the lemon juice over them. Roughly chop the watercress and quarter the oranges. Combine them in the bowl with the remaining ingredients, season and toss well. Serve immediately.

Seaweed

VITAMINS B1, B2, B3, B5, B6, B12, C, E, K, BETA-CAROTENE, FOLIC ACID; CALCIUM, COPPER, IODINE, IRON, MAGNESIUM, MANGANESE, PHOSPHORUS, POTASSIUM, SELENIUM, SODIUM, ZINC; LIGNANS; OMEGA-3 ESSENTIAL FATTY ACIDS; COMPLEX CARBOHYDRATE, FIBER; PROTEIN

Seaweed is a marine algae, the oldest form of life on the planet, and it contains a host of health-giving properties, particularly minerals. These gifts from the ocean could help to soothe away stress and put an end to insomnia by promoting peaceful sleep.

Seaweed, or sea vegetables, can be found both in salt water and in freshwater lakes and seas. Best known for their use in Japanese cuisine, they offer an unrivaled range of nutrients that promote emotional health and keep the brain alert. They contain a wide range of minerals: magnesium helps to relieve stress-related symptoms, such as heart palpitations; calcium helps to stabilize moods; and iron provides energy to the many people—especially young women—whose iron stores are low. The wide range of sea vegetables now available are rich in iodine, which supports metabolic and thyroid function. A slightly underactive thyroid, which is fairly common, especially among women, often causes depression and lethargy before any other signs lead to diagnosis.

Seaweed is among the foods credited with helping Japanese women to keep their legendary composure through life's changes. It contains phytonutrients called lignans, which work as a gentle form of hormone-replacement therapy. Eaten regularly, seaweed could help to reduce stress-inducing symptoms of the perimenopause, such as hot flashes. The plentiful nutrients found in sea vegetables could relieve sleeplessness. The calming effects of magnesium, in particular, might counteract insomnia, as well as ease anxiety. Along with calcium, it can also prevent the leg cramps and restlessness that keep many women awake at night after menopause.

Filled with mucilaginous gels that alkalinize the blood, seaweed can treat rheumatic complaints. It also helps to clear liver stagnation, treating PMS, headaches, and skin problems.

Agar-agar: Rich in trace minerals, agar-agar is used to soothe the digestive tract and relieve constipation. Its high fiber content helps to lower cholesterol and suppress the appetite, making it an ideal food for dieters. Its main culinary function is as a gelling agent.

Kombu: Laden with protein and minerals, such as calcium, magnesium, potassium, iodine, and iron, kombu improves the nutritional value of any meal. A substance in kombu called fucoidan has been found to make cancer cells self-destruct, and is now available as a nutritional supplement. Owing to kombu's excellent nutrient profile and cleansing abilities, it can offer relief in a range of health conditions from rheumatism, arthritis, and high blood pressure to an under-active thyroid.

Nori: Used in sushi-making, this "fishy"-tasting seaweed has been cultivated in Japan for more than 1,000 years. An excellent source of protein, nori helps with growth and tissue repair, and its calcium and iron content nourishes the bones and blood. Particularly high in beta-carotene, nori might help to promote skin health, boost the immune system, and slow down eye disease. It also contains vitamin B12, which is rarely found in the plant world, making it an ideal food for strict vegetarians.

Wakame: Traditionally added to miso soup, wakame is mild in flavor. It's an excellent source of potassium and might improve heart health by keeping high blood pressure in check. It's also an outstanding source of calcium, needed for bone maintenance, and magnesium for relieving stress and muscle tension. In Japan, wakame is used as a blood purifier and is also valued for its nourishing effect on the hair and skin.

Dulse: Full of potassium, which helps to relieve fluid retention, dulse is also the most iron-rich of the edible seaweeds, making it an excellent food for combating anemia. Like most sea vegetables, it's high in iodine, which is needed to regulate the thyroid gland.

Hijiki: High in minerals, hijiki is thought to play a contributory role to the thick, shiny hair enjoyed by many Japanese people. It's a superb bone-builder, containing more calcium than any other sea vegetable, and it might help prevent osteoporosis.

SEAWEED RICE

2 tbsp. wakame
2½ cups warm water
½ onion, chopped
2 large garlic cloves, minced
1 cup brown rice

Rinse the wakame, the soak in the warm water 5 minutes. Squeeze dry and chop. Save the water and heat 1 tablespoon in a pan. Simmer the onion slowly 2 minutes, stirring. Add all the other ingredients and the remaining water. Bring to a boil, then simmer 35 minutes. Serve.

LAVER CAKES

1 lb. laver or rehydrated cooked nori,
  chopped
1¾ cups oatmeal
1 tsp. ground black pepper
3 tbsp. vegetable oil
1 lb. portobello mushrooms

Mix together the laver, oatmeal, and pepper in a bowl. Using your hands, shape into 12 balls and flatten slightly to make cakes. Heat 2 tablespoons of the oil, add the laver cakes and fry 2 to 3 minutes. Brush the mushrooms with the remaining oil and broil until brown. Serve with the laver cakes.

WAKAME AND NOODLE BROTH

2 tbsp. sesame oil
1 garlic clove, crushed
2 celery ribs, trimmed and chopped
4 cups vegetable stock
1 tbsp. miso
2 carrots, peeled and diced
8 strips wakame, chopped
1¾oz. dried noodles

Put all the ingredients, except the noodles, in a large saucepan over high heat. Bring to a boil, stirring, until the miso dissolves. Simmer, covered, over low heat 30 minutes. Add the noodles and cook until they are cooked through and tender. Serve immediately.

REAL FRUIT JELLY

14 oz. soft fruits, such as grapes, peaches,
strawberries, seeded, stoned, or hulled,
as necessary, and chopped
2½ cups white grape juice
4 tbsp. agar-agar flakes

Place the chopped fruit in a large heatproof glass bowl and set aside. Put the grape juice and agar-agar in a saucepan, bring to a boil, then simmer a few minutes, stirring, until the agar-agar dissolves. Pour the liquid over the fruit and leave to cool. Once the set, store in the refrigerator.

MISO SOUP

4 tbsp. chopped dulse
2 tbsp. wakame
1-inch piece gingerroot, finely chopped
½ cup firm tofu cut into cubes
3 tbsp. miso

Pour 5 cups water into a saucepan over high heat. Add the seaweeds, ginger, and tofu and bring to a boil, then simmer 5 minutes. Stir in the miso and simmer 2 minutes longer, then serve.

CANNELLINI AND KOMBU BEANPOT

1 cup dried cannellini or haricot beans
1 strip dried kombu
½ leek, trimmed and chopped
½ red bell pepper, deseeded and chopped
7 oz, spinach leaves, chopped

Soak the beans overnight in plenty of cold water. Next day, drain, place in a saucepan, and cover with 4 cups water. Add the kombu, then bring to a boil and simmer, covered, about 2 hours until the beans are tender. Add the leek, red pepper, and spinach, and simmer 15 minutes longer until the beans and vegetables are tender. Mix well and serve.

KOMBU-TOMATO STOCK

1 strip dried kombu
6 sun-dried tomatoes in oil, drained

Soak the kombu and tomatoes in 4 cups water 30 minutes, then bring to a boil over high heat. Lower the heat and simmer 5 minutes. Remove the kombu and tomatoes. Use the liquid in any recipe that calls for stock. The kombu can be reused to make more stock or added to beans or casseroles during cooking to enhance the flavor.

NORI-POTATO FRITTERS

2 large potatoes, peeled and
  coarsely grated
1 onion, finely chopped
4 eggs
5 tbsp. nori flakes
1 tbsp. ground mustard seeds
olive oil, for shallow frying

Using your hands, squeeze as much
of the juice from the grated potatoes
as possible, then put them in a bowl.
Add the onion, eggs, nori, and
mustard seeds and mix together.
Warm the oil in a skillet, adding the
mixture when the oil is hot. Flatten
each fritter with a fork and cook
on both sides until golden brown.

SEA SALAD

3 tbsp. dulse, rinsed
2 handfuls mixed salad leaves
½ cucumber, peeled and chopped
1 scallion, trimmed and chopped
2 tbsp. sesame oil
1 tbsp. rice vinegar
1 tbsp. sesame seeds

Soak the dulse in water to cover
about 3 minutes, then drain and cut
it into pieces with scissors. Put
it in a large bowl along with the salad
leaves, cucumber, and scallion. Add
the sesame oil and rice vinegar, toss
well, and serve immediately sprinkled
with the sesame seeds.

SCRAMBLED EGGS WITH HIJIKI

heaping 2 tbsp. hijiki
1 tbsp. olive oil
4 eggs
6 cherry tomatoes, sliced
2 tbsp. finely chopped chives
1 tsp. ground mustard seeds
1 garlic clove, crushed
salt and ground black pepper,
  to taste

Soak the hijiki in water to cover
15 minutes, then drain and sauté
in the oil in a skillet about 8 minutes.
Meanwhile, beat the eggs in a bowl
and add the remaining ingredients.
Pour the mixture over the hijiki
and cook, stirring frequently, until
the eggs have thickened but are
still soft.

CRAMMED WITH PROTEIN,
THE BUILDING BLOCK
FOR OUR BONES, TISSUES,
AND TEETH, MEAT AND
DAIRY PRODUCTS KEEP US
STRONG AND HEALTHY

03 | wonder
MEAT & DAIRY

L a m b

VITAMINS B1, B2, B3, B6, B12; IRON, PHOSPHORUS, SELENIUM, SULFUR, ZINC; PROTEIN

A staple of Greek cuisine, lamb has valuable nutritious properties. Lean lamb is an excellent source of protein and easily absorbed iron.

Like other red meat, lamb is rich in protein, as well as being an excellent source of two vital minerals: iron and zinc. Iron helps to boost the oxygen-carrying capability of blood, preventing anemia and fatigue from setting in, while zinc is necessary for optimum functioning of the immune system, helping to fight colds, infections, and other invaders. According to the Chinese, eating lamb improves circulation, overcomes coldness, and might even treat postnatal depression.

Lamb is a rich source of B-vitamins, including vitamin B3, which is thought to stave off age-related memory problems, and vitamin B12, which helps in the production of red blood cells and plays an important role in cell metabolism. The meat is also rich in easily absorbed iron, which is fundamental for preventing anemia. The selenium in lamb protects the eyes from disease and the heart from muscle damage.

The high protein content in lamb, which is necessary to repair aging cells, helps to suppress the appetite for longer and prolongs satiety more than foods high in carbohydrate or fat. Lamb is also rich in sulfur, a mineral good for the hair and nails, and a key component of chondroitin sulfate, a complex molecule that gives cartilage the elastic, spongelike quality that joints need to act as shock absorbers between the bones.

LAMB KOFTA

1 lb. finely ground lamb
1 large onion, grated
1 tsp. salt
1 cup finely chopped parsley
¼ tsp. ground black pepper
1 tsp. ground allspice

Combine the ingredients and chill
1 hour. Divide the mixture into
8 equal portions and shape into balls,
then thread the balls onto skewers.
Cook under a preheated broiler until
brown on all sides.

LAMB SHANKS IN TOMATO-ORANGE SAUCE

oil, for greasing
4 lamb shanks
1¾ cups canned crushed tomatoes
1 cup plus 2 tbsp. water
1 tbsp. crushed garlic
juice and grated zest of 1 orange
2 tbsp. mint leaves,
  finely chopped

Lightly grease a large saucepan. Add
the lamb shanks and cook, turning
as needed, 10 minutes, or until lightly
brown all over. Add the tomatoes,
water, garlic, and orange juice and
zest to the pan. Cover and simmer
2 to 3 hours until the meat is tender.
Stir in the mint, then serve.

BAKED LAMB AND POTATO

1 lb. 2 oz. new potatoes
8 bay leaves
2 red onions, sliced
2 tbsp. olive oil
juice of 1 lemon
8 lamb loin chops
handful mint leaves, chopped

Preheat the oven to 425°F. Put the
potatoes, bay leaves, and onions
in a roasting pan. Sprinkle with
a little olive oil and the lemon juice,
cover with foil and roast 40 minutes.
Meanwhile, brown the chops on both
sides in the remaining oil in a skillet.
Remove the foil, add the chops and
mint, and roast 15 minutes longer,
or until the chops are as desired.

Beef

VITAMINS B1, B2, B3, B5, B6, B12; IRON, SULFUR, ZINC; CONJUGATED LINOLEIC ACID; PROTEIN

A popular meat for millennia in many ancient cultures, beef is a flavorful meat with many therapeutic attributes. It is particularly high in iron, which boosts the oxygen level in the blood.

Rich in protein, beef is also full of B-complex vitamins, including B1, B2, B3, B5, and B6, which collectively help to protect against chronic fatigue syndrome, weak digestion, eye disease, depression, and mood swings. It is also an excellent source of vitamin B12, which helps to prevent fatigue and protect against memory loss.

Beef is loaded with iron, which is needed for the production of red blood cells and staves off conditions such as anemia. Full of zinc to boost immunity and aid the healing of wounds, this flavorsome red meat also contains sulfur, which we need to maintain youthful hair and nails.

According to the Chinese, eating beef lifts body metabolism, treats hypoglycemia, and strengthens the bones. Organic beef is free from pesticides and contains conjugated linoleic acid (CLA), a fatty acid that has cancer-fighting properties and helps those trying to lose weight by stimulating the conversion of stored fat in the body into energy.

PEPPER STEAKS

4 filet mignons
2 tbsp. olive oil
6 tbsp. assorted cracked peppercorns
2 garlic cloves, crushed
3 tbsp. butter
salt and ground black pepper

Coat the steaks with the olive oil. Press down on the peppercorns with a knife, then press them into the steaks. Coat the steaks thoroughly with the garlic. Melt the butter in a large skillet. Cook the steaks over medium heat 3 to 4 minutes on each side. Season to taste with salt and pepper and serve.

Duck

VITAMINS B1, B2, B3, B6, B12; COPPER, IRON, PHOSPHORUS, SELENIUM, ZINC; PROTEIN

Duck is delicious roasted or stir-fried and is an excellent source of the stress-busting vitamin B2 and an energy-rich way for athletes to hit their daily protein target.

Ducks were first domesticated in China, where they are appreciated for their eggs. Today, duck is a popular and uniquely flavorsome variety of poultry as well as a wonderful source of immunity-boosting nutrients.

Although duck has a reputation as a fat-laden meat, its saturated fat content is five times lower when all the skin is removed—in fact, a skinless duck breast is leaner than a skinless chicken breast. Duck meat provides plenty of the protein and iron needed to repair body tissue and build new red blood cells, as well as phosphorus, necessary for strong bones. Its copper content is needed for healing wounds and for the formation of collagen and elastin, which keep the skin looking and feeling youthful, while its selenium helps to neutralize the aging effects of free radicals on the body.

Duck is high in a host of B-vitamins, which help to fight fatigue, regulate metabolism, and lift the mood. Eating duck will also help you to combat stress, as it contains the vitamin B2 and aids the production of infection-fighting immune cells.

DUCK STIR-FRY

1 red onion, finely chopped
1 tbsp. sesame oil
2 tbsp. soy sauce
4 Long Island duck breasts, skinned and cut into strips
2 carrots, peeled and cut into batons
4 oz. mung bean sprouts
juice and grated zest of 1 orange

Fry the onion in a wok in the oil and soy sauce. Add the duck breast strips and carrots and fry 5 minutes, then add the bean sprouts and orange juice and zest and cook 1 minute longer. Serve immediately.

Turkey

VITAMINS B2, B3, B5, B6, B12, D, BIOTIN, FOLIC ACID; CALCIUM, IODINE, IRON, MAGNESIUM, PHOSPHORUS, POTASSIUM, SELENIUM, TRYPTOPHAN; ZINC; PROTEIN

One of the leanest forms of animal protein, this traditional festive food makes a healthy everyday alternative to other meat and poultry.

Turkey is rich in immunity-fortifying zinc in a form that is easy for the body to use. It also contains a significant amount of selenium, which is usually found only in small amounts in many foods. This mineral helps to repair cell DNA and lower the risk of cancer. The meat is also a good source of anemia-preventing iron.

Turkey is dense in B-vitamins, which are crucial for normal metabolism and necessary for maintaining a healthy nervous system. They are vital for keeping down levels of homocysteine, a toxic substance in the blood formed as a breakdown product of amino acids and linked with heart disease. Turkey is an excellent source of tryptophan, which boosts immunity, as well as helping in the treatment of insomnia.

Research shows turkey contains one of the highest concentrations of muscle-building dipeptides. In tests, athletes who regularly eat five-ounce portions of turkey breast meat show an increase of 40 percent in muscle concentration. Their performance improves greatly, especially for runners, rowers, cyclists, and speed skaters.

DELUXE TURKEY SANDWICH *serves 1*

½ avocado

2 slices wholegrain bread

fresh spinach leaves

2 cooked turkey slices

1 scallion, trimmed and finely chopped

1 tomato, sliced

a little whole grain mustard (optional)

Scoop out the avocado flesh and spread over the bread like butter. Layer the spinach and turkey slices on one slice and top with the scallion, tomato, and mustard, if desired. Sandwich together and eat immediately.

TURKEY AND PEPPER BURRITOS

2 turkey breast halves, diced

1 red onion, chopped

1 red bell pepper, seeded and cut into
    strips

1 tbsp. sunflower oil

6 tbsp. store-bought salsa

4 large flour tortillas

handful grated cheese, such as cheddar

Preheat the oven to 350°F. Stir-fry the turkey, onion, and pepper in the oil 5 to 6 minutes. Add the salsa and heat through. Warm the tortillas in the oven, then place the mixture in the middle of each. Roll them up and place them seam-side down on a baking sheet. Top with the cheese and bake 10 to 12 minutes until it melts, then serve.

TURKEY SCHNITZEL

4 turkey breast halves, about 6 oz. each,
    flattened

3 tbsp. all-purpose flour

1 extra-large egg, beaten

4 cups cornflakes, finely crushed

green salad, to serve

Preheat the oven to 350°F. Coat the turkey pieces lightly in the flour, shaking off any excess. Dip them in the egg and then coat in the cornflakes. Place the turkey breasts on a baking sheet, then bake 25 minutes, or until the juices run clear when you pierce a piece. Serve hot with a green salad.

Chicken

Vitamins A, B2, B3, B6, B12, K; iron, magnesium, phosphorus, potassium, selenium, sodium, zinc; lysine; tryptophan; protein

This hugely versatile and popular meat has a host of health-boosting properties. Dating back to the ancient Egyptians in the fourteenth century BC, chicken has become an everyday food full of goodness.

A useful source of protein, and low fat if the skin is removed, chicken contributes to the growth and repair of all the body's cells. The meat is a good source of B-complex vitamins, which also help to regulate metabolism, and is rich in absorbable iron and zinc—with twice as much in the dark meat as in the breast—fighting anemia and boosting immunity, while the breast is particularly high in vitamin B6, which protects the heart and fights premenstrual syndrome. Chicken's vitamin B3 and B6 content also help to maintain a healthy nervous system and work together to make the most of food's energizing potential.

Chicken contains magnesium to help reduce the risk of cramps during exercise, and potassium to balance the fluid levels in the body, as well as selenium, which helps to prevent wrinkles and keep hair glossy, and zinc to bolster immunity. Zinc is also known to have energy-boosting properties. In addition, chicken has the antiviral amino acid lysine, helpful for suppressing the cold-sore virus.

Another nutrient found in chicken is tryptophan, an essential amino acid that helps to control the brain's serotonin levels, which are linked to appetite and mood. Chicken promotes circulation and invigorates the kidneys, thus treating diarrhea and edema. Made into a soup, chicken is known to be soothing and restorative. Chicken soup is an effective remedy for colds and infections of the upper respiratory tract.

A high intake of saturated fats increases the risk of heart disease and piles on the pounds, significantly slowing an athlete down. Lean meat is a top choice for anyone doing regular exercise, and chicken is one of the leanest, as long as you resist eating the skin. Always buy organic chicken, which is now widely available, as it offers all the nutritional benefits without the possible drug residues.

ZESTY CHICKEN CASSEROLE

3 tbsp. olive oil

2 onions, sliced

8 skinless chicken thighs

1 tbsp. all-purpose flour, seasoned with
a little salt and pepper

1¼ cups vegetable stock

grated zest of 1 orange

juice of 2 oranges

⅔ cup white wine

5 portobello mushrooms, sliced

hot cooked rice, to serve

Heat 2 tablespoons of olive oil in a skillet. Add the onions and sauté 10 minutes, then transfer to a plate. Toss the chicken in the flour, heat the remaining oil, and fry the chicken until brown. Add the stock, onions, orange zest and juice, and white wine. Bring to a boil, reduce heat to low, cover, and simmer 25 minutes. Stir in the mushrooms and cook 5 minutes longer. Serve with rice.

GRANDMA'S CHICKEN SOUP

2¼ quarts chicken broth

6 garlic cloves, minced

1-inch piece gingerroot, peeled and cut
into 2 or 3 chunks

8 oz. skinless, boneless chicken breast
meat, diced

4 scallions, trimmed and chopped

Bring the broth, garlic, and ginger to a boil in a large saucepan, then lower the heat and simmer 10 minutes. Add the chicken and simmer 5 to 7 minutes. Discard the ginger. Top with the onions to serve.

SWEET-AND-SOUR CHICKEN DRUMSTICKS

8 chicken drumsticks, skinned

4 tbsp. honey

2 tbsp. sesame oil

6 tbsp. soy sauce

4 tbsp. lemon juice

4 tsp. whole grain mustard

Preheat the oven to 400°F. Put the drumsticks in a baking dish and pierce with a fork. Mix the honey, sesame oil, soy sauce, lemon juice, and mustard together, then pour over the chicken. Cook 20 to 25 minutes. Serve hot or cold.

EASY MARINATED CHICKEN

3 tbsp. soy sauce

3 tbsp. rice wine or sherry

1 tsp. sugar

2 garlic cloves, crushed

1 lb. chicken breasts, cut into

    bite-size pieces

Mix together the soy sauce, rice wine, sugar, and garlic. Place the chicken in a nonmetallic dish, pour the marinade over, cover, and refrigerate 2 hours, turning occasionally. Cook as desired until the juices run clear.

BALSAMIC-BARBECUED CHICKEN

6 tbsp. balsamic vinegar

2 tbsp. sunflower oil

1 tsp. Dijon mustard

1 tsp. honey

½ tsp. salt

1 tsp. ground black pepper

8 large chicken drumsticks

Mix the vinegar, oil, mustard, honey, salt, and pepper together. Coat the drumsticks, then chill in a shallow nonmetallic dish 2 hours, turning occasionally. Meanwhile, heat the barbecue coals. Grill the chicken 15 to 20 minutes, turning every 5 minutes, until cooked through and the juices run clear. Serve hot or at room temperature.

Live yogurt

VITAMINS A, B2, B3, B5, B12, C, D, BIOTIN, FOLIC ACID; CALCIUM, IODINE, IRON, MAGNESIUM, MOLYBDENUM, PHOSPHORUS, POTASSIUM, SELENIUM, SODIUM, ZINC; PROTEIN; BACTERIA CULTURES

Also known as probiotic or bio yogurt, live yogurt is an immune-system savior, positively brimming with "friendly" bacteria and many health-promoting nutrients.

Live yogurt contains health-boosting lactobacillus and bifida bacteria. A healthy gut should be teeming with these, but stress, antibiotics, and a poor diet can allow "unfriendly" bacteria to take over. Eating one pot of live yogurt a day can help redress the balance, aiding the body to fight off infections, as well as allowing the gut to absorb other immunity-boosting nutrients efficiently. Yogurt also stimulates the production of antiviral agents, which enhance immune response and help to ward off cancer.

Live yogurt can help to prevent constipation and alleviate the bloating, gas, and vaginal thrush often caused by an overgrowth of candida yeast, which produces itching, burning, and other uncomfortable symptoms. It can also avert antibiotic-related diarrhea and keep invading organisms in check, and it is thought to offer some relief from stomach ulcers. Some studies have found that the probiotics present in yogurt produce enzymes that are absorbed directly through the gut wall, which farther strengthens the body's immune defenses.

Live yogurt has a high calcium content, as well as traces of vitamin D, which help us to absorb calcium. It also contains other bone-building minerals, such as magnesium and phosphorus. Eating it regularly reduces the risk of developing the bone-thinning condition, osteoporosis.

YOGURT WITH NUTS AND HONEY

1¾ cups plain yogurt
handful walnut halves
4 tbsp. honey
4 tbsp. almonds

Mix the yogurt with the walnuts in a bowl. Drizzle the honey in a spiral around the top. Sprinkle with the almonds, then serve.

SEEDED APPLE YOGURT   *serves 1*

⅔ cup plain yogurt

2 tbsp. sunflower seeds

1 green apple, cored and seeded

Chop the apple into bite-size chunks and place in a small bowl. Spoon the yogurt over the top, then sprinkle with the seeds and eat immediately. This can be enjoyed as a breakfast or as a snack at any time of the day.

*YOGURT AND EVENING PRIMROSE FACE MASK

for revitalizing & replenishing tired skin

2 capsules evening primrose oil

2 capsules vitamin E oil

3 tbsp. plain yogurt

1 tsp. honey

2 tbsp. potato flour

Extract the oil from the capsules and combine it in a bowl with the other ingredients. Add extra potato flour to achieve the desired consistency, if necessary. Apply the mask evenly to the face and leave approximately 20 minutes. Wash off with water and pat dry. Repeat the process each evening, as desired.

LASSI

1 cup plus 2 tbsp. plain yogurt

2½ cups cold water

1 tsp. cumin seeds

½ tsp. salt

½ tsp. finely chopped mint leaves

Put all the ingredients in a blender and whiz a few seconds, or until well mixed. Serve cold.

AMBROSIA FRUIT SALAD *serves 2*

2 tbsp. slivered almonds

2 tbsp. shredded coconut

7 oz. canned crushed pineapple, drained

1 banana, chopped

1 cup cherries, pitted

6 tbsp. live yogurt

2 tbsp. pure maple syrup

1 tsp. cinnamon

½ tsp. ground nutmeg

Toast the almonds and coconut in a dry skillet for a few minutes, then transfer to a bowl and leave to cool. Add the fruit and yogurt and mix together so all the ingredients are well combined. Spoon into individual dessert bowls, top with the maple syrup, cinnamon, and nutmeg, and serve.

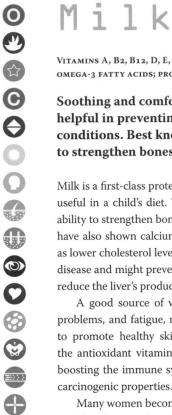

Milk

VITAMINS A, B2, B12, D, E, K; CALCIUM, IODINE, PHOSPHORUS, POTASSIUM; OMEGA-3 FATTY ACIDS; PROTEIN

Soothing and comforting, milk provides liquid nutrition helpful in preventing and treating a great many conditions. Best known for its calcium content, it helps to strengthen bones and fight off heart disease.

Milk is a first-class protein, providing building blocks that are especially useful in a child's diet. The abundance of calcium in milk gives it the ability to strengthen bones and to help to stave off osteoporosis. Studies have also shown calcium might help to reduce blood pressure, as well as lower cholesterol levels. Its potassium content is key in fighting heart disease and might prevent strokes, and it might contain substances that reduce the liver's production of cholesterol and lower blood pressure.

A good source of vitamin B12, which combats memory, hearing problems, and fatigue, milk also contains vitamin B2, which is known to promote healthy skin and good vision. Another of its nutrients, the antioxidant vitamin E, also benefits the skin and eyes, as well as boosting the immune system. Skim milk is also believed to have anti-carcinogenic properties.

Many women become irritable, forgetful, or depressed just before a period starts—the well-known symptoms of premenstrual syndrome (PMS). A glass of milk can be the simplest remedy, as it contains many nutrients that can lift and stabilize mood. It's rich in calcium and vitamin D, which together have been found to reduce or even prevent PMS symptoms. Cold milk can also be useful when you need to stay awake, because it triggers the brain's production of dopamine and norepinephrine, two substances that keep you alert.

As with other animal foods, it's best to buy organic milk. This has been found to contain up to 70 percent more omega-3 oils than ordinary milk, helping the brain to function at optimal efficiency.

Studies show drinking chocolate milk improves endurance more than conventional carbohydrate-only sports drinks, because it contains the ideal ratio of carbohydrates to protein to help refuel tired muscles. Try a homemade milkshake, a smoothie, or a cup of cocoa within two hours of exercise. The body converts these postexercise calories into glycogen to deliver carbohydrate straight to fuel-depleted muscles.

---

*MILK AND HONEY BATH LOTION
to nourish the skin

2 eggs	In a bowl, beat together the eggs and
3 tbsp. carrier oil	oil. Add the other ingredients, mix
⅔ cup milk	and pour into a glass bottle. Add
2 tsp. honey	2 to 3 tablespoons to bath water.
2 tsp. shampoo	Keep the remaining lotion chilled
1 tbsp. vodka	and use within 3 or 4 days.

BEDTIME MILK *serves 2*

2¼ cups milk	Gently heat the milk, saffron, and
tiny pinch saffron	honey in a pan, stirring until the
2 tbsp. honey	honey dissolves. Pour into cups,
1 tsp. ground nutmeg	sprinkle with the spices, and serve.
½ tsp. cinnamon	

CEREAL SOOTHER

scant 4 cups wholegrain breakfast cereal	Mix together the cereal and the
4 tbsp. sunflower seeds	seeds in a bowl. Divide between four
2 bananas, sliced	bowls, top with the bananas, and
1 cup skim or 1% milk	pour the milk over the top. Serve
	immediately while still crunchy.

Egg

Vitamins A, B2, B3, B5, B6, B12, D, E, K, biotin, choline, folic acid, lutein, zeaxanthin; calcium, chromium, copper, iodine, iron, lecithin, magnesium, manganese, molybdenum, phosphorus, potassium, selenium, sodium, zinc; omega-3 essential fatty acids; protein

The perfect complete protein, these little capsules of nutrition are an excellent low-fat, slow-release energy food, stabilizing blood sugar levels and keeping hunger pangs at bay. Low in fat and extremely versatile, eggs contain all the essential amino acids needed for peak fitness, staving off aging and boosting brain power.

Eggs are a superb source of B-vitamins, zinc, iron, and phospholipids—fats required for cell membranes and a healthy brain. They're also one of the few nonmeat sources of vitamin A, which supports vision; vitamin D, which we need for healthy bones; and B12, which aids many of the body's processes. The vitamin E contained in eggs is a powerful antioxidant, which thins the blood, benefits the heart, and fights harmful free radicals. They also contain omega-3 fats and a B-vitamin called choline, both of which are required for normal brain function, and lutein, which can help to reduce the risk of eye disease. Moreover, eggs are rich in vitamin K, which helps to heal bruises and minor sports injuries by making sure blood is able to clot normally, so it can also reduce the danger of blood clots in arteries. In addition, eggs are a valuable source of selenium, which rejuvenates the immune system and protects the heart.

Low in saturated fats and high in protein, eggs have been shown by research to improve brain function. It is thought their high lecithin content not only enhances memory and the ability to concentrate but also promotes a healthy emotional state. Egg yolk is the richest known source of choline, the B-vitamin that makes up cell membranes, helping the body to convert fats to acetylcholine, an important memory molecule needed in the brain.

Eggs are a concentrated source of muscle-building amino acids and other body-building nutrients. Their high zinc content boosts immunity and is beneficial for liver function, as well as tissue repair and healing. It is also vital for the production of collagen, which is needed for healthy, youthful skin. Because eggs contain all eight essential amino acids, thus helping to make up the building blocks for the entire body, they benefit everything from skin to hair, and bones to muscles.

Many of us worry about the apparently high cholesterol content of eggs, but studies suggest this might be unfounded as the cholesterol in eggs doesn't circulate in the blood. In fact, of the 5g fat contained in an egg, most is monounsaturated, which is the type that helps to lower the risk of heart disease. The nutritional value of eggs has been found to vary, so it is best to choose the organic free-range variety, which contain more vitamins and good fats than eggs laid by battery hens.

---

*EGG YOLK MASK *to nourish dry skin*

1 tbsp. honey
1 extra-large egg yolk
1 tsp. potato flour

In a bowl, combine the honey, egg yolk, and potato flour, stirring to create a fine paste. Apply evenly to your face and neck and leave about 20 minutes. Rinse off with cotton balls and water, then pat dry. Repeat 2 or 3 times a week, making a fresh mask for each treatment.

SMOKED SALMON WITH SCRAMBLED EGGS

6 eggs
1 tsp. olive oil
3 oz. smoked salmon
4 tbsp. chopped dill or chives
salt and ground black pepper, to taste
lemon wedges, to serve

Beat the eggs with salt and pepper. Heat the oil in a skillet, then add the eggs and fry, stirring all the time, until just cooked. Pile on plates with the smoked salmon, sprinkle with the herbs and garnish with lemon wedges and more black pepper.

LEEK AND PEPPER OMELET

1 tbsp. peanut oil
1 leek, trimmed and finely chopped
1 sweet bell pepper, seeded and diced
4 eggs
salt and ground black pepper

Heat the oil and slowly fry the leek 2 to 3 minutes until half cooked. Add the pepper and cook 2 minutes longer, then remove the vegetables with a slotted spoon and set aside. Beat the eggs in a bowl and add 2 tablespoons cold water. Season well, then pour the egg mixture into the pan. Add the vegetables and cook about 5 minutes until the egg is set.

POTATO FRITTATA

3 cups peeled and diced potatoes
1 tbsp. olive oil
4 eggs, beaten
1 tbsp. soy sauce
5 tbsp. chopped parsley leaves
ground black pepper. to taste

Preheat the broiler to high. Steam the potatoes 15 minutes, or until tender. Transfer to a ovenproof skillet greased with the olive oil. Stir the remaining ingredients together and pour into the skillet. Cook 3 to 4 minutes until the underside is set. Place the pan under the broiler until the top is golden and set.

FROM HUMBLE SARDINES
TO LUXURIOUS OYSTERS,
FISH AND SEAFOOD OFFER
A WEALTH OF BENEFITS
IN TANTALIZING TASTES
AND TEXTURES

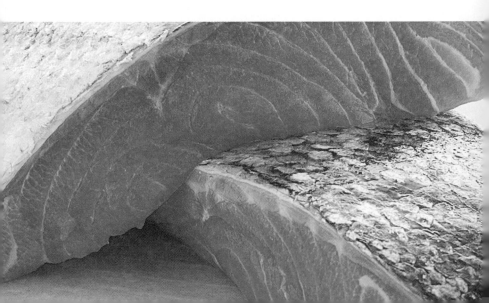

04 | wonder FISH

Tuna

VITAMINS B1, B3, B6, B12, D, E; IODINE, MAGNESIUM, PHOSPHORUS, POTASSIUM, SELENIUM, SODIUM; OMEGA-3 FATTY ACIDS; PROTEIN; TRYPTOPHAN

A member of the mackerel family, tuna is rich in healthy oils and immunity-boosting minerals.

Popular sources of protein, such as meat and hard cheese, are often high in fat. Yet, high-protein foods keep you going longer before flagging energy levels send you in search of a snack. Tuna is an excellent high-protein, low-fat option, providing more protein than even the healthiest meat. Lean sources of protein are key for anyone who's physically active, as they prevent slumps in energy without sending your calorie intake soaring. The best choices are albacore, skipjack, or yellowfin tuna.

Like other oily fish, fresh tuna is exceptionally rich in omega-3 fatty acids, which play an important role in energy production and helping to burn excess fat. Among their many other benefits, omega-3s stimulate the production of leptin, a hormone that controls the appetite. Essential fatty acids can help to prevent heart disease, cancer, and depression and support the immune system. They are also anti-inflammatory, calming conditions such as rheumatoid arthritis and eczema.

Tuna contains vitamin E and selenium, which are needed for the production of disease-fighting antibodies, and many B-vitamins, which boost energy levels.

TUNA NIÇOISE

juice of 1 lemon
½ tsp. salt
1 tsp. Dijon mustard
5 tbsp. olive oil
a pinch of ground black pepper
4 tuna steaks
4 potatoes, cooked and sliced
4 oz. green beans, cooked
4 oz. mixed salad greens
4 tomatoes, cut into segments
handful black olives

Whisk together the lemon juice, salt, mustard, olive oil, and black pepper. Place the tuna steaks on a large plate and coat in the vinaigrette mixture. Cover and refrigerate 1 hour. Meanwhile, preheat the broiler. Broil the tuna steaks 4 to 6 minutes, or until cooked as desired. Combine all the vegetables in a bowl and drizzle the remaining vinaigrette over. Top with the tuna and serve.

BAKED TUNA

4 fresh tuna steaks
ground black pepper, to taste
3 tbsp. olive oil
2 onions, chopped
½ cup dry white wine
4 tomatoes, chopped

Preheat the oven to 425°F. Put the tuna in a baking dish and rub with pepper and 1 tablespoon of the oil. Heat the remaining oil in a skillet over medium heat and sauté the onions 3 to 5 minutes until soft. Add the wine and tomatoes, and bring to a boil. Pour over the tuna and bake 15 minutes, or until cooked through as desired. Serve immediately.

TUNA WITH SALSA

4 fresh tuna steaks
2 tomatoes, chopped
2 red onions, finely diced
2 tbsp. finely chopped chives
1 tbsp. chopped parsley leaves
2 tsp. red wine vinegar

Broil the tuna 3 minutes on each side. Meanwhile, mix together the tomatoes, onions, chives, parsley, and vinegar in a bowl. Place the tuna on four plates, spoon some salsa next to each steak, and serve immediately.

Salmon

VITAMINS A, B1, B2, B3, B5, B6, B12, D, E, BIOTIN, FOLIC ACID; CALCIUM,
IODINE, IRON, MAGNESIUM, PHOSPHORUS, POTASSIUM, SELENIUM, ZINC;
OMEGA-3 FATTY ACIDS, DIMETHYLAMINOETHENOL, DOCOSAHEXAENOIC ACID,
EICOSAPENTAENOIC ACID; PROTEIN; TRYPTOPHAN

Containing a wealth of omega-3 fatty acids, vitamins, and minerals, salmon is essential to a good diet.

Being an oily fish, salmon is an excellent source of omega-3 fatty acids in the form of eicosapentaenoic acid (EPA) and docosahexaenoic acid (DHA), which counteract many of the effects of aging and help to reduce postexercise joint stiffness. The DHA is especially important for the brain and nervous system, keeping the memory working well, and is believed to boost intelligence in children. By preserving brain and cell functions, the fatty acids protect against numerous diseases including cancers, stroke, and dementia. They regulate the activity of white blood cells and exhibit anti-inflammatory properties.

Omega-3 fatty acids also help to control cholesterol and fat levels, thereby protecting the cardiovascular system and reducing the risk of heart disease. They aid blood flow through the arteries, prevent arrhythmia, lower blood pressure and make the blood less likely to clot. Essential fatty acids are also good for keeping the skin and hair youthful, and for combatting skin conditions, such as psoriasis and eczema.

Salmon provides plenty of low-fat protein, making it a wonderful food for regular exercisers and athletes, who need a plentiful supply of protein to help recovery time after training and to build up their muscles and stamina.

This fish contains many antioxidants, including vitamin A, which helps to keep the blood and nervous systems healthy; vitamin D, which aids calcium absorption and is good for general bone health; and selenium, a powerful antioxidant mineral, that also helps to produce antibodies and boosts immunity.

It is advisable to buy wild rather than farmed salmon to maximize the benefits from eating this flavorsome fish. Wild salmon is rich in astaxanthin, one of the most potent antioxidants ever discovered.

SALMON FISH CAKES *serves 2*

2 small skinless and boneless salmon fillets
4 small potatoes, peeled and chopped
1 onion, finely chopped
2 tbsp. olive oil
1 egg, beaten
handful parsley leaves, chopped

Bake or steam the salmon until it is cooked through as desired. Meanwhile, boil and mash the potatoes. Sauté the onion in 1 tablespoon of the oil until soft. Mix all the ingredients, except the remaining oil, then form into 8 fish cakes and chill 1 hour. Slowly fry the fish cakes in the remaining oil until crisp on both sides. Serve hot.

SIZZLING SALMON

1 lb. 2 oz. boneless salmon fillet
½ tsp. crushed dried chilies
¼ tsp. paprika
4 tsp. olive oil
salt and ground black pepper
4 tsp. chopped cilantro leaves,
* to serve*

Cut the salmon into 4 equal pieces. Place skin-side down on a ridged grill pan, sprinkle with the chilies, paprika, and oil, and season with salt and pepper. Add to the pan and cook 6 to 8 minutes until cooked through. Sprinkle the salmon with the cilantro. Serve immediately.

SALMON PATTIES

½ cup long-grain rice

1 egg

1 garlic clove

1 onion, halved

2 tsp. sunflower oil, plus extra for frying

1 lb. 2 oz. salmon fillets, skinned and
    chopped

1 tbsp. chopped parsley leaves

In a saucepan, bring 1 cup water
to a boil. Add the rice, reduce the
heat, and simmer 10 minutes. Drain
the rice and leave to cool. In a food
processor, purée the egg, garlic,
onion, and oil. Mix these ingredients
with the rice, salmon, and parsley,
then form into 8 patties. Fry
in batches in the oil 4 to 5 minutes
on each side. Serve immediately.

WATERCRESS SALMON STEAKS

4 salmon steaks

4 tsp. extra virgin olive oil

juice of 1 lemon

a bunch watercress, chopped

4 tbsp. mayonnaise

1 tsp. hot pepper sauce (optional)

salt and ground black pepper

Put the salmon on a broiler pan. Drizzle 1 teaspoon of olive oil and lemon over each. Broil each side under medium heat 5 minutes. Put the watercress, mayonnaise, and remaining lemon juice in a blender and whiz until smooth. Season and add the hot pepper sauce, if using. Spoon over the salmon and serve.

SALMON IN GRAPE SAUCE

2 tsp. mustard

2 tsp. dried thyme

2 tsp. honey

4 salmon fillets

1 tbsp. olive oil

8 oz. seedless red grapes, halved

½ cup red wine

Preheat the oven to 300°F. Mix together the mustard, thyme, and honey and rub onto the fish. Heat half the oil in a skillet and brown the salmon on both sides. Transfer to a greased baking sheet and bake 10 minutes. Heat the remaining oil in the pan and fry the grapes 2 minutes. Add the wine, bring to a boil, and reduce by half. Pour over the salmon and serve immediately.

BAKED SALMON WITH CAPER AND TOMATO DRESSING

4 salmon fillets

2 tbsp. olive oil, plus extra for greasing

1 tbsp. capers, drained and chopped

4 cherry tomatoes, chopped

1 shallot, chopped

1 tbsp. lemon juice

Preheat the oven to 400°F. Put each fillet on a piece of greased aluminum foil. Combine the other ingredients in a bowl, then spoon over the fillets. Fold the foil to form parcels. Bake on a baking sheet 10 minutes, or until cooked through. Serve immediately.

Sardine

VITAMINS B3, B6, D, E; CALCIUM, IODINE, IRON, PHOSPHORUS, POTASSIUM, SELENIUM, ZINC; OMEGA-3 ESSENTIAL FATTY ACIDS; PROTEIN

Fresh and canned sardines contain a host of age-defying and health-promoting fatty acids and antioxidants.

Some of the most beneficial nutrients for keeping our skin looking young and radiant are omega-3 fatty acids, and sardines are an excellent source. Research suggests they might also help to protect the skin against sun exposure and ultraviolet radiation. The benefits of omega-3 fats, however, are more than skin-deep. Several studies show they help to make the blood less liable to clot and so reduce the risk of heart disease. They also keep the eyes healthy and boost brain function.

Packed with protein, iron, and zinc, sardines are exceptionally rich in calcium. Being one of the few nondairy sources of easily absorbable calcium makes them a first-rate food for athletes. Sardines are also an excellent source of vitamin D, which is vital for healthy bones because it increases the body's ability to absorb calcium. In addition, sardines are high in selenium, a powerful antioxidant that helps to prevent wrinkles and heart disease. Selenium is anticarcinogenic and neutralizes toxic metals in the body.

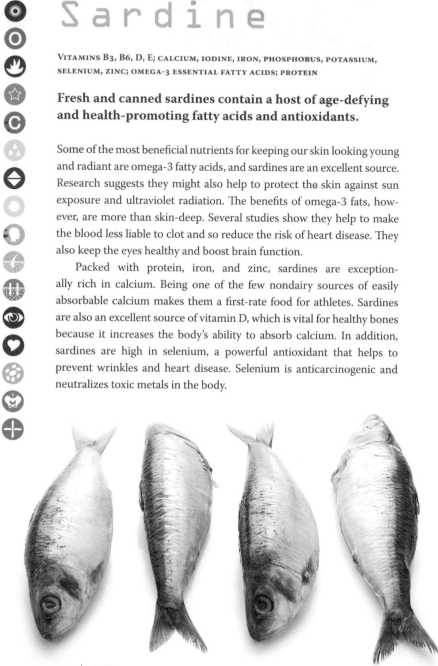

BROILED SARDINES WITH SALSA VERDE

2 large onions, chopped

2 garlic cloves, peeled

2 large green bell peppers, seeded and chopped

½ cup extra virgin olive oil

2 oz. canned anchovies, drained

2 small green chilies, seeded

juice and grated zest of 2 lemons

2 tbsp. capers, drained

8 tbsp. chopped basil leaves

4 tbsp. chopped parsley leaves

12 fresh sardines

In a saucepan, gently fry the onion, garlic, and peppers with half the oil. Put in a food processor with the anchovies, chilies, lemon juice and zest, capers, and herbs and whiz into a chunky purée. Broil the sardines on foil under a preheated broiler 5 to 7 minutes on each side. Place the sardines on a serving plate, drizzle with the salsa, and serve.

JAPANESE SARDINES

1 lb. sardines, washed and dried

½ cup soy sauce

4 tbsp. white wine vinegar

juice and zest of 1 lime

1 lemon grass stem, chopped

1-inch piece gingerroot, peeled and chopped

2 garlic cloves, crushed

1 tsp. cayenne pepper

Arrange the sardines in a shallow, nonmetallic dish. Mix together the remaining ingredients in a bowl and pour over the sardines, then cover and refrigerate 3 hours. Meanwhile, preheat the broiler to high. Discard the marinade and broil the sardines, turning once, 5 minutes on each side, or until the flesh flakes. Serve immediately.

Shrimp

VITAMINS B3, B12; CALCIUM, IODINE, MAGNESIUM, PHOSPHORUS, POTASSIUM, SELENIUM, SODIUM, ZINC; PROTEIN

The world's most popular and versatile crustaceans, immunity-boosting shrimp work well in sandwiches, salads, stir-fries, and seafood stews.

Shrimp are a great source of protein, which is necessary for building healthy bones and muscles, as well as for boosting energy. They are rich in vitamin B3, which is crucial for preserving the memory, and vitamin B12, which promotes brain function and prevents fatigue.

Shrimp contain high levels of immune-essential minerals, including zinc, which we need to produce the enzymes that keep cancer at bay, and to help to develop other disease-fighting cells. This mineral also boosts fertility. Shrimp also contain selenium, a potent antioxidant mineral that helps in the production of antibodies and improves the efficiency of white blood cells at recognizing unwanted invaders, as well as fighting off wrinkles. In addition, shrimp supply iodine, which is vital for the proper functioning of the thyroid gland, and calcium and phosphorus for strong bones. Phosphorus also regulates red blood cell metabolism.

Shrimp are a particularly good food for athletes, and sportsmen and -women. They are loaded with vital minerals, including potassium, magnesium and sodium, that all help balance the body's water levels and restore the electrolyte balance after a session of exercise or a sport's game. As shrimp are higher in sodium content than most food (although not in harmful levels), they can also help to prevent the mineral imbalance that can result from drinking too much water during an energetic workout.

SHRIMP WITH BELL PEPPER SAUCE

4 red bell peppers, seeded and chopped
1 tomato, chopped
2 garlic cloves, crushed
2 tbsp. chopped parsley leaves
1 tbsp. white wine vinegar
1 lb. 12 oz. shelled cooked shrimp
1 iceberg lettuce

Place the peppers on a baking sheet and bake 10 minutes, or until soft. Mix together in a bowl with the tomato, garlic, parsley, and vinegar. Shred the lettuce and divide among four bowls. Place a few shrimp in each bowl and top with the pepper mixture.

SHRIMP PÂTÉ

1 lb. shelled cooked shrimp
3 tbsp. butter
3 tbsp. cream cheese
1 tbsp. sour cream
2 drops hot pepper sauce
½ tsp. ground nutmeg
1 garlic clove, crushed
1 tbsp. lemon juice
salt and ground black pepper

Put all the shrimp, except one, in a blender with all the other ingredients and whiz until smooth. Place the pâté in a serving dish and decorate with the whole shrimp. Cover and chill at least 2 hours, then serve with French bread or hot toast.

SHRIMP AND BULGAR WHEAT

heaping 1 cup bulgar wheat
2¼ cups hot vegetable stock
1 red onion, finely diced
14 oz. shelled cooked shrimp
2 handfuls basil leaves, chopped

Place the bulgar wheat in a pan, pour the stock over, and let sit 30 minutes. Stir in the raw onion, shrimp, and basil, then serve.

Oyster

Vitamins A, B3, B12, C, D, E; calcium, copper, iodine, iron, magnesium, potassium, selenium, zinc; omega-3 fatty acids; protein

Oysters are a type of shellfish that is not only a renowned aphrodisiac, but is also full of health-promoting vitamins, minerals, and other nutrients.

A versatile food, oysters can be cooked in many ways, including roasting, baking, broiling, frying, stewing, boiling, and steaming. They are also available canned, smoked, and pickled. Oysters are, however, traditionally eaten raw with a pinch of salt or a dash of lemon juice.

The nutritional value of oysters and their flavor and texture can vary according to the type of water in which they grow, and they are affected by factors such as salinity levels and mineral content.

A great source of energy for athletes, oysters are an excellent form of low-fat protein. They are loaded with vitamin E, which is also good for the skin and for preventing heart disease, as well as conditions such as arthritis. The shellfish are a very rich, low-fat source of omega-3 fatty acids, which are vital for heart health and make us feel happier and livelier by supporting the brain's healthy functioning.

Oysters are also full of B-vitamins, essential to mind and mood, including B12, which helps to fight fatigue. They are an excellent source of the mineral iodine, vital for the proper functioning of the thyroid gland, which, if underactive, can lead to debilitating bouts of exhaustion. These shellfish also contain vitamin D, which is needed for healthy bones and teeth, as well as potassium and iron, which combat anemia. In Chinese medicine, shellfish supplement the liver and kidneys, and treat insomnia, restlessness, and agitation.

Packed with nutrients, oysters act as a general health tonic as well as enhancing sexual well-being. They have a well-documented affinity with the reproductive system. Research also indicates that certain sterols are present in oysters, from which the sex hormones are derived. They are used regularly by Chinese women to increase estrogen in their body, and are useful for infertility and for treating menopausal disorders.

Oysters are a rich natural source of nutrients, including zinc—just six raw oysters provide excellent amounts of this important nutrient. Zinc is essential for the production of sperm, and restores libido to people who don't enjoy sex any more. When the body is short of vital nutrients, sex is low on the list of functions it needs to maintain. Zinc also helps to boost immunity, maintain youthful skin, and prevent hair loss.

OYSTERS AU PARMESAN

1 cup fresh breadcrumbs

1 tbsp. butter, plus extra for greasing

36 fresh oysters, shelled

½ cup chopped fresh parsley leaves

1 cup freshly grated Parmesan cheese

½ cup white wine

salt and cayenne pepper

Preheat the oven to 350°F. In a pan, brown the breadcrumbs in the butter, reserving 1 tablespoon of the crumbs. Grease a shallow baking dish, then dust with the fried breadcrumbs. Season the oysters with salt and cayenne and place them on top of the breadcrumbs. Scatter the parsley and Parmesan over, followed by the reserved breadcrumbs. Pour the wine over the entire dish. Bake 15 minutes, or until golden brown and bubbling. Serve hot.

OYSTER BISQUE

24 fresh oysters, shelled
2 cups vegetable stock
4 cups milk
1 cup light cream
salt and white pepper, to taste
1 tbsp. potato flour
1 tbsp. butter

In a saucepan, simmer the oysters in the stock about 30 minutes. Strain, then add milk, cream, and salt and pepper and simmer 2 minutes longer. Mix the potato flour with the butter, add to the pan, and stir to thicken the soup. Serve immediately.

GREEN OYSTERS

24 fresh oysters
1 lb. spinach, chopped
4 cups chopped parsley leaves
4 tbsp. white wine

Preheat the oven to 425°F. Discard any open or cracked oysters. Shuck the remainder and wash the shells. Place the oysters on the half shells in a baking dish. Mix together the spinach, parsley, and white wine, then spread this over the oysters. Bake 6 to 7 minutes, until the oysters are cooked through, then serve.

ROASTED OYSTERS

16 fresh oysters
1 tbsp. sesame oil
1 tbsp. white wine vinegar
1 tbsp. lemon juice
½-inch piece gingerroot, peeled
    and grated
1 tsp. salt

Preheat the oven to 400°F. Discard any open or cracked oysters. Place the remainder in a roasting pan, deep shell side down, and roast 5 minutes, or until they open; discard any that remain closed. Whisk the sesame oil, white wine vinegar, lemon juice, ginger and salt in a bowl. Remove the top shells, and add a drizzle of dressing to each oyster. Serve the oysters in their shells as a first course.

LITTLE POWERHOUSES
OF GOODNESS, NUTS AND
SEEDS ARE BRIMMING
WITH ENERGY, MAKING
THEM FANTASTIC SNACKS
AT ANY TIME

05 | **wonder**
NUTS, SEEDS
& OIL'S

Walnut

Vitamins B1, B2, B3, B5, B6, E, biotin, folic acid; calcium, copper, iodine, iron, magnesium, manganese, phosphorus, potassium, selenium, zinc; omega-3, -6 and -9 fatty acids; glutathione; arginine; ellagic acid; protein; tryptophan; fiber

Walnuts are a wonderful snack food, providing many nutrients, as well as a healthy oil. With their two-lobed appearance resembling a brain, it's no surprise walnuts aid cognitive function and sharpen the memory.

One of the richest sources of antioxidants, walnuts protect the heart in numerous ways, preventing arrhythmia, as well as lowering cholesterol and protecting the arteries. Walnuts contain glutathione, an important antioxidant that aids the development of lymphocyte cells and, thereby, boosts immunity.

Walnuts and walnut oil contain protein, vitamins B6 and E, potassium, magnesium, copper, and zinc, all of which help to keep us youthful. Vitamin B6 helps to prevent memory loss and protect the heart, while vitamin E maintains healthy skin and hair. Both potassium and magnesium are good for the heart, and copper helps to prevent varicose veins. Zinc has a miraculous ability to rejuvenate the thymus gland and to boost immunity.

One of walnut's most valuable effects is in fighting inflammation. This means a lot more than just relieving sore skin and painful joints, especially as you grow older. Inflammation plays a role in many of the most debilitating conditions of aging. It hardens the arteries, causing high blood pressure, stroke, and heart disease. It speeds up thinning of the bones, leading to osteoporosis. The damage caused by chronic inflammation has been linked to the development of cancers. And it is implicated in degenerative diseases of both brain and body. Eating just six walnuts a day is enough to reduce your risk. Additionally, scientists have found that eating walnuts at the end of a rich meal can counter the potentially harmful effects of the fat you've eaten by reducing inflammation and keeping the arteries clear.

Walnuts might reduce the risk of developing diabetes, but if you already have it, they provide the right balance of fats in your diet. They are not only a good source of heart-healthy monounsaturated fats but also contain alpha-linolenic acid, an omega-3 essential fatty acid, which makes them unique among nuts. Omega-3 fats provide cardiovascular protection and aid brain function and positive mood; they're also anti-inflammatory and so are useful in the treatment of asthma, rheumatoid arthritis, and skin disorders, such as eczema and psoriasis. In addition, walnuts contain the amino acid arginine, which helps to keep blood vessels flexible, and ellagic acid, an antioxidant that research has shown to have powerful anticancer properties.

WALNUT AND PASTA SALAD

4 tbsp. chopped walnuts,

3¾ cups wholewheat pasta spirals, cooked

3 large tomatoes, cut into wedges

handful arugula

2 tbsp. chopped basil leaves

1 garlic clove, crushed

4 tbsp. walnut oil

2 tbsp. balsamic vinegar

In a large bowl, combine all the ingredients, except the garlic, oil, and vinegar. Whisk these remaining ingredients together, then drizzle over the salad. Serve immediately.

WALNUT AND BANANA WHIRL

2 bananas, chopped

1 cup plain yogurt

8 tbsp. chopped walnuts

2 tbsp. honey

Place the bananas in a blender. Add the yogurt, half the walnuts, and the honey and blend, on a low speed at first, until smooth. Serve immediately, sprinkled with the remaining walnuts.

WALNUT, APPLE, AND CELERY STUFFING

1 large onion, chopped

2 celery ribs, trimmed and chopped

6 tbsp. butter

2 cooking apples, peeled, cored, and
chopped

3 cups fresh breadcrumbs

2 cups chopped walnuts

½ tsp. dried thyme

1 large egg, beaten

½ cup milk

Preheat the oven to 350°F. Fry the onion and celery in the butter in a skillet. Mix the apples, breadcrumbs, walnuts, and thyme in a bowl, then stir in the vegetables, egg, and milk. Spoon into a baking dish and bake 30 minutes, then serve alongside roasted chicken or turkey.

SPICY WALNUTS

1 tbsp. curry paste

1 tsp. mango juice

1 tsp. ground cumin

1 cup walnuts

Preheat the oven to 350°F. Mix together the curry paste, mango juice, and cumin into a paste. Coat the walnuts and put on a greased baking sheet and roast 5 to 10 minutes until crisp. Serve as a snack.

Pine nut

VITAMINS B1, B2, B3, E; COPPER, IRON, MAGNESIUM, MANGANESE, ZINC;
PINOLEIC ACID; OMEGA-6 ESSENTIAL FATTY ACIDS; PROTEIN

Full of protein and minerals, these aromatic kernels can aid the prevention of disease. They are perfect with pasta, in stir-fries or salads, or as an energy-boosting snack.

The small edible seeds of the pine tree, pine nuts are lower in fat content than most other nuts, which means they're a brilliant choice for weight-conscious athletes who need to get plenty of muscle-building protein and joint-friendly essential fats in their diet without overloading on calories.

As well as being rich in the immunity-boosting antioxidant zinc, pine nuts contain high levels of anti-inflammatory polyunsaturated fats, which help to maintain low cholesterol and promote a healthy heart. They are high in immunity-boosting vitamin E, which helps to protect against damage caused by pollution and other toxins, and is needed by the immune system's antibodies to fight disease. In addition, pine nuts are a good source of magnesium, which helps to calm allergic reactions.

Pine nuts are also nature's only source of pinoleic acid, which stimulates the secretion of a hormone in the gut that sends messages to the brain indicating you are full. The brain then switches off the appetite. Pinoleic acid also slows the rate at which food leaves the stomach, leaving you feeling fuller for longer.

RED BELL PEPPER BRUSCHETTA

4 red bell peppers, seeded and sliced
1 garlic clove, crushed
1 tbsp. balsamic vinegar
5 tbsp. olive oil
1 wholewheat loaf of bread, thickly sliced
7 oz. goat cheese, sliced
⅓ cup pine nuts, toasted

Broil the peppers until soft, then place in a bowl and toss with the garlic, vinegar, and 4 tablespoons of the oil. Drizzle the remaining oil over the bread and place in a hot oven to bake until golden on each side, turning once. Top each slice with goat cheese, peppers, and pine nuts.

Almond

VITAMINS B1, B2, B3, B5, B6, E, BIOTIN, FOLIC ACID; CALCIUM, COPPER, IODINE, IRON, MAGNESIUM, MANGANESE, PHOSPHORUS, POTASSIUM, SELENIUM, ZINC; MONOUNSATURATED FATS, OMEGA-6 ESSENTIAL FATTY ACIDS, OMEGA-9 FATTY ACIDS; LAETRILE; PLANT STEROLS; PROTEIN; FIBER

These delicately flavored nuts contain healthy oils and other vitality-enhancing nutrients. Nibbling on almonds provides nutrients and energy for people who work out, with less risk of piling on unwanted pounds.

Almonds are one of the top sources of cancer-preventing antioxidant vitamin E, containing 24mg per 100g. This plays an important role in maintaining healthy skin both internally and externally, helping to preserve elasticity and repair damage, and protect cells from free radicals, hence slowing down the aging process. Almond oil, especially, is wonderfully soothing for the skin and effective in healing postoperative scars. Vitamin E also boosts immunity and protects the heart by keeping "bad" LDL cholesterol from oxidizing and sticking to artery walls.

The nuts also contain monounsaturated fats and plant sterols, which help to reduce the risk of heart disease, and the phytochemicals quercetin and kaempferol, which might protect against cancer, as well as laetrile, thought to be a powerful tumor-fighting compound.

Almonds are a good source of protein, needed for healthy growth and the repair of cells, making these nuts great for vegetarians. The nuts also contain more fiber than any other nut, which helps almonds to promote healthy digestion through the efficient elimination of waste matter. They are full of calcium, which aids muscle function and helps to keep bones strong and to stave off osteoporosis. Almonds also provide zinc, magnesium, and potassium. While zinc strengthens immunity and improves wound healing, magnesium increases energy and potassium reduces blood pressure, protecting against heart disease.

Almonds are a useful food for dieters. They might seem an odd weight-loss choice because they contain quite a lot of fat, but when scientists put two groups of people on low-calorie diets, one of which included almonds, the almond-eating group lost 50 percent more weight and fat than the others. Almonds are rich in monounsaturated fat, which helps you feel fuller for longer, and their high fiber content helps to keep blood sugar levels steady and prevent hunger pangs. A dozen almonds contain just 90 calories along with a burst of protein and nutrients that combine to increase energy levels, so they are a great snack food for athletes, and sportsmen and -women.

ALMOND AND RAISIN MILK

2 cups whole blanched almonds (not
   roasted or salted)
handful raisins
2 cups water

Cover the almonds with water and leave to soak 24 hours, then drain and rinse. Soak the raisins in water to cover 2 hours, then drain. Put the almonds, raisins, and the water in a blender and whiz, then strain through a fine strainer and drink. Cover and chill up to 4 days.

ALMOND AND BANANA SMOOTHIE

1 cup blanched almonds
2 small bananas
2¼ cups water
2 tsp. vanilla extract
2 tsp. honey
a pinch of cinnamon

Place the almonds, bananas, and water in a blender and whiz until smooth. Add the vanilla extract, honey, and cinnamon and whiz again. Serve immediately.

ALMOND MACAROONS

2 extra-large egg whites

1¾ cups very finely ground blanched
  almonds

⅓ cup sugar

1 tsp. almond extract

a pinch of salt

Preheat the oven to 350°F. In a bowl, beat the egg whites until firm peaks form. Fold in the almonds and sugar, then the almond extract and salt. Roll out and cut into 20 circles. Place on a greased baking sheet and bake 20 minutes, or until golden. Cool on a wire rack.

RASPBERRY AND ALMOND BAKE

1 jar raspberry jam

1 egg, beaten

5 tbsp. brown rice syrup

1 cup very finely ground almonds

4 tbsp. sunflower oil

5 tbsp. rice milk

½ tsp. vanilla extract

4 drops almond extract

Preheat the oven to 375°F. Spread the jam over the bottom of a baking dish. Put the remaining ingredients in a bowl, mix well, and spoon the mixture evenly over the jam. Bake 40 to 45 minutes until golden and firm to the touch. Leave to cool for a couple minutes, then serve hot.

*TRADITIONAL ALMOND MILK
to nourish the skin

4 tbsp. very finely ground blanched
  almonds

2 tbsp. honey

2 cups plus 2 tbsp. still mineral water

In a bowl, combine the almonds, honey, and water and stir well, until the honey dissolves, then set aside 2 hours. Filter and pour into a bottle with a lid. Apply generously to your face and neck with a cotton ball and leave on 20 minutes. Use in the morning and evening. This keeps up to 3 days in the refrigerator.

Cashew nut

VITAMINS B2, B3, B5, B6, BIOTIN, FOLIC ACID; CALCIUM, COPPER, IODINE, IRON, MAGNESIUM, MANGANESE, PHOSPHORUS, POTASSIUM, SELENIUM, ZINC; TRYPTOPHAN; OMEGA-6 ESSENTIAL FATTY ACIDS; PROTEIN; FIBER

The seeds of the Brazilian cashew apple, cashew nuts are full of healthy fats, vitamins, and minerals, making them an ideal instant, nutritious snack.

Cashew nuts are a great source of omega-6 essential fatty acids, which protect against heart disease by helping to keep cholesterol levels down. Rich in B-vitamins, which aid the maintenance of nerves and muscle tissue, and boost resistance to stress, they also provide iron to help to prevent anemia.

Loaded with minerals important for immune health, cashews are high in the antioxidant selenium, which is crucial in the production of antibodies. Selenium also has potent antiaging properties, staving off wrinkles and promoting glossy hair. The nuts are also high in virus-fighting zinc, which helps to fight common infections, such as colds and flu, as well as to keep cancer cells at bay.

Cashew nuts are also rich in many of the minerals that active people need—30 cashews provide one-fifth of an average woman's recommended daily iron intake, while 20 nuts provide more than one-tenth of an average man's daily zinc requirement. The phosphorus in the nuts works with the calcium to form and maintain strong bones, while the copper has healing properties, and might help to rid the body of infections.

Cashews are packed with the minerals essential to fitness: magnesium keeps bones strong while combating muscle fatigue and soreness. They also aid the function of the heart and enable the metabolism of calcium, which prevents osteoporosis. In addition, the copper in cashews not only increases energy and protects joints from injury but also helps the body to utilize iron.

There is no handier snack than a package of nuts after you've worked up an appetite exercising. The body is still burning calories faster than usual up to an hour or so after a workout, so make the most of this and enjoy some healthy cashews rather than an empty-calorie snack.

SUMMER BERRIES WITH CASHEW CREAM

1 cup cashew nuts
7 tbsp. water
1 tsp. ground nutmeg
2 tbsp. honey
1¼ cups raspberries
1⅓ cups strawberries, hulled
  and halved

Blend the nuts and water in a food processor until smooth, then add the nutmeg and honey and whiz again until thoroughly blended. Divide the berries into four bowls, top with the cashew cream, and serve.

CHICKEN WITH CASHEWS

1 tbsp. peanut oil
2 bird's-eye chilies, seeded and chopped
2-inch piece gingerroot, finely chopped
1 lb. skinless chicken breast meat, cubed
2 scallions, trimmed and chopped
2 tsp. white wine vinegar
2 tsp. sesame oil
heaping 2 tbsp. cashew nuts
rice, to serve

Heat the peanut oil and stir-fry the chilies and ginger. Add the chicken and stir-fry 2 to 3 minutes longer. Add the scallions, vinegar, and sesame oil and fry 5 minutes, or until the chicken is cooked through, then transfer to a bowl. Stir-fry the cashews 1 minute and sprinkle over the chicken. Serve with rice.

CASHEW NUT DIP

⅔ cup cashew nuts
1 tbsp. crunchy peanut butter
3 garlic cloves, crushed
3 tbsp. olive oil
juice of 1 lemon
⅓ cup tahini
a pinch of paprika
pita bread, to serve

Blend all the ingredients in a food processor until smooth. Serve with pita bread.

Brazil nut

VITAMINS B1, E, BIOTIN; CALCIUM, COPPER, IRON, MAGNESIUM, MANGANESE,
PHOSPHORUS, SELENIUM, ZINC; OLEIC ACID; OMEGA-3 AND -6 FATTY ACIDS;
GLUTATHIONE, FIBER, PROTEIN

Large seeds of giant trees that grow in South America's Amazon jungle, Brazil nuts provide a plethora of healing nutrients. High in the antioxidant mineral selenium, the Brazil is one of the most nutritious of all nuts.

The Brazil nut grows wild in the Amazonian rainforest, where it was sacred to ancient tribes. It is the kernel of a fruit that loosely resembles a coconut, and the nuts grow in clusters of up to 24 within this shell. When ripe, the shells fall to the ground. The kernels are then removed, dried in the sun, and washed before being exported.

This nut is one of the best sources of selenium, an antioxidant mineral that strengthens the immune system's antibody response and helps to prevent cancer, heart disease, and premature aging, as well as having great mood-boosting properties. It is a key component in the action of glutathione, an enzyme that suppresses free radicals and helps to halt the development of tumors. Just a couple of Brazil nuts a day are enough to meet the selenium levels needed by most people.

They also contain other important minerals, including iron, crucial for healthy blood, and magnesium, essential to the nervous system and important for the formation of protein and for boosting energy.

Brazil nuts are packed with vitamin E, which works with selenium to provide a super-boost to the immune system, and also contain vitamin B1, which is essential to the nervous system.

Brazil nuts are about 70 percent fat. Half of this is oleic acid, the building block for the omega-9 fatty acids that are excellent for the skin and have anti-inflammatory properties. The rest is made up of omega-6 and omega-3 essential fatty acids, which promote healthy skin, glossy hair, and a good memory, ease inflammation, and enhance digestion.

Rich in protein, a handful of Brazil nuts eaten raw makes a satisfying snack. They can be processed into nut milk or butter, and can be used in stir-fries and salads to add a crunchy protein kick.

GREEN BEAN AND BRAZIL NUT STIR-FRY

2 tbsp. sesame oil

1 onion, chopped

1 tbsp. peeled and grated gingerroot

2 garlic cloves, crushed

7 oz. asparagus stalks

7 oz. green beans

¾ cup Brazil nuts, sliced

2 tbsp. soy sauce

hot, cooked brown rice, to serve

Heat the sesame oil in a wok over high heat until it is sizzling hot. Add the onion, ginger, and garlic and stir-fry 2 minutes, then add the asparagus stalks, green beans, and Brazil nuts. Continue to stir-fry 5 minutes, then add the soy sauce. Reduce the heat and cook slowly 8 to 10 minutes until the asparagus and beans are tender. Serve immediately on a bed of hot brown rice.

BRAZIL NUT BRITTLE

heaping 2 cups sugar

¼ tsp. baking soda

1½ cups finely ground Brazil nuts

6 oz. milk chocolate, melted

In a heavy skillet, melt the sugar over low heat, stirring. Add the baking soda and 1 cup of the nuts and mix together. Roll out on a greased baking sheet until about ¼ inch thick. When cold, cover with the melted chocolate and sprinkle with the remaining nuts. Once set, break into pieces.

Coconut and coconut oil

VITAMINS B1, B2, B3, B5, B6, C, E, FOLIC ACID; CALCIUM, COPPER, IODINE, IRON, MAGNESIUM, MANGANESE, PHOSPHORUS, POTASSIUM, SELENIUM, ZINC; FIBER; PROTEIN; CARBOHYDRATE; MEDIUM CHAIN FATTY ACIDS

Traditionally the staple food on many tropical islands, this health-giving nut has potent healing properties.

Although coconut is high in saturated fats, they're a different type to those found in meat and dairy and don't pose the same health risks. Known as medium chain fatty acids (MCFAs), they are soluble and easily digested and metabolized by the body, and are used as an energy source rather than being stored as fat. MCFAs have been shown to assist the absorption of calcium, magnesium, and some amino acids, as well as supporting the healthy function of the thyroid. They also stimulate metabolism, benefit the heart, and promote weight loss.

Rich in vitamins, coconut oil's vitamin E keeps the skin's connective tissues strong and supple, which helps to prevent wrinkles.

Coconut water—the liquid inside young coconuts—is known to be one of the most balanced electrolyte sources in nature, making a wonderful rehydration drink following intense exercise or when fluids and electrolytes have been lost through diarrhea or fever.

*COCONUT BODY OIL _to moisturize the skin_

1 tub (2½ oz.) coconut oil

15 drops of your favorite essential oil

Remove the lid from the coconut oil and place the tub in a large pan with water and heat slowly until the oil liquefies. Add your favorite essential oil and stir well. Replace the lid and put the tub in the refrigerator 15 minutes. Apply generously all over your body (but not to your face). Beware that the oil can stain your clothes, so avoid dressing until the oil has soaked well into the skin.

NON-ALCOHOLIC PIÑA COLADA

2 cups pineapple juice

¾ cup coconut water

7 oz. canned pineapple in fruit juice

2 oz. creamed coconut, crumbled

Put all the ingredients in a blender and whiz until smooth. Pour into a glass pitcher and stir well before serving with ice.

COCONUT RICE

1 cup brown rice

1 onion, chopped

1 tbsp. ground coriander

1 tbsp. ground cumin

2 tbsp. coconut oil

2 large tomatoes, chopped

3 tbsp. shredded coconut

Place the rice and 2¼ cups water in a saucepan and bring to a boil. Reduce the heat and simmer 45 minutes, or until the rice is tender. In another pan, fry the onion and spices in the oil 3 minutes. Add the tomatoes and coconut and simmer 10 minutes. Mix well with the rice. Serve as a side dish.

Flaxseed

VITAMINS B1, B2, B3, B5, B6, E, FOLIC ACID; CALCIUM, COPPER, IRON, MAGNESI-
UM, MANGANESE, PHOSPHORUS, POTASSIUM, SELENIUM, ZINC; FIBER; PROTEIN;
OMEGA-3 AND OMEGA-6 ESSENTIAL FATTY ACIDS; LIGNANS; FIBER

With abundant and balanced levels of essential fatty acids, flaxseed is acclaimed in history for its ability to prevent and combat many conditions. This tiny wonderfood, also known as linseed, can lift depression, aid concentration, increase energy levels, and smooth hormonal changes.

Today, the amazing, health-giving virtues of flaxseed are recognized throughout the world. Whatever your age or sex, flaxseed can make you feel happier and help you to think more clearly. This superseed contains nutrients that are vital to brain functioning but often lacking in people's everyday diets.

Flaxseed is one of the richest sources of alpha-linolenic acid (ALA), an omega-3 essential fatty acid renowned for its benefits to both mind and body. One of the ways in which omega-3s help to keep the brain and nervous system working smoothly is by allowing cells to function and communicate with each other properly. This can prevent many disorders that we think of as psychological. It also increases mental alertness and boosts memory. Our ability to use omega-3s is reduced by saturated and hydrogenated fats, which compete for the same receptors in our bodies. So cut down on these fats and eat foods rich in vitamins B3, B6, and C, plus zinc and magnesium, which help the body to absorb ALA.

High in omega-6 essential fatty acids (EFAs) in addition to omega-3s, flaxseeds are involved in systematic energy production, oxygen transfer, and transportation of fats, and might, therefore, help to maintain the body's tissue cells, reproductive organs, glands, muscles, and eyes. Flaxseed is thus traditionally used to treat everything from malnutrition and skin diseases to arthritis, PMS, and fertility problems. For women aged over 35, it can also alleviate stressful perimenopausal symptoms, such as hot flashes, insomnia, and mood swings, as it is rich in compounds called lignans, which the body converts into substances that smooth out fluctuating hormone levels. Lignans are special compounds that are converted by friendly bacteria in the gut into phytoestrogens called enterolactone and enterodiol. These health-giving compounds have also been found to offer protection against breast cancer. (Flaxseed oil, while rich in omega-3s, however, does not contain lignans and loses much of its value if used in cooking.)

Essential fatty acids are also needed to make prostaglandins, hormonelike substances responsible for stamina, circulation, and metabolism. These are anti-inflammatory, and might benefit conditions such as asthma and arthritis. They also promote heart health by reducing cholesterol, blood pressure, and plaque formation in the artery walls. Not only this, prostaglandins encourage weight loss by removing excess fluid from tissues and boosting metabolism, thereby helping to burn calories.

Flaxseed is expectorant and dissolving by nature and can help to treat conditions such as coughs and bronchitis, as well as other respiratory ailments. The seeds also have a mild purgative action and can be capable of tonifying the bowel, easing constipation.

Another great feature of flaxseed is mucilage, a type of soluble fiber that lowers cholesterol, stabilizes blood-sugar levels, and alleviates constipation. Flaxseed's laxative effect is gentle, helping to keep intestinal contents moving smoothly along.

The benefits of flaxseed do not stop there. Its Vitamin E content helps to keep the skin looking youthful and the hair glossy. Flaxseed also contains antiviral, antibacterial, and antifungal properties. Its zinc and selenium, two powerful antioxidant minerals, boost the immune system to protect against infections, while its iron and copper help in the production of hemoglobin, needed to keep red blood cells healthy. Copper aids wound healing and the formation of collagen in the skin. In addition, the seeds provide calcium and magnesium, which together support strong, healthy bones, while magnesium also helps to ward off muscle cramps and release energy.

As flaxseeds and their oils are easily oxidized, which causes them to go rancid, keep them in dark jars or tubs with sealed lids, and store them in the refrigerator no longer than a year.

TROPICAL FLAX SHAKE

1 tbsp. flaxseeds
2½ cups pineapple juice
¾ cup apple juice
2 kiwifruit, peeled and chopped
2 passion fruit, halved

Grind the flaxseeds in a coffee grinder and put them in a blender along with the fruit juices and kiwifruit. Scoop out the seeds from the passion fruit and add them to the juice mixture. Blend well and drink immediately.

FLAXSEED MUFFINS *makes 12*

½ cup golden flaxseeds, ground
1¼ cups wholewheat flour
1 tbsp. baking powder
2 tsp. ground allspice
1 cup light brown sugar
1 egg, beaten
1 cup plus 2 tbsp. milk

Preheat the oven to 350°F. Mix the dry ingredients in a bowl. Add the egg and milk and stir together. Spoon into 12 paper muffin cases in a muffin pan and bake 25 minutes, or until a toothpick inserted in the middle of one comes out clean. Turn out on a wire rack to cool.

*FLAXSEED FACE MASK *to smoothe wrinkles*

2 tsp. flaxseeds
water, enough to cover
1 drop neroli oil

In a small bowl, combine the flaxseeds and water. Allow to sit until the seeds swell and the water turns to gel, then add the neroli oil. Using your fingers, spread the gel over your face and neck. Leave to dry, then rinse off with cool or tepid water. Pat your face dry.

BREAKFAST BOOSTER

4 tbsp. flaxseeds
2 bananas, sliced
½ small cantaloupe melon, peeled, seeded, and chopped
4 tsp. pumpkin seeds
2 tsp. sesame seeds
½ cup plain yogurt
¾ cup strawberries, hulled and chopped

Place all the ingredients, except the strawberries, in a bowl and mix together well. Divide between bowls and serve topped with the strawberries.

PEANUT AND FLAX BARS

heaping ⅓ cup flaxseeds
10 cups puffed rice cereal
5 tbsp. crunchy peanut butter
5 tbsp. brown rice syrup

Grind the flaxseeds in a grinder and put them in a large bowl. Add the puffed cereal, peanut butter, and rice syrup and mix well using your hands. Press the mixture very firmly into a nonstick baking sheet and allow to set and set for several hours before cutting into bars.

Sesame seed and oil

VITAMINS B1, B2, B3, B5, B6, E, BETA-CAROTENE; CALCIUM, COPPER, IODINE, IRON, MAGNESIUM, MANGANESE, PHOSPHORUS, POTASSIUM, SELENIUM, ZINC; FIBER; PROTEIN; OMEGA-6 AND -9 ESSENTIAL FATTY ACIDS

These tiny seeds can add both taste and essential nutrients to a variety of sweet and savory dishes. A fantastic source of calcium, sesame seeds are brilliant nondairy bone-builders.

Sesame seeds have a nutty flavor and are slightly crunchy in texture to eat. Valuable health-boosters, they are made into a number of products, such as sesame oil, which is highly resistant to rancidity, and tahini, a sesame-seed paste, or can be sprinkled over stir-fries, salads, and pasta.

Rich in zinc and antioxidant vitamin E, sesame seeds are powerful immunity boosters. They also contain a host of B-vitamins to support the nervous system and to help the body to cope with stress, as well as selenium to stave off wrinkles and keep the skin looking youthful. The seeds and oil are rich in calcium and magnesium—two important minerals, which are necessary for bone and heart health.

A good source of vegetarian protein, sesame seeds are packed with omega-6 fatty acids for healthy skin and hair, while sesame oil contains omega-9 fatty acids, which offer great benefits to the heart by reducing the risk of atherosclerosis and lowering cholesterol levels. Omega-9s also help to balance blood sugar levels and enhance immunity.

CRUNCHY SESAME STIR-FRY

3 tbsp. olive oil

2 tbsp. sesame seeds

2 tbsp. peeled and grated gingerroot

2 garlic cloves, crushed

½ broccoli head, cut into small florets

3 carrots, peeled and cut into long thin
    slices

½ cabbage, cored and shredded

In a wok, heat the oil and sesame seeds until the seeds start to toast. Add the gingerroot and garlic, followed by the remaining ingredients, and combine well. Turn the heat down to low and fry 5 to 10 minutes longer until all the vegetables are tender. Serve.

SESAME TAHINI DIP

1¼ cups sesame seeds

4 tbsp. peanut oil

roasted vegetable pieces, to serve

Preheat the oven to 350°F. Sprinkle the sesame seeds onto a baking sheet and toast in the oven 20 minutes. Whiz the seeds in a blender about 3 minutes, then add 1 tablespoon of the oil and whiz 30 seconds longer before adding the remaining oil. Whiz again until a smooth paste forms. Serve with a selection of roasted vegetable pieces.

SESAME CHEWS

6 oz. dried dates

½ cup chopped pecans

2 tbsp. tahini

2 tbsp. peanut butter

4 tbsp. sesame seeds

Put 1 cup plus 2 tablespoons water and the dates in a pan and simmer, covered, 10 minutes, or until soft and the liquid has been absorbed. Mash the dates and mix together with the pecans, tahini, and peanut butter. Leave to stand about 30 minutes so the mixture firms, then form into small balls and coat with the sesame seeds.

Sunflower seed and oil

Vitamins B1, B2, B3, B5, E, folic acid; calcium, copper, iron, magnesium, manganese, phosphorus, selenium, zinc; omega-6 essential fatty acids; protein

Power-packed with a whole host of nutrients, sunflower seeds are one of the finest energy "pick-me-ups" nature provides. Although small, they are loaded with life-enhancing antioxidants.

Sunflower seeds are a valuable source of B-vitamins, which means they are nourishing to the adrenal glands and, thus, might help to combat energy slumps and many symptoms associated with stress.

Sunflower seeds are a diuretic and expectorant, and have been used in the treatment of bronchial, throat, and lung infections. The seeds and oil are full of vitamin E, omega-6 essential fatty acids, and monounsaturated fats, which help to keep the skin elastic and minimize heart disease. Omega-6s also help to fight inflammation, thus relieving arthritis. The essential fatty acid content might be beneficial in treating eczema.

The seeds and oil are rich in the minerals calcium and magnesium, needed for the contraction of muscles as well as a healthy bone structure. Magnesium is used in producing energy and calming allergic reactions. Sunflower seeds and oil also contain immunity-boosting zinc, a powerful antiviral, and selenium, which has potent antioxidant properties to fight the free radicals that harm the body's cells.

SUNFLOWER SEED AND OAT BREAD

makes 2 small loaves

5 cups oat flour
1 envelope (¼ oz.) instant active dry yeast
2 tbsp. sunflower seeds
2 tbsp. malt extract
1 tsp. salt
¾ cup warm water (100° to 110°F)
1 tbsp. sunflower oil

Preheat the oven to 350°F. Mix the flour, yeast, seeds, malt extract and salt in a bowl. Mix in the water and oil to form a dough. Knead 10 minutes, then divide, shape, and place in 2 bread pans. Cover and leave to rise 30 minutes. Bake 50 minutes, or until loaves sound hollow when tapped.

SUNFLOWER SEED TOPPING

1 tbsp. peanut oil
4 tbsp. sunflower seeds
1 tbsp. sesame seeds
2 tbsp. walnut halves
1 tbsp. soy sauce
1-inch piece gingerroot, peeled

Heat the oil in a wok until very hot. Add the seeds and walnuts, and fry 30 seconds, stirring constantly. Add the soy sauce, then transfer to a bowl. Chop and add the ginger. Serve sprinkled over rice or stir-fries.

MUESLI

1½ cups rolled oats
2 tbsp. chopped dried dates
2 tbsp. chopped dried apricots
1 tbsp. pecans, chopped
1 tbsp. slivered almonds
1 tbsp. sunflower seeds
1 tbsp. flaxseeds
1 tbsp. wheat germ
1 tbsp. wheat bran
2 apples, peeled, cored,
   and chopped
unsweetened soy milk,
   to serve

Combine all the dry ingredients in a bowl and top with the apple. Serve with the soy milk.

Pumpkin seed

VITAMINS B2, B3, B5, E, K, BETA-CAROTENE; CALCIUM, COPPER, IRON, MAGNESIUM, MANGANESE, PHOSPHORUS, POTASSIUM, SELENIUM, ZINC; OMEGA-3 AND -6 ESSENTIAL FATTY ACIDS

Tasty pumpkin seeds are full of essential fatty acids and many health-enhancing micronutrients. Boasting the highest iron content in the seed world, they make a very nutritious snack.

Packed with nutrients, pumpkin seeds are full of omega-3 fatty acids, which are anti-inflammatory, so they protect joints and also promote the healing of sports-related injuries. Along with omega-6 fatty acids in the seeds, they are crucial for good immune function, as well as for healthy skin, blood clotting, digestion, and nerve function. The essential fatty acids (EFAs) are also vital for youthful skin and glossy hair.

The EFAs in pumpkin seeds boost memory and are central to a healthy brain. Studies show that they can boost children's brainpower and are important for babies in the womb to avoid the risk of developing eye and nerve problems.

Pumpkin seeds might help to fight cardio-vascular and immunodeficiency disorders. The seeds are one of the richest natural sources of phytosterols, plant compounds that reduce the risk of arteries becoming narrowed by cholesterol. Phytosterols are also thought to boost immunity and have anticarcinogenic properties.

The seeds are also rich in B-vitamins, which are vital for moderating stress and its damaging effects on the immune system. These vitamins play an important role in converting carbohydrates into energy, as well as being essential for cell reproduction, which makes them beneficial for the tissues that grow and renew themselves, such as the hair and nails.

Pumpkin seeds contain many health-giving minerals including the antioxidants selenium and zinc, which support the immune system, helping to fight off diseases and infections. Selenium helps to neutralize the damaging effects of harmful free radicals and is thought to have anti-cancer activity. Owing to their high zinc content, pumpkin seeds have a reputation as a male sexual tonic and studies have shown that they can also help to reduce an enlarged prostate gland. A combination of zinc and essential fatty acids has been found to be particularly effective in combating prostate problems.

Pumpkin seeds are a good source of calcium and magnesium, which are needed for healthy bones, nerves, and muscles. The magnesium ensures the calcium is properly absorbed in the body. They also provide a valuable source of energy through the presence of digestible iron, which encourages the formation of red blood cells and helps guarantee oxygen is pumped around the body efficiently, making fatigue and low energy levels during exercise less likely. Exercise requires good circulation, and pumpkin seeds are rich in a compound that can help. Pumping oxygenated blood rapidly around the body puts pressure on the arteries, which need to remain flexible and clear.

The seeds also make an effective dewormer and have been used to help to treat roundworm, tapeworm, and other intestinal parasites.

PUMPKIN FRITTERS *serves 2*

1 small pumpkin, peeled and sliced
heaping 1 cup wholewheat flour
½ tsp. salt
½ tsp. baking powder
2 tsp. ground cumin
1 egg, separated
¾ cup water
1 onion, chopped
2 garlic cloves, crushed
2 tbsp. olive oil
2 tbsp. pumpkin seeds

Steam the pumpkin 10 minutes, then let cool. In a bowl, combine the flour, salt, baking powder, and cumin, then add the egg yolk and the water, a little at a time, stirring to form a smooth batter. Add the onion and garlic, then whisk the egg white and fold it in. Heat the oil in a skillet, then dip the pumpkin slices in the batter and fry a few at a time, turning, until crisp and brown. Sprinkle with the seeds and serve warm.

PUMPKIN SOUP

1 tbsp. olive oil
1 tbsp. butter
1 onion, chopped
2 cups peeled, seeded and diced pumpkin
2 cups peeled and diced parsnips
2 cups peeled and diced carrots
4 cups chicken or vegetable stock
1 to 2 tbsp. lemon juice
2 tbsp. pumpkin seeds

Heat the oil and butter in a saucepan and sauté the onion until soft. Add the pumpkin, parsnips, and carrots, and stir. Cover and cook over low heat 5 minutes. Add the stock, bring to a boil, cover, and simmer 30 minutes. Leave to cool, then blend until smooth. Reheat, add lemon juice to taste, and serve sprinkled with pumpkin seeds.

PUMPKIN SEED MUFFINS

scant 3 cups all-purpose flour
2 tsp. baking powder
1⅔ cups raisins
½ cup pumpkin seeds
2 carrots, peeled and grated
4 eggs, beaten
⅔ cup maple syrup
¾ cup plus 2 tbsp. milk
¾ cup plus 2 tbsp. sunflower oil

Preheat the oven to 350°F. Combine the flour, baking powder, raisins, and seeds in a mixing bowl. Add the remaining ingredients and mix well to form a batter. Spoon the mixture into the holes on a muffin pan and bake 20 minutes, or until the muffins are a light golden color and peaked. Immediately turn out on to a wire rack and leave to cool.

PUMPKIN SEED PORRIDGE

1½ cups pumpkin seeds
2¼ to 3 cups milk
honey, to taste

Grind the pumpkin seeds in a food processor or spice grinder. Add 2¼ cups of the milk and blend to form an oatmeal consistency. Add additional milk, as desired. Transfer to a saucepan and bring to a boil. Add honey to taste, and serve.

GREEK PEAR DESSERT *serves 2*

2 pears, cored and chopped
¾ cup Greek or thick plain yogurt
3 tbsp. pumpkin seeds
1 tbsp. sunflower seeds
1 tbsp. manuka honey

Divide the chopped pears between two bowls and top with the yogurt. Sprinkle the seeds in a layer over the yogurt, then drizzle with the honey and serve.

PUMPKIN SEED BRITTLE

½ cup pumpkin seeds, toasted
1 tsp. olive oil
a pinch of salt
⅓ cup sugar
4 tbsp. water

Preheat the oven to 250°F. Toss the pumpkin seeds in a bowl with the oil and a pinch of salt. Spread them out evenly on a baking sheet in the middle of the oven and roast 1 hour, stirring occasionally. In a skillet, combine the sugar and water, stirring continuously over low heat, until the mixture is a deep caramel color. Add the seeds and stir until well coated. Spread on to a greased sheet of foil. Leave to cool completely, then break into pieces.

TASTY, VERSATILE, AND NUTRIENT DENSE, GRAINS, LEGUMES, AND BEANS FORM THE CORNERSTONE OF A HEALTHY DIET THE WORLD OVER

06 | **wonder**
GRAINS,
LEGUMES
& BEANS

Wheat and wheat germ

VITAMINS B1, B2, B3, B5, B6, E, FOLIC ACID; IRON, MAGNESIUM, MANGANESE, SELENIUM, ZINC, OMEGA-6 FATTY ACIDS, CHOLINE; PYRODOXINE; PROTEIN, FIBER

A staple food in the Western diet, wheat is protein-rich, providing B-vitamins and minerals. Wheat germ, the sprouting part of wheat grain, is a super source of free-radical-fighting vitamin E.

Whole wheat is a nutritious and healthy cereal grain. A valuable source of protein, it provides important constituents for youthful skin, hair, and nails. It also provides a valuable source of energy, thus combating fatigue. Whole wheat is rich in B-vitamins, including B6, which maintains the nerves, prevents adult-onset diabetes, and also enhances the ability to register, retain, and retrieve information. The grain is a good source of zinc, which boosts immunity and aids eye health.

Found inside the wheat grain, wheat germ is the heart of the cereal, containing many of its most valuable nutrients. It is rich in the antioxidant vitamin E, which helps to detoxify the body by neutralizing harmful free radicals and has been shown to help to prevent heart disease. The high vitamin-E content is especially good for keeping hair glossy and skin glowing. Wheat germ is a very high-fiber food, so helps to guarantee an efficient digestive system, as well as to reduce cholesterol levels.

Used topically, wheat germ's slightly granular texture gently exfoliates sensitive or dry skin.

Wholewheat bread and flour contain wheat germ. But it is missing from white bread and standard baking products, which is why these provide a quick energy rush followed by a slump.

HONEY AND WHEAT GERM SMOOTHIE
serves 1

¾ cup plus 2 tbsp. soy milk
¼ cup plain yogurt
scant 1 cup strawberries, hulled
1 large banana
2 tsp. wheat germ
2 tsp. Manuka honey

Whiz all the ingredients together in a blender, then serve immediately.

SIMPLE WHOLEWHEAT PIZZA CRUST

heaping 3¾ cups wholewheat flour
2 tbsp. instant active dry yeast
1½ tsp. salt
2 cups plus 2 tbsp. warm water
    (100˚ to 110˚F)
2 tbsp. extra virgin olive oil
2 tsp. honey
toppings of choice

Preheat the oven to 400˚F. Combine the flour, yeast, and salt in a bowl. Add the water, oil, and honey and mix well. Cover with a moist cloth and leave to rise in a warm place 10 minutes. Knead and press into a greased large pizza pan. Add the toppings, then bake 15 to 20 minutes until the crust is crisp and golden.

*WHEAT GERM LOTION *for exfoliating the skin*

1 cup plus 2 tbsp. milk
1 cup dried chamomile
4 tbsp. honey
8 tsp. wheat germ

Pour the milk into a cup and add the chamomile, then leave to infuse a few hours. Strain the liquid and discard the chamomile. Add the honey and wheat germ, and mix well. Pour the lotion into a bottle and refrigerate up to a week. Apply to your face and neck, then rinse off with warm water. Use as needed.

Barley

Vitamins B1, B2, B3, B5, B6, E, K, beta-carotene, folic acid; calcium,
copper, iron, magnesium, manganese, phosphorus, potassium, silica,
selenium, zinc; tocotrienol; lignans; fiber; protein; carbohydrate

**Used by the ancient Romans as a strengthening food,
barley is the oldest cultivated cereal. Today, it is largely
neglected, but it has amazing nutritional properties.**

With its unique ability to act on the mucous membranes, barley might
help to soothe inflammatory conditions of the intestines and the urinary
tract. The grain is rich in minerals, with high levels of calcium and potassium and plenty of B-complex vitamins, making it useful for people suffering from stress or fatigue. It also contains beta-glucan, a gummy fiber
that has dramatic cholesterol-lowering abilities.

Barley is one of the richest sources of the antioxidant tocotrienol,
which studies have shown to be even more potent than some forms of
vitamin E in preventing heart disease. It works in two ways. First, it helps
to stop free radical oxidation, a process that makes "bad" cholesterol
stick to artery walls. And second, it acts on the liver to reduce cholesterol production. The grain also contains lignans, which help to prevent
blood clots from forming, farther reducing the risk of heart disease. In
addition, barley is exceptionally high in vitamin E, which keeps the
skin and hair healthy and young looking, and selenium, which is
especially effective in fighting viral infections.

✦ LEMON BARLEY WATER
for cystitis, constipation & diarrhea

⅔ cup pearl barley

4 cups water

grated zest of 1 lemon

honey, to taste

In a pan, combine the the barley and 1 cup plus 2 tablespoons of the water and bring to a boil. Strain, then add the remaining water and the lemon zest. Simmer until the barley is soft, adding water as needed. Strain the liquid, sweeten with honey, and cool. Drink at once or chill up to 4 days.

✦ BARLEY LOTION *to improve blood circulation*

½ cup pearl barley,
  soaked for 24 hours in cold water and
  drained

4 cups water

generous handful fresh rosemary
  leaves, or 3 tbsp. dried rosemary

Put the barley in a pan with the fresh water. Bring to a boil, then cover and simmer 30 minutes. Strain and discard the barley. Add the rosemary to the water, cover and leave to infuse until cool. Strain into a bottle. Using cotton balls, apply twice daily. Refrigerate up to 4 days.

BARLEY AND VEGETABLE SOUP

¼ cup wholegrain barley, soaked
  overnight in cold water

2 tbsp. olive oil

1 onion, chopped

1 garlic clove, crushed

2 celery ribs, trimmed and chopped

1 tomato, chopped

1 tbsp. paprika

½ cup chopped green beans

6 cups vegetable stock

1 tsp. Italian seasoning

Drain the barley and put it in a large saucepan with all the other ingredients. Bring the water to a boil over high heat, then reduce the heat to low, cover, and simmer about 1 hour until the barley is tender.

Oats

VITAMINS B1, B2, B3, B5, B6, E, K, BIOTIN, FOLIC ACID; CALCIUM,
COPPER, IRON, MAGNESIUM, MANGANESE, PHOSPHORUS, POTASSIUM,
SELENIUM, SILICA, ZINC; SAPONINS; TOCOTRIENOL, FERULIC ACID, CAFFEIC
ACID; FLAVONOIDS; FIBER; PROTEIN; COMPLEX CARBOHYDRATE

**Comforting and sustaining, oats bring a host of health
benefits. For blood sugar maintenance, sustained energy,
and staving off hunger, there's no better breakfast than
a steaming bowl of delicious oatmeal.**

Although wild oats are thought to have originated in the Near East, domesticated oats first appeared in Europe in the Bronze Age. Today, the grain is particularly suited to the cool, wet summers of northwest Europe, where it is particularly popular.

Oats can be used in several ways, including being "rolled" to make a commercial foodstuff, or kiln dried, stripped of their husks and delicate outer skins, and then coarsely ground to make steel-cut oats, or finely ground to constitute oat flour.

A cornucopia of nourishment, oats are a good source of protein, and are incredibly high in calcium, potassium, and magnesium, which, like the B-vitamins, act as a nerve tonic, as well as promoting strong bones and teeth, and can aid weight loss because they release energy slowly, staving off hunger pangs. Oats have plenty of silica, which is anti-inflammatory and helps to maintain healthy arterial walls, as well as to keep nails strong and hair glossy. Their selenium and zinc increase the body's immune system and the ability to fight off infectious diseases.

These remarkable grains are also rich in fiber and singularly digestible, as well as having a demulcent quality that protects the duodenal surfaces, stomach, and intestines. Oats are especially good for irritable bowel syndrome as they are antispasmodic.

High in immunity-boosting vitamin E, oats contain flavonoids called avenanthramides—potent antioxidants that help to break down cholesterol buildup and are thought to help prevent some cancers, especially colon cancer. Other powerful, youth-promoting antioxidants found in oats include tocotrienol, ferulic acid, and caffeic acid to fight against free radicals and protect against everything from heart disease to obesity and eye disease. Oats also have a mild tranquillizing effect, and boost mood, making them the perfect comfort food.

Research shows oats can be helpful in staving off heart disease, diabetes, and strokes. Eaten regularly, all kinds of whole grains are associated with good health in older people, but oats have special qualities. They contain a form of fiber called beta-glucan, which has an exceptional ability to reduce cholesterol—cutting the risk of stroke and heart disease from blocked arteries—and stabilize blood sugar. Oats are a complex carbohydrate with a very low glycemic index. They, therefore, provide sustainable energy, alleviating insomnia and improving insulin sensitivity in people with diabetes.

As well as being the prime ingredient in oatmeal, oats are a mainstay of other breakfast cereals, such as muesli and granola. They are also used in a variety of baked goods, such as oat bread, crackers, granola bars, and oatmeal cookies. Oat milk is now widely available as a drink and makes a useful alternative to cow's milk for people who are lactose intolerant.

Used topically, oats have an emollient and anti-inflammatory effect on the skin, which makes them a common ingredient in beauty preparations. They can be used as a skin cleanser and exfolliant to remove the surface layer of dead skin cells. Oats are also found in bars of soap and when combined with water in the bath, they can help to alleviate and soothe skin irritations.

* OATMEAL HERBAL SCRUB *to cleanse the skin*

⅔ cup boiling water
3 tbsp. dried parsley, lemon balm,
   or fennel seeds
1 tbsp. ground oatmeal
2 drops almond oil

Make a herbal infusion by pouring the water over the herbs and leaving 15 minutes, then strain and discard the herbs. Leave the infusion to cool, then add enough to the oatmeal to form a pastelike consistency. Add the almond oil. Smooth the scrub mixture on your face and neck and leave 20 minutes, then rinse off with warm water and pat your face dry.

OATCAKES

¾ cup fine steel-cut oats
a pinch of baking soda
a pinch of salt
1 tbsp. olive oil

Preheat the oven to 350°F. Mix together the oats, baking soda, and salt. Add the oil and 2 tablespoons hot water and mix well to form a firm dough. Roll out on a lightly floured surface. Cut into 8 circles and place on a greased baking sheet. Bake 8 to 10 minutes until light brown. Serve at room temperature.

OATMEAL RAISIN BARS

3 cups oatmeal
¾ cup raisins
⅔ cup margarine
8 tbsp. honey
6 tbsp. fruit sugar
1 tbsp. vanilla extract

Preheat the oven to 375°F. Put the oats and raisins in a bowl and set aside. Melt the margarine in a pan, then add the remaining ingredients. Stir into the oats. Press into a nonstick baking pan and bake 15 to 18 minutes. Cool on a wire rack, then cut into bars.

✦ OATEN JELLY *for gastric problems*

½ cup oat flour
2 cups water
1 tbsp. butter
sugar or honey, to taste

Blend the oat flour with a little water. Boil the rest of the water in a pan and slowly pour onto the flour, stirring until thick. Return the mixture to the pan and add the butter. Bring to a boil, then simmer 7 minutes, stirring continuously, until thick. Add the sugar or honey.

FRUITY OATMEAL *serves 2*

3¾ cups unsweetened soy milk
1½ cups oatmeal
1 tsp. cinnamon
1 small banana, chopped
1⅓ cups blueberries
2 tbsp. slivered almonds

Put the soy milk and oatmeal in a saucepan and cook over low heat, stirring regularly, 5 minutes. Add the cinnamon and banana, stir, and cook 2 minutes. Divide the mixture into two bowls. Serve topped with the blueberries and slivered almonds.

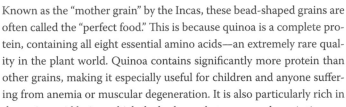

Quinoa

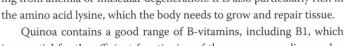

VITAMINS B1, B2, B3, B5, B6, E, FOLIC ACID; CALCIUM, COPPER, IRON,
MAGNESIUM, MANGANESE, PHOSPHORUS, POTASSIUM, ZINC; FIBER; PROTEIN;
SAPONINS; CARBOHYDRATE

Pronounced "keenwa," and introduced from the South American Andes, quinoa is rich in unique health-sustaining properties, packed with goodness.

Known as the "mother grain" by the Incas, these bead-shaped grains are often called the "perfect food." This is because quinoa is a complete protein, containing all eight essential amino acids—an extremely rare quality in the plant world. Quinoa contains significantly more protein than other grains, making it especially useful for children and anyone suffering from anemia or muscular degeneration. It is also particularly rich in the amino acid lysine, which the body needs to grow and repair tissue.

Quinoa contains a good range of B-vitamins, including B1, which is essential for the efficient functioning of the nervous, cardiovascular, and muscular systems, and vitamin B2, which controls the buildup of cholesterol in the body by destroying harmful free radicals. Among the other B-vitamins found in quinoa are B5, which is essential for a healthy response to stress, and folic acid, which aids the reproductive organs and is crucial for the healthy production of red blood cells.

The grain is a useful source of antioxidant vitamin E, needed for the body's healing processes and to keep the skin youthful, as well as a number of health-enhancing minerals, including calcium, iron, manganese, magnesium, and zinc. Calcium, magnesium, and manganese are all vital for strong bones and for staving off osteoporosis, while iron helps to prevent fatigue, as well as hair loss and anemia. Magnesium is also thought to play a role in averting migraines and headaches, and in lowering blood pressure. Zinc is a powerful antioxidant mineral that fights infections and is also necessary for the health of the thymus gland, the regulator of immune cell production.

In Eastern medicine, quinoa is used to strengthen the kidneys and revitalize the liver, as well as for everything from reproductive health and urinary problems to detoxification and skin disorders.

QUINOA PILAF

3¾ cups water
1¾ cups quinoa
⅔ cup olive oil
4½ cups thinly sliced okra
3 tbsp. tomato paste
1 onion, chopped
2 garlic cloves, crushed
2 tsp. cumin seeds
1 tsp. black pepper
2 tbsp. chopped cilantro leaves

Boil the water in a saucepan. Add the quinoa and return to a boil again, then lower the heat and simmer 15 minutes. Drain and set aside. Heat the oil in a wok, add the okra, and stir-fry 3 minutes. Add the remaining ingredients, except the cilantro, and stir-fry 5 minutes. Lower the heat and cook 10 minutes longer. Stir in the quinoa and cilantro. Serve.

SOUTHWESTERN QUINOA AND CHICKPEA SALAD

½ cup quinoa
2¼ cups water
4 tsp. olive oil
1 cup canned chickpeas, drained and
   rinsed
1 tomato, seeded and chopped
3 tbsp. lime juice
2 tbsp. chopped cilantro
½ tsp. ground cumin
1 garlic clove, minced
a pinch of salt

Bring the quinoa and water to the boil in a pan, then lower the heat, cover, and simmer 15 minutes. Drain and transfer the quinoa to a bowl. Drizzle with the oil and toss. Add the remaining ingredients and mix well.

Brown rice

VITAMINS B1, B3, B5, B6, E, K, BIOTIN, FOLIC ACID; CALCIUM, COPPER, IODINE,
IRON, MAGNESIUM, MANGANESE, PHOSPHORUS, POTASSIUM, SELENIUM, ZINC;
ORYZANOL; FIBER; PROTEIN; CARBOHYDRATE; TRYPTOPHAN

**First cultivated in China more than 6,000 years ago,
brown rice is a folk remedy for soothing the digestive
and circulatory systems. It is an excellent source of fiber,
as well as many valuable youth-preserving nutrients.**

Thought to be indigenous to Southeast Asia and parts of Africa, rice is
the most important dietary staple for a large part of the world's population. While in many places, white rice is the traditionally available and
established type, brown rice is becoming increasingly popular as more
people become aware of its superior nutritional benefits.

Brown rice contains abundant amounts of fiber, which promote
healthy digestion. It also has a soothing effect on the entire intestinal
tract, helping to ease conditions such as irritable bowel syndrome. Short-
grain rice varieties are good for colon function, helping to clear toxic
waste. The outer layer of the grain, the bran, contains oryzanol, which
lowers cholesterol and aids in the relief of gastritis and other gastrointestinal complaints. Rice's rich fiber content is excellent for the digestive system and helps to lower cholesterol, so is important for a healthy
heart. It is a complex carbohydrate, so it releases energy slowly, and is
ideal for keeping hunger pangs at bay.

Dense in B-vitamins, brown rice is good for keeping the brain and
nervous system healthy, and helps to relieve anxiety, fatigue, and depression. Its protein is a building block for the bones and muscles, as well as
soft tissues, such as the skin and the hair. Brown rice is also a good source
of trace minerals, such as phosphorus and copper, which build resistance
to infections. Brown rice is also rich in magnesium, which plays a major
role in bone health, as well as reducing mood swings and easing stress,
lowering high blood pressure, preventing muscle cramps, and helping
the body to turn food into energy. Containing iron to combat anemia
and hair loss, brown rice is also high in zinc, which is antiviral and excellent for warding off colds.

Many of the nutrients that can improve mood more effectively are lost when rice is processed to become white. Brown rice still contains all its nutrients and provides selenium, which counters depression but is lacking in most people's diets. Brown rice takes longer than white varieties to digest, preventing a sudden rise and fall in blood sugar levels and making you feel comfortably full. It also makes a wonderful convalescing food as it is gentle on the stomach. Packed with phytonutrients, it is particularly useful in countering mood swings and other symptoms associated with the perimenopause.

According to the macrobiotic philosophy, brown rice is considered to be the most balanced of all foods and people who follow this dietary regime often eat it on a daily basis.

The processing of wholegrain rice into white rice removes many of its key nutrients and all of its fiber. So, although brown rice takes longer to cook than white rice—about 45 minutes as opposed to 15 minutes—it's well worth the extra time. Brown basmati rice is not rapidly absorbed into the body, providing a steady stream of energy for exercisers, rather than a spike followed by a slump.

BROWN RICE SALAD *serves 1 to 2*

¼ cup brown rice, cooked
  and cooled

2 scallions, trimmed and sliced

4 tomatoes, cut into segments

½ cup black olives, pitted
  and halved

2 garlic cloves, crushed

3 tbsp. basil, roughly chopped

3 tbsp. olive oil

Combine all the ingredients together in a large salad bowl. Leave at room temperature 1 hour to let the flavors mingle, then serve.

PILAU RICE

1 onion, finely chopped

1 tbsp. olive oil

2 green cardamom pods

5 cloves

½ cinnamon stick

a pinch of saffron threads

1 cup brown basmati rice

3½ cups vegetable stock

2 bay leaves

Sauté the onion in the oil until soft. Add the spices and cook 2 minutes longer. Add the rice and stir until the grains are coated in the oil before adding the stock and bay leaves. Bring to a boil, then lower the heat and simmer, covered, 50 minutes, or until the rice is soft and all the liquid is absorbed. Leave to stand 5 minutes, then fluff with a fork.

✦ GROUND RICE POULTICE
for skin inflammation

¼ cup brown rice flour

¼ cup milk

gauze or cotton strip

In a bowl, mix the rice and milk to make a paste. Apply to the affected area. Wrap securely in place, using the gauze or cotton strip. Leave on 3 hours, as required.

SPICED BROWN RICE

4 cups water
1½ cups short-grain brown rice
2½ cups soy milk
4 tbsp. rice syrup or date syrup
1 tsp. cinnamon
¼ nutmeg, grated
4 cloves
2 small handfuls raisins
4 shavings orange zest

Preheat the oven to 350°F. Put the water in a pan and bring to a boil. Add the rice, lower the heat and simmer 15 minutes. Strain and return the rice to the pan. Add the remaining ingredients and simmer 20 minutes. Transfer to a lightly greased baking dish and bake 40 minutes. Serve hot.

RAISIN RICE PUDDING

1½ cups brown rice
4 tbsp. raisins
1 cup plus 2 tbsp. milk
2 tbsp. honey
2 tsp. cinnamon

Boil the rice 15 minutes, or until tender. Preheat the oven to 325°F. Mix the rice and raisins in a baking dish. In a pan, gently heat the milk and honey, stirring until the honey dissolves. Pour over the rice and sprinkle with the cinnamon. Bake 30 minutes and serve immediately.

COCONUT MILK RICE PUDDING

1 cup short-grain brown rice
3 tbsp. raisins
2 tbsp. agave syrup
1 cinnamon stick
10 green cardamom pods
1¾ cups coconut milk
½ tsp. natural vanilla extract
ground cinnamon, to serve

Put the rice, raisins, agave syrup, cinnamon stick, and cardamom pods in a pan with 4 cups water and bring to a boil. Lower the heat and simmer, covered, 90 minutes, or until the water is absorbed. Add the coconut milk and vanilla extract. Cook 5 minutes longer. Sprinkle with the cinnamon and serve.

Buckwheat

VITAMINS B1, B2, B3, B5, B6, E, K, FOLIC ACID; CALCIUM, COPPER, IRON, MAGNESIUM, MANGANESE, PHOSPHORUS, POTASSIUM, SELENIUM, ZINC; RUTIN; CHIRO-INOSITOL; FIBER; PROTEIN; CARBOHYDRATE

This unique-tasting grain blends well when mixed with other grains and is marvelous for strengthening blood vessels and improving a sluggish circulation.

Thought to have originated in China, buckwheat spread to northern Europe and Russia in the fourteenth century. In spite of its name, buckwheat is not related to wheat and can ve eaten by those on a wheat- or gluten-free diet.

Buckwheat's main asset is its rutin, a bioflavonoid compound that helps to strengthen weakened blood capillaries, thus preventing the formation of thread veins. In turn, the strenthening of capillaries might improve circulatory problems, such as chilblains and high blood pressure. Buckwheat also appears to aid the management of diabetes and glucose intolerance by controlling blood sugar balance through the action of a substance called chiro-inositol.

Buckwheat contains fiber and all eight essential amino acids, and is a good source of protein for the brain. Rich in magnesium, which is vital for bone health, the grain also contains several B-vitamins, which help to maintain the nervous system. It also lowers blood cholesterol levels.

Buckwheat is today widely consumed in Eastern Europe, especially in Poland and Russia, where it features in many traditional dishes.

BUCKWHEAT MUESLI

2½ cups buckwheat flakes
1 cup oatmeal
½ cup sunflower seeds
1 cup dried apricots
⅓ cup raisins
milk or soy milk, to serve

Chop the apricots into bite-size pieces. In a large mixing bowl, combine the ingredients thoroughly. The muesli keeps well in a sealed plastic container. Serve with milk or soy milk.

Millet

MAGNESIUM, POTASSIUM, SILICA; PROTEIN

Millet is a highly nutritious grain that supplies fantastic support to the digestive system, especially the stomach, spleen, and pancreas.

Grown in Asia and Africa for thousands of years, millet was one of the first cereals to be cultivated by mankind. It is even mentioned in the Bible. Today, millet is gaining in popularity in the West.

High in protein, low in starch, and containing all eight essential amino acids, millet is one of only a few alkaline-forming grains, thus helping to counteract overacidity in the stomach and joints. It has antifungal and antimucus properties, which help to prevent ailments such as candida and premenstrual discomfort.

Millet is rich in silica, the great cleansing, mending, and eliminating mineral that is essential for hair, skin, teeth, eye, and nail health, as well as the growth and maintenance of tendons and bones. Silica also supports arterial health, prevents cardiovascular disease, and plays an important role in memory function. The grain has high levels of potassium and magnesium, useful for treating arthritis and osteoporosis.

MILLET PILAF

1 large onion, finely chopped

4 tsp. olive oil

2 tbsp. ground coriander

2 garlic cloves, crushed

2 cups millet

1 lb. 5 oz. tomatoes, chopped

2½ cups vegetable stock

1 cup plus 2 tbsp. white wine

2 tsp. slivered almonds

4 or 5 dashes soy sauce

Preheat the oven to 350°F. Slowly sauté the onion in oil 4 to 5 minutes. Add the coriander and garlic, and cook 5 minutes longer. Add the millet and sauté 2 minutes. Add the tomatoes, stock, and wine. Bring to a boil, then simmer, uncovered, 20 minutes until tender. Add the slivered almonds and soy sauce. Serve immediately.

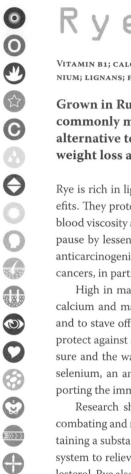

Rye

VITAMIN B1; CALCIUM, IRON, MAGNESIUM, PHOSPHORUS, POTASSIUM, SELE-
NIUM; LIGNANS; FIBER; PROTEIN

Grown in Russia for more than 2,000 years, rye is commonly milled into flour and is used as a nutritious alternative to wheat. This high-fiber, low-GI grain aids weight loss and combats fluid retention.

Rye is rich in lignans, plant phytonutrients that have many health benefits. They protect against heart disease and stroke by helping to reduce blood viscosity and help women approaching or experiencing the menopause by lessening hot flashes and other symptoms. Lignans also have anticarcinogenic properties and are thought to prevent breast and colon cancers, in particular.

High in many health-enhancing minerals, rye is a useful source of calcium and magnesium, both of which are needed for healthy bones and to stave off osteoporosis. Its iron content helps to fight fatigue and protect against anemia, while its potassium helps to control blood pressure and the water balance in the body's cells. Rye is also packed with selenium, an antioxidant mineral that plays an important role in supporting the immune system.

Research shows that rye is useful for balancing blood sugar and combating and managing diabetes, as it improves insulin response. Containing a substantial amount of dietary fiber, rye stimulates the digestive system to relieve constipation and is also thought to help to lower cholesterol. Rye also contains sucrose and fructooligosaccharide, which have prebiotic properties that are useful to digestive health.

Wholegrain cereals play an important role in weight loss. Full of insoluble fiber, they score low on the glycemic index (GI), meaning they release sugar into the blood slowly, whereas refined versions have little nutritional value and cause a sudden spike in energy, then a slump. Low-GI foods have long been known to benefit health, but they are now believed to aid fat loss, too, even when you eat the same number of calories as on a higher-GI diet. Rye is one of the lowest GI cereals. It's also rich in compounds that food to water, which prevents bloating.

COTTAGE CHEESE ON RYE

8 slices rye bread
½ cup cottage cheese
1 tsp. finely sliced lemongrass
4 tomatoes, roughly chopped
4 gherkins, sliced

Toast the bread. Mix together the cottage cheese and lemongrass. Pile onto the toast and top with the tomatoes and gherkins. Serve immediately.

RYE PANCAKES

½ cup rye flour
1 extra-large egg
7 tbsp. water
⅔ cup milk
1 tbsp. olive oil

Whiz the rye flour, egg, water, and milk in a food processor, then let sit 10 to 15 minutes. Drizzle some oil into a heavy skillet and heat. Carefully ladle in the batter, allowing 2 to 3 tablespoons per pancake. As the batter for each pancake begins to bubble on the surface, flip it over, and cook for another 4 to 5 minutes or until cooked through.

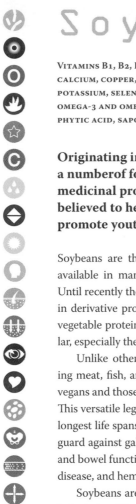

Soybean

VITAMINS B1, B2, B3, B5, B6, E, K, BETA-CAROTENE, BIOTIN, FOLIC ACID; CALCIUM, COPPER, IODINE, IRON, MAGNESIUM, MANGANESE, PHOSPHORUS, POTASSIUM, SELENIUM, ZINC; FIBER; PROTEIN; COMPLEX CARBOHYDRATE; OMEGA-3 AND OMEGA-6 ESSENTIAL FATTY ACIDS; LECITHIN; ISOFLAVONES; PHYTIC ACID, SAPONINS, PROTEASE INHIBITORS

Originating in the Far East, soybeans are made into a numberof food products with a wealth of ancient medicinal properties. Eating a diet rich in soybeans is believed to help to prevent heart disease, as well as to promote youthfulness and longevity.

Soybeans are the most widely grown beans in the world. They are available in many forms, including dried, canned, fresh, and frozen. Until recently they have perhaps been best known in Western countries in derivative products, such as tofu, soy milk, soy sauce, and textured vegetable protein. The fresh beans, however, are becoming more popular, especially the young beans in their pods, known as edamame.

Unlike other legumes, soy is a source of complete protein, rivaling meat, fish, and eggs, making it an ideal alternative for vegetarians, vegans and those who simply wish to reduce their consumption of meat. This versatile legume is central to the diet of the Japanese, who have the longest life spans in the world. Plant-derived protein is also said to help guard against gallstones. They are excellent in promoting healthy colon and bowel function, and are protective against constipation, diverticular disease, and hemorrhoids.

Soybeans are an excellent source of dietary fiber and complex carbohydrates. They are known to have a cholesterol-lowering effect and to prevent high triglyceride levels, which can cause heart disease. In addition, soybeans contain youth-preserving antioxidants, such as phytic acid, which can help to prevent the clogging of the arteries that can lead to a stroke or heart attack.

Perhaps the most useful attribute of soybeans, however, is that they are extremely rich in micronutrients, such as saponins and isoflavones. A type of flavonoid, isoflavones are converted by the body into phytoestrogens and have anticarcinogenic properties as well as the ability to reduce the risk of cardiovascular disease and to promote bone health. The isoflavone genistein is thought to stop the breakdown of bone and to help to increase bone mass, offering protection against osteoporosis and it might also increase the flexibility of blood vessels. Phytoestrogens can also mimic the effects of the hormone estrogen in the body. This makes them useful for helping to control menopausal symptoms, such as hot flashes. Studies have shown that isoflavones can help to prevent the hormone-linked diseases of breast and prostate cancers.

These beans contain vitamin E, which is vital for preserving youthful skin and hair, and B-vitamins, which maintain the nervous system and keep stress from causing premature aging.

Having an extremely low glycemic index (GI) score, soybeans are great blood sugar and insulin regulators, which makes them useful for helping to prevent diabetes, as well as for maintaining energy levels in people who already have the disease.

Soybeans are rich in lecithin, a natural emulsifier of fats, which helps them to assist in lowering cholesterol levels. Their omega-3 essential fatty acids stimulate blood circulation, reduce blood pressure, and lower the risks of heart disease. Omega-3s also boost brain power, improve the quality of the skin, and protect against cancer.

SOY CRÊPES

1 cup soy flour
2¾ cups all-purpose flour
3 tbsp. baking powder
3 tbsp. sugar
½ tsp. salt
3 large eggs
3 cups soy milk
6 tbsp. soy oil
1 tbsp. butter

Combine all the ingredients, except the butter, in a bowl and beat to form a batter. Melt a little of the butter in a skillet and add ½ cup of the batter. Cook on both sides until golden brown. Remove from the pan and keep warm while you cook the remaining batter. Fold the crêpes and serve.

BANANA, AVOCADO, AND SOY SMOOTHIE *serves 2*

1 banana, peeled
1 avocado, pitted and peeled
3½ oz. silken tofu
1¾ cups soy milk
a generous sprinkling of slivered almonds

Whiz together the banana, avocado, tofu, and soy milk in a blender until smooth. Sprinkle the almonds over and serve immediately.

SOYBEAN PÂTÉ

1 cup soybeans, cooked
1 tbsp. olive oil
1 onion, finely chopped
2 tbsp. tomato paste
10 black olives, pitted and chopped
2 tbsp. chopped parsley leaves
1 tbsp. sesame seeds, lightly toasted
a pinch of salt

Put the soybeans in a bowl and mash them with a fork. Heat the olive oil in a skillet and sauté the onion until it is clear and soft. Add to the beans, then stir in the tomato paste, olives, parsley, sesame seeds, and salt. Cover and chill at least 30 minutes before serving.

SCRAMBLED TOFU

2 garlic cloves, crushed

½ large red bell pepper, seeded and diced

2 tbsp. olive oil

10 oz. firm tofu

½ tsp. ground turmeric

½ tsp. salt

pinch of ground black pepper

1 onion, chopped

1½ tsp. soy sauce

salsa and corn tortillas, to serve

In a skillet, sauté the garlic and red pepper in the olive oil 2 minutes. Crumble the tofu and add it to the pan, then add the turmeric, salt, black pepper, onion, and soy sauce. Cook 3 minutes, stirring occasionally. Remove from the heat. Serve with salsa and corn tortillas.

Adzuki bean

VITAMINS B1, B2, B3, B5, B6, E, BETA-CAROTENE, BIOTIN, FOLIC ACID; CALCIUM, COPPER, IODINE, IRON, MAGNESIUM, MANGANESE, PHOSPHORUS, POTASSIUM, SELENIUM, ZINC; FIBER; PROTEIN; CARBOHYDRATE

These nutty beans, known as the "king of beans" in Japan—where they have been used for their healing properties for more than 1,000 years—are packed with energizing nutrients.

According to Oriental medicine, adzuki beans help to disperse stagnant blood, which can be the cause of many diseases. They have a tonifying effect on the kidney-adrenal function and, therefore, help to regulate the stress response. Adzuki beans are drying in nature, and are useful in the treatment of diarrhea, edema, and boils. They are also good for the urinary tract and a drink made from the water in which adzuki beans have been boiled is a traditional remedy for kidney and bladder complaints.

Adzuki beans are high in fiber, making them useful for speeding up the elimination of waste and helping to detoxify the body. They contain good levels of B-vitamins, which are needed for steady energy production and to repair body tissues. Adzuki beans are also a useful source of protein, which helps to build muscle and maintain healthy skin, and are rich in immunity-boosting minerals, including antiviral zinc, calcium, and magnesium.

They contain more fiber and protein and less fat than most other beans, making them useful for anyone trying to lose weight. They are diuretic and their high potassium content helps to control water balance by heping to rid the body of excess fluid.

ADZUKI BEAN SOUP

1 cup dried adzuki beans
2½ cups vegetable stock
1 onion, sliced
1 carrot, diced
1 celery stick, diced
soy sauce, to taste

Put all the ingredients, except the soy sauce, in a pan. Bring to a boil, then lower the heat and simmer 1 hour, or until all the beans and vegetables are tender. Add the soy sauce to taste. Blend in a food processor, if desired, or serve chunky.

ADZUKI BEAN CHILI

½ cup dried adzuki beans
1 onion, chopped
1 garlic clove, crushed
2 tbsp. olive oil
15 oz. canned crushed tomatoes
½ green chili, seeded and finely chopped
½ tsp. cayenne pepper
1 tbsp. tamari soy sauce

Soak the beans overnight in cold water. The next day, drain, put in a pan with water to cover and bring to a boil. Simmer, covered, about 1 hour until tender. Drain and set aside. In another pan, gently sauté the onion and garlic in the oil, add the remaining ingredients and the beans, and simmer, covered, 25 minutes.

ADZUKI BEAN HOTPOT

½ cup dried adzuki beans
1 large onion, chopped
3 carrots, peeled and diced
2 parsnips, peeled and diced
2 sweet potatoes, peeled and diced
2 bay leaves
1 tbsp. tomato paste

Soak the beans overnight in cold water. Drain, put in a pan, and cover with water. Bring to a boil, lower the heat, and simmer 45 minutes. Drain. Put all the ingredients with water to cover into a large baking dish with a tight-fitting cover. Bake in a preheated oven at 375°F 1½ hours.

Kidney bean

VITAMINS B1, B6, K, FOLIC ACID; COPPER, IRON, MAGNESIUM, MANGANESE, MOLYBDENUM, PHOSPHORUS, POTASSIUM, ZINC; FIBER, PROTEIN

Thought to originate from Peru, these soft beans are high in protein, vitamins, and minerals. This small but powerful food provides an armory of nutrients to keep your mind and body in top form.

Popular in Central and South America, kidney beans are an excellent source of protein, which helps to keep energy levels steady as well as maintaining and repairing cells. One average serving of kidney beans provides lots of protein and one-third of the recommended daily intake of fiber for most adults. This is beneficial for regular exercisers who want to lose weight, because fiber curbs hunger for longer, while the protein gives energy. The soluble fiber keeps blood sugar levels steady, giving you plenty of vitality while preventing energy spikes and slumps. This means these beans are especially useful for people with diabetes or hypoglycemia, too. Fiber also protects the heart and cardiovascular system by lowering blood cholesterol, and it encourages good digestion and the efficient elimination of toxins and waste matter.

The humble kidney bean provides an impressive array of nutrients for combating low moods and strengthening brain function. Rich in vitamin B1, it keeps the memory sharp and its rich magnesium content promotes physical and mental relaxation. Kidney beans contain iron—crucial for the production of the immune system's antibodies and white blood cells. They also provide an iron top up for the many women whose periods leave them short of this essential mineral.

Kidney beans are also rich in folic acid, a B-vitamin that is important for good reproductive health, especially in early pregnancy for protecting the developing fetus from spina bifida. Folic acid also combats heart disease and helps to speed up wound healing.

QUICK KIDNEY BEAN CASSEROLE *serves 2*

2 tbsp. olive oil

1 onion, chopped

1 red bell pepper, seeded and chopped

1 zucchini, sliced

4 portabello mushrooms, sliced

3 large tomatoes, chopped

2 garlic cloves, crushed

15 oz. canned red kidney beans, rinsed

2 tsp. chopped basil

1 tsp. salt

Heat the olive oil in a large saucepan, then add the onion and stir-fry until golden. Add the pepper, zucchini, mushrooms, tomatoes, and garlic, continue stir-frying 5 minutes, then add the kidney beans and enough water to cover. Add the basil and salt, then cover and simmer until the vegetables are soft.

KIDNEY BEAN GUMBO

1 red onion, chopped

1 red bell pepper, seeded and diced

1 celery stick, trimmed and chopped

2 garlic cloves, crushed

1 tbsp. olive oil

6 cups vegetable stock

1½ cups chopped tomatoes

1 tsp. dried thyme

a pinch of cayenne pepper

1½ cups canned kidney beans, rinsed

In a saucepan, sauté the onion, red pepper, celery, and garlic in the oil 5 minutes. Add the stock, tomatoes, thyme, and cayenne pepper, cover, and simmer until soft. Add the kidney beans and simmer 10 minutes until the flavors blend. Serve hot.

CHILI BEANS

1 tbsp. peanut oil

2 onions, chopped

1 tsp. cayenne pepper, or 1 fresh chili, seeded and chopped

8 oz. lean ground beef (optional)

2¼ cups canned kidney beans, drained and rinsed

1⅔ cups canned crushed tomatoes

Heat the oil in a saucepan and sauté the onions 2 to 3 minutes. Add the cayenne and fry 1 minute. Stir in the beef, if using, and cook until brown. Add the beans and tomatoes and bring to a boil. Lower the heat and simmer 10 minutes. Serve hot with brown rice.

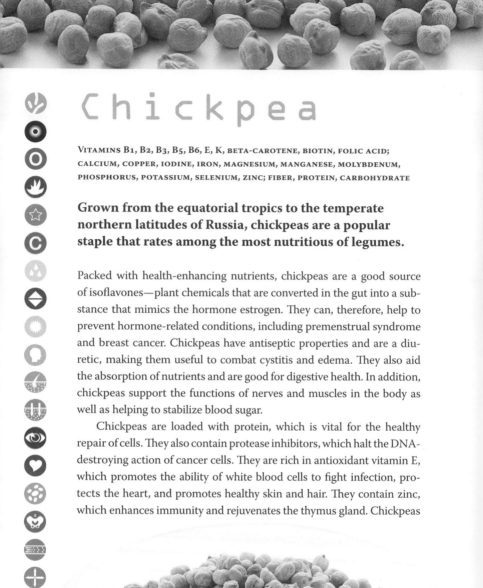

Chickpea

VITAMINS B1, B2, B3, B5, B6, E, K, BETA-CAROTENE, BIOTIN, FOLIC ACID;
CALCIUM, COPPER, IODINE, IRON, MAGNESIUM, MANGANESE, MOLYBDENUM,
PHOSPHORUS, POTASSIUM, SELENIUM, ZINC; FIBER, PROTEIN, CARBOHYDRATE

Grown from the equatorial tropics to the temperate northern latitudes of Russia, chickpeas are a popular staple that rates among the most nutritious of legumes.

Packed with health-enhancing nutrients, chickpeas are a good source of isoflavones—plant chemicals that are converted in the gut into a substance that mimics the hormone estrogen. They can, therefore, help to prevent hormone-related conditions, including premenstrual syndrome and breast cancer. Chickpeas have antiseptic properties and are a diuretic, making them useful to combat cystitis and edema. They also aid the absorption of nutrients and are good for digestive health. In addition, chickpeas support the functions of nerves and muscles in the body as well as helping to stabilize blood sugar.

Chickpeas are loaded with protein, which is vital for the healthy repair of cells. They also contain protease inhibitors, which halt the DNA-destroying action of cancer cells. They are rich in antioxidant vitamin E, which promotes the ability of white blood cells to fight infection, protects the heart, and promotes healthy skin and hair. They contain zinc, which enhances immunity and rejuvenates the thymus gland. Chickpeas

also provide plenty of iron, a mineral that women in particular, tend to be deficient in until after menopause.

It is thought that chickpeas also help the body to deal with preservatives, found in some processed foods, that can cause headaches. Canned chickpeas (without added sugar or salt) are just as nutritious as dried.

CHICKPEA SALAD

1½ cups dried chickpeas
10 scallions, trimmed and sliced
7 oz. watercress
7 oz. arugula
a handful mint leaves
3 tbsp. olive oil
2 tbsp. balsamic vinegar
1 cup Parmesan cheese shavings

Soak the chickpeas overnight. Drain, place in a pan and cover with water. Bring to a boil, lower the heat, and simmer 2 hours, or until soft. Once cool, mix well with the scallions, watercress, arugula, mint, oil, and vinegar in a large bowl. Top with the cheese and serve.

HUMMUS

2¼ cups canned chickpeas
2 garlic cloves, crushed
3 tbsp. lemon juice
2 tbsp. tahini
2 tbsp. olive oil

Drain the chickpeas and blend with the garlic and lemon juice, or mash them in a bowl. Stir in the tahini and oil, then add a little water for smoothness, if wished.

CHICKPEA CURRY

⅔ cup dried chickpeas, soaked in water
   overnight and drained
1 onion, chopped
2 garlic cloves, crushed
2 tsp. curry powder
2 tbsp. olive oil
2 cups tomato purée

Put the chickpeas in a saucepan and cover with water. Bring to a boil, lower the heat, and simmer, covered, 2 hours. Drain and set aside. Sauté the onion, garlic, and curry powder in the oil. Add the tomato purée and chickpeas and simmer, covered, 25 minutes. Serve hot.

Lentil

VITAMINS B1, B2, B3, B5, B6, B9, B12, E, K, BETA-CAROTENE, BIOTIN, FOLIC
ACID; CALCIUM, COPPER, IODINE, IRON, MAGNESIUM, MANGANESE,
PHOSPHORUS, POTASSIUM, SELENIUM, ZINC; FIBER; PROTEIN; CARBOHYDRATE

The humble lentil, one of our oldest foods and a staple in many countries, is antioxidant-rich and one of the single most nutritious and digestible foods of all.

Whether red, green, or brown, lentils are a good source of protein, which we need to keep our skin, hair, teeth, and nails strong and healthy. They contain high levels of B-vitamins, particularly B3, deficiency of which can lead to poor memory and irritability, and B12, which helps to prevent everything from arthritis to tinnitus. Along with the antioxidant selenium, the B-vitamins also help to boost the body's immune system, aiding the fighting of bacteria and other invaders. They are rich in iron and are recommended for pregnant and lactating women, as well as people suffering from anemia. As with all other legumes, lentils contain anticarcinogenic phytochemicals and are also a good source of plant estrogens, which can help to reduce menopausal symptoms.

Lentils are loaded with fiber, which promotes a healthy digestive system and can help to regulate colon function as well as boosting heart health and the circulatory system. Lentils are also great for stabilizing blood sugar levels, making them a useful food for diabetics.

Providing the perfect combination of nutrients to allay hunger pangs and spark energy, lentils are an ideal snack to have before exercising or playing sports. A spoonful of dhal on bread, for example, is sustaining but not heavy, so it won't slow you down or cause indigestion. Lentils are rich in complex carbohydrates, which the body turns into glucose, providing a steady source of energy to maintain stamina. In fact, one study found that eating lentils three hours before exercise could help to increase endurance significantly more than other carbohydrates. Lentils also contain very little fat.

Lentils are crammed full of folic acid, an energy-boosting vitamin that plays a key role in the production of serotonin, the neurotransmitter in the brain associated with feelings of happiness.

SPICY LENTIL BURGERS

1 onion, finely chopped
1 tbsp. olive oil
1 to 2 tsp. curry powder
scant 1 cup red lentils
2 cups vegetable stock
1 cup wholewheat breadcrumbs

Sauté the onion in the oil, then stir in the curry powder and cook 2 minutes. Add the lentils and stock and bring to a boil, then simmer 20 to 25 minutes. Add the breadcrumbs and shape into four burgers. Broil on a lightly greased baking sheet until crisp and brown.

WARM LENTIL SALAD

1½ cups red lentils
4 tbsp. olive oil
2 onions, chopped
1 garlic clove, crushed
1 red bell pepper, seeded and finely
    chopped
1 zucchini, finely chopped
1 carrot, peeled and finely sliced
1 celery stick, finely chopped
2 large ripe tomatoes, seeded and chopped
2 tbsp. balsamic vinegar
1 tbsp. finely chopped mint leaves

Cook the lentils in a pan of boiling water 30 minutes, or until tender, then drain. Heat the oil in a wok, add the vegetables, and stir-fry until tender. Remove the wok from the heat, add the lentils, vinegar, and mint, combine thoroughly, and serve.

SWEET-AND-SOUR LENTILS

1¼ cups red lentils
2 tbsp. vegetable oil
2 dried red chilies, chopped
½ tsp. mustard seeds
2 tbsp. soy sauce
1 tbsp. sugar
4 tbsp. pineapple juice
1 tbsp. white wine vinegar

Place the lentils in a saucepan, cover with water, and bring to a boil. Cover the pan, lower the heat, and simmer 40 minutes, then drain. In another pan, heat the oil and fry the spices 3 minutes. Add the soy sauce, sugar, juice, vinegar, and lentils. Stir in ½ cup water and simmer 10 minutes, then serve.

LENTIL AND CUMIN SOUP

2 onions, roughly chopped

4 garlic cloves, crushed

4 tsp. cumin seeds

3 tbsp. vegetable oil

1 bay leaf

½ tsp. dried oregano

3 quarts chicken stock

3 cups canned green or brown lentils,
   drained

In a saucepan, sauté the onion, garlic, and cumin seeds in the oil. Add the bay leaf, oregano, and stock. Bring to a boil, then lower the heat and simmer 10 minutes. Add the lentils and cook 10 minutes longer. Remove the bay leaf and purée the soup in a food processor.

DHAL

1 tbsp. peanut oil

1 tsp. mustard seeds

1 large onion, finely chopped

2 garlic cloves, crushed

1 tsp. ground cumin

1-inch piece gingerroot, peeled and finely
   chopped

1 cup lentils

Heat the oil and fry the mustard seeds until they pop. Add the onion, garlic, cumin, and ginger and stir-fry 3 to 5 minutes until the onion is soft. Add the lentils and 3 cups water and bring to a boil. Lower the heat and simmer 30 to 40 minutes. Serve with bread or rice, or leave to cool, cover, and refrigerate overnight.

RED LENTIL DHAL

2 tbsp. olive oil

1 onion, chopped

2 garlic cloves, crushed

1 tsp. ground mustard seeds

1 tsp. ground cumin

½ tsp. cayenne powder

½ tsp. turmeric

2 tomatoes, chopped

1 cup red lentils

Heat the oil in a pan and slowly fry the onion until soft. Add the garlic, spices, and tomatoes and simmer a few minutes, stirring. Add the lentils and 2 cups plus 2 tablespoons water and bring to a boil. Lower the heat and simmer, covered, 20 minutes. Serve hot.

HERBS, SPICES, AND
FOODS SUCH AS HONEY
AND APPLE CIDER
VINEGAR PUNCH WELL
ABOVE THEIR WEIGHT IN
THE NUTRITION STAKES

07 | wonder
HERBS,
SPICES
& OTHERS

Parsley

VITAMINS A, B1, B3, B5, C, K, BETA-CAROTENE, BIOTIN, FOLIC ACID; CALCIUM, COPPER, IODINE, IRON, MAGNESIUM, MANGANESE, PHOSPHORUS, POTASSIUM, SELENIUM, ZINC; LIMONENE, MYRISTICIN; LUTEOLIN

One of the world's most popular culinary herbs, parsley has much more to it than its use as a garnish. Parsley is full of youth-enhancing nutrients and is a natural healer.

A great source of disease-fighting antioxidants, parsley is high in vitamin A and its precursor, beta-carotene, as well as vitamin C. Vitamin A is known for its ability to keep the arteries clear from the build up of plaque and for protecting against eye disease. It is a potent anti-inflammatory agent, which, along with vitamin C and the flavonoid luteolin, is thought to be useful in combating asthma and arthritis. Vitamin C fights the harmful free radicals that encourage the development of many diseases, such as cancers, diabetes, and heart conditions. A powerful immunity-booster, vitamin C also staves off day-to-day illnesses, such as colds, flu, and ear infections.

Parsley is the richest herbal source of the mineral potassium, which reduces high blood pressure—the number one cause of heart attacks. A natural diuretic, parsley encourages the excretion of sodium and water. Its potassium helps to balance fluid levels in the body, which can be disturbed by exercise, and also stimulates the kidneys to eliminate waste matter. Potassium is destroyed in cooking, so eat parsley raw to obtain maximum benefits.

The herb is also an excellent source of magnesium and calcium to protect the bones and the nervous system, as well as manganese, which boosts the memory, iron to prevent fatigue, and copper and zinc, which aid the healing of wounds.

Parsley contains several substances, including limonene, that exhibit anticancer properties, particularly against tumors. They also are believed to neutralize the carcinogens in cigarette smoke.

Chewing on a parsley sprig after a meal can help to freshen the breath. When applied topically to the skin, the herb is said to relieve irritation caused by insect bites.

PARSLEY SAUCE

2 tbsp. butter
1 tbsp. all-purpose flour
1¾ cups milk
2 tbsp. heavy cream
juice and grated zest of ½ lemon
4 tbsp. finely chopped parsley leaves
ground black pepper

In a small pan, melt the butter over low heat, then stir in the flour to form a smooth paste. Gradually stir in the milk, then bring the sauce to a boil, stirring. Lower the heat and simmer 3 minutes, whisking constantly. Add the cream, lemon juice and zest, and parsley and season with black pepper.

PARSLEY PASTA SAUCE

2 tbsp. olive oil
½ onion, chopped
1 garlic clove, crushed
1 tsp paprika
1¾ cups tomato purée
3 tbsp. chopped parsley leaves
salt and ground black pepper

Heat the oil in a pan and slowly sauté the onion until soft. Add the garlic and paprika and continue to cook 1 minute longer, stirring. Add the tomato purée and simmer, covered, 20 minutes. Add the parsley and seasoning toward the end of cooking time. Serve over pasta.

Sage

VITAMINS B3, B6, C, E, K, BETA-CAROTENE, BIOTIN, FOLIC ACID; CALCIUM, IRON, MAGNESIUM, MANGANESE, PHOSPHORUS, POTASSIUM, ZINC; FLAVONOIDS; TANNINS, SAPONINS, POLYPHENOLS; VOLATILE OILS

A native of the Mediterranean, this common garden herb is popular both used in cooking, and for its many curative properties.

With its rich array of nutrients, sage has antiseptic, antibacterial, and antiviral properties, and is a traditional ingredient of cough, cold, and respiratory remedies. Sage is antimucosal, so it is useful for beating colds as it helps to clear catarrh as well as fight off germs, and it is particularly successful in the treatment of bronchitis. Its antiseptic properties make it excellent for healing gum problems and sore throats when drunk as a tea or used as a gargle, and its antioxidant and anti-inflammatory action can help to ease arthritis. It also clears sluggish skin and firms tissues.

Sage has several ways of improving mind and mood. Recent research has shown that the herb can increase brain power, particularly short-term memory—for example in word-recall tests. It contains compounds similar to those in drugs that are used to combat the formation of plaques in the brain, and research is now under way to find out if it can help to slow the progression of Alzheimer's disease. The herb is also thought to soothe emotional distress.

Thanks to its success in reducing perspiration, sage is now a popular remedy for hot flashes during menopause. By preventing hot flashes and night sweats, it promotes healthy sleep patterns. Sage stimulates the intestines and is a digestive tonic. In Germany, it has been approved for the treatment of mild gastrointestinal complaints. A sage infusion drunk after eating can ease indigestion and bloating, as it is an antispasmodic herb.

SIMPLE SAGE STUFFING

8 oz. onions
1½ cups fresh breadcrumbs
1 tsp. dried sage
ground black pepper
2 tbsp. butter, melted, plus extra
    for greasing

Preheat the oven to 400°F. Quarter the onions and cook in boiling water until tender, then drain and chop them finely. Place them in a bowl, stir in the breadcrumbs, sage, and pepper, then add the melted butter to help the mixture stick together. Grease a baking dish and place scoops of stuffing in it, then bake 15 minutes. Suitable for serving with meat and vegetables.

✦ SAGE GARGLE *for respiratory ailments*

1 large handful sage leaves
1 small handful thyme leaves
2 cups boiling water
2 tbsp. apple cider vinegar
2 tsp. honey
1 tsp. cayenne pepper

Roughly chop the herb leaves and place in a pitcher. Add the boiling water, cover, and leave 30 minutes. Strain the liquid and stir in the vinegar, honey, and cayenne. Gargle with the mixture at the first sign of symptoms, or drink 2 teaspoons 2 or 3 times a day. Use within a week.

SQUASH SOUP WITH SAGE

4 cups seeded and chopped squash
2 cups plus 2 tbsp. vegetable stock
1 tbsp. olive oil
2 onions, chopped
4 tbsp. chopped sage leaves
ground black pepper

Boil the squash 10 minutes, and drain. Place in a blender, add the stock, and purée until smooth. Heat the oil in a pan. Sauté the onions 3 minutes, adding half the sage for the last minute. Add the squash and bring to a boil. Lower the heat and simmer 10 minutes. Add the pepper and remaining sage. Serve hot.

Peppermint

VITAMINS A, B2, B3, C, E, BETA-CAROTENE, FOLIC ACID; CALCIUM, COPPER, IRON, MAGNESIUM, MANGANESE, PHOSPHORUS, POTASSIUM; FIBER; OMEGA-3 FATTY ACIDS; VOLATILE OILS

A well-known digestive aid, peppermint has many other benefits and is one of the most popular traditional remedies used today. This dark green, strongly flavored variety of mint can help to beat colds and flu.

Native to Europe but now grown all over the world, peppermint is not a species in its own right but a hybrid of spearmint and watermint. Often known as the world's oldest medicine, peppermint may have been used as a remedy for more than 10,000 years.

Peppermint contains menthol, a substance useful for clearing congestion in the nose and chest from colds and infections. It is calming and anti-inflammatory, and also a good source of the minerals iron, needed for healthy blood, and calcium, necessary for strong bones and teeth.

This useful herb also improves circulation, and can help to treat both chills and fevers. In addition, it has analgesic properties, which are useful for headaches, inflamed joints, neuralgia, and sciatica. Its volatile oils are antibacterial, antiparasitic, antifungal, and antiviral. They also have antiseptic qualities, which make it ideal for use in toothpastes and mouthwashes to protect teeth and gums, as well as to freshen the breath. Traditionally it has been used to treat toothache.

From a bunch of fresh leaves to a tube of candy, any form of peppermint can relieve digestive upsets fast. It soothes the burning pain of indigestion, counteracts nausea, kills bacteria, relieves wind, and regulates intestinal movement. Its ability to stop muscle spasm makes it a useful remedy for irritable bowel syndrome and for the abdominal cramps felt during painful periods. It has also been found to inhibit the growth of several types of bacteria, including *Helicobacter pylori*, which has been identified as being the main cause of stomach and duodenal ulcers. Use it with caution, however, if you suffer from heartburn (when stomach acids rise into the throat), because although peppermint helps many sufferers, others find that it makes their heartburn worse.

PIPERADE *serves 1*

1 yellow bell pepper, seeded and sliced
1 onion, sliced
3 tbsp. olive oil
2 tomatoes, sliced
a pinch of cayenne pepper
1 tbsp. finely chopped peppermint leaves
1 egg

Sauté the pepper and onion in the oil over low heat until the onion is soft. Add the tomatoes, cayenne, and mint. Stir 2 minutes, then break the egg over the vegetables and cook until the yolk is cooked as desired. Serve immediately.

✦ PEPPERMINT FOOTBATH *for tired feet*

2 cups roughly chopped peppermint leaves
4 cups boiling water
7½ cups hot water
1 tsp. borax
1 tbsp. Epsom salts

Combine the herbs with the boiling water in a large bowl and leave to cool 1 hour, then strain. Add to a bowl or footbath filled with the hot water. Stir in the borax and Epsom salts. Soak your feet 15 to 20 minutes.

MINT TEA

4 tbsp. finely chopped peppermint leaves
1-inch piece gingerroot, peeled and finely
   chopped
2 tsp. honey

Boil 2 cups water and pour over the mint and ginger in an heatproof bowl. Allow to steep until cool enough to drink. Stir in the honey and drink when dissolved.

Rosemary

BETA-CAROTENE; CALCIUM, IRON, MAGNESIUM, MANGANESE; SAPONINS; CAFFEIC ACID; FLAVONOIDS; VOLATILE OILS; FIBER

This wonderfully fragrant and intensely flavored herb has a range of health-enhancing properties. A potent, stimulating herb, rosemary is an old-fashioned remedy for everything from colds and colic, to nervousness, stress, and eczema.

Rosemary has antiseptic, antioxidant, antispasmodic, and astringent qualities, proving useful for circulatory conditions, stiff muscles, coughs and colds, mouth and gum infections, and irritable bowel syndrome. An invigorating herb, rosemary fights fatigue. It is also a nervine and is excellent for female complaints and headaches.

Rosemary has traditionally been prized for its ability to improve memory, and it's not a myth: this herb can help to counteract a tendency to forgetfulness. A compound called rosmarinic acid improves blood circulation, increasing the flow of oxygen-rich blood to the brain. This improves all kinds of brain functions, aiding concentration and alertness. People perform better in memory tests, and have been found to be more alert, when they work in a room smelling of rosemary. And at the same time they also feel more relaxed and contented.

Recent studies on rosemary have shown that rosmarinic acid and another powerful antioxidant and anti-inflammatory agent known as caffeic acid might have the ability to help to prevent cancer. Current research shows that they might be particularly effective against breast cancer. The compounds also counter age-related skin damage, such as wrinkles, as well as boost liver function and act as a mild diuretic. Together with vitamin E, they have significant abilities to fight the free radicals that cause premature aging and are thought to increase the risk of cancer.

Traditionally, rosemary essential oil has been used as an insect repellent. Applied topically, it helps to strengthen the blood capillaries and has a rejuvenating effect on skin and hair, making it a popular ingredient in many beauty products, including skin lotions, creams, toners, soaps, and hair shampoos and conditioners.

✦ TONIC WINE AND LINIMENT
for stiff muscles, headaches, etc.

handful rosemary leaves
5 cloves
2 small cinnamon sticks
1 tsp. ground ginger
a bottle of good-quality red wine

Lightly crush the rosemary, cloves, and cinnamon in a tall jar, using a pestle. Add the ginger and the wine, then seal the jar and leave in a cool place 7 to 10 days. Strain and store in a sealed bottle. Drink a glass daily, or dip a cotton ball in and apply to the affected area.

ROSEMARY POTATOES

1 lb. potatoes, cut into wedges
2 tbsp. peanut oil
1 garlic clove, crushed (optional)
black pepper, to taste
1 tbsp. chopped rosemary leaves

Boil the potato wedges 10 minutes, or until tender, and drain. Heat the oil and sauté the garlic and potatoes until the potatoes are brown and crunchy. Add the pepper and rosemary for the final minute of cooking time and serve immediately.

SOOTHING ROSEMARY TEA *makes 1 cup*

1 tsp. dried rosemary
1 tsp. dried marjoram
1 tsp. dried feverfew
1 tsp. dried peppermint

Mix the herbs well and place in a teapot. Add 1 cup boiling water, and leave to infuse 10 minutes, then strain and drink.

Garlic

VITAMINS B1, B3, B5, B6, C, BIOTIN, FOLIC ACID; CALCIUM, COPPER,
GERMANIUM, IODINE, IRON, MAGNESIUM, MANGANESE, PHOSPHORUS,
POTASSIUM, SELENIUM, SULFUR, ZINC; AMINO ACIDS, S-ALLYLCYSTEINE,
VOLATILE OILS; PROTEIN; FIBER

**An ingredient few cooks would be without, this pungent
bulb has many therapeutic properties. Acclaimed as a
superfood, garlic guarantees extra protection for over-
worked joints and helps to keep the heart healthy, too.**

Originally from Asia, garlic is part of the onion family. It was known
in ancient Egypt and Greece, where it played a role in rituals as well as
being an important medicinal food. Widely used today in cooking
throughout the world, garlic is versatile and tasty, and can be added to
virtually any savory dish to boost its flavor—add one clove per person
for its full health-boosting effects. It gives a kick to stir-fries, casseroles,
and sauces, and can be chopped and added raw to salads and dressings.
For those who find the taste of garlic overpowering, it can also be taken
in supplement form.

Known for its powerful smell and taste, garlic's protective powers are
even stronger, ranging from fighting cancer to promoting weight loss. Its
most potent properties stem from a rich supply of compounds containing sulfur, which is what creates that distinctive smell. The sulfur helps in
the formation of new cells, keeping skin, nails, and hair young-looking.
It is also said to treat cellulite.

Garlic has been found to aid weight loss even if you make no other
changes to your diet. It helps to make low-calorie meals more flavorsome,
providing added flavor with virtually no calories. At the same time, it lowers blood levels of insulin, reducing the risk of weight-
related problems, such as metabolic syndrome
and diabetes. Garlic doesn't just discourage your
body from putting on weight from fats—even
more importantly, it helps to prevent fatty
deposits forming in your arteries, where
they gradually harden and restrict

blood flow, and it lowers blood pressure. People who are trying to lose weight often eat high-protein diets and do extra exercise. These actions can result in an inflammatory response in the body, which can compromise immunity and reduce resistance to disease. In such cases, adding a clove of garlic a day to your diet has been proved to be very effective in counteracting inflammation.

Traditionally, garlic has been used to fight a range of diseases, from gastrointestinal conditions to respiratory infections. A potent antimicrobial, garlic boosts the production of white blood cells and fights off bacteria, parasites, fungi, and viruses. These properties make it a useful weapon against many conditions, from yeast infections to the common cold. It is also a powerful antioxidant, thanks to its amino acids, helping it to enhance overall immune function. This amazing food is useful for combating bladder and kidney problems, as well as ear infections. It also improves digestion and enhances the absorption of food.

Garlic contains a volatile oil called allicin, which is released when it is crushed, encouraging the elimination of cholesterol from the body, lowering triglyceride levels, detoxifying the liver, and acting as a potent anti-inflammatory. It also inhibits blood-platelet stickiness, which is associated with the formation of blood clots, and heart attacks, and strokes. In addition, garlic contains a compound called s-allylcysteine, which appears to have an anticarcinogenic action. Ajoene, which is produced from allicin, might be useful in the treatment of skin cancer when applied topically. Other anticancer compounds in garlic include the powerful antioxidant minerals germanium and selenium.

✦ GARLIC SYRUP *for colds*

1 garlic bulb, cloves peeled and crushed
1 cup water
juice of ½ lemon
2 tbsp. honey

Put the garlic and water in a pan and bring to a boil. Lower the heat and simmer 10 minutes. Add the lemon juice and honey and simmer 2 to 3 minutes longer. When cool, strain into a dark glass bottle. Drink 2 to 3 tablespoons 3 times a day. Store in the refrigerator 2 to 3 weeks.

GARLIC MUSHROOM SALAD

4 garlic cloves, crushed
12 large open mushrooms
3 tbsp. olive oil
4 handfuls arugula leaves
4 oz. feta cheese, drained

In a skillet, slowly sauté the garlic and mushrooms in the oil. Arrange the arugula leaves in 4 piles on four plates. Put 3 mushrooms on each pile, crumble the feta cheese over, and serve.

GARLIC-INFUSED OLIVE OIL

1 cup extra virgin olive oil (see method)
8 garlic cloves
1 tsp. crushed dried chilies

Buy a 1-cup bottle of extra virgin olive oil and add the whole garlic cloves and chilies. Some of the oil might have to be removed before infusing so it doesn't spill over. Secure the lid and leave in a cool, dark cupboard for several days to let the flavors mingle. Use the oil as required for cooking or as a salad dressing.

TOMATO, BASIL, AND GARLIC SALAD

1 lb. 12 oz. large tomatoes, sliced
4 tbsp. roughly chopped basil
2 garlic cloves, finely chopped
6 tbsp. olive oil
2 tbsp. balsamic vinegar
salt and ground black pepper

Arrange the tomatoes flat on a large plate and top with the remaining ingredients. Serve immediately.

GARLIC SOUP

2 tbsp. olive oil
4 garlic cloves, crushed
2 cups fresh breadcrumbs
4 cups hot vegetable stock
4 large eggs (optional)
crusty bread, to serve

Heat the oil in a pan over low heat and fry the garlic about 30 seconds. Add the breadcrumbs and fry 1 minute longer. Stir in the stock and bring to a boil, then lower the heat and simmer 10 minutes. Break the eggs, if using, into the soup and poach about 3 minutes, or until done as desired. Serve with crusty bread.

REFRIED BEANS

1¼ cups dried red kidney beans
3 tbsp. olive oil
3 garlic cloves, crushed
1 tsp. cayenne pepper
1 tsp. ground cumin
1 tsp. ground mustard seeds
1 tsp. tamari soy sauce

Soak the beans in cold water overnight. Drain, then put in a pan with water to cover. Bring to a boil, lower the heat and simmer, covered, 2 hours until tender. Drain and set aside. Put the remaining ingredients and 7 tablespoons water in another pan and sauté a few minutes. Add the beans and mix well. Mash until creamy.

Chili

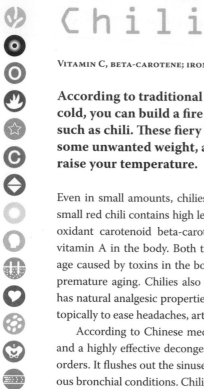

VITAMIN C, BETA-CAROTENE; IRON, POTASSIUM, CAPSAICIN; FIBER

According to traditional Oriental theory, "If you have a cold, you can build a fire in your stomach" with a spice such as chili. These fiery hot peppers can also burn away some unwanted weight, as they boost metabolism and raise your temperature.

Even in small amounts, chilies are a helpful addition to the diet—one small red chili contains high levels of the antiviral, anticancer, and antioxidant carotenoid beta-carotene, some of which is converted into vitamin A in the body. Both these nutrients help to prevent the damage caused by toxins in the body, and can help to stave off cancer and premature aging. Chilies also contain capsaicin, a plant chemical that has natural analgesic properties, which can be used both internally and topically to ease headaches, arthritis, and sinusitis.

According to Chinese medicine, chili is a hot, pungent yang spice and a highly effective decongestant for colds as well as respiratory disorders. It flushes out the sinuses and clears the lungs, thus treating various bronchial conditions. Chili also acts on the circulatory and digestive systems, and is used to treat a wide range of complaints, ranging from arthritis and chilblains to colic and diarrhea.

Some experts say chilies increase the body's fat-burning ability for about 20 minutes after a meal, so you are literally burning up the food you've just eaten faster than normal. Others say the fiery taste simply makes you eat more slowly, or the tastiness makes food more satisfying. Whatever the reason, adding some of these hot peppers to your everyday diet does seem to aid weight control.

A recent Australian study seems to indicate that chilies could help diabetics, as they seem to significantly reduce the amount of insulin needed to lower blood sugar levels after a meal. Chilies also alleviate chronic indigestion and kill the bacteria that cause stomach ulcers, although eating too many chilies is to be avoided, as research suggests it can increase the risk of stomach cancer.

ROASTED CHILI RELISH

7 oz. chilies, seeded
1 tbsp. olive oil
4 garlic cloves, crushed
1 cucumber, finely chopped

Broil the chilies 4 to 5 minutes until the skins blister, then put in a sealed plastic bag 10 minutes. Rub the skins off and finely chop the chilies. Mix with the remaining ingredients. Keep in the refrigerator up to 2 weeks. Use sparingly.

SPICY RICE *serves 2*

1 cup long-grain rice
grated zest of 1 lime
1 garlic clove, peeled
1 red chili, sliced
juice and grated zest of 2 lemons
1 tbsp. whole grain mustard
4 tbsp. olive oil

Place the rice, lime zest. and garlic in a pan, cover with water, and bring to a boil, then lower the heat and simmer until the rice is tender. Drain and remove the lime zest and garlic. Combine the remaining ingredients in a bowl, then stir the mixture into the rice. Serve as a side dish.

✦ CHILI PASTE *for colds & bronchial conditions*

3 small Thai dried chilies
2 garlic cloves, halved
1 small onion, chopped
2 tbsp. sugar
3 tbsp. lemon juice
3 tbsp. water
½ tsp. salt

Put the ingredients in a blender and whiz until finely chopped. Pour the mixture into a pan and cook slowly, stirring occasionally, 10 minutes. Makes scant ½ cup of paste.

Cayenne pepper

Vitamins A, B1, B3, B5, B6, C, carotenoids; calcium, iron, manganese, potassium; capsaicin; flavonoids, volatile oils, fiber

The name "cayenne" derives from the name of a town in French Guiana. A fiery spice, cayenne pepper is a variety of chili, which was first introduced to the West in the sixteenth century.

A rich source of vitamins A and C, as well as many of the B-vitamins, cayenne pepper is useful for everything from eye health to immune function, and healthy skin to good memory. It is strongly antibacterial, can break down catarrh, and has antioxidant properties that boost immunity and aid the body in fighting the damage caused by free radicals. Cayenne is also very high in calcium, which staves off osteoporosis, and potassium, which helps to regulate the body's fluid levels.

Its active constituent capsaicin is a warming stimulant and a powerful remedy for poor circulation, helping to dilate blood vessels and increase blood supply to all parts of the body. This makes it useful for people experiencing general debility and malaise, such as postviral fatigue (ME) sufferers. Capsaicin, which also gives cayenne its anti-inflammatory properties, has been widely studied for its pain-reducing effects and its ability to help to prevent stomach ulcers. .

Cayenne pepper also offers great cardiovascular benefits by helping to revitalize the veins and arteries so they regain youthful elasticity. It also strengthens the heart and regulates blood pressure, helping to prevent strokes and heart attacks.

Taken to relieve wind and colic and to stimulate secretion of the digestive juices, cayenne encourages the process of waste elimination in the gut. It is also known to boost metabolism and to aid weight loss.

When applied topically to the skin, capsaicin desensitizes nerve endings and acts as a counterirritant, helping local blood flow. It might help psoriasis, neuralgia, headaches, and arthritis.

✴ CAYENNE-INFUSED OIL *for the skin*

scant 1 cup finely chopped cayenne pepper

2¼ cup vegetable or olive oil

Place the cayenne and oil in a large heatproof bowl. Bring a large pan of water to a boil, then lower the heat and simmer gently. Set the bowl over the saucepan and leave 2 to 3 hours. Remove from the heat and let the oil cool completely. Pour the infused oil, using a funnel, into a dark glass bottle. Apply as needed.

✦ WARMING CAYENNE WAX
to treat painful, inflamed joints

8 oz. beeswax

2 cayenne peppers, or 1 dried cayenne pepper

⅔ tsp. St.-John's-wort

In a pan, melt the beeswax and add the cayenne peppers. Simmer 10 minutes, then remove the peppers. Stir in the St.-John's-wort. Pour the warm mixture into empty ice-cube trays and freeze. Melt 1 cube as needed. As it melts, lay out some paper tissue and, using a pastry brush, paint on the wax in a strip. Wrap the tissue strip around the painful area. To retain heat, cover with plastic wrap, then leave 20 minutes. Repeat 3 times a week.

Turmeric

Vitamins B3, B6, C, E, K, folic acid; calcium, iron, magnesium, manganese, phosphorus, potassium, selenium, zinc; curcumin

Grown for its root, which has a host of beneficial properties, turmeric is the most commonly used flavoring and coloring agent in Eastern cuisine.

Many spices would have stronger medicinal effects if they were not eaten in such small quantities. Turmeric, however, is such a potent anti-inflammatory that the small amount used in a curry is enough to reduce the risk of many illnesses and conditions.

Turmeric is used in traditional Chinese medicine to treat the liver and gallbladder. Elsewhere, it is a useful remedy that might help everything from gallstones and jaundice to premenstrual discomfort and skin conditions. It is also an anticoagulant, and appears to prevent platelet stickiness, which helps to guard against heart disease and strokes.

The potent ingredient is curcumin, which gives turmeric its vivid golden color. It has been shown to protect against inflammatory bowel disease and several forms of cancer , including prostate cancer and childhood leukemia. In addition, turmeric might counteract the carcinogenic effects of some additives found in processed food. Its anti-inflammatory properties are also very effective in relieving the pain and stiffness of arthritis and rheumatic problems.

Curcumin is a powerful antioxidant that is very effective at fighting free radicals and, therefore, protects the skin, eyes, and hair, and keeps them youthful. It also has antibacterial and cholesterol-lowering properties. Research shows curcumin might also protect against memory deterioration, and recent studies suggest it might one day form the basis of a treatment for cystic fibrosis.

✦ TURMERIC POULTICE *for skin inflammation*

dried piece turmeric root
gauze bandage

Grind the turmeric in a blender to make a powder. Mix 1 teaspoon of the powder with a little water to make a paste. Wrap the paste in a gauze bandage and tie to the affected area. Leave 20 minutes, then discard. Repeat 3 times a day.

SPICED CAULIFLOWER

1 large cauliflower, broken into florets
1 tbsp. peanut oil
1 tsp. ground coriander
1 tsp. ground black pepper
1 large onion, chopped
1 tsp. salt
1 tbsp. ground turmeric

Steam the cauliflower 10 minutes. Meanwhile, heat the oil in a pan over low heat and briefly sauté the coriander and pepper. Add the onion and stir-fry 3 to 5 minutes until translucent. Add the salt and turmeric. Stir in the cauliflower until well coated, then serve.

THAI CURRY SAUCE

1¾ cups coconut milk
2 green chilies, seeded and chopped
2 garlic cloves
2 tsp. grated gingerroot
1 tbsp. olive oil
2 shallots, chopped
1 lemongrass stalk, peeled
1 tsp. ground turmeric
2 tbsp. chopped cilantro leaves
hot, cooked rice, to serve

Put the coconut milk, chilies, garlic, and ginger in a blender and whiz. Heat the oil, then add the shallots and sauté over low heat until soft and golden. Add the coconut mixture and the remaining ingredients. Bring to a boil, then lower the heat and simmer 5 minutes. Serve hot with a side of rice.

Ginger

VITAMINS B3, B6, C, E, FOLIC ACID; CALCIUM, COPPER, IRON, MAGNESIUM, MANGANESE, PHOSPHORUS, POTASSIUM, SELENIUM, ZINC; GINGEROL; PHENOLS, VOLATILE OIL

Said to have derived from the Garden of Eden, ginger is a favorite spice and flavoring, and one of the world's greatest medicines. With its soothing, pain-relieving, and anti-inflammatory properties, ginger is invaluable as a food remedy.

Used in India and China since 5000BC, ginger is grown throughout the tropics and used extensively as both a culinary and therapeutic spice. It contains an active constituent, gingerol, which has anticancer properties and is responsible for much of its hot, pungent taste and aroma, as well as its stimulating properties.

Ginger is useful for anyone feeling sluggish because it is stimulating and promotes detoxification by increasing perspiration and circulation. Recognized by scientists as a fast-acting cure for all kinds of nausea, it relieves complaints such as motion and morning sickness, reducing all associated symptoms, including dizziness and vomiting. Keeping ginger cookies to hand during early pregnancy is a piece of advice that has been handed down for generations.

Ginger's volatile oil works on the digestive system by encouraging the secretion of digestive enzymes. Ginger is a wonderful remedy for indigestion, wind, and colic. It protects the digestive system against premature aging, thus aiding the general absorption of nutrients. It also invigorates the stomach and intestines, easing constipation and removing the accumulation of toxins, including fungal infections, thus increasing vitality and well-being. The root helps to regulate blood sugar, both by stimulating pancreas cells and by lowering cholesterol levels.

Ginger is particularly rich in the mineral zinc—essential for a healthy immune system. The spice is warming and soothing, and is a favorite home remedy for colds and influenza. It promotes perspiration, reducing a fever and clearing congestion, and has a stimulating and expectorant action in the lungs, expelling phlegm and relieving coughs.

It is a potent antiseptic. Ginger is also a useful remedy for pain and inflammation, helping cramps, peptic ulcers, allergies, and asthma. Its gingerol, which suppress the substances that trigger joint pain and swelling, make it one of the most respected foods for the treatment of joint problems, such as osteoarthritis and rheumatoid arthritis.

Ginger has a stimulating effect on the circulation, lowering high blood pressure. Ginger supports heart health by preventing blood platelets from sticking together and lowering cholesterol levels, thereby offering protection against heart attacks and strokes.

To gain the strongest benefits, pour hot water on a thumb-size piece of peeled, crushed fresh gingerroot and drink it as a tea.

GINGER-TOFU STIR-FRY

serves 2

6 garlic cloves, crushed

1-inch piece gingerroot, peeled
    and grated

cayenne pepper, to taste

7 oz. firm tofu, diced

soy sauce, to cover

4 tbsp. olive oil

1 broccoli head, cut into florets

1 green bell pepper, seeded and chopped

4 oz. bean sprouts

1 cup slivered almonds

Place the garlic, ginger, cayenne pepper, and tofu in a bowl and drizzle enough soy sauce to cover over, then allow to marinate 10 minutes. Heat the oil in a wok, add the marinated tofu with any marinade, vegetables, and bean sprouts, and stir-fry until cooked. Add the almonds and stir through, then remove the wok from the heat and serve.

✦ GINGER & LEMON DECOCTION
for sore throats

4 oz. gingerroot
2¼ cups water
juice and grated zest of 1 lemon
a pinch of cayenne pepper

Slice the ginger (there is no need to peel it) and put it in a pan with the water, lemon zest, and cayenne pepper. Bring to a boil, then lower the heat and simmer, covered, 20 minutes. Remove the pan from the heat and add the lemon juice. Drink 1 cup according to symptoms. This will keep 2 to 3 days.

GINGER BEER

2 quarts bottled still mineral water
1¼ cups sugar
¼ tsp. active dry yeast
juice of 1 lemon
1½ to 2 tbsp. grated gingerroot

Decant the water into another container. Pour the sugar into the empty bottle through a funnel, then add the yeast. Mix the lemon juice with the ginger, then pour into the bottle through the funnel. Add the water (leaving a 1-inch gap at the top). Re-cover the bottle, shake well, and leave in a warm place 24 to 48 hours, then chill overnight. Strain into glasses and serve chilled.

RASPBERRY AND GINGER WHIP

2 tsp. grated gingerroot
1⅔ cups raspberries
2 cups crème fraîche or sour cream
handful crystallized ginger, chopped

Put the gingerroot and raspberries in a food processor and whiz. Add the mixture to the crème fraîche and stir. Serve chilled in individual dessert glasses, sprinkled with a few pieces of chopped crystallized ginger.

CREAMY GINGER DRESSING

4 tbsp. tahini

2 tsp. grated gingerroot

1 garlic clove

1 tsp. tamari soy sauce

2 tsp. brown rice syrup

Put all the ingredients in a blender with 5 tablespoons water and whiz until creamy. Serve stirred into hot noodles or as a salad dressing.

GINGERADE *serves 2*

1 tbsp. sugar

2 oz. gingerroot, peeled
   and grated

1 cup plus 2 tbsp. sparkling
   mineral water

juice of ½ lemon

ice, to serve

Place the sugar, ginger, and 1 cup water in a saucepan and bring to a boil. Lower the heat, cover, and simmer 10 minutes. Leave to cool, then strain. Stir into the sparkling mineral water, add the lemon juice, and serve with ice.

Cinnamon

Vitamins B2, B3, B5, B6, E, K, beta-carotene, biotin; calcium, copper, iodine, iron, magnesium, manganese, phosphorus, potassium, selenium, zinc; fiber

Highly prized since antiquity, cinnamon was regarded as a gift fit for kings and it is said wars were even fought over it. With a long history of use in India, cinnamon is now one of the world's most important spices, with a plethora of healing properties.

Stimulating and warming, cinnamon is a traditional remedy for digestive problems, such as nausea, vomiting, and diarrhea, as well as for aching muscles and other symptoms of viral conditions, such as colds and flu. Owing to its heating properties, it can promote sweating, thus helping to lower body temperature during a fever. It can also be used for treating mild food poisoning, and is good for bleeding gums and as a mouthwash to counter halitosis.

Cinnamon has a surprisingly strong effect on the brain and moods, scientists have found. Its distinctive smell works directly on the brain to increase alertness. It has been found to help students concentrate more effectively in exams, and might slow down the onset of cognitive decline in old age. Research has shown that compounds in cinnamon stabilize blood sugar levels, which, in turn, prevent mood swings and dips in blood sugar postexercise—a time when even the most health-conscious athlete might be tempted to succumb to calorie-laden chocolate and candy. As little as half a teaspoonful a day—sprinkled on oatmeal for breakfast or used to sweeten a cup of herbal tea—can make a difference and, say scientists, even help to control type-2 diabetes.

Cinnamon also has antibacterial and antifungal properties that have been found to inhibit organisms such as *Candida albicans*, a yeast responsible for causing candidiasis and thrush.

This powerful healing spice is also good for the heart and the circulatory system. Research has shown that it can significantly lower cholesterol levels. It also has a positive effect on blood platelets, preventing them from clumping together too much.

CINNAMON-POACHED FRUIT

1 cup plus 2 tbsp. white wine
juice and grated zest of ½ lemon
2 tbsp. cinnamon
4 pears, peeled, cored, and chopped
8 apricots, pitted and chopped
4 tbsp. chopped dried fruit of choice
yogurt, ricotta cheese, or ice cream to serve

Place the wine, lemon juice and zest, and cinnamon into a large pan. Bring to a boil, then add the fruit and return to a boil. Lower the heat and simmer 2 minutes, then set aside and allow to stand 10 minutes. Serve with yogurt, ricotta, or ice cream.

CINNAMON CREAM

9 oz. silken tofu
⅔ cup apple juice
3 tbsp. brown rice syrup
3 tbsp. sunflower oil
½ tsp. cinnamon

Put all the ingredients in a food processor and whiz until smooth and creamy. Use as a substitute for dairy cream on desserts.

APPLE AND CINNAMON OATMEAL

2 cinnamon sticks
5 cloves
2 tsp. sugar
2 apples, peeled and sliced
1¼ cups instant oatmeal

In a large saucepan, bring 3 cups water to a boil. Lower the heat, add the cinnamon, cloves, sugar, and apples and simmer 10 minutes. Remove the spices, stir in the oatmeal, and serve.

Green tea

VITAMINS C, E, K; FLAVONOIDS; TANNINS

Not just a refreshingly different brew, green tea is also packed with powerful healing nutrients. This health-giving drink can help weight reduction while protecting against a wide range of diseases.

Tea is the most popular beverage in the world. It is grown in high areas in countries with warm, wet climates, such as Japan and India, but China is the biggest producer. Green tea comes from the same plant, *Camellia sinensis*, as ordinary black tea, but is processed differently, leaving important nutrients intact. Its leaves are lightly steamed when cut, rather than left to dry out like black tea. The medicinal properties of green tea have been recognized in the East for more than 4,000 years and it is fast becoming recognized all over the world for its youth-enhancing properties. It has a fresh, astringent flavor.

Green tea is available both loose and in teabags, with added natural flavorings, such as lemon and apple, and herbs, such as digestion-soothing peppermint and brain-boosting ginkgo biloba, to enhance the health benefits even more. Choose high-quality gunpowder green tea if possible, preferably organic. Green tea is best drunk without milk, but you can add lemon or honey to taste.

Few foods excite scientists as much as green tea, with its phenomenal range of health benefits. This humble hot drink is a powerhouse of polyphenols—potent antioxidant flavonoids that neutralize damaging free radicals, helping to prevent diseases such as cancer and helping the body to stay youthful. Tea's polyphenols include catechins, which counteract cancer-causing agents. It is also anti-inflammatory and can prevent flare-ups of allergic conditions such as asthma. Its antibacterial abilities mean it can fight tooth decay and gum disease.

Green tea plays a dual role in helping you to shape up: firstly by increasing exercise endurance and secondly by inhibiting the action of enzymes that help to turn food into fat, especially around the midriff, where stored fat increases the risk of heart disease and diabetes.

This wonderdrink contains phenolic compounds that help to strengthen blood vessels, which makes it excellent for treating conditions such as thread or varicose veins, as well as cold hands or feet. It also contains good amounts of vitamin E to help boost immunity, promote healthy, glowing skin, and protect the eyes and the heart. The tannins in green tea offer additional benefits for the eyes, as they act as an anti-inflammatory to relieve puffiness.

Green tea can help to lower blood pressure and cholesterol and stop the hardening of the arteries, reducing the risk of heart disease and strokes. The antioxidant flavonoids in green tea offer fantastic protection against heart and circulatory problems and have anticarcinogenic properties. They lower "bad" LDL cholesterol and triglyceride levels and raise "good" HDL cholesterol levels. They also help to ward off wrinkles and preserve eye health.

You can enjoy the benefits of green tea by drinking three or four cups a day. Use boiling water to gain the full health benefits, or slightly cooler water if you prefer a less-bitter taste. To take advantage of all its nutrients, you need to brew it five minutes and drink it strong. Some people, however, find this too bitter and compromise by drinking it weaker.

GREEN TEA AND PEACH REFRESHER

2 peaches, pitted and sliced
6 cups cold water
6 green tea teabags
honey, to taste
mint sprigs, to serve

Put the peaches in a saucepan, add the water, and bring to a boil. Put the teabags in a large pitcher. Pour the water and peaches over them, then allow to steep 6 minutes. Remove the teabags, add the honey and allow to cool. Chill until required. Pour into glasses and garnish with mint when ready to serve.

MORROCAN MINT TEA

2 tbsp. gunpowder green tea
4 cups boiling water
large bunch fresh mint
brown sugar, to taste (optional)

Place the tea in a teapot, cover with boiling water, and allow to steep 3 minutes. Pull out a few mint sprigs to save for each serving, then add the rest to the pot and steep 5 minutes longer. Pour into glasses, adding sugar, if desired, and decorate with the saved mint sprigs.

Chamomile

FLAVONOIDS, TANNINS, COUMARINS, VALERIANIC ACID

Best known as a relaxant, this medicinal plant is one of the most widely used healing herbs, and is a popular remedy for insomnia and digestive complaints.

There are two main species of chamomile, which are known as Roman and German chamomile. While both have great therapeutic properties, German chamomile is more widely available.

Usually made into a tea, chamomile relaxes the muscles throughout the body. Its bitters stimulate the flow of bile and the secretion of digestive juices, enhancing the appetite and improving sluggish digestion. The herb has sedative properties and is very soothing, helping to induce relaxation and sleep.

Chamomile contains antioxidant flavonoids, which help to fight harmful free radicals and protect against infection. One of these flavonoids, quercetin, also has powerful anti-inflammatory properties.

Used topically, chamomile treats inflamed joints and stiff muscles. It also has cosmetic benefits—when used in face creams, it promotes a youthful, glowing complexion. Chamomile is also known for being a powerful conditioner that leaves the hair softer and shinier.

✳CHAMOMILE TREATMENT *to condition the hair*

handful chamomile flowers
5 tbsp. olive oil

Combine the chamomile and oil in a jar with a lid. Cover tightly, then place on a sunny windowsill and shake at least once a day. After 2 weeks, strain and discard the herb. Brush out your hair and apply to the hair ends, avoiding the scalp, using 2 to 4 teaspoons, depending on the length of your hair, and leave on 10 minutes. Shampoo as normal.

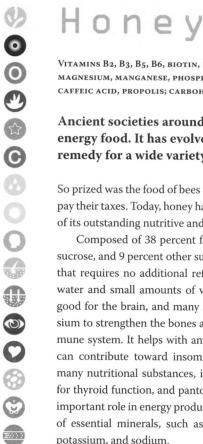

Honey

VITAMINS B2, B3, B5, B6, BIOTIN, FOLIC ACID; CALCIUM, COPPER, IRON,
MAGNESIUM, MANGANESE, PHOSPHORUS, POTASSIUM, SELENIUM, SODIUM, ZINC;
CAFFEIC ACID, PROPOLIS; CARBOHYDRATE

Ancient societies around the world used honey as an energy food. It has evolved as a unique and powerful remedy for a wide variety of complaints.

So prized was the food of bees that the Romans used it instead of gold to pay their taxes. Today, honey has become known as "liquid gold" because of its outstanding nutritive and healing properties.

Composed of 38 percent fructose, 31 percent glucose, one percent sucrose, and 9 percent other sugars, honey is the only natural sweetener that requires no additional refining or processing. The rest comprises water and small amounts of vitamins, including vitamin B6, which is good for the brain, and many minerals, including calcium and magnesium to strengthen the bones and selenium and zinc to support the immune system. It helps with any tendency toward hypoglycemia, which can contribute toward insomnia and mood swings. It also provides many nutritional substances, including vitamins B2 and B3, necessary for thyroid function, and pantothenic acid (vitamin B5), which plays an important role in energy production. Honey is also rich in trace amounts of essential minerals, such as copper, iron, manganese, phosphorus, potassium, and sodium.

A recognized antioxidant, honey is a powerful, broad-spectrum antibiotic with both antifungal and antimicrobial properties, acting against organisms that encourage *Staphylococcus* bacteria as well as candida fungal infections. Honey also contains an amazing substance called propolis, which helps to prevent and treat coughs and colds, as well as stomach disorders—recent research suggests that it can counteract food-poisoning bacteria.

The extraordinary antibacterial content found in the Manuka honey of New Zealand has been shown to inhibit the growth of many bacteria, including *Helicobacter pylori*, which is associated with causing most stomach and duodenal ulcers. The antibacterial activity of this honey is also proving to be an effective weapon in combating superbugs, such as MRSA (Methicillin-resistant *Staphylococcus aureus*), strains of which have become particularly resistant to conventional antibiotic treatment. Moreover, because it also has potent antifungal properties, this special honey has been used effectively to treat athlete's foot and other fungal infections. Unfiltered honey contains pollen grains and helps hayfever.

Honey also contains phytonutrients, such as caffeic acid, which has anticarcinogenic properties. As an energy source, it enhances sports performance by providing a welcome boost both during and after exercise. No wonder honey is considered a general pick-me-up!

Used topically, honey has a powerful antiseptic effect for the treatment of ulcers, burns, and wounds. It has an anti-inflammatory action, reducing swelling and pain, and by stimulating the regrowth of tissue under the skin's surface, honey helps the healing mechanism. It is also a humectant, attracting and retaining water, which keeps the skin soft and supple. This makes it a popular ingredient in beauty creams.

HONEY AND CITRUS JUICE

2 grapefruit, peeled and broken into
segments
3 lemons, peeled and quartered
1½-inch piece gingerroot, peeled and
cut into chunks
1 tbsp. honey

Press alternate chunks of grapefruit, lemon, and ginger through a juicer. Add the honey, stir well, and drink immediately.

✦HONEY DRESSING *for wounds*

honey
gauze bandage

Spread some honey onto a gauze bandage and apply it to the wound. The amount of honey used depends on the amount of fluid exuding from the wound. Large amounts of exudate require substantial amounts of honey. Reapply the dressing as necessary.

HONEY AND ALMOND CUP

2¼ cups rice milk
1⅓ cups blanched almonds
2 tbsp. honey
1 tbsp. vanilla extract

Put the rice milk, almonds, and 1¼ cups water in a blender and mix well. Pour the liquid through a strainer into a glass pitcher. Stir in the honey and vanilla extract, then refrigerate until required. Serve well chilled.

*HONEY FACE MASK
to firm the skin

1 tbsp. honey
1 egg white
1 tsp. glycerin
¼ cup all-purpose flour

Mix the honey, egg white, and glycerin together in a small bowl. Add enough of the flour to make a paste. Smooth the mask over your face and throat. Leave 10 minutes, then rinse off.

HONEY VINAIGRETTE

2 tbsp. honey
2 tbsp. apple cider vinegar
3 tbsp. extra virgin olive oil
1 tsp. French mustard (optional)
a pinch of salt

Pour the honey and apple cider vinegar into a saucepan and place over low heat until just warm. Gently stir in the olive oil, beating with a fork. Remove the pan from the heat, then add the mustard, if using, and the salt. Serve with a warm salad, such as chicken.

BANANA, HONEY, AND PEANUT BAGELS

4 wholeheat bagels
6 tbsp. crunchy peanut butter
4 bananas
4 tsp. honey
½ tsp. cinnamon

Carefully cut the bagels in half and spread each side with peanut butter, then set aside. Chop the bananas and mash them in a bowl, then mix in the honey and cinnamon. Spoon the mixture on top of the peanut butter. Broil the bagel halves a few minutes under a preheated broiler, topping side up, and serve immediately.

Apple cider vinegar

VITAMINS B1, B2, B6, C, E, BETA-CAROTENE; CALCIUM, CHLORINE, FLUORINE, IRON, MAGNESIUM, MANGANESE, PHOSPHORUS, POTASSIUM, SELENIUM, SODIUM, SILICA, SULFUR, ZINC; MALIC ACID, ASCETIC ACID; PECTIN; FIBER

Made from fermented apple juice and rich in enzymes, apple cider vinegar has been used for centuries to aid digestion. It is thought Hippocrates, the father of modern medicine, used apple cider vinegar as a healing elixir to treat his patients.

More than 90 different beneficial substances have been discovered in apple cider vinegar, including carbolic acids, enzymes, and trace minerals, which help to balance the body's acid-alkaline levels. Through its alkalizing effect, it is reported to alleviate a number of complaints, such as rheumatism, headaches, heartburn, and muscle cramps.

The malic acid content of apple cider vinegar helps to dissolve calcium deposits in the body and eases arthritis. It also helps to balance the body's acid-alkaline pH levels and oxygenates the blood, thus aiding digestion and boosting the immune system. Enzyme-rich, apple cider vinegar contains a perfect balance of minerals, as well as apple pectin, the water-soluble dietary fiber that binds to toxins in the body and assists in their removal, thus improving the elimination of waste. Pectin also lowers cholesterol levels, so it helps to stave off heart disease.

Drinking a few drops of apple cider vinegar with or before a meal has been proved to help people lose weight. It has the added benefit of reducing the indigestion that can accompany a change in diet, which can cause pangs that feel like hunger even when you've just eaten. Vinegar's acetic acid content makes you feel full up sooner and for longer. This feeling of satiety stems from a reduction in the glycemic index (GI) of the food you eat. Foods with a high GI, including most highly processed items, go through your system quickly, leaving you wanting more. Vinegar reduces the GI and lets food stay longer in your stomach. It also reduces the risk of a midafternoon slump sending you in search of a snack.

✦ OXYMEL *for respiratory ailments*

apple cider vinegar
honey
water

Combine equal amounts of cider vinegar and honey in a glass jar and shake to combine. Drink 1 teaspoon when you have specific symptoms, or add eight times the amount of water to create a juice for regular sipping.

*APPLE CIDER VINEGAR HAIR RINSE
to restore dull, lifeless hair

2 tbsp. apple cider vinegar
3 cups water

Mix the cider vinegar and water in a pitcher. After shampooing and conditioning your hair as usual, pour the apple cider vinegar mixture over your hair as a final rinse.

CREAMY SALAD DRESSING

2 tbsp. apple cider vinegar
2 tsp. apple juice
4 tbsp. plain yogurt
1 garlic clove, crushed
1 tsp. chopped thyme

Place all the ingredients in a bowl and whisk together. Chill and serve the dressing on your favorite salad.

Tofu

Vitamins A, K; calcium, copper, iron, magnesium, manganese, phosphorus, potassium, selenium; omega-3 and -6 essential fatty acids; fiber; protein; tryptophan; isoflavones

One of the best vegetarian forms of protein, tofu works well in everything from smoothies to stir-fries. This wonder-working soy product can protect your organs while also helping you to lose weight.

Made fom the curds of soy milk, which gives it its alternative name "bean curd," tofu is a versatile, low-fat food jam-packed with nutrients. It is available in traditional Chinese block form or in the smoother Japanese silken form. Both come in a range of textures from soft to extra-firm. Soft tofu blends easily in smoothies and desserts, while firm tofu works well in main meals.

While it is perhaps best known for its beneficial effects on women's hormones, tofu might also help both sexes to maintain a healthy weight. Among soy's many healthy components is an isoflavone that seems to promote fat loss by reducing the size and number of fat cells. Women using tofu to treat menopausal symptoms have found it also prevented weight gain, especially on the abdomen, which is an area commonly affected by the changes in the body's reproductive hormone levels after the menstrual cycle stops.

Research has shown that people who regularly eat tofu can lower their "bad" (LDL) cholesterol levels by as much as a third, making it a powerful protector of the heart and cardiovascular system. Tofu is also a good source of omega-3 fatty acids and fiber, which both support heart health as well as helping to stave off food cravings. Like all soy products, tofu is rich in calcium and magnesium to build strong bones.

Although tofu has been shown to reduce the risk of many serious diseases, including cancers, heart disease, osteoporosis, and diabetes, its powerful effects on hormones can also stimulate hormone-dependent cancers or thyroid problems, so it should not be overused. Traditional tofu is the healthiest option—the long-term effects of new products are not known, so it is best to avoid them.

TOFU SKEWERS

4 tbsp. soy sauce

1 tbsp. sesame oil

1 tbsp. apple juice

a pinch of cayenne pepper

1 lb. firm tofu, drained and cubed

4 sweet bell peppers, seeded and chopped
into chunks

Mix together the soy sauce, sesame oil, apple juice, and cayenne, add the tofu, and marinate 1 hour. Thread the tofu and peppers alternately onto skewers. Broil or bake the skewers 5 to 10 minutes until brown, basting often with the remaining marinade.

TOFU SMOOTHIE

7 oz. tofu

8 tbsp. orange juice

8 tbsp. mango pulp

4 apples, cored and chopped

4 tbsp. chopped walnuts

Put all the ingredients, except 1 tablespoon of walnuts, in a blender and whiz on low speed until mixed, then on a high speed until smooth. Pour into glasses, sprinkle with the remaining walnuts, and serve.

BLUEBERRY AND TOFU MOUSSE

7 oz. silken tofu

1⅔ cups blueberries

¾ cup finely ground blanched almonds

1 tsp. cinnamon

1 tsp. lemon juice

2 tsp. slivered almonds, toasted

Whiz the tofu and blueberries in a food processor. Add the almonds, cinnamon, and lemon juice. Spoon the mousse into four bowls. Sprinkle over the slivered almonds and serve.

Ailments
directory

ANEMIA

This condition occurs when there is a decrease in the amount of oxygen-carrying hemoglobin in our red blood cells. The first sign is usually weakness or exhaustion. Symptoms include feeling tired all the time, pale skin, breathlessness, and pale inner lower eyelids. The likeliest cause is lack of iron or vitamin B12. Young women, in particular, are at risk, especially if they have heavy periods and eat little or no meat, as the body absorbs iron more easily from meat or fish than from any other source. Foods rich in vitamin C help the body to absorb iron. If the exhaustion continues, see your doctor.

Foods to eat: apple (p.26); pineapple (p.36); papaya (p.42); strawberry (p.52); plum (p.56); apricot (p.58); asparagus (p.78); globe artichoke (p.80); beet (p.82); sweet potato (p.90); broccoli (p.94); spinach (p.100); cabbage (p.104); fennel (p.124); alfalfa (p.130); watercress (p.132); seaweed (p.134); lamb (p.142); beef (p.144); turkey (p.146); live yogurt (p.151); milk (p.154); egg (p.156); salmon (p.164); oyster (p.172); flaxseed (p.192); quinoa (p.214); millet (p.221); rye (p.222); chickpea (p.232); lentil (p.234); chili (p.252); cayenne pepper (p.254); turmeric (p.256); apple cider vinegar (p.272)

ARTHRITIS

Osteoarthritis is caused by wear and tear of the joints, so most people have at least a few twinges by the time they reach their fifties. It can also happen earlier at the site of an injury. The degenerative disease rheumatoid arthritis is much less common but often starts in younger people. They're different conditions, but both may respond to the anti-inflammatory effects of foods rich in omega-3, especially oily fish although oily fish is not recommended for anyone with the form of arthritis called gout). Calcium, iron, and vitamin D have shown some good effects on arthritis. A diet rich in fruit and vegetables provides many other phytonutrients that are believed to be helpful.

Foods to eat: pineapple (p.36); papaya (p.42); cherry (p.48); raspberry (p.54); pomegranate (p.60); olive and olive oil (p.72); beet (p.82); broccoli (p.94); cabbage (p.104); onion (p.108); celery (p.110); squash (p.116);

eggplant (p.118); mushroom (p.120); seaweed (p.134); salmon (p.164); walnut (p.178); sesame seed and oil (p.196); oats (p.210); parsley (p.240); turmeric (p.256); ginger (p.258); apple cider vinegar (p.272)

ASTHMA AND LUNG DISEASE

Asthma sufferers experience inflamed air passages of the lungs. This can cause extra-sensitivity to "triggers" or allergens, including milk, wheat, nuts, and fish, which might be best avoided.

Foods rich in vitamin C have long been known to fight asthma and other chest diseases. Other nutrients are now known to help in different ways: magnesium, for example, helps prevent an asthma attack.

Foods to eat: *orange (p.18); kiwifruit (p.38); papaya (p.42); raspberry (p.54); olive and olive oil (p.72); carrot (p.86); sweet potato (p.90); broccoli (p.94); kale (p.98); onion (p.108); bell pepper (p.112); squash (p.116); mushroom (p.120); fennel (p.124); seaweed (p.134); salmon (p.164); walnut (p.178); flaxseed (p.192); peppermint (p.244); rosemary (p.246); garlic (p.248); cayenne pepper (p.254); green tea (p.264)*

CANCER

Healthy eating could prevent up to one-third of all cancers, according to the World Health Organization. There are a huge number of naturally occurring phytonutrients shown to reduce cancer risk. Fruits and vegetables of every kind offer slightly different beneficial compounds.

Foods to eat: *lemon (p.14); orange (p.18); grapefruit (p.20); apple (p.26); pear (p.30); grape (p.34); blueberry (p.44); cherry (p.48); cranberry (p.50); strawberry (p.52); raspberry (p.54); prune (p.56); pomegranate (p.60); cantaloupe melon (p.62); tomato (p.68); olive and olive oil (p.72); asparagus (p.78); globe artichoke (p.80); beet (p.82); carrot (p.86); potato (p.88); sweet potato (p.90); yam (p.92); broccoli (p.94); kale (p.98); spinach (p.100); Brussels sprout (p.102); cabbage (p.104); cauliflower (p.106); onion (p.108); celery (p.110); bell pepper (p.112); squash (p.116); eggplant (p.118); mushroom (p.120); fennel (p.124); lettuce (p.126); cucumber (p.128); alfalfa (p.130); watercress (p.132); seaweed (p.134); beef (p.144); turkey (p.146); live yogurt (p.151); salmon (p.164); shrimp (p.170); walnut (p.178); almond (p.182); Brazil nut (p.188); flaxseed (p.192); oats (p.210); brown rice (p.216); rye (p.222); chickpea (p.232); garlic (p.248); turmeric (p.256); ginger (p.258); green tea (p.264)*

COMMON COLD AND FLU

Flu is a viral infection with extreme coldlike symptoms. Avoiding dairy products, and eating fruits and vegetables can help to fight both types of virus. Use foods and herbs that help to boost immunity.

Foods to eat: lemon (p.14); orange (p.18); grapefruit (p.20); blueberry (p.44); cranberry (p.50); raspberry (p.54); pomegranate (p.60); tomato (p.68); carrot (p.86); potato (p.88); sweet potato (p.90); broccoli (p.94); onion (p.108); bell pepper (p.112); mushroom (p.120); lettuce (p.126); watercress (p.132); seaweed (p.134); shrimp (p.170); oats (p.210); sage (p.242); peppermint (p.244); rosemary (p.246); garlic (p.248); chili (p.252); ginger (p.258); cinnamon (p.262); honey (p.268)

COUGHS AND BRONCHITIS

If you have a cough or bronchitis—an infection of the bronchial tube lining—it is best to avoid dairy products, which are mucus-creating.

Foods to eat: lemon (p.14); orange (p.18); apricot (p.58); carrot (p.86); sweet potato (p.90); onion (p.108); watercress (p.132); flaxseed (p.192); sunflower seed and oil (p.198); adzuki bean (p.228); sage (p.242); rosemary (p.246); garlic (p.248); chili (p.252); ginger (p.258); honey (p.268)

CYSTITIS

Urinary tract infections, such as cystitis, cause pain and difficulty in passing urine. They must always be treated promptly, as they can spread fast and affect the kidneys. Vitamin C combats infection, and some foods discourage bacteria from sticking to the bladder wall. These foods are a backup to medical treatment, and they reduce the risk of recurrence.

Foods to eat: blueberry (p.44); cherry (p.48); cranberry (p.50); raspberry (p.54); asparagus (p.78); Brussels sprout (p.102); celery (p.110); fennel (p.124); alfalfa (p.130); live yogurt (p.151); sesame seed and oil (p.196); barley (p.208); quinoa (p.214); adzuki bean (p.228); chickpea (p.232); garlic (p.248)

DEPRESSION (MILD)

Characterized by tearfulness, anxiety, and feelings of hopelessness, mild depression is a condition experienced by one in four people at some stage in their lives. Cutting out alcohol, cigarettes, and sugary foods, and eating those high in omega-3 fatty acids and B-vitamins is thought to help.

Exercise is also known to increase the feel-good factor. The body converts nutrients into message-carrying chemicals that have a direct effect on our emotions. Cheer yourself up with foods rich in tryptophan, selenium, B-vitamins, and protein.

Foods to eat: banana (p.23); raspberry (p.54); apricot (p.58); avocado (p.64); sweet potato (p.90); spinach (p.100); seaweed (p.134); milk (p.154); egg (p.156); tuna (p.162); salmon (p.164); oyster (p.172); walnut (p.178); almond (p.182); Brazil nut (p.188); flaxseed (p.192); sunflower seed and oil (p.198); oats (p.210); quinoa (p.214); brown rice (p.216); buckwheat (p.220)

DIABETES

Diabetes is a disease in which the body either fails to produce enough insulin or doesn't respond properly to the insulin produced. Foods that release glucose slowly into the bloodstream help to keep diabetes under control, and might also reduce the risk of developing this condition. Avoid processed foods and, although dried fruit and juices are healthy foods, limit these as they are rich in sugars.

Foods to eat: orange (p.18); grapefruit (p.20); apple (p.26); blueberry (p.44); avocado (p.64); globe artichoke (p.80); carrot (p.86); sweet potato (p.90); yam (p.92); mushroom (p.120); seaweed (p.134); turkey (p.146); walnut (p.178); almond (p.182); barley (p.208); oats (p.210); quinoa (p.214); brown rice (p.216); buckwheat (p.220); millet (p.221); chickpea (p.232); lentil (p.234); garlic (p.248); cinnamon (p.262); green tea (p.264); tofu (p.274)

DIGESTIVE COMPLAINTS *see also Irritable Bowel Syndrome, p.282*

The key to keeping the digestive system in good shape is to eat plenty of fiber-rich foods and drink lots of water. If you suffer from indigestion —discomfort, or a burning feeling in the esophagus—reduce your intake of acid-forming foods, such as cheese and red meat.

Foods to eat: banana (p.23); grape (p.34); papaya (p.42); globe artichoke (p.80); carrot (p.86); Brussels sprout (p.102); fennel (p.124); watercress (p.132); live yogurt (p.151); almond (p.182); coconut and coconut oil (p.190); wheat and wheat germ (p.206); barley (p.208); brown rice (p.216); buckwheat (p.220); millet (p.221); chickpea (p.232); peppermint (p.244); garlic (p.248); cayenne pepper (p.254); ginger (p.258); cinnamon (p.262); chamomile (p.267); apple cider vinegar (p.272)

ECZEMA

Eczema describes a group of inflammatory skin conditions that make the skin itchy, irritated, and red, sometimes with blisters. There are a number of causes, ranging from household cleaning products to certain foods to stress. To manage the condition it is important to identify and avoid any common allergens. A diet rich in essential fatty acids, vitamin A, and zinc can help.

Foods to eat: papaya (p.42); avocado (p.64); tomato (p.68); olive and olive oil (p.72); carrot (p.86); cucumber (p.128); seaweed (p.134); salmon (p.164); walnut (p.178); pine nut (p.181); flaxseed (p.192); sunflower seed and oil (p.198); pumpkin seed (p.200); oats (p.210); quinoa (p.214); rosemary (p.246); cayenne pepper (p.254); turmeric (p.256); chamomile (p.267)

EYE DISEASE

If you want to keep your eyes shiny and bright, remember the old adage about eating your carrots—or, in fact, any brightly coloured fruits and vegetables. Studies suggest the antioxidants they contain, including vitamins A, C, and E and lutein, benefit the eyes by helping the lenses to adjust to changes in light; maintaining the macula (the part of the eye that enables clear vision); and keeping the eyes moist.

Foods to eat: kiwifruit (p.38); blueberry (p.44); cherry (p.48); apricot (p.58); pomegranate (p.60); asparagus (p.78); beet (p.82); carrot (p.86); broccoli (p.94); kale (p.98); spinach (p.100); bell pepper (p.112); watercress (p.132); seaweed (p.134); lamb (p.142); live yogurt (p.151); egg (p.156); sesame seed and oil (p.196); pumpkin seed (p.200); barley (p.208)

FATIGUE *see also Postviral Fatigue, p.284*

If you're getting seven to eight hours' sleep a night but feel exhausted most of the time, you might not be eating all the many nutrients you need, including protein, B-vitamins, and an array of minerals. This often happens when you're busy and living on fast food.

Unexplained fatigue can be a sign of something more serious, such as Postviral Fatigue, so if cutting down on stress, working sensible hours, and eating well doesn't help, seek medical advice.

Foods to eat: orange (p.18); banana (p.23); raspberry (p.54); prune (p.56); avocado (p.64); asparagus (p.78); globe artichoke (p.80);

potato (p.88); sweet potato (p.90); yam (p.92); spinach (p.100); celery
(p.110); squash (p.116); mushroom (p.120); cucumber (p.128); lamb
(p.142); beef (p.144); tuna (p.162); sardine (p.168); oyster (p.172); almond
(p.182); cashew nut (p.186); Brazil nut (p.188); coconut and coconut oil
(p.190); sunflower seed and oil (p.198); pumpkin seed (p.200); barley
(p.208); oats (p.210); quinoa (p.214); brown rice (p.216);
millet (p.221); soybean (p.224); kidney bean (p.230); chickpea (p.232);
lentil (p.234); rosemary (p.246); honey (p.268)

HEADACHES AND MIGRAINE

These can be triggered by many different stimuli, from fatigue to expansion of blood vessels in the head. They can be prevented, or relieved, by foods rich in omega-3 fats, vitamin B2, magnesium, or calcium. Some migraines are triggered by eating preserved meat, strong cheeses, pickles, fatty foods, coffee, or the artificial sweetener aspartame.

Foods to eat: *seaweed (p.134); milk (p.154); rye (p.222); chickpea*
(p.232); peppermint (p.244); rosemary (p.246); cayenne pepper (p.254)

HEART DISEASE

One of the main causes of heart disease is the blockage of arteries by cholesterol. Following an exercise regime and eating monounsaturated fats (found in olive oil, nuts, seeds, and fish), instead of saturated fats (found in animal products and processed foods), can make a dramatic difference to your heart health.

Healthy eating is proven to play a major role in preventing or alleviating heart disease. All kinds of fruit and vegetables are especially valuable because of their flavonoids and fiber content, particularly when they are replacing high-fat foods or heavily processed items that are low in nutritional value.

Foods to eat: *grapefruit (p.20); apple (p.26); pear (p.30); grape (p.34);*
kiwifruit (p.38); papaya (p.42); blueberry (p.44); cherry (p.48); cranberry
(p.50); raspberry (p.54); apricot (p.58); pomegranate (p.60); cantaloupe
melon (p.62); avocado (p.64); tomato (p.68); olive and olive oil (p.72);
asparagus (p.78); globe artichoke (p.80); carrot (p.86); broccoli (p.94);
spinach (p.100); cabbage (p.104); onion (p.108); celery (p.110);
bell pepper (p.112); squash (p.116); eggplant (p.118); mushroom (p.120);
fennel (p.124); watercress (p.132); seaweed (p.134); tuna (p.162); salmon
(p.164); sardine (p.168); oyster (p.172); walnut (p.178);

almond (p.182); cashew nut (p.186); coconut and coconut oil (p.190); flaxseed (p.192); sesame seed and oil (p.196); sunflower seed and oil (p.198); pumpkin seed (p.200); barley (p.208); oats (p.210); quinoa (p.214); brown rice (p.216); buckwheat (p.220); millet (p.221); soybean (p.224); chickpea (p.232); lentil (p.234); garlic (p.248); turmeric (p.256); ginger (p.258); green tea (p.264); tofu (p.274)

HIGH BLOOD PRESSURE

Hypertension, or high blood pressure, means the heart has to work harder to pump blood around the body, and increases the risk of heart disease and stroke. You can bring it down through exercise, stress reduction, and losing excess weight.

It also helps if you avoid high-fat and salt-laden dishes and instead choose foods loaded with magnesium, vitamin C, essential fatty acids, and fiber, such as fruit and vegetables.

Foods to eat: *orange (p.18); banana (p.23); apple (p.26); fig (p.32); grape (p.34); pomegranate (p.60); avocado (p.64); olive and olive oil (p.72); potato (p.88); broccoli (p.94); spinach (p.100); celery (p.110); mushroom (p.120); seaweed (p.134); salmon (p.164); flaxseed (p.192); sesame seed and oil (p.196); oats (p.210); buckwheat (p.220); lentil (p.234); parsley (p.240); garlic (p.248)*

IRRITABLE BOWEL SYNDROME (IBS)

This distressing and sometimes painful condition can involve constipation, diarrhea, flatulence, nausea, or all of these afflictions. Bouts of irritable bowel syndrome can be triggered by stress or by certain foods, such as dairy products, gluten, spicy foods, or the artificial sweetener sorbitol. Tea, coffee, and alcohol can also have an irritating effect.

As irritable bowel syndrome sometimes develops from chronic constipation, it might be relieved by the same remedies: exercise every day, plenty of fluids, regular meals not too late in the evening, and unhurried bowel movements. If flatulence is a problem, avoid eating a lot of legumes.

Foods to eat: *apple (p.26); pear (p.30); fig (p.32); raspberry (p.54); prune (p.56); asparagus (p.78); globe artichoke (p.80); fennel (p.124); cucumber (p.128); live yogurt (p.151); flaxseed (p.192); oats (p.210); brown rice (p.216); millet (p.221); peppermint (p.244); rosemary (p.246); ginger (p.258); chamomile (p.267)*

JOINT PROBLEMS

Regular exercise can place a strain on the joints. Knee pain, for example, is a common running injury. It's possible to protect joints from injury and wear and tear by maintaining the correct weight for your height and by alternating periods of heavy activity with periods of rest to avoid repetitive stress on your joints. Research also shows eating foods rich in essential fatty acids can help to protect the cartilage cells that facilitate joint movement.

Keep your joints supple by eating antioxidant-rich fruits and vegetables, along with nuts, seeds, and oily fish. Some spices, such as cayenne pepper, can be used topically to help to relieve aching joints.

Foods to eat: apple (p.26); pineapple (p.36); cherry (p.48); avocado (p.64); olive oil and olive (p.72); fennel (p.124); salmon (p.164); oyster (p.172); walnut (p.178); flaxseed (p.192); sesame seed and oil (p.196); sunflower seed and oil (p.198); wheat and wheat germ (p.206); lentil (p.234); parsley (p.240); garlic (p.248); cayenne pepper (p.254); turmeric (p.256); ginger (p.258); chamomile (p.267); apple cider vinegar (p.272)

MEMORY LOSS

As we get older, our bodies start to make fewer of the chemicals our brain cells need to work, making it harder to recall information. Studies have shown vitamin E, magnesium, and other nutrients might help to counteract this, thus preventing memory loss. Researchers are also studying the possibility that foods rich in antioxidants—particularly vitamins C and E and silica—might help keep our brains active in later life.

Forgetfulness, inability to concentrate, and "brain fog" can stem from many causes, often including stress and tiredness. Some nutrients are known to help keep your brain sharp at any age, including omega-3 oils and compounds in certain herbs. These might also delay or prevent mental deterioration in later life.

Foods to eat: fig (p.32); mango (p.40); blueberry (p.44); olive and olive oil (p.72); beet (p.82); kale (p.98); spinach (p.100); cabbage (p.104); bell pepper (p.112); watercress (p.132); seaweed (p.134); milk (p.154); egg (p.156); salmon (p.164); shrimp (p.170); oyster (p.172); walnut (p.178); flaxseed (p.192); sunflower seed and oil (p.198); pumpkin seed (p.200); wheat and wheat germ (p.206); millet (p.221); kidney bean (p.230); parsley (p.240); sage (p.242); rosemary (p.246); cayenne pepper (p.254); turmeric (p.256); cinnamon (p.262); green tea (p.264)

MENOPAUSAL SYMPTOMS

Levels of the reproductive hormone estrogen can rise and fall sharply during the few years leading up to menopause, and then decline steeply afterward. This sometimes causes disruptive symptoms, which can be alleviated through healthy eating. Depression, fatigue, and memory loss can also occur during this time.

Phytoestrogens help to replace some of the missing estrogen. Foods rich in vitamin E can reduce the severity of hot flashes and prevent night sweats causing insomnia.

Foods to eat: olive and olive oil (p.72); alfalfa (p.130); seaweed (p.134); flaxseed (p.192); sunflower seed and oil (p.198); brown rice (p.216); rye (p.222); soybean (p.224); sage (p.242); tofu (p.274)

OSTEOPOROSIS

Osteoporosis causes bones to become weak and brittle, so you are more prone to fractures and breaks. Eating foods rich in calcium, as well as phosphorus and magnesium, can help to prevent the disease. Making sure you spend plenty of time outside also helps, as the sun triggers the production of vitamin D in the body, which helps to turn the calcium you eat into bone.

Building strong bones before you reach your 30s reduces the risk you'll suffer from this condition in later life. Weight-bearing exercise is another vital way in which to protect bone health for the future.

Dairy foods and oily fish also provide vitamin D. Vitamin K and several other minerals are also important. All of these can also delay the progression of osteoporosis if you already have it.

Foods to eat: fig (p.32); pineapple (p.36); cherry (p.48); olive and olive oil (p.72); broccoli (p.94); kale (p.98); spinach (p.100); onion (p.108); lettuce (p.126); cucumber (p.128); watercress (p.132); seaweed (p.134); beef (p.144); chicken (p.148); live yogurt (p.151); milk (p.154); sardine (p.168); shrimp (p.170); oyster (p.172); cashew nut (p.186); flaxseed (p.192); sesame seed and oil (p.196); pumpkin seed (p.200); oats (p.210); quinoa (p.214); millet (p.221); rye (p.222); soybean (p.224); parsley (p.240); cayenne pepper (p.254); ginger (p.258); tofu (p.274)

POSTVIRAL FATIGUE (ME)

Although the specific cause of postviral fatigue is still unknown, it often follows on from a viral illness and is more likely to occur in athletes who